DESIGNS
in Affective Education

DESIGNS
in Affective Education

**A TEACHER RESOURCE PROGRAM
FOR JUNIOR AND SENIOR HIGH**

*by ELIZABETH W. FLYNN
JOHN F. LAFASO*

Edited by RICHARD J. PAYNE

PAULIST PRESS
NEW YORK, N.Y./PARAMUS, N.J.

Psychology - study + teaching
affective education

Design by Joanne Cossa
Interior Photos by Charles Gatewood

Library of Congress Catalog Card Number: 73-90085

ISBN: 0-8091-1811-4

Published by Paulist Press
Editorial Office: 1865 Broadway
                     New York, New York 10023
Business Office: 400 Sette Drive
                     Paramus, New Jersey 07652

Printed and Bound in The United States of America

ACKNOWLEDGEMENTS

ADDRESS TO THE INDIANA STATE BAR ASSOCIATION, April 15, 1971, by William D. Ruckelshaus. Reprinted with permission.

ALIENATION AND FREEDOM: THE FACTORY WORKER AND HIS INDUSTRY by Robert Blauner. Copyright © 1964 by The University of Chicago Press. Reprinted with permission.

"The American Family: Future Uncertain". Reprinted by permission from *TIME, The Weekly Newsmagazine*; copyright © TIME, Inc., December 28, 1970.

AMERICAN HERITAGE DICTIONARY OF THE ENGLISH LANGUAGE. Copyright © 1969, 1970, 1971, 1973 by American Heritage Publishing Co, Inc. Reprinted by permission.

BHAGAVAD-GITA. Translated by Swami Prabhavananda and Christopher Isherwood. Copyright © Vedanta Society of Southern California, Hollywood, copyright holder. Published by Mentor, New York, 1951.

THE BIOLOGICAL TIME BOMB by Gordon Rattray Taylor. Published by The New American Library, New York, 1968.

"The Biology of Behavior" by Robert J. Williams. Copyright © January 30, 1971 by Saturday Review, Inc. Used with permission.

"Blacklist" by Dan Herr. Reprinted from THE CRITIC, vol. XXX no. 1. Copyright © 1971 by The Thomas More Association, 180 N. Wabash Avenue, Chicago, Illinois, 60601.

THE BODY HAS A HEAD by Gustav Eckstein. New York, Harper & Row, 1970. Reprinted by permission of the copyright owner.

Book Review in CHEMICAL AND ENGINEERING NEWS, 48, July 27, 1970, p. 39. Copyright © 1970 by The American Chemical Society. Reprinted by permission of the copyright owner.

"The Brain: Part III" by Will Bradbury. Copyright © Will Bradbury, *LIFE Magazine*, 1972, Time, Inc.

"Breathing Therapy" by Magda Proskauer from WAYS OF GROWTH ed. by Herbert A. Otto and John Mann; copyright © 1968 by Herbert A. Otto and John Mann; all rights reserved; reprinted by permission of Grossman Publishers.

THE BRIDE AND THE BACHELORS by Calvin Tomkins. Copyright © 1962, 1964, 1965, 1968 by Calvin Tomkins. Reprinted by permission of The Viking Press, Inc.

THE BROTHERS KARAMAZOV by Fyodor Dostoyevsky. Translated by Constance Garnett. New York, Random House, 1950.

CELEBRATION OF AWARENESS, A CALL FOR INSTITUTIONAL AWARENESS by Ivan Illich. Copyright © 1970 by Ivan D. Illich. Reprinted by permission of Doubleday & Company, Inc.

THE CHALLENGE OF WORLD POVERTY by Gunnar Myrdal. New York, Pantheon Books, A Division of Random House, Inc., 1970. Reprinted by permission of the copyright owners.

CHILDHOOD AND SOCIETY, 2nd. ed., by Erik H. Erikson. New York, W. W. Norton & Company, Inc., 1963; London, The Hogarth Press, Ltd. Used with permission.

"The City as Environment" by Kevin Lynch from CITIES. New York, Alfred A. Knopf, 1965. Originally published in *Scientific American*, September, 1965. Used with permission.

COLOR: A GUIDE TO BASIC FACTS AND CONCEPTS by Robert W. Burnham, Randall M. Hanes and C. James Bartleson. Copyright © 1963 by John Wiley and Sons, Inc.

COLOR IN YOUR WORLD by Faber Birren. Copyright © The Crowell-Collier Publishing Company, 1962.

COMMUNES IN THE COUNTER CULTURE by Keith Melville. New York, William Morrow & Co., 1972. Reprinted by permission of the copyright owner.

THE COMPLETE WORKS by O. Henry. New York, Doubleday and Company, 1953.

"Composition in Pure Movement" by Mary Wigman from THE CREATIVE PROCESS, ed. by Brewster Ghiselin. New York, Mentor, 1952. Originally published by The University of California Press, reprinted by permission of The Regents of The University of California.

CONVERSATIONS WITH IGOR STRAVINSKY by Igor Stravinsky and Robert Craft. New York, Alfred A. Knopf, Inc. Reprinted by permission of Random House.

"Counsel to the Commission of Pornography"; Paul Bender in an interview by Lillian R. Kohn in the PENNSYLVANIA GAZETTE, December, 1970. Reprinted by permission.

THE CREATIVE ATTITUDE by Eric Fromm quoted in WALKING THROUGH YOUR COMMUNITY WITH YOUR SENSES TURNED ON by Inez Seagle. Philadelphia, Lutheran Church of America Youth Ministry. Reprinted by permission of the copyright owners.

"Death of a Demon" from HOMICIDE TRINITY by Rex Stout. Copyright © 1961 by Rex Stout. Reprinted by permission of The Viking Press, Inc.

"Die Like a Dog" from THREE WITNESSES by Rex Stout. Copyright © 1954 by Rex Stout. Reprinted by permission of The Viking Press, Inc.

"Distinguishing Features of Adolescence" from NORMAL ADOLESCENCE: ITS DYNAMICS AND IMPACT by The Group for the Advancement of Psychiatry is used by permission of Charles Scribner's Sons. Copyright © 1968 Group for the Advancement of Psychiatry.

A DOCUMENTARY HISTORY OF ART by Elizabeth Gilmore Holt. Copyright © 1947, 1958 by Princeton University Press. Reprinted by permission of Doubleday & Company, Inc., and The University of London Press, Ltd.

DORLAND'S POCKET MEDICAL DICTIONARY, 21st ed. Philadelphia, Pa., W. B. Saunders, 1968. Used with permission.

"Dusk Before Fireworks" from THE PORTABLE DOROTHY PARKER. Copyright © 1933, 1961 by Dorothy Parker. Reprinted by permission of The Viking Press, Inc. London, Gerald Dudworth & Co., Ltd. Used with permission.

ETHICS AND THE NEW MEDICINE by Harmon L. Smith. New York, Abingdon Press, 1970. Reprinted by permission of the copyright owners.

EXISTENCE AND THE WORLD OF FREEDOM by John Wild. Englewood Cliffs, N. J., Prentice-Hall, Inc., 1963. Reprinted by permission of the copyright owner.

"Explanation of the 'Black Psyche' " by John Oliver Killens from THE REBEL CULTURE, ed. by Robert S. Gold. Copyright © 1964 by John Oliver Killens. First appeared in *The New York*

5

WHY USE THIS BOOK WITH YOUR HIGH SCHOOL STUDENTS?

1. *Integration of the affective and cognitive domains*
    —encourage and assist student in examining his feelings, attitudes and values and integrating these with his cognitive learnings.

2. *Motivation*
    —interest—fun—success, minimal willingness to participate insures student's success, cooperative rather than competitive.

3. *Increased depth of learning—active experience leads to questions in student's mind*
    —ample opportunity for challenge in depth.

4. *Practice in self-expression, creativity, improved communication skills.*

5. *Variety*
    —change of pace—different approaches
    —exercises capable of rearrangement and restructuring to fit needs, interests, abilities of students
    —opportunity to develop others as you work with these exercises.

6. *Development of community in class*
    —peer learning and work in small groups leads to development of cooperative working teams.

7. *Relationship to world outside classroom*
    —content of exercises helps relate student to neighborhood and global community.

INTRODUCTION

For many years our systems of education have sought to help students invade and conquer the cognitive domain, and there has been a corresponding decrease in pursuing affective objectives. The general feeling was that, although a value-free education was not really possible, it was probably a suitable ideal toward which to strive. In this way indoctrination would be avoided, the individual would be free to make his own choices, and things which were a matter of "taste" would not be arbitrarily imposed upon the student. Educators seemed to hope that the student would become aware of good literature, would appreciate, or at least tolerate the customs and beliefs of visitors from other countries, would recognize a difference between news presented in a scandal sheet and in a journal of opinion. They hoped that he would not only know about immunization, but choose to obey laws concerning it; that he would care enough about politics to inform himself and cast his vote, or even rise above these minimal affective responses and develop a passion for fine art, or give indications that he would find ways to achieve better education for all or to reduce violence in our country.

Our educational methods, however, seemed to move farther from the realization of these hopes. All these hopes concerned matters of taste, preference, choice, attitudes, values and decisions; they involve feeling and emotion. Since society continued to count these matters as important and respectable, our schools made vague references to them in statements of purpose, course descriptions, and curricula studies, but textbooks, lesson plans, examinations and grades clearly reflected the persistant belief that if the cognitive were taken care of, the affective would follow.

This book deals primarily with something very old-fashioned that's been around a long time—the human being. Although man is a unit, or is so designed, he has become increasingly split, divided, dichotomized, even fragmented. He thinks of his body as separate from "himself," or of his mind as separate from his emotions, or of his "reason" as separate from his "feelings." There are times when this is useful and legitimate, but modern man in Western society has carried this fragmentation too far. He is often almost totally out of touch with his body, with his emotions, with "himself." He tends to disbelieve that his body affects his feelings and ideas, that his feelings affect his ideas, and that his ideas affect his body. Despite our awareness of psychosomatic illness, despite our "mood pills," despite our knowledge of the effect of color, for instance, on our buying habits, we seem not only to have continued the Platonic dichotomy of body-soul, but to have intensified and augmented this partitioning of self.

We have somehow lost our natural, human sense of joy in sensation. We have developed a sense of guilt or shame as a basic attitude toward our body and its physical sensations; we have developed a feeling of fear or distaste for much of the data presented to us by our senses. We school ourselves and are schooled to ignore these bodily signals. We develop a belief that unless we can translate a response into strictly cognitive terms, it is of little value, or is even harmful or "bad" in some way. We intellectualize that the cognitive is "superior" to the emotional or feeling level. But do we really believe this? Do our lives show this to be true? Is "love" cognitive? Do we understand or express love best in words? Does a mother teach her baby or her child love through an intellectual process? Does a husband express his love for his wife in logical speeches? We recognize the artificiality of such attempts; language is inadequate to meet the needs of intense emotion. At the same time, we seem to doubt the value of nonverbal expressions—we feel we "should" be able to express our emotions in words, that then the emotions would be "better," or we would be more "human" for being able to express them in this way.

We have long talked about teaching the "whole child" and "whole person" learning, but have usually meant the inclusion of other cognitive factors, or a recognition of "background" such as the child's concepts from sources other than the school or his intellectual experiences in other classes. When we considered his body, we thought in terms of training it, disciplining it, schooling it through athletics. We have worried about the problem of controlling it, of "making the child sit still," of "keeping him from jiggling about." The child's body has been a nuisance, a hindrance to learning, a problem to be overcome. All too often we have set about teaching him how to ignore his body, to conquer his emotions, to suppress his feelings.

When we try to teach and learn we are too quick to intellectualize our reactions, to leap to higher levels of abstraction without allowing interim stages of recognition and acceptance. We eliminate portions of received data; we filter input to suit our preconceived categories, or to channel it into acceptable, limited mental boxes. We tend to think this approach is better and even more virtuous. We fear the unclassified emotion, the uncategorized reaction. We believe that the more quickly we leap from the original sensory impression to the final translation to abstract or nominalistic statement, the better off we are. We take our shears and trim off what doesn't fit —the ragged edges, the fringe, the trailing threads. We discard them and quickly forget them as of no value.

Our more intimate acquaintance with the computer will probably intensify this tendency. From objective tests to computerized tests we hurry eagerly along a road which compresses data into yes-no groups, often squeezing out all the human juice along the way. If it cannot be answered "yes" or "no," it cannot be recorded, it is not "verifiable," it has "no validity," it doesn't exist! If it cannot be "quantified," it is without value. If it cannot be translated into statistics, it is useless. The student mind must learn to imitate the computer, avoid sloppiness, be definite and definitive. Philosophers and mathematicians have dreamed of inventing a mathematical language which could be used in solving all problems, a language which would be "purely rational" and thus eliminate the messiness now obvious in much human problem solving. Some people think that language is already available. We ask our students to act as if they already knew this language.

Much philosophical, scientific and religious thought has reinforced this avoidance of physical and emotional response, this refutation of the body. Much, but not all. There have always been those who sought to preserve the whole person, who refused to ignore any part of the human being. The field of education has begun to reinvestigate the importance of the affective domain, and in so doing has recognized the need for accepting the body as part of the student.

In 1948 a group of psychologists at an American Psychological Association convention discussed their mutual interest in achievement testing. They began an intensive study of educational objectives, meeting regularly with a large number of educators over a period of years. They developed a classification of these objectives under three general "Domains": the Cognitive, the Affective and the Psychomotor. Detailed study began with the Cognitive Domain, since they found that most educational objectives at the secondary school and college level fell within this category. The results of this work were published in 1956 (B.S. Bloom (ed.), M.D. Englehart, E.J. Furst, W.H. Hill and D.R. Krathwohl, *A TAXONOMY OF EDUCATIONAL OBJECTIVES: HANDBOOK I, THE COGNITIVE DOMAIN,* New York: Longmans, Green Co.).

Some of the members of the original team, plus others, continued work, developing a similar taxonomy of the affective domain. They had found that while all objectives could be classified in one of the three domains, each objective contained some elements of the other two. In 1964 the second Handbook was completed and published (David R. Krathwohl, Benjamin S. Bloom and Bertram B. Masia, *TAXONOMY OF EDUCATIONAL OBJECTIVES: HANDBOOK II: AFFECTIVE DOMAIN,* New York: David McKay Co.).

Meanwhile, behavioral science research had indicated that thinking by the living individual could not be separated from feeling and acting. As abstractions these elements could be considered separately, but in practice the individual operated as a whole, and educational practice began to take this fact more seriously. Many studies in group dynamics and communication contributed further data emphasizing the importance of affective elements in any learning situation.

In addition to these ongoing studies, trends in our society have been forcing educators to rethink their total program. Dionysian elements in Christianity have begun to receive more attention, and many young American Jews are engaged in a renewal of spirituality and a search for elements of love and fantasy within society. A developing interest in Eastern thought has shown that it is not all cold Confucianism and ascetic Buddhism, but often includes a concern for the senses and their use and appreciation. The Counterculture has been saying that school, as well as war, was not good for living things, and the rising Black Culture points out a lack of Soul.

Volumes of criticism of our educational practices augmented by student complaints attracted increasing interest during the 1960's. Many attacked the schools for being inhuman, uncaring, mechanistic and irrelevant. Humanistic psychology expressed many of the same criticisms and recommended some of the same cures. Most recommendations involved greater attention to the affective domain. Psychiatrists and others interested in mental health made similar recommendations. All these factors have contributed to the increasing stress on finding ways to strengthen affective education.

How is this particular book going to be useful to you?

WHERE? WHO?

Where should a teacher use these exercises? They may be used within the usual class periods in a secondary school, an alternative school, a school of religion, a summer camp, or other educational setting. They are particularly suitable for 11th and 12th grade, although many are usable with younger students or adults. The exercises can be done satisfactorily by students of various levels of ability, competence and academic preparation, although different levels of production will result.

If you have the opportunity of working with a "learning cell" situation, where children and adults of different ages come together to help one another learn, you will find many of the exercises excellent for this. It should not, of course, be thought of as a situation in which "adults play with children to help children learn." Rather, it is a situation in which all engage in serious play so that all may learn. There should be no attempt on the part of older children or adults to pretend to something they do not feel or believe in, or to pretend ignorance of information which younger members may not possess, but the feelings and observations of all should be valued. All should contribute, all should gain.

The exercises are useful in a variety of traditional secondary school subject areas, as outlined in the *appendix,* as well as in interdisciplinary programs, particularly those which involve the teaching of values or of religion. They can be arranged and expanded to structure a syllabus, or used in conjunction with a pre-determined syllabus or curriculum.

WHEN?

Although most exercises may be completed in a single class session, some are divided in "parts" to accommodate themselves to a 45—60 minute time-slot, and yet allow for sufficient depth to be meaningful. Schools using modular scheduling may be able to complete more than one part of these subdivided exercises in a longer session. Some exercises offer sufficient optional material for many additional sessions, and a few are short enough to be combined with other activities.

WHAT?

We recognize today's teacher as one who is willing to try innovative approaches, who is usually well prepared in his subject area, but who is sometimes discouraged by the seeming apathy of many students or by their rather standardized demands for "relevance," or by their unwillingness to deal with material presented. We hope teachers will see these exercises not as gimmicks simply to catch the student's attention or arouse his interest, but as valid educational procedures through which the teacher may also discover new things about himself and the world around him.

Each of the 125 sections of this book describes a basic exercise and, in most cases, suggests a number of variations. Each exercise consists of an experience for the student which provides some learnings and serves as the basis for investigation through discussion, research or exploration of resources that you can provide. The exercises presume the value of experiential, peer group learning, but do not presume that the experience is sufficient without guided reflection and usually the provision of additional information. The exercises presume that affect is an essential ingredient in internalizing new information, clarifying values and modifying behavior. The exercises are united primarily by their (1) experiential approach; (2) stress on affective learning; (3) emphasis on group activity, cooperativeness and peer group learning; (4) common thread, sometimes distinct and clear, sometimes a very faint line in the background—the human body, the student's own body. Attention is paid to helping the student become comfortable with his own physical self.

Non-threatening exercises help him become aware of and sharpen the receptivity of his senses, to recognize muscular tension and hear what it says to him. He is helped to find ways to achieve greater relaxation, freedom, grace and poise as a by-product of exercises which are often directed toward other subject matter. He is helped to get in touch with his own feelings and emotions and those of others, and to recognize their part in his decision making and the establishment of his values. We feel this element is needed to help make his education more human, less impersonal. It concerns aspects of man strangely neglected in education for a society which both over-emphasizes and simultaneously devalues all but the "intellectual."

WHAT IS THE SUBJECT MATTER?

The exercises are arranged under six themes: Communication, Freedom, Love, Peace, Happiness and Life—all areas of concern to the secondary school student. With the exception of Communication, however, these are seldom the titles of the "subjects" offered, although most teachers recognize the student's need to deal with these matters and therefore try to weave them into the fabric of their particular discipline. The outline in the *appendix* shows how the exercises may be incorporated into seven of the more usual high school course offerings. The location of a particular exercise under one theme is sometimes rather arbitrary. The exercise on "Apparel as Symbolic Speech," for instance, is in the section on Communication, but could be placed under Freedom or Happiness.

HOW IS THE BOOK ARRANGED?

The exercises are described in a simple and

consistent format to help you find the right one for your needs at the moment. Each exercise begins with a *purpose,* offers some explanatory and usually informational *comment,* suggests a suitable total *group size* and a *time* span, provides *general directions* and gives the *materials required.* It then gives a step by step *procedure,* which usually includes some suggested questions for discussion. This is usually followed by *variations* and *suggested resources.* As you work with these patterns you will find they can serve as the basis for many similar exercises in which the content or subject matter could vary considerably. With few exceptions each exercise can be used independently.

PURPOSE:

Most exercises can serve a variety of purposes related to the subject matter dealt with and to your class's life and needs. In some cases you may wish to make the purpose known to the class in advance, but usually it is better to let students develop their own "purposes," or to introduce the purpose in your own words toward the end of the exercise. Sometimes to announce the purpose in the beginning would distort the experience, as in the exercise "Peace: American History."

In planning a group of exercises to structure a unit on a particular subject, the purpose may be modified through modifying the *comment,* the questions used during the *procedure,* or the *resources.*

COMMENT:

Usually this gives some factual data concerning the subject matter and sometimes indicates things which may come up in class during the exercise. You may wish to share some of this material with your students, and sometimes it is useful to reproduce the Comment as a "Fact Sheet."

GROUP SIZE AND TIME SUGGESTED:

Although we have included our suggestions as to the optimum group size, we have somewhat arbitrarily placed the top limit at twenty. Usually, larger classes can work satisfactorily with the exercises but only after students have become familiar with working in subgroups. Considerable subgrouping is suggested, and although here again specific group sizes are recommended, you will be the best judge as to subgroup size for your own students.

The time span suggested for the parts of the exercises may seem very short. Depending on the group and its experience and needs, you may wish to lengthen portions of the exercise. We have found that setting short, announced time limits is usually helpful in moving groups to productive work, avoiding boredom, and developing goal orientation and interaction in groups. Short periods are particularly helpful in working with subgroups without trained leaders, as such groups quickly get off the track, develop participation problems or degenerate in other ways if left alone too long in a single activity. When students protest that they need more time it is sometimes a good idea to offer them a choice of a few more minutes. A small group will move through more material in a given time than a large one, and the size of subgroups may be varied to adjust the time to your needs.

Some exercises involve work done outside the class, either before or after the initial part of the exercise. When this is the case it is indicated.

If you have a large class you may want to offer a choice of alternative exercises in some cases. This is a bit like running a three-ring circus, but it is not impossible, particularly after your students gain experience in working in their subgroups. Some exercises lend themselves to this possibility. In the section of the Introduction titled "Working Groups" suggestions are offered to help develop subgroups into effective working teams.

MATERIALS REQUIRED AND SUGGESTED RESOURCES:

Since the teacher is usually well informed about textbooks and other standard educational materials, almost all the "Suggested Resources" come from other fields—government, business, industry, science or the mass media—and are often classified as "adult" material. Students may find it a welcome change. We have tried to indicate what you will need in addition to this book for yourself and your students, but you may vary these materials considerably. You will find most materials suggested are simple, inexpensive and readily available, and many exercises need no materials at all.

Sometimes you may wish to use materials in "Suggested Resources" as a substitute for portions of the exercise, or for additional related sessions. Only occasionally have we separated these Resources into those suitable for the teacher and those suitable for the student. In most cases we believe them equally applicable, although our presumption is that you would wish to examine in advance any materials you recommend to your class. Not all Resources suggested are of equal value, and we have noted where we felt special problems should be brought to your attention. We have chosen some controversial and conflicting materials to provide more than one kind of input, to encourage free discussion, and to broaden perspective.

GENERAL DIRECTIONS:

This includes a very brief description of the exercise and sometimes conditions for its use. At times you may find other exercises suggested which may precede or follow. Occasionally, suggestions are made as to whether the exercise is suitable for a "new" group or best used with a group that has worked together for some time.

DISCUSSION AND QUESTIONS FOR DISCUSSION:

This material is included in the *Procedure*. Ideas, concepts, feelings developed through the activity become the basic material for discussion and reflection or for the development of an inquiry or research project. In this way student questions usually arise before any attempted answers. Students already possess considerable information. The fact that some of it may be "wrong" is not a reason to avoid or ignore it, but an additional reason to bring it into the open for examination. The kinds of questions suggested for exploring issues or problems are not those to which easy, pat answers are available, but those to which many possible answers may be given, answers which reflect affective and attitudinal response, personal beliefs and feelings. There is seldom an attempt to arrive at a single "right" answer, although group consensus is sometimes sought. The young people for whom the exercises are designed need to be able to find their own answers, the answers that satisfy them.

During the exercise and discussion it will sometimes become obvious that more "facts" are required. This provides you, the teacher, with the opportunity to help students find these facts at a time when they are sincerely interested in discovering them. It is important to help students recognize these points in their discussions, and to realize that further discussion on a particular matter will be a waste of their time until more input is available. Some further suggestions are given on handling discussions in the following sections of the Introduction.

WORKING GROUPS:

"The class" and "the group" are used interchangeably throughout to indicate the total number of students physically present and for whom you are responsible. Occasionally, when a subgroup is being discussed, the term "group" refers to a subgroup, but this will be obvious in the context. The terms "teacher," "instructor" and "group leader" are used interchangeably for "you." When another leader is intended, we use "subgroup leader" or "student leader" to designate this individual.

In a large class it is usually desirable to divide the total group into smaller groups or *subgroups*. Sometimes, particularly when rather personal matters are to be discussed, it is best to allow students to choose their own group members. Such groups are called "self-selected." There are obvious advantages and disadvantages to such groups. In most cases it will be best if you pre-select the membership of each group. You may want to re-form groups at various times to provide variety and insure certain kinds of input or behavior in a group, but it is often best to keep a group together long enough to develop into a cohesive, productive working team. The size of subgroups should be kept small—from two to eight members. Much depends on the size of the class, its experience in discussion and in working together, the material considered, the procedures and the ability of the student leaders. As a rule, the more self disclosure expected, the smaller the group, and the larger the group, the more necessary some training will be for the student leaders.

A *plenary* is a bringing together of all subgroups for a general discussion or for reporting. In a plenary it is usually important to be sure that everyone present can see the face of everyone else, and that someone act as leader, facilitator or moderator.

The following suggestions will help you develop your subgroups into productive, effective working teams. For convenience we have arranged this material in alphabetical order.

ALTER EGO:

Sometimes groups are hampered by the "hidden agenda" of their members. Such felt, but unspoken feelings and ideas hinder open discussion and prevent progress. An exercise that can help your groups with this problem is "Communication: Alter Ego."

COHESIVENESS:

A feeling of oneness, or of "*my* group" is of value in promoting effectiveness and productivity. A group which works together satisfactorily over a period of time will develop cohesiveness, but the process can be hastened. One way to do this is the exercise "Happiness: Meal, Variation No. 1". See also "Ice Breakers" and "Responsibility" below.

COMMUNICATION PROBLEMS:

In addition to hidden agenda, other common problems are lack of clarity in statements, listening and speech problems. One way to work with the last named is the use of the exercise "Life: Senses: Audition: Tapes and Voices." See also "Listening" and "Perception Check" below.

CONSENSUS:

Sometimes you will want your subgroups to make a decision. They can be helped by an exercise such as "Happiness: What Is Community?", or "Love: Defining Peace, Step No. 2." These help a group experience consensus, and the latter also provides the possibility of including a "minority report" in decision making.

Another exercise to help a class examine consensus is "Understanding a Different Point of View." Using any issue on which there is a known difference of opinion in the class, ask two members holding opposite opinions if they will hold a five minute discussion on this topic in front of the class. Ask someone who is "undecided" to join this discussion. The three members are seated in front of the class and asked to try to reach consensus about the issue. It is highly unlikely that consensus will be reached, but if they are asked to try for it there will be an effort to persuade, particularly to persuade the "neutral" member. After five minutes ask the discussants how they felt about their efforts at consensus. It is quite possible that they have forgotten this was the "goal," and were thinking primarily of winning the argument. You may then help the class explore what would have helped achieve consensus.

COOPERATION VS. COMPETITION:

We believe that in the long run groups that work cooperatively are usually more effective and productive than those which work competitively. Most of the exercises in this book are based on this belief. Students may be interested in examining this idea through a number of the exercises, but one which can be used specifically for this purpose is "Peace: Conflict: Scavenger Hunt."

ENVIRONMENT AND PLACEMENT:

Groups work best when the seating arrangement allows comfortable seeing and hearing of all other members. A table provides a rather formal arrangement, and is often helpful in promoting a "let's get down to work" attitude, as well as being a convenience. A group that has been working at an oblong table and moves to a round one usually comments on the "improvement" because of the greater ease in seeing and hearing one another. Ideally, your room should allow groups to work with or without tables of various shapes and sizes. Modular triangular tables are often very useful. Naturally, groups work better in an attractive setting, and an attractive setting for young people is one they have arranged and decorated to their own taste. In experimenting with placement a useful exercise is "Communication: and Position Change."

FISHBOWL:

Often used to help a group examine its methods of working together is the Fishbowl, variously known as "cluster design," "goldfish bowl" and "micro lab." The purpose is to see a group in operation, to observe its behavior carefully, to give helpful suggestions to that group, and in turn to accept and use suggestions for one's own group.

Procedure:
1. Two groups are paired. One group sits in a closed ring in the center; the paired group sits in another outer ring. The inner group is active, the outer group observes.
2. The inner group has a topic assigned for discussion, or they may choose one. The only restriction should be that the topic does not call for a decision. The regular discussion planned for the session may be used.
3. The outer group of observers note which contributions seem to help the movement of the active group and which have a negative or blocking effect.
4. The instructor is time-keeper, or asks someone else to see to this. He may encourage the reporting of observations, or ask that these be deferred until Step No. 5.
5. The two groups get together in one large circle and talk over the experience. Which suggestions were resented? . . . why? Which were accepted and helpful? . . . .why?
6. The process is repeated with the groups' roles reversed.

An exercise which can be used for a first experience with the fishbowl is "Communication: Apparel as Symbolic Speech."

ICE BREAKERS:

When a group first forms, particularly at the beginning of a semester or term, it is important that those who are going to work together have a quick and simple way to become acquainted. To many persons a gathering, class or group is threatening. It takes great effort for some to break into a group and get acquainted. To free oneself from shyness or a retiring attitude one may need help.

Interview: Ask the members to seek out someone they don't know and interview this person with the task of presenting him or her to the others (3—5 minutes). Depending on the size of the class you may have several subgroups of 6—12 members. The advantage of this procedure is the immediate involvement of all. Persons who normally never talk will not find the one-to-one conversation threatening and are usually able to give a brief introduction of their partner. The one interviewed becomes the interviewer within the original 3—5 minutes, or half the group may be introduced and then more interviews conducted and introductions continued. You may wish to indicate that "no note-taking" is allowed.

Better Acquainted: The procedure for this is a variation of the Interview:

1. What information about persons in your group would you like to know? What one question could you ask that would add to your understanding?
2. Write several questions down, then choose the one you prefer.
3. Pair with a member and answer each other's question as frankly as you can.
4. Report to your subgroup on the success of your question. What did you learn? Listen to the others.
5. Pair with another person. Ask a new question.
6. Repeat this several times.

The Adjective Game: Subgroup members sit in a circle. Each person describes the member to his right by one adjective. Everyone gets up and then sits down in a different chair, at random, and the procedure is repeated.

After the "game," help the class see that it is difficult to summarize a person's complex character by one word. Warn the group that "first impressions" are often wrong, but that it does help individual members to recognize the first impression they make on others.

The following exercises are recommended as "ice breakers": "Communication: Voice and Intelligibility, Session I"; "Communication: Paraverbal and Silent Communication, Steps Nos. 1 and 2"; "Happiness: Meal, Variation No. 1"; "Life: Memory"; "Life: Senses: Olfaction: 'Smells of Childhood' ".

INSTRUCTIONS:

When the class is divided in subgroups you may wish to vary the ways in which you give procedural directions. In addition to simply making a general announcement you may use a tape recorder for one or more groups, you may post directions on newsprint or use chalkboards, you may hand group members or subgroup leaders a sheet of paper outlining procedures or recommending questions for discussion, or you may give each member a slip of paper or a file card. In some cases you may wish to have one group prepare such directions for another. You will want to wander about among the groups at times to be sure all directions have been understood.

LISTENING:

One of the most important skills, if not *the* most, for your members is listening. If the class receives some training in discussion their listening skills will improve. (See "Discussion" in section of this Introduction titled "Techniques.") In addition, an exercise that may be used early in the year is "Peace: Conflict." The listening exercise contained in this may be used in connection with other exercises, or independently with other material.

Another listening exercise may be used when a group has been working for a while. Interrupt the group and say, "In any group you will find that some people seem to listen to you more than others. They may listen better because they agree with you or are unusually interested in what you say. Write down the names of the two people in your subgroup that you believe really listen to you . . . Now write down the names of the two people whom you usually listen to most carefully. Now check your results and score yourself as follows: 2 —if both people you wrote down as listening to you wrote your name as one to whom they listen; 1 —if one person does; 0 —if neither person wrote your name . . . Talk over your scores . . . What is happening to the people who score 0? . . . to those who score 2? . . . What is involved in successful listening? . . . What role does eye contact play?"

OBSERVERS:

The use of observers may be introduced at times and will be helpful if not allowed to become a means of threatening or punishing groups or group members. One simple introduction to this procedure is "Communication: and Position Change."

PERCEPTION CHECK:

Another cause of communication problems is the faulty or inaccurate assumptions we often make about others' views or feelings. A helpful means of sharpening our perceptions is included in "Peace: War and Peace: Perception Check." This technique may be used with many other exercises.

PROCESS DISCUSSION:

One of the most helpful techniques to promote group growth is the "process discussion." This refers to any interchange among the members following their regular discussion, which enables them to talk about "How did it go?" The group investigates how it works together, what helped, what hindered, how they can have a better discussion next time. This may be done very informally or with reports from observers or the use of various forms. It is important to stress any problem as a *group problem,* rather than try to blame one or more individuals.

RECORDERS:

This well-known method allows a group to have some permanent record of what they did and said or of reporting their findings to the class at large. The greatest danger with recorders is the necessary editorializing of the person reporting. (See comments on "recorders" in "Discussion" below.)

An exercise which demonstrates one use of recorders is "Mass Media: and 'Good' and 'Bad' Bodies."

RESPONSIBILITY:

Group cohesiveness depends in part on the degree of responsibility group members take for one another. One way to further this is to be sure each member of a semi-permanent subgroup has the name, address and phone number of every other member, and that the group accepts the responsibility of contacting absentees and filling them in on what they missed and what is coming up. Once such subgroups have been established it is a good idea to start this procedure. Check out the subgroups for a week or so until this is automatically taken care of by the group. An exercise specifically helpful in promoting mutual responsibility is "Happiness: Group Excursion." Another one which can be helpful is "Freedom: from Prejudice: Group Rejection."

TECHNIQUES:

It is possible to develop an almost endless repertoire of exercises by switching techniques or approaches, by combining exercises, and by developing the "Variations" or using the "Suggested Resources" with various techniques. After the students have experienced a number of exercises, they will be able to assist in planning others.

BUZZ GROUPS:

This somewhat overworked technique is used to involve a large group in something which has been presented "up front." It can be used when a class has brought up a problem in which all are interested but a few members would dominate in a general discussion, or when there seems to be differences of opinion which are not being adequately expressed. It aids the free flow of ideas and exchange of opinions in an informal atmosphere. It can stimulate critical thinking and analysis. When used carefully, buzz groups provide variety and are helpful.

1. Explain the procedure and set a time limit.
2. Make the topic for discussion clear. A copy of questions on the topic may be distributed. You may wish to word the same question in a number of ways if a problem needs clarification, or you may divide a list of questions surrounding the problem so each buzz group has 1—3 different questions.
3. Arrange for a leader and recorder for each buzz group.
4. Attention must be given to keeping discussion on course.
5. Each recorder makes a report in a plenary.

BRAINSTORMING:

This is often fun, can unclog log jams of thought and encourage creativity, and is a good technique when a group is fearful of criticism. It uses group ideation and group problem solving. Members are encouraged to produce as many ideas as possible on a problem. No critical remarks are tolerated and the process of idea-production and evaluation are separated in time.

1. Define and limit the problem.
2. Form suitable subgroups of 6—15.
3. Set a time limit.
4. Determine ahead of time a system for recording the ideas, e.g., a tape recorder, listing on chalkboard or paper. Explain system to selected recorder.
5. Criticism is not allowed. Forbid negative or critical remarks.
6. Accept all ideas, no matter how fantastic. Quantity and speed are encouraged. The greater the number of ideas, the more the likelihood of winners.
7. Permit hitch-hiking—the adding to, or building on one another's contribution.
8. Evaluate the list of suggestions at another session, or assign a committee to organize and/or do a preliminary screening. The committee reports to the class, at which time a final evaluation and selection are made.

NOTE: If the class is unfamiliar with the method, try a warm-up such as "the extraordinary uses for paper-clips," or "how to improve life inside a ping-pong ball." There's no need in a warm-up to keep a record. Allow about 3—5 minutes.

CREATIVE ACTIVITIES:

In addition to activities suggested in such exercises as "Happiness: Faces," "Happiness: Photographs," and "Happiness: Montage of Physical Self," the following general suggestions may be incorporated in many exercises or used in developing new ones.

1. *Written material:* Students may be asked to write a few sentences, a paragraph, an essay, a short story, or a brief skit. These may form the basis of a discussion, may be used to clarify a problem or issue or a viewpoint during an exercise, be used as part of the input at the beginning, or form a personal summary at the end. At times you may wish to make these available to all members (see "Reproducing Student Work" below).

A technique used by Joan Dickstein of the Human Resources Center of the University of Pennsylvania is to have everyone write a letter to himself at the conclusion of an exercise that may develop a desire for changed behavior or specific action. Each member is given a sheet of paper and an envelope. About fifteen minutes is allowed, and members are asked to seal their letter in the envelope and address it to themselves. The sealed envelopes are collected with the understanding that they will be mailed on a specific date, such as "in two months," "at the end of the semester," etc.

A graffiti board or several sheets of heavy paper or newsprint can offer students the opportunity of brief written statements, quotations, slogans, sketches or cartoons when an exercise seems to lend itself to this sort of response. Heavy wrapping paper or discarded rolls of wallpaper may be used.

Students often enjoy writing poems in the Haiku style. Read a few to the class and then give them an opportunity to compose their own. The rule for the mechanics of this style is simple: three lines of 5, 7 and 5 syllables respectively. This is a good technique to combine with meditation, and can be used with such exercises as "Life: Senses: Touch: Water," "Life: Senses: Audition: Background Music, Variation No. 7," "Love: Learning to Love, Step No. 7," or "Love: Meditation." For further information on the haiku, and also on a variation, the *tanka*, see *POETRY HANDBOOK: A DICTIONARY OF TERMS*, by Babette Deutsch, New York: Funk & Wagnalls, 1957, pp. 59-60, or other recent handbooks.

Students may also be interested in trying their hand at composing a myth, as in "Life: Senses: Kinesthesis: Social Space, Variation No. 3."

2. *Posters:* The poster has developed a number of offspring very useful for the expression of ideas and feelings. Many students find such activities an excellent way to express themselves and a means to communicate with others. The *collage* consists of words, pictures, designs, etc., cut or torn from other printed materials, such as magazines, newspapers, advertisements, colored papers, and placed in a meaningful arrangement on a backing such as poster board, construction paper, or other surface. Glue, tape, staples, etc., may be used for attaching the components to the backing. A variation of the collage is the *box* construction. The outer and inner surfaces of the box are used in the same way as the collage backing.

Boxes may be large or small, planned as individual objects or parts of a larger structure, may be hung by a corner, sealed and pierced with a light-hole and a peep-hole. Objects may be suspended within them, sections cut away or folded in or out as shelves or windows, or they may be partially opened up as folding screens. When students work with boxes it is helpful to provide some sharp knives such as craft knives or penknives and additional sturdy cardboard boxes to form a cutting surface.

Four people may use the four sides of a box to mount elements of a collage, all of which may be visible to them only when it is completed. This may be done by allowing all to know the theme in advance, or by allowing each to know only his own element, or all may know the theme and titles of the others. Each side may be a different color, either by asking that objects of the selected color be used or by covering each completed side with a colored transparent plastic sheet.

Collages may be mounted on many shapes and forms such as blown-up balloons or bottles or jars, or they may be mounted on glass or reflected in mirrors. A supply of cork squares and push pins provides the base for many quickly assembled collages. If greater permanence is desired, these may be photographed.

A *montage* usually signifies a collage-like object in which some of the components are not flat or printed surfaces. Objects are mounted or otherwise attached or arranged in the area, often combined with typical collage materials. As in the poster or collage, additional original elements may be contributed by the designer such as lines, words, colored areas, etc. Tactile as well as visual elements may be included, such as sandpaper, seeds, textured fabrics or even small water-filled plastic bags.

A *mobile* may be thought of as an animated poster, collage or montage, as well as an abstract art form. The suspending strings or threads may be attached to a loop, coat hanger, bar, box, etc. The simplest consists of a single string of cards, forms or objects suspended one above another, each object attached by a thread to the one directly above. Elaborate and complex ones have many parts and branches and in form and construction may resemble an inverted tree or bush. For students unfamiliar with the form, the easiest introduction is to be shown a few examples, or even pictures of various kinds of mobiles. Calder's variation of the *stabile* could also be used, although its miniaturization destroys the essence of the form.

The best introduction to the concept of *found art* is to show the students some slides or pictures from museum catalogues or magazines. The results will often be similar to those of a montage, but students may select just a few objects and arrange them to convey a viewpoint, summarize a discussion, or report on findings. Although both mobiles and found art are usually abstract, conveying moods, feelings or simply line and color, both modes allow a statement to be made, if desired.

3. *Group pictures and murals* may be single paintings, drawings, cartoons or murals. Line, color, shape, can all be used to communicate something to others to help a group consolidate its own ideas. The resulting products may be demonstrated and explained in a plenary.

4. Wire, including pipe cleaners, plaster of paris or clay may be used for the creation of individual *sculpture,* or as components of mobiles, montages, etc. Foam plastic of various kinds may be cut, painted and glued to form portions of a sculpted piece, as a base, or for an entire object. Excellent catalogs, instructions and suggestions for the use of clay and other modeling and sculpting materials, as well as paints, colored chalks, etc., are available to teachers on request from the American Art Clay Co., Inc., 4717 W. 16th St., Indianapolis, Ind. 46222. Information on working with Styrofoam is available from Literature Inquiry Service, Dow Chemical Co., 2030 Dow Center, Midland, Mich. 48640.

5. Chalk, crayon, felt-tip markers, pastels as well as the usual paints, pencils and pens add variety and excitement to *designs, sketches, cartoons* and *pictures.* When using colored chalks on paper, it is helpful to wet the paper or to dip the chalk in water as it is used. If an overhead projector is available, an erasable series of pictures or cartoons may be made on the transparency roll with suitable colored pencils, and projected for all to see. Scraps of colored papers or fabric of various types may be pasted on paper or laid on the transparency to incorporate certain features in a drawing or sketch.

6. Fabric variations on the poster or collage make for variety. With a strong burlap backing it is possible to incorporate heavier objects in a *wall hanging, banner* or *scroll* than could be mounted on paper or poster board. Some objects may be provided with string slings and tied in place. A macrame-like hanging may be created with dowels, flat doughnuts of plastic or wood, and string or heavy wool yarn, and may also be used as a mounting for a picture or object.

7. *Slides* are considerably less expensive than films for student use, and are often neglected. In addition to the common use of the commercially prepared "set," a good deal can be done with purchased slides. Beyond this there is a great opportunity for creative work by students in photographing local scenes, people or objects for use as slides by the class, and slides may also be made by painting and drawing on developed film.

A helpful illustrated guide which includes instructions for making and using slides and which includes a bibliography is "Slides with a Purpose: for Business and Education," available from the Eastman Kodak Company. For materials for teachers address requests to Motion Picture and Education Markets Division, Eastman Kodak Co., 343 State St., Rochester, N.Y. 14650.

Another way in which slides may be used creatively by students is to make available to them a selection of commercial slides from which they can put together a presentation with or without an accompanying talk, taped script, or musical background. Commercial slides may also be combined with slides students have made. The National Gallery of Art is a good source of fine and inexpensive art slides. Slides are 35¢ each, and schools and other educational institutions receive a 20 percent discount. The National Gallery is also a good source of reproductions, post cards and other visual aids. Write for their current catalog, The National Gallery of Art, Washington, D.C. 20565.

If your school has a transparency copier that reproduces in color you can make a supply of slides using small colored pictures or parts of pictures from magazines and advertisements. Rule off a sheet of 8½ x 11 paper in 1½ inch squares, cut the pictures to fit, paste on the sheet with a bit of rubber cement, and run through the copy machine. The resulting transparency is cut in squares which are then mounted in purchased slide frames.

8. Student made *films* as well as commercial ones are becoming standard equipment in most classrooms. "Movies with a Purpose" from Eastman Kodak (see address above) will give considerable assistance in planning and producing 8 mm. movies, and BEHIND THE CAMERA by William Kuhns and Thomas F. Giardino, Pflaum, 1970, gives clear, explicit and detailed information for those who wish to go more deeply into the subject.

9. Many students own or have access to *tape recorders* and several exercises suggest the use of audiotapes for data gathering, or for creating background music or other sounds. It is sometimes helpful for students to record a discussion and then play it back, and sometimes subgroups may wish to record discussions and trade tapes for replay. Some students have achieved considerable skill in the use of recording equipment and will prove very helpful.

10. Some schools have *videotaping* equipment available that is seldom used. If portable equipment is available to you, and you have not used it, arrange to have someone come in and give a brief lesson to you *and* your students. Tapes are reusable and videotape recording and playback can offer a wealth of creative experiences and an excellent learning tool. The company that manufactured the equipment used in your school will usually send you suggestions for its use, and once you have done a bit of experimenting with it you and your students will find many ways in which it can be helpful.

A helpful paperback on audiotape, film, TV, etc., is *PRACTICAL GUIDE TO CLASSROOM MEDIA* by Dolores and David Linton, Dayton,

Ohio: Pflaum Standard, 1971. You may also get some helpful ideas from a free pamphlet, "Video-tape Recording Applications," Ampex Corporation, 2201 Estes Ave., Elk Grove Village, Ill. 60007.

DATA GATHERING:

Students will have occasion to collect data from fellow class members and from others in the school, home and community. Learning appropriate and successful ways of doing this is a valuable experience. In addition to the usual reading of materials distributed or recommended by the teacher, many methods are described in the exercises. Among these are the following:

—researching maps, newspapers, telephone books etc., using forms prepared by others, "Life: Urban Design: Study Your Community,"

—using community governmental services as sources, "Life: Urban Design: 'Get the Facts',"

—using a game to gather data on attitudes of class members and parents, "Happiness: Body as 'Good' or 'Bad',"

—designing and using questionnaires, "Freedom: and Work,"

—use of Public Interview, "Love: Public Interview,"

—developing and using charts and forms, "Life: Ecology, Conservation and Pollution, Part II, 12."

Polls: Newspapers and magazines frequently publish the results of public opinion surveys and polls. Students may wish to experiment with some of the questions used in these polls and collect data in their class, school, homes or community. Sampling techniques may be discussed as part of this procedure. After practice with some of the "tested questions," students may devise polling questions of their own.

Interviews may be constructed by preparing a set of questions, or a set of statements with blanks, such as incomplete sentences. Without such tools, interview data is apt to be difficult to collate and compare. Students may write down answers in full, make notes, or use and transcribe from a tape recorder or play it back in class. All these methods have certain advantages and disadvantages which students will discover as they collect and analyze the data gathered.

Opinion statements in class may be gathered anonymously by asking students to reply to a question in writing on a file card or slip of paper. These may be collected, read back to the class, redistributed or reproduced for distribution of all statements. Questions should be simple and clear, and brief responses requested.

Students may be interested in knowing that in scientific research, a "finding" is commonly

thought of as a statistically significant difference. At times they may wish to try to devise data-gathering instruments which aim at this degree of precision, asking respondents to circle numbers on a scale, place a number on a continuum, or circle or underline words to which a key provides previously assigned numbers. From such data various kinds of charts and graphs may be prepared.

DISCUSSION:

Most of the exercises are designed to include group discussion. This is an option that you need not always use. Some exercises require it, but at times you may wish to reduce the length of the discussion, use discussion only in dyads or pairs, or eliminate it altogether. Many of the discussions are very brief, and you may wish to extend some of them if you find student interest high. It is usually best, however, to end discussions before they become tiresome or interest lags. There are some people who do not enjoy or even profit from discussion, including some very creative people who simply work better alone.

The exercise preceding the discussion forms a common ground and reference point to help keep discussion on the track. Some side-trips in discussion will be very worthwhile, but there will be times when students wander into an area where they are seriously handicapped by lack of necessary information, or where the subject introduced is of interest to only a few. You can help by asking questions which relate back to the original discussion. If the sidetrack is potentially valuable, suggest a later discussion when some input can be provided so that all can enjoy the conversation.

The well-formulated, well-timed question is your key to success in helping students benefit from discussion. Most exercises include suggested questions. We believe that these questions can be productively handled by secondary school students and often prove interesting to you, as well. They are not "quiz" questions, but questions to which more than one answer can be given. Avoid asking questions to which you are sure you know the answer, and encourage your student leaders to do the same. Write questions in advance, and help your students to do this. You may change the wording as you use them, drop some and introduce others. Listen carefully to what is said and rephrase questions to relate to previous statements, while keeping the goals and purposes of the discussion in mind.

Students may be reluctant to speak because of unfortunate experiences in the past. They must learn to trust you and their group. Encourage respect for one another, listening, the expression of minority opinions, and help your student leaders to do the same. Ask questions, rather than make state-

22 ments or give opinions. Be receptive to the statements of others, even when you disagree. Do not argue. Do not bias or slant questions to try to convince the participants that your ideas are correct or theirs incorrect. Avoid allowing one or two to monopolize. Serve the group by helping others to express themselves, not by instructing, providing "information," or approving or disapproving particular answers. Once your students become accustomed to such open-ended discussions in which you will not "rate" answers as right or wrong, they will discuss more freely, introduce questions of their own, and begin to follow your example in questioning others.

It is not always necessary to have a leader for short subgroup discussions. Before using student leaders, set the pattern by leading some discussions yourself. Also, give the class some help in working together as a group by using some of the exercises suggested above in the section of the Introduction titled "Working Groups."

When classes are subgrouped, the common practice is to have all groups "report" to the class. This is usually done to share the greatest amount of input, correct misunderstandings, and keep a check on class activity. This practice has many disadvantages as well as advantages. If students are bent on "fooling around," it is simple for them to assign one member to prepare a statement, while they talk about whatever they please. It is true that it often increases input, but the summarizing of the reporter often distorts the discussion, discourages subgroup members, and can lead to increased misunderstanding. There are times when "reporting" should not be used. Some exercises in this book recommend such a procedure, but *what* is to be reported is usually limited to a few statements on which the group is asked to reach agreement, and an attempt is made to avoid situations in which the reporter will tend to editorialize.

On the other hand, it is sometimes a good idea to give a sheet of newsprint and a felt-tip marker to subgroups doing data gathering. Ask them to put down key words or phrases as they come out in discussion, telling them they can "cross it out if you get a better idea later, or think it doesn't fit." In untrained groups, putting something down helps focus discussion.

Some students who are particularly interested in leadership may be given a few extra sessions to help them develop the necessary skills, or the entire class may be helped to do this. Discussion and question formulation are valuable techniques which deserve study. We suggest our own books on this, being biased! (*GROUP DISCUSSION AS LEARNING PROCESS: SOURCEBOOK,* and also the *GUIDEBOOK* of the same name, both by Flynn and LaFaso.

MEDIA:

Excellent materials are on the market giving help in the selection, use and discussion of commercially available slides, films, records and TV programs. May we simply suggest that you enlist the help of your students in the selection of material, preview or hear it with a few students, particularly those who will lead subgroups and, when possible, offer a choice of two or more possible selections? Sometimes vary the way the material is used, turning off the sound on a film, substituting different sound-tracks, using "live" music, etc. Also, try some mixed media experiences with slide and film projector used simultaneously with two screens or a "split screen" effect, combine with tapes or records, a "light show," or whatever suitable experiments your students can help you plan and execute.

REPRODUCING STUDENT WORK:

Sometimes student input should be available for the entire class. In addition to the usual means of compiling and reproducing such material, the less expensive ditto master is helpful. Students may write, draw or type directly on the master, and these may be run off very quickly, sometimes even within the class session in which they are being used. Other means of reproduction are films, including stills, Polaroid shots, filmstrips and slides, tapes, overhead transparency and opaque projectors and videotape. Early in the year investigate the facilities available in your school and among your students. Sometimes nearby public libraries or even commercial firms will make available to you some of their facilities on a limited-use basis.

SIMULATIONS:

Games, dramatizations, skits and role plays are particularly useful when attitudes and feelings are being explored. They offer the opportunity of active participation by students playing a specified role in a simulated environment in which they make decisions and experience consequences without real danger. In each case, simulations should be followed by discussion.

The original simulation or educational games derived from war games and presumed a conflict, a winner and a loser. Many such games exist today, but others strive for a "win-win" situation. The word game is used so loosely these days that some educators would call all the exercises in this book "games." Some commercial games are close to the war games or to popular board games such as *Monopoly,* others are scripts for role plays. Try some of the games already available in your school before purchasing any commercial games for your class. Many of the good ones are quite expensive. You may be able to construct games of your own after you have used a few with your class. Two books which are helpful on education games are *SERIOUS GAMES* by Clark C. Abt, Viking, 1970, and *SIMULATION GAMES IN LEARNING* by Sarane Boocock and E.O. Schild, Sage Publishing Co., 1968. There are helpful suggestions for the use of "games" in the classroom in *REALITY GAMES* by Saville Sax and Sandra Hollander, Macmillan, 1972, but the activities described are closer to sensitivity or communications training exercises than the games in the other two books.

Dramatizations used as simulations involve the spontaneous acting out of a story. This may be done as a play or skit in which an outline of the story is given but the dialogue is spontaneous. In dramatization it is possible to have a director, either the teacher or a student, who coaches from the sidelines, introduces new events or characters into the situation, and more or less "walks the actors through" the play. Students may dramatize something they have read, or may enact a "new scene" which might be inserted in a play, novel or short story with whose characters they are familiar. Dramas may combine characters from one or more stories set in a new situation, bring to life situations in songs or poems, add episodes to a TV serial, or convert essay material into drama form.

Pantomimes, tableaus or dances may be used to express attitudes, feelings, values or ideas. Individuals or groups may "take off" from a picture, written material, or recommendations from a director or the audience. The following suggests one possible procedure for tableaus:

1. Students assume pose and "think themselves into" designated attitude as they understand it.

2. Change pose as they prefer, to express attitude, as a new thought comes to them.

3. Allow "audience" to recommend and explain changes.

4. Go into motion either from point "2" or "3", spontaneously or upon direction from the audience.

Improvisational theater is similar to dramatization and also to role playing. It presents a situation or environment, and sometimes a task or characters with freedom to create their own task. A feeling, emotion or incident may be specified. It strives to present these realistically and convincingly to an audience, although it is possible to involve an entire class simultaneously in improvisational work, eliminating the audience.

Role playing may or may not involve an audience, and may be loosely or tightly structured. A situation is always presented, usually a problem of some sort, and characters or roles designated. The following outline shows the usual differences between dramatizations or improvisations and role plays.

DRAMATIZATIONS

The director is active before and sometimes during the play, suggesting ways to do things.

Some lines may be "written" in advance. The speeches and actions are planned to some extent. Either (a) actors are not "taken by surprise" at what is done by other actors, no sudden changes are demanded during the performance by the director, all know conclusion; or (b) director may add or subtract actors, give directions during the play, provide some "surprises."

The play runs along preordained lines to a preordained conclusion. It does more than simply present a problem, as a rule.

Length varies, but is usually predetermined.

The play is seldom re-run for the same audience. Audience and role players never reverse roles.

Players may sometimes read lines. Players are "acting," may ham it up, if they wish. There is no need for sincerity, only the appearance of sincerity.

"Good acting" is received as such, and applause is encouraged. There is nothing for actors to reveal after play.

Props, sets, lighting and costumes may be used to enhance effect. A 35 mm. slide projector, for instance, makes a good "spotlight," and colored or mottled effects achieved with colored slides, projected out of focus. It is helpful to keep on hand a box of hats, scarves, few hand props. Folding screens or panels create instant-sets and signs such as a menu to indicate a restaurant, "Buy Tickets Here" for a race track, or "Shower before entering pool area" aid in setting scene. Director avoids verbal description, if possible.

ROLE PLAYS

The director assigns roles, describes the situation, but is otherwise inactive.

No "lines" are given players. No speeches or actions are planned in advance. There are frequent "surprises." The conclusion is unknown and not anticipated.

Even the director does not know how the role play will "turn out," or when he will stop it until the moment comes—he stops the role play when he feels the problem is made obvious.

Role play may last 3—7 minutes. Occasionally longer role plays are used to attempt to solve a problem or for training purposes.

The play may be re-run with new players or slight change in the situation, and with the same audience. Audience and role players may reverse roles.

24 No player ever reads lines. Role players should not ham it up but be as sincere as possible, trying to feel empathetically their roles, but being "himself" as much as role allows.

"Good acting" is incidental bonus, and applause discouraged. Role players may sometimes reveal information about their roles unknown to other players and audience, when role play ends.

No props, set, costumes or lighting are used, other than perhaps a table and chairs. Any necessary information about the setting is quickly given verbally by the director, or even by one of the players. Even in role reversal, a man playing a woman would not wear any article of woman's clothing.

Two books you will find particularly helpful are *DISCOVERY IN DRAMA* by Clifford Frazier and Anthony Meyer, Paulist Press, 1969, and *IMPROVISATION FOR THE THEATER* by Viola Spolin, Northwestern University Press, 1963.

VALUING:

In addition to the numerous approaches to value clarification suggested in many of the exercises, helpful suggestions are found in "A Theory of Values" by Louis E. Raths, Merrill Harmin and Sidney S. Simon, in *DISCOVERY PATTERNS:* BOOK 2, by Robert J. Heyer and Richard J. Payne, Paulist Press, 1969, pp. 80-88, and in *VALUES AND TEACHING* by Raths, Harmin and Simon, Charles E. Merrill, 1966.

COMMUNICATION

COMMUNICATION AS LEARNING

PURPOSE:

To discover the different forms of communication by which we learn, or to examine learning as it takes place through different modes of communication.

COMMENT:

Learning depends on communications picked up by our nervous system in many different ways. All our senses are involved in one way or another in learning, but one or another sense predominates at various times in receiving the input. Students may be able to see the actual process of learning in a younger child more readily than they could in themselves or their peers. Many students have small brothers and sisters or nieces or nephews, others have experience with small children through babysitting or with children in the neighborhood. By helping a small child to learn something they can observe the process in operation. Whatever we learn, we learn with our bodies. Whatever we learn is communicated to our bodies in some way. Whatever we teach we must teach in some way by our bodies.

GROUP SIZE:

Up to 25 in subgroups of 5—6.

TIME SUGGESTED:

Three sessions, two of approximately 30 minutes, one of 45—60 minutes. These minimum times allow for other activities during the first two sessions.

GENERAL DIRECTIONS:

A preliminary discussion on "how children learn," and "learning and communication" is followed by individual field work in teaching a two- or three-year old a new learning. At the following sessions these experiences are examined and discussion focuses on communication and learning. Some findings are gathered and fed back to the class in written form. Relationships to their own learning experiences are discussed.

MATERIALS REQUIRED:

Hectograph or ditto masters for each subgroup.

PROCEDURE:

FIRST SESSION:

1. Depending on class size, this may be handled with the entire class. Ask the students to think about two- and three-year old children they know, and suggest different types or categories of learning or ways of learning experienced by these children. How do they learn to talk? . . . to ride a tricycle? . . . to stay out of the street? . . . to draw a picture? . . . to slide down a sliding board? What kinds of communication are involved? After the discussion begins to produce a variety of kinds and ways of learning, you may wish to subgroup the class.

2. Distribute hectograph or ditto masters and explain their use. Ask a recorder in each subgroup to list the "kinds of learnings," with an example of each, e.g., "observation and imitation—small child puts on make up, imitating mother without encouragement," or "physical and nonverbal—small child puts on makeup, imitating mother without encouragement."

3. Ask each subgroup to decide which of their members is to teach a specific type of learning to a two- or three-year old, e.g., to model something in clay; to recognize the letter "S," to sing a song, to enjoy the beauty or wonder of a flower, a new taste, a sound. Each student is to report on the results of this teaching/learning experience at the next session. Ask the students to be particularly observant of how the child looks, how he handles his body during this experience, his attention span, what ways of teaching were successful and which were unsuccessful. Ask them to make brief notes, being as objective as possible. These notes will be for their own use.

SECOND SESSION:

1. Depending on the size of the class, you may wish to conduct this session in subgroups. Ask each member to explain and, if possible, demonstrate to his group his teaching experience, allowing 2—3 minutes for each student.

2. Each subgroup holds a 15—20 minute discussion on the kinds of communication involved in the teaching/learning experience with the small child—verbal, nonverbal; visual, auditory, muscular; tactile, taste, smell. While they are doing this, post or write on the chalkboard some suggestions for step No. 4.

3. Distribute a fresh set of ditto masters and secure one recorder for each group.

4. Ask the groups to discuss the elements that went into each teaching/learning experience with their young "students." Ask the recorders to list the names of the members of the group, and opposite each name a brief record of specific learning, and selected elements. Indicate that the material on the board is "suggested" categories.

The following are suggested, but you must determine what kind of listings that pertain to "communication and learning" would be most helpful for your group:
   a. How was the learning communicated?
      —use of senses—which ones?
      —emotions and feelings involved
      —muscles, or muscular learnings
      —role of memory, and previous experiences built on, if any
      —approach or method of teaching used and the kind of interpersonal relationship with child.
   b. What kind of learning was it?
      —cognitive—new information acquired
      —attitudinal or affective—fear, pleasure, interest
      —skill or muscular ability.
   c. Successes and failures. What worked? What didn't work? What helped? What hindered?
SAMPLE: Mary Jones—to drink through a straw—muscles (muscular skill)—senses: touch, taste, vision—observation, imitation, verbal directions—playful, friendly relationship.
THIRD SESSION:
1. Distribute to all class members the reproduced copies of lists and descriptions from Sessions I and II. Allow 5—10 minutes for reading.

2. In original subgroups, ask each group to plan which 2—3 experiences they wish to report to the entire class. In reporting they should explain the kinds of communication involved, amplifying the written report and answering questions from the class.

3. In a plenary (with entire class), each group reports its findings.

4. General discussion. Focus on *communication in learning.* The class may explore some of the following:

—Are there differences in the teaching methods reported?

—What things helped the small children to learn? What hindered?

—What role was played by emotions or feelings in this experience?

—What role was played by past experience in some of the learnings?

—What difficulties did they experience in communicating with the children? How did they overcome these difficulties?

—Are there differences in the way they themselves learn, compared to the small children? Are these differences in kind, in degree, both?

—How would they describe their own ways of learning?

—Can you analyze some of the ways in which you have recently learned something? (to play a game, use a particular tool, cook something, learn a part for a play, learn about city government, learn a foreign language, learn to play an instrument, to create in an art medium, to get along with someone)

—What kinds of communication were involved in these learnings?

—What helps and hinders the kinds of communication necessary?

—What role is played by emotions or feelings in these experiences?

—What part is played in communication by attention? (interest, involvement)

—What do they think is the best way to learn specific things?

VARIATIONS:

1. In a small class the exercise may be completed in two sessions, conducting sessions in a single group and eliminating the second written report.

SUGGESTED RESOURCES:

Robert J. Heyer/Richard J. Payne (eds) DISCOVERY PATTERNS, BOOK 2: PATTERNS OF DYNAMICS AND STRATEGIES, New York: Paulist Press, 1969. See p. 30, "A Difference of Degree."

Students may be interested in reading or hearing something about the development of small children such as Eric Erikson's theory of personality development. In Robert J. Heyer/Richard J. Payne (eds) DISCOVERY PATTERNS, BOOK 1: PATTERNS OF SITUATIONS, you will find suitable material on pp. 114-117.

RECOGNITION

PURPOSE:

To discover how we recognize people—how we "tell people apart."

GROUP SIZE:

10—20

TIME SUGGESTED:

Two 60 minute sessions

GENERAL DIRECTIONS:

Either of the two Sessions may be used independently. Either may be used as a preface or sequel to the exercise on "Physiognomy or Facial Analysis," or may be combined with a portion of that exercise if time allows. Members attempt written descriptions of their own faces and attempt to recognize one another from the written descriptions. Members write a description of another well-known face. Members attempt recognition of classmates under conditions of limited information. Discussion focuses on the means of visual recognition of others, the uniqueness of the individual. Exercise may be used early in a group's life, and will help the members to get acquainted.

MATERIALS REQUIRED:

SESSION I:
None

SESSION II:
A shoulder-high screen or solid room divider; large brown paper bags to fit over and conceal the entire head; an old sheet torn into squares large enough to tie around the head to conceal the hair.

PROCEDURE:

SESSION I:
1. Each member writes a brief description of his own face, such as he might send to a stranger who is to meet him somewhere a month from now. Tell the class, "Do not put your name on the paper. Write or print clearly so others in the class can read your description." Collect and shuffle the papers, number each with a large visible number, "1," "2," etc., and post all of them on the wall around the room.

2. Each member takes a sheet of paper and goes around the room, reading each description and writing down the number and names of the persons described on the posted sheets, guessing wherever necessary. Each student may start at a different number to keep the line from piling up. When all have completed the circuit, each student stands beneath his own description, and the others check their lists. (Each person may take home his self-description and check it with a mirror for accuracy.)

3. Students close their eyes and think about a particular face they believe they know fairly well—a parent, another relative, a public figure such as the President of the United States, a film star, a rock musician, etc. Ask them to try to get these mental images as clear as possible. What details would they want to include to reconstruct a "police portrait" if this person were missing and no photograph available? What is the shape of the ears? Are the ears placed high or low on the side of the head? How long is the nose? Is the hair parted? If so, on which side? Are the teeth regular? Students now open their eyes and write a brief description.

4. The class may be subgrouped for this step, if desired. The group now discusses their findings. They may share their written descriptions from Step No. 3, if desired. Why do some people know their own face fairly well, while others do not? Why is it sometimes very hard to describe the face of someone we know well? Is it easier to describe the face of someone we see frequently, or the face of someone we see in political cartoons? Why? What do we notice first about a face? Why? Why do different people notice different things? When we look at someone do we notice: the eyes, nose, mouth, hairline, ears, forehead, jawline, hair, skin color, general shape and size of the face or head? How much are we influenced by "faces"? What kinds of "instant judgments" do we make? Why?

SESSION II:
1. Place the screen at right angles to a door into the room, so that those entering the room will be concealed if they crouch down a bit. Briefly explain the procedure, and then send half the class out of the room. The members remaining "inside" are to take a sheet of paper and write down a number on the left side for each "outsider." You will call these "outsiders" in, one at a time, but those in the room

will be able to see only the back of their heads. They will try to identify each member, writing down the name opposite the number in the order of appearance. Those waiting outside are to count off, "1, 2, 3" etc., and remember their number!

2. Each member comes into the room just far enough to be concealed by the screen. He crouches down until in position, and then shows the back of his head *only* to those in the classroom, keeping his shoulders below the top edge of the screen. No one completely reenters the room. "Insiders" must make individual judgments or decisions.

3. After each "outsider" has been viewed in this way, the process is repeated except this time each person shows his face to those in the classroom, still keeping his shoulders below the top of the screen. "Insiders" may correct their lists if they believe it necessary.

4. "Outsiders" now enter one at a time, in order, coming fully into the room and speaking their name as the "insiders" check their lists.

5. Former "insiders" now become the "outsiders," and the process is repeated, with the following changes:

First time behind screen: the head covered with a brown paper bag.

Second time behind screen: the face and ears are exposed, but the hair is tied in the square of fabric.

6. If desired, the results may be charted on the chalkboard, showing the number of correct answers in each of the four tries: (1) back of head; (2) face and hair exposed; (3) head concealed, body revealed; (4) face only, hair concealed. In which were the fewest correct answers? In which were the most? Is it possible to determine which features are most helpful in recognizing a familiar face? When we come face to face with someone, why are we usually immediately aware of whether we know the person or not? Why don't we have to look him over carefully and make a decision about it? Why are we occasionally unsure? Why do some people have a better "memory for faces" than others? Why do we sometimes have a good memory for "faces," but "forget the name"? What would it be like to live in a society where everyone wore a mask all the time? What would it be like if all the masks were alike? When we recognize someone from a distance too great to distinguish the face, how do we do it?

VARIATIONS:

1. In most groups of teenagers, one or more may be troubled with acne and is apt to be sensitive about it. However, in a group free of skin problems or any real malformations, an experience in recogni-

tion through the sense of touch will be interesting. Use the head scarves again and also wrap the person to be identified in a sheet to avoid recognition by clothing. Blindfold the "identifiers" and allow them to gently feel each face in turn. Since this could be too drawn out, arrange to have only 3—4 persons identified by each class member.

2. Around Halloween, when half masks are readily available, the following may be tried. Using the screen again, bring in those to be identified one at a time wearing a half-mask. Bring them in the second time in the same order, but this time with the "head scarf" squares tied across the bridge of the nose under the eyes, as worn by some women in the Middle East. Or, half the class may use masks, the other half the scarfs.

PHYSIOGNOMY OR FACIAL ANALYSIS

PURPOSE:

To explore what "faces" tell us—how much we rely on this information, how valid it is.

COMMENT:

Many of us learned in psychology classes that in analyzing character, the face was of no value. We were shown a group of pictures and asked to "pick the criminals" or the "low I.Q.'s" or the "geniuses," only to find afterward that our judgments were inaccurate. On the other hand, our literature is full of references to the "noble brow," the "strong jaw," the "coarse mouth," or the "eye as the window of the soul." Are the poets wrong? Are the psychologists? Which psychologists?

Employers, lovers, school teachers, salesmen and purchasers, judges, spies, statesmen and psychiatrists recognize how helpful it would be if character and personality could be identified by simply looking at a person's face. Hippocrates and Aristotle believed they had found ways to judge a man's character and ability from his physical appearance and particularly from his face. During the Middle Ages and the Renaissance psychology depended heavily on physiognomy. In the late eighteenth century the Rev. Johann Lavater devised a system of "character analysis" from the face, and Franz Gall moved a bit higher and introduced phrenology for this purpose. In the nineteenth century an Italian anthropologist, Cesare Lombroso maintained that criminal types could be identified by physiognomy. In the 1920's Ernst Kretschmer in Germany and W. H. Sheldon in the United States developed a system of classification of body types—the thin type, the muscular type, and so forth, and tried to show correlations with personality. More recently Sheldon and Eleanor Glueck have found correlations between body build and delinquency. Eric Berne believed fortunetellers often unconsciously base successful predictions on learned relationships between such factors as body build or skin texture, and the probabilities about present troubles and likely futures. Some cultures pay more attention to the face than others. In some European countries there seems to be greater stress on showing children pictures of the faces of men and women whose work they are studying in history, literature, mathematics or music. In Japan respectability is granted in some circles to the study of the face in character analysis.

However, most contemporary psychologists give little credence to such relationships because first, there seem to be as many "exceptions" to such rules as there are cases which "prove" them and second, the expectations of any culture or society tend to define and treat individuals in ways that create self-fulfilling prophecies.

We look at a face and make a number of judgments, depending on our interests or needs. First, we may look to see if it is someone we know, or for (1) recognition. Second, we watch people to see what emotions or reactions they are registering, or for an aid in (2) communication. (3) We look at strangers to see "what he is like," or for character assessment. We actually use all three assessments or judgments in communicating with one another.

Gustav Eckstein, Eric Berne, Margaret Mead and many others point out that we can tell a good deal about someone's thoughts and feelings by observing muscle contraction, particularly around the eyes and mouth, and such things as flushing or blushing and the expression of the eyes. This seems to be common sense. But how accurate are we? How far beyond this do we go in practice? A man's face seems unlikely to have a relationship to his ability to conduct an orchestra, yet Jean Amery in *PREFACE TO THE FUTURE*, New York: Frederick Ungar Publishing Co., 1964, p. 284, points to the success of Herbert von Karajan as an example of contemporary society's tendency to prefer and hence promote artists who are "good-looking" according to our standards.

GROUP SIZE:

10—20, using dyads and other subgrouping

TIME SUGGESTED:

Two sessions of 45—60 minutes

GENERAL DIRECTIONS:

Exercise may be used sequentially with "Communication: Recognition," and portions may be combined. Students compare, evaluate and discuss photographs of faces and parts of faces. In Session I individual judgments are made. In Session II judgments are by group consensus. Discussion follows each session.

MATERIALS NEEDED:

SESSION I.

Each member of the class receives a set of four photographs cut from magazines or newspapers and mounted on cards or sheets of paper. Use only the heads, preferably full front face, and no captions. Select people not readily recognizable by students, but about whom some information is available to you, for instance from the accompanying text in the magazine. Have a variety—actors, convicted criminals, businessmen, teachers, politicians, etc. Number each picture and keep a record of relevant information coded to the number.

SESSION II.

Each subgroup will need one or more sets of the photographs, consisting of sections cut apart and mounted separately. It may be convenient to use photographs approximately 5—9 inches high and to use 3 x 5 file cards for mounting. Each face is cut apart as follows: (a) draw a line with the ruler resting at the top of the eyebrows, giving a "slice" of forehead and hair; (b) draw another line with the ruler resting immediately under the nose, touching the tip of the nose, resulting in a picture which includes the eyes and nose; (c) the remaining slice includes the mouth, chin, and jawline. This set may be made up of people who are better known to students, if desired. Number the slices and keep the record of relevant information. Mount so the slices may be overlapped to form a complete face.

PROCEDURE:

SESSION I.

1. Each student receives four photographs from the Session I set. Using a separate sheet of paper for each photo, the students write several "assessments" about each face. Have them spread the photographs out in front of them . . . "Which person would you most like to have for a friend? . . . Which person would you least like to know? . . . What occupations do you think they have . . . do they look like . . . a dentist? . . . teacher? . . . lawyer? . . . thief? . . . retail sales clerk? . . . baseball player? . . . truck driver? . . . What else can you tell about them?" Allow about 5—8 minutes.

2. Form subgroups of 2—6. Subgroup members compare assessments. Dyads might want to trade pictures and compare assessments, or groups might want each member to show his pictures and state his assessments. Why are there differences in assessments? Why are there similarities? Allow 8—12 minutes.

3. Read to the class a short description of each person whose photographs are held by the students, reading the code number and having the holder of the photo display it to the rest of the class. If the class is large, subdivide the descriptions and have a student in each group read the pertinent sections to his group only. Allow 5—8 minutes.

4. General discussion focuses on, "What can you tell about a person from his face?"

SESSION II.

1. Describe and demonstrate the location of the "three areas" of the face, as described in "Materials Required: Session II." Ask each group to choose which area they believe is most revealing of a person's character. Subgroups may have the same membership as Session I, or different. Distribute to each group one or more sets of their chosen area *only,* placing the "slices" of the other areas in piles to indicate to *you* which sets belong to which group. Each group tries to reach a consensus on some assessments of character or personality of the individual photographed. The Group Recorder notes beside the code number the assessments made. Allow 10—15 minutes.

2. Distribute the remaining slices to the appropriate groups. Groups arrange the cards to form a complete face; re-examine assessments; make any changes desired.

3. If the photos are not of very well known people, read the identifying descriptions as in Session I, Step No. 3.

4. General discussion. What helped or hindered them in making assessments? How accurate do they think they were? Did their judgments change when they had all three "slices"?

You may wish to provide further input for the discussion by reading some material from the "Comment" section above, or from the "Suggested Resources" or other materials.

VARIATIONS:

1. Parts of this Exercise may be used as games. Session I, Steps No. 1 and No. 2 may be followed, but at No. 3 ask the Group Recorder to list after each code number the group's "best judgment" as to "occupation." When the descriptive sentences are read, the Recorder checks the answers, and the group with the largest number of correct answers wins. Other assessments may be used.

2. A set of pictures of well-known people may be prepared by mounting them on construction paper and temporarily blocking off all but the eye-nose area with "curtains" of paper. Number them and post them on the wall. Each member writes his guess as to "occupation." Students may also be asked to write one or two words descriptive of the "character" of the person. Do not tell the group these are "well-known" people, although occasionally someone will recognize a face. Individual or group competition may be used if a game is desired.

3. Distribute old magazines for cutting up. Ask the students to select faces that illustrate for them specific characteristics such as "honesty," "friendliness," "reliability," "aggressiveness," "phoniness," etc. In subgroups each student shows his pictures, explaining the characteristics they see illustrated. Students discuss the points of agreement and disagreement in their subgroups. Have some students chosen faces of those they recognize and know something about? If so, do they think they would have recognized these characteristics in the face of someone who was unknown to them? How much reliance do we place on our assessments of people made by looking at their faces? Do some features tell us more than others?

4. In times of social stress and change traditional institutions and beliefs suffer a loss of adherents. Very new or very old ideas enjoy a sometimes faddish ascendance. Today, many young people turn away from traditional beliefs in science as well as in religion. Shamanism and the occult present them with possibilities, and global perspectives recommend beliefs and practices alien to our Western institutions. Students may be interested in doing individual or group research and presenting to the class findings on currently popular ways of determining personality, character, ability or the future, by means of examining some portion of the body—palmistry, phrenology, physiognomy, etc. There is considerable literature on these topics on the market, and the public libraries can be helpful.

SUGGESTED RESOURCES:

Body build and personality
W.H. Sheldon *et al, THE VARIETIES OF HUMAN PHYSIQUE,* New York: Harper & Bros., 1940.

W.H. Sheldon and S.S. Stevens, *THE VARIETIES OF TEMPERAMENT,* New York: Harper & Bros., 1944.

Eric Berne, *A LAYMAN'S GUIDE TO PSYCHIATRY AND PSYCHOANALYSIS,* 3rd ed., New York: Simon and Schuster, 1968. (A brief summary of some of the above listed material may be found on pp. 25-28; 349-350; 357-358.)

Body build and criminal behavior
Sheldon and Eleanor Glueck, *PHYSIQUE AND DELINQUENCY,* New York: Harper & Bros., 1956.

George B. Vold, *THEORETICAL CRIMINOLOGY,* New York: Oxford University Press, 1958, ch. 4 "Physical Type Theories," pp. 43-74.

Paul B. Horton and Gerald R. Leslie, *THE SOCIOLOGY OF SOCIAL PROBLEMS,* 2nd ed., New York: Appleton-Century-Crofts, 1960. (A brief summary of some of the material in this section is given on p. 141.)

Franz Joseph Gall, 1758-1828, and phrenology
Gustav Eckstein, *THE BODY HAS A HEAD,* New York: Harper & Row, 1970, p. 406.

Franz G. Alexander and Sheldon T. Selesnick, *THE HISTORY OF PSYCHIATRY,* New York: Harper & Row, 1966, pp. 124-25.

Cesare Lombroso, 1836-1909; *Johann Kaspar Lavater,* 1741-1801.
Alexander and Selesnick, *HISTORY OF PSYCHIATRY,* pp. 82, 131, 162.

Fortune-tellers and physiognomy
Eric Berne, *A LAYMAN'S GUIDE TO PSYCHIATRY AND PSYCHOANALYSIS,* 3rd ed., New York: Simon and Schuster, 1968, pp. 348-50; 357-58.

Facial expression and personality
Gustav Eckstein, *THE BODY HAS A HEAD,* pp. 657-58.

Eric Berne, *A LAYMAN'S GUIDE TO PSYCHIATRY AND PSYCHOANALYSIS,* pp. 65-66.

Margaret Mead, *SOVIET ATTITUDES TOWARD AUTHORITY,* New York: McGraw-Hill, 1951, pp. 65-66.

Contemporary physiognomy
Hachiro Asano, *FACES NEVER LIE: THE NEW ART OF JAPANESE PHYSIOGNOMY,* Tokyo: Rikugei Pub., 1964. (By a "believer.")

OUR
MULTIPLE
SELVES

PURPOSE:

To discover the kinds or types of communication applicable and appropriate to our different "selves."

COMMENT:

Each of us is many people. Each of our personal selves communicates with the outside world in a number of different ways at different times. Our group memberships, interests, and occupations create the petals of our "field flower" which exert force upon the center of the "flower," or the "I," and which interact with that center. Upon examination, we find that our ways and means of communicating vary a good deal with the particular "petal." Another image which can be used instead of the flower is a segmented wheel. The central "I" communicates in different ways along the spokes or within the segments of that wheel. The form and level of this communication help to develop and establish the type of persons we are.

GROUP SIZE:

8—20

TIME SUGGESTED:

45—60 minutes

GENERAL DIRECTIONS:

Class members fill in their own "wheel," including the type or kind of communication they believe they use most commonly in each segment. Subgroups classify the types of communication, rank them according to level or depth, importance, involvement, etc. Classification and ranking can be done in various ways, according to the group's needs and interests. The class should have had some pre-

vious work in communication to enable recognition of the variety of meanings and possibilities in human communication. Discussion includes consideration of the possibilities of changing the characteristics of communications in some situations.

MATERIALS REQUIRED:

A blank wheel chart of 12—20 segments should be prepared and reproduced for each student.

PROCEDURE:

1. Distribute the wheel charts and explain how they are to be filled in. You may put a chart on the board, your own or that of a hypothetical student. This will serve as a model and simplify the explanation. In each segment place a "field" or "self," such as "teacher," "member of a religious congregation," "member of bowling team," "actor in a little theatre," "United States citizen," "uncle," "a reader," etc. Add verbs indicating the type of communication involved in each, e.g., in the "United States citizen" segment, you might put "write" (tax returns, letter to Congressman); "speak" (recite the Pledge of Allegiance); "gesture" (salute the flag); "pull lever" (to register vote). Ask the students to fill in the chart, limiting the number of fields to the number of segments in the wheel even if they find they should have more.

2. When the wheels are completed ask the students to underline the one word *in each segment* that they feel is the most important—"Which one would you save if you had to sacrifice all but one?" This is difficult to do.

3. Form subgroups of 5—6. Students then explain their wheel to the subgroup.

4. Ask the students to re-examine the underlined words in their wheels and make any changes they wish. Next, each student writes a word or two around the outer edge of his wheel over each segment to describe the part of the body most important in that form of communication, e.g., "voice apparatus," "skin," "muscles," etc. Tell them it is presumed that the brain and nervous system will be involved in some way in all communication, so they need *not* write that in.

5. Select a discussion leader for each subgroup. His task will be to help his group explore the relationship between the physical means of the communication used and its effect on the individual communicating. Give each leader a sheet of paper with some questions, such as the following, but tell him they are only suggestions to help the group to get started—he is free to use others.

Give the groups five minutes to think about how their *means* of communication in each segment affect them, how they feel about it. You may want to give them an example, e.g., "How do you communicate with team members on the field?" "How do you feel about this?"; "How do you feel about kissing someone as a form of greeting? . . . an aunt? . . . a friend?"

SUGGESTED QUESTIONS:

Your task as leader is to help your group explore how their *physical means of communication,* in the various segments of their lives, affect them as individual persons. These questions are only suggestions. Reword them or change them as you wish to accomplish your task.

—Did you find it difficult to choose only one or two words for each segment?

—Did all the segments seem to come out alike?

—What would happen if you switched around some of your words to different spots on your wheel? Would this improve or worsen communication? Would it be more helpful to you as a person? less helpful? Do you wish you *could* change some of the words around? why? Do you think you, as a person, would be different if your means of communication in some segments were different?

—How could your total communication *within* a given segment be improved? Would this mean a different mode, or means, of communication, or a deepening of the present mode? How might this change you as a person?

—How much communication goes on by physical touch? (one person to another)

—How much is visible movement of some part of the body? (nodding agreement, pointing your finger, smiling)

—How much is by spoken or visible symbols? (talking, writing, photographs)

—How do you feel about switching from one of the above three modes to another in one of your segments, or of increasing one type more than another?

SUGGESTED RESOURCES:

Kaiser Aluminum *NEWS,* Vol. 23, Number 3, 1965, on "Communication." You will be interested in reading this issue which deals with the subject in a lively, informative and attractive way. If you wish to purchase copies for use by the class, bulk orders should be sent to Mr. Frank Urbanowski, the Glencoe Press, 8701 Wilshire Blvd., Beverly Hills, California 90211. They are $1.25 per copy, but educational discounts apply.

EFFECT ON OUR BODIES OF GROUP MEMBERSHIP

PURPOSE:

To discover some of the ways we are affected by membership in groups, including groups which are "communities."

COMMENT:

All of us belong to many groups and organizations. These affect and involve our bodies, although because of our culture we often think of them as having relevance only to our "minds." In what ways do these various groups relate to our bodies? In what ways do our bodies relate to these groups? In what ways would we be different, or behave differently, if we belonged to other groups, rather than to those in which we actually hold membership? There are groups of which we are not members, but to membership in which we aspire. Do these affect our bodies? If so, how? Do they affect the way we dress, for instance? Which of these groups are "communities"? Is there a correlation between degree or kind of effect on us and the nature of the group—whether or not we regard it as a "community"?

GROUP SIZE:

8—15

TIME SUGGESTED:

45—60 minutes

GENERAL DIRECTIONS:

This exercise may be used with a fairly new group, and may be used as an introduction to developing ideas about "community." Class members work individually preparing lists of the groups to which they belong. They try to distinguish "communities" from other kinds of groups, exploring dif-

ferences in effect, if any. There is a final plenary session for data gathering.

MATERIALS REQUIRED:

chalkboard or newsprint

PROCEDURE:

1. Class members are asked to jot down the names of as many groups and organizations of which they are members as they can in one minute. If necessary, remind the students that sociologically speaking, groups would include "this class," "this school," "your family," etc.

2. Students are to examine their own lists and think of ways in which membership in these various groups affect or involve their bodies—the physical effects on them of such membership. Suggest that they make a few notes on this for their own use, e.g., "school—wear uniform, gym suit, sit in desk-chairs, eat lunch, play football, ride bus to school." Another student's list might focus on the senses, e.g., "school—see things, hear things, touch things, smell things, taste things," or "school—hear talking, singing, bells; see people, books, films, building," etc. It is better not to offer examples unless necessary.

3. Form subgroups of 2—6 to compare and discuss the lists. Ask the students to talk about the *most important* effects on their bodies of membership in these groups. If they need some suggestions, you might put a few on the chalkboard:
   —What are the most important effects of membership in your particular family?—How does membership in your family affect your nutrition, appearance, what you wear?—Think about it in terms of belonging to another family—what would be the difference?
   —Suppose you belonged to another national group—were a citizen of another country—went to a different school—compare the physical effects to determine the effects of your actual membership.

4. After about 10—15 minutes, ask the subgroups to focus on those groups they have listed which, for them, are "communities." Do these "communities" affect you physically more than other kinds of groups? Does a group that is a community necessarily affect its members more in physical ways? Why or why not? There will be difficulty in making these distinctions. It will be necessary for the subgroups to arrive at some working definition of "community." Suggest that if they have difficulty in doing so, they compromise and accept someone's

definition temporarily, or that they simply vote on which groups to call "communities." They will have time at a later date to consider this point more carefully.

5. Bring the class together in a plenary session to gather its findings. Using newsprint or the chalkboard develop brief answers to some of the following questions, or to others you think helpful to your group:

—Do "communities" of which we are members affect our bodies more, less, or the same as our other groups?

—Does the answer depend on the nature or character of the group?

—What words describe the most important effects on our bodies of membership in these communities?

—What distinguishes a "community" from another kind of group?

—Can we belong to a community which has no effect on our bodies?

6. The data gathered may be reproduced for distribution to the class at a later session in which "community" is to be discussed. It may serve as a background for the refinement of a definition of "community" satisfactory to the class or to individual subgroups, and the material may be used in other exercises concerning happiness, freedom, etc.

COMMUNITY

PURPOSE:

To explore the relationship of "communication" and "community."

COMMENT:

"If I talk to another person, I communicate with him. Such a communication implies a revelation of my inner life, my thought and my feeling, to another. As soon as this is recognized, it becomes evident that the human use of words implies mutual trust.

"I would not reveal my thought unless I felt it would be welcome and understood; indeed, I express it because I desire to be welcome and understood. In so doing, I reveal myself to another, who is thereby made to share something of myself and my life. By the same token, I also share his self and his life. For my word that has entered his thought through the channel of sensation and perception, becomes his, a part of his world, while remaining mine, a part of my world. Thus we enter into an ineffable communion together, each becoming part of the other's interior world. This communion is deeper than any other that man may experience." (George H. Tavard, "Meditation on the Word," DISCOVERY PATTERNS, BOOK 1: PATTERNS OF SITUATIONS, Robert J. Heyer/Richard J. Payne, eds., p. 176.

GROUP SIZE:

6—20

TIME SUGGESTED:

One hour 20 minutes to one hour 50 minutes; or 2 sessions of 50—60 minutes.

GENERAL DIRECTIONS:

May be used as a follow-up to Exercise "Effect on Our Bodies of Community Membership," or may be used independently. Exercise includes individual introspection, sign making, the design and performance of role plays, and discussion. The group should have had several previous experiences with role playing. May be used as an early session on "communication."

MATERIALS REQUIRED:

Paper strips, 4 x 11 inches or larger
newsprint and felt-tip markers or chalkboard

PROCEDURE:

1. Ask the class to think individually of what they mean by "community." Suggest that they write down a few phrases which help them to understand the term. These are for their own use.

2. Distribute to each member paper strips large enough to make signs. Ask them to print on their strip, "Community means _____," filling in the blank with a single word.

3. Arrange the group in dyads to compare the signs and for a 10 minute discussion of the reasons why they chose the word they did, and for permitting each individual to reconsider his decision as to whether he wishes to keep his original word or change it. If they wish to change the word, they may turn the paper over and print a new sign. It is not necessary for them to agree on the same word.

4. Dyads may now combine in groups of six, or, if the total group is small, convene the entire group for a plenary. Post the completed signs where all subgroups can see them. Ask each person to jot down how *communication* is related to the descriptive word they have chosen to complete the sign. Subgroups discuss the relationship between "communication" and "community." For this discussion it is best to have a leader for each subgroup. Ask them to use the chalkboard or newsprint and marker to put down "key words." Allow about 15 minutes.

5. Each group designs a role play to show situations in which *lack* of communication destroys a feeling of community. For instance, one might concern a group of close friends who have been separated by circumstances for five years, and then meet again for the first time. Another could be a family dinner table at which two teenagers are discussing a new musical group, the parents are discussing a situation in the father's place of business, and neither pair participates in or understands the other's conversation.

Each group writes a brief description of the situation and, on separate sheets of paper, role descriptions for each of the characters. Each group selects one member to serve as role play director for one of the other groups, using the role play his group has designed. Allow about 15 minutes.

6. Role play directors have five minutes to instruct their players, giving them time to read their lines. Each group performs its role play for the class, with the role play director interrupting role play after about 5 minutes, when he believes the communication-community problem has been made obvious. Some subgroups may wish to work on nonverbal communication, if their role play allows for this.

7. After each role play allow the role players to comment on their own feelings about their roles and the situations before the general discussion takes place. Allow 5—10 minutes of discussion after each role play, seeking to identify the communication problem and its source and how this affected the feeling or sense of community. The object at this time is not to see how communication may be improved in such situations, but simply to seek causes and effects.

8. Discussion may now move to consideration of all role plays together, as well as the input from the signs posted earlier. What kinds of communication were used in the role plays? What is the relationship between communication and community? When breakdowns in communication damages a sense of community, are all three modes of communication equally affected—touch, visible bodily movement, and symbolic communication? Does one mode have more effect on community than another? Can community exist if only one mode of communication is used?

You may wish to save the signs and newsprint sheets to use as input at a later session.

VARIATIONS:

1. The exercise may be divided between Step No. 5 and No. 6. Or the first session may end with Step No. 4, and the role plays may be prepared outside of class time by individuals or groups.

2. Each subgroup may tape its discussions up to and including Step No. 5. For Step No. 6, groups trade tapes and listen to one another's tapes, then continue at the following session by performing the role plays, etc.

SUGGESTED RESOURCES:

You may be interested in reading the entire selection by Tavard quoted in "Comment" above. You may want to share it with the class.

Film: "Have I Told You Lately That I Love You?", 16 min., 16 mm., black and white. University of Southern California, Film Distributing Section, 1958. Good, though exaggerated, depiction of automatized, non-communicating family life. The problem is current, although the clothing is unfortunately out of style and the film is therefore too dated for some groups.

APPAREL AS SILENT SPEECH

PURPOSE:

To investigate apparel as symbolic speech demonstrating group membership, and how this relates to a sense of community.

COMMENT:

"Actually, all uniforms are enemies. Just another extension of machine living. The way we dress —in costumes—is in direct opposition to a uniform culture. Costumes are the opposite of uniforms. Since the cops' uniforms also include clubs, handcuffs, guns, etc., they are particularly hated uniforms" (Abbie Hoffman, "Talking in My Sleep—An Exercise in Self-criticism," *THE REBEL CULTURE,* Robert S. Gold, (ed), New York: Dell, 1970, p. 214).

GROUP SIZE:

20—25, in subgroups of five

TIME SUGGESTED:

45—60 minutes

GENERAL DIRECTIONS:

Small groups plan a uniform or similar apparel, explain the designs to the class, discussion follows. Further input may be provided with pictures, slides, film.

MATERIALS REQUIRED:

This may vary from paper on which to write descriptions through art media for depicting design (crayons, paint, colored papers for cut-and-paste collage).

Optional additional input:
—a few photos or posters showing pictures of various kinds of uniforms, identifying clothing, pins, badges, etc.
—slides showing pictures of past and present apparel of the above type
—a film showing the history of uniforms, crown jewels, protective clothing, etc.

PROCEDURE:

1. Form subgroups of 4—6. Each subgroup is to choose a particular profession, organization or type of person for whom they will design an identifying uniform, insignia, hair style, or combination of these. Allow 3—5 minutes for the subgroups to decide on the people for whom they will design.

2. Groups have 15 minutes for the designing project. The only requirement is that another person who is a member of the same "club" would be able to identify his fellow member on sight by the article(s) they have designed. Tell them they will have an opportunity to explain their design to the class, and their reasons for the selection of the article, color, pattern or design.

3. One member of each subgroup shows and explains the subgroup's design. All designs are posted after being described.

4. If you wish additional input, the class may discuss other uniforms, etc., or examine and discuss slides, pictures, etc.

5. General discussion. NOTE: Discussion is likely to change direction, involving students in a discussion of police, the military, etc. A decision should be made as to the goals of the session and what areas will be covered.

If the group is quite large, it may be better to handle it by fish-bowling, having an inner circle explain their design to the outer circle, and then reverse. The class may become restless if more than three subgroups are involved, and time may be limited. In this case, the discussion may be in subgroups.

The following questions may be considered:
—How and when does the wearing of special, identifiable clothing, accessories, jewelry, etc., aid in developing a feeling of "belonging"?—of being part of a cohesive, supportive community? When does it not? Why?
—Why was each garment or article chosen in the subgroup designs? What does it mean to the viewer?—what might it mean to the wearer? Is it suitable, in your mind? Would you have preferred something else? Does it serve a practical function other than to identify the wearer? Is this important?

Is its presence of contemporary value, or is it a reminder of a useful past?

—If you have ever been a hospital patient, have you sometimes mistaken one group of employees for another? Were you always sure who was a trained nurse? a student nurse? laboratory assistant? orderly? technician? physician? physical therapist? volunteer? Would you have preferred being able to tell? Why? Why have nurses usually worn white? Why do some now wear other colors? Why are male hospital nurses given armbands instead of caps? Operating room personnel often wear green (easier on the eyes, cuts down glare) instead of white —as a potential patient, does this matter to you? If you were a hospital employee, would it matter to you?

—Why have religious habits usually been black, dark blue, brown or white? Do you think it is a good thing that many religious no longer wear habits?

—Some apparel is passing out of fashion such as the shroud, headsman's hood, butcher's straw hat —what is coming in?

—Some apparel, originally intended as protective garb, now function primarily as status regulators or identifiers, such as the nurse's cap. Why are such things continued? What purposes do they serve? Whom do they help?

—If you wear or have worn a school uniform, are you glad or sorry? Did you like the school uniforms you have seen on others? Do you think school uniforms are a good idea? Does this apply to school blazers, sweaters, rings, athletic uniforms, band uniforms? Why? What are the good and bad points about students wearing uniforms?

—Why would someone want to wear a non-protective uniform or insignia? Why do many people wear green on St. Patrick's day? Is this like a uniform?

—Why does the wearing of such articles sometimes aid in developing a feeling of belonging to a group? Does a uniform ever operate against a sense of community among its wearers? Some young men say their long hair is a "badge of identity"—how? What does it say to them? to others who see them? Do you feel more a "member" when you wear identifying articles? Why? If you were to start a new organization, profession or institution would you want its members to have some mark of membership? Why? Have you ever worn an armband or a button in support of some person, cause or movement? Why? When you saw a stranger with the same button, how did you feel? Did you speak to him? Why?

—If the American Nazi Party offered its uniforms free to any student who would wear them to your school, plus $10.00 a day if the student kept the payment a secret, do you think any students would take up this offer? How would other students react to the sight of these uniforms? Would their wearers feel a sense of community?

VARIATIONS:

1. Instead of choosing a group for which they will design, subgroups are each given a description of a group or of a kind of people and asked to design a uniform or insignia for them. Or, a picture of a familiar uniform could be given to each group with instructions to design a completely new uniform to replace it.

2. Give each member of the class an envelope. These envelopes have been prepared as follows:

¼ are empty

¼ contain identical buttons with the same design

¼ contain identical buttons with a different design from the above

¼ contain assorted buttons which do not match each other or the above.

These envelopes are shuffled and distributed.

Tell the class, "Please open your envelopes, and if there is a button enclosed, wear it." The class is then asked to get up, move about, form subgroups, without being specifically told to use buttons as the means of group selection. They may talk to one another quietly, if you wish. When the groups are formed, if they have formed according to button design, they may sit together and discuss why they did so. If groups formed on some other basis, ask them to discuss this basis, and why buttons were not used as the basis. Either discussion could then continue into exploration of such questions as given in the exercise.

3. Each person is to write down as many groups as he can think of in two minutes who wear on one or more occasions a uniform or identifying insignia or jewelry. The lists are compared in subgroups, and discussion begins with exploration of reasons why the groups listed wear particular articles, which uniforms etc., are liked, which disliked, whether reasons are aesthetic, practical, ideological, etc. Discussion then continues as above.

4. Blank buttons in white or solid color are available in some local stores and wholesalers. Students may be given blank buttons at some point during the exercise and asked to design a button for the class, their subgroup, or some other group, using felt-tip markers. This may be done on an individual basis, and the products shared and discussed in the subgroups.

5. Blank buttons may be used as in "4" above, but this may be used as an exercise in consensus, with each small group agreeing on and producing a single design for their group. A theme may be offered, but if possible it is better if the group is allowed to decide upon its own theme.

SUGGESTED RESOURCES:

Nat Hentoff, "Why Students Want Their Constitutional Rights," *SATURDAY REVIEW OF LITERATURE,* May 22, 1971, pp. 61-62. This article contains information on the 1969 Supreme Court decision on the armband as "symbolic speech" in the *TINKER* case, on *BURNSIDE V. BYARS* (1966) in U. S. Court of Appeals for Fifth Circuit concerning the "Freedom Now" buttons, and the 1970 case in the U. S. Court of Appeals for the Seventh Circuit *(CREWS V. CLONCS, 1969)* concerning rights of the long-haired student.

COMMUNICATION AND POSITION CHANGE

PURPOSE:

To examine the discussion behavior of a group as it is affected by changes in physical positioning.

COMMENT:

When other variables in the physical environment are held constant, but group members change their "seating" arrangements so that individual position, spatial relationships and physical position in the group change, noticeable changes may occur in such group operations as participation patterns, communication level, procedure, norms and content of the discussion.

GROUP SIZE:

5—15. May be used with a larger group if assistant leadership is available for subgrouping.

TIME SUGGESTED:

One to two hours

GENERAL DIRECTIONS:

This exercise may be introduced unexpectedly or may be planned for by the group if additional materials are needed. It may be introduced early in a group's life, and may be used as one of their first experiences in "process discussion."

The particular changes to be made and the times at which they are to be made should be selected by the Leader. It is possible that group members may begin to make other suggested changes, and these should be accepted if possible, but the pace at which changes are made should not be increased. After each of these changes, or after several of them, the group should shift temporarily to a "process discussion" (see Step No. 3) and talk about what effects, if any, their change in position made on their group and its discussion.

MATERIALS REQUIRED:

1. More floor space may be required for this exercise than is normally occupied by the group, but by pushing unused furniture to the walls most rooms will be quite adequate. In addition to the usual chairs, which must be movable, a reasonably clean rug or carpet will help. If this is not available, the floor area to be used may be swept clean before the group meets.

2. Discussion materials: The discussion content may be based on an issue, problem or subject which arose in a previous discussion, proved of interest, but for which time for adequate exploration was not available. A new topic of known interest may be used, for which the group has had some preparation or for which a brief presentation has been made at the beginning of the session prior to the start of the exercise. If necessary, it is possible for the group members to have a book or paper in their hands during most, but not all, of this discussion time. A discussion in which frequent reference must be made to projected slides, chalkboard material, or posted or displayed materials would not be suitable.

PROCEDURE:

1. The group starts discussing a topic of general interest seated in usual way, with the Leader seated among them, facilitating the discussion by his questions.

2. After discussing for 10—15 minutes, the Leader recommends a change in position, moving himself into the new situation. Changes should be made as quickly and easily as possible, and the new position tried for another 10—15 minutes to allow any possible effects to be noticed. The following possibilities may be tried:

—a group which normally sits in chairs around a table may abandon the table, but remain seated in the same positions

—a group seated in chairs may pull their chairs very close together, even squeezing together so that knees are touching

—a group seated in chairs may stand in the same locations in which they have been sitting

—the group may move and sit on the floor in the same relative position

—the group may sit on the floor spacing themselves further apart or closer together

—the group may stand, pushing close to-

gether so that shoulders are touching

—the group may stand facing outward, in a tight circle with backs touching

—the group may kneel, facing each other

—the kneeling group may pull in closer, placing their hands on one another's shoulders, or holding hands

—the group, seated on the floor, may face outward, sitting back to back in a tight circle

—the group may lie prone, forming the spokes of a wheel, with their heads close together

—the group may lie on their backs, forming the spokes of a wheel, with their feet touching

—during any of the above position changes, the Leader may recommend that several people in the group trade their relative position in the circle.

3. After each of these changes, or after several of them, the group should shift to process discussion. The Leader may assist the group with questions such as the following:

Which position tried seemed to elicit the most laughter? Why?

Which position seemed to provide the "best" discussion? Why?

When did you feel most comfortable? least comfortable? why?

Did some people talk more than usual this time? less than usual? why?

Did some people refuse to change their position? why? how did the rest of the group accept this? why?

Was there a change in "who talks to whom"? why?

Did the quality or content of the discussion change in any way? how?

4. The Leader may find that his own tendency will be to change his style or manner of leadership in some way as he moves with the group. He, too, should reflect on the experience and express his feelings and ideas as to what he notices about this, why this happened.

5. If desired, the discussion may be continued by thinking about other "discussion" situations in the broad sense of the term, and how they are affected by seating arrangements, physical arrangement of the group, and physical positioning of the Leader in relation to group.

VARIATIONS:

1. One or two members may be asked to serve the group as Observers, remaining outside the group during the discussion proper, and rejoining it during the "process discussions." Particularly in a "new" group, Observers should be asked to make general observations about the group and "what happened,"

without referring to people by name.

   2. Instead of performing all the variations on the basis of a circle pattern, single or multiple row patterns may be introduced, with many of the above variations introduced.

SUGGESTED RESOURCES:

   In preparation for this exercise, the Leader may wish to read some background material concerned with social space and nonverbal communication, such as: Argyle, Michael, *THE PSYCHOLOGY OF INTERPERSONAL BEHAVIOUR*, Baltimore, Md.: Penguin Books, 1967, pp. 32-37; 80-82; 105-116. Birdwhistell, Ray L., *KINESICS AND CONTEXT: ESSAYS ON BODY MOTION COMMUNICATION*, Philadelphia, Pa.: University of Pennsylvania Press, 1970, pp. 180-190. Goffman, Erving, *INTERACTION RITUAL: ESSAYS ON FACE-TO-FACE BEHAVIOR*, Garden City, N.Y.: Doubleday & Co., 1967, pp. 33-40; 64-75; 90-95; 97-136. Goffman, Erving, *STRATEGIC INTERACTION*, Philadelphia, Pa.: University of Pennsylvania Press, 1969, pp. 31-36. Hall, Edward T., *THE SILENT LANGUAGE*, Greenwich, Conn.: Fawcett Premier, 1959, pp. 146-168. Hall, Edward T., *THE HIDDEN DIMENSION*, Garden City, N.Y.: Doubleday Anchor, 1966.

   See also: "Life; Touch: Social Space" exercise.

GRAPHOLOGY

PURPOSE:

To look at handwriting as paralinguistic communication, as an expression of the person, and to examine a "fringe" science, our reactions to it, and to "science" as a guide in life.

COMMENT:

At one time much despised as superstitious nonsense, enjoying great popularity as a parlor game in the late 1920's, graphology, or the analysis of personality by handwriting, has recently grown to greater respectability first in Europe and then in the United States. It is now used by many firms in making decisions about employment, promotion and transfer of personnel. Whether or not such analyses are accurate measures of personality or character, handwriting is accepted by most psychologists and psychoanalysts as being in some way an expression of the personality, though not all agree that we know how to decipher this code. Handwriting is one of the ways in which our body functions in communication, and carries with it more of the individual than, for instance, the typewritten message.

GROUP SIZE:

Up to 25

TIME SUGGESTED:

2 sessions of 50—60 minutes

GENERAL DIRECTIONS:

Depending on materials and personnel available, students can begin their investigation of this subject through listening to a lecture or doing individual reports, or by using a popular text for laymen to examine their own handwriting. They discuss ideas, findings and feelings about the subject and about science. Sessions are interchangeable.

MATERIALS REQUIRED:

A qualified speaker (or several students report on the subject).

Using a book such as Meyer's in "Suggested Resources," "A" through "F" scales may be reproduced on tracing paper, plastic overlays, etc. Students may use any previously written material of at least fifty words written on unlined paper. For these simpler scales, it does not matter if a ball point pen is the writing instrument. If desired, only one set of scales may be prepared per subgroup, letting groups take turns in this activity.

PROCEDURE:

SESSION I.

1. Contact the personnel departments of large local firms and ask if someone can speak to the class on this subject. If they do not use graphology, ask them if they would care to tell you why, or if they could suggest another company that does use this as part of their personnel work. Students should be able to make these inquiries through parents or other adults they know, or they can approach a company "cold." It may be that a company has its own graphologist, who might speak with the class.

2. Students can discuss in small groups their reactions to the talk, or a plenary may be held with the entire class. Such questions as following may be examined:

—Do you believe what the speaker said? Why? Do you think that the use of graphology is "good for man"? . . . "bad for man"? . . . "neutral"?

—Can a science be "bad"? Do you think graphology is a science? Should it be taught in school? Why? How should a school decide what is "scientific knowledge," and therefore worth including in a curriculum? Should knowledge which is not "scientific" be taught in schools? What is "special" about science, if anything?

—Would you like to be a graphologist? Why? Would you like to learn more about the subject? Do you think it differs from phrenology, for instance, or palmistry? How? Would you want to be hired for a job on the basis of a graphologist's report? Would you want to choose your friends in this way?

SESSION II.

1. Working with a simple book on graphology or material prepared as suggested in "Materials Required," students make some initial determinations about their own handwriting. This will be less threatening to them than having others examine their handwriting in this way.

2. In subgroups, students share their feelings about this exercise, and those findings which they wish to discuss with others. IT IS IMPORTANT TO STRESS THAT PEOPLE SHOULD BE ENCOURAGED TO MAKE WHATEVER STATE-

MENTS OR JUDGMENTS THEY WISH ABOUT THE EXPERIENCE, AND *NOT* REQUIRED TO REVEAL ANYTHING ABOUT THEMSELVES OR THEIR HANDWRITING UNLESS THEY WISH TO DO SO.

3. Read aloud some material on the subject, such as that in the "Suggested Resources." Discuss it in light of their previous experiences and findings. Re-examine some of the questions suggested in Step No. 2, Session I.

VARIATIONS:

1. If it is not feasible to have a graphologist or psychologist talk to the class, perhaps some students would like to make reports to the class on the subject, using some of the suggested resources or others of their own choosing. Your school librarian may be of assistance. Remind the students to identify the sources of their information and explain why they selected these particular sources. This is part of the exercise—to investigate how we decide to believe one source of communication, or one "authority" rather than another. They may wish to illustrate their reports using an opaque overhead projector, plastic sheets in a non-opaque overhead one, or photographed slides or filmstrips of their own making.

2. If it is felt that harmful information or misinformation may result from the procedure as outlined in Session II, give the students samples of the handwriting of famous (or infamous!) people, photographically reproduced from various books, to use for their "handwriting analysis."

3. Some students may have been studying the subject on their own, and might be glad of an opportunity to address the class on this subject and demonstrate their skills. If the class is interested, these "student experts" might be willing to analyze the handwriting of several volunteers. In general, unless the information is made public to the rest of the class, students will feel little threat from the analysis of a student, and can be asked to share with the class only a few pieces of information at their own discretion. The "student expert" might be willing to provide the class with materials so that each student could analyze his own handwriting, as in Session II above.

SUGGESTED RESOURCES:

Jerome S. Meyer, *THE HANDWRITING ANALYZER,* New York: Simon and Schuster, 1927, 1953, pp. 25-36; 57-70.

Klara G. Roman, *HANDWRITING: A KEY TO PERSONALITY,* New York: Pantheon, 1952.

Eric Berne, *A LAYMAN'S GUIDE TO PSYCHIATRY AND PSYCHOANALYSIS,* 3rd ed., New York: Simon and Schuster, p. 362.

Corbett H. Thigpen and Hervey Cleckley, "A Case of Multiple Personality," *BASIC CONTRIBUTIONS TO PSYCHOLOGY: READINGS,* ed., Robert L. Wrenn, Belmont, California: Wadsworth Pub., 1966, pp. 221-231; abridged from C. H. Thigpen and H. Cleckley, "A Case of Multiple Personality," *JOURNAL OF ABNORMAL AND SOCIAL PSYCHOLOGY,* 49 (1954), 136-149.

James A. Brussel, George La F. Cantzlaar, *THE LAYMAN'S DICTIONARY OF PSYCHIATRY,* New York: Barnes & Noble, 1967, p. 101.

PARAVERBAL— "HARRY"

PURPOSE:

To examine our accuracy in conveying and understanding paraverbal communication.

COMMENT:

Much of the reliability of our communication depends upon our ability to interpret or decode the meanings intended by those speaking to us, and much of this meaning is conveyed by nonverbal or paraverbal means, such as facial expression, bodily position, voice pitch and tone. When we speak, our brain supplies the word, but most of our body is involved in conveying it to others.

GROUP SIZE:

6—20

TIME SUGGESTED:

20 minutes to two or more sessions of 45—60 minutes.

GENERAL DIRECTIONS:

A volunteer speaks a single word, "Harry," in a variety of ways, attempting to convey different feelings or emotions. The group tries to interpret these, and then checks their accuracy against the interpretations of others and against the speaker's intentions.

It should be noted that this is *not* role playing, but a form of "acting" or "dramatization," and is more difficult for the Speaker (actor). A group in which some of the members are interested in acting or in the theater in general may find this exercise of particular interest if this is pointed out, and if the selections in "Suggested Resources" are read to them or recommended for reading in advance of the class. It is possible to try the exercise once without this preliminary instruction, and then spend some time discussing acting "methods." Repeat the exercise following the discussion.

MATERIALS REQUIRED:

supply of "tally sheets" for class members.
supply of "Speaker's" sheets for all Speakers.
A Speaker's sheet should look something like this:

"You are to say the single word, "Harry" about once every five seconds, trying to express the following emotions or feelings, in the order given. You may use any facial expression, body posture, gesture, or voice tone you believe suitable to convey the meaning. Do *not* announce the emotion you are conveying."

1. distaste
2. joy
3. pleased surprise
4. anger
5. simple greeting
6. uncertain recognition
7. worry
8. mock annoyance
9. fear
10. disbelief
11. pleading
12. firm conviction

Tally sheets consist of a column of numbered lines and another column of the list of words on the Speaker's sheet, in scrambled order (e.g., 10, 7, 9, 3, 8, 2, 1, 4, 6, 5, 12, 11). Do not number the words on the tally sheets.

You retain a copy of each Speaker's sheet. See also step No. 5 below.

PROCEDURE:

1. You may ask for a volunteer, or ask someone you know likes to act to be the "Speaker." Tally sheets are distributed to the rest of the class, and they are told that, as in a "matching test," they are to write down one of the words on their descriptive list each time the Speaker says the word, "Harry." If in doubt, they may' write two words or phrases per line, but no more.

2. The Speaker goes down his list, pausing to allow the group to find and write the word they believe suitable.

3. Chart all interpretations from the tallies on chalkboard. Each individual checks the "correctness" of his own list in comparison with the majority decision on each line. This gives the Speaker some indication of his paraverbal communication ability, and listeners an indication of how they compare with others in "decoding"—interpretation of signals from a Speaker.

4. The Speaker's actual list-order is put on the board.

5. The exercise may be repeated with another Speaker using a second Speaker's sheet, varying the order (e.g., 10, 11, 7, 3, 5, 12, 9, 6, 2, 4, 1, 8). Listeners receive another tally sheet, or more than one may be reproduced on their original sheet.

6. The class may wish to prepare another list, using different "feelings." They may write this directly on the chalkboard. The Speaker copies, scrambling the order.

7. General discussion of "cues" used in making decisions in decoding. Which cues helped the most? How could the Speaker have more clearly conveyed his meaning? Which cues were most easily misinterpreted? The class may be interested in knowing that this is a training exercise used by some schools for actors.

VARIATIONS:

1. Two Speakers may be used simultaneously after the group has tried the exercise with one Speaker. This is a vaudeville act which they may have seen on TV. Two Speakers' lists may be prepared in such a way as to logically correlate some of the emotions, as in the vaudeville act, or they may be illogically arranged, grouping strong emotions together and weak emotions together. Another way to use two Speakers is to give them identical lists, without informing the listeners. The Speakers, of course, alternate, whichever variation is used.

2. The exercise may be repeated with more serious examination of each expression. Instead of continuing after the five-second pause, the Speaker stops until the group has a chance to discuss what they felt he was expressing, what cues they used in making the decision, and then to check with the Speaker. This provides a much richer experience for those interested in improving nonverbal ability, and can be very helpful for those interested in acting or public speaking. It provides useful feedback as to how their "effects" come across.

3. The following quotations are reproduced on tally sheets for the listeners, and as before, in scrambled order on the Speaker's sheet. The procedure is as in the original exercise, still using "Harry" or some other single word in place of the quotation, but the word may be repeated 3—4 times, if the Speaker thinks this would be helpful, for each quotation. The Speaker follows the "intention" as described in the quotation.

1. John Cheever, THE WAPSHOT CHRONICLE, ch. 7: "He had that spooky bass voice meant to announce that he had entered the kingdom of manhood, but Rosalie knew that he was still outside the gates."

2. Henry Fielding, TOM JONES, Bk. XVI, ch. 5: "He speaks all his words distinctly, half as loud again as the other. Anybody may see he is an actor."

3. F. Scott Fitzgerald, THE GREAT GATSBY, ch. 6: "Her voice is full of money."

4. O. Henry (W. S. Porter), THE DEFEAT OF THE CITY: "There was always something in her voice that made you think of lorgnettes, of accounts at Tiffany's, of sledges smoothly gliding on the trail from Dawson to Forty Mile, of the tinkling of pendant prisms on your grandmother's chandeliers, of snow lying on a convent roof; of a police sergeant refusing bail."

5. John Keats, THE FALL OF HYPERION, I, 162: "They seek . . . /No music but a happy-noted voice."

6. George Linley, POEMS: "Ever of Thee": "Thy gentle voice my spirit can cheer."

7. Dorothy Parker, DUSK BEFORE FIRE-WORKS: "His voice was intimate as the rustle of sheets, and he kissed easily."

8. William Shakespeare, MUCH ADO ABOUT NOTHING, II, 1: "Speak low, if you speak love."

9. Shakespeare, THE MERRY WIVES OF WINDSOR, I, 1: "She . . . speaks small like a woman."

10. Shakespeare, ROMEO AND JULIET, II, 1: "How silver-sweet sound lovers' tongues by night, /Like softest music to attending ears!"

11. Shakespeare, HAMLET, II, 2: ". . . this player . . . /Tears in his eyes, distraction in 's aspect,/a broken voice."

12. Shakespeare, KING LEAR, V, 3: "Her voice was ever soft,/gentle and low, an excellent thing in woman."

13. Shakespeare, AS YOU LIKE IT, II, 7: ". . . the whining schoolboy, . . /then the lover/Sighing like furnace, with a woeful ballad/ Made to his mistress' eyebrow . . . /The sixth age . . . his big manly voice,/Turning again toward childish treble, pipes / And whistles in his sound."

14. Logan Pearsall Smith, ALL TRIVIA:

"What is more enchanting than the voices of young people, when you can't hear what they say?"

15. Rex Stout, *THREE WITNESSES*, "Die Like a Dog," III: " 'I'll discuss it with you,' she said, in a voice that could have been used to defrost her refrigerator."

16. Rex Stout, *HOMICIDE TRINITY*, "Death of a Demon"; "Handshakes can be faked and usually are, but smiles can't. It isn't often that a man gets a natural, friendly, straightforward smile from a young woman, with no come on, no catch, and no dare, and the least he can do is return it if he has that kind in stock."

17. Igor Stravinsky and Robert Craft, *CONVERSATIONS WITH IGOR STRAVINSKY*: "Rachmaninov's immortalizing totality was his scowl. He was a six-and-a-half-foot-tall scowl."

18. Alfred, Lord Tennyson, *MAUD*, Pt. I, V, 2: "Maud with her . . . wild voice pealing up to the sunny sky."

19. Lewis Carroll (Charles Lutwidge Dodgson), *ALICE IN WONDERLAND,* ch. 6: "Speak roughly to your little boy . . ."

SUGGESTED RESOURCES:

American Medical Association, "The Muscles of Expression" (illus.), *THE WONDERFUL HUMAN MACHINE,* A.M.A., Chicago, Ill.: 1970, p. 13.

Argyle, Michael, *THE PSYCHOLOGY OF INTERPERSONAL BEHAVIOUR*, Baltimore, Md., Penguin, 1967, pp. 37-38; 81; 84.

Cole, Toby (ed.), *ACTING: A HANDBOOK OF THE STANISLAVSKI METHOD,* rev. ed., New York: Bonanza Books, 1971. Especially pp. 34-36; 52-55.

Coleman, James C., "Facial Expressions of Emotion," *PSYCHOLOGICAL MONOGRAPHS,* Vol. 63, No. 1, 1949. Some useful material from this is included in George A. Lundberg *et al., SOCIOLOGY,* 3rd ed., New York: Harper & Row, 1963, p. 214.

Sapir, Edward, "Communication," *READER IN PUBLIC OPINION AND COMMUNICATION,* 2nd ed., Bernard Berelson and Morris Janowitz, (eds.), New York: The Free Press, Collier-Macmillan, 1966; reprinted from *ENCYCLOPEDIA OF THE SOCIAL SCIENCES,* Edwin R. Seligman, (ed.), Vol. IV, New York: Macmillan, 1931, pp. 78-80.

VOICE AND INTELLIGIBILITY

PURPOSE:

To explore ways to: (a) increase control of the voice, mouth movements; (b) develop concentration; (c) loosen up with humorous exercises in speaking.

COMMENT:

There are times when it does not matter whether or not our words are understood. A good deal of our daily verbal interchange is at such a primitive level that, as long as our gestures, facial expressions and voice tone remain appropriate, we could speak to others in a foreign language and the same meaning would be conveyed. We agree, disagree, say "hello," "goodbye," and exchange pleasantries about the weather. These are communications of friendly intent rather than of information. We point or nod to something we want on the dinner table as we ask for it, or hand the salesperson the article we wish to purchase. If we do not hand him the money at the same time, he will interpret almost any garbled sound as "How much is this?", and give us the answer. There are even times when we hope our spoken words will not be clearly understood. For instance, if I am asked a question, do not know the answer but do not wish to admit it, I may either quite clearly and distinctly give an ambiguous answer, hoping the matter will end there, or I may mutter or slur the sound of my words, hoping the questioner will somehow extract a satisfactory reply.

However, not all of life will support communication at this level without grave problems. When we move beyond this sort of thing, understandable speech acquires importance. We want people to understand both our words and the intention behind them. The "Harry" exercise may have demonstrated that we can convey a good deal of irritation, for instance, without "speech." But we sometimes want to explain the reason for our irritation or recommend changed behavior in others to lessen it. Then we need words.

Beyond content, intelligibility requires appropriate loudness, syllable duration and distinctness. Pronunciation varies with locality and group, but distinctness includes pronunciation quickly understandable in that group. Substandard pronunciation may confuse the hearer. The pronunciation used on the local radio and TV station is often a better guide than the dictionary. Appropriate loudness varies with both distance and accompanying noise. Syllable duration may need to vary both with content and those factors affecting loudness requirements. The jaw, the tongue, the lips must all work well for us, as must the voice box and the lungs.

GROUP SIZE:

6—25

TIME:

One or more 30 minute sessions. NOTE: Portions of this exercise may be used in 10 minute segments at various times, if desired.

GENERAL DIRECTIONS:

Tongue-twisters and maxims are repeated by class members individually and in concert. Students experiment with reading lists of words to others under various conditions, striving for intelligibility. Tape records and microphones may also be used.

MATERIALS REQUIRED:

SESSION I:
   None

SESSION II:
   Word lists

SESSION III:
   Tape recorders, microphone and amplifier, absorbent cotton to use as ear-stops

PROCEDURE:

1. Individuals take turns repeating tongue twisters. The class may contribute ones they know for use. Following are a few suggestions:

   a. Rubber baby-buggy bumpers.

   b. National Shropshire Sheep Association.

   c. He sawed six long, slim, sleek, slender saplings.

d. She sells sea shells on the seashore.

e. Big black bugs bleed blood.

f. "Are you copper-bottoming them, my man?" "No, I'm aluminuming 'em, mum."

g. "B-A, Ba; B-E, Be; Ba Be;
B-I, Bi; Ba Be Bi;
B-O, Bo; Ba Be Bi Bo;
B-U, Bu; Ba Be Bi Bo Bu!"

2. Using the following maxims, or similar ones, take one line at a time and have the entire class repeat it after you. Keep repeating over and over, each time encouraging the class to speak *louder.* As you do so, express yourself with hand movements, demonstrating and encouraging the class to imitate you, as indicated below.

a. "I am only one
(point to self)

But I am one
(hands outstretched)

I can't do everything
(point out and upward)

But I can do something
(wave hand in emphatic movement)

What I can do I will Do."*
(emphasize: hammer right fist in open left hand)
*Edward Everett Hale (1822-1909): A maxim written for the "Lend-a-Hand Society."

b. "I cannot lose. Why?
I'll tell you why.
Because I have faith,
courage and enthusiasm."
Gabriel Richard Institute

SESSION II

1. Copies of the following word lists are prepared for each member of the class. An additional copy is made and cut apart so that one copy of each separate group of 16 words may be given, one at a time, to the Speakers.

2. Begin by giving the first Speaker one of the cut-apart list sections, such as "A". Ask him to read the first four words consecutively, then to allow a long pause for the rest of the class to write down the four words as they heard them—no repeats are allowed. After the pause he reads the next four, etc.

3. When all twenty Speakers have been heard, distribute the complete set of word lists to each student, who then checks and adds the number of words correctly understood. To obtain the Speaker's intelligibility score add together the number of words correctly understood by each listener and di-

vide this total by the number of listeners times 16 (the number of words spoken).

4. If desired, this test may be repeated varying the conditions of noise. You may introduce background noise by having one or more students read aloud from a book while the test is being carried on, or play a record in the room at the same time, or have students stuff their ears with cotton to simulate greater distance from the Speaker. This test was used by Gayland L. Draegert on military personnel who averaged 38.2% of the words understood correctly before training and 46.3% after training. The experiment was reported in SPEECH MONOGRAPHS, Vol. 13, No. 2, p. 50ff.

WORD LISTS FOR INTELLIGIBILITY

A. Three, flap, switch, will—resume, cold, pilot, wind—chase, blue, search, flight—mine, area, cleared, left.

B. Iron, fire, task, try—up, six, seven, wait—slip, turn, read, clear—blue, this, even, is.

C. Nan, flak, timer, two—course, black, when, leave—raise, clear, tree, seven—search, strike, there, cover.

D. List, service, ten, foul—wire, last, wish, truce—power, one, ease, will—teeth, hobby, trill, wind.

E. Flight, spray, blind, base—ground, fog, ceiling, flame—target, flare, gear, low—slow, course, code, scout.

F. Tall, plot, find, deep—climb, fall, each, believe—wing, strip, clean, field—when, chase, search, select.

G. Climb, switch, over, when—this, turn, gear, spray—black, flare, is, free—runway, three, off, red.

H. Thing, touch, marker, sleeve—find, top, leave, winter—skip, free, have, beach—meet, aid, send, lash.

I. Try, over, six, craft—green, victor, yellow, out—trim, X ray, ramp, up—speed, like, believe, sender.

J. Dim, trip, fire, marker—wave, green, rudder, field—climb, to, plot, middle—speed, like, straight, lower.

K. Smooth, mike, four, catch—strip, park, line, left—leg, wheel, turn, lift—time, baker, orange, look.

L. Wake, other, blue, been—size, wish, black, under—field, down, empty, what—ship, strip, land, fire.

M. Leg, on, strip, leave—ground, trip, plot, area—speed, blue, will, ramp—wheel, blind, sector, Nan.

N. Tail, when, through, at—climb, off, tower, rain—time, gear, cloud, pass—loaf, three, crash, direction.

O. Station, left, reply, read—final, blue, field, out—wind, west, marker, fire—tower, ground, gear, time.

P. Sighted, toward, finder, search—red, blind, each, weather—tall, after, while, wide—close, hole, mark, signal.

Q. Neat, warm, beam, where—side, leader, bell, map—view, face, trap, well—seem, feed, clutch, vine.

R. Circle, beach, up, that—port, even, catch, pad—reach, heat, break, safe—still, put, enter, iron.

S. Chamber, wait, hair, open—wind, keep, sector, free—light, home, take, will—base, eleven, headphone, by.

T. Service, flat, have, on—bay, wait, fade, cold—tire, horn, bill, sad—feel, cave, set, limit.

SESSION III

1. Reproduce the word lists given below and distribute one copy of the complete set to each student at the beginning of the session. This exercise may be carried on in a number of ways. If you have a microphone and amplifier, place the amplifier near the front of the room and the student with the microphone at the back of the room with his back to the class. If you wish to use a tape recorder the student speaks into the tape recorder. In both cases the Speaker checks the word he is saying on his sheet while the listeners check the word they believe he is saying on their individual sheets. In the case of the tape recorder method, the recording Speaker then has an opportunity to listen to his own tape, at a later time, and to write down the words he thinks he is hearing. These lists are taken from standardized tests designed by C. Hess Hagen and published in *INTELLIGIBILITY MEASUREMENT: TWENTY FOUR-WORD MULTIPLE CHOICE TESTS,* OSRD Report No. 5567 (P.B. 12050), Office of Technical Services, Department of Commerce, p. 21. It has been found that when there is noise interference it is difficult to distinguish these words from others in their foursome.

2. The student announces which column or which row he will read from. He then selects and reads one word from each foursome in that column or row, pausing after each word to allow listeners to check the word they believe they are hearing.

SUGGESTED RESOURCES:

Monroe, Alan H., PRINCIPLES AND TYPES OF SPEECH, 5th ed., Chicago, Ill.: Scott, Foresman and Co., 1962, chs. 3-6.

Davis, Hallowell, HEARING AND DEAFNESS, New York: Murray Hill Books, 1947, pp. 475-476 gives additional word lists used by the Psycho-Acoustic Laboratory of Harvard University.

Hagen, C. Hess, OSRD Report No. 5414, Office of Technical Services, Department of Commerce, describes another test which may be adapted for classroom use.

Similar materials may often be found in current issues of the following periodicals: *SPEECH MONOGRAPHS,* the *QUARTERLY JOURNAL OF SPEECH,* the *SPEECH TEACHER,* the *JOURNAL OF SPEECH AND HEARING DISORDER,* and the *JOURNAL OF SPEECH AND HEARING RESEARCH.*

MULTIPLE CHOICE TESTS FOR INTELLIGIBILITY MEASUREMENT

	A	B	C	D	E	F
1	system	firm	banner	puddle	carve	offer
	pistol	foam	manner	muddle	car	author
	distant	burn	mother	muzzle	tarred	often
	piston	term	batter	puzzle	tired	office
2	heave	detain	cream	porch	fable	cross
	heed	obtain	screen	torch	stable	cough
	ease	attain	green	scorch	table	cloth
	eve	maintain	stream	court	able	claw
3	Roger	pure	petal	vision	bubble	thrown
	rupture	poor	battle	bishop	tumble	drone
	rapture	tour	meadow	vicious	stumble	prone
	obscure	two	medal	season	fumble	groan
4	art	sponsor	game	cape	texture	eye
	heart	spotter	gain	hate	lecture	high
	arch	ponder	gage	take	mixture	tie
	ark	plunder	gang	tape	rupture	hide
5	comment	exact	made	process	glow	single
	comic	retract	fade	protest	blow	jingle
	cannon	detract	vague	profess	below	cycle
	carbon	attack	may	possess	low	sprinkle
6	bumper	cave	pier	divide	kitchen	baker
	number	cake	pierce	devise	mission	major
	lumber	cage	fierce	define	friction	banker
	lover	case	spear	divine	fiction	maker
7	gale	glamour	ward	leap	second	rich
	jail	slimmer	wart	leaf	suction	ridge
	dale	swimmer	wash	lease	section	bridge
	bail	glimmer	war	leave	sexton	grip
8	danger	enact	hold	crater	seaport	joy
	feature	impact	old	traitor	keyboard	going
	nature	relax	ode	trainer	piecework	join
	major	intact	hoed	treasure	eastward	dawn

PARAVERBAL AND SILENT COMMUNICATION

PURPOSE:

To improve our ability to use our whole body freely and expressively in communication.

COMMENT:

In his book, *THE HIDDEN DIMENSION,* Edward T. Hall says, "It is essential that we learn to read the silent communications as easily as the printed ones. Only by doing so can we also reach other people . . . as we are increasingly required to do" (p. 6). Ray L. Birdwhistell says, ". . . (B)ody motion and spoken 'languages' do not constitute independent systems at the level of communication. By a logic, not yet known, they are interinfluencing and probably interdependent" *(KINESICS AND CONTEXT).* As with many findings of the sciences of man, the poets said something about these matters first. In *TROILUS AND CRESSIDA,* IV, 5, Shakespeare says, "There's language in her eye, her cheek, her lip,/Nay, her foot speaks; her wanton spirits look out/At every joint and motive of her body."

GROUP SIZE:

Up to 20

TIME SUGGESTED:

45—60 minutes. Portions of this exercise may be done independently.

GENERAL DIRECTIONS:

The students perform special exercises to relax the head and neck muscles, others to limber up the hands, arms, shoulders and torso, and begin to combine "speech" with these. Students react to assigned "situations," using body movements including facial expression and gesture. Brief sentences are repeated expressing various emotions, noting pitch, stress, etc.

MATERIALS REQUIRED:

Lists of "situations" for Step No. 3 may be prepared for distribution, if desired, or these may be read to the students or written on newsprint or chalkboard.

PROCEDURE:

1. Exercises to relax and stimulate the head and neck muscles:
   a. Sit in a comfortable position, back comfortably straight, both feet on floor.
   b. Gently lower your head until your chin touches your chest. Swing your head slowly from side to side, as an elephant swings its trunk. Do not "lead with your chin"—think of motion as beginning at the back of the neck, just below your head.
   c. Let swinging slowly subside.
   d. Let your head flop gently back—your mouth will open slightly.
   e. Gently turn your head as though to look over your shoulder, bringing your chin down to touch your shoulder on the left side.
   f. Push a little harder, forcing your head around as far as it can go.
   g. Reverse procedure "e" to look over your right shoulder, finishing with a push as in "f".
   h. Lie down, let your head roll gently back and forth on the mat—do not lift your head or shoulders from the mat. Do this slowly.
   i. Stop and let your jaw drop.
   j. Sit up and do yoga "lion stretch": lean your head slightly forward, opening your eyes very wide.
   k. Now, open your mouth, stick out your tongue, tensing the muscles of your face and neck. Be very fierce! Hold this position at least 15 to 30 seconds.
   l. Slowly, slowly—relax your muscles, allow your face to subside to a comfortable, relaxed expression.

2. Exercises to limber up the head, arm and shoulder muscles:
   a. Stand up, hold your arms away from the sides of your body about 12—18 inches.

Pretend that you have something stuck to your hands that you are trying to shake off —milkweed plumes, contact tape or whatever. Shake your hands and arms hard, being as free and energetic as possible. Gradually let one arm relax at your side while continuing to shake the other. As you do this, repeat a nonsense phrase, such as "Apple babbit," or a tongue twister such as "Put the bitter pat of butter in the bottle," or "Abel Rable the rabble rouser," or a jump rope rhyme such as "One two, buckle my shoe,/Three four, shut the door, /Five six pick up sticks, /Seven eight, lay them straight, /Nine ten, a big fat hen."

b. After a minute or two, switch to reciting the alphabet, continuing the arm shaking, but beginning to use the relaxed arm to gesture with. Recite the alphabet with feeling and expression, as though you were arguing with a friend or trying to persuade someone to do something. Be increasingly vigorous in your gestures. Now bring the formerly "shaking" arm into action in this conversation. Exaggerate your gestures.

c. Continue your persuasive recitation, but join a partner. Both of you continue simultaneously to gesture and argue, facing one another, and using only the alphabet as your speech.

3. React physically to the following situations. If you want to react verbally also, you may do so. This part of the exercise may be done by one person at a time in front of the class, or in subgroups, taking turns.

a. Someone approaches you with a mug of hot coffee. They drop the cup in such a way that it spills in your direction.

b. You receive a telephone call telling you that you have won $1,000.00 in the supermarket "sweepstakes."

c. You are walking along the pavement and someone behind you shouts, "Watch out!"

d. At a folk festival you are surprised to see your best friend in the middle of a dense crowd. You try to attract his attention.

e. You are standing on a dock and see a large motorboat about to run into a small rowboat. You try to signal the motorboat to turn.

f. Your mother walks into the room just as you accidentally smash her favorite lamp.

g. At a party you realize a friend opposite you is giving away a secret. You try to stop him without letting others know what you are doing.

h. You just made a nasty remark about an acquaintance, not realizing he is standing behind you, whereupon he says, "Hello."

4. Using the sentence, "I hate you," the Speaker tries to express a range of specific feelings or emotions by pitch, stress (loudness) and juncture (the rise or fall, together with the elongation of sound commonly found at the end of a sentence or before a pause). He tries to show his feeling in his facial expression and in any movement of the head, but he may not use his hands or arms. Emotions are: (a) hate; (b) love; (c) surprise and disagreement; (d) teasing; (e) fear; (f) total disagreement or negation.

The listeners analyze the clues and try to chart them, using written descriptions or a pre-determined set of simple symbols to indicate the various factors. The following sample deals only with the sounds and breathing in several "tries," but eyes, mouth, forehead and chin may also be noted.

a. (Hate). Stress is on "hate." The pitch rises slightly on "hate" and falls slightly on "you." The stress on "you" is midway between that on "I" and on "hate." Considerable breath is expelled on "hate." If the palm of the hand is held about one inch from the Speaker's mouth as these phrases are uttered, the difference in breath quantity or force is noticeable. Moistening the palm increases the ability to detect differences.

b. (Love). The stress is on "hate," but the pitch starts slightly lower than on "I" and falls on the second half of word. On "you," the pitch starts lower than in "a" above, but rises slightly on the last part of word. The pitch is usually lower on "hate" than in "a".

c. (Surprise and disagreement). The stress is on "I" and "you," being slightly stronger on "you." The pitch is much higher on both these words than in "a" or "b", and rises sharply on the latter part of "you," as in typical interrogatory statement. More breath is used on "you" than on "hate."

d. (Teasing). This differs from "a" in that the pitch on "I" is higher than on "a" and falls on the first part of "you," but rises on the second part. There is noticeably less breath used on "hate."

e. (Fear). The pitch usually starts high and continues to rise to the end of the sentence. The stress is fairly equal throughout.

f. (Total disagreement or negation). The stress tends to be equal throughout, the pitch falling steadily from the beginning to the end of sentence.

SUGGESTED RESOURCES:

Birdwhistell, Ray L., *KINESICS AND CONTEXT*, Philadelphia, Pa.: University of Pennsylvania, 1970, pp. 128-130.

Gunther, Bernard, "Sensory Awakening and Relaxation," *WAYS OF GROWTH*, Herbert Otto and John Mann (eds.) New York: Viking Press, 1968, pp. 60-68.

Monroe, Alan H., *PRINCIPLES AND TYPES OF SPEECH*, 5th ed., Chicago, Ill.: Scott, Foresman and Co., 1962, chs. 3 and 5.

GIVING DIRECTIONS AND "SUCCESSFUL" COMMUNICATION

PURPOSE:

To examine nonverbal communication used in giving directions, and to explore the ways in which nonverbal behavior may contribute to the success of other kinds of communication.

COMMENT:

"People in direct association depend to a considerable degree upon gestures for communication. All physical movements or postures to which meaning is ascribed constitute this form of communication. Gestures range from the subtle raising of an eyebrow to the gross thrashing of the arms." (George A. Lundberg *et al.*, SOCIOLOGY, 3rd ed., New York: Harper & Row, 1963, p. 212.)

GROUP SIZE:

6—20

TIME SUGGESTED:

30—60 minutes

GENERAL DIRECTIONS:

Students try various ways of giving directions to a place, with and without nonverbal or paraverbal assistance. The implications of this are discussed. Students make lists of that day's attempts at communication and rate them as "successful" or "unsuccessful," and discuss possible ways in which nonverbal behavior might have improved the less successful encounters. Role playing may be used.

MATERIALS REQUIRED:

None

PROCEDURE:

Select several of the following experiments.

1. Ask two students to volunteer to demonstrate different ways of giving directions, or call on two students who will feel comfortable in this. Ask #1 to think of a place which #2 does not know—a park, store, the home of a friend or relative. Ask him to choose a place that is not too easy to find. He is to clasp his hands behind his back and give #2 directions for getting there by driving, walking, or public transportation. #2 may not ask questions or nod or shake his head to indicate understanding or lack of it.

2. Ask #2 to repeat the directions. If he has trouble, ask him what would help him most to understand the directions—gestures?—let #1 repeat the directions with gestures. A map?—let #1 draw a map on the chalkboard or a piece of paper. Would it help if #1 wrote them down for #2?—Let him do so.

3. Ask for two more volunteers to repeat the experiment with variations. This time let #1 select whatever means he wishes for giving the instructions, and #2 may question him at any point, or ask him to give the directions in a different way if he thinks it would be more helpful.

4. Ask four members of the class to leave the room while #1, in front of the group, explains the directions to #2 in any way he chooses. After #2 has received the directions, and destroyed the paper or erased the board if these were used, he calls in #3 and repeats the directions in front of the class, and so forth until #5 has received the directions. This is another use of the "Whisper Down the Lane" game. It can be a useful experience if discussed to determine some of the causes and cures of communication problems.

5. Number 1 and #2 stand back to back while the directions are given; #1 is not told that he may not use his hands, and #2 is told that he may not turn around until #1 has finished giving the directions; #1 then repeats the directions.

6. Number 2 is blindfolded while the directions are given. He may experience some low-level anxiety as to "what is going on" and be discomfited by laughter from the class which probably would not bother him if he were not blindfolded.

7. General discussion for 10—15 minutes on "What's the best way to give directions?" Explore the possibility that one person will understand directions better if given in one way, while another prefers them in a different form.

8. Now ask the students to take a minute or so to make a list of those people with whom they have talked since they got up this morning. Ask them to think about the relative "success" of these communication experiences, and put a plus beside those they consider successful and a minus beside those they feel were unsuccessful.

9. General discussion follows, focusing upon "How does nonverbal behavior improve the communication process?" Some of the following questions may be explored:

—In less successful communications, did you feel you were being understood? Did your message get through in the way you intended it? What sort of feedback did you get? Did it indicate agreement, disagreement, disapproval, acceptance, hostility . . . ?

—Do you believe you are best understood when you write something down for someone else to read?—Talk to someone on the telephone?—Talk to them in a group?—Talk to them on a one-to-one basis, in person?—Does it make a difference what kind of message you are trying to communicate?

—What kinds of nonverbal behavior might have improved your less successful communication attempts?—tone of voice?—facial expression?—touch?—gesture? . . .

—Do you think you were sufficiently aware of the nonverbal signals the other person was sending?

10. If desired, some of the unsuccessful communicative attempts may be role played with a view to finding ways in which they might have been improved. They may first be role played as they happened, and then with the changes suggested by the class.

ALTER EGO

PURPOSE:

To increase awareness of "hidden" feelings in persons and groups.

COMMENTS:

Committee meetings and discussions are sometimes unproductive because, for one reason or another, people are not clearly stating their real feelings or others are not picking up such clues as restlessness indicating boredom, withdrawal indicating disagreement, or tenseness indicating irritation. All of these "clues" may, of course, be signs of something quite different, but if not "checked out" by others in the group such feelings may be ignored or misinterpreted. Very often we remain unaware of the body language "spoken by others," and sometimes are even unaware of our own underlying feelings. The following exercise allows members of the group to "guess" what others may be feeling, and then to check with them for their accuracy of perception.

GROUP SIZE:

10—20

TIME SUGGESTED:

50 minutes

GENERAL DIRECTIONS:

The fishbowl arrangement is used, in which the outer circle consists of alter ego for members of the inner circle during a discussion. Comments of alter ego are reviewed in a plenary.

MATERIALS REQUIRED:

None

PROCEDURE:

1. Form two circles with the same number of members. The inner circle is seated. Each outer circle member stands behind a seated member. The outer circle members are told that in the discussion they are to represent the ego of the person in front of them. When the alter ego believes his person is really feeling something he doesn't express, the alter ego speaks up with what has been left unspoken.

2. Begin a discussion on a topic of interest, perhaps a controversial one.

3. After five or ten minutes, stop the discussion and regroup into a single circle. Review and discuss the interpretations offered by the alter egos.

4. Switch the groups to allow all to have both experiences, and repeat Steps No. 2 and No. 3.

VARIATIONS:

1. Two other physical arrangements are possible. One, the outer circle may observe the person directly opposite them, rather than in front of them. This allows observation of facial expressions. Two, both circles are seated. Alter egos may observe any person in the circle. When an alter ego feels a person in the inner circle is not expressing his true feelings, he goes and stands behind him.

If the group is particularly interested in working on their ability to pick up clues from paralinguistics alone, that is from voice sounds, it is preferable for alter egos to work with the person seated immediately in front of them, so they cannot see the face. If other nonverbal clues are being investigated, alter egos may sit to one side of the persons they are working with, or observe them across the circle.

NONVERBAL: HANDSHAKE, FIST

PURPOSE:

To examine the symbolic use of the body in nonverbal communication through a few such uses of the hand.

COMMENT:

"Bodily contact is . . . the most primitive kind of social act, and is found in all animals . . . There are symbolic contacts, such as patting on the back, and the various ways of shaking hands . . . The same gesture may have a quite different meaning in two cultures. Sticking out the tongue means an apology in parts of China, the evil eye in parts of India, deference in Tibet, and simple negation in the Marquesans" (Michael Argyle, *THE PSYCHOLOGY OF INTERPERSONAL BEHAVIOUR*).

"(T)o shake someone by the hand is not only a way of putting oneself symbolically in their power, it also means that one is prepared to put the most mobile and naturally dominating part of one's body at the other person's service" (Francois Duyckaerts, *THE SEXUAL BOND*).

"Most human gestures are highly conventionalized and take on their meaning through cultural definitions. Americans, for example, shake hands as a form of greeting. Polynesians stroke their own faces with the other person's hands, and in some Eskimo tribes the friendly way to greet a visitor is to lick one's own hands, draw them first over one's own face and then over that of the visitor . . . American politicians, when waving to the populace, are careful about the placement of arm and hand (the 'democratic' gesture) lest they imitate the clenched fist of the communists and the straight-armed salute of the fascists . . . The Niam Niam of Central Africa (beckon approach) by waving their arms in a way which we might take for withdrawal" (George A. Lundberg *et al*, *SOCIOLOGY*).

GROUP SIZE:

10—15

TIME SUGGESTED:

60 minutes

GENERAL DIRECTIONS:

The short short story which begins this exercise may be read in advance of the session, or the first ten minutes of the session may be used for reading it. The group as a whole discusses the story very briefly, and then works together in various subgroups, finishing with a plenary of the entire group, if desired. This session may be used early in a group's life, and may serve as an introduction to nonverbal and paraverbal communication.

MATERIALS REQUIRED:

1. One copy of the short story or parable by F. Kafka, "The City Coat of Arms" for each member of the class.

2. A collection of pictures of various people using hand gestures of salutation. These should be collected in advance either by students or teacher, and may be used mounted or unmounted, posted about the room or distributed to the subgroups. There should be a minimum of ten pictures.

PROCEDURE:

1. If the short story has not been read before the group meets, allow about ten minutes reading time. It would be advisable for each member to read the story silently to himself, but if this is not practical, it may be read aloud.

There are many discussible elements in this story and the group might wish to go into them at some future time, but for this session the concentration is on the appearance of the fist described as being shown on the City Coat of Arms. Ask the group what they think this fist looks like—ask them to hold their hands in the position they believe is shown on the Coat of Arms. Are the knuckles toward you (back of hand or front)? How is the wrist held? Is the arm upright? on a slant? at right angles across the Coat of Arms? Is it coming down from the top of the Coat of Arms? It is not necessary for the class to reach any consensus on this, but ask some members why they believe that their position is probably the "way it would look." Ask all the members of the class to make a closed fist, and then slowly open their hands and spread their fingers. Ask them to do it again, and think about how it feels.

2. Subgroup the class in dyads to discuss

58

what they think a "closed fist" can mean. Ask them how they usually feel when their fist is clenched—when their hand is spread out. How do they feel when they see a member of their family or a friend with clenched fists? Are "both fists" different in the impression they make, as opposed to "one fist"? What are the many things a "fist" can mean? Ask them to try several fist positions and see how they feel about them, and what comes to their minds.

3. Distribute or point out the previously prepared pictures of hand gestures of salutation—Hitler, Stalin, Queen Elizabeth II, the President of the United States, previous Presidents, revolutionary groups, the "peace sign," the old "V for Victory" sign, the prize fighters "salute," the military salute, the Indian "How!" gesture, the British Royal wave, the TV wave, the folded hands in the Japanese bow, etc. Ask the dyads to combine to form groups of six, and talk together about the hand salutations in the pictures. What do they mean to them? How do they react to the various types? How do they differ from each other? Why? After a few minutes ask them if they can think of other hand gestures of salutation not shown in any of the pictures. (You may have some problems here with "rude gestures" —"figs," "the horns of the cuckold," etc. Decide in advance how you are going to handle these. If the class would be comfortable with it, you may want them to explore the meaning and use of some of these.

4. Ask for volunteers to demonstrate "handshakes" before the entire group, such as:

   a. the usual "political" handshake

   b. the "sincere" political handshake (one hand on the forearm, the other clasping the hand)

   c. the "cold fish"

   d. the clasp for Indian wrestling

   e. "secret handshakes"

   f. Hindu greeting—looking into each other's eyes—hands raised close to the face, palms joined (accompanying the phrase, "I recognize the God in you")

   g. the "kiss of peace" handshake (various types)

   h. the on-stage comedian's handshake

   i. the European man's kiss on a woman's hand

5. With the entire group, discuss the various handshakes. Why do people shake hands at all? Why do they think the custom arose? With whom do they shake hands? Why? How do they feel about the demonstrated handshakes?

6. Ask how actors use handshakes on stage to convey the sort of character they are portraying. Ask for volunteers to demonstrate. Ask a volunteer to demonstrate a handshake without naming it, and let

the group guess the kind of character they are "playing." Why is such a handshake characteristic of such a person? How important do they think gestures of salutation and "handshakes" are? Do they think they are more, or less "important" than spoken greetings, salutations etc? Within their lifetime they have seen the development of the "peace sign" salute or greeting—how do they think this came about? Why did it become popular? Is it important?

Do you agree with Max Black when he says, "What smiles, grimaces and nods can do, words can do infinitely better."

SUGGESTED RESOURCES:

Argyle, Michael, *THE PSYCHOLOGY OF INTERPERSONAL BEHAVIOUR*, Baltimore, Md.: Penguin, 1967, pp. 32, 81.

Black, Max, *THE LABYRINTH OF LANGUAGE*, New York: Mentor, 1968.

Lundberg, George A., *et al.*, *SOCIOLOGY*, 3rd ed., New York: Harper & Row, 1963, pp. 212, 213, 214.

Duyckaerts, Francois, *THE SEXUAL BOND*, New York: Delta, 1970, p. 195.

WALKING

PURPOSE:

To examine what is communicated by bodily attitude, posture, walk, relative position, to think about what creates these and why they convey these meanings to us.

COMMENT:

Although in watching pantomime or viewing old silent films we may be consciously aware of attaching meaning to bodily attitudes, we usually are unconscious of the effect on our assessments of others caused by such things as a person's walk and posture. Actors watch others carefully and think through their own movements in preparing to play a role, and physicians, psychologists and psychiatrists are accustomed to making conscious assessments of such things. Models, dancers and West Point Cadets are trained to move in a stylized way when on the job, and many occupations require temporary specific alterations in "normal" or "everyday" posture and motion. Almost all of us, however, see people every day whom we immediately and almost unconsciously categorize as "old," "poor," "dangerous," "afraid" and so forth—much of which we determine from their walk or posture. Also, we ourselves change our walk and posture from time to time in accordance with the situation.

GROUP SIZE:

10—15

TIME SUGGESTED:

60 minutes.

GENERAL DIRECTIONS:

This exercise is best done following some advance individual field work, but film may be used as a substitute. Students observe, record, demonstrate and discuss samples of bodily attitudes, talking over the possibilities of cause and effect. This presumes a class which has had at least some experience with

the investigation of nonverbal communication, and of role playing.

MATERIALS REQUIRED:

If film is desired, a series of very short films should be used, some of which may be old TV commercials, obtainable free of charge from local TV stations, short noncommercial films, or clips of commercial films, if available. It is also possible to prepare your own films or slides for this, or students may prepare them. In advance of the session, the total amount of film desired should be edited and wound on a single reel. Ten or fifteen minutes of viewing is sufficient or, if the material is particularly rich, five to seven minutes of film may be used, running it through twice. To assist in concentrating on the motion, it is best to turn the sound down, if you are using sound film, but remember NOT to run sound film on a silent projector as you will usually ruin the film.

If film is not used and you wish to enrich the data provided by the students, the "frozen action" of still photographs may be used, but it will offer much less than a motion picture or "live" field work. Students may wish to augment or fortify their own field work by still photographs of their own making, or by bringing in photos from magazines and newspapers.

All pictures used should be selected to show full length shots of many different kinds of people in many different situations—people of differing status in conversation with each other, the gang on the corner, the priest on the altar, the "delinquency strut," the officer reviewing the troops and the troops being reviewed, a child squatting on his haunches, an old man sitting down, an old woman waiting for a bus, a wealthy woman getting into a car, a poor woman waiting in a line, a child running for fun, a child running in fear.

PROCEDURE:

1. A week prior to the session, ask each student to spend at least fifteen minutes in each of two locations observing and recording the walk and posture of those he sees. Suggest that one of these locations be a busy local intersection. The other may be one of his own choosing that he believes will furnish good opportunities for investigation. Give the students a few suggestions as to what to look for and how to record these so that they can explain and demonstrate them in class. They may work in pairs, if desired.

NOTE: If for some reason the field work does

not seem desirable or the class is not particularly interested in working with the medium, film may be used.

2. On the day of the session, ask for volunteers to explain their observations. If they do not voluntarily demonstrate the positions as they describe them, ask if "you can show us what you mean." After a few volunteers have given their observations, ask if others have observations of similar types, and if so, if their observations coincided with those already given, or if there were differences. At this point, the discussion should be kept to the objective observation and demonstration, without going into causes or effects. If the students have brought pictures to class, ask them to show them to the group, explaining what they see in them. The demonstrations by the students are important to validate the effect of posture and walk apart from clothing, facial appearance, etc.

3. Form subgroups of 5—6
(a) What *causes* the bodily attitudes shown?
(b) What *causes* their own reactions to these attitudes? Why do we interpret them the way we do?

4. Bring the group back together to share their findings.

5. Ask for volunteers, or assign roles if the class has not done much role playing, to role play a few situations in which it is common to find contrasts in bodily attitude.

For instance:
—a student called to the principal's office because of misbehavior
—two students going voluntarily to the principal's office to ask a favor
—a young boy passing a gang of older boys on a street corner
—a policeman talking with a young person he has just stopped for speeding
—a man who has been out of work for 6 months sitting on a park bench reading the want ads, and a man on his way to work walking through the park.

In these role plays it will be more natural for the role players to speak, as an attempt at carrying on most of these roles without speaking will result in exaggerated action and unrealistic positions. Observers will be asked to concentrate on and observe walk and posture rather than words or facial expressions. Gestures should be seen as part of the total body position. It is also important to note how close together the role players stand in the various situations. If no mention is made of this in advance, the role players will probably assume natural distances, although this is not always the case. Allow each role play to go on for only a few minutes, and then encourage the class to discuss their observations, again asking for ideas on "causes" as in their previous discussion. If the role players have provided suitable material, some discussion may also take place on "social distance."

VARIATION:

1. "The Walk." Select a few members to walk around in front of the class. Ask them to do the following:
a. Walk as naturally as you can.
b. Walk as if you are going to catch a bus.
c. Walk as if you are angry.
d. Walk as if you are going to meet someone you haven't seen for a long while.
e. While walking, do the following multiplication problem: (e.g., 3 x 35; 2 x 50; 5 x 777).

Then ask the "walkers" how they felt about this. Their walking will probably change as the concentration on multiplication begins. Did they feel embarrassed?—self-conscious?—tense? Did they forget the audience as they did the arithmetic? How does tension work against us and affect our bodily movements?

HANDCLAPPING, DANCE

PURPOSE:

To observe and experience some of the ways we use our bodies to communicate and celebrate.

COMMENT:

"Since the drum is often the only instrument used in our sacred rites, I should perhaps tell you here why it is especially sacred and important to us. It is because the round form of the drum represents the whole universe, and its steady strong beat is the pulse, the heart, throbbing at the center of the universe. It is as the voice of *Wakan-Tanka,* and this sound stirs us and helps us to understand the mystery and power of all things" (Joseph Epes Brown [ed.], *THE SACRED PIPE: BLACK ELK'S ACCOUNT OF THE SEVEN RITES OF THE OGLALA SIOUX.* © 1953 by the University of Oklahoma Press).

Japanese *sumo,* a form of wrestling, is of ancient origin and stems from a religious ceremony. In Japan today one still sees remnants of the religious origin in the ceremonial clapping of hands before the match, to call the attention of the gods to the wrestling. This same handclapping takes place in Shinto and Buddhist temples.

"I can at this moment clearly recall the origin of my 'Festlicher Rhythmus.' Coming back from the holidays, rested, restored by sun and fresh air, I was eager to begin dancing again. When I stepped into the studio and saw my co-workers there waiting for me, I beat my hands together and out of this spontaneous expression of happiness, of joy, the dance developed . . ." (Mary Wigman, "Composition in Pure Movement", *THE CREATIVE PROCESS*).

"Another ancient educational medium which might be revived is dance. In primitive cultures dance was a central way of exhibiting and celebrating values and beliefs. As Arthur Darby Nock, the Harvard historian of religions, was fond of saying, 'Primitive religion is not believed. It is danced.' Even Plato knew that dance and gymnastics were essential for political education; if the values of a culture are to be deeply rooted they must be celebrated with all the faculties—reason, emotion and sensation. The body has wisdom to teach that the mind knows not of. It understands much of rhythm and timing which is easily forgotten when life is ruled too exclusively by ideas. Such fundamental themes as the relation between activity and passivity, strength and weakness, tension and relaxation, disease and grace are more easily learned from bodily movement than from conceptual analysis. As Zorba knew, there are times when only dance can say what must be said. There are certain emotions which are difficult to entertain without motion. We are moved by joy, or shaken by grief. It may be that the sparsity of joy in contemporary life is closely related to the loss of dance as a central vehicle for the education and articulation of values and beliefs. We do not share the same dances. Perhaps corporate bonds are strongly forged only when bodies join together in celebration. If so, re-education of the body is essential for creating a community. Is it really possible to be in touch without touching, to be moved without moving?" (Sam Keen, TO A DANCING GOD).

GROUP SIZE:

12—20

TIME SUGGESTED:

90—120 minutes. The exercise may be abridged. A group used to working together may be able to do the first half at one session and the second half at a following session.

GENERAL DIRECTIONS:

Using films, records or tapes, students experience rhythms and patterns of movement and dance. The semi-darkness in which the film is shown, and their focus on the screen as the center of attention make it easier to begin to express rhythms themselves.

MATERIALS REQUIRED:

One or more short films and records or tapes (see "Suggested Resources")

PROCEDURE:

1. Seat the students on the floor or in chairs against the wall, but in a semicircle to allow space for Step #4.

2. Show one or more of the films. It is best if these show less familiar dances, such as American Indian, African, etc., with a strong although perhaps unfamiliar beat.

3. After the film has been running a few minutes, ask the students to clap their hands in time with the beat. Where more than one rhythm is discernable, divide the group so the different sections keep time with different beats, or so that half the class claps once on every beat, the other half joining in on the major stress beat. Careful watching and listening may uncover more than one beat pattern.

4. Ask the students to stand and begin to sway or move their feet in time to the music, while continuing to clap. They may or may not choose to imitate some of the movements they see in the film, but the sensing of the rhythms is the first step.

5. As soon as the film ends, start the recorded music and ask the students to try to pick up the new beat and continue with Steps No. 3 and No. 4.

6. Ask the class to sit down in pairs and talk about what they remembered seeing in the film, and how they felt while clapping out the beat and moving with the beat.

—Would they have preferred to just watch the film, and just listen to the record?—why?

—Would they have preferred to move with the beat without clapping?—why?

—What did they see as the purpose of the dance in the film?

—What are the purposes of dances?

7. After about five minutes, ask the pairs to team up to form groups of six to discuss handclapping and dancing as communication. Ask them to make a list showing *who is communicating what to whom* in their examples.

—How does the handclapping of applause differ from the handclapping in a dance?

—What difference does it make to them if they just sit and listen, or if they actively participate in clapping, dancing, or moving in time to a beat?—why?

8. After about 10—15 minutes, ask the groups to post their lists where all can see them, and ask someone from each group to explain their group's list to the class. Help the students classify their lists. Some classifications might be "applause," "voting," "attracting attention" for handclapping, and for dancing, "entertainment," "celebration," "education" (some of the African dances are used as a means of moral education for the young), "worship," "appeasement or petitionary dances," "story telling," "social."

9. Ask each group to select one of the dance categories and choreograph a story, theme, or idea in that category. Explain that it is sometimes hard to put things into words, particularly feelings. Suggest that when they decide on their theme they try out a few beats by clapping hands, and then begin to put a few motions with the beat. They might try something such as, "A Child's Sixth Birthday," or "Saying Goodbye to a Friend Going Far Away," or "Praising the Springtime Day," or "Praying for Peace." It is not necessary to use any melody, though if they wish they may do so. They may wish to vary the sound of their clapping by clapping hands, then clapping the palm of one hand against the back of the other hand, then against the knee, thigh, top of the head, then tapping their feet, then using some surface as a drumhead. Give them about twenty minutes to prepare their dance.

10. Ask the groups to demonstrate their "dance" for the benefit of the class.

VARIATIONS:

1. If you feel that the class will be disinterested in Steps Nos. 9 and 10, or hesitant about performing, there may be one or two dance students in the class who would be interested in working out this portion of the exercise and performing their dance for the rest of the class at another session. The performers could take a few minutes to instruct class members in handclapping as an accompaniment to their dance.

2. The class might be interested in inviting a dance instructor or choreographer to talk to them and demonstrate a few of the ways in which feelings, emotions and ideas are expressed.

3. You may want another session on dances as part of religious ceremonies, viewing and discussing films or making independent reports on the dances of particular groups or countries. Students with a special interest in theater, music or dance will be helpful here, and may be able to bring in pictures, slides, films or music and give brief talks.

4. Students may be interested in studying the use of masks in connection with story telling and ritual dances of the Orient, of Africa and of the American Indian and Eskimo. The mask helps the audience to recognize the performer at a distance and see him as the person he portrays. It gives the dancer a single "expression," and thus all the rest of his communicating is through body motions. Even without the mask, many dancers wear a masklike expression in ritual and classic dances. After looking at pictures of masks used in various kinds of dances and discussing their use and suitability, they may be interested in designing masks suitable for use in a dance for a specific purpose or performance. A local museum or private collector may be able to lend you masks or replicas of masks.

SUGGESTED RESOURCES:

FILMS:

    African Rhythms. 13 minutes, color. Associated Films, Inc., 1621 Dragon St., Dallas, Texas, 75207.

    The Strollers, 6 minutes, color. The Moiseyev Dance Company in a Russian folk dance.

    Negro Spirituals, 17 minutes. Helen Tamiris performing to spirituals.

    Dancer's World, 30 minutes, NET. Martha Graham discusses dancing as her students dance the emotions of hope, fear, joy, and love.

RECORDS:

    Authentic Afro-Rhythms, LP 6060, Kimbo Educational, P.O. Box 246, Deal, N.J. 07723. (Although done by Montego Joe, a Latin and Caribbean percussionist, this record includes rhythms from Africa, Cuba, Haiti, Brazil, Trinidad and Puerto Rico. A teacher's guide giving historical background is included.)

    Authentic Indian Dances and Folklore, choreographed and researched by Carole Howard, Dance Instructor at Central Michigan University. Includes drumming and story-telling by Michigan Chippewa Chiefs, who narrate the history of the dances. LP 9070, Kimbo Educational, (see above for address).

    Authentic Music of the American Indians (3-records), Everest, 3450/3, Chesterfield Music Shops, Inc., 12 Warren St., New York, N.Y. 10007.

    The Lark in the Morning. Songs and Dances from the Irish Countryside, Everest, Chesterfield Music Shops, 1004 (see above).

    The Real Flamenco, Everest, 1008. Chesterfield Music Shops (see above).

BOOKS:

    Brown, Joseph Epes, (ed.), *THE SACRED PIPE: BLACK ELK'S ACCOUNT OF THE SEVEN RITES OF THE OGLALA SIOUX,* Baltimore, Md.: Penguin, 1953, 1971, p. 69.

    Wigman, Mary, "Composition in Pure Movement," *THE CREATIVE PROCESS,* Brewster Ghiselin (ed.), New York: Mentor, 1952, p. 78.

    Keen, Sam, *TO A DANCING GOD,* New York: Harper and Row, 1970, pp. 51-52.

EXAMINING NONVERBAL BEHAVIOR

PURPOSE:

    To increase facility in expressing and interpreting nonverbal communication.

COMMENT:

    "Gestures are hard to classify and it is difficult to make a conscious separation between that in gesture which is of merely individual origin and that which is referable to the habits of the group as a whole . . . we respond to gestures with an extreme alertness and, one might almost say, in accordance with an elaborate and secret code that is written nowhere, known by none, and understood by all" (Edward A. Sapir, "The Unconscious Patterning of Behavior in Society", *SELECTED WRITINGS OF EDWARD SAPIR IN LANGUAGE, CULTURE, AND PERSONALITY*).

    ". . . (O)ut of the vast range of possible combinations of muscular adjustments, perhaps a quarter of a million in the facial area alone, each society 'selects' certain ones for recognition and utilization in the interaction process" (Ray L. Birdwhistell, *KINESICS AND CONTEXT*). Birdwhistell goes on to list a number of temptations experienced by the investigator of nonverbal or paralinguistic behavior, such as that each gesture "has a 'real' meaning," that "body movement is somehow . . . closer to biological nature than is verbal behavior," or that infantile behavior is "more natural than adult behavior," or that "words carry meaning and . . . all other non-word behavior merely modifies it," or that one can fruitfully ask the communicator "what the movement meant." (See note concerning Birdwhistell's work under "Suggested Resources.")

    "FATHER: . . . The point is that the messages which we exchange in gestures are really not the same as any translation of those gestures into words.

    DAUGHTER: I don't understand.

    FATHER: I mean—that no amount of telling somebody in mere words that one is or is not angry is the same as what one might tell them by gesture or tone of voice.

DAUGHTER: Would it be a good thing if people gave up words and went back to using only gestures?

FATHER: Hmm. I don't know. Of course we would not be able to have any conversations like this. We could only bark, or mew, and wave our arms about, and laugh and grunt and weep. But it might be fun—it would make life into a sort of ballet —with the dancers making their own music" (Gregory Bateson, "Why Do Frenchmen?", *THE USE AND MISUSE OF LANGUAGE*).

We often pay very little attention to the nonverbal and paraverbal signals of someone who is trying to communicate with us. Not only does our rejection of this sort of communication lead to misunderstanding, but it deprives us of much of the richness and depth of our world. It is possible to improve our ability to receive and to send nonverbal communication.

GROUP SIZE:

6—20

TIME SUGGESTED:

2 sessions of approximately 5—60 minutes

GENERAL DIRECTIONS:

Each of the four parts of this exercise consists of a different approach to a deliberate attempt at nonverbal communication. In the first, dyads attempt nonstructured communication. In the second, individuals seek to express genuine feelings or emotions, and may be joined by others who wish to try to share their feelings. The third consists of the attempt by subgroups to build an object with construction toys without using speech. The fourth is a role play, which is a paraverbal, not nonverbal, experience. All of these are followed by discussions.

MATERIALS REQUIRED:

For part III one set of construction toys is required for each subgroup.

GENERAL DIRECTIONS:

PART I.

1. Form dyads, asking students to move out to the edge of the room to sit in chairs or on the floor. Each pair is to spend 3—5 minutes communicating without words, written messages, or the "sign language" of charades, etc.

2. Ask them to remain seated where they are and talk over their experience with their partner. Allow 3—5 minutes. (If desired, Steps Nos. 1 and 2 may be repeated, asking the students to choose another topic [nonverbally], to see if they can improve their communication).

3. General discussion in a plenary session: Was it easier or more difficult than usual conversation? What made the difference? Can they remember what sort of clues were most helpful? Did any not participate at all, or give up very quickly? How did they feel about the experience? Did they feel it was a waste of time? When they began to speak, did they continue to remain aware of nonverbal communication? Did they pantomime action or try to show feelings or emotions?

PART II.

1. Explain to the class that in this part of the exercise group members are going to try to express feelings. It is important to be sincere, and not try to express any feeling or emotion which they do not clearly feel. Ask the entire class to wander slowly around the room, while thinking over events of the past few days. Ask them to think about anything at all that they did, that happened, or that they thought about. When they remember a feeling or emotion they experienced, they are to slow down their mind and give this feeling some serious thought. If the feeling comes through clearly they are to try to give it expression in some way. They may continue to walk about, but at this point it may be better if they go to the edge of the room and sit down, concentrating on their feeling and its expression.

2. When others see someone expressing an emotion, they may go to them to see if they can share that feeling. The person expressing the feeling is free to wave them away if they do not wish to share. Sharing is to be nonverbal.

3. After a few minutes, if most of the group is paired off, stop the exercise and allow the pairs or small groups to discuss their feelings together, if they wish. They may check the accuracy of their interpretation, discover misunderstandings, or give a fuller explanation of their behavior, if they wish. Those who did not participate in a "feeling sharing" pair or small group may form a group of their own to discuss the experience—how they felt, what they thought of it, what they noticed.

4. The exercise may be started up again, and more pairing take place. Stress again the importance of sincerity of feeling, rather than the attempt to communicate it. This is not role playing or acting,

and it is important not to pretend or exaggerate the feeling.

5. In a plenary hold a rather brief discussion of the experience. You may find that they will not wish to talk about it very much, but on the other hand, some may have felt more like "observers" than "participants," and want to talk about what they noticed.

—A baby is not afraid to let people know how he feels—why are we? What makes the difference? What do we think will happen? Why do we feel this way? How can you "listen" to someone else when no words are being spoken?

PART III

1. Form subgroups of 5—7. Seat each group at a table or on the floor in a circle. Dump a package of construction toys in the middle of each group. Tell the subgroups that, without speaking in any verbal way they are to decide on something to build, and build it. They must use every piece. Tell them the time limit allowed. (Allow 10 or 15 minutes.)

2. When the time is up, allow about 5—8 minutes for each subgroup to discuss its experience.

3. In a plenary, hold a general discussion of the experience.

—How did they decide what to build? Did everyone agree on the decision? Were other members aware of disagreement? Were there any conflicts or disagreements during construction? How were they manifested? How were they handled? Did any member not participate? Did others try to get them involved? How did they do this? What was the result? Was the group focus on the object being constructed, or on the group members?

PART IV.

1. Select two role players and instruct them separately and secretly. The situation: two people meet and engage in a conversation. The roles: "A"—relaxed and comfortable, but eager to tell the other an experience he has had recently. "B"—has another engagement and is eager to get away quickly, but tries to be polite, to give the appearance of interested listening, to not mention the fact that he must leave or he will be late for his appointment. Be sure "A" knows what experience he wants to relate and "B" knows what engagement he is hurrying toward —they need not tell you, but must be clear about this themselves before they start. In this case they are to talk—this is not a nonverbal, but a paraverbal experiment.

2. Explain to the "audience" that they are to look for paraverbal clues in the following role play. Tell them the situation, but *not* the roles.

3. Allow the role play to run 3—5 minutes, until some frustration or irritation becomes obvious.

4. Start the general discussion of the experience by asking the role players how they felt in their roles. Ask them to tell the group their roles.

—How did "B's" muscles feel? How does he feel now? Can he recreate the muscular sensations he felt then?

—Was "A" aware of his partner's eagerness to leave? How did he feel about this? How did his muscles feel? Did he believe "B" was "really listening" to him? What did he notice about his own physical behavior?

—What did the observers notice about the gestures and facial expressions of the role players? How did they think the role players were feeling? What clues made them think this?

If desired, following this or other parts of the exercise, the students may make individual lists of the ways in which we communicate nonverbally. They may share these lists in subgroups and discuss ways in which we encourage or discourage others by nonverbal communication. Ask them to think about the kinds of nonverbal communication that accompany words (paraverbal or paralinguistic communication) and the kinds we act out without words. Are there some things which can be better expressed verbally?—some which are better expressed nonverbally?—some which require both? Is there really such a thing as verbal expression without nonverbal or paraverbal accompaniment? Does the nonverbal accompany the verbal, or does the verbal accompany the nonverbal?

VARIATION:

To try to experience ways to communicate feelings.

1. Divide the class in half. Form two rows facing one another across the room.

2. Ask the students to begin moving very slowly toward someone. Tell them that when they are aware of a clear feeling they are to express it in a movement or posture, e.g., hold their head in their hands, dance, jump. Tell the students it is important to keep all expressions as authentic or genuine as possible.

3. Tell the students, "If you are approached, you may respond cooperatively or antagonistically, or even ignore the person and walk away.—Do not 'play-act'."

4. After 10—15 minutes, seat the group to discuss "what happened."

SUGGESTED RESOURCES:

Amidon, Peggy, *NONVERBAL INTERAC-*

TION ANALYSIS: A METHOD OF SYSTEMAT-ICALLY OBSERVING AND RECORDING NON-VERBAL BEHAVIOR, Minneapolis, Minn.: Paul S. Amidon & Associates, Inc., 1971. (An extension of the work of Paul Amidon and others in interaction analysis in the classroom.)

Birdwhistell, Ray L., *KINESICS AND CON-TEXT,* Philadelphia, Pa.: University of Pennsylvania, 1970. (We would like to strongly recommend the reading of this important book, particularly pp. 173-191. Not a popularizer, but a sound scholar in a field in which there are very few experts, Dr. Birdwhistell presents in this volume a collection of essays written for various audiences, some of which are quite technical, but many of which make delightful reading.)

Sapir, Edward A., "The Unconscious Patterning of Behavior in Society," *SELECTED WRITINGS OF EDWARD SAPIR IN LANGUAGE, CULTURE AND PERSONALITY,* (ed.) David G. Mandelbaum, Berkeley, Calif.: University of California Press, 1949, p. 556.

Bateson, Gregory, "Why Do Frenchmen," *THE USE AND MISUSE OF LANGUAGE,* (ed.) S. I. Hayakawa, Greenwich, Conn.: Fawcett Premier, 1958, pp. 190-191.

"MIRROR, MIRROR ON THE WALL . . ."

PURPOSE:

To exercise the facial muscles and continue the investigation of nonverbal communication.

GROUP SIZE:

6—20

TIME SUGGESTED:

30—45 minutes

GENERAL DIRECTIONS:

This exercise may be used as an introduction to nonverbal communication, or it may be used as part of a series on the subject. All students participate in dyads in showing emotions by facial expression. Two students then demonstrate "The Mirror" in front of the class. The latter may be repeated by others, if desired.

MATERIALS REQUIRED:

None

PROCEDURE:

1. Form dyads, partners face one another, one is "A", one, "B".

2. Tell the students that as you call out different "emotions," all "A's" are to express the emotion by their facial expression. All "B's" are to mirror this expression. No one is to speak.

3. Call out such emotions as joy, happiness, sadness, disappointment, etc.

4. Give dyads about three minutes to discuss

the experience.

5. Ask for two volunteers to do a variation of this in front of the class. Take volunteers aside and instruct them together. They are to sit facing one another, sideways to their "audience," and each pretends to be looking into a mirror. One is to be the "instigator," one the "mirror." They are to decide before they go "onstage" which is which and also the general nature of the incident they are to act out, such as "receiving a sad letter," "deciding to go out," "remembering a pleasant evening," "worrying about an exam." Warn them to make all moves slowly and deliberately, to see if they can "fool" the audience as to which is the instigator, which the mirror. Their whole body should be involved in this, rather than just the face.

6. Following the "performance," you may wish to have other pairs repeat "The Mirror" before a short general discussion on how we show our feelings.

NONVERBAL CONCEALMENT

PURPOSE:

To explore nonverbal communication in situations of deliberate concealment, recognizing our own and others' ways of revealing and concealing feelings.

COMMENT:

"FATHER: There are lots of people who smile in order to tell you that they are *not* angry—when they really are.

DAUGHTER: But that's different, Daddy. That's a sort of telling lies with one's face. Like playing poker.

FATHER: Yes." (Bateson, "Why Do Frenchmen?", *THE USE AND MISUSE OF LANGUAGE*.)

Poker is a game in which winning and losing can depend in good part on the ability of the player to conceal the "truth" and project useful "falsehoods." One can win by outbluffing others, and, without displaying one's actual hand, collect from others who may have better hands.

In our everyday lives we sometimes win by outbluffing and collect from those who, indeed, do have "better hands." Why and how we do this is usually unexamined and often unnoticed—unless we are caught in the act! How many times this week have you told lies with your face?

Sidney M. Jourard says, "In a society which pits man against man, as in a poker game, people do keep a poker face; they wear a mask and let no one know what they are up to. In a society where man is *for* man, then the psychological iron curtain is dropped" (*THE TRANSPARENT SELF*).

GROUP SIZE:

6—20. In most variations of poker, 2—8 players are involved. Groups of observers may be equal in size.

TIME SUGGESTED:

45—60 minutes.

GENERAL DIRECTIONS:

Some subgroups play a game of poker, others observe the players. More than one round may be played and groups may switch roles. In discussion the group examines the nonverbal communication and concealment here and in other situations in which we deliberately "distort" our communications in order to conceal our feelings.

MATERIALS REQUIRED:

Packs of cards and poker chips

PROCEDURE:

1. Establish subgroups of poker players and observers. Playing groups play poker or some variation of the game while observing groups watch for nonverbal communication. (If time allows, players and observers change places for another game.)

2. Observers report their findings at the end of the game.

3. General discussion centers on such questions as the following:

—How did you feel about yourself in this situation? About your opponents?

—What nonverbal clues did you pick up as players?—as observers?—How accurate did they prove to be?

—What are some of the characteristic clues given by particular players?—What do these clues normally mean in games?—in other life situations?

—Which people seem more aware of these expressions? Why?

—What situations in your lives call for specific types of concealment of expression? Why? Do you normally conceal more at home than at school? At school than among friends?

—How do you normally effect or achieve concealment? What are the most successful ways? why?

—How do people you encounter in your life try for concealment?

—When you are with someone who bores or annoys you, how do you conceal this?—why do you conceal it?

VARIATIONS:

1. Players are individually instructed in advance. Some are told to look "consistently triumphant" during playing, others "consistently dis-heartened," etc. Depending on the size of the playing group, one role may be given to more than one player, but a role should not be assigned to every player. Observers may be informed of roles or not. The same group of players may be observed during two games, one without "assigned roles" and the other with such roles.

Game is played.

During the ensuing discussion, observers report on the players' actions, noting apparent lapses in "consistent attitudes." Players are asked how maintaining a "consistent expression" affected their playing. How did the consistency of expression affect opponents? How quickly did players recognize the roles of others?

2. Experiment with such possibilities as:

a. Play entire game "back-to-back," all moves being made by "aides." For this, the simpler child's game of "I Doubt It" may be preferable. An additional aide reports to all players on the cards shown face-up on the table.

b. Players all wear masks, half masks, or dark glasses, or some players are masked, others not.

3. At the same or a later session role play various concealment situations brought up in the discussion following the game. Situations selected should be those involving face-to-face interaction. These may start with situations in which the need for concealment is exaggerated and unfamiliar, such as "spy trying to get information out of someone at a party," and go on to such things as "an athletic team member trying to get information about another team," "a coach seeking such information," "a situation in which cheating on exams is attempted," or "social situations in which the 'white lie' is used." Discussion should include an examination of the good and bad points from the view of "success" and of "values."

4. The Argentinean game of *truco* would be a very interesting example to use but unless some members of the class happen to be familiar with the game, its difficulty precludes its use. Roger Caillois describes *truco* as follows: "The whole emphasis is upon guile and even trickery, but trickery that is codified, regulated and obligatory. In this game, related to poker and manilla, it is essential for each player to let his partner know the cards in his hand, without his opponents learning them. The cards are symbolized by various facial expressions, appropriate pouts, grimaces, and winks, always identical, to correspond to different high cards. These signals, part of the rules of the game, must be meaningful to one's partner, without enlightening one's adversary. The good player rapidly and discreetly profits from the least inattention of his opponents. An imperceptible sign alerts his partner. Various card combinations are named after flowers. Skill is required to

communicate them to the partner's mind without pronouncing them, merely suggesting them in so far-fetched a manner that only one's partner can understand the message." (Roger Caillois, MAN, PLAY, AND GAMES, translated by Meyer Barash, N.Y.: Free Press of Glencoe, Crowell-Collier, 1961, pp. 83-84.)

SUGGESTED RESOURCES:

Frazier, Clifford, and Anthony Meyer, *DISCOVERY IN DRAMA*, New York: Paulist Press, 1969, pp. 111ff. (Improvisational dramatization of "To Cheat or Not to Cheat".)

Goffman, Erving, *STRATEGIC INTERACTION*, Philadelphia, Pa.: University of Pennsylvania, 1969. (Students may enjoy this work of Goffman's using the international spy as the basis for a discussion of nonverbal behavior. They may then be interested in reading some of Goffman's other works.)

Bateson, Gregory, "Why Do Frenchmen?", *THE USE AND MISUSE OF LANGUAGE,* (ed.) S. I. Hayakawa, Greenwich, Conn.: Fawcett Premier, 1958, p. 189.

Jourard, Sidney M., *THE TRANSPARENT SELF*, rev. ed., New York: Van Nostrand Reinhold, 1971, p. 6.

FILM: *Somebody's Cheating,* 2 filmstrips with record. Pleasantville, N.Y.: Guidance Associates, 1967.

PANTOMIME

PURPOSE:

To increase poise, grace, freedom of expression; to develop keener powers of observation and greater awareness of the feelings of others.

GROUP SIZE:

10—20

TIME SUGGESTED:

One or more 60 minute sessions. Portions of this exercise may be used separately or in combination with other exercises.

GENERAL DIRECTIONS:

These suggestions are all useful in serious training for the performing arts. It is helpful to follow such practice with a discussion in which an effort is made to pinpoint and understand how specific actions, expressions, gestures and so forth conveyed the communication. A "grammar of gesture" will develop, and much understanding of how various postures, actions and expressions affect others about us.

Two general rules in pantomime are (1) silence, (2) few or no props. Silence should be total on the part of the mimers, so that actions which involve speech should be performed with typical movements of the face, including the mouth and tongue, but without the use of any "real" words, and noises such as coughing, sighing, groaning, screaming, are actively but silently carried out. A chair, perhaps a desk or table is allowable and, if desired, an occasional sign may be posted if one might appear in the situation which is being mimed, e.g., "Menu," "No Tipping," "Ladies," or "Stop," "Blink Lights for Service."

The fewer specific directions given in the early stages of a group's work with pantomime, the better.

MATERIALS REQUIRED:

Almost any area in which a group might meet would contain more than enough "materials."

PROCEDURE:

1. With the group seated comfortably in a circle, lead them through some simple pantomime, stating the action, demonstrating it yourself, perhaps in a rather exaggerated fashion, and then asking the entire group to mime the action or behavior.

a. disagreement with a speaker (shake head as in "No!")

b. applause (clap hands vigorously, smile, perhaps rise)

c. listen to (imaginary) lively music (tap foot, move hands back and forth at wrist, nod head from side to side, or anything else which seems natural)

d. express misunderstanding of a speaker (wrinkle forehead, perhaps squint eyes, cock head to one side, open mouth as though to speak, but do not form a word, perhaps scratch head)

e. express misunderstanding of a speaker as in "d", but this time, the speaker is giving you directions to somewhere you must go (point, shake head, show "sheet of paper with directions," throw hands up in the air, etc.)

f. you are impatiently waiting for someone who is late for an appointment—use only your feet to express this

g. you are very unhappy—use only your shoulders to express this

h. you are running very fast down hill—use only your arms and shoulders to express this

i. smell something good cooking—use only your nose and eyes to express this

j. beckon someone to "come here," using only your eyes

k. warn someone to "go away," using only one finger

2. As in "i" above, all the group enacts the following simultaneously, but in this exercise you do not demonstrate for them, but simply give them the instructions, allowing 20—30 seconds after each statement:

a. you are worried about an examination you must take tomorrow

b. you are happy because a friend is moving back to the city

c. you are excited because you have received tickets to a concert

d. you are frightened by a sound when alone in a house at night

e. you are angry because someone has taken your favorite record

f. you are jealous because you have just seen a friend off for Europe

g. you are annoyed because you have lost a phone number

h. you are pleased because you have just learned you are to receive an award

i. you are embarrassed because someone has just paid you a compliment

j. you feel terrible because you have accidently insulted your best friend

k. you feel wonderful because you are going to go somewhere you just love going

l. you are very sad

m. you are in love

You will notice that the items from "h" through "m" are increasingly "vague," thus increasingly difficult and requiring more imagination.

3. As in "2", all the group enacts the following simultaneously, without your demonstration. Remind them that these "sounds" must be made in total silence. Allow about 5 seconds after each word:

a. sigh

b. laugh

c. giggle

d. sneeze

e. sing

f. hum

g. snore

h. groan

i. stutter

You may add as many as you wish, but the exercise should not last more than fifteen minutes.

4. After one or more experiences of this type, a group is usually sufficiently relaxed and self-consciousness sufficiently reduced to allow individuals or small groups to perform for the rest of the class. Groups or individuals may be given slips of paper on which are written *brief* descriptions of pantomimes, and allowed a few minutes to plan their action. You may introduce each "act" either by stating the situation, or part of the situation or background, or by simply announcing the names of the mimers, and allowing the "audience" to guess what is portrayed. These brief descriptions may consist of one word describing an occupation, sport or hobby, for instance, or they may describe a situation, an occurrence or an historic event. Newspaper headlines may be clipped out and distributed, or pictures cut from news magazines may be used as starters. See "Suggested Resources" for many possible suggestions.

SUGGESTED RESOURCES:

FILMS

Occurrence at Owl Creek Bridge, 27 min., 16mm, black and white, 1961. Available from Contemporary Films, 828 Custer Ave., Evanston, Ill., 267 W. 25th St., New York, N.Y. 10001, 1211 Polk St., San Francisco, Calif. 94109; also from Mass Media Ministries, 2116 N. Charles St., Baltimore, Md., 21218 or 1714 Stockton St., San Francisco,

Calif. 94133. Fine film with many discussion possibilities on the value of life, peace, love, justice, and symbolism of water, but used with this exercise is demonstration of communication without dialogue.

Parable. 22 min. 16mm film, color, 1964. Mass Media Ministries (see above). This well known film on the Christian life has perhaps been seen by most people, but deserves examination as an example of pantomime.

Red Balloon, 34 min., 16 mm., color, 1956. Available from Brandon Films, 221 W. 57th St., New York, N.Y. 10019, Film Center, Inc., 20 E. Huron St., Chicago, Ill. 60611, Western Cinema Guild, Inc., 244 Kearny St., San Francisco, Calif. 94108. As with the *Parable,* this delightful film is well known and useful for discussions in human relationships, but can be examined here as pantomime and nonverbal communication.

New Born Again, 30 min., 16 mm., black and white, 1965. Available from Grailville, Loveland, Ohio 45140. All black cast shows the story of salvation in various ways, including dance and pantomime.

Two Men and a Wardrobe, 15 min., black and white, 1958. Directed by Roman Polanski (Poland), Contemporary Films, Inc. Polanski made this film while a student at the Polish Film Academy. An obscure film without dialogue, and one which lends itself to a discussion of the actual physical actions of each character, their expressions and gestures.

A Chairy Tale, 10 min., black and white, 1957. Norman McLaren and Claude Jutra, National Film Board of Canada, Contemporary Films. Classic film pantomime, in which a chair is one of the mimes. Students may concentrate on posture and gesture of the human mime to see how he creates his effects.

Run, 16 min., black and white, 1965. Available from Mass Media Ministries. An excellent discussion film on man's relationship with himself and today's society, discussed elsewhere in this book. For this exercise, demonstrates nonverbal communication.

BOOKS:

Howard, Vernon, *PANTOMIMES, CHARADES AND SKITS*, New York: Sterling Publications, 1959. This and the following book by Howard are written primarily from the point of view of entertainment or "parlor games," but have many excellent suggestions simply presented.

Howard, Vernon, *MORE CHARADES AND PANTOMIMES*, New York: Sterling Publications, 1961.

Cole, Toby, (ed.) *ACTING: A HANDBOOK OF THE STANISLAVSKI METHOD,* New York: Bonanza, 1955. Many suggestions for exercises in pantomime. See especially pp. 35-38; 52; 55; 113-115; 118; 121-123; 213.

Spolin, Viola, *IMPROVISATION FOR THE THEATER,* Evanston, Ill.: Northwestern University Press, 1963.

FREEDOM

BREAKTHROUGH

PURPOSE:

To experience a struggle for physical freedom and to consider the implications.

COMMENT:

"Man's freedom is born in the moment of his contact with God. It is really unimportant whether God forces man out of his limits by the sheer distress of much suffering, coaxes him with visions of beauty and truth, or pricks him into action by the endless hunger and thirst for righteousness that possess his soul. What really matters is the fact that man is called and he must be sufficiently awake to hear the call" *(THE PRISON MEDITATIONS OF FATHER DELP).*

"Ere the base laws of servitude began,
When wild in woods the noble savage ran."
(John Dryden, 1631-1700,
"The Conquest of Granada", Pt. 1, I,1)

"Necessity is the plea for every infringement of human freedom. It is the argument of tyrants; it is the creed of slaves."
(William Pitt, 1759-1806,
"Speech, House of Commons, Nov. 18, 1783")

"But though my wing is closely bound,
My heart's at liberty
My prison walls cannot control
The flight, the freedom of the soul."
(Jeanne Guyon, 1648-1717,
"A Prisoner's Song, Castee of Vincennes, France",
    Stanza 4)

"I only ask to be free. The butterflies are free. Mankind will surely not deny to Harold Skimpole what it concedes to the butterflies."
(Charles Dickens, 1812-1870,
BLEAK HOUSE, Ch. 6.)

"Man is born free, and everywhere he is in chains."
(Jean-Jacques Rousseau, 1712-1778,
DU CONTRAT SOCIAL, Ch. 1.
"L'homme est né libre, et partout il est dans les
    fers.")

"Hereditary bondsmen! know ye not
Who would be free themselves must strike the
    blow?"
(Lord Byron, 1788-1824,
CHILDE HAROLD, Canto II, lxxvi)

"Let me point out to you that freedom is not something that anybody can be given; freedom is something people take and people are as free as they want to be."
(James Baldwin, *NOBODY KNOWS MY NAME,* Dell, 1961, p. 125)

"No human being, however great, or powerful, was ever so free as a fish"
(John Ruskin, 1819-1900,
THE TWO PATHS, Lecture 5).

"If you continue in my word, you are truly my disciples, and you will know the truth, and the truth shall make you free"
(*GOSPEL ACCORDING TO JOHN,* 8:31-32).

"The second mark of freedom is *activity* as opposed to the passive and receptive. Insofar as I am pushed about by alien forces, I am not free. Any obstacle, in fact, that impedes my action also restricts my freedom. Thus obsessions that force me to think of one thing only, as well as physical imprisonment, which restricts my movements, interfere with my freedom. I become free only by acting in some way"
(Wild, *EXISTENCE AND THE WORLD OF FREEDOM).*

"Opinion, we all instinctively feel, is vastly important for freedom. Nothing brings tyranny home to us so vividly as the stifling of opinion, and all the great political prisoners of history, from the Prisoner of Chillon down, have always boasted that their bodies might be in chains but their minds were free. That fact marks the superiority of a dungeon in the past over 'liberty' in a modern totalitarian state. The new millennium promises the better life, but it turns ordinary men into suspicious, terrified and cruel beasts, in whom the possibility of political democracy has died, because the cultural source of freedom has been quenched . . . (D)emocracy is a way of living and thinking which is pre-requisite to all the other freedoms we want to attain."
(Jacques Barzun, *OF HUMAN FREEDOM)*

GROUP SIZE:

8—20

TIME SUGGESTED:

One or more sessions of 45—60 minutes

GENERAL DIRECTIONS:

Group members try to break out of a circle to

"freedom." Members participate both as individuals who try to gain physical freedom and those who band together to prevent another's physical freedom. In this exercise we experience ourselves as physical beings. We recognize our tensions and relate these to other situations. This serves as a basis for brainstorming, reflection and discussion.

MATERIALS REQUIRED:

None. Clear enough floor space for the group to work comfortably in a circle, realizing that the entire circle will move about to some extent, and insuring that those who "break through" will not hurt themselves on objects outside the circle.

PROCEDURE:

1. Members form a tight circle, arms around one another's shoulders or waists. If the group is larger than fourteen, form two circles.

2. One at a time the members go to the middle of the circle. The member in the center is to regard the circle as a problem that stands between him and his freedom. He is to break out, doing everything he can to escape by using force, if he wishes, but not violence—he may not kick or strike anyone, for instance. Members of the circle are to do everything they can, short of violence, to retain him within their circle.

3. After the first member breaks through, ask him to wander around outside the group long enough for another person to break through. Propose to him these questions for consideration: How do you feel? Do you enjoy your feeling of freedom? Stand at a distance, look at the group, think of yourself as free from the group—remember how you feel for discussion later. Someone else now volunteers to try to "reach his freedom." It is not necessary for everyone to have a turn. After the second person breaks through, the first person out rejoins the group, etc.

4. General discussion. Consider such questions as:

—How did you feel when you were trying unsuccessfully to break out? How did you finally manage to break through? How did you feel then? How do your muscles feel now? How did they feel during the exercise?

(Other things may come out in the discussion, such as feelings of aggression or frustration, or a discussion of violence, group membership, or physical "belonging." Keep the focus on "bodily freedom," if that is the direction of exploration desired.)

5. Brainstorming. Form subgroups of 5—7. Appoint a Recorder. Groups spend about ten min-utes brainstorming the question, "What limits man's PHYSICAL freedom?" (Many of the ideas may actually deal with other kinds of freedoms. Some of these, however, may be viewed in more than one way, and students may begin to see the difficulty of distinguishing the "physical" from other aspects of the "self" or "person."

6. Individual list making. Ask the Recorder to read back or post the list in each group. Lists may include such things as physical handicaps, clothes, need to eat, classroom, traffic, fears, parents, no car, jail. They may also include such things as advertising, drugs. Each member chooses one word from the list which he really cares about—one term which seems important to him. They are to write that word at the top of a sheet of paper, and under this to list ways in which the "limits" might be expanded. Ask them to jot down as many ways as possible in 3—5 minutes.

7. Sharing lists. Subgroup members share the list and discuss it.

—why these particular limitations on their freedom bother them;

—how they would use the greater freedom their lists from Step No. 6 would provide.

8. After about ten minutes, gather the groups for a general discussion. Put on the board, "How can I be more free?" Encourage contributions from previous steps, and also new thoughts which come to them during the discussion. Discussion will be rather scattered, due to the considerable variety of the data.

After a few minutes, focus in on ways in which their freedom could actually be expanded at this point in their lives. Help them find ways in which the "impossibles" on their lists may be changed to "possibles." Depending on the group and time available, this may be a brief "idea sharing," or an in-depth discussion. Some questions which may be discussed are:

—What kinds of physical restraint make a person most un-free? In what ways do physical handicaps limit freedom? Can anything replace this lost freedom?

—How do emotional handicaps limit physical freedom?

—Which animal is most free? why? which least free? What do we mean when we use the phrase, "free as a bird"? If we have "free will," are we more or less "free" than a bird?

—Do clothes limit freedom? How? Do you think clothes sometimes increase freedom? In what kind of clothing do you feel most free?

—How free are we to think as we please? What helps? What hinders? How do we choose which freedoms we prefer to seek? What freedoms are you most willing to give up? why?—least willing

76 to give up? Why do people willingly give up "freedoms" at times? (If the class has read such books as Huxley's *BRAVE NEW WORLD,* or Orwell's *NINETEEN EIGHTY FOUR,* they can talk about why some of these people gave up their "freedoms.")

VARIATIONS:

1. Following Step No. 4, the group may move directly into a discussion of "freedom." There will be many ideas as to what the term means, and you might ask, "What are some of the things 'freedom' means to different people? . . . to you?". This discussion may involve the entire class, or start with dyads or small groups, moving into larger group after about ten minutes.

2. If you ask "What is freedom?", you may get a variety of answers such as, "to be able to do as I please," or "not having to follow rules or laws." Sometimes this problem is best approached indirectly by such questions as:

—What limits should be placed on a person's freedom?

—If everyone in the world were really "free," how would you behave tomorrow?

—Are all kinds of freedom equally desirable?

—If not, what kinds of freedom are best?

—What causes "conflicts" of freedoms?

—What is the opposite of freedom?

—Do you think it is possible to define "freedom"?

—Is freedom "breaking out" or "breaking in," or "breaking through"?

—How is it that we have been able to talk about "freedom" at all?

—Is freedom connected with "destiny"?

—What freedoms are people most worried about today?

—What freedoms are usually stressed in a "Student Bill of Rights"? . . . How are these related to Franklin Roosevelt's Four Freedoms: Freedom of speech, Freedom of everyone to worship in his own way, Freedom from want, and Freedom from fear? . . . What happens to people when they lose any of these freedoms? . . . When they never have them to begin with?

—What are the differences between "being free *from*" and "being free *to*" or "being free *for*"?

2. Following Step No. 4, sheets of quotations on "freedom" may be distributed to the subgroup members. Members are asked to rank these quotations from "1. Strongly agree with this," to "6. Strongly disagree with this." This may be done individually, and then subgroups may try to reach a consensus on rank order. To simplify this procedure,

the groups may be asked to try to at least agree on "the 3 you most agree with," and "the 3 you most disagree with." Dictionaries and collections of quotations will supply a suitable collection.

3. Following Step No. 5 the group may rank the freedoms brought out in brainstorming. This may be done individually at first, or in dyads, and then subgroups may try to arrive at a consensus on priorities.

4. Students may gather definitions of "freedom" outside of class. This may be done by a literature search, or by interviews with parents, friends, or "street corner" interviews. Interviews may be taped, if desired. Ask the students to select several brief definitions they like and print them on sheets of newsprint to post in the classroom. Tapes and interviews may be shared and discussed in class.

SUGGESTED RESOURCES:

Arendt, Hannah, *THE HUMAN CONDITION,* Garden City, N.Y.: Doubleday Anchor Books, 1958.

Aristotle, "The Republic", *INTRODUCTION TO ARISTOTLE,* Bk. I, pp. 558-563.

Berdyaev, Nicolai, *SLAVERY AND FREEDOM,* trans. T. M. French, N.Y.: Charles Scribner's, 1944. See especially pp. 59-72; 215; 219.

CONSTITUTION OF THE UNITED STATES AMENDMENTS. See particularly Amendments IV, V, VIII and XIII.

DECLARATION OF INDEPENDENCE. Among the "repeated injuries and usurpations, all having in direct object the establishment of an absolute tyranny over these States," some deal specifically with physical freedom.

Epictetus, *THE DISCOURSES OF EPICTETUS WITH THE ENCHEIRIDION,* trans. George Long, Philadelphia, Pa.: Henry Altemus (n.d.), pp. 239, Numbers 14, 28.

Delp, Alfred, S. J., *THE PRISON MEDITATIONS OF FATHER DELP,* New York: Macmillan, 1963.

Wild, John, *EXISTENCE AND THE WORLD OF FREEDOM,* Englewood Cliffs, N.J.: Prentice-Hall, 1963, p. 127.

Barzun, Jacques, *OF HUMAN FREEDOM,* rev. ed., Philadelphia, Pa.: J. B. Lippincott, 1964, pp. 8-9.

TRUST
(BLIND WALK)

PURPOSE:

To experience the necessity of trust in achieving freedom.

COMMENT:

Erik Erikson, in describing the "Eight Ages of Man," lists the first age as "Basic Trust vs. Basic Mistrust." He lists the eighth as "Ego Integrity vs. Despair," and says, "Webster's Dictionary is kind enough to help us complete this outline in a circular fashion. Trust (the first of our ego values) is here defined as 'the assured reliance on another's integrity,' the last of our values." (p. 269) Erikson points out that it is a mistake to assume that the "sense of trust (and all the other 'positive' senses postulated) is an *achievement,* secured once and for all at a given state. . . . The personality is engaged with the hazards of existence continuously, even as the body's metabolism copes with decay" *(CHILDHOOD AND SOCIETY).*

Trust is a necessary ingredient or prerequisite for freedom. The person who is totally without trust in others is totally unfree—he cannot move physically, emotionally, mentally. He also needs trust in himself for freedom. The "blind walk" is an exercise used for many purposes, but always the factor of trust is involved.

GROUP SIZE:

10—20

TIME SUGGESTED:

45—60 minutes

GENERAL DIRECTIONS:

The exercise may be done anywhere at any time and can be carried on with no equipment at all or with a number of added objects (see "Variations"). It is helpful to caution the "guides" in the presence of the "blind" to be as careful as possible of their charges. Remind them that the safety and well being of the "blind" are in their care. If they have not done this sort of thing before, the guides will tend to hurry the "blind" at first, not realizing how hesitant they will be to step out.

MATERIALS REQUIRED:

Blindfolds. These must be comfortable but efficient.

If desired, various pieces of furniture and other objects may be imported into the situation, or removed (see "Variations").

PROCEDURE:

1. Form dyads. Assign one member of each pair to be blindfolded. They will be led from here on by their "sighted" partner or "guide."

2. Tell the guides to take their charges on an exploratory tour of the assigned area. Suggest they take their partner's hand. (This may change as the exercise continues. The blindfolded member may clutch his guide by both hands or around the neck and shoulders, the guide may steer his partner by the shoulders, take both his hands to pull him along, or reach down and move his feet or legs at times.)

3. Allow the exercise to continue for at least fifteen minutes. The blindfolds are now removed and the group sits down for a general discussion, or if the group is large, subgroups of 6—8 may discuss together. Some questions considered may be:

—What was it like not to see?

—What was it like to be the guide?

(Effect of various spacial relationships:)

—Were the led able to determine "how far" it was from one point of their walk to another? . . . how high or low something was? . . . Did their posture or natural walk change in any way? . . . Were they aware of any muscular tensions? (Usually shoulders and neck, sometimes knees, thighs, entire leg)

—Was some other contact used beside "holding the partner's hand"? What was the effect of this? . . . on both partners? . . . Why was it done? . . . Was discomfort increased or decreased? . . . Was the sighted partner aware, if he instituted the change?

(Experience of lapsed time)

How long did the time seem to those led? . . . to those leading? What part of the experience seemed longest? . . . shortest? why?

—As the guide, were you more conscious of yourself, or of the person you were leading?

—As the blind, were you more conscious of yourself, or your guide? Did you "worry" about your guide? how? why? Were you aware of others in the room? . . . in what ways?

—Did the blind trust their guides? . . . all the time? . . . If not, when did you feel a lack of trust? . . . why? What helped you feel trust?

—If you were to repeat this exercise, how would you change it?

—If girls led boys, did this seem like role reversal?

VARIATIONS:

1. The usual procedure is to reverse the guides and the guided, so that both may have the experience. This may be done before the discussion.

2. Explain the exercise in advance and ask for volunteers for the "blind." Some may not want to participate in the exercise. If so, they may help rearrange the environment. During the discussion, ask them why they did not want to participate. If the option is offered, and all volunteer, ask them if they felt they had a choice. Did they feel free to *not* participate?

3. During the course of the walk some portions of the environment are changed, creating "ups and downs," "crawl-throughs," "duck-unders," etc. Students may be told to leave the room and make a round trip to a named location.

4. The exercise is conducted in silence, with the guides and the blind able to communicate only in nonverbal ways.

5. A single guide is made responsible for two or more blindfolded members. Also partners or chains may be led by a girl with blind boys, or vice versa.

6. At a signal, the guides are asked to leave their blind partners and go to another part of the room, leaving the blind to their own devices. Their former guides watch them and see what happens to them, and how they feel about their blind partners in this situation. If desired, certain verbal signals may be given by the guides.

7. Final discussion may include an exploration of the relationship of trust and freedom in many situations. For instance:

—What are the ingredients of trust?

—In order to be free, what kinds of trust must we have?

—In order to free others, what kind of trust must we have?

—In order for parents to allow their children to be free, what kind of trust is needed?

—How do we feel when we lead others? . . . How do we try to develop their trust? . . . Can we develop their trust and their freedom at the same time?

—Under what circumstances do we "follow blindly"?

—On what basis do we decide a person is "trustworthy"? In what ways are we more free with someone whom we believe to be trustworthy? Why are some individuals usually considered more trustworthy than others? If you say of a six-year old, "I can trust him," how does your meaning differ from such a statement about an adult?

—What is the relationship between "trust" and "faith"?

SUGGESTED RESOURCES:

Erikson, Erik H., *CHILDHOOD AND SOCIETY,* 2nd ed., rev., New York: W. W. Norton, 1963, pp. 72ff; 247ff, 252, 273-274.

Erikson, Erik H., *IDENTITY: YOUTH AND CRISIS*, New York: W. W. Norton, 1968, pp. 82, 95-96; 103-104; 106.

BREATHING

PURPOSE:

To experiment with, to explore and to enjoy some aspects of breathing.

COMMENT:

When our parents and grandparents were children they were exhorted to "breathe deeply," and told that it was important to get as much "nice fresh air" deep down in their lungs as possible, and also to exhale deeply to "get rid of all that stale air." Later it was decided that our lungs functioned very well without conscious help, and that tinkering with natural breathing patterns was useless and sometimes harmful.

Current interest in yoga has revived faith in the benefits of breath control (pranayama) and even in prolonged breath retention (kevala). Work with troubled individuals whose normal breathing has been disturbed by emotional problems has caused some psychotherapists to stress "correct" breathing. The psychiatrist Alexander Lowen believes deepened breathing so important that he downgrades worries about sensations regarded as symptoms of hyperventilation, stating that they will "diminish and disappear . . . as the patient's capacity to tolerate higher levels of excitation and oxygen increases." (PLEASURE). Another therapist, Magda Proskauer, points out that her aim is to help the patient "concentrate on the act of breathing, observing its inner movement until the breath, left to itself, can find the way back to its own rhythm" ("Breathing Therapy", WAYS OF GROWTH).

Robert S. de Ropp, biochemist, while approving many yoga practices, opposes some extremes. He agrees that man can learn, with great effort, to suspend normal breathing for increased periods, but that the practice is dangerous and of doubtful value. (THE MASTER GAME).

Respected Zen Master Yasutani-roshi insists on classic zazen training in which "attention" to one's normal breathing is of critical importance. At no time does he advocate the strenuous athletic feats of breathing common in much yoga, and sometimes confused with normal Zen practices (THE THREE PILLARS OF ZEN).

Breathing is so obviously a "vital" function that it has always fascinated man. For many centuries it represented the difference between "life" and "death." Since it was an unconscious function which could to a great extent be consciously controlled, it also seemed to be the doorway between these two aspects of man's body. The relaxed but alert and healthy body breathes very well, with no need for attention. On the other hand, freedom from muscular tension as well as freedom from mental distractions may increase with exercises which include awareness of and even some mild control of our breathing patterns.

GROUP SIZE:

Up to 20

TIME SUGGESTED:

One or more sessions of approximately 30 minutes

GENERAL DIRECTIONS:

We recommend that you select one or two of the following seven exercises for any given session, rather than using all of them serially. NOTE: Students with respiratory diseases or with chronic cardiac disease may be damaged by hyperventilation. Hyperventilation is an unusual occurrence, but can be brought on by deep breathing exercises, and therefore students with such problems should be asked not to engage in ANY breathing exercises. They should be encouraged to experiment with one of the exercises for muscle relaxation when the rest of the class is performing the following.

MATERIALS REQUIRED:

For "1" below, a wrist watch with a second hand for each dyad will be helpful, although a wall clock may be used.

For "6" and "7", floor mats are desirable, although not essential.

PROCEDURE:

1. Experimental breathing.

a. Form dyads. One member of each pair is the "experimenter," one is "observer."

b. For one minute, or more if desired, the experimenter is to breathe very, very slowly, inhaling only four or five times a minute. They will need to watch the second hand to control their breathing. The observer watches closely, observing whether the breathing is deep or shallow.

c. For one minute, the experimenter breathes very rapidly, inhaling thirty or more times per minute. Again the observer looks for deep or shallow breathing.

d. The partners switch roles, and the observer is now the experimenter. Repeat "b" and "c".

e. Tell the experimenters, "Take twelve breaths, inhaling and exhaling both deeply *and* quickly. Now relax." The observer should notice the pattern of the breathing during the period of relaxation—is it slower than usual, faster than usual, deeper or more shallow than usual?

f. Tell the experimenters, "Take four slow, shallow breaths. Now relax." The observer makes a note of the rate and depth of the breathing during the period of relaxation.

g. Partners switch roles, repeat "e" and "f".

h. Partners exchange findings.

i. Explain to the class that, unlike most exercises they do, the results of these are predictable. Fortunately for our health and life, the breathing "computer" in the lower part of the brain works very well, making necessary compensatory adjustments for our breathing gymnastics. In "b", breathing automatically becomes "deeper"; in "c", "shallower," in "e" the period of relaxation will be one of slower and shallower breathing, and in "f" of more rapid and deeper breathing. Eventually, despite attempts to distort breathing and "fight the computer," nature will win. *"Under almost all circumstances the way you* automatically *breathe is the* best *way to breathe"* (Brecher, BREATHING: WHAT YOU NEED TO KNOW).

The musician may be taught special ways of breathing by his music teacher, but this is to improve his breathing for the sake of the musical effect in singing or blowing a wind instrument, not for health reasons. Special breathing exercises are taught to emphysema patients and to pregnant women. Patients confined to bed for long periods of time need to be helped to sit up to allow more internal room for lung expansion. Underwater swimmers learn to take very deep, quick breaths before diving. Even these "special cases," however, must be approached with respect for our body's own "good sense." The diver's "trick" breathing can result in death, as hyperventilation has led to "blacking out" of fine swimmers in excellent health. The National Tuberculosis and Respiratory Disease Association warns, "Never take more than two or three deep breaths before diving and swimming under water." Dr. Gustav Eckstein states that "Blowing night after night against the resistance of a horn might cause a rip (in the pleura) from inside" (THE BODY HAS A HEAD).

2. Emotion and breathing. Ask for a few volunteers to demonstrate the relationship between breathing and emotion. Explain that they will be role playing or dramatizing situations, not experiencing these emotions! Instruct role players in front of the class, and ask the class to note the varying effects, if any, on the breathing patterns of the role players.

a. You are a member of the track team, and are trying very hard to take first place. Think of yourself in the final stretch, with one competitor ahead of you. Stand up, and "run" in place, without moving across the room.—How would you be breathing?—Is this effect caused by emotion? . . . need for more oxygen? . . . both? How would he really be breathing if he actually were coming down the last lap? why?

b. You are alone in a house at night. It is three o'clock in the morning and you hear stealthy footsteps approaching the room in which you are.— How would you be breathing?—What causes this effect? What other emotions might cause the same kind of breathing?

c. You have worked all summer and saved your money to buy a motorcycle. You were finally able to purchase it yesterday. Today you arrive home just in time to see a neighborhood boy ride it across the street, jumping off just before it crashes into a wall.—How are you breathing?—What causes this kind of breathing? Do you think you would breathe this way?

d. You are in an extremely dull class. It is a hot Friday afternoon, and the teacher has been reading a boring book aloud for forty-five minutes.— How are you breathing?

e. You have a summer job lined up at a vacation resort. Your best friend is also going to be working there with you, and you are really looking forward to it. You had not realized your marks were slipping badly but you now realize you may not pass one of your major subjects. If you flunk you will have to go to summer school. In a few minutes you will know whether you passed.—How are you breathing?

—(Ask each person to think now of some problem in their lives which really causes worry or tension. Ask them to really concentrate on it for a minute or two. After a minute or so ask them to try to let a part of themselves "stand aside" and watch their own breathing.) The class may now discuss what they noticed about their breathing. (Real worry or tension usually results in shallow breathing, often in hurried breathing, sometimes even in panting.) Because of the close connection between our bodily behavior and our emotions, it is possible to relax our emotional tensions somewhat by relaxing our physical tensions. At any rate, it will make us more comfortable physically for a while. This is the basis of the many exercises for "good" breathing. Some of the following exercises may be helpful to try when students find themselves tense, worried or sleepless.

3. Relaxation exercises.

    a. Breathe out, then breathe in quickly through the nose, keeping the mouth closed.

    b. Pause.

    c. Now breathe out through the nose very, very slowly.

    d. Inhale comfortably.

    e. Repeat for a total of six inhalations, alternating fast and slow breathing.

4. Yoga alternating breathing, often used as preparation for sleep.

    a. Sitting comfortably upright on the floor or a chair, hold the nose gently between thumb and forefinger, using only enough pressure to close one nostril and then the other.

    b. Start by breathing through the left nostril only, and releasing the air through the right nostril.

    c. Now breathe in through the right nostril, exhale through the left.

    d. Repeat for a total of seven inhalations. Breathe deeply, steadily, rhythmically, concentrating completely on the course of the breath through the nose, down the throat, into the lungs. (Some students who have studied yoga may object to this somewhat less than orthodox version.)

5. Sitting in a comfortable position, hold the phrase "It breathes me" in your mind. Be aware of your breathing. Shut out everything else from your mind except this phrase and the sensation and rhythm of your breathing. Make no attempt to alter your breathing in any way. Continue for three minutes. This may be used as a preliminary to meditation.

6. Zen breathing. The beginning student of Zen Buddhism starts his practice of zazen (pronounced "zah-zen" with equal stress on both syllables) by counting his exhalations while seated quietly in the correct position. He may continue this for some weeks before changing to counting his inhalations instead, which is considered more difficult. He is often instructed to take two or three deep breaths at first, and then to allow his breathing to take its normal pattern as he counts each exhalation, "one . . . two . . ." etc., up to "ten," and then to start over again. Philip Kapleau says, "This is the first step in the process of stilling the bodily functions, quieting discursive thought, and strengthening concentration." Hours of practice in this are required of the serious Zen student, and the formal aspects of zazen—sitting, breathing, and concentration—are included in all Buddhist teaching and practice, regardless of the sect, and are considered to have value beyond "training." In itself, zazen is not meditation, but the practice of zazen aids meditation.

Various positions for "sitting" may be considered correct, but all involve the straight back and the hands loosely arranged in the lap with thumbs touching, pointed upwards, the rest of the fingers slightly curved, the back of the left hand resting lightly on the palm and fingers of the right. If sitting in a chair, the knees should be spread, the feet flat on the floor.

If you are interested in helping your students explore Zen breathing, we recommend Philip Kapleau's book listed in "Suggested Resources." The above information, based primarily on this book, is sufficient to help your students enjoy a "first taste" of beginning Zen training.

SUGGESTED RESOURCES:

The following two booklets are among materials available to teachers without charge from the National Tuberculosis and Respiratory Disease Association. These are usually obtainable from your local Christmas Seal Society who can also supply charts of the respiratory system. Some of the material in this exercise is based on their publications.

Brecher, Ruth and Edward, *BREATHING: WHAT YOU NEED TO KNOW*, National Tuberculosis and Respiratory Disease Association, 1968, p. 42, 45.

(no author given) *INTRODUCTION TO RESPIRATORY DISEASES*, 4th ed., National Tuberculosis and Respiratory Disease Association, 1969.

American Medical Association, *THE WONDERFUL HUMAN MACHINE*, 1970.

Eckstein, Gustav, *THE BODY HAS A HEAD*, New York: Harper & Row, 1970. See pp. 181, 188-192, 194-195, 392, 525.

Gamow, George, and Martynas Ycas, *MR. TOMPKINS INSIDE HIMSELF: ADVENTURES IN THE NEW BIOLOGY*, New York: Viking Press, 1967.

Kapleau, Philip, *THE THREE PILLARS OF ZEN*, Boston, Mass.: Beacon Press, 1965, rev. 1967. pp. 11-13, 32, 38, 40, 124-133.

Proskauer, Magda, "Breathing Therapy", *WAYS OF GROWTH*, Herbert A. Otto and John Mann, (eds.) New York: Viking, 1968.

Schultz, J. H., and W. Luthe, *AUTOGENIC TRAINING: A PSYCHOPHYSIOLOGICAL APPROACH IN PSYCHOTHERAPY*, New York: Grune and Straton, 1959.

Lowen, Alexander, *PLEASURE*, New York: Lancer, 1970, p. 45.

de Ropp, Robert, *THE MASTER GAME*, New York: Dell, 1968, p. 238.

STRETCH

PURPOSE:

To discover ways to "free-up" our bodies when we are tired or tense.

COMMENT:

When we are tired, distressed or worried we sometimes are conscious of the tightening of muscles across the back of the neck and shoulders. Sometimes our jaws are so tense that we become aware of an ache. At other times we are unaware of physical tenseness, but vaguely aware of "tension"—which always translates itself into tenseness in some part of our body. In a more Platonic age we often thought of "the soul in the cage of the body." Far too often tensions in our bodies *do* form a "cage." When our muscles are "tight" and not "free," we are unable to do many things, such as reach, swim, dance, move gracefully and with pleasure. We become increasingly more tired. Sometimes we cannot fall asleep. To free ourselves of this "cage" the best way is often, paradoxically, to "tense up" or deliberately contract our muscles. Certain exercises seem to help a good deal.

GROUP SIZE:

Up to 20

TIME SUGGESTED:

45 seconds to 25 minutes

GENERAL DIRECTIONS:

Some or all of the following may be used at any time. They need not necessarily lead into or precede any particular activity and may be used more than once, as the occasion seems to indicate. The exercises should be done with force and concentration. Some should be done with grace and rhythm but always with enough energy to achieve a thorough stretch. Except for the first and last, these should be done on the floor with shoes removed. Most people will have a sense of well-being when they achieve muscular relaxation, but occasionally someone who has been very worried or depressed may become tearful.

MATERIALS REQUIRED:

Mats, beach towels, or carpeting.

For the first and last exercise, no mat is required.

PROCEDURE:

1. Stand up and stretch—just any way you please. Yawn a few times—wide, slow yawns. Now, take a deep breath through the nose—slowly blow it out through your mouth. Stand loose—not so loose that you fall down, but almost!

2. Lie flat on your back on your mat and think of your left foot. Curl it up tight, making a "fist," and hold it for the count of five. Now, relax that foot completely. Now tense the calf muscles in your left leg the same way. Move up this leg to the hip, and then start with your right foot. As you move up the body, concentrate on one area at a time, allowing the other muscles to lie still on the mat. Finish with the muscles of your face and scalp. Each time, after the count of five, let the muscle contraction relax as completely as possible.

3. Lie on your back on the mat, close your eyes. Picture in your mind a cat, asleep. Now he is waking up—he has a good stretch. Watch him on your mental screen as he puts his head back and yawns, squeezing his eyes closed and pushing one leg out stiffly in front of him, claws spread wide. Follow him as he stretches the other forepaw, humps his back and begins to stand up, stretching one leg out stiffly behind him, then the other. Now he gives himself a good shake, all over. Play this through in your mind again, following him with whatever motions seem comfortable and natural to you. You are built differently and will want to move somewhat differently, but try to achieve the same graceful freedom.

4. Sit on the mat and draw your knees up to your chest. Cross your arms around your legs, push your face down against your knees. Now, contract all those muscles at once which you slowly and carefully contracted and relaxed in Step No. 2. Squeeze yourself into a tight, rigid little package, holding your position until it is painful . . . Now, bang! Immediately, flop down on your back again and stretch all ways at once—wide and free, head back, arms and legs out. Stretch your arms up over your head, and bend your head back . . . Now go completely limp and just lie quietly for a moment.

5. Still lying on the mat, check out all parts of your body, looking for any remaining tensions. Your hands should be lying comfortably at your sides, palms up, fingers slightly curled. Your heels should be resting on the mat with the toes turned slightly outward. Your face should be as limp as the rest of you, eyes partly closed, mouth partly open. If there are still any tensions left, contract that area again, and then relax.

6. This exercise takes only forty-five seconds, but can be very helpful if you have been sitting or working in one position for a long time. You will return to work more energetically.

    a. Stand with your feet about eighteen inches apart, knees slightly flexed.

    b. With the right hand, reach upward and slightly forward, as though to pick a piece of fruit from a high branch—stretch for it! Your heels will probably leave the floor.

    c. Let the right hand fall back at your side, and reach up and forward with the left. Repeat three times, alternating right and left.

    d. Return to position and raise both arms sideways, palms down, to shoulder height—stretch out a bit.

    e. Bend forward and down, allowing your arms to swing downward until your head is hanging down and your fingers brush the floor. In this position, "bounce" your head downward 5—6 times, gently.

    f. Stand upright again and place your hands behind you on the buttocks or upper part of your thigh, and lean gently backward from the waist, sliding your hands down your legs and dropping your head backward.

VARIATIONS:

NOTE: Students may have some favorite relaxing exercises and be glad to show them to the class.

1. For legs. If the legs are tired and tense, try this. Lie flat on your back, legs straight, feet a few inches apart. Slowly draw up one knee, keeping your foot on the mat. Now let your foot slide back into its original position. Repeat with your other leg. Now put your arms over your head, resting on the mat. Pull your feet together so they gently touch and stretch as tall as you can—push—in both directions. Raise one leg, push against the air with the heel, continuing to stretch with your arms. Repeat with your other leg.

2. For arms. Make a tight fist, squeezing fingers and thumb together until your whole arm begins to shake. Now, relax entirely. Repeat with your other arm. Begin again, but this time concentrate only on your fist, avoiding involving the upper arm. Your forearm muscles will tighten, as they are needed to contract your fist. Now move the contractions up your arm through the elbow, upper arm and shoulder. Relax the areas one at a time, reversing the direction, starting with the shoulder, moving to the upper arm, etc. Stop with limp hand, fingers in slightly curled position. Repeat with the other arm.

Another approach is to lie flat on the back and force the lower arms up tight against the upper arms, making a fist at the same time with both hands. Now let the arms fall back on the mat. Stretch the arms straight out at the side—stretch—stretch—now go limp.

SUGGESTED RESOURCES:

(see also: "Communication: Paraverbal and Silent Communication" for additional stretch exercises.)

Kohler, Mariane, and Jean Chapelle, *101 RECIPES FOR SOUND SLEEP,* translated by Joan Hills, New York: Walker and Co., 1967.

Lewis, Howard R., and Dr. Harold S. Streitfeld, *GROWTH GAMES,* New York: Harcourt, Brace, Jovanovich, 1970.

Ask a physical education or dancing teacher for suggestions. Additional exercises may be found in the above from which some of these exercises were adapted.

PURPOSE:

To explore the extent of our physical freedom in making choices, and to examine the relationship between these physical freedoms and other aspects of freedom.

COMMENT:

Using some of the value clarification techniques of Raths, Harmon and Simon, group members are helped to examine their values, to explore which are "real" values as opposed to those to which they might give lip service without action, and to explore the relationships of their physical actions and reactions to situations in which they believe they are free or unfree. "(T)here can be no question of anyone concerned with child care, or education, abdicating responsibility for moral development. . . . We are furthering or hindering a child's moral progress every time we foster his self-respect by giving real responsibility, or remain uninterested in trivial problems that loom large to him, or make arbitrary decisions overriding his developing ability to think for himself. We are all moral educators, whether we like it or not" (Williams, *INTRODUCTION TO MORAL EDUCATION*).

GROUP SIZE:

Up to 20

TIME SUGGESTED:

15—60 minutes

GENERAL DIRECTIONS:

The following exercises may be used at various times alone or in connection with other exercises or class activities. It is not suggested that all of the following be carried on in any one session. Individual decision making precedes discussion.

MATERIALS REQUIRED:

No. 1 does not require any materials.

No. 2 This may be done without any previous preparation, if desired, or lists may be duplicated in advance for distribution.

No. 3 A chalkboard may be used for this, or a long paper strip, somewhat like a "time-line."

PROCEDURE:

1. VOTING consists of a series of questions which begin with the same words, "How many of you . . . ?" Raise your hand when you are in favor of the statement. If you are very much for it, wave your hand vigorously. Turn your thumb down when you are against it. If you are very much against it, turn your thumb down and move your hand up and down. Make your opinion known. Fold your arms if you honestly do not have an opinion. Look around and see how much spread of opinion there is.

Examples:

—How many of you enjoy watching TV regularly?

—How many of you would like to learn how to fly?

—How many of you have experienced a time when you did not have enough money to buy necessary items?

—How many of you have gone without food for an entire day?

—How many of you like to work on a farm?

—How many of you like to talk with children?

—How many of you enjoy camping? sleeping outdoors?

—How many of you have friends who are of a different ethnic or socio-economic background?

—How many of you would welcome a family from a different racial background into your neighborhood?

2. RANKING involves arranging several items in an order of preference. You are asked to arrange three possibilities. It might involve choices of what you would like to do. Your first choice would be what you like best, and the third choice what you like least. You can reverse this order by listing the least liked first and the best last.

Examples:

Sports: What do you like?

1. La Crosse	1. Bowling	1. Surfing
2. Tennis	2. Bridge	2. Hunting
3. Archery	3. Ice Skating	3. Basketball

Reading: What do you like to read?

1. Magazine-pictorial	1. Science fiction
2. Novel	2. Newspaper
3. Biography	3. News periodical

Socializing: What do you like to do on a night out?

1. Go to movies	1. Drama—play	1. Picnic
2. Go to dinner	2. Shakespeare	2. Basketball game
3. Go to musical	production	3. Visit relatives
	3. TV show, live	

Chores: Which would you rather do?

1. Do dishes	1. Wash dishes	1. Wash clothes
2. Cut grass	2. Iron clothes	2. Wash windows
3. Mop floor	3. Dust furniture	3. Vacuum carpet

On the move: Which would you rather do?

1. Walk in the country	1. Ride in the country
2. Window shop	2. Visit a shut-in
3. Walk on the beach	3. Visit a friend in the hospital

Emotions: (Hardest, easiest to express)

1. Anger	1. Show anger at your teacher
2. Love	2. Show affection in public
3. Hurt	3. Cry in public

Situation: Which would you rather do?

1. Wear a formal dress to an informal, casual party (or reverse)
2. Tell a white lie to a friend (you don't want to go out with him)
3. Tell a friend he has bad breath

1. Sign a petition for open-housing legislation
2. Live in a neighborhood that is racially mixed
3. Demonstrate in an anti-war rally

3. A CONTINUUM is simply a line with the extreme positions placed at either end. You decide where you belong between the extremes. Compulsive moderated belong in the middle. You put your initials on the continuum at the point which you think fits your position.

Examples:

Sex Education

1 _____ 1
1 _____ 1
Sexy Sam   Prudish Peter

SS: Feels very strongly that everything and anything goes. More interested in biological than personal relationships.

PP: No sex in school. This is left completely to the individual. Even as a parent, he wouldn't instruct his children in this vulgar stuff.

Nuclear War

1 _____ 1
1 _____ 1
Cynical Cindy   Optimistic Otto

CC: So scared of war that she has built two bomb shelters. Everytime a plane flies overhead, she ducks. This is a rotten world.

OO. Organizes campaigns to do away with the military services. Advocates an open-door policy. No fear of nuclear bombs.

Public Assistance

1 _____ 1
1 _____ 1
Miserly Mary   Generous Gene

MM: Feels that if they can't work, let them starve. The government shouldn't give taxpayers' money away.

GG: Feels that nobody should work, let the machine do it. We should all share the wealth equally.

DISCUSSIONS:

In regard to this decision, are you physically free to do what you want? If not, can you identify the part or parts of your body which hinder your freedom? or which are not free to do this?

Can you physically act on your choice? why or why not? How could you increase your freedom in this matter?

Do your own physical reactions interfere? those of others?

Do you feel there is no relation to physical freedom in this choice? In what nonphysical way are you free or unfree here?

Where choices differed in the class, what caused the differences? What physical factors are involved?

Are you physically more or less free than a younger person to do this?

Are you physically more or less free than your parents? Are there physical reasons for this?

Do our values change as we change physically? How? Why?

VARIATIONS:

Variations on these topics, suggested choices and methods are almost endless. They should be selected in accordance with class needs and interests. At times you may wish to spread your "continuum" all the way across the floor, allowing members to "stand on what they believe," and then giving them another chance to "take a stand" after the discussion, or halfway through. At other times you may wish to distribute sheets at the end of a session, following a related topic, and ask them to think about them and fill them in and bring them to the following session. You may wish to use voting before an exercise or discussion, and then again, afterwards, either with or without pursuing the reasons for any shift in opinions. Some students may volunteer their reasons for changing their minds—others may not feel sufficiently comfortable with the group to do this. Sometimes you may wish to use one of these techniques with a single subgroup, or with all subgroups working only within their group, or with the entire class in a plenary. The same value clarification techniques may be used in connection with other themes, the discussion itself determining the focus of the questions to be asked.

SUGGESTED RESOURCES:

Raths, Louis E., Merrill Harmin and Sidney B. Simon, *VALUES AND TEACHING,* Columbus, Ohio: Charles E. Merrill, 1966. Although this book seems to address itself primarily to elementary school teachers, the approach was used in the fifties by Simon with high school teachers testing some of the techniques. It has also been tried by others at the college level and in adult education. If you are not already familiar with this book you will find it very rewarding and full of practical suggestions. The authors tend to warn against discussion at times (see pp. 106-107), in part because of the frequent mis-handling of discussion in classroom situations (see p. 113), and in part because of the focus on the younger child, but at other times they give some helpful and wise suggestions for discussion.

Wilson, John, Norman Williams and Barry Sugarman, *INTRODUCTION TO MORAL EDUCATION,* Baltimore, Md.: Penguin, 1967, p. 307.

RESPONSIBILITY

PURPOSE:

To examine the relationship between freedom and responsibility through several problem experiences.

COMMENT:

"The acting out of every impulse is often mistakenly taken for freedom. In practical work it is important to know the difference between acting out and befriending the suppressed instincts" (Proskauer, "Breathing Therapy", *WAYS OF GROWTH*).

"Freedom is a partial, negative aspect of responsibility which is richer and more complete in meaning. We may become free from the immediate and yet remain irresponsible. We cannot become responsible, however, without also becoming free" (Wild, *EXISTENCE AND THE WORLD OF FREEDOM*).

"We like the eagles, were born to be free. Yet we are obliged, in order to live at all, to make a cage of laws for ourselves and to stand on the perch" (William Bolitho, 1890-1930, *TWELVE AGAINST THE GODS*).

GROUP SIZE:

Up to 20

TIME SUGGESTED:

60 minutes

GENERAL DIRECTIONS:

A series of role plays are used as the basis of the discussion of freedom as the right and the ability to make responsible decisions about our own behavior. Whatever situations are chosen, it is important to follow each role play with a discussion which explores in some depth the relationship between freedom and responsibility, growth in freedom and responsibility, and also usurpation of freedom and responsibility. Situations selected should in each case involve all three elements in some way, although the "answer" or "solution" of the problem may seem to be a simple one initially. See, for instance, the first role play described below. This exercise may be used with a group which has had little or no previous experience in role playing.

MATERIALS REQUIRED:

For the first role play: a few pieces of facial tissue.

For most role plays: a table and a few chairs will probably be sufficient.

PROCEDURE:

1. For first role play, explain the situation to the entire class as follows: "Here we have a family dinner table, Joe, you are the father—will you sit here? (Call on someone you believe will put himself into the role without stage fright)—and the mother —Mary, you be the mother—Jane, you are the daughter. Now, Jane and Mother have not seen each other today until just now. Jane is discovered as having symptoms of a heavy cold (hand Jane a few pieces of facial tissue). Jane is blowing her nose, . . . sounds hoarse and stuffy. Mother is upset . . . Jane wants to go out this evening . . . Mother, what are you thinking? . . . what do you say to Jane, now that you see she has a cold?"

As the role play proceeds you may find that Mother may suggest that Jane go to bed, that she is at fault for catching cold, etc. Mother may drag Father into the argument, or he may come in voluntarily. Jane may try to conceal her cold, or may make it very obvious, meanwhile making a strong pitch for going out. Mother and Father may or may not yield, Jane may say something about "making her own decisions," or Father may say, "You think you're free to do anything you please, no matter what the consequences." Stop the role play after 3—5 minutes when the argument has reached a pitch and before any solution has been reached.

2. Discussion. Ask the role players to tell the class how they felt in the situation and then help the class discuss the implications here of freedom and responsibility. Some of the following questions may be used:

—Who is responsible for what? . . . for whom? . . . Is Jane "responsible" for catching cold? . . . Are her parents responsible for "allowing her to catch cold?" Should Jane be "free" to catch cold? . . . to go out, if she wants to, with a cold? . . . Are these foolish uses of the word "free" or "freedom"? Suppose her going out that evening

included visiting her married sister who has an infant—does this affect Jane's "freedom"? How? Why? Whose responsibility should this decision be?

Since this situation involves communication and conflict, you may wish to help the students search for better ways to communicate with their own parents. Pay particular attention to the way statements are made by all role players. In the above role play, does Mother say, "I am upset because I feel responsible for you, and don't see how I can take care of you properly." Or does she say, "You never pay any attention to your health" or "You have no respect for our opinion"? Does Jane say, "I want to go out and I'm mad because you are telling me I shouldn't go," or does she say, "You don't ever want me to have any fun"? In other words, are the speakers "owning" their own feelings, or are they imputing feelings to the other? Are they taking responsibility for their own feelings and allowing others to be free to say how they really feel?

Students may find it helpful to repeat this role play, changing their statements of imputation to statements of "my own feelings," to see if it will be helpful in working out this problem. The same or different role players may take the roles.

3. For subsequent role plays use current and live issues. Role plays involving decisions among peers on questions involving freedom and responsibility, and among students and various authority figures may be prepared before the session and written out for distribution to selected role players. Role players may be given their situation and role sheets during the latter part of the preceding discussion. Role players may go to a corner of the room for five minutes to read their sheets and decide a few things among themselves about their supposed relationships. Remind them not to prepare lines or solutions in advance. Some suggested role plays follow:

a. 2—3 boys belong to a rock group and have scheduled a practice session for this evening. They have a gig (paid performance) at a wedding in two weeks and not too much rehearsal time is left. One boy has suddenly decided he is going somewhere with a friend this evening and won't be able to make the practice session. The others are angry and try to convince him that he can't do this. He insists he's free to do as he pleases.

b. John's father and mother have found a cache of marijuana in John's room and removed it. John discovers it is gone, but doesn't know whether they have found it or a friend has taken it. Father and Mother come to John's room determined to find out as much as they can and to get John to promise to "stop smoking grass." John feels he should be free to keep what he wants to in his room and to use grass.

c. Mary has been called to the office of the

vice-principal because instead of going to a study hall, she used that time to go to the student lounge to work on a school assignment with a friend. The vice-principal knows Mary has "cut study hall" before, and she also feels responsible for the whereabouts of the students, and for keeping the building quiet during class hours. Mary feels she can study much better away from the "distractions" in the study hall, that it is her responsibility to decide when and how to do her assignments, and that this is true of the other students also.

d. Harry and Jane have been picked up by the police because they built a bonfire on a public beach where "open fires" are forbidden by law. They are discussing with their parents the forthcoming hearing in front of the magistrate (justice of the peace). Harry and Jane feel (1) there wasn't any sign on the beach saying you couldn't build a fire, so how were they supposed to know there was such a law; (2) on public property the public should be free to do as they please as long as they're not hurting anyone; (3) they have done enough camping and picnicking to know how to handle a simple bonfire. Their parents are angry because they feel disgraced and worried because they believe their children deliberately disobeyed the law and the police told them that Harry and Jane were "fresh and argumentative—a couple of smart-alecks."

The above case presents a number of problems which deserve discussion. Although Harry and Jane are quite definitely at fault, just what is the responsibility of (a) the community: in properly and adequately posting property signs and promulgating the law; (b) their parents and the school: in making clear to them the meaning of "public property," and providing sufficient information on available public property, the uses for which it is intended, the places, if any, where fires may be built and under what conditions? . . . Did their parents, the school and the community help or hinder the freedom of Harry and Jane? . . . If you were Harry and Jane's parents would you believe they were capable of being "free"? . . . If you were Harry and Jane, how would you react? . . . What kinds of laws should be made regarding the use of public property? . . . why? . . . Whose responsibility is it to see that such laws are passed? . . . How does "public property" enhance the freedom of members of a community? . . . How does it usurp their freedom? . . . Is there enough park and recreation space within easy distance of the homes of students in your school? . . . Why or why not? . . . What would have to happen to make some (or more) available? . . . How would this be done? . . . Would it involve a loss of freedom for someone? . . . How free are students to use the public property in their own area? . . . for what purposes?

SUGGESTED RESOURCES:

Proskauer, Magda, "Breathing Therapy," WAYS OF GROWTH, Herbert A. Otto and John Mann, (eds.), New York: Viking, 1968, p. 32.

Wild, John, EXISTENCE AND THE WORLD OF FREEDOM, Englewood Cliffs, N.J.: Prentice-Hall, 1963, pp. 154-155.

WORK

PURPOSE:

To examine our ideas of freedom in connection with occupations or job situations.

COMMENTS:

". . . Workers all over the world refuse to be treated as objects without intelligence or freedom, to be used according to the will of others; they want to be regarded as men with a share in every area of society, in social and economic matters, as well as in public life and education . . ." (Pope John XXIII, *PACEM IN TERRIS*).

"A person is powerless when he is an object. . . . The non-alienated pole . . . is freedom and control. Freedom is the state which allows the person to remove himself from those dominating situations that make him simply a reacting object. . . . These individual task-related freedoms—control over pace, freedom from pressure, freedom of physical movement, and the ability to control the quantity and quality of production and to choose the techniques of work—together make up control over the immediate work process" (Blauner, *ALIENATION AND FREEDOM: THE FACTORY WORKER AND HIS INDUSTRY*).

Physical freedom can be an important part of job satisfaction. Men and women who are free to move about, to leave their usual place on the job, or whose normal job activity enables them to move about in a large area, who can eat when they are hungry, talk, and change the pace of their actions— these people experience a greater sense of freedom, power and self-determination than those nailed to one spot, one speed, one set of motions. What other kinds of freedom are important in considering careers or occupations? How important are these elements of freedom in selecting a job?

The following exercise investigates these questions in various ways. It also gives some experience in preparing a questionnaire, administering it, and analyzing and reporting the data.

GROUP SIZE:

12—25

TIME SUGGESTED:

This exercise is divided into three sessions which should be spread over at least a week, and may extend over three weeks or longer.

GENERAL DIRECTIONS:

Students listen to a sociologist's report and compare the "case of the worker's soup" with their own experiences in school, part-time or summer jobs, and their knowledge of other employment. They prepare a questionnaire and use it in field interviews, as well as in conducting an informal interview or conversation with an adult about his work. Results of the field work are reported, examined, dramatized and discussed.

MATERIALS REQUIRED:

A means of reproducing the student-prepared questionnaire.

PROCEDURE:

SESSION I

1. Read "The case of the worker's soup" to the class:

"When work activity does not permit control, evoke a sense of purpose, or encourage larger identifications, employment becomes simply a means to the end of making a living. For Marx himself this was *self*-estrangement, the very heart of the alienation idea . . . (p. 3) . . . The work environment with the most alienating consequences, the automobile assembly line, has been the favorite research laboratory for the sociologist of the manual worker . . . Yet assembly-line workers in all industries probably constitute no more than five percent of the entire labor force (p. 5).

"An apparently trivial situation, the homely 'case of the worker's soup,' strikingly illustrates how a continuous-process technology restores the personal freedoms of the employee. This incident also points out the disparity in atmosphere between assembly-line and automated work environments. When asked about the possibilities of setting his own work pace, a chemical operator mentioned that the men often warm up a can of soup on a hot plate within the automated control room where they are stationed. Suppose this soup is on the stove, ready to eat, just at the time that's officially scheduled for the operator's round of instrument readings, an activity that takes about thirty minutes. 'You can eat the soup first and do the work later, or you can take the readings earlier than scheduled, in order to have the soup when it's hot,' reported this operator. In other words, the nature of production work in an automated technology makes it possible for the employee to satisfy personal and social needs when he feels like it, because he can carry out his job tasks according to his own rhythm. The automobile assembly-line worker who gets a craving for a bowl of soup is in an entirely different situation. He must wait for his allotted relief time, when another worker takes his place on the line, and if he still wants soup at the time he will probably drink it hurriedly on his return from the lavatory. Ironically but fittingly, his will be the 'automated' soup, purchased from a commercial vending machine, since there is no room and no time for hot plates and cans of soup on an automotive conveyer belt" (Blauner, *ALIENATION AND FREEDOM: THE FACTORY WORKER AND HIS INDUSTRY*).

2. Discussion: You may wish to start with a discussion of "physical freedom in school," and move from there to students' work experiences in part-time and summer jobs. Students often tend to think of "freedom" as a state or condition rather than as a personal characteristic, or mental, spiritual or emotional quality, and therefore this is a good place to start the discussion. You might want to ask such questions as:

—In comparison with this worker who could heat and drink his soup when he chose, how free are you in school?

—What limits your freedom? why?

—Would you be happier if you could choose your own lunch time each day? why? How could a school make arrangements for such a lunch system?

—Is there any time during the day when you can eat a few crackers or something, other than lunch time? If not, why not? If yes, what makes this possible? Is this of any importance to you?

—How long does your school day last, in comparison with this worker's day? Do you have free time to eat or talk which he does not? If you have an after-school job, can you eat between school and job? If you combine in-school hours and on-the-job hours, is your "work-day" longer or shorter than his, do you think?

—How much control do you have over your total time schedule, as compared to this worker? Do you think you are physically more, or less, free than he? why?

—What sort of time schedule do your parents have?

—What kinds of jobs do you think give the most freedom? the least?

3. Form subgroups of 5—7 to prepare ques-

tionnaires. Each group should try to prepare about 6—8 questions that they could ask adults which would help them determine the amount of physical freedom allowed on jobs held by these people. Explain that the class will arrive at a composite questionnaire which they will be asked to use in interviewing adults in various occupations. Give them a time limit of 10—20 minutes.

4. In a plenary session help the class arrive at a common set of questions to be reproduced for class use at a later time. Some students may state that they believe other freedoms are more important in a job, and some questions may deal with aspects of decision-making, power, creativity, etc.

5. In preparation for the next session ask each student to talk with at least one adult who has a full-time job. He is to ask him about the "worker's soup" story, and how he sees his own job in terms of physical freedom. The student should prepare brief notes indicating whether he interviewed a man or a woman, their job title, the kind of work they do, the profession, business or industry in which they work, and a note or their reply to the question as to whether they could follow the example in the "case of the worker's soup."

SESSION II

1. In the same subgroups as in Session I, Step No. 3, students report on their interviews, and subgroups make a decision on the "most" and "least" free jobs described.

2. In a plenary session each subgroup reports its "most" and "least" free jobs.

3. A short general discussion may be focused on some of the other kinds of freedoms they would want in a job—freedom from fear (job security as well as hazardous conditions may be considered), freedom from boredom, or some of the aspects mentioned in Session I, Step No. 4. If desired, the following items may be helpful in furthering discussion:

a. In his book, *THE SANE SOCIETY*, Erich Fromm quotes from the "Rule of the R. G. Workshops," a Community of Work which manufactures picture frames: "A man is really free only under three conditions: . . . *Economic Freedom.* Man has an inalienable right to work. He has to have absolute right to the fruit of his work from which he should not part except freely. . . . *Intellectual Freedom.* A man is free only if he can choose. He can choose only if he knows enough to compare. *Moral Freedom.* A man cannot be really free if he is enslaved by his passions. He can be free only if he has an ideal and a philosophical attitude which makes it possible for him to have a coherent activity in life . . . Moral freedom is to be found only within strict observance of the group ethics freely accepted."

b. A few years ago *THE NEW YORK TIMES* carried this brief article:

"MOSCOW (AP). A sociological study shows that only one of five Soviet unskilled workers is satisfied with his job, *IZVESTIA,* the Government organ reports.

"Among skilled workers, half were found to be satisfied with their jobs.

"The four-year study was made by a group of University of Leningrad sociologists, who questioned 2,665 young workers in that city.

"The sociologists concluded that one of the main problems in worker satisfaction was the increased level of education in the Soviet Union in recent years."

c. In an article titled, "On the Pinnacles of Power—The Business Executive," Kenneth Underwood wrote, "The executive-manager is the one level of work the corporation permits general freedom from the desk and the time clock, because the nature of the work so deeply involves the whole person that he attends to it in all circumstances. His problem is that he can't get away from it enough to see it in perspective as not the whole of his life . . . the major substance of his life is the life of the corporation" *(THE HUMAN SHAPE OF WORK).*

d. Robert Blauner, from whom we quoted the "case of the worker's soup," gives the following report on the "alienation curve": "In the early period, dominated by craft industry, alienation is at its lowest level and the worker's freedom at a maximum. Freedom declines and the curve of alienation (particularly in its powerlessness dimension) rises sharply in the period of machine industry. The alienation curve continues upward to its highest point in the assembly-line industries of the twentieth century . . . But with automated industry there is a counter-trend . . . Automation increases the worker's control over his work process and checks the further division of labor and growth of large factories. The result is meaningful work in a more cohesive, integrated industrial climate . . . as employees . . . gain a new dignity from responsibility and a sense of individual function" *(ALIENATION AND FREEDOM).*

4. Distribute the reproduced copies of the questionnaire prepared at the previous session. In the light of their discussion, do they wish to amend the questionnaire in any way before it is used? Some time may be spent in discussing the problems of creating a satisfactory questionnaire. Questions should be clear, cover as many possibilities as are essential, and omit questions the answers to which the person being interviewed might object to having made public knowledge. The problem on "objective vs. essay" questions may be discussed, and the students should be satisfied that they will be able to

handle the interviewing using the questionnaire as it is finally approved.

5. Students are to interview at least one person engaged in full time employment, using the questionnaire, and bringing results to the next session.

SESSION III

1. In the original subgroups all completed interview questionnaires are shared and discussed. Again, subgroups are to decide on "most" and "least" free jobs, but they are also to prepare to put on a 3—4 minute skit illustrating the "freedom" aspects on these two jobs. They should also be prepared to make a statement based on an examination of the following questions:

—What kind of freedom does this job offer? What kind of freedom is curtailed by this job?

—Would they rather have the "most" free or the "least" free job which they have selected as their two "poles"?

—Is the group in agreement on these choices, or are there differences of opinion? If there are, why?

2. In a plenary, each group presents its skits of the "most" and "least" free jobs, and makes a brief statement of its feelings about these jobs. After each skit allow a few minutes for questions to the interviewers by the class.

VARIATIONS:

1. Role playing or dramatization may be introduced in Session I if a number of the students have had job experience. Ask the student-worker to think about his own degree of freedom on the job, and to create a short role play or skit, directing another class member so that he can illustrate the amount and kind of freedom offered by that job. Following each role play or skit the player may be asked to give his own feelings about the job, and the class may discuss the situation briefly.

2. The quotations given in this exercise may be prepared and distributed to the class members in one of the following ways:

a. Each member of the subgroup receives a different quotation.

b. Identical sets of 4—5 quotations may be given to each subgroup member.

c. A different set of quotations is given to each subgroup, but each member of the subgroup receives the same set as others in his group.

The entire class is given about ten minutes to examine their quotations and decide on their meaning to them. If "a" is used, subgroup members share their quotations and discuss their feelings about them. If "b" or "c" is used, they may begin at once to rank the quotations in order of "importance," of "meaningfulness," trying to reach a consensus within their subgroup in about 15—20 minutes.

Subgroups report their decisions, explaining their reasons, in a plenary session. Post all "first choices" on the wall, and engage the class in general discussion focusing on the kinds of freedom important to them in the work situation, whether or not these are covered by the quotations chosen.

3. At Session II sample questionnaires are distributed together with the questionnaire prepared by the students at the previous session. These samples may be developed by the individual research and study based on materials such as those recommended in "Suggested Resources," or the Guidance Counselor in your school may be able to provide some materials. A session may be devoted to the comparison of various questionnaires and to further discussion of the subject of "questionnaire making."

SUGGESTED RESOURCES:

Berger, Peter L., *THE HUMAN SHAPE OF WORK*, New York: Macmillan, n.d., p. 192.

John XXIII, Pope, "Pacem in Terris," April 11, 1963, *THE TEACHINGS OF POPE JOHN XXIII*, (ed.) Michael Chinigo, trans. Arthur A. Coppotelli, New York: Grosset and Dunlap, 1967, p. 153.

Fromm, Erich, *THE SANE SOCIETY*, Greenwich, Conn.: Fawcett Premier, 1955, p. 277.

Blauner, Robert, *ALIENATION AND FREEDOM: THE FACTORY WORKER AND HIS INDUSTRY*, Chicago, Ill.: University of Chicago, 1964, pp. 16, 22, 171, 183, 210-212. Blauner reproduces the Roper-Fortune Survey Questionnaire, an excellent instrument for the study of freedom on the job.

Cantril, Hadley, *THE PATTERN OF HUMAN CONCERNS*, New Brunswick, N.J.: Rutgers University Press, 1965. Considerable material in this excellent book is relevant to questionnaire making, although students will not find a complete questionnaire on the subject such as appears in the Blauner study.

Campbell, Don G., *WHAT DOES DADDY DO ALL DAY?*, Indianapolis, Ind.: Bobbs-Merrill, 1963. Despite the title, this is not a children's book, but a collection of humorous newspaper columns dealing with the business world. The author is business and financial editor of the Indianapolis *STAR*, author of a book on the stock market, and editor of the weekly stock market newsletter, *THE DOW THEORY TRADER*. Students will probably enjoy his jibes at advertising practices and the retail trade.

Oppenheim, A. N., *QUESTIONNAIRE DE-*

SIGN AND ATTITUDE MEASUREMENT, New York: Basic Books, 1966.

A number of industrial and professional associations publish pamphlets to recruit young people for their field. These provide some information about jobs and are often available to teachers without charge in quantities sufficient for class distribution. A few suggestions follow:

American Chemical Society, 1155 16th St., N.W., Washington, D.C. 20036.

American Council on Education for Journalism, School of Journalism, University of Missouri, Columbia, Missouri 65201.

American Dental Association, Council on Dental Education, 211 E. Chicago Ave., Chicago, Ill. 60611.

American Institute of Architects, 1735 New York Avenue, N.W., Washington, D.C. 20006.

American Management Association, 135 W. 50th St., New York, N.Y. 10020.

American Physical Therapy Association, 1740 Broadway, New York, N.Y. 10019.

American School Counselor Association, 1607 New Hampshire Avenue, N.W., Washington, D.C. 20009.

American Society of Medical Technologists, Suite 1600, Hermann Professional Building, Houston, Texas 77025.

American Society of Radiologic Technologists, 645 N. Michigan Ave., Chicago, Ill. 60611.

Council on Medical Education, American Medical Association, 535 N. Dearborn St., Chicago, Ill. 60610.

Data Processing Management Association, 505 Busse Highway, Park Ridge, Ill. 60068.

Engineers' Council for Professional Development, 345 E. 47th St., New York, N.Y. 10017.

National Association of Accountants, 505 Park Ave., New York, N.Y. 10022.

National Association of Purchasing Management, 11 Park Place, New York, N.Y. 10007.

National Commission on Teacher Education, National Education Association, 1201 16th St., N.W., Washington, D.C. 20036.

Nursing Careers Program, American Nurses Association, 10 Columbus Circle, New York, N.Y. 10019.

Manufacturing Chemists Association, 1825 Connecticut Ave. N.W., Washington, D.C. 20009. In addition to their own material, M.C.A. will send you a booklet, "Sources of Career Information in Scientific Fields" which, in the 1971-1972 edition, lists 65 organizations, institutions and companies, the names of the booklets offered, and the addresses. Where there is a charge this information is also included. A school or other educational institution may ask for up to six copies of this useful guide without charge.

There are three standard works on occupational opportunities which should be available in your school and public libraries. These supply sound information for serious inquirers.

THE ENCYCLOPEDIA OF CAREERS AND VOCATIONAL GUIDANCE, William E. Hopke (Editor-in-chief), Vol. 1: *PLANNING YOUR CAREER:* Vol. 2: *CAREERS AND OCCUPATIONS,* Chicago, Ill.: Ferguson, 1967.

OCCUPATIONAL LITERATURE (1964 edition), Gertrude Forrester (comp.), New York: H. W. Wilson, 1964.

OCCUPATIONAL OUTLOOK HANDBOOK. Prepared by the Bureau of Labor Statistics, U.S. Department of Labor. Department of Labor, Bulletin 1550, (available from Superintendent of Documents, United States Government Printing Office, Washington, D.C. 20540. If ordering, request the current edition. It is updated regularly by the *OCCUPATIONAL OUTLOOK QUARTERLY.*) Students may also request without charge a copy of "Occupational Outlook Handbook—in Brief", from Office of Publications, Bureau of Labor Statistics, United States Department of Labor, Washington, D.C. 20212.

PREJUDICE: IDENTITY AND DIFFERENCE

PURPOSE:

To explore physical differences, to recognize and rejoice in the fact that we are all different, and must strive for the freedom to be ourselves.

COMMENT:

Another prejudice which cripples many of us is our own worry about "being different," and society's seeming desire to cast us all in a very limited number of molds. Dr. Roger J. Williams, professor of biochemistry at the University of Texas, and past president of the American Chemical Society has spent many years studying "biochemical individuality" and has found amazing anatomical and physiological differences which show that each person really is unique, and should be expected to vary in character traits, ways and degrees of perception, likes and dislikes, abilities, interests, and life styles. Government and education as well as other social structures seem, in many ways, to be devoted to the ideal of stamping out differences. The results are unfortunate not only in the way we see others, but in the way we perceive ourselves. Not only do we look different on the outside, but we are different inside. Think of it—all the millions of people alive today, all the millions who have lived in the past—all truly individuals, all truly different, all truly unique— custom made, each one! We are naturally fascinated by identical twins, and the studies which have demonstrated strikingly similar incidents in their lives. The reason we are fascinated is that these "identical" features are so few and so rare! Even "identical twins" are very far from identical. Even a litter of armadillos, a relatively simple creature compared to man, proved upon study to vary enormously anatomically after careful raising under laboratory conditions which guaranteed identical diets and environmental conditions.

GROUP SIZE:

TIME SUGGESTED:

45—60 minutes

GENERAL DIRECTIONS:

This is a slow moving, non-threatening exercise which can be used with a new group. The experiences themselves are very simple, but involve interaction with a number of different people. This is a time when soft music playing in the background might be useful during Steps Nos. 1, 2 and 4.

MATERIALS REQUIRED:

Ink pad, paper, facial tissues and a cleaning fluid of some kind, one magnifying glass for every five or six students, copies of the prayer given in "Procedure: 6," if desired, record or tape player with suitable music.

PROCEDURES:

1. Have the students take turns in pairs, comparing the palms of their hands. Let them spend about 2—3 minutes with each partner, exploring differences in configuration, color, texture, and last, the lines beloved of palmistry. Have each student examine the hands of about five other persons—more than this will become tiresome. Ask them to jot down a few notes as they go along, writing a few words or sentences on what strikes them about the differences.

2. As the students complete the palm comparisons, ask them to "take their own fingerprints," using the ink pad and a piece of paper. Provide facial tissues and a liquid cleanser of some type to clean the fingers. A thumb and forefinger print will be sufficient. In groups of five or six, using a magnifying glass, members examine and compare the prints of the members of their subgroups.

3. Ask one group member at a time to close his eyes, while the other members of his group change places. Ask each member of the subgroup in turn to now say aloud "Oh, oh, oh," and ask the member with his eyes closed to simply listen to the differences in tone, timbre, and voice quality in general. He may or may not be able to identify each person by the sound, but he will recognize the fact that there is some difference in each case.

4. Ask them to form dyads and talk to one another about how they feel regarding these differences. What about other kinds of differences? Ask them to talk about how "being different" from other people makes them feel in specific situations. Ask them to discuss whether they think this is a good thing or a bad thing.

5. Bring the group together in a plenary to discuss the question of "difference," how it makes them feel, its values and problems. Suggested questions: When and how are you free to be different? When and how is your freedom to be different hampered? How does knowledge of the fact of physical differences affect your thinking about yourself as a person?

6. The session may close with the distribution for quiet reading of the following prayer by Michel Quoist from *THE MEANING OF SUCCESS* (Notre Dame, Ind.: Fides, 1963, pp. 78-79):

"Don't seek to live
somebody else's life;
it's just not you . . .
You have no right
to put on a false face
to pretend you're what you're not,
unless you want to rob others.
Say to yourself:
I am going to bring something new
into this person's life,
because he has never met anyone like me
nor will he ever meet anyone like me,
for in the mind of God
I am unique and irreplaceable."

NOTE: If desired, a class member may be asked to read this aloud, rather than distributing copies to the class.

SUGGESTED RESOURCES:

Williams, Roger J., "The Biology of Behavior," *SATURDAY REVIEW OF LITERATURE,* Jan. 30, 1971, p. 61.

PREJUDICE: FIRST-HAND IMPRESSIONS

PURPOSE:

To understand and recognize our feelings toward others; to see through the eyes of another; to increase appreciation for individual differences.

COMMENT:

Prejudice is pre-judging—judging others on the basis of stereotypes, second-hand impressions, which we allow to blunt and blind our senses and our understanding, and prevent us from seeing and knowing the reality of another human being. This exercise approaches the problem of prejudice indirectly by dealing with "stereotypes" and "prejudices" which carry no emotional freight. It also points up the difference that involvement makes. We "look" at others, we think we "examine" them, but we are not free to *see* them. Unless we have some sort of interaction with them, we really don't *know* them. Empathy requires involvement.

GROUP SIZE:

6—20

TIME SUGGESTED:

30—45 minutes

MATERIALS REQUIRED:

A bag of lemons (oranges) in sufficient number for each class member.

PROCEDURE:

1. Each member selects a lemon (orange) from the bag.
2. Class members are told: "For five minutes, get acquainted with your lemon. Study it, feel it, smell it, etc."
3. Form small groups of no more than six. Ask the students to compare their lemons. "Suggest a name for your lemon." Allow about five minutes.
4. Put all lemons in a pile, mix them up.
5. Each member goes up, in twos or threes, and picks out his own lemon.
6. In small groups members share their feelings about the happening. Some of the following questions may be considered:
   —Why were you able to pick out your lemon?
   —What is special about your lemon? (discuss similarities, differences)
   —Why is it that, with even more time, we fail to build up relationships with others?
   —Why was it easy to build up a relationship with that lemon?
   —How does this experience compare with our efforts to get to know other people, especially those from other races, socio-economic backgrounds, faiths?
   —How can we use what we have experienced in this happening as we try to get to know others?

VARIATION:

Other objects may be substituted for the fruit, such as a stone, and the exercise can be incorporated in a nature walk, in which it provides a quiet, restful, thoughtful interlude. It is important, however, to follow it immediately by the discussion if the purpose is lessened prejudice and increased understanding of our feelings toward others and appreciation of them. This exercise may also be used in developing sensory awareness, and variations for this purpose have been suggested by Bernard Gunther in *SENSE RELAXATION BELOW YOUR MIND,* New York: Macmillan Collier, 1968.

IMPRESSION

COMMENT:

This exercise requires caution: use the exercise after the experiencing of the *Lemon Exercise.*

GROUP SIZE:

Approximately 12

TIME SUGGESTED:

Approximately 45 minutes

PROCEDURE:

1. One person at a time stands before the group.

2. In no particular order of starting, members of the group express their first impression of the person standing in front.

3. Focus first on appearance: take notice of the body structure, posture, facial expression, body movement.

4. Go up and touch the person. Note the feel of his skin—firm, soft; feel his muscles, touch his hair.

5. Push him—let him push you. Do you resist? (resistance/compliance) Does he?

6. Smell him.

7. Reaffirm or amend your first verbal reaction to him.

After each person has had a chance to stand before the group, discuss what has happened, your feelings both as a giver and as a recipient.

MALE/FEMALE ROLES

PURPOSE:

To examine some of the ways in which prejudice and stereotyping of male/female roles limit our freedom to select an occupation.

COMMENT:

Edward T. Hall says, "The fact that behavior in animals is predominately sex-linked has led to certain misconceptions concerning the role of sex in man. It is a great mistake to assume that the behavior which is observed in man is linked to physiology. Studies of culture have shown us that this is usually not the case. Behavior that is exhibited by men in one culture may be classed as feminine in another. All cultures differentiate between men and women, and usually when a given behavior pattern becomes associated with one sex it will be dropped by the other" *(THE SILENT LANGUAGE).*

In the long struggle for identity, for Maslow's "self-actualization" or Rogers' "fully functioning person," many things interfere, including role stereotypes and prejudices. The American male stereotype gives little opportunity to the poet, the ballet dancer or the artist to feel fully "masculine," and to provide a variety of models of "maleness." The female stereotype does not include leadership, business acumen, political skill or technical ability. Even though two-fifths of all married women living with their husbands are employed outside the home, the woman very rarely looks upon her career in the same way as her husband views his. In addition to these problems, many people have difficulty in feeling a sense of "self," of an identity apart from their roles, activities and relationships.

GROUP SIZE:

12—25

TIME SUGGESTED:

At least two sessions of 45—60 minutes.

The first exercise is a modification of one designed by Dr. Claudio Naranjo and helps us to look for the essential features of the self. The class then explores the specific problem of the economics of the "working wife" or "working mother," as an example of stereotyping of male/female roles. Job opportunities and recruitment materials are examined as typical examples of stereotyping.

MATERIALS REQUIRED:

Each student will need a copy of the chart, "Homekeeping: What is its dollar value?"

An assortment of literature available from industrial and professional associations and from individual companies used for recruitment. (see "Suggested Resources")

PROCEDURES:

A. "WHO ARE YOU?"

1. Select six participants, preferably three male, three female, and ask them to leave the room. Admit them back one at a time.

2. After they have left the room, instruct the class that they are to ask of each person, "Who are you?", wait for an answer, and then ask the question again for a total of ten times. Without varying the wording, the voice tone, stress and gesture will be varied each time the question is asked. Repeat this procedure with each participant. Before bringing in the first participant, give the class a few suggestions, demonstrating ways in which the question may be asked. Warn the class that the effect of this repeated questioning may be frustration and confusion on the part of the participants, and that it is important that the class show that they *care* about this person, and are going through this process to help them, not to make fun of them or make them unhappy.

3. Admit the participants, one at a time, repeating the question ten times to each person.

4. Entire class discusses experience.

—What differences in responses occurred? . . . what similarities?

—Which answers were sex-linked? . . . what kinds of differences were there between males and females?

—Do we think of the "self" as physical? . . . as nonphysical?

—Is the "real me" something totally separate from our total person, our self, our physical self?

—Are our bodies unimportant to our "selves"?

—What are some of the relationships between "body" and "career" that come to your mind?

—What kinds of jobs do you believe are suitable for men? . . . for women?

B. "WORKING WIVES"

1. Distribute the "Homekeeping" charts (see below). Determine in advance the current pay rate by calling your local employment office—for instance, in Philadelphia, Pa., June, 1971, the minimum rate for domestic workers was $3.00 per hour for meal preparation (or $75.00 per week for a live-in cook), and $2.00 per hour for other domestic services.

2. Each student fills out a chart on the basis of an estimate of the work load in their own home. Point out that the chart includes time spent with children under ten, but no time is allotted for "helping with homework," chauffeuring, helping girls with sewing, taking telephone messages, etc., for older children. Ask them to estimate the amount of time their own mothers spend with children of various ages. NOTE: If desired, these charts may be filled in by small groups working together, or students may take the charts home to fill them out, saving class time for more discussion.

The following chart is reproduced from "Can Wives Afford to Work," Home Economics Extension Leaflet 11, with permission of the New York State College of Human Ecology at Cornell University.

HOMEKEEPING: What is its dollar value?

JOB & DESCRIPTION	AVERAGE TIME TAKEN*	YOUR WORK LOAD**	VALUE OF YOUR WORK LOAD FOR ONE WEEK
MEAL PREPARATION (table setting, cooking, serving each meal of the day)	Pickup meal, all raw or heat-and-serve ...... 15 min. a meal Simple meal, some preparation ...... 30 min. a meal Typical family dinner ...... 45 min. a meal More elaborate meal ...... 1 hr. a meal	***Average hrs. daily _____ X 7 = _____ av. hrs. weekly Average hrs. weekly _____ X $ _____ an hour = $ _____	
DISHWASHING (the whole cycle from clearing table to cleaning sink, counters)	2 person family ...... 55 min. a day 3 person family ...... 1 hr. a day 4 person family ...... 1 hr. 10 min. a day 5 person family ...... 1 hr. 30 min. a day	Average hrs. daily _____ X 7 = _____ av. hrs. weekly Average hrs. weekly _____ X $ _____ an hour = $ _____	
PHYSICAL CARE OF CHILDREN (all physical care including help with homework and chauffeuring, but not just playing with or checking on them)	If only one child under 10 years: child under 2 years ...... 2 hrs. a day child 2 to 5 ...... 1 hr. a day child 6 to 10 ...... 35 min. a day If additional children under 10: Add for second child under 6 ...... 30 min. a day Add for second child 6 to 10 ...... 20 min. a day Add for third child under 6 ...... 10 min. a day	Average hrs. daily _____ X 7 = _____ av. hrs. weekly Average hrs. weekly _____ X $ _____ an hour = $ _____ (This hourly rate for a baby sitter is too low a measure of the value of a mother's care.)	
ROUTINE CARE OF HOME (daily pickups plus heavier weekly jobs, not seasonal projects)	For homes without children ...... 4 hrs. a week For homes with children ...... 7 hrs. a week	Average hrs. weekly _____ X $ _____ an hour = $ _____	
CLOTHES WASHING (gathering, sorting, spot removing, washing, rinsing, starching, drying)	Each load washed ...... 20 min. each	Average hrs. weekly _____ X $ _____ an hour = $ _____	
IRONING (sprinkling, ironing, folding, putting away)	1 to 9 pieces done at a time ...... 10 min. each 10 to 29 pieces done at a time ...... 5 min. each 30 or more pieces done at a time ...... 4 min. each (2 towels or napkins = 1 piece; 6 handkerchiefs = 1 piece)	Average hrs. weekly _____ X $ _____ an hour = $ _____	
		Total value of the above 6 jobs	$ _____
		Add 25 percent for miscellaneous work	+ _____
		TOTAL DOLLAR VALUE OF HOMEKEEPING FOR ONE WEEK	$ _____
			X 52
		DOLLAR VALUE OF HOMEKEEPING FOR ONE YEAR	$ _____

***Table for changing minutes to nearest tenths of an hour

Minutes	Hours
5	0.1
10	0.2
15	0.3
20	0.3
25	0.4
30	0.5
35	0.6
40	0.7
45	0.8
50	0.8
55	0.9
60	1.0

*The average times given are based on a study of the use of time for household work in 250 New York State families. If you hired the work done, this is about the amount of time these jobs would require.

**Check with the employment office in your community to secure current pay rates.

A PAID JOB:

What is its dollar value?

MONTHLY EXPENSES RESULTING FROM THE JOB	
TAXES, DEDUCTIONS (income, social security, pension)	$_____
PERSONAL EXPENSES (clothes, lunches away from home, personal care, transportation)	$_____
OFFICE EXPENSES (contributions, gifts, coffee breaks, parties)	$_____
FAMILY EXPENSES (services: child care, cleaning, laundry food: meals out, prepared foods, less home preserving)	$_____
OTHER	$_____
TOTAL EXPENSES FOR ONE MONTH	$_____

Gross income for one month	$_____
Total expenses for one month	$_____
NET INCOME FOR ONE MONTH (Gross income minus expenses)	$_____
	X 12
YEARLY NET INCOME FROM PAID JOB	$_____

3. Using the charts as part of input, subgroups of 5—6 discuss pros and cons of working wives and mothers.

4. In a plenary session, subgroups report their findings. Using the chalkboard, help the group arrive at suggested figures for:

"reasonable salary" for working wife

cost of taxes, other deductions such as social security, pension plan, etc.

cost of such expenses as additional clothing, cleaning of clothes, lunches, transportation, office expenses for coffee breaks, gifts, parties, etc.

possible increases in the cost of family food—purchase of prepared dishes and meals eaten away from home.

5. In subgroups as in No. 3, discuss the findings from Nos. 3 and 4. Consider such questions as:

—Would the boys want their wives to work? . . . why?

—Would the girls want to work when they are married? . . . why?

—Why are expenses calculated on the basis of "replacing" the wife, rather than the husband in the home?

—What do they think of the idea of husband and wife working part-time, and performing household tasks part-time? How could this be done? Why is it not done more often? Do the boys believe the girls are better suited to care for children? . . . Do the girls share this view? Is there a physical difference that enters into this?

—In some places in the U.S.S.R. and Israel nursing mothers work, with time off at regular intervals to nurse their babies—do you think this is a good plan?

—In some youth communes in the United States some mothers work while fathers stay home and take care of the children—would you prefer this?

—Do the girls believe it is "unfeminine" or "physically impossible" for them to do heavy work, such as digging, as some women do in the U.S.S.R.? . . . How do the boys feel about this?

—Do the boys feel that occupations such as typist, stenographer, nurse, nursery school teacher are "unmasculine"? . . . How do the girls feel about this?

6. Ask the subgroups to make lists of jobs or occupations which they think are suitable ONLY for women and others suitable ONLY for men, and be prepared to explain their lists.

7. In a plenary, subgroups display and explain their lists.

—Do any subgroups feel that all jobs can be done equally well by either sex?

—What effect have our prejudices or stereotypes had on our list making?

—What physical considerations are involved? Which decisions are based on known anatomical or physiological differences, and which are based on cultural habits?

—What changes do they think would occur in our society if there were total equality in employment? . . . What would happen when the wife was "transferred" to another city? . . . What would happen when the wife was sent overseas on combat duty? . . . What would be the effect on such unions as the electrician's or plumber's unions? . . . Should pregnant women be allowed to work on high steel? . . . as riggers? . . . as telephone linesmen?

C. EMPLOYMENT RECRUITMENT PROCEDURES, AND EDUCATION.

1. Distribute an assortment of employee recruitment pamphlets such as those suggested in "Suggested Resources." Also distribute or ask the students to bring to class the "Help Wanted" sections of the newspaper.

2. Ask the students, working individually or in small groups, to make a "head count" of the men and women pictured in their pamphlets, and to try to identify the kinds of jobs these men and women hold. Ask them to read through the text and decide on its intended audience.

3. General discussion in a plenary can focus on such questions as:

—What job opportunities are offered to men? . . . to women?

—Is some of the material slanted more toward one sex than the other? . . . How can you tell?

—In TV programs that you have seen, what kinds of jobs are held by men? . . . by women?

—In advertisements in the mass media, what work are women usually doing? . . . men?

—How do these findings relate to your "lists" from "B. 7.?"

—How do schools affect the job expectations of men and women?

—Are there any reasons which make sense to you to separate the sexes in school? . . . Does the fact that high school boys develop more slowly than girls make co-ed high schools unfair to boys? . . . Why do you think most schools in the world are segregated by sex? (UNESCO reports: Europe, 35 percent co-ed; South America, 33 percent; North America, 28 percent; Australia and New Zealand, 25 percent; Asia, 12 percent; Africa, 7 percent. Only the U.S.S.R. is 100 percent co-ed.) . . . Do you think this sexual segregation violates the equal protection clause of the 14th Amendment? . . . How do you think segregation affects employment? . . . Or do you think employment practices affect school sexual segregation? . . . Do you think the fact that many formerly all-girls colleges are now admitting boys, and vice versa, is good? . . . Do you know how many students in your community attend sexually-segregated high schools or colleges? . . . Suppose all your community schools became co-ed, what would be the effect? . . . Should this be demanded by law? . . . Who should decide?

VARIATION:

Put a short list of categories on the chalkboard: "Explorers, Rulers and Statesmen, Scientists, Painters, Poets, Philosophers, Inventors, Novelists, Industrialists," or a similar list.

Ask the students to write down as many names as they can in three minutes which fit in one or more of these categories. Ask them to try to think of at least one name in each category, but to write as many names altogether as possible, regardless of category.

Ask them now to go back over these names and note how many are women. Ask them in which category or categories the women should be listed.

Following this, a general discussion may be held, such as that in "C" above.

SUGGESTED RESOURCES:

THE FAMILY AND EDUCATION:

Blitsten, Dorothy R., *THE WORLD OF THE FAMILY*, New York: Random House, 1963. This book may be used for a start, and includes helpful bibliographies on a number of countries.

Kiell, Norman, (ed.), *THE UNIVERSAL EXPERIENCE OF ADOLESCENCE*, Boston, Mass.: Beacon Press, 1964.

Friedenberg, Edgar Z., *COMING OF AGE IN AMERICA*, New York: Vintage, 1965.

Jourard, Sidney M., *THE TRANSPARENT SELF*, rev. ed., New York: Van Nostrand Reinhold, 1971, pp. 30ff. (On "Who am I?" and "Sickening Roles".)

Hall, Edward T., *THE SILENT LANGUAGE*, New York: Fawcett Premier, 1959, p. 49.

Erikson, Erik H., *IDENTITY: YOUTH AND CRISIS*, New York: W. W. Norton & Co., 1968.

King, Edmund J., *OTHER SCHOOLS AND OURS*, rev. ed., New York: Holt, Rinehart & Winston, 1963.

Grant, Nigel, *SOCIETY, SCHOOLS AND PROGRESS IN EASTERN EUROPE*, New York: Pergamon Press, 1969.

Jacoby, Susan, "Who Raises Russia's Children?", *SATURDAY REVIEW*, August 21, 1971, pp. 40ff.

de Rham, Edith, *THE LOVE FRAUD*, New York: Pegasus, 1971. (Examines children's programs and day-care centers in Sweden, Israel and Russia, and urges similar systems for the United States.)

EMPLOYMENT RECRUITMENT MATERIALS

Public Relations Staff, General Motors Corporation, 3044 W. Grand Boulevard, Detroit, Mich. 48202. Write for free "career" leaflets in classroom quantities. Among these, for instance, is one titled, "In Planning Your Future, Look First at the Retail Automobile Business: Sales/Service/Parts/Office/Management." Illustrations show sixty-two male figures, including customers, passersby and personnel, one female standing working at a filing cabinet, and one shadowy background figure which is possibly female. Another pamphlet, "Can I Be an Office Worker?" shows twenty-four females at work, eight as students, and five whose activity is not immediately apparent. It shows two men apparently in executive positions, six as students, and two others whose activity is not determinable.

American Red Cross. (for details on ordering, see "Happiness: Back to Nature"). *LOOKING FOR A FUTURE?* (ARC 872); *EMPLOYMENT OPPORTUNITIES* (ARC 893); *STENOGRAPHERS—A JOB FOR YOU OVERSEAS WITH THE AMERICAN NATIONAL RED CROSS* (ARC 875); *CAREERS IN FIRST AID, SMALL CRAFT, AND WATER SAFETY PROGRAMS* (ARC 898); *BE A DISASTER REPRESENTATIVE* (ARC 874).

American Petroleum Institute, Publication and Distribution Section, 1271 Avenue of the Americas, New York, N.Y. 10020. *PETROLEUM MARKETING—A FUTURE FOR YOU*, 2nd ed., 1965, Publ. 1526, ($.20); *A FIRST STEP*, 1966, Publ. 1563 (service station employees).

Manufacturing Chemists Association, 1825 Connecticut Ave. N.W., Washington, D.C. 20009, *A DOZEN REASONS: WHY YOUNG PEOPLE CHOOSE CHEMICAL INDUSTRY CAREERS. CAN YOU ADD TO THEM?; A BRIGHT FUTURE: FOR YOU AS A CHEMICAL TECHNICIAN; CAREERS AHEAD IN THE CHEMICAL INDUSTRY; SOURCES OF CAREER INFORMATION IN SCIENTIFIC FIELDS.*

American Chemical Society, 1155 16th St., N.W. Washington, D.C. 20036, *CHEMISTRY AND YOUR CAREER*, and *IS CHEMICAL TECHNOLOGY THE CAREER FOR YOU?* (1—5 copies free)

Pfizer Laboratories Division, 235 E. 42nd St., New York, N.Y. 10017, *YOUR CAREER OPPORTUNITIES IN HOSPITALS: YOUR CAREER OPPORTUNITIES IN PHARMACY: YOUR CAREER OPPORTUNITIES IN MEDICINE.*

GROUP REJECTION

PURPOSE:

To experience group rejection on the basis of physical differences, discover our feelings about rejecting and being rejected.

COMMENT:

"Attraction" and "avoidance" are constant phenomena in human behavior. Prejudices constantly prevent our freedom of choice, cloud our judgment and in the case of prejudices against groups of human beings, damage our lives. Skin color is, of course, the case which springs to mind, and in today's world, is the most obviously harmful. There is hardly anyone in the United States who would not agree that this is a "problem," but many have not personally experienced it *as* a problem, or have a variety of views as to "what the problem *is*".

"Most of us came here in chains and most of you came here to escape your chains. Your freedom was our slavery, and therein lies the bitter difference in the way we look at life . . . We are not fighting for the right to be like you. We respect ourselves too much for that. When we fight for freedom, we mean freedom for us to be black, or brown, and you to be white and yet live together in a free and equal society. This is the only way that integration can mean dignity for both of us" (Killens, *THE REBEL CULTURE*).

"You look upon these times as the Atomic Age, the Space Age, the Cold War era. But I believe that when the history of these times is written, it will not be so important who reached the moon first or who made the largest bomb. I believe the great significance will be that this was the century when most of mankind achieved freedom and human dignity. For me this is the Freedom Century" (Killens, *THE REBEL CULTURE*).

GROUP SIZE:

12 or more

TIME SUGGESTED:

This exercise may be carried on over a period

of several days, may be completed in one session of approximately one hour, or may be repeated in different versions on several occasions, building toward a knitting together of the findings at a final discussion. Enough material is included for a series of sessions.

GENERAL DIRECTIONS:

This exercise provides one or more brief experiences in rejection on the basis of physical characteristics, and serves as a basis for discussion. The actual choice of the characteristic to be used depends on the group's composition, their experiences in the past, and their needs in the present. It is important to stress the seriousness with which the experience should be approached. With proper handling of the situation, real tensions will build. The teacher or group leader should enter into the experience whole heartedly, and encourage the class to do so. A single one-hour session will obviously have less impact and provide less data than an experience which can be carried on over a full day or longer.

MATERIALS REQUIRED:

As a rule, no materials will be required, but in some cases it may be desirable to provide different colored armbands to distinguish groups or, if this is impractical, patches of paper or material may be pinned to the clothing. Some additional materials may be used to augment the experience such as films, posters, pictures or records.

PROCEDURES:

1. The first step is to decide on how the group is to be divided. This may be done on the basis of male/female, brown eyes/blue eyes, over 5 ft.2/under 5 ft.2, etc. You may wish to make the division one which is not easy to determine at first glance, such as height or eye color. Make the original decision without consulting the class. Assign students to a group either by saying "You are Group I," "You are Group II," or by sending them to a particular corner of the room.

2. Take Group II out of the room and tell them, "Because of your (height, blue eyes or whatever) we are going to ask you to wait here for a few minutes. I will call you in when it is time." Then instruct Group I by telling them that Group II has a certain undesirable physical feature, telling them what this is, and that for Group I's own sake it will be best if Group II people are treated as very un-

desirable. Explain that this is an exercise which will benefit Group II by helping them to see the results of extremely prejudicial treatment. Group II is to be made to feel unwelcome in the classroom by any means, short of physical mistreatment, which Group I feels will be effective. Group II is to be treated with dislike, distrust, suspicion and disdain, their ideas and suggestions ignored, made fun of, or contradicted. They are to be physically avoided, their company shunned. Explain that because of their extreme undesirability, you will countenance whispered comments about them and even rudeness in a way you would not ordinarily want to see in the class. Tell them that this behavior is to continue until you feel that Group II has thoroughly learned its lesson, and you will tell them when these individuals are to be welcomed and the situation explained.

3. Group II is now brought back into the room without any further explanation or instruction. See that your own manner is "correct," but distant. Ignore their questions, if any.

4. From here on, any activity which involves supposed interaction may be carried on by the class. If it is a procedure in which you are active, be sure to treat Group I and Group II in an obviously different manner. Convince yourself that Group II is undesirable, disruptive, unpleasant, harmful to the other class members, stupid, irresponsible, or whatever will help you. Be your usual pleasant, accepting, interested self with Group I. Group II members will probably try to make friendly contact with personal friends in Group I and, finding themselves rebuffed, will at first treat it as an amusing game, but their pleasure will usually soon fade and be replaced by discomfort, possibly even anger. You may wish to hold a discussion on some topic unrelated to freedom or prejudice, continue part of a previously begun project, work on a valuing exercise, do a role play on some other subject following it with a discussion. The more the activity would normally involve considerable friendly interaction of all group members, the more quickly the effect will be observable, but if you are able to carry the exercise on for a long period of time, it is acceptable to allow the effect to arise more subtly. If possible, at the close of the session, ask the group to "continue the exercise as they were instructed until the next time this class meets." Some will not, of course, follow directions, particularly if the class will not meet again the following day, but some residual behavior will take place.

5. *If* it is necessary to complete the exercise on the same day, "break the spell" by explaining the instructions you gave Group I, and opening the discussion by asking the Group II people how they felt, and then allowing the Group I people to get involved in the discussion. The Group I people will realize

that the exercise was as much for their "benefit" as it was for Group II's. It will be helpful to ask students to recall specific incidents and remember their feelings as accurately as possible.

—Ask Group II members what they first noticed, and how it affected them.

—Did it influence their behavior?

—What did they want to do?

—How did they handle the situation?

—Did Group II people begin to feel a fellowship among themselves, or were they too concerned with their personal reactions.

—Did they resent mistreatment of their fellow Group II people?

—Can they trace a succession of different feelings as the exercise continued?

—Did they become angry, apathetic, disinterested?

—Did they feel as though they were waiting for something to happen?

—Did Group I people begin to enjoy the exercise, or did they feel the same way Group II people did?

If the exercise is to be continued at another session, begin the session as in "4" above, with no reference to this exercise other than saying something to the effect that "We will continue the exercise with Group I and Group II as at the last session. Today we are going to . . ." After enough time has elapsed so that you see the groups are "into their roles," break the spell as above, and hold a discussion.

6. The last part of the discussion should focus in on the whole problem of prejudice and how it limits freedom—both Group I and Group II were unfree, both suffered in one way or another, both were victims of prejudice.

—In what way was Group II a special kind of victim?

—What other freedoms were affected?

—How was your own freedom affected?

It is important to relate any actual feelings experienced to the cognitive level of this discussion, and to build on these feelings by asking such questions as:

—How would you have felt if we had continued the exercise for the rest of this year?

—How would you handle this situation if the same attitudes and behaviors were expressed toward you in all other situations outside this classroom?

—What happened to your original feelings about (eye color, height, etc.)?

—Were you increasingly or decreasingly aware of this as a factor?

—Did you think of this when you were outside the classroom?

—What feelings, if any, did you have

about any people other than members of this class?

—If you did not continue the exercise outside of class, what were your feelings when you changed your behavior?

—How alike were "all members of Group I" (II)? How unalike?

The class can continue this discussion with an exploration of their own ideas on how their prejudices have been developed, etc.

7. The class may suggest reversing roles and continuing the exercise, but the effects may be different. It might be best to repeat the experience at some future date, perhaps using different criteria for division. In this case, some class members will be in "Group II" or "Group I" on both occasions, some will not, and a variety of differences will be noticed in the discussion.

VARIATIONS:

1. The group may be divided arbitrarily, without regard to any physical characteristics, by the use of armbands, or circles may be drawn on the forehead with waterproof mascara or eyeliner.

2. A session on the language of prejudice will be useful. Students may develop their own lists of words or speech patterns which show various degrees of prejudice, from the outright "insult" words to the much more subtle and often unconscious phrases of paternalism. A useful, although dated, booklet is available from The Palo Alto Fair Play Council, 180 University Ave., Palo Alto, Calif., called "Prejudice Won't Hide: A Guide for Developing a Language of Equality," 1960, $.20. Dan Herr, writing in the *CRITIC* of September-October, 1971, includes the following "Black List," saying, "I think it proves beyond question that we have been raised in and live in a racist climate that equates white with good and black with evil. It helps to explain us."

Blackguard	Black and Tan
Black Maria	Black bile
Black hand	Blackhead
Black cloud	Black hearted
Blackmail	Blackjack
Black Tuesday	Black magic
Black rage	Blackleg
Blackball	Black Mass
Black flag	Black measles
Black Death	Black rot
Black Hole	Black sheep
Black eye	Black Friday
Black lie	Black deed
Black mood	Black humor
Blackout	Blackdamp
Black outlook	Blacken
Black words	Black depression

Black market	Black curse
Black mark	Black Sox

3. Students may start their work on prejudice and group rejection by writing a paragraph starting with, "I would describe the typical foreigner as . . ." After writing their paragraphs individually, small groups may try to prepare a list of phrases which they think would properly describe "typical foreigners." In the course of this, they will find considerable disagreement within their groups, and begin to see the stereotyping and prejudicial attitudes so common among us. A plenary session can then discuss our prejudices against "foreigners," how they have developed, and their effect on our society.

4. Follow-up sessions may use films, records, readings, or monitoring of the mass media.

SUGGESTED RESOURCES:

Check with your school and local libraries to find materials available in your community. Students may be able to recommend books and other materials. There is a great deal of suitable material available, and only a few suggestions follow, illustrating the range of recent works and a few older books of lasting value.

Baldwin, James, *NOBODY KNOWS MY NAME*, New York: Dell, 1961.

Binzen, Peter, *WHITETOWN, USA*, New York: Vintage, 1970.

Brown, Claude, *MANCHILD IN THE PROMISED LAND*, New York: Macmillan, 1965.

Ellison, Ralph, *INVISIBLE MAN*, New York: Modern Library, 1947, 1952.

Elman, Richard M., *THE POORHOUSE STATE: THE AMERICAN WAY OF LIFE ON PUBLIC ASSISTANCE*, New York: Delta, 1966.

Flannery, Edward H., *THE ANGUISH OF THE JEWS: TWENTY-THREE CENTURIES OF ANTI-SEMITISM*, New York: Macmillan, 1965.

Glazer, Nathan, and Daniel Patrick Moynihan, *BEYOND THE MELTING POT: THE NEGROES, PUERTO RICANS, JEWS, ITALIANS, AND IRISH OF NEW YORK CITY*, Cambridge, Mass.: M.I.T. Press and Harvard University, 1963.

Graham, James J., *THE ENEMIES OF THE POOR*, New York: Random House, 1970.

Killens, John Oliver, "Explanation of the 'Black Psyche'," *THE REBEL CULTURE*, Robert S. Gold, (ed.), New York: Dell, 1970, pp. 35, 38.

Knowles, Louis L., and Kenneth Prewitt (eds.) *INSTITUTIONAL RACISM IN AMERICA*, Englewood Cliffs, N.J.: Prentice-Hall, 1969.

*Lewis, Oscar, *LA VIDA: A PUERTO RICAN FAMILY IN THE CULTURE OF POVERTY—SAN JUAN AND NEW YORK*, New York: Random House, 1966.

Liston, Robert, *THE AMERICAN POOR*, New York: Dell, 1970.

Moore, Truman, "Slaves for Rent: The Shame of American Farming," *THE TRIPLE REVOLUTION: SOCIAL PROBLEMS IN DEPTH*, Robert Perrucci and Marc Pilisuk (eds.), Boston, Mass.: Little, Brown and Co., 1968.

* Lawson, Fusao Inada, *BEFORE THE WAR: POEMS AS THEY HAPPENED*, Morrow, 1971. (Poems by an American-born Japanese poet, illustrating prejudice against his people in the United States.)

Nash, Gary B., and Richard Weiss, *THE GREAT FEAR: NINE HISTORIANS PROBE THE HISTORICAL ORIGINS OF WHITE RACIAL ATTITUDES AND THEIR EFFECT ON TODAY'S RACIAL CRISIS*, New York: Holt, Rinehart and Winston, 1970.

*Richette, Lisa Aversa, *THE THROWAWAY CHILDREN*, New York: Dell, 1969.

Szasz, Thomas S., *PSYCHIATRIC JUSTICE*, New York: Macmillan, 1965.

Szwed, John F., (ed.), *BLACK AMERICA*, New York: Basic Books, 1970.

*transACTION, "A Special Supplement: Crusade against Children", July/August, 1971, Vol. 8, Nos. 9/10. A series of articles concerned with mishandling of children in various ways, in part stemming from an apparent prejudice against children.

(NOTE: Works marked with an asterisk contain some materials which may be considered in questionable taste for school assignments, or even of possible harm to some young people. If you are unfamiliar with this material it would be best to read it yourself first.)

Carson, Hampton L., *HEREDITY AND HUMAN LIFE*, New York: Columbia, 1963. (A sound introduction to genetics and also a presentation of the evidence opposed to racism.)

Vanderwerth, W. C., *INDIAN ORATORY: FAMOUS SPEECHES BY NOTED INDIAN CHIEFTAINS*, Norman, Okla.: University of Oklahoma Press, 1971.

Black, Elk, *THE SACRED PIPE:* Black Elk's Account of the Seven Rites of the Oglala Sioux recorded and edited by Joseph Epes Brown, Baltimore, Md.: Penguin, 1971.

McLuhan, T. C., *TOUCH THE EARTH: A SELF-PORTRAIT OF INDIAN EXISTENCE*, New York: Outerbridge & Dienstfrey/E. P. Dutton & Co., 1971. (A beautiful collection of about equal parts of

106   Indian writings and speeches from the sixteenth to the twentieth century, and the photographs of Edward S. Curtis, taken early in the twentieth century.)

The following materials may have special usefulness to educators:

Abrahams, Roger D., *DEEP DOWN IN THE JUNGLE: NEGRO NARRATIVE FOLKLORE FROM THE STREETS OF PHILADELPHIA*, 1st. rev. ed., Chicago, Ill.: Aldine, 1970.

Allport, Gordon W., *THE NATURE OF PREJUDICE*, Garden City, N.Y.: Doubleday Anchor, 1958.

Brink, William, and Louis Harris, *THE NEGRO REVOLUTION IN AMERICA*, New York: Simon and Schuster, 1963.

Decker, Sunny, *AN EMPTY SPOON*, New York: Harper & Row, 1969.

Fish, Kenneth L., *CONFLICT AND DISSENT IN THE HIGH SCHOOL*, New York: Bruce, 1970.

Kozol, Jonathan, *DEATH AT AN EARLY AGE*, New York: Bantam, 1967.

Mack, Raymond W., (ed.), *PREJUDICE AND RACE RELATIONS*, A New York Times Book, Chicago, Ill.: Quadrangle, 1970.

Miel, Alice, with Edwin Kiester, Jr., "The Shortchanged Children of Suburbia: What Schools Don't Teach about Human Differences and What Can Be Done about It", Institute of Human Relations Press, Pamphlet Series, #8, 1967, The American Jewish Committee, 165 E. 56th St., New York.

Myers, Gustavus, *HISTORY OF BIGOTRY IN THE UNITED STATES*, ed. by Henry M. Christman, New York: Capricorn, 1960.

Wallerstein, Immanuel, and Paul Starr (eds.), *THE UNIVERSITY CRISIS READER*, Vol. I, Section IV, "Racism and the University"; Vol. II, Section V, "The Counterattack against the Student Movement", New York: Vintage, 1971.

You may also write for literature and bibliographies to the following organizations:

American Council for Judaism, 309 Fifth Ave., New York, N.Y. 10016.

Anti-Defamation League of B'nai B'rith, 315 Lexington Ave., New York, N.Y. 10016.

Association on American Indian Affairs, Inc., 432 Park Ave. South, New York, N.Y. 10016.

Association for the Study of Negro Life and History, 1538 Ninth St. N.W., Washington, D.C. 20001.

Indian Rights Association, 1505 Race St., Philadelphia, Pa. 19102.

National Association for the Advancement of Colored People, 1790 Broadway, New York, N.Y. 10019.

National Congress of American Indians, 1346 Connecticut Ave. N.W., Washington, D.C. 20036.

National Association for Retarded Children, 2709 Avenue E East, Arlington, Texas 76011.

National Conference of Christians and Jews, 43 W. 57th St., New York, N.Y. 10019.

FILMS:

Picture in Your Mind. 16 min., 16 mm., color. International Film Foundation, 1949. Despite its age, this provocative film stresses in animated symbols the growth of prejudice and the importance of trying to see things as they really are. Sophisticated music and impressionistic art will appeal to students who might be annoyed by more simplistic moralizing.

Who Do You Kill? 51 min., 16 mm., black and white. CBS-TV, 1964. This moving TV drama is still up-to-date, and despite its length is worth using if possible. Racial prejudice and prejudice against the poor are both illuminated.

Willie Catches On. 24 min., 16 mm., black and white. National Film Board of Canada, 1962. Available from Contemporary Films. As Willie grows, so grow his prejudices, assembled from those around him.

The Woodpile. 27 min., 16 mm., black and white. Paulist Productions, Insight Series. Previously unrecognized prejudices come to light when an electronics firm considers hiring a black employee.

Night and Fog. 31 min., 16 mm., black and white and color. Argos Films (French), 1955. Mass Media Ministries. Man's inhumanity to man is shown in this excellent film on the unrelieved horror of Nazi concentration camps. Results can be disappointing if students are unprepared for the emotional impact and are not helped to see an application to themselves.

Flatland. 12 min., 16 mm., color. Robert Gardner, Howard University, 1955. Contemporary Films. A very cheerful and delightful animation about an intellectual prejudice—which leads to jailing for the young square who is converted to a belief in the third dimension.

An American Girl. 29 min., 16 mm., black and white. Anti-Defamation League, 1958. ADL regional offices. Although dated in part, the film is still an appealing presentation to girls of the theme of prejudicial rejection of a young girl by her "own group" because she wears a bracelet of Jewish religious symbols. For unsophisticated groups.

Ku Klux Klan: The Invisible Empire. 47 min., 16 mm., black and white, CBS News, 1965. This film and the following filmstrips are for groups which desire some factual input about the black/white situation in the United States. This documentary shows the history of the Klan, interviews with klansmen and some actual filming of their activities.

Crescendo. Not a film, but a well made filmstrip in color, 76 frames, with guide and record, National Council of Churches, Department of Education for Mission, 1967. Friendship Press. The black protest movement from revolts on slave ships to the Black Muslims and S.C.L.C.

Let the Rain Settle It. 15 min., 16 mm., color. St. Francis Productions, 1970. The meeting between two boys, one Caucasian, one negro, is actually an encounter between poor and middle-class, between rural and urban cultures, between black and white.

EYEBALL TO EYEBALL

PURPOSE:

To explore and enlarge our personal awareness and ability to be comfortable in situations of physical proximity.

COMMENT:

How comfortable do you feel when you look at another person for any length of time? When you are talking with someone else, how aware are you of their physical presence? Does this awareness make you comfortable, or uncomfortable? Why? Most of the interaction in this exercise is on a one-to-one basis, and although more personal and intimate than the usual classroom situation, is fairly low key. There may be some giggling, but this will not damage the experience. The dyads move briefly into a small subgroup, then each person works individually, the final results being shared by the large group in what will be a rather lighthearted and amusing finish.

GROUP SIZE:

Any number. Groups of more than six are subgrouped. If the total number is uneven, you may participate in dyad or use one triad.

TIME SUGGESTED:

45—60 minutes

GENERAL DIRECTIONS:

This exercise may be used with a fairly new group, and may be used immediately following "Freedom: Break Through," if desired. It will help a new group become more cohesive.

MATERIALS REQUIRED:

Crayons, felt tip markers or paints; shelf paper or newsprint.

PROCEDURE:

1. Ask class members to think of a time in their life when they remember feeling really free. Break the class into dyads, and ask each person to tell his partner about it. Encourage them to explore a bit why they felt free in that situation, and whether they were alone or with others.

2. In the same dyads, ask them to sit silently for two minutes, gazing into each other's eyes. Can you tell each other something with your eyes? Do you feel the other is telling you something important with his eyes?

3. In the same dyads, ask them to discuss how they felt in "2".

4. Combine the dyads in groups of six, asking them to stand in a circle. In asking them to form a circle, do not specify what they are to do with their hands. They may spontaneously put their hands on one another's shoulders, or about one another's waists. If they do not, after a few moments, ask them to do one or the other. How do they feel now? More, or less comfortable? Why? Do they feel part of a group? More, or less free? After a few more moments, ask them to "let go of each other" and while remaining in approximately the same position, turn their backs so that they face outward from the circle. How do they feel now? More, or less free? Do you still feel part of the group? Is there any difference in the way you now feel about the group (standing looking outward)?

5. Using shelf paper or newsprint and crayons, felt tip markers or paint, ask each member of the class to draw "What do you think is the group's identity? (If this question stumps them after a minute or two, help them a bit by asking "What do you think of right now when you think of this group today?")

6. Members then share the pictures with either the entire class, or if the class is large, with their subgroup from "4". Ask them to decide which picture best represents the group.

7. Encourage the group to discuss the picture for a few minutes in the light of what has happened in this session. Does the picture represent the physical reality of the group members? Are "eyes" or a "circle" visible? What is left of their first discussion on "remembering when you were really free"? Is the group "free"? Are they "free" in the group? Did they feel free enough with each other to be comfortable when looking into one another's eyes?

VARIATIONS:

1. After "3", ask each member to turn away from his partner and "gaze into space" for two minutes, just thinking his own thoughts, about anything he wishes, but without catching the eye of anyone else. Ask all to compare this experience with that of "2". What made the difference?

2. After "3", ask them to talk quietly with each other about a memory of a time when they felt very restricted, limited, unfree. During this exchange they are to gaze steadily at their partner's hands. Ask them to discuss this experience and compare it with "2". Were they more, or less comfortable? Why?

3. Ask them to place both their hands on their partner's face, one hand on each cheek, fingertips just touching cheekbones. While doing this they are to tell their partner what the word "free" makes them think of. Tell them they do not have to come up with a definition—just to say what other words and ideas come into their minds when they think of the word "free." Ask them to talk about how they felt doing this. Did they look at each other all the time? Did they feel silly? comfortable? uncomfortable?

4. If they have done the original Steps Nos. 1, 2 and 3 in the "Procedure" and then the above three "Variations," ask them to sit quietly for a moment or so thinking about these experiences. Ask them to combine the dyads in groups of six, and compare their experiences, feelings and ideas about what they have done so far.

PHYSICAL HANDICAPS

either of two ways. The film may be used first, as a change of pace, with the carrying out of the physical experiment deferred until another session, or the experiment can be the first step, followed by the film at the next session. In either case, discussion follows both the film and the experience. You may wish to ask the students in advance to bring in certain specific food items for this session.

PURPOSE:

To see how physical handicaps limit our freedom, and at the same time how handicapped people can greatly expand their freedom through retraining and community acceptance.

COMMENT:

Severely handicapped people are usually identified early, and retraining instituted promptly. Many people with minor handicaps are never identified, and their freedom to do, act, and be is impeded. Through work with the handicapped, many untapped resources and potentials of the human body have been identified and means of developing them found. In a sense, we all are "handicapped" by underdevelopment. As a matter of interest and concern, the training of the severely handicapped is a subject worthy of study. In addition, throughout our lives we are often in contact with people with physical disabilities, and our reactions to them are often not helpful to them. Sometimes we are afraid or uncomfortable when working or associating with handicapped people. This limits our freedom as well as theirs, in the same way that other prejudices do. We can deepen our appreciation of those senses and abilities which we have, and be alerted to the possibilities of expanding and developing dormant capabilities.

GROUP SIZE:

6—20

TIME SUGGESTED:

This is planned for two sessions of about one hour each.

GENERAL DIRECTIONS:

Decide on other activities to be used in Step "3" in "Procedures". This exercise may be started in

MATERIALS REQUIRED:

1. Blindfolds for half the class.
2. "Children of the Silent Night," a 27-minute color film available from Guidance Information Center, Academy Avenue, Saxtons River, Vermont 15154. This is a documentary made at the Perkins School for the Blind in Massachusetts, and deals with the children in the deaf-blind department. This film is available without charge.
3. Something to eat and drink, such as canned or bottled soda, fruit, small individual cans of pudding which are now available in many food stores.
4. Plastic spoons for the pudding or knives for the fruit, if desired.

PROCEDURE:

1. If the film is to be shown first, explain to the class before screening the film what the students are to watch for. There are many aspects that you might suggest the students watch for and you may wish to suggest they make a few notes. Ask them to note their own reactions to the children—would they want to get to know these children? How do they feel about them? If there were children like this in the homes of their friends or in their neighborhood, how would they feel about baby-sitting for them when they were young, or having them as friends in their teens? What methods are used to compensate for the senses they lack? Can these children do anything they can't do? What? How? What can they do that these children cannot? How does their day differ from the day of these children?

2. After the film, conduct a discussion, working with questions such as above, and helping the class explore the limitations on freedom suffered by the children in the film, their own relative freedom, and ways in which their freedom could be expanded by some of the means used in training these children. How well could they manage at night in the event of a power failure? How would they spend their time? How well can they identify surroundings by touch?

3. At the following session, ask half the class

110

to volunteer to be blindfolded for the duration of the class. Ask the other half to volunteer to use only their left hand (if they are right-handed), doing everything they normally would do with their right hand as well as they can with the left—writing, picking things up, etc. They will have to help the blindfolded members do such things as write their names, check off answers or tallies, eat, etc. For the first part of this session provide a variety of activities which will bring the handicaps to light, such as (a) give them something to eat and drink which is not too easy to manage; (b) ask them to fill out a short questionnaire on something of interest to them; (c) create a number of situations in which they must move about, regroup, walk to the chalkboard and write something, re-arrange the furniture, climb up and stand on a chair to speak briefly to the group.

4. Save ten or fifteen minutes at the end of the session to discuss how they felt in these situations. During the discussion, ask the blindfolded students to keep their blindfolds on, and the one-handed students to sit on both their hands during this discussion, thus inhibiting their gestures. Help them express their frustrations. As in any sensory deprivation exercise, this will at least temporarily increase their appreciation of the normal functioning of the deprived sense, but will also begin to open up to them the possibilities of increasing their freedom through increasing all sensory awareness.

VARIATIONS:

1. If feasible and/or desirable, the experiment may be continued over several sessions or, if the circumstances allow, throughout a single day.

2. This exercise may be part of a series concerned with physical handicaps, in which some of the exercises or materials given in the section "Happiness: Physical Handicaps" are used, and field trips and speakers arranged. Opportunities for service may be explored, the question of birth defects and their causes and prevention investigated. If the students are particularly interested in finding out more about the blind and the partially sighted, the section on "Life: Senses: Vision" may be used.

3. A study of minimal physical handicaps may be made, investigating the limitations on freedom made by such relatively small problems as near-sightedness, deafness in one ear, etc., or of those problems which are far from minimal, but which are often unseen, such as diabetes, heart disease, and so forth. Some students in the class may suffer from a number of these problems and, depending on the individual and the group, may be willing to speak for themselves on this matter, once

the subject has been brought up by an impersonal film, exercise or discussion of the problem.

SUGGESTED RESOURCES:

ACTIVITIES:

A field trip may be arranged to a local school for the deaf, blind, or crippled.

A speaker may be brought in who works either as a volunteer or professional staff member with an institution or organization working with the physically handicapped. For instance, a staff person from the local branch of the Crippled Children's Society may be able to come and show a film and talk about his own work.

LITERATURE:

Yunge, Gloria, "White Cane," *GOOD HOUSEKEEPING,* Vol. 172, No. 6, (June, 1971) p. 71, 160-163. A first person account of a young girl who gradually lost her sight, but managed to keep a job in the same advertising agency in New York. It tells of her experiences, her feelings, and her initial rejection and later use of "the white cane." The brief article is excellent to develop empathy and help us experience second-hand her physical, emotional and intellectual responses to her situation.

Mehta, Ved, *FACE TO FACE,* Boston, Mass.: Little, Brown & Co., 1957. Fascinating autobiography of the author's childhood in India, his efforts to overcome his sightless condition, culminating in his university days in England and his beginning success as an author. It is quite possible to read his *FLY IN THE FLYBOTTLE,* a series of interviews with philosophers active on the "Oxbridge" scene today without being aware of his blindness. He has since written other books, including an account of his temporary return to India and his experiences of changes in that country since his childhood.

ORGANIZATIONS:

American Diabetes Association, 18 E. 48th St., New York, N.Y. 10017.

Epilepsy Foundation of America, 733 15th St. N.W., Washington, D.C. 20005.

March of Dimes (The National Foundation), 1275 Mamaroneck Ave., White Plains, N.Y. 10605.

National Association for Retarded Children, 2709 Avenue E East, Arlington, Texas 76011.

National Easter Seal Society for Crippled Children and Adults, 2023 W. Ogden Avenue, Chicago, Ill. 60612.

National Association of Hearing and Speech

Agencies, 919 18th St. N.W., Washington, D.C. 20006.

National Federation of the Blind, 524 Fourth St., Des Moines, Iowa 50309.

National Health Council, Inc., 1740 Broadway, New York, N.Y. 10019.

United Cerebral Palsy Association, 66 East 34th St., New York, N.Y. 10016.

PHYSICAL DEPENDENCIES

PURPOSE:

To discover ways to remain or achieve freedom from physical dependencies, both for oneself and for others in society.

COMMENT:

"When Christ freed us, he meant us to remain free. Stand firm, therefore, and do not submit again to the yoke of slavery" (GAL. 5:1). Probably 200,000 children in the United States receive amphetamine and stimulant therapy, another 100,000 receive tranquilizers and antidepressants. In addition, an unknown number of high school students are using the same sedatives or tranquilizers as their parents—all on the doctor's prescription (transACTION, July/August, 1971, Vol. 8, No. 9/10). Chemotherapy has largely replaced "restraints" in our mental institutions and allowed thousands of patients to return to their homes, and as of March, 1971, there has been a reduction in the number of admissions for schizophrenia and depression. Length of stay has been reduced, although readmissions apparently have increased.

Although cigarette smoking dropped in 1971 for the fourth consecutive year, there are still millions physically or emotionally dependent on tobacco.

It is etimated that there are 300,000 cases of alcoholism in New York City alone, where it is the fifth leading cause of death. The problem is compounded by the fact that many commonly used tranquilizers, sedatives, antihistamines and antidiabetic agents interact with alcohol with harmful and sometimes fatal results.

Drug abuse, although far down this list, is seriously damaging the lives of many, and on June 17, 1971, President Nixon declared that drug abuse "has assumed the dimensions of a national emergency," and set up a new White House office on drug abuse. The U.S. Bureau of Narcotics and Dangerous Drugs lists a total of only 68,864 known active addicts as of Dec. 31, 1970, but in 1969 and again in 1970 about 3,000 new addicts under 21 were reported.

GROUP SIZE:

6—25

TIME SUGGESTED:

This exercise calls for a series of discussions, field trips, lectures, individual research, or some combination of these elements. More than one session is involved, but the exact number would depend on group needs and interests.

GENERAL DIRECTIONS:

The exercise starts with a discussion seeking to discover areas of needs and interests in the class as well as investigating the knowledgeability of members. NOTE: It is quite possible that some members of your class are using drugs prescribed by their physicians. It is necessary to be careful that these students are not unduly upset by the discussions. The exercise should be introduced by a statement that, given the present state of our medical knowledge and our societal problems, chemotherapy, or the use or such drugs as tranquilizers has been of great benefit to many people, but that it is important that some questions be raised.

MATERIALS REQUIRED:

Speakers, films, literature, sources of information.

PROCEDURE:

1. An initial discussion session explores the field broadly to determine the most immediate concern of the class. Some questions which may help to open up the problems are:

—What do you see as the difference between the physical dependency of all men on air, food and water, and the special kinds of dependencies of some people on drugs, alcohol and tobacco?

—What organizations and institutions in your area are dealing with the "problem" kinds of dependencies?

—What are the laws in your State governing the sale and use of these substances? . . . What legislation is being considered?

—What is the Federal government doing about research, control, and information in these matters?

—What do you know about how these various things affect the human body (mind)?

—Why do you think some people have these special dependencies? . . . Why doesn't everyone? . . . What other means are available for handling the needs and desires which lead to such dependencies? . . . Are these alternatives good, or bad, in your view?

—Do you think there are other dependencies or addictions or ways of escape which are comparable, such as TV, some kinds of movies, behavioral modification or control training? . . . In what ways do these differ from drugs, alcohol, tobacco?

2. Depending on class interests, various programs may be arranged, with the help of the students, to further investigate answers to the above. Field trips, knowledgeable speakers, individual interviews, carefully selected films, tapes and reading materials may form the basis of individual reports and group discussions. Your area may provide few suitable field trips, but investigate the possibilities of: a mental health center, a college or university, sources listed in the telephone directory under "alcohol," "alcoholism," "drug abuse," "smoking clinics," etc. Literature and speakers are often available through such sources. Also, professional people working with some centers or agencies may be helpful, for instance, those working with counseling, social work, community health, or hospitals.

We would recommend that you *not* start with "drug abuse by the young," unless this is clearly the primary interest of the class, and that when you do work on this part of the project you are very careful in your selection of material. A young "ex-addict" may be a very helpful speaker, but try not to have your material all from one point of view.

3. Make your approach as positive as possible, helping the students to seek viable alternatives, "better ways to turn on," to calm down, to find closeness, warmth, excitement. Help the students to look for ways to be free from the need for chemical agents, to look for ways in which their own community can help prevent, as well as try to remedy, these problems. You will find some of the exercises in this book helpful. Students may want to help get a teen-center started where such things as yoga may be taught, or may be interested in doing volunteer work to help publicize or assist in other ways, agencies in the community seeking alternatives for young people.

SUGGESTED RESOURCES:

TOBACCO:

For literature contact your local branch of the National Tuberculosis and Respiratory Disease Association.

FILM:

Smoking and You, 11 min., color, produced in England for the Central Office of Information. Illustration of relationship between cigarette smoking and lung disease, particularly cancer.

ALCOHOL:

LITERATURE:

(See also "organizations" listed below for sources of pamphlets, bibliographies, etc.)

Sherburne, Zoa, *JENNIFER,* New York: William Morrow, 1959. Good novel about a girl with an alcoholic mother.

Horton, Paul B., and Gerald R. Leslie, *THE SOCIOLOGY OF SOCIAL PROBLEMS,* 2nd ed., New York: Appleton-Century-Crofts, 1960, pp. 479-485. Although dated, suitable on sociological approach to problem.

"Alcoholism," Health and Welfare Division, Metropolitan Life Insurance Co., One Madison Ave., New York, N.Y. 10010. Free booklet, addressed to adults but suitable.

FILMS:

To Your Health, 11 minutes, color, World Health Organization.

(For the following films, contact the Chapter nearest to you of the Mental Health Association, or write National Association for Mental Health, 10 Columbus Circle, New York, N.Y. 10019, or Midwest, 828 Custer Ave., Evanston, Ill. 60202, or Western, 1211 Polk St., San Francisco, Calif. 94109.)

David—The Profile of a Problem Drinker, 27 minutes, black and white, 1958. National Film Board of Canada. Some basic insecurities and danger signals leading to alcoholism are illustrated in this story of a young architect. Use of drugs, psychotherapy and hospitalization to combat the addiction are shown.

Problem Drinkers, 19 minutes, black and white, 1962. Shows work of Alcoholics Anonymous, the Research Council on Problems of Alcohol, and Yale School of Alcohol Studies. Somewhat dated.

Mental Health, Alcohol, Narcotics, Part III of the National Health Test series, 1968. Nine scoring questions and one opinion question form good discussion basis.

ORGANIZATIONS:

For literature, films, and sources of speakers or suitable subjects for interviews, contact your local branch of Alcoholics Anonymous. If there is no listing in your telephone directory, ask doctors, hospitals or clergy if they know how you can contact the local branch. If there is no local branch, write to Alcoholics Anonymous, Box 459, Grand Central Post Office, New York, N.Y. 10017, or one of the follow-ing nonaffiliated organizations:

Al-Anon Family Group Headquarters, P.O. Box 182, Madison Square Station, New York, N.Y. 10010. This is also the address for Alateen Headquarters.

National Council on Alcoholism, 2 East 103 St., New York, N.Y. 10029.

North American Association of Alcoholism Programs, Room 323, Dupont Circle Bldg., Washington, D.C. 20036.

FACT SHEETS:

You may want to prepare such sheets for your students containing information such as the following geared to your own locality.

Alcoholism is a cause or contributing factor in many kinds of illness, in homicide, suicide and divorce. In business and industry it causes absenteeism, lateness, accidents, wasted materials and damaged products. It is considered by experts in many fields to be one of the major social problems in the United States today.

AMERICA magazine recently pointed out that there are more than 85,000 fatalities a year due to alcohol abuse. They also noted that although the mass media made much of drug abuse among the military, little attention was paid to the disclosure that there are 120,000 alcoholics among military personnel (*AMERICA,* Jan. 15, 1972, Vol. 126, no. 2, pp. 32-33). There are almost 55,000 fatal car accidents a year. It is known that alcohol abuse is a causative factor in a large percentage of these.

The Ford Foundation sponsored a study of drug abuse which states, "Of all the potential drugs of abuse, alcohol is one of the most damaging, since even relatively light consumption clearly causes some damage to such organs as the brain and liver and heavy consumption causes serious damage and sometimes death." The authors state that the alcoholism of the nine million Americans who abuse alcohol affects a total of well over thirty million people (Philadelphia *INQUIRER,* Jan. 10, 1972, p. 5).

A study made in Montgomery County, Pa., of student abuse of drugs and alcohol was reported Nov. 30, 1971, in the Philadelphia *INQUIRER.*

"The $17,000 study which took nine months to compile, used information from 5 parochial schools, 10 private schools, 8 colleges and 20 public school districts. Nearly 4,000 students participated." Among the conclusions were that "Catholic school students tend to use drugs less than those in public schools but that the parochial youths are heavier drinkers . . . Fred Streit, study consultant, said he couldn't explain why there was a lower drug incidence in Catholic schools. The study did conclude, however, that drug abuse is directly related to the lack of a formal religious attachment."

Medically approved use of drugs:

Dowling, Harry F., *MEDICINES FOR MAN: THE DEVELOPMENT, REGULATION AND USE OF PRESCRIPTION DRUGS,* New York: Alfred A. Knopf, 1970.

Eckstein, Gustav, *THE BODY HAS A HEAD,* New York: Harper & Row, 1970, pp. 749-754.

Witter, Charles, "Drugging and Schooling," *transACTION,* July/August, 1971, Vol. 8, No. 9/10, pp. 31ff.

Drug abuse and addiction:

Gorodetzky, Charles W., and Samuel D. Christian, *WHAT YOU SHOULD KNOW ABOUT DRUGS,* New York: Harcourt Brace Jovanovich, 1970.

"Life on Two Grams a Day," *LIFE,* Vol. 68, no. 6, Feb., 1970.

Lingeman, Richard R., *DRUGS FROM A TO Z: A DICTIONARY,* New York: McGraw-Hill, 1969.

Marin, Peter, and Allan Y. Cohen, *UNDERSTANDING DRUG USE: AN ADULT'S GUIDE TO DRUGS AND THE YOUNG,* New York: Harper & Row, 1971. (Excellent. Useful for students as well as adults. See particularly ch. 3, "Prevention—The Provision of Alternatives."

The following articles document the increased popularity of marijuana among middle-class adults: Gaeton Fonzi, "The Socialization of Pot", *PHILADELPHIA MAGAZINE,* Nov., 1969, Vol. 60, No. 11, pp. 82ff.; John Keats, "The New American Pastime: Appraising Marijuana: Has grass replaced alcohol as the lifeblood of the party, and if so what does it mean?", *HOLIDAY MAGAZINE,* April, 1970, pp. 52ff.

Schwartz, Berl, "Drug Story", *THE PHILADELPHIA GAZETTE,* April, 1971, Vol. 69, No. 6, pp. 19ff. Heroin and the college student.

Blum, Richard, "Drug Pushers: A Collective Portrait," *transACTION,* July/August, 1971, Vol. 8, Nos. 9/10, pp. 18-21.

Wilson, John Rowan, *THE MIND, A TIME-LIFE BOOK,* New York: Time-Life Books, 1969, ch. 7, "Manipulations of Mentality: Hypnosis, Drugs and 'Thought Control'," pp. 152ff.

Wolfe, Tom, *THE ELECTRIC KOOL-AID ACID TEST,* New York: Bantam, 1968. Semi-fictionalized account of the psychedelic experience.

Treatment:

May, Edgar, "Drugs without Crime: A report on the British success with heroin addiction," *HARPER'S MAGAZINE,* July, 1971, Vol. 243, No. 1454, pp. 60ff.

Yablonsky, Lewis, *THE TUNNEL BACK: SYNANON,* New York: Macmillan, 1965.

"Drug abuse education is the subject of a guide for teachers written by teachers of Stamford, Conn., public schools. The guide was used throughout the Stamford schools in grades four through twelve in the past year. It takes the behavioral approach toward drug problems, outlines discussion and study, and suggests activities. The book will be distributed early this fall and will cost about $4.00. For further information, write J.G. Ferguson Publishing Co., 277 Park Ave., New York, N.Y. 10017". (*CAEN,* July 27, 1970, p. 39.)

Fringe areas, and possible futures:

Clark, Walter Houston, *CHEMICAL ECSTASY: PSYCHEDELIC DRUGS AND RELIGION,* New York: Sheed and Ward, 1969.

Harman, Willis W., "The Psychedelic Experience," *WAYS OF GROWTH,* Herbert A. Otto and John Mann (eds.), New York: Viking, 1968.

Schoen, Stephen M., "LSD and Creative Attention," *WAYS OF GROWTH,* Otto and Mann, as above.

Taylor, Gordon Rattray, *THE BIOLOGICAL TIME BOMB,* New York: World Publ., 1968, "New Minds for Old," pp. 125-57.

Records:

Many records include references to drugs. Ask your students to recommend some which are current. One which has been popular for some time is "Mr. Tamborine Man," available in a Bob Dylan recording under the Columbia label and by the Byrds, also Columbia.

Films:

Peter Hammond, director of the National Coordinating Council for Drug Abuse and Information, says that many of the films designed for "drug abuse education" undermine drug education efforts through their inaccuracies. The Council report states that the review panel judged thirty-six out of a hundred drug abuse films "scientifically unacceptable." The report originally requested by the National Institute of Mental Health, is available from them or from the National Coordinating Council for Drug Abuse and Information, Washington, D.C., for $2.00.

Alternatives:

The following are a few suggestions to help in the continuing search for alternatives to chemical dependencies:

Cox, Harvey, *THE FEAST OF FOOLS,* New York: Harper Colophon Books, 1969.

de Ropp, Robert S., *THE MASTER GAME: BEYOND THE DRUG EXPERIENCE,* New York: Delta, 1968.

Gunther, Bernard, *SENSE RELAXATION BELOW YOUR MIND,* New York: Macmillan-

Collier, 1968.

Lewis, Howard R., Harold S. Streitfeld, *GROWTH GAMES: HOW TO TUNE IN YOUR-SELF, YOUR FAMILY, YOUR FRIENDS,* New York: Harcourt, Brace and Jovanovich, 1970.

Maslow, Abraham H., *RELIGIONS, VALUES, AND PEAK-EXPERIENCES,* New York: Viking, 1964, 1970.

Peterson, Severin, *A CATALOG OF THE WAYS PEOPLE GROW,* New York: Ballantine Books, 1971.

Rogers, Carl, *CARL ROGERS ON ENCOUNTER GROUPS,* New York: Harper & Row, 1970.

Stern, E. Mark, and Bert G. Marino, *PSYCHOTHEOLOGY,* New York: Newman, 1970.

FREEDOM AND NUDITY

PURPOSE:

To seek freedom from distorted perceptions and conceptions of nudity, and to develop our own values in regard to nudity.

COMMENT:

All societies or cultures have standards of decency, modesty, and propriety in connection with the clothing of the human body. Apparently these are always linked in some way with sexual behavior, that which is immodest being that which suggests or stimulates some kind of behavior considered wrong or improper in the particular situation. Some concept of obscenity is usually found. However, what is considered immodest, sexually stimulating, or obscene varies from one culture to another and even among subgroups within a culture. Following World War II, Americans in Japan found that they shocked the Japanese by their use of semi-nude women in art, advertisements and entertainment, and that the Japanese found their custom of privacy in the bath as peculiar. On the other hand Americans were shocked by the Japanese custom of mixed nude bathing. At one time a Japanese emperor had ordered that men and women must cover their genitals while bathing in public. The people dutifully followed his order, enjoying themselves on the beach as naked as ever, but putting on bathing suits at the moment they entered the water. In the Israeli kibbutzim boys and girls share dormitories and showers until they begin high school, but kibbutz sex taboos are so strong that in later life these same young people often suffer embarrassment in relationships with those of the opposite sex. The Kwoma girl in New Guinea wears a net bag which hangs down her back almost to her knees, being suspended from a band across her forehead. It serves her as pockets and purse, since it is her only article of clothing. However, she would be considered quite indecent if she were to bend over in the presence of men or leave her own village without it. Americans are still startled by the bare breasts of a troop of dancers from West Africa which tours the country each year, although these women are considered entirely modest within their own culture. Chinese women who still wear the classic gown are quite comfortable with the side slit to show several inches of thigh, but the collar is high and they would feel very immodest in the low-cut dresses common for generations in the United States. At one time in Bali where women did not cover their breasts in public, the prostitute wore a scarf over hers, and in one of the New Britain tribes a scrap of clothing was a similar uniform of the trade among her naked people.

GROUP SIZE:

10—25

TIME SUGGESTED:

45—60 minutes

GENERAL DIRECTIONS:

Examining pictures of various kinds of nudity, students write and then discuss their reactions. Associations, implications, and language about nudity are explored and values investigated. Picture selection and discussion must be guided by the teacher's knowledge of his group.

MATERIALS REQUIRED:

With the help of students, make a collection of pictures of "nudes," seeking as wide a variety of types as possible. Some "partial nudes" should be included in the collection. Suggested categories follow:

—reproductions of paintings, prints and sculpture, such as reproductions of figurines from the Minoan civilization of Crete, African and ancient Greek sculpture; Bonnard, *"Nude at the Fireplace, 1917,"* in Musee de l'Annonciade, Saint Tropaz; Cassatt, *"La Toilette,"* 1891, print; Cezanne, *"The Negro Scipio, 1866-1868,"* in Sao Paulo Museum; Pearlstein, *"Untitled,"* in Allan Frankin Gallery, New York (see *DISCOVERY IN ART,* p. 124); Ramos, *"Rhinoceros"* (see *DISCOVERY IN ART,* p. 130); Kienholz, *"State Hospital,"* in Dwan Gallery, New York (see *DISCOVERY IN ART,* p. 158); reproductions of the crucifix or the Crucifixion.

—artistic photographs of nudes

—photographs of people in cultures where little or no clothing is worn, from sources such as *NATIONAL GEOGRAPHIC* (a Japanese family bathing together, Australian aborigines, etc.)

—medical photographs—some full-length or almost full length are available—many demonstrate such things as acromegaly, generalized dermatitis, gigantism, etc.

—photographs from such women's magazines as *VOGUE* and *HARPER'S BAZAAR*—soft, romantic views of models to advertise cosmetics, etc.

—photographs of poor slum children in South America, etc.

—photographs or reproductions of graphic art depicting nudity as "punishment," as in Nazi concentration camp

—photographs of people in nudist camps

—pictures from magazines such as *PLAYBOY* or *PENTHOUSE*

—pictures from newspaper advertisements of "adult movies."

PROCEDURE:

1. Distribute three pictures from different categories to each student.

2. Ask the students to examine the pictures carefully and write down their feelings about each picture, and about the group of three as a whole.

3. In dyads or small groups, ask the students to share their pictures and talk about their reactions.

4. Ask for volunteers to show their pictures and read what they have written.

5. Post all the pictures around the room, and have the students vote on the picture they like most and the one they like least.

6. Put the following words on the chalkboard and ask the students to comment on which word or phrase seems most suited to the pictures they voted for (either individually or as a group, depending on the size of group).

bare
nude
undraped
stripped
in the altogether
naked
raw
exposed
peeled
in a state of nature
unclothed
without any clothes on
undressed
unclad
with nothing on
in his birthday suit
in the buff

7. General discussion may focus on such questions as the following:

—Which pictures look "sexy"? . . . why?

—Which pictures look most warmly human? . . . which least? . . . what do you think creates this effect? . . . What part is played by the pose, skin texture, facial expression, age, other physical features, surrounding elements?

—Do you feel sorry for any of the persons pictured? . . . why?

—Which people would look better with clothes on? . . . why?

—In those pictures in which there is some article of clothing, what is the effect? . . . If this were removed, would the effect change?

—What do you think the mass media tell us to think about nudity?

—Why have artists often painted nudes?

—What do you think is the purpose of nudity in movies? . . . the effect?

—Why do you think there is often a difference in the effect of, or response to, pictures of nude children vs. nude adults?

—Why do you think cultures or societies differ in what they consider "nudity" or "immodesty in dress"?

—Why does increased "civilization" increase the amount of clothing worn?

—Which pictures might be embarrassing to some people? . . . to whom? . . . why? . . . Are any of them somewhat embarrassing for you?

—Do you think a discussion such as this one is appropriate for school? . . . why or why not? . . . Do you think it would be more, or less appropriate at some other grade level? . . . Do you think it has any value for you? . . . Would the discussion have been better or worse if your parents had been here?

SUGGESTED RESOURCES:

Local museums may have post cards or other inexpensive reproductions for sale, or may be able to arrange a "loan show" of reproductions or even prints. Your local library will also be helpful, the school art department and perhaps your friends and those of your students. You may wish to use slides or an opaque overhead projector for part of this exercise.

Bush, Roger, *PRAYERS FOR PAGANS*, Dayton, Ohio: Pflaum Press, 1968, "The Body," pp. 24-25.

MASS MEDIA AND "GOOD" AND "BAD" BODIES

117

PURPOSE:

To examine the possible effects of the mass media on our freedom in making value judgments about the human body.

COMMENT:

"On the day God created Adam he made him in the likeness of God. Male and female he created them. He blessed them and gave them the name 'Man' on the day they were created." (GEN. 5:1-2). For thousands of years Western man has repeated these words. What have they meant to him? What do they mean now? In PSALM 139:12-14 we find, "It was you who created my inmost self, and put me together in my mother's womb; for all these mysteries I thank you: for the wonder of myself, for the wonder of your works." Is this the way we look at man? This creature, made in the likeness of God, put together in his mother's womb—do we regard him as a "wonder"? Do we think of the human body as "good" or "bad"? Do we think of some bodies as "good" while we regard others as "bad"? How do we decide such things? When St. Paul wrote to the Hebrews he quoted Psalm 8, "Ah, what is man that you should spare a thought for him, . . . you have made him little less than a god, you have crowned him with glory and splendor." Are "man" and his "body" different things? Are the views of the mass media an accurate reflection of our society's values? What effect have the mass media on our thinking about the value or relative quality of the body? Why are we so eager to change this creature? . . . to conceal it? . . . to disguise its natural qualities? Do we think the product design is basically bad?

GROUP SIZE:

10—20

TIME SUGGESTED:

60 minutes, plus possible additional time for

GENERAL DIRECTIONS:

Students spend a few minutes writing their own ideas on important aspects of the physical appearance of men and women, and then investigate the mass media images. Discussion focuses on the effect of mass media on our value judgments about our bodies and how these impinge on our freedom to decide what is "good" or "bad."

MATERIALS REQUIRED:

You may either make a collection of advertisements from current popular magazines and newspapers, or you may have the class do this, working with publications in class or gathering the material outside of class. Ads should be sought which emphasize the human body or some part of it. Choose some which stress the product's ability to "change you for the better," make you "more desirable," "give you machismo," etc. Clothing ads, cosmetic ads are most obvious here, including such things as ads for hair shampoos and rinses that "give great body" to your hair, or dishwashing liquids that "don't just do the dishes . . . they soften your hands." Other products use the human form in selling, as in the case of the cigarette ad which states, "You've come a long way, baby." Full color, full page ads are preferable, but others may be used. See also DISCOVERY IN ADVERTISEMENT for materials.

PROCEDURE:

1. Ask the students to take a piece of paper and write three possible endings for each of the following sentences. Each ending should contain a different idea.

"The most important thing about a woman's appearance is . . ."

"The most important thing about a man's appearance is . . ."
Ask them to put these papers away temporarily.

2. If the class is larger than ten, form subgroups of 5—8, and distribute 5—10 advertisements to each group. Ask the students to disregard the particular product for the moment and to concentrate on what the ad says about the human body. You may want to put on the chalkboard or on sheets of newsprint some of the following incomplete sentences to help the investigation. Allow for about 10 minutes of discussion.

"The human body is . . ."
"A woman (man) ought to look . . ."
"A woman is not attractive unless . . ."
"No one wants to bother with a man who . . ."
"A good body is . . ."
"A bad body is . . ."

3. In a plenary session, ask the class to consider HOW the advertisers have tried to put across this image of the "correct" physical characteristics of men and women. Some points will be very obvious to the students, and rejected by them as "typical selling." Others will be unconsciously accepted as "true" and "important." Using one ad at a time, start with questions such as:

—Can you tell what this man is doing?
—Why is she dressed (or undressed) in this way?
—What do these words make you think of?
—Why are (other things visible) in this picture?
—What part of her body seems most important in this picture? Why (or how) is it emphasized?
—What colors are used? . . . why?

Encourage investigation of statements, particular words, colors, camera angles, layout. Try to keep the focus on the advertisers' attempts to persuade their audience that this is the way a person *should* look, rather than on their attempt to persuade you that their product will produce this look. Ask someone to serve as Recorder, and put down some of these phrases indicating the qualities of a "good" body on the chalkboard.

4. Ask the students to get out the papers they wrote in Step No. 1, and compare what they wrote with the statements or phrases on the chalkboard. Ask them to consider silently for a moment whether their thinking about the human body has been affected by advertisements. Ask them to close their eyes and think of a man or woman (girl or boy) they like or love. Ask them to think whether he (she) matches their written statements . . . the advertisers' statements. (These questions are not to be answered aloud.)

5. In a plenary or subgrouped as in Step No. 2, assist the students in the consideration of the effect of the mass media in general on our valuing of the human body. Allow about 10—15 minutes discussion.

—Aside from advertising, how do the media present the human body?

—In the press, TV, and the movies, is the human body respected? . . . valued?

—Is there an "ideal body" valued by the media? . . . Is this the same as, or different from, bodies valued by advertising? . . . How are the "less than ideal" bodies presented to us?

6. In a plenary, spend about 15 minutes discussing the groups' findings, focusing on the question, "How free are young people in this country to develop their own concepts (images, thinking, valuing) of the human body?

—How have advertising and the other media affected these views?

—How have other experiences affected these views?

—How have your parents' views of or beliefs about the body affected your values?

—What sort of values do the media present in regard to the human body?

—What is a "good" body . . . a "bad" body? . . . why?

—How much are people influenced by these values?

—How free are you to form your own values on this?

—Is it desirable that you be free to form these values? . . . why? On what basis should such values be formed?

—Suppose almost everyone in our society agreed with this view of the human body . . . what would be the effect? . . . Would it change our society? In what way?

VARIATIONS:

1. Instead of using ads, use films, including, if possible, used advertising videotapes from commercial broadcasting stations, commercial and educational films. Other input may be used, such as contemporary literature, even textbooks, or news presentations on TV or in the press.

2. If the students have done previous work with advertisements, they might benefit more from creating ads. Subgroup the class and distribute art materials suitable for various techniques, such as photography (Polaroid), cutting-and-pasting from old magazines, drawing, painting, use of felt tip markers, etc. Each subgroup may be asked to create a particular kind of ad, such as:

—to sell an expensive perfume

—to sell a lipstick

—to sell a man's after shave lotion or cologne.

A second round of ad-making may concentrate on trying to "sell a value you think is good and important," or "to combat racism," or to "discourage cigarette smoking."

After ads are completed, each group shows its ad, and the class discusses "values" and "persuasion."

—How do people arrive at their values?

—What persuasion is justifiable, and what is not? . . . from whose point of view? . . . Who should decide?

—What values about the body should be promoted? . . . why?

—What current value judgments about the body do you dislike?

—Does the "credibility gap" force us to choose opposing values?

—How do such values affect our self-image? . . . our judgments (and prejudices) about others?

SUGGESTED RESOURCES:

Payne, Richard J., and Robert Heyer, S.J., *DISCOVERY IN ADVERTISING,* New York: Paulist Press, 1969.

Rasschaert, William M., "Appeals to Selected Emotions: A Semantic Study of Advertising Techniques," *CRITICAL READING,* Martha L. King *et al.* (eds.), Philadelphia, Pa.: J.B. Lippincott, 1967.

Hovland, Carl I., "Effects of the Mass Media of Communication," *CRITICAL READING,* Martha L. King *et al.* (eds.), Philadelphia, Pa.: J.B. Lippincott, 1967.

Brown, J.A.S., *TECHNIQUES OF PERSUASION,* Baltimore, Md.: Penguin, 1963.

HAPPINESS

PHOTOGRAPHS

PURPOSE:

To develop acceptance of ourselves as physical beings and to be comfortably accepting of a realistic image of our physical selves.

COMMENT:

The mass media have produced a standard of "beauty" and have so stressed it that achievement of an approximation of this standard is highly valued in our society. In actual fact, young people and adults usually choose and enjoy their friends on other bases, and yet feel a lack in themselves insofar as they do not achieve this "plastic perfection" held up as a valued goal. They may even be apologetic about their friends' appearance, and describe them in negative terms. Even the success of some people in the entertainment field who do not reflect this image has not greatly altered the national belief that to be happy you must look like the "standard product."

GROUP SIZE:

6—25

TIME SUGGESTED:

45—60 minutes

GENERAL DIRECTIONS:

The class is photographed individually, and these shots used as the basis for small group discussion. Students may begin the exercise by filling out privately a brief "questionnaire" or writing a self-description. The questionnaire helps them compare their "idealistic" or "imaginary" self-image with the somewhat more realistic one, and a final discussion seeks to clarify values concerning appearance.

MATERIALS REQUIRED:

Polaroid cameras and film (it is possible to conduct this with a single camera, but with a class larger than six, the exercise will move more easily with one camera for every 3—6 persons).

Questionnaire forms (optional).

PROCEDURE:

1. Each student is asked to fill in a "questionnaire." He is told that this is for his own use, and he need not share the information unless he so desires. Any of the three following questions may be used, or more than one may be used, if desired. Question sheets may be duplicated in advance and distributed at the beginning of the session, or questions may be written on the chalkboard. Other questions may be substituted, of course.

   a. Write a short paragraph describing the physical appearance of your ideal male or female (phrase to suit the group).

   b. Complete the following sentence: "I would like the way I look much better if I could change my . . ."

   c. Check one of the following to complete the sentence: "If I could change one thing about my body it would be . . ." height__; weight__; voice__; hair__; skin__; teeth__; eyes__; mouth__; nose__; shape of face__; shape of body__.

2. Subgroups of three are now formed, and a Polaroid shot taken of each member. These are not "candid" photographs, but rather each member is asked to "pose" for his portrait. Each person is given his photo as it is completed, and is asked to think about whether it seems to him to be an "accurate" representation.

3. Members of each subgroup now discuss their pictures among themselves. In each case each member first discusses his own photograph before inviting comments from other members of his group. How does he feel about being photographed? How does he feel about this photo? What are his immediate reactions to it?

   Other group members now react to the photo and to the original comments of its owner.

4. Ask each person to look over what he wrote originally and, if he wishes, share any of these thoughts with the members of his subgroup. This may lead to a discussion of "the ideal type," or to individual discussions of real or imagined flaws. Ask them to talk briefly among themselves about what they think is most important in "appearance."

5. After a few minutes, convene a plenary to discuss such questions as the following:

   —Why are a person's "looks" important? . . . How do they affect his feelings about himself as a person? . . . How does this affect his life?

—Is "attractive" the same as "pretty" or "handsome" or "beautiful"?

—What does it mean to be "good-looking"? What makes a person *not* good-looking? Are they, then, "bad-looking"?

—Is it necessary for someone to be good-looking in order for him to be liked or admired?

—Is it necessary to be good-looking in order to like yourself?

—Why are many people dissatisfied with their appearance? . . . What difference does it make?

—Do we often think about "how we look"? . . . when . . . how . . . why?

—Do we often think about how our friends look?

—Do we use the same *kind* of standards in judging other people as we would if we were judging a dog show? . . . why or why not?

—Do we judge our own appearance with the same standards we apply to friends? . . . to strangers? . . . Do we accept our own physical appearance in the same way we accept the appearance of our friends? . . . If there are differences, what are they? . . . why?

VARIATIONS:

1. Instead of Step No. 1, each student writes a brief, unsigned personality sketch of himself, including any data he is willing to reveal to others. After the photographs are taken, two triads work together, exchanging photographs and personality sketches which have been shuffled. Each triad, working as a group, then tries to attach the right photo to the right personality sketch. The triads combine for a discussion of their choices and the reasons for them. (In a class which has been together for a while, this may be very easy to do in some cases, as strong clues based on known "interests" may appear in the personality sketches.) The rest of the discussion follows as from Step No. 3.

2. Instead of Step No. 2, the three photographs are temporarily concealed from *all* members of the subgroup. They are placed face down, at random, on a table or desk. Two members of each triad are blindfolded. The third member selects one of the three photos (which includes his own) and *without identifying the subject*, talks to the members of his subgroup about what he sees in the picture he picked up. The blindfolded members are asked which of the three subgroup members fits the description, and how they feel about the description. Blindfolds are removed, and the exercise procedes as from No. 3.

3. If videotape equipment is available, each triad may have a five minute "spot" discussion, in which they may comment on something they wrote in Step No. 1, or talks about "Why physical appearance is important," or "Why people care about what they look like," or another similar topic. Ask one member to start the conversation, but be sure each has a chance to speak. Discussion after viewing the tape includes comment on voice, posture, gesture and motion characteristics, as well as features that would be obvious in a still photo, but seek to focus on physical aspects. In a large group this variation presents considerable difficulty if all groups work on the exercise on the same day. A short portion of several sessions may be devoted to taping and replaying one group at a time, while the rest of the class works on other things. Discussion within the subgroup follows immediately. It is much less satisfactory to do all taping at one session, and replay at several successive sessions, as the immediacy of replay while feelings about the experience are fresh in the members' minds is more helpful.

FACES

PURPOSE:

To discover our own faces, what we think of as our "best" and "worst" features, to try to understand why these seem to matter to us, what value we place on them, and the effect of all this on our happiness.

GROUP SIZE:

6—25

TIME SUGGESTED:

45—60 minutes

GENERAL DIRECTIONS:

This exercise may be done in a number of ways—three possibilities are suggested. Knowledge of the group will probably indicate the best approach—"one-feature" masks, photographs, or selected features from magazine pictures.

MATERIALS REQUIRED:

A. clean brown paper bags, large enough to wear as hoods or masks; drawing materials, such as crayons, paints, felt-tip markers

B. camera and film

C. a supply of old magazines with pictures

PROCEDURES:

A. MASKS.

1. Each person is given a paper bag which he puts on to determine where he needs to cut or tear eye slits to allow him to see, and makes these slits. He is also given drawing materials.

2. Each person is asked to draw ONE feature on his "mask." This may be EITHER his "best" or "worst" feature—eyes, forehead, nose, ears, chin, mouth, facial shape, hair-line, neck. Explain that artistic skill is not necessary. If the "eyes" are the selected feature, explain that these may be drawn above the actual cut-out eye slits.

3. Each person puts on his mask and wears it during Step No. 4.

4. The class is divided into triads, with the third person in each subgroup serving as Observer or Moderator. The other two talk about their own and their partner's "feature." The Observer encourages them by asking questions, if necessary, such as:

—Why do you like or dislike the feature you drew?

—Do you think others notice or are more aware of that feature than of other things about you?

—Do you think your life would be different if that feature were changed?

—If you two traded your worst, or best features, what would happen?

The two partners may then discuss with the Observer *his* selected feature.

5. Ask everyone to try to remember exactly how the others in their triad actually look without their masks.—Masks are now removed.

6. Triads combine in groups of six, or, if the class is smaller than twelve, a plenary is called to discuss the findings. Discussion may be started by asking the class to think of the face of someone *not* in the class, and select a feature they like best. This may be difficult at first, but "eyes," or "mouth," etc. will be mentioned.

—Why do you find it appealing?

—Would it "fit" your own face? . . . the face of someone else in the class?

—Would you like to adopt this feature? . . . Would you feel "at home" with this new feature?

—Would your friends like this new feature?

—How would it contribute to your happiness?

B. PHOTO FACES.

This confrontation with a photo which is simultaneously "me and not-me" is helpful in awakening a deeper exploration of how one feels about oneself. The exercise is based on the fact that the two sides of a person's face are different. It is best done with advance preparation. Ask a student interested in photography to take a full face photo of each member and make two prints of each face. Photographs are cut in half and pasted on a sheet of paper, resulting in two photographic portraits—one of "two left sides," the other of "two right sides." The same effect can be achieved by holding a pocket mirror upright down the center of a photo, but this is less satisfactory for this exercise.

1. The photographic studies are returned to

the class members, and dyads are formed to study the photographs. NOTE: Since some students will be interested in seeing the pictures of others in the group, they may be told, before the dyads begin their discussion, that there will be an opportunity to see the other pictures later on.

2. Dyads discuss which of the "faces" they like best, and why, and how they feel about their own and their partner's "two faces." They may consider questions such as:

—Which of your portraits seems most like your "true self"?

—Might your life be different if you looked like either of these?

—If these "two people" met, would they like each other?

If desired, some fantasizing may be encouraged.

3. The photos may be posted around the room, or the students regrouped to discuss their photos with others.

C. MAGAZINE FEATURES

1. Give each student one or more old picture magazines, and ask him to select a single feature he would be willing to trade for his own.

2. Form subgroups of 5—6. Each member shows his selected feature to others in his group, explaining why he would like or accept this change.

3. The subgroups discuss how this might affect their lives.

4. A plenary session shares their findings, and discusses such questions as:

—Which features are most frequently selected for change? . . . why?

—What features are most often mentioned or remarked upon when someone is described? . . . why? . . . Which features are usually ignored?

—How much influence does any one feature have on an individual's happiness?

The question of facial scarring or disfigurement may be discussed, if desired. Some members of the class may have minor scars of which they are extremely conscious, others may have considerable scarring and ignore it, at least at the conscious level, or may be affected by it so that they "unconsciously" try to present their "good" side to others. Some students with braces on their teeth actually avoid smiling, while others are able to ignore their braces. Some worry about a tiny scar which their friends are quite unaware of. Such questions as the following may be explored:

—How much of such disfigurement is necessary before someone is actually shunned? . . . *Why* are they shunned? . . . Why does such disfigurement affect us in selecting our friends? . . . What happens after we get to know such people?

—Why is a very small blemish of great importance for some people?

—How important are these things to our happiness? . . . To the happiness of those about us?

—Do we pick our friends on the basis of such things?

SUGGESTED RESOURCES:

Lowery, Bruce, *SCARRED,* New York: Vanguard, 1961. Novel of a boy with a scar remaining from an operation for harelip tormented by adolescent peers.

MONTAGE OF PHYSICAL SELF

PURPOSE:

To gain perspectives on our personal views of our bodies.

GROUP SIZE:

6—25

TIME SUGGESTED:

60 minutes

GENERAL DIRECTIONS:

Each student works individually to complete a meaningful montage which represents in some way his own views of his physical appearance or his body. Discussion follows in the subgroup and then in a plenary.

MATERIALS REQUIRED:

A large sheet of heavy paper or bristol board for each student.

A supply of "tools," such as paste or glue, paper clips, rubber bands, paper fasteners, a few pairs of scissors, contact tape, a stapler.

A large supply of materials. For this, collect several cartons of "junk"—odds and ends of leftovers from such sources as the school Art Department, Sewing class, "Shop," or cafeteria. You will want to have new, clean scraps of such things as patterned paper, fabrics and trims, nuts and bolts, wire, wood scraps, plastic scraps, construction paper, string, etc. It is best to have few or no complete objects, e.g., a tin can, a paper flower, a complete picture, but paper plates, cups and straws are acceptable.

PROCEDURE:

1. Dump the "junk" on tables, providing one table of junk for every six students. Tell the students they are to "construct or arrange a montage which can be titled, "This Is the Way My Body Seems to Me." Explain the general procedure, and indicate that such things as the glue bottles should not be appropriated for use in the montages. Explain that students may simply pile their materials on their poster board, if they wish, as construction will be viewed from above, not mounted vertically. Stress that the "portrait" is of "physical characteristics," rather than "personality." Each student places his poster board on the floor and gets to work. If desired, music may be played as a background for this step.

2. After about twenty minutes, members of each subgroup of about six members will describe their montages to other members of each subgroup. Ask the members to comment on their group members' work, indicating whether they "see" their classmate as he sees himself.

3. Call the class together for a general discussion, asking such questions as the following:

—Are the particular features an individual has chosen to describe himself the ones most noticeable to others?

—Do you feel your montage was primarily dictated by the materials available, or by other factors? . . . What else would you have used had it been available? . . . Why?

—Do you feel your montage is accurate? . . . important, or irrelevant? . . . Do others see it this way?

If a student has constructed nothing at all, or only made a small start, why was this? . . . Does he think his body is unimportant? . . . Does he see the material available to him for construction as totally unsuitable? Does he see something in one of the completed montages which he feels would be more suitable for himself?

NOTE: You may find your students are interested in looking at others' work and having others look at their's, but not anxious to discuss the experience. If you wish, eliminate the plenary, but move around among the groups and ask some of these questions as the occasion arises.

4. If time permits, members of subgroups may experiment with changing one another's montages, trading pieces with one another, or suggesting possible trades or rearrangements.

VARIATIONS:

1. The exercise may be varied by controlling the materials or their distribution in a number of

ways. (a) Each student is allowed to take a specific number of objects (5, 6, 7), no more, no less, to create his montage. (b) One student per group may be asked to distribute a given number of objects from the box at random, before the exercise is explained. (c) Each student may make his selection, but instead of creating his own montage with these, he may immediately be asked to trade his entire collection with "the person on his left." (d) Instead of poster board, students may have the option of using a cardboard carton, composing their montage either *in* or *on* this box.

    2. Halfway through Step No. 1, a short period for "trading" may be called, with a limit put on the time or the number of objects or the number of persons with whom trading is allowed. This may be announced in advance, or be a "surprise."

    3. Students may work in pairs instead of individually, each student creating a montage of himself, but with conversation and trading allowed throughout the exercise between partners.

    4. As an exercise in "seeing," one member of a subgroup may be asked to look carefully at one of the montages, giving a verbal description as he does so. In giving this description he should *avoid naming* any of the materials in the composition, or any of the "parts of the body" he believes they symbolize, but instead should describe what he sees in terms of color, line, form and texture.

SELF-IMAGE: ART MEDIA

PURPOSE:

To express feelings about our self-image and to fantasize about our physical appearance.

COMMENT:

Through the use of art media some degree of freedom is provided for gathering data about one's self-image, and developing the ability to talk about it with someone else in a situation of growing trust. Since the exercise is fun and "artistic ability" is unnecessary and since it is possible to talk only to one other person if desired, there is little threat. Using the idea of a portrait of one's self at various times introduces an element of fantasy and permits some thought of the body as a changing thing or a being-in-process.

GROUP SIZE:

8—24

TIME SUGGESTED:

45—60 minutes

GENERAL DIRECTIONS:

Students make a chronological series of self-portraits using some art medium and then discuss these in dyads. If the class desires, dyads combine to form foursomes, or may involve others in discussion on free basis. This exercise may be one of a series, including other exercises such as "Photographs," or may be used alone. It is suitable for use in the early stages of a group's life.

MATERIALS REQUIRED:

Selection of art materials: crayons, charcoal,

paints (especially finger paints), felt-tip markers, etc., and paper.

PROCEDURE:

1. Each person is asked to draw two pictures of himself, one as a small child and one as he sees himself now. Do not specify whether the portraits are to be full length, face only, whether anything else is to be shown in the picture, etc. If questions are asked, simply answer that the individual is free to draw the picture however he wishes. Stress that they are not to worry about "art"—this is for fun, and those who feel they have no "talent" can enjoy it.

2. When most of the class has completed its drawings, announce that a minute or two is left to finish them up. Form dyads. Depending on the group and its history, dyads may be self-selecting or selected by you. Ask the dyads to share their portraits and discuss them with each other. It is unlikely that intervention to promote conversation will be necessary at this stage.

3. Dyads may self-select another dyad to talk with, or dyads may be combined to form groups of four or six. If the class has done other exercises on self-image, the physical body and its relation to happiness, these subgroups may compare this exercise with others previously performed, or with data from previous discussions.

Discussion may now focus on the relation between happiness and the way we feel about our own bodies and those of others. Points considered in the dyad discussions about comparisons between the "small child" and the "today person" may be shared. Comparisons may be examined of the differences between "full length portraits" and "faces," or between an "empty stage" and an environment peopled by others or including various objects. A few questions may help, such as:

—Have some people drawn full-length portraits for their "child," and only a face for "today's person," or *vice versa*? . . . why?

—Have some people drawn only faces for both?

—Do some pictures show action?

—Are the figures clothed?

VARIATIONS:

1. Students are provided with art materials as above. Give the following directions: "In a small area in the corner of your paper draw a stick figure of yourself. Use any color or colors you wish for the various parts of your body such as your legs, your feet, your head . . . Now, consider this drawing . . . Is there any color you want to change?

"Re-draw your figure, making it as large as the remaining space permits, and thickening the figure by using "balloons" or "sausages" instead of sticks (demonstrate on the chalkboard as below). Fill in, using any changes in color you wish from your first drawing.

In dyads discuss your two drawings, trying to decide why you chose the colors you did, what your changes implied, etc. If you were drawing your partner, instead of yourself, what colors would you use? . . . why?"

2. "Variation 1" above may be used without giving any instructions about color, but distributing art materials including a variety of colors. Students may be asked to draw a "balloon" figure immediately. Dyads discuss questions such as:

—Which colors were used? . . . why?

—Why did some people use only one color?

—Where different colors were used for different parts of the body, why were these selected? . . . Do you see these parts of the body in these colors when you think of other people? . . . when you think of your own body?

—What do these colors mean to you?

3. Students are shown 6—8 color samples, or a list of the names of 6—8 colors, including black and white is put on the chalkboard. The students are asked to rank these colors in order of preference. Remind them to think about the colors just *as* colors, rather than as colors they would want to wear, for instance. Colors may be identified by name or number. These lists are then put away until later, and either "Variation 1" or "Variation 2" is used. The lists are brought out and included as part of the data for the latter part of the discussions.

SUGGESTED RESOURCES:

See materials in the section on "Life: Senses: Vision."

THE HANDICAPPED

PURPOSE:

To help us accept as fellow human beings those about us who have noticeable or known physical or mental handicaps, and to develop an interest on the part of some in working to make life happier for such people. It may also help some students to accept their own handicaps, known or unknown to other class members.

COMMENT:

Real acceptance of any group includes assumption of responsibility by the community for seeing that environmental conditions allow maximum possible participation in community life. Students may say they are perfectly willing to "accept" the handicapped, but that they "don't know any." It is almost certain that such people live in your community, and such a statement by students indicates a lack of community acceptance and should warrant prompt investigation. The physically and mentally handicapped constitute the largest "minority group" in the country: there are 24 million disabled or physically handicapped, or 12 percent of the population, and 20 million more who require psychiatric treatment. Each year 250,000 more people become disabled. 1972 marked the 25th birthday of the President's Committee on Employing the Handicapped, established by President Truman and housed in the Labor Department building in Washington. The work of this Committee has resulted in considerable improvement in training and employing the handicapped and this in turn has increased society's acceptance of their right to the happiness which comes from active productive participation, but much more needs to be done.

GROUP SIZE:

6—20

TIME SUGGESTED:

60 minutes, although the problem may interest the group and be continued over several sessions.

GENERAL DIRECTIONS:

This exercise may be initiated in a number of ways: using student research and presentations on the day appointed; a guest speaker; a general discussion. Subgroups then discuss findings, explore possible action and may organize further investigation. This exercise may follow the one on "Freedom: and Physical Handicaps," or one of the "Life" exercises.

MATERIALS REQUIRED:

Some literature should be available to students from organizations serving the handicapped, which will usually stress the importance of community acceptance.

PROCEDURE:

1. One of the following three presentations may be used:

    a. Speaker. Have someone speak to the class who is active in a voluntary association or organization or professional group working to improve conditions for people with specific handicaps, e.g., epilepsy, blindness, crippling conditions.

    b. Literature and student research. Prior to the planned session, distribute literature to selected class members, asking them to prepare a presentation, either as individuals or as small groups, which will help the class to understand the facts about a particular handicap, how these people see their own needs, and in what ways their happiness is affected.

    c. Discussion. In a plenary, talk with students about "What is and what isn't a 'physical handicap'?" Almost everyone would agree that having to wear glasses is something of a nuisance, and yet not usually thought of as a "handicap" or a serious bar to happiness. In addition to the nuisance and occasional danger involved in wearing glasses, however, some people feel more attractive without them and wear contact lenses. At the same time, since dark glasses are commonly used on vacations outdoors in the summer or in the winter snow, few people would say of someone, "She would be pretty if she didn't have to wear sunglasses." Impaired vision, like any other handicap may be considered a deterrent to "happiness" by some . . . Why? . . . Is it a matter of degree? . . . of individual personality? . . Are there "handicaps" which invariably make happiness impossible?

Not all medically recognizable defects are generally considered by the public to be "handicaps." For instance, persons with diabetes, with slightly impaired hearing, are not usually spoken of as "physically handicapped," whereas someone who is "lame" or "blind" is almost immediately categorized as "physically handicapped."

—What about people with epilepsy? . . . with heart ailments? . . . alcoholics? . . . drug addicts? . . . people with scars or birthmarks visible under normal, everyday conditions? . . . pregnant women? . . . people who have a red nose because of a head cold? . . . How do we categorize these people? . . . why? If they are not "handicapped," what elements make the difference? . . . How do these things affect "happiness"? . . . why? . . . Does "not having any handicaps" result in "happiness"?

Many people, including many students, live happy, productive lives with quite serious physical problems. Others, with minimal defects or ailments, are miserable and suffer considerable rejection by others.

—What makes the difference?

—How much unhappiness is caused by the limitation of activity? . . . How much by the reaction of society?

—Why do many people tend to fear the epileptic, yet not fear the person with a serious heart ailment?

—Why do people tend to avoid someone with a facial birthmark, and be happy in the presence of a diabetic?

2. Subgroup the class in groups of about six to discuss their own experiences with handicapped people, their own feelings about the handicaps discussed in Step No. 1, their feelings about needed changes in the laws, in society's handling of the handicapped, and so forth. Some of the following questions may be recommended for consideration:

—What can be done to insure the possibility of happiness and well-being of handicapped people in your own community? . . . What *is* being done?

—What are the real needs of the handicapped? . . . What are their problems?

—How would you feel if you had a child with cerebral palsy? . . . What would you want for that child? . . . . Is it possible for such a child to attend your school? . . . What special physical arrangements are there for such children in your school? . . . Does your school have ramps as well as steps to allow for a wheelchair, for instance?

—Do stores in your neighborhood have doors which allow someone in a wheelchair to get in by himself?

—Do you know anyone who spends time in the office of a blind person reading their business

correspondence to them? . . . What are others in your community doing to help the blind find and retain employment? . . . What businesses in your community employ the handicapped?

—What can you, as students, do to help with these problems?

SUGGESTED RESOURCES:

Epilepsy Foundation of America, Suite 1116, 733 15th St., N.W., Washington, D.C. 20005. Write for leaflets: "Epilepsy, The Teacher's Role"; "Facts about Epilepsy and the Many Groups Concerned with Its Medical and Social Management," and other materials. In States where applicable, they will also send information regarding your own State's laws regarding Drivers' Licenses, Marriage, Workmen's Compensation and Sterilization. Literature is also available on electroencephalography, occupational information, and a brief survey on various State laws.

The President's Committee on Employment of the Handicapped, Washington, D.C. 20210. Much valuable information on ways to assist the handicapped educationally, occupationally and socially. Includes information on the mentally retarded, the mentally restored, the crippled and those with such handicaps as hearing and vision limitations.

National Society for the Prevention of Blindness, Inc., 16 East 40th St., New York, N.Y. 10016. Their booklet "Classroom Lighting" discusses ways in which partially seeing and deaf children can be aided in normal classrooms by adequate lighting.

FILM:

Thursday's Children. 22 min., 16 mm., black and white. World Wide Pictures and Morse Films, 1952. Contemporary Films. Excellent film showing how deaf children are taught in Margate School in England. See also the discussion of this film in DISCOVERY IN FILM, by Robert Heyer and Anthony Meyer, New York: Paulist Press, 1969, pp. 96-97.

LITERATURE:

Chevigny, Hector, *MY EYES HAVE A COLD NOSE*, New Haven, Conn.: Yale University, 1946. Blinded at forty, Chevigny goes back to work with his Seeing Eye Dog. Makes a plea for acceptance as a human being.

Green, Hannah, *I NEVER PROMISED YOU A ROSE GARDEN*, New York: Holt, 1964. Novel about a 16 year old institutionalized schizophrenic's start back up the hill. Many students may have read this popular book.

Greenberg, Joanne, *IN THIS SIGN*, New York: Holt, 1970. Abel and Janice Ryder suffer from isolation, frustration and sometimes anger as they raise their "hearing" daughter.

Killilea, Marie, *KAREN*, New York: Dell, 1952. Growth in understanding by the parents and friends of Karen, a child with cerebral palsy.

VALUES AND LIFE STYLES

PURPOSE:

Examination of various life styles as expressive of values, with special reference to the body and to physical appearance.

GROUP SIZE:

20—24

TIME SUGGESTED:

90 minutes, or two sessions of approximately 45 minutes. A class of 6—10 could probably complete the exercise in 60 minutes.

GENERAL DIRECTIONS:

Primarily this exercise operates by discussion and list making, but it will be improved by some dramatization. Subgroups and plenaries discuss the relationships of life styles, appearance, and values. It might be helpful to use first "Happiness: Body as 'Good' or 'Bad'."

MATERIALS REQUIRED:

Chalkboard or newsprint and felt-tip markers.

PROCEDURE:

1. In subgroups of 5—6 discuss and decide upon a life style "all of you definitely do *not* wish to follow." Each group is to make a presentation to the class, either:

a. acting out a short illustrative skit, ad-libbing the lines

b. several members describe the thinking of the group.

At this time the subgroups need not express

their reasons for disliking this particular life style, nor support their own opposing values. Allow about 15—20 minutes.

2. Each subgroup has 5—6 minutes to explain or demonstrate the selected life style to which they are opposed. About 20—25 minutes.

3. In a plenary discussion look for similarities in life styles depicted by subgroups, seeking what is devalued by the groups. A list of these "bad," "poor" or "undesirable" values should be put on chalkboard or newsprint. About 15 minutes should be sufficient.

4. The class returns to subgroups of Step No. 1 to discuss each subgroup member's own desired life style. Groups should examine the relationship between life styles they prefer and physical appearance. How does your present appearance match your desired life style? . . . why? Group members may produce individual or group lists which show: (a) items of apparel, hair style, posture, etc. which characterize people living the life style their group *de*valued (as in Step No. 2); and (b) a similar list which would characterize their chosen life styles. If they feel that particular foods or activities affect the physical appearance of the valued and/or devalued life style, this can be noted in their lists. Allow about 20 minutes.

5. Bring groups together in a plenary to discuss relationships between life styles, values and appearance. A second list may be developed and put on the chalkboard showing "good" or "desirable" values. The following questions may be discussed:

—How do these chosen life styles demonstrate their "owner's" values?

—What, if anything, is the relationship between appearance and values?

—What people in the public eye, if any, exemplify some of these values? Does their life style show this? . . . How does their appearance reflect their life style?

—What is the effect of people "in" such groups on others "outside"? How much does this have to do with appearance?

—Is the physical appearance characteristic of this life style of greater importance to those "in" or "out" of the group?

VARIATIONS:

1. Step No. 5 may start with skits demonstrating desired life styles, with students freely interacting in a situation of their own design. This will require at least another 30 minutes. If the exercise is divided over two sessions, data in the first session may be put on newsprint for re-posting at the second session.

2. A collage or montage of the "chosen life style" may be made at the beginning of Step No. 4, and each "self-portrait" discussed within the subgroups preliminary to completing that step. Requires an additional 35—50 minutes.

SUGGESTED RESOURCES:

Frazier, Clifford, and Anthony Meyer, *DISCOVERY IN DRAMA,* New York: Paulist Press, 1969, pp. 31ff. Description of a scenario and technique for improvisational theater such as might be used in this exercise. This particular drama concerns a "Cocktail Party," and variations would be helpful for demonstrating various life styles. See also Viola Spolin's *IMPROVISATION FOR THE THEATER,* Evanston, Ill.: Northwestern University, 1963.

CLOTHING: THE INSURANCE COMPANY

PURPOSE:

To examine the relationship between our clothing and our happiness.

COMMENT:

Clothing, as an extension of our bodies, serves many purposes, not all of them physical. The clothing we choose, or would choose if we could, is often not directly related to what we think of as "physical needs." What does our clothing mean to us? What controls our choices? Would we be happier if our choices were made on another basis?

GROUP SIZE:

6—25

TIME SUGGESTED:

60 minutes

GENERAL DIRECTIONS:

This exercise consists of a series of letters from "the insurance company," which results in lists of desired clothing, necessary clothing, etc., and then in a discussion of the role of clothing in our lives and its relation to our happiness.

MATERIALS REQUIRED:

The letters from the insurance company may be reproduced and distributed, or they may be read aloud to the class. The former is preferable. Suggested letters are included below in "Procedure."

PROCEDURE:

1. Tell the class that they have just returned from a very long journey, in the course of which they lost all their luggage when a fire destroyed the baggage room where their trunks and suitcases were waiting to be transferred for the last leg of the trip home. The insurance company has sent each member of the class the following letter:

"We were very sorry to learn that, except for what you are now wearing, your entire wardrobe was lost when the baggage room burned. We believe you will be happy to hear of a way in which you can replace it with a "wardrobe of your dreams"! We are involved in a research project and are therefore able to offer you an unusual opportunity.

"We will pay for a complete and UNLIMITED wardrobe for you, provided you are willing to abide by the following conditions of the experiment:

a. You will have only five minutes in which to prepare a list of your needs. Give the number and general type or style of the garment desired. It is not necessary to give prices or detailed descriptions. For instance, you may list shoes as follows: "3 prs. shoes, 1 pr. boots, 1 pr. sneakers."

b. You must not purchase any other clothing for twelve months.

c. You may not give away, lend or sell any of the clothing you receive as a result of our offer.

d. At the end of the year our inspector will examine your wardrobe and take back all of the clothing, giving you an *equal* amount of *new* clothing without restrictions "2" or "3" above, *provided* all of the clothing you had this year shows reasonable signs of wear."

2. Class members have five minutes in which to prepare their lists.

3. Form the class into dyads or other small groups. These subgroups discuss one another's lists, deciding such things as: —What important items were omitted, if any? . . . Why were these particular choices made? . . . How will you feel with your new wardrobe? . . . Which of these items of clothing are most important to you, and why?

4. Tell the class that another letter has just been received from the insurance company. It reads as follows:

"Due to circumstances beyond our control, we cannot carry out our experimental program as originally outlined. Instead, we would like to make you the following offer:

"You may select only the fifteen most important and necessary items, following the conditions as laid down in Step No. 1 through Step No. 3 in our first letter. Each separate article counts as one item with the exception of "pairs" such as shoes or socks.

"As a token of our appreciation of your cooperation, if you abide by the terms of this agreement for one year, you will receive an equal value of clothing of your own selection each year for the following ten years without, of course, any restrictions."

5. Class members have five minutes in which to prepare their new lists.

6. Subgroups again share their lists and discuss them. How do these lists differ from the original ones? What do clothes mean to us when our choice is unlimited? . . . when it is limited? . . . why?

7. Tell the class that a year has gone by, and another letter has come from the insurance company:

"We know you will be glad to hear that as a result of your fine cooperation we have been able to complete our research project and the report has been very favorably received. In fact, as a result we have obtained a government contract, and would like to solicit your assistance once again. Naturally, as in the past, we will try to make it worth your while.

"A government committee working on 'possible futures' would like the opinion of young people on the following economic measure:

A committee will be charged with the responsibility of issuing all the clothing to be used by an entire population. They are to produce a list of the minimum number and type of garments to be issued to your age group in your part of the country. It is essential to be as economical as possible and yet cover all real needs. This committee wishes to consider your list, and will expect you to be ready to defend your choices."

8. Give the subgroups about ten minutes to prepare lists which they will then explain to the class.

9. Each group, or its representative, explains his subgroup's list to the class, mentioning minority opinions if there were any.

10. A general discussion may follow in which clothes as extensions of our bodies are considered in their relation to our happiness. Such questions as the following may be discussed:

—What role does clothing play in our lives? . . . in our society?

—What clothing is useful? . . . useless? . . . beneficial? . . . harmful?

—If everyone were always dressed in exactly the same clothing, what differences would it make in our lives?

—Which garments do we wear because they make us happy? . . . more comfortable? . . . Which do we wear because "society" demands that we do so?

—Can you remember the garment or article of clothing that has meant the most to you in your entire life? . . . Why was this so important? . . . Was it "practical"? . . . beautiful? . . . With what do you associate it? . . . What bearing does this have on its importance to you?

133

MONEY AND WORK

PURPOSE:

To examine our ideas and feelings about work, money, values and happiness and their interrelationships.

COMMENT:

Most students do not earn, have or spend a great deal of money, and the money they do have is largely what is known as "discretionary income"— that is, they are not required to spend it for necessities, but may spend it at their own discretion. Many students will continue in this state beyond high school; food, shelter, clothing, medical expenses and often tuition and books being paid for by their parents while they continue their education.

Students are growing up in a time of affluence and in a country with a welfare program, however inadequate. Their parents are products of "the Depression years." The result is a difference in the perspective from which students and parents view the relationship of "money" and "work." Other factors are involved in student attitudes toward these things, but this single factor has considerable importance.

Although people who want a job are unhappy to be unemployed, being happy in one's job depends on many things besides money. Young people are aware that a large percentage of people in the United States are basically dissatisfied or unhappy with their jobs, even when they are members of a profession. This unfortunate state of affairs may not be new in the history of the world, but people seem particularly distressed because of the shock of finding out how often a position long desired and striven for is unrewarding when achieved. Many young people oppose the materialistic striving they see around them, and yet get caught up in it as they mature, adding a burden of guilt for abandoned dreams to their other frustrations. To those from less affluent homes this "idealism" seems foolish, and yet they find their own increasing possessions inadequate to insure happiness.

GROUP SIZE:

5—13. Larger classes may be subgrouped if assistant leaders are available.

TIME SUGGESTED:

60 minutes. If interest in work opportunities is present, several more sessions are possible and suggestions are included.

GENERAL DIRECTIONS:

The "Money Game" is used as the introduction for a discussion in the first part of the exercise, and a very short anonymous questionnaire on "jobs and income" for the second discussion. This exercise might follow "Happiness: Body as 'Good' or 'Bad,' " since some of the differences between students' values and those of their parents will have been discussed.

MATERIALS REQUIRED:

None

PROCEDURE:

1. a. The group sits around a table or on the floor. Every member is asked to put all the money he has with him on the floor or the table directly in front of him.

b. The group is encouraged to talk about how much they have with them, how they feel about it, and how they feel about how much others have at this time.

c. Each person is asked to put in a "kitty" in the middle of the table as much money as he is willing to pool with the rest of his group. He may keep in front of him as much as he wishes, and this will remain his.

d. The group is told that each member may take from the "kitty" as much as he wishes, until it is all gone.

e. The group discusses how much each took, why, how they felt about taking it. They may go on to discuss how they feel in general about giving money to others.

f. The group moves into a discussion of how they have felt about past experiences with money—having it, not having it, earning it, losing it, giving, lending or borrowing money.

2. a. Ask each student to write on a slip of paper, without signing his name, two items: (1) the kind of work he would like to do when he finishes school; (2) the amount of money he would want to earn the first year he worked full time and supported himself.

b. Collect these slips, shuffle them, and re-distribute them so that no one has his own slip.

c. Help the group discuss the jobs or the kinds of work described, and the relation of the suggested income to the work. The group should investigate such things as the life style the suggested income would permit, the likelihood that the work selected would yield the income desired, and the length of time before this "first year of work" could be realized. The group may find it is lacking in factual information and may wish to have some data, statistical or other, available to them at a future session.

Follow-up Sessions: If the group is interested in further discussion of jobs, careers or employment, subgroups may form for other sessions, preparing for these by research in available literature or through individual or group interviews of people working in these fields. Many students may not have any idea either of what they want to do, or of how much money they want to earn. Your school guidance department may be able to provide literature or recommend sources. Roger J. Williams has said, "In our complex society a multitude of ways (of making a living) exist—an estimated 23,000 . . . Some (people) might function well in any one of a large number of capacities, many others might be highly restricted in their capabilities and yet be extremely valuable members of society" (*SATURDAY REVIEW*, Jan. 30, 1971, p. 18, "The Biology of Behavior").

The group might also be interested in discussing jobs and money from the point of view of contrasting values—their values, the values of their parents, or of "the Establishment." In this connection the article by Peter F. Drucker in "Suggested Resources" could provide some interesting data for discussion. They may agree with his statistics, but differ with his "necessary conclusions." If it is possible in your school, the students might be interested in reading and discussing a different view of the subject in *REVOLUTION FOR THE HELL OF IT*. The language is hardly that normally offered in "school textbooks," but it is that used and read by many students in their free time. Less colorfully presented opinions which still differ from Drucker's are presented by Fromm and McLuhan in their books listed in "Suggested Resources."

Students may also be interested in a discussion of work which contributes to the good of society. If the class has read and discussed such readings as the Fromm or Hoffman works, they might be interested in comparing the proposals in these with the recommendations in Vatican II's Pastoral Constitution on the Church in the Modern World *(GAUDIUM ET SPES)*, especially sections 34, 35, and 66-71, in which work, man's economic life, money and private property are considered. If desired, some of these paragraphs could be reproduced and distributed. The class may examine various kinds of work in the light of these guidelines. Subgroups may wish to role play various job situations, to examine how they feel in these roles, and to offer them for discussion by the class. A panel presentation by students, or by outside speakers, might also precede a general discussion on kinds of work in relation to personal happiness and societal needs. Some questions which may be considered are:

—What kinds of jobs would you feel you would not want because such work is destructive of your own values?

—What sort of work would promote your values?

—What sort of work would you find personally fulfilling, regardless of the money involved?

—What sort of work do you believe is necessary to society, and yet unappealing to everyone? . . . How can such work get done?

—What is an "ideal job"?

—Should everyone have a job?

—What kinds of jobs are most frequently advertised in your local paper? Is the kind of job you want ever advertised?

SUGGESTED RESOURCES:

Drucker, Peter F., "The Surprising Seventies", *HARPER'S MAGAZINE*, July 1971, Vol. 243, No. 1454, pp. 35ff.

Fromm, Erich, *THE SANE SOCIETY*, Greenwich, Conn.: Fawcett Premier, 1955, especially pp. 268-284.

Hoffman, Abbie, *REVOLUTION FOR THE HELL OF IT*, by "Free," New York, N.Y.: Dial Press, 1968.

McLuhan, Marshall, "Guaranteed Income in the Electric Age", *THE GUARANTEED INCOME*, Robert Theobald (ed.), Garden City, N.Y.: Doubleday Anchor, 1966, pp. 194ff.

"Pastoral Constitution on the Church in the Modern World" *(Gaudium et spes)*, *THE DOCUMENTS OF VATICAN II*, Walter M. Abbott (ed.), New York: Guild Press, America Press, Association Press, 1966, especialiy pp. 232-233; 274-282.

Sandman, Peter M., *THE UNABASHED CAREER GUIDE*, New York: Macmillan, 1969.

U.S. Atomic Energy Commission, P.O. Box 62, Oak Ridge, Tenn. 37831 has some materials available for teachers, such as "Careers in Atomic Energy" by Loyce J. McIllhenny," and "The Creative Scientist: His Training and His Role" by Glenn T. Seaborg.

see also: References suggested elsewhere in this book, as under "Freedom: and Work."

SELF-CONFIDENCE, POISE, AND SELF-IMAGE

PURPOSE:

To examine ways of increasing self-confidence and poise.

COMMENT:

Some people are self-confident, others are not. Some people who are shy or lack poise and self-confidence can, in some situations, overcome these problems and appear "poised." For almost everyone there are certain conditions in which we feel ill at ease. Even persons in positions of high authority have their moments of discomfort. What makes the difference? What can help us in these situations? What happens to other people when we demonstrate a lack of self-confidence?

Appearing poised helps us *feel* poised. If we know we are projecting to others a lack of self-confidence we become even less self-confident. It is difficult for young people to express to others their own good qualities, and sometimes difficult for them to even recognize such qualities in themselves. There are both cause and effect in developing self-confidence and poise. It is possible, as students will realize, to be "poised" and yet to carry out "bad" rather than "good" acts, e.g., to lie and yet be calm and cool. Some students may suggest that this is the sort of "poise" they admire, but in general the class will be more receptive to the idea of behavior that they actually value for both its intrinsic worth and the manner of its performance.

GROUP SIZE:

10—20

TIME SUGGESTED:

One or two 60 minute sessions, depending on the class size.

GENERAL DIRECTIONS:

This exercise examines some factors which help and hinder self-confidence and poise. It starts with a nonverbal which allows at least one positive, nonqualified statement to be made by each person about himself—often difficult to achieve in other ways. It continues with role plays or dramatization and discussion seeking to uncover the ways in which poise is conveyed to others and self-confidence achieved.

MATERIALS REQUIRED:

None

PROCEDURE:

1. Subgroup the class in dyads. Tell the class that for the next five minutes they will have an exercise in nonverbal communication during which each person is to convey to his partner what he thinks is *his own* most positive quality—his best quality. No restrictions are placed on whether this is physical, characteriological, etc. Discourage questions. Remind the students that this must be done without talking and should *not* be "spelled out" as in some versions of charades, but conveyed nonverbally as a total quality. Tell them that no one is to speak until you give the signal following the completion of this part of the exercise. Five minutes will actually be rather a long time for this experience, and when your dyads "run dry," call time.

2. Each dyad discusses what they were trying to convey, and talks about these qualities and their helpfulness, usefulness, etc. Wander about among the groups and, if necessary, stress that this part of the exercise is to concentrate on the positive—the good qualities, whatever they are. No one should talk about any qualities he dislikes in himself or others at this point.

3. Each person writes down on a slip of paper, anonymously, a brief description—one word, if that is adequate—of the quality expressed by his partner. Neither his name nor his partner's is to be put on the paper.

4. Collect and shuffle these slips and re-distribute them to the class. Ask each member to think about the question, "How does a self-confident, poised person actively demonstrate this quality in interaction with another person?"

5. The dyads discuss the qualities written on their slips and plan a very brief skit or a role play situation in which they can show the class both these qualities.

6. Each dyad performs for the group, announcing the qualities being demonstrated. As these qualities are announced, ask someone to write them on the chalkboard. When each dyad completes its performance, the class may discuss briefly other ways in which self-confident, poised people show these qualities. Each dyad should have a chance to perform, even if there are duplications. The class now has a "bank" or list of qualities or values written on the chalkboard, plus the experience of acting out and seeing manifestations of these qualities in a fashion they see as that of a "poised" person.

7. It is now time to attempt to role play some situations in which the class sees potential embarrassment or discomfort. In the role plays they can "try-out" behavior in accordance with some of the values they have listed while striving for "a self-confident manner." Ask the students to suggest situations and role play them. Keep the situations and roles fairly simple, role plays brief, and allow time for a short discussion after each role play. You may wish to insert some very simple role plays yourself which are not necessarily embarrassing, e.g., entering a room full of strangers, shaking hands, introducing a house guest to friends, or some more difficult situation, such as "turning down a date." It is better to talk about "friendliness," "efficiency," "usefulness" and "self-confidence," rather than "etiquette" or "good manners."

8. In a plenary, discuss the ways in which physical posture, gestures, voice tone and so forth convey self-confidence or its lack. The group may also wish to discuss the root causes of self-confidence, rather than simply its exterior physical manifestations. Some of the material from the role plays may be used as input for this discussion. Discussion may also focus on the differences between self-confidence, vanity, self-complacency and arrogance, using the students' own terms as they appear during this discussion.

POISE: TRYING ON

PURPOSE:

To experiment with new ways of behavior to achieve the desired modifications in physical appearance and the presentation of the self.

COMMENT:

Poise and self-confidence are greatly aided when we feel confident that we "look good." This involves aspects of physical appearance and behavior which are usually subject to modification. We may be dissatisfied with our complexion, with our tendency to lose our temper or worry excessively. We may be uncomfortable about inviting friends home because of the way our room looks. All of us have at least one area of appearance or behavior which we would like to change in some way. We may want to be thinner, or less thin, stronger, or more graceful. We think we would be happier if our clothes were different. All these things are part of the visible self we present to others. We often have difficulty getting started on a program of change, or wish we could talk it over with someone before starting.

Most students would hesitate to share their desire to lose weight, improve the appearance of their hair or their posture, with the entire class, but would feel fairly comfortable about doing so with a friend. Mutual sharing of some personal dissatisfactions and desires is more apt to bring positive efforts to carry out a program of change, particularly if there is some sort of deadline and check-up system.

GROUP SIZE:

This exercise is conducted entirely in dyads with perhaps an occasional triad. The total number is unimportant.

TIME SUGGESTED:

30 minutes once a week for 4 (or 7) weeks.

GENERAL DIRECTIONS:

After introducing the idea, the instructor remains in the background, on call for individual conferences or as a resource person. The dyads should be seated so that they can talk quietly with one another without feeling they are eavesdropping on another pair. This exercise is possibly best used at "beginnings"—the beginning of a term or semester, or after a vacation, but could be used any time. Soft background music might be helpful.

MATERIALS REQUIRED:

Depends on individual needs. It may help to have available some literature on diet and nutrition, magazines with articles on women's hair styles, material on mental health and exercise for both men and women.

PROCEDURE:

Speak to the class briefly, explaining some of the ideas as presented above in "Comment," and explain that you think an experiment might be helpful.

1. Each member makes a short list of things about himself that he would like to change, and which he thinks it might be possible to change. This list is for his own use—no one else will see it unless he wishes.

2. Ask the class to pair off with a friend, and discuss the one or two items on the list which he most wants to change, and is willing to talk over with his partner. (If you are afraid somecne will be "left-out" in self-selected pairing, assign pairs.) Give the pairs 5—10 minutes for conversation.

3. Tell the class that over the next three weeks (or six weeks) they will be able to spend some time each week talking to their present partner about their program for change. This will be a mutual progress report, and problems and suggestions may be discussed. Ask them not to discuss their partner's program with anyone else without his permission.

4. Allow dyads another 10—15 minutes to write down some specific suggestions as to how they plan to go about making the change, talking this over with their partner. Suggest that they set some actual deadlines and write down some specific goals, objectives, or criteria for success.

Schedule and announce regular "conference times" over the next few weeks. Make literature available, and offer to assist in obtaining other materials, or perhaps resource persons, on request.

SUGGESTED RESOURCES:

Your schools Physical Education and Guidance departments, as well as the library, may have some suitable materials available for your "resource table." You may also wish to obtain brochures from local organizations such as the YM/YWCA, YM/YWHA, local Yoga classes, little theater groups, etc.

You can send for some free materials to such sources as the following:

Best Foods: a Division of CPC International Inc., P.O. Box 307, Coventry, Conn. 06238. Ask for a selection of literature available in classroom quantities on such subjects as tie-dying and batiking for clothing, home decorating, etc., and for a teacher's booklet, "A Guide to Good Nutrition."

Educational Service, Standard Brands Incorporated, P.O. Box 2695 Grand Central Station, New York, N.Y. 10017. Ask for student materials on diet and nutrition.

The following agencies can supply some materials on mental health suitable for teenagers interested in improved mental hygiene:

Child Study Association of America, 9 E. 89th St., New York, N.Y. 10003.

Family Service Association of America, 44 E. 23rd St., New York, N.Y. 10010.

Mental Health Materials Center, Inc., 419 Park Avenue South, New York, N.Y. 10016.

Health and Welfare Division, Metropolitan Life Insurance Company, 1 Madison Ave., New York, N.Y. 10010; or 600 Stockton St., San Francisco, Calif. 94120. (One booklet, "Stress—and your health," although addressed to adults, is sound, interesting and a brief 15 pages.)

FILM:

Metropolitan Life Insurance Company, at the above addresses, has two films, available on loan without charge, which might be helpful. The first, "Mr. Finley's Feelings," is a 10 minute animated color film addressed to adult audiences, but of interest to many teenagers. "A Song of Arthur" is a 16 mm. musical film in color, 21 minutes, which deals with checking overweight and promoting fitness.

The Florida Citrus Commission offers three leaflets, one for boys, "How to Get in Shape and Stay There!" and two for girls, "The Road to Beauty," and "The Beauty Habit or How to Be a Doll." These offer suggestions on food, exercise, grooming, posture and complexion care. Florida Citrus Commission, Production Mgr., P.O. Box 1720, Lakeland, Fla. 33802.

Schifferes, Justus J., WHAT'S YOUR CALORIC NUMBER? A PRUDENT GUIDE TO LOSING WEIGHT, New York: Macmillan, 1966. (Not too technical but still sound on nutrition facts and fallacies, exercise and dieting for weight loss.)

POISE: CONTRARY DIRECTIONS

PURPOSE:

To experiment with contrary and contradictory situations—problems that have to be worked out. To develop poise, confidence and control.

COMMENT:

Simultaneously performing two contradictory actions causes a state of tension. It takes much concentration and practice to "master" a simple motion such as lifting a chair while performing an entirely different function with one's "mind." It is usually even more difficult to do two quite different things simultaneously with the right and left hand, witness the old game of "patting your head and rubbing your stomach."

GROUP SIZE:

6—20

TIME SUGGESTED:

20—30 minutes

GENERAL DIRECTIONS:

This exercise may be carried on by two or three people in front of the class, or by individuals in each subgroup, or, in some cases, by the entire class at the same time.

MATERIALS REQUIRED:

Coffee in a pot, coffee cups; or bottles of soda and glasses.

Other objects in the room will suffice for various modifications of the following suggestions.

PROCEDURE:

1. Give the student directions for a very simple action: pouring a cup of coffee, holding a cup of coffee, etc. AT THE SAME TIME give him a "contrary motion": pick up with one hand some heavy object, e.g., a chair, a stack of books, etc.

2. Give the student a mathematical problem to figure out mentally. AT THE SAME TIME ask him to lift a chair.

BODY AS "GOOD" OR "BAD"

PURPOSE:

To consider and compare some of our values.

COMMENT:

Although many young people today share a majority of their values with their parents, there are a large and probably growing number who do not. This has been extensively documented and discussed by such authors as Margaret Mead, Kenneth Keniston, Edgar Friedenberg and Theodore Roszak. Most of these authors would agree that at least one important and underlying cause has been the accelerated rate of social change which has given this generation of teenagers and their parents a prediction of an unpredictable future. Both realize that "tomorrow" is going to be very different from "yesterday"—the world of the children very different from the world the parents knew. Writing in the early 1960's, Keniston said, "No valid models exist for the as-yet-to-be-imagined world in which they will live. Not surprisingly, their very sanity and realism sometimes leads them to be disaffected from the values of their elders" ("Social Change and Youth in America", *THE CHALLENGE OF YOUTH*). The kind of literature these young people have been reading reflects the inversion of parental values, or simply their destruction. Such books as Kurt Vonnegut's *CAT'S CRADLE* or publications such as *MAD* magazine point out and devastatingly illustrate for them not only the hypocrisy of the parental generation, but the inhumanity resulting from many values they successfully pursued.

Many of the best educated and most aware young people come from the homes of liberal, well-educated parents and they often find at home no refutation of their accusations, but rather a somewhat despairing acquiescence. Their parents may still "value their values," but find an adequate explanation or defense of them almost impossible. The two generations may reach mutual tolerance, an armed truce, or open warfare, but very seldom a coherent, articulated system of mutual values. Even though this particular group of young people often disavow leadership, their influence among their peers is strong. They model a range of attitudes from apathy through nihilism to generalized rage against "things as they are." Their negation of adult values does not necessarily imply an opposing set of positive values. They have difficulty in finding any values to which they can give real adherence, and a distrust of any valuing decisions they do make. Much of the generational conflict in values relates, not surprisingly, to the human body—what it is, what is good for it, how it should be treated. There are differences of opinion among young people themselves, extremes at both ends of the scale, but between these poles lies a large group characterized by uncertainty and insecurity about values relating to the body and consensual primarily in a generalized feeling that the values of the adult world around them are inadequate at best, and probably destructive.

GROUP SIZE:

About 12

TIME SUGGESTED:

60 minutes

GENERAL DIRECTIONS:

Class members categorize a list of topics as "good" or "bad" as they believe the adult world sees them, and then as they see them. They compare and discuss their findings.

MATERIALS REQUIRED:

1 set of topic cards for each student. The cards may be made very simply by using 3 x 5 file cards, cut in half from top to bottom. You may use perforated sheets of address labels, making four carbon copies of each item, tearing the labels apart and pasting them on the cards, repeating this process until enough labels are obtained. There must be one complete set of twenty-two cards for each student. Each card contains one of the following items:

long hair, beards (men)
the mind
the human body
money
a nice home

attending church or synagogue
capitalism
football, baseball
sex
see-through clothes
astrology
religion
alcoholic beverages
patriotism
socialism
drugs
work
the study of history
marriage
a professional career
big business
academic achievement

PROCEDURE:

1. Distribute one pack of cards to each member of the class. Ask them to shuffle the cards. On the chalkboard put the following three headings:
   "good, valuable, important",
   "neutral or unimportant, not bad or good",
   "bad, unwholesome or dangerous".
Leave room to the left to fill in the list of 22 terms. Under each of the above headings you will have two columns to be filled in when "votes" are tallied.

Ask the students to think how most adults they know well—their parents, friends' parents, teachers, etc.,—would arrange these cards. Under which of the three headings would they place each card? Ask them to arrange their cards in front of them in three piles, as they believe these adults would place them. Ask them to take just a few minutes to make the three piles.

While they are arranging their cards, write the twenty-two terms on the board to the left of the three headings.

2. Take a tally of the class votes by asking, "How many put 'money' under the first heading— 'Good, valuable, important'? . . . How many put it under 'neutral'," etc. Put the total number of votes opposite the term in the first column under each heading.

3. When all the votes are tallied, ask the students to shuffle their cards again, and this time lay them in three piles as they themselves want to rank or classify them.

4. Explain to the students that they may change their vote later, if they should so wish, but that an initial tally of their decisions will be taken now. Tally their votes as above, placing the numbers in the second column under each heading.

5. Subgroup the class in dyads or triads, and ask them to discuss their own decisions with those shown on the class tallies for about ten minutes.

6. In a plenary, ask the class to identify those items which they believe are connected with our bodies. Put a check or asterisk beside those so identified. (NOTE: Some groups may include "the mind," "academic achievement," "astrology," etc.; others may exclude "drugs," "marriage," etc. As the discussion progresses, more items may be so identified, or dropped, as the class sees fit.)

Using the tallies as a basis, examine similarities and differences between classifications of students and their judgments as to adult classifications. Help the class examine the reasons for their choices in both instances. Some of the following questions may be explored:

—Do you see your understanding of the human body as the same or different from the adults?

—Do the things you believe they rate as "bad" affect the body in some way? . . . What about the things you think they rate as "good"?

—Does the way the adult sees the human body affect his decision on these things?. . . . What other factors are involved?

—Where do you think the adults would draw the line between "body" and "not body"? . . .Where would you draw the line?

—How does your view of the human body affect your values?

—What influences do you think have most affected your values?

7. Give students 3—4 minutes to make any changes they wish in their three piles of cards, before taking another tally on student values.

8. Repeat the tally, making any changes necessary in the appropriate column.

9. Allow a few more minutes for a plenary discussion of these changes. NOTE: As discussion progresses, many more mature students will move all their cards to the center pile, if the discussion has involved many statements such as, "it all depends. . . ."

VARIATIONS:

1. The above method may be used with a variety of topics other than those suggested above. In some instances you might prefer to eliminate the tallying, and form small subgroups for discussion of choices.

2. Students may take their cards home with them and use them in the family to check their "guesses." Remind them to ask those whom they "test" to work quickly at the task. If the students so

142 desire, their findings could be tallied and discussed.

SUGGESTED RESOURCES:

The first three of the following are recommended primarily for the teacher; the fourth will probably be of interest to the students as well.

Erikson, Erik H., (ed.), *THE CHALLENGE OF YOUTH,* Garden City, N.Y.: Doubleday Anchor, 1963, p. 203.

Friedenberg, Edgar Z., *COMING OF AGE IN AMERICA,* New York: Vintage, 1965.

Roszak, Theodore, *THE MAKING OF A COUNTER CULTURE,* Garden City, N.Y.: Doubleday Anchor, 1969.

Mead, Margaret, *CULTURE AND COMMITMENT: A STUDY OF THE GENERATION GAP,* Garden City, N.Y.: Doubleday, 1970.

See also "Freedom: Mass Media and 'Good' and 'Bad' Bodies."

ACCEPTANCE/ REJECTION

PURPOSE:

To explore acceptance and rejection by experiencing, observing and discussing the nonverbal aspects of such behavior.

COMMENT:

Young people have an intolerance of "difference," a tendency to reject the outsider, and to adopt clothing and behavior which help them identify with their chosen group, toward which they will demonstrate the loyalty which they greatly admire. Erik Erikson speaks of this clannishness as "unavoidable," given the special stresses of adolescence, and says that this intolerance "may be, for a while, a necessary defense against a sense of identity loss." He adds, however, that this does not mean that one should condone all of its manifestations (*IDENTITY: YOUTH AND CRISIS,* New York: W. W. Norton, 1968, pp. 132-133).

Experiencing it themselves in many instances, young people are not unaware of the unhappiness caused by being the rejected one, but tend to counter this by finding a group in which they can be accepted. Since at this age there is apt to be considerable shifting and changing of values, there is apt to be a concomitant shifting of groups. To the more secure and stable adult this may place the depth of their loyalty in doubt, and make the young people seem both less sincere and more unreasonable in their intolerance. A truly healthy maturation should eliminate the problem, but our society and our world bear witness to the continuance of problems of intolerance, stereotyping and group rejection, and presents at least as many models of the continuation of these attitudes as of their resolution.

GROUP SIZE:

10—20

TIME SUGGESTED:

60 minutes

GENERAL DIRECTIONS:

This exercise will be more profitable for a group with some previous experience in role playing and/or pantomime. A series of role plays forms the basis for an examination of the results of nonverbal behavior exhibited in situations of rejection and acceptance. If possible, use role play situations suggested by the students.

MATERIALS REQUIRED:

None

PROCEDURE:

1. Ask the class to suggest a role play situation of peer acceptance or rejection. For example, "Sam has deliberately lied, and as a result Dave has been unfairly punished. Sam, the troublemaker, now wants to go to a party with three close friends of Dave." If you wish to add "acceptance" to this role play, add, "While Sam is talking with the three, Dave joins them." After a few situations have been suggested, select the role players and ask them to go to another room for five minutes to prepare the selected situation.

2. While they are out of the room, explain to the class that they are to pay particular attention to the *nonverbal* aspects of acceptance or rejection demonstrated in the role play.

3. Bring the role players in and have them perform in front of the class.

4. When you have stopped the role play, ask the role players how they felt in their roles. Then explain that you have asked the audience to pay particular attention to the nonverbal behavior, and ask the class to mention and demonstrate the nonverbal communications. As they do so, stop them occasionally and ask them how their muscles *feel* in the positions and gestures they are demonstrating. You may wish to ask one of the role players to use a new posture or gesture, one not actually used in their role play but which now occurs to them as suitable to the situation. Ask them what feelings or emotions they associate with the particular muscular tensions or contractions involved. Allow a few minutes to explore the relationship between striking a particular pose or using a particular gesture, and the resulting feelings within the acting individual.

5. Ask the class to suggest another role play situation in which rejection is by an authority figure. For instance, "Two students go to the principal's office to request permission to distribute handbills for the Resistance, and are "rejected" by the principal."

6. Role players are selected, given a few minutes to prepare, and the role play performed for the class.

7. After the role play has been stopped, ask the class to concentrate on discussing some of the more subtle ways in which rejection was shown in this situation. If the role play has been done very broadly, ask, "In what other small, less obvious ways is rejection often shown?" They may also discuss differences between rejection by peers and by authorities, as shown nonverbally.

8. Ask for four volunteers or assign role players and give them a previously prepared scenario which indicates a shift either from rejection to acceptance or vice versa. Use a fairly topical situation involving perhaps 3—5 people, such as the following:

SITUATION: Three members of the football team meet with a boy who has recently transferred to their school. (NOTE: All role players receive a sheet headed by this "Situation," but are *not* to share the other data on their role sheets.)

RICHARD: You have just transferred to this school and are very interested in getting on the football team, as you played for two years in your old school, enjoyed it very much and were well liked by your team. You run into three members of the team and want some tips from them on how to get on the team. You are anxious to have them like you, and avoid correcting any mistakes they make; for instance, they apparently think your last name is "Anderson," but you let this ride for several minutes before telling them that it is actually "Bates."

THREE MEMBERS OF TEAM: (All receive identical role sheets.) Richard Anderson and Richard Bates have just transferred to your school. *Bates* was a star football player, well liked by his team mates, but Anderson, although constantly boasting of his ability, was thrown off the team both because of poor playing and also because he stole small articles from the locker room. Anderson has asked to meet with the three of you. You have not seen him before, but you are at least willing to speak with him. As he approaches, you say, "Hello, Richard," but are not eager to converse with him.

9. Following the role play and, in this case, before the role players discuss their own roles and feelings, ask the audience what change in attitude they noticed and what nonverbal behavior indicated this shift.

—What did you "see," or hear in the voice tone or pitch, which indicated a shift in attitude on the part of any of the role players? Help the group discuss the perceptual and conceptual bases for rejection and acceptance, and how these are translated into nonverbal behavior.

—Short of hitting someone, what is the

most clear-cut physical rejection? . . . What is less clear-cut, but still important?

—How do these behaviors affect the one rejected? . . . The ones demonstrating such rejection?

—What do you think "hurts" the most? . . . why?

—Why is genuine "acceptance" sometimes rebuffed? . . . Does it make people "happy" to reject another? . . . why? . . . how?

—Does it ever make people unhappy to be accepted?

—Why is acceptance important? . . . Must you be accepted by *every* group in order to be happy?

—Do you think there is any difference in the effect of verbal *vs.* nonverbal acceptance or rejection? . . . Is one more important than the other? . . . Does it depend on the individual? . . . on the group or culture?

BELONGING

PURPOSE:

To think in terms of our physical self and its relation to others. To accept our physical form, or think about why we do not do so.

GROUP SIZE:

6—12

TIME SUGGESTED:

25—45 minutes

GENERAL DIRECTIONS:

This exercise is the reverse of the "Freedom: Break Through" exercise. In a larger class, subgroup for circles. Clear sufficient floorspace to allow the formation of groups standing in tight circles, with several feet of free space outside each circle. Encourage volunteers, but do not insist that everyone take a turn at "breaking in." Discussion should be easygoing, following the direction of student concern.

MATERIALS REQUIRED:

None

PROCEDURE:

1. Form a circle(s). One at a time a member steps outside the circle and then tries to break in to become a part of the group. Members in the group are to form a tight circle and try to keep the person from breaking in. Force may be used, but not excessive force or violence.

2. Share and discuss feelings about what has happened. What does this exercise tell us about physical belonging? . . . about rejection? . . . acceptance? If the group has done the "Freedom: Break Through" exercise, compare experiences. How do you feel about this kind of rough contact? . . . why? . . . Is there a difference in this between men and women? . . . why? . . . Did anyone try to "talk" their way in? . . . why? . . . What happened? . . . why? . . . Did anyone use threats or trickery? . . . If so, how did people feel about that?

GIVING

PURPOSE:

To explore or express our physical relationships with others and the use of the body to express feelings.

COMMENT:

As in "Happiness: Belonging," this involves an exploration of feelings in situations of close physical contact. However, this is a sensitivity training exercise, and is recommended ONLY for a cohesive group of mature students who have worked together for a long time. The instructor should use this only when he believes group members can handle rejection, and talk about it, or when he feels sure that no rejection will occur.

GROUP SIZE:

6—10

TIME SUGGESTED:

30—60 minutes

GENERAL DIRECTIONS:

If you use this exercise, you may find that expressions of feeling are apt to be imitative—one or two members really expressing something, the rest just "following the leader." If this happens, it should be discussed. The exercise may be used without discussion as a concluding action following other exercises or experiences which you believe might lead naturally to a suitable climate in the group. You may wish to use a reading before or after this exercise, such as the selection from Gibran in "Suggested Resources."

PROCEDURE:

1. Members form a circle. One at a time each member goes to the center and closes his eyes. Each other member of the circle then goes to him in turn and expresses in a nonverbal manner some positive regard or feeling he has for him. The member in the center receives the expression of regard without re-

turning it or reacting to it.

2. After each member has had his turn in the center, the group discusses the experience, sharing particularly the feeling of receiving without giving back or reacting to this experience. What were the different expressions of feeling? . . . the reactions to them?

SUGGESTED RESOURCES:

Gibran, Kahlil, *THE PROPHET,* New York: Alfred A. Knopf, 1951, pp. 19-22.

GROUP EXCURSIONS

PURPOSE:

(1) To promote group feeling, sense of mutual responsibility, imagination and sharing. (2) To become aware of the unconscious. (3) To know other aspects of the personalities of members of the group.

COMMENT:

It would be a distortion of the experience to overstructure the discussions following each of these possible approaches to fantasy. Keep in mind the possible purposes given above, but do not drive the group toward explorations of particular elements in which you are interested and they are not.

GROUP SIZE:

6—20

TIME SUGGESTED:

Times for the four possibilities given vary from 15—60 minutes.

GENERAL DIRECTIONS:

Use one of the following when the time seems appropriate. The first three could be done in an ordinary classroom situation, although the experience may be a deeper one if conditions such as are prescribed for "4" exist. Number "3" could be used early in a group's life, the others are better for a group that has been meeting for some time.

MATERIALS REQUIRED:

For "2" only: crayons and paper.

PROCEDURE:

1. Future Get-together.

a. Everyone takes the first 15—20 minutes of the session and writes about an imaginary get-together of this group at some future date, in some other location. The story may be in outline form. Tell the students to let their imagination have free play as to when and where they will meet, what they will look like, and what they will do. They should write their stories without recounting any conversations, but include lots of action or activity. Their stories should have a definite ending or conclusion.

b. Have someone volunteer to read or tell his story to the group.

c. Group now talks about the story. Are the people the same? If not, how have they changed? Have relationships among members changed? Who changes most? . . . least? Allow discussion to follow student interest.

2. Picture. Either several groups or one large group can participate. Provide crayons and paper.

a. Everyone draws with crayons a "fantasy picture." No prior decision is made about what it will be—just let it emerge. Start with one line, and let the group members choose colors and draw. Usually the group members will put themselves and others in the picture without being so instructed. If so, they may show what, to them, is the strongest physical characteristic of that person.

b. Share and discuss the picture.

3. Song.

a. Everyone just begins to hum . . . Let it drift, without conscious choice, into a tune or song.

b. Share and discuss the experience.

4. Group Fantasy. An appropriate atmosphere is important: evening is preferable; semi-lighted room; relaxed posture; no time restriction; you may wish to have soft music in the background, but this may be distracting. Ask the participants to close their eyes for this exercise.

a. The teacher or some other member may start. Let the imagination work freely. Begin a story. Place and events are freely imagined, but the people in the group must be in the story. One way to start might be to say, "Let's continue this story together . . . I'll start . . . 'At some future date, Jim graduates first in his class from medical school. John is released from prison after a two-year term for armed robbery. Bob returns from Vietnam, and is discharged from the Army. Mary is not married, and will have a baby within a few weeks. Jeanne is the mother of five kids, is pregnant, the family is financially struggling. Besides the doctors warned her against any more children . . .' (etc.)"

b. Once the story has begun, anyone in the group may pick it up. Don't try consciously to shape the story—just let it emerge.

   c. When most of the group have had a chance to contribute, or after an appropriate amount of time, stop.

   d. Discuss the aspects of the story that impressed the people. Generate discussion on the choice of place, time, activities, who was included and who was not.

WHAT IS COMMUNITY?

PURPOSE:

  To explore the ingredients necessary for community.

COMMENT:

  "Left entirely to himself man is unhappy and intrinsically insincere. He needs other people to give him a sense of completeness; he needs the community. He needs the world and the duty of serving it. He needs eternity, or rather, he needs the eternal, the infinite" *(THE PRISON MEDITATIONS OF FATHER DELP)*.

GROUP SIZE:

  8—10

TIME SUGGESTED:

  This will probably best be considered as spread out over several sessions. Other activities may intervene without destroying the effectiveness of the exercise.

GENERAL DIRECTIONS:

  This exercise should be used following one or more such as "Happiness: Meal," or "Happiness: Group Excursion Fantasy," in which some discussion has arisen about community. "Community" is here used in the sense of a viable support community, a primary community, a sharing community, a "primary group" feeling.

  It is also an exercise in consensus building, which is one reason it is apt to take longer than one session. Students should understand that in attempting to reach consensus, they must not simply "vote" and let the majority rule, they must defend those things they believe important, and they must try not to exclude any person who wishes to participate. It is possible that, if the group is larger than 8 —10 persons, more than one "community" will result. Adjunctive material on communes, the extended family, "communitarian communities of work," utopian societies etc., may be included in this total exercise, if student interest is shown. It is also possible that the class may wish to explore the idea of their own geographical community, how it serves their needs and the needs of others who live there. The basis of the experience is the actual relationships and interactions of the members of the community, no matter which kind of community is under discussion. Depending on time and student interest, further developments from this basis may be explored.

This exercise may be used in a number of ways. (1) "Permanent" subgroups of the class may be formed during the course of this exercise, which will last until a set time, e.g., the end of the term. (2) It may be used as preparation for a week-long retreat, camping expedition, or a one or two week experiment in communal living, if facilities and staffing personnel are available. If this is the option, every effort should be made to allow the students to make their own plans and rules and they should be responsible for obtaining parental permission and an acceptable live-in staff (supervision). (3) It may be used as a hypothetical situation, in which the groups plan "an ideal community life."

MATERIALS REQUIRED:

Chalkboard or newsprint and chalk or felt-tip markers.

Large paper strips or squares of bristol board and felt-tip markers.

In connection with some of the further developments listed under the "Variations," additional materials—literature, games, etc.,—may be required.

PROCEDURE:

I. 1. Talk briefly to the students, recalling some of the group's previous experiences, and proposing that the group investigate the needs met by a "community." Encourage them to start with the idea of a small group, living in close proximity and trying to serve all the needs of its members. Explain that they need not include air, water, food, shelter and clothing, since these may be presumed to be essential to support life for the individual, whether or not he lives in community with others. However, they might want to include items which *relate* in some way to the distribution or management of these items. If it is difficult for them to approach this abstractly, suggest that they think in terms of a commune, a village, a group shipwrecked on an island, etc. As "essential ingredients" are suggested, put these on the chalkboard, including all suggestions at present. Explain that they can go over the list later, making adjustments and changes. Avoid suggesting "things you have forgotten," and avoid being the "judge" as to whether or not an item is important or relevant, placing the burden for the decision on the group.

2. If the group is larger than twelve, divide the class in subgroups of 7—10, explaining that each group must now reach a consensus on the items they consider most important from the list on the board. At this point, each group should decide what it wants to "be"—a commune, a small village, a group air-crashed on an island, a work community, etc. Each group is given large paper strips or bristol board "posters" and asked to place one item on each, their finished product to represent all the essential ingredients for a community which would be sufficient for all their needs—psychological, psychological, sociological—for one year.

3. Give them about twenty minutes to prepare their "community." NOTE: If any group has not reached a true consensus at the end of this time, tell them that it is better to continue this at a later time, rather than accept an unsatisfactory decision. If a group feels that the number of paper strips is insufficient, allow them to have more, giving them additional strips or posters, but only AFTER they have identified the consensually agreed upon item.

4. Mount each group's "community" somewhere on the wall, and, if more than one group is operating, allow some time for inspection.

II. 1. Each group is now to consider the nature of the physical, emotional, or social relationships of their own members in this community, presuming that the community would exist for the one year suggested in Step Nos. 1 and 2.

What are the *kinds* of physical relationships of people in an "average community"?

Various classifications might be used, such as:

A. *Physical Contacts*
   People we ignore
   People we bow to or nod to
   People we shake hands with
   People to whom we give a friendly pat or slap on the back
   People whom we hug or kiss
   People whom we take care of physically, either because they are infants or small children, or because they are ill
   People with whom we have sexual relationships

OR

> People whose physical needs we care for
>
> People who care for our physical needs
>
> Reciprocal combination of the preceding two.

What kinds of relationships would occur in your hypothetical "community"? Which would not? What would be the effect of these relationships on other aspects of community?

> B. *Emotional and Social*
>
> People who give orders
>
> People who obey orders
>
> How will decisions be made?
>
> How will deviations from group norms be handled?
>
> Will there be any rules? . . . If so, how will these be arrived at? . . . How will they be enforced?
>
> Will some people give orders, and others obey? . . .Will someone be in charge?
>
> How will the community decide who is to be in charge? Will others be allowed to join the community? . . . If so, under what circumstances?

2. (a) Each group trades one member with another group. (This may mean a change of two persons, depending on the number of groups.) "Trading" is to be done by chance, using dice, straws, etc.

(b) Each group explains to the new member what they think is important about their community—the elements decided upon in I. 2. and the relationships decided upon in II.1.

(c) The "outsider" may decide whether he wants to remain in this "new" community, or to return to the one he left, but if he wishes to return, he must persuade some member of his "old" community to take his place instead in the "new" community, explaining the "new" one and offering whatever features he thinks might appeal to the person he is trying to persuade to take his place. If he has decided to remain in the "new" community, he must win their acceptance by demonstrating his agreement with their principles, telling their group members why he thinks their community is preferable to his old one.

3. Each group now writes three "laws" or "rules" which they think are essential to maintaining their community as they would want it to be, remembering that they are to stay in existence at least one year. The groups may make any laws they wish except one which dissolves their community or restricts immigration or emigration. Agreement on these rules should also be reached by consensus. These laws should be printed on cards and posted.

4. Another "trade" is arranged, again by chance, with the same procedures as in "2", but this time the newcomer must also consider the "laws" as well as the elements or principles and the physical relationships. The "newcomer" is not included as one of the possible people to be traded.

III. 1. By this time each group will have been exposed to two "other cultures," beside its own community, and each person should now decide in which of the three he would prefer to "spend the year." All those who wish to move to another group must present their "case" to the group they are leaving—even if *all* members are leaving that group, all cases must first be heard. Those wishing to emigrate must explain why they believe they would be better off in the group they wish to enter, and the group they wish to leave may grant or withhold permission for emigration according to whether they believe their group can survive without the departing members.

2. If a group grants permission for emigration to one or more members, these members must then win acceptance into the group of their choice, again presenting their reasons for believing that they would be better off in the group they wish to enter. The "accepting" group is also free to grant or withhold permission to immigrants on the basis of whether the group believes they will be benefited by accepting the new members.

IV. The final step in the total exercise should be a discussion of "community and communities," in which the family as community is a possible point of departure. Various kinds of family structures may be examined, including communes, religious communities, utopian work communities, etc., in accordance with student interest. Their own learnings from previous parts of the exercise may be very helpful in examining desires and needs, and the importance of the actual interpersonal relationships, the necessity for regulation, and the difficulties of group decision making involving such communities. The group should have enough previous knowledge to draw on to see the close connection between the physical and emotional as well as the intellectual and spiritual needs of the individuals. A serious gap in their learnings will be the actual working out of the responsibilities which must be accepted by various members in order for their hypothetical community to work. If it is possible to discuss this problem, it might be helpful for the groups to have a "planning session," in which they try to map out the time available during a week's life of the community, the work which must be done, the resources available to them and the assignment of responsibilities. In urban areas some students may have experienced communal life, and many other students will have experienced camping or vacation trips where there was some degree of independence, but when they begin to examine these possibilities, they will find major requirements unfilled, and some decisions would have to be made as to who was to get a job, the amount of money needed, the actual possibilities of finding a place to live, and so forth. Very few students will have had any experience of being even partially financially independent, or of trying to make a community function successfully as a community for as long as a year.

VARIATIONS:

Some groups may want to substitute for part of Sections II and III some readings, with a discussion of them. The usual ones found helpful and interesting are listed below.

SUGGESTED RESOURCES:

Golding, William, *LORD OF THE FLIES*, New York: Capricorn, 1955.

Heyer, Robert J., Payne, Richard J., (eds.), *DISCOVERY PATTERNS, BOOK 1: PATTERNS OF SITUATIONS*, New York: Paulist Press, 1969, p. 193ff.

Hilton, James, *LOST HORIZON*, New York: Morrow, 1933.

Huxley, Aldous, *BRAVE NEW WORLD*, New York: Bantam, 1932.

Orwell, George, *NINETEEN-EIGHTY-FOUR*, New York: Signet, 1949.

Skinner, B. F., *WALDEN TWO*, New York: Macmillan, 1948.

Delp, Alfred, S.J., *THE PRISON MEDITATIONS OF FATHER DELP*, New York: Macmillan, 1963, p. 90.

SOUND

PURPOSE:

To explore the possibilities of various sounds as contributing to our happiness, or unhappiness.

COMMENT:

There is silence, and there is sound. City dwellers rarely hear silence, or even hear a single sound—usually they hear layers of sound of many kinds from many sources. Even listening to a record or tape with the "ear muff" type earphones is an interesting experience for many people who seldom hear music in isolation. The all encompassing sound of a rock group is a very different experience—we do not so much "hear" it as we are overwhelmed by it. Alone in a relatively quiet house at night fear may make us very aware of a small sound we would not notice in the daytime. The factor of "attention" plays a large role in our listening and hearing. Sometimes we hear a sound, and smile—are we happy because the sound pleases us, or because it tells us something else is happening, or going to happen? Would we hear *more* happy sounds if we "paid attention"? Is there any way to increase our ability to obtain happiness from sound?

GROUP SIZE:

6—20

TIME SUGGESTED:

60 minutes. This session requires advance preparation at one or more previous sessions, where the purposes and design of the exercise are explained and assignments made for various articles and materials to be brought to the class for the session itself.

GENERAL DIRECTIONS:

Students are encouraged to produce their own tapes, music or other sounds, or at least to bring in their own records, as well as to experiment with sound in various ways in the classroom. The "sound session" is a sort of happening or party or "sound tasting" event.

MATERIALS REQUIRED:

Encourage the students to be innovative in bringing in a wide variety of materials. The most obvious things, such as a "recording I like to listen to because it makes me happy" are not to be discouraged, but more creative and less obvious choices should be looked for. Any member of the class who has a portable musical instrument should be asked to bring it with him for his particular session, and other articles not normally thought of as "musical" should be considered. Some selected items may need associated equipment to be usable, e.g., a whistling teakettle needs an electric hotplate. If you think the class is apt to be unimaginative or limited in what they will produce, have some back-up materials available.

PROCEDURE:

1. At a previous session ask the class to take 5—10 minutes to jot down a list of "sounds" that make them happy—no limit on type. These lists are not to be handed in, but retained by them for another session. When the lists are completed, ask the class members to call out items which you will list or have listed on the chalkboard. You will probably find some things such as "the last class bell," "the electric mixer running in the kitchen," "sea gulls," "birds singing," "a fountain" as well as the expected "favorite songs." Explain that you want to have a session in which as many happy sounds as possible can be heard by the class. Sounds which are "happy" for one person may, of course, not produce this feeling in anyone else. Ask the class for suggestions as to how some of these sounds may be brought into the classroom. Most students will suggest tapes and records, a few will suggest an instrument, person or object. Plan with the class for the tape recorders, record players, etc., required, and ask for volunteers to bring in specific tapes etc. Put the lists down on newsprint and post them in the classroom for reference. Explain that they may add to these lists during the next week, provided they can find a way to practically implement their ideas.

2. On the day of the session have as much space available as possible, as well as the necessary equipment and your own back-up supplies. If you have a large class and a good bit of material, try to arrange to use more than one room, and run your "sound experience" like a fair, with more than one sound producer available for use at the same time. The session itself may operate like a "Happening," with a certain amount of randomness, or it may be planned in some detail so that there is a definite sequence, an explanation by the selector of the sound, a reaction from the entire group or subgroup. The particular arrangements may be the work of a committee, or several coordinated committees, or of the class as a whole, if the number is fairly small.

3. Time should be allowed at the end of the session for a very brief reaction to the experience as a whole. A formal discussion of the relationship between the particular sensory experience and the feeling of happiness may follow, or may be postponed. If there is not at least thirty minutes for this discussion, it is best postponed, rather than rushed or shortened.

4. Using the data of the sound experiences, encourage the class to discuss why certain sounds result in "happy" or "sad" feelings. This discussion may go in the direction of aesthetics or psychology or both. Students may describe sounds as "naturally more pleasing" or "naturally happy," or they may talk in terms of their associations with the sounds. Music students may discuss the major as opposed to the minor chords as being "happier," or may talk of the tempo or rhythm as productive of differing emotions. It would be helpful if both foci could be included in the discussion, but students will usually find it more productive to pursue one aspect at a time.

VARIATIONS:

1. Some students particularly interested in music might wish to prepare a short program to present to the class which would experiment with individual instruments, individual notes, or individual chords, asking the class to vote on which ones strike them as "happy" or "not happy." The votes may be tallied and examined for significant findings. What variables, if any, affect the judgments? For instance, do most votes for high notes come from girls? for low notes from boys? vice versa? is there no difference? Do students who are either studying music or regularly play an instrument vote differently from those who do not? Do more students find chords "happy" than find any individual notes "happy"? Can they see any reasons for any of these choices? The music students might then try 3-tone melodies, and see what variations in voting reactions they can obtain in this way. They may also try the same 3-tone melody with variations in tempo, loudness, etc.

2. The exercise may be introduced by means of the public interview technique, if desired. (See "General: Techniques: Public Interview"), or this may be used as a later exercise after the class has begun to look for and experience new happy sounds.

3. If some students have portable tape recorders or casette recorders, they may be delegated by the class to make a collection of brief samples of

152 favorite happy sounds of people who are not members of the class. The class may make a list of possible people whom they would like "interviewed" in this fashion, but the actual taping would be of the sounds themselves. The suggested list might include such people as "an elderly Lady," "a small child," "a young mother," "two college students," "a policeman," "a professional dancer," etc.

4. The class may decide to constitute itself a study group for a period of 3—4 weeks, during which they will make an effort to collect "happy sounds," keeping a diary of these or some other records and either reporting and discussing these at the end of the designated period or running another "sound show." They may find that there are many previously unnoticed sounds which actually produce happy feelings in them, and also discover certain sounds which they can arrange to reproduce at will when they need a change in mood. They will undoubtedly find that some sounds will cheer them at certain times, but not at others—the dinner bell is a happy sound when you are hungry, but merely a nuisance when you are not hungry and are busy with something else. Some people may find a cuckoo clock normally a happy sound, but be annoyed by it when they are late. Some people may believe they are made happy by the sound of the ocean, but find that, by itself, this sound has no effect—it is successful for them only in combination with other things.

SUGGESTED RESOURCES:

Some of the "sounds" recommended in "Life: Senses: Hearing" may be useful here. Also recommended are records of poetry, such as some of the Caedmon Poets series, the "Environment" records or sound effects used by theaters, which may be purchased or rented from companies such as Thomas J. Valentino, Inc., 150 W. 46th St., New York, N.Y. 10036, tapings you or friends have made of ordinary street noises, or groups of children at play, or storms, or fountains, or other sound effects. Some people like the sound of an orchestra "tuning up," some people even like the sound of a piano being tuned—a sound unpleasant to many others. Some people like bells ringing, or carillons, others like train whistles, fog horns, crickets, a purring cat, a roaring lion, a high wind blowing through tree branches—the possibilities are endless. Many sounds may be taped from sound tracks of films, TV or radio, from other tapes or records as well as from actual live performances or auditory experiences. Many sounds, of course are "happy" when heard for a few seconds, but merely tiresome or even annoying if prolonged over several minutes. The reasons for this deserve exploration.

FOR YOUR OWN READING:

Maslow, Abraham H., *RELIGIONS, VALUES, AND PEAK-EXPERIENCES*, New York: Viking, 1964, 1970.

Otto, Herbert A., and John Mann, *WAYS OF GROWTH: APPROACHES TO EXPANDING AWARENESS*, New York: Viking, 1968.

Keen, Sam, *TO A DANCING GOD*, New York: Harper & Row, 1970.

Cooper, Grosvenor W., *LEARNING TO LISTEN: A HANDBOOK FOR MUSIC*, Chicago, Ill.: University of Chicago, 1957.

Carpenter, Edmund, and Marshall McLuhan, "Acoustic Space," *EXPLORATIONS IN COMMUNICATION*, Boston, Mass.: Beacon, 1960.

DREAMING

PURPOSE:

To practice a kind of "tripping without drugs" which can be used to temporarily escape unhappiness and worry or to take a "happiness vacation."

COMMENT:

To be able to escape the tensions of contemporary life on occasion, to seek for beauty and peace within the mind or person—these are valuable goals. Many people seek such escape through alcohol, drugs or long absorption in TV or loud rock music. The total time required is often excessive and the results are not always predictable and may be undesirable. The means are not always at hand, and also have unfortunate side-effects. Many people who are able to accomplish unusual amounts of work and, day after day, put forth energetic effort, are able to do this because they have learned to relax quickly and thoroughly when an opportunity presents itself. Rather than contributing to lethargy, such ability to relax on demand can revitalize us and help us be more aware and alert.

One of the reasons for the current popularity of yoga is its ability to produce a state of peaceful relaxation. The first step along the threefold path of "union" in yoga is "hatha yoga," the complete control of the body by the mind. Although some parts of hatha yoga are contrary to accepted Western medical beliefs and practices, others are not only harmless but can be very beneficial. This exercise is based on the yoga *asana*, *"savasana,"* and consists of gradually deepened relaxation, followed by deliberate "daydreaming." As practiced by those skilled in yoga, this is a deceptively easy process, but actually is difficult to do properly.

GROUP SIZE:

Up to 20

TIME SUGGESTED:

20—30 minutes

GENERAL DIRECTIONS:

In a quiet, confident manner, talk your class through the steps of this exercise. If some of your students are studying yoga, you may wish to ask their help in directing this exercise. It will be helpful if the students have previously gone through the exercises in "Freedom: Stretch," or Steps Nos. 4, 5, or 6 in "Freedom: Breathing."

MATERIALS REQUIRED:

Clear sufficient floor space for everyone to lie down comfortably. Floor mats, beach towels, or carpeting are helpful.

PROCEDURE:

1. Tell the class in your own words something such as the following: "When you are unhappy or depressed it is often possible to take a refreshing 'vacation' in a short period of time. This requires some discipline, will-power and self-control, but it is a skill or technique worth spending time acquiring. "Daydreaming" is often condemned, but sometimes can have great value. "Positive daydreaming," deliberately and purposefully evoked or created, can bring us some measure of happiness, some relief in periods of stress, making us more able to return to active work."

2. The exercise is carried out as follows: Lie flat on your back, arms at sides, feet together, but in a relaxed position. Allow your eyelids to partially close, and roll your eyes slightly upward and slightly toward the nose—a position they tend toward in sleep. Without tensing muscles first (as was done in "Freedom: Stretch," for instance), gradually relax all of your muscles, starting with the feet and legs and working upward. Allow your facial muscles to go slack, and be sure to get the tension out of your neck muscles.

3. Students who have had some practice in following the progress of their natural breathing may spend a few minutes doing this. Others may concentrate on slow, regular, deep abdominal breathing during these few minutes. Now, think of all your strength and energy as flowing gently away from you, washed away by a gently rolling series of shallow waves or ripples, as though you were lying at the edge of the ocean in very shallow water as the tide recedes.

Allow 5—15 minutes for the stages of relaxation, depending on class experience—more experienced students may require the longer period of time, as more complete relaxation will be sought than by students with little practice.

4. Tell the students, "Deliberately send your mind on a little trip. You may re-create a time you

remember when you were peacefully comfortable and happy, enjoying a beautiful place—you may envision a lovely spot where you have been happy in the past. Or you may create a scene remembered from a painting or photograph in which you think you would be happy . . . Create this scene with careful detail, in your mind's eye, as though you were looking out a window at a garden, or view, or as though you were looking in through a window at a room . . . Now, slowly, allow yourself to enter this scene and sit quietly and peacefully there, looking about, hearing whatever soft sounds there are—absorbing the beauty, the tranquility, the peaceful happiness around you. I will be quiet now, and let you enjoy your dream."

VARIATIONS:

If desired, prior to Step No. 1 give the class an assortment of reproductions of paintings and photographs from art books or catalogues, magazines such as NATIONAL GEOGRAPHIC or nature magazines. Ask them to browse through these and select one picture which particularly appeals to them and which shows a place where they would like to sit quietly and relax—a place where they think they would be happy and peaceful. Ask them to study the picture carefully, so that they will be able to re-create it in their mind later on. When you continue with the exercise, starting with Step No. 1, you may or may not wish to suggest that they remember this particular picture in Step No. 4. You may wish to mention it simply as a possibility.

SUGGESTED RESOURCES:

Phelan, Nancy, and Michael Volin, GROWING UP WITH YOGA, New York: Harper and Row, 1967.

Koestler, Arthur, THE LOTUS AND THE ROBOT, New York: Macmillan, 1961. Koestler's very negative views on yoga are based on considerable study, and are an antidote to any over-enthusiastic reliance on such techniques.

BACK TO NATURE

PURPOSE:

To discover and enjoy some of the experiences of a re-creational "going back to nature."

COMMENT:

"Three themes in the new naturalism of the student movement stand out—the stress on community, the apparent anti-intellectualism, and the search for what is sacred in nature. . . . The essence of the idea is that we must initiate a new stage in man's relatedness to nature and the natural . . . Our sons and daughters on campus are urging us to stop our frantic rush to bend nature to the human will and in its place to restore a vital, more harmonious—and more humble—balance with nature" (Yankelovich, "The New Naturalism," SATURDAY REVIEW).

Many urban young people increasingly make use of opportunities for outdoor recreation, but many do not know how to go about it. Some think only in terms of organized sports, formal camp or vacation situations, or hunting and fishing. Many outdoor activities benefit from "know-how," and some, such as skiing, surfing and mountain climbing demand a grasp of safety rules. Long-distance hiking and camping should not be undertaken without some knowledge of "wilderness survival." Some students are interested in camping trips by automobile, and some plan to hitch hike across country in the United States or Europe. All these can be either marvelous, or disastrous experiences.

Are your young people aware of the available facilities? Do they know how and when they may be enjoyed? Do they know what to take with them? When they get there, what do their senses tell them? Are they tuned in? Turned on to the outdoors?

GROUP SIZE:

Up to 20

TIME SUGGESTED:

Some of the following exercises may be completed in an hour, others involve field trips of varying lengths.

GENERAL DIRECTIONS:

If the group has experienced the "Life: A Sense of Wonder" exercise, they may be interested in some outdoor experiences. It is probably best to start your "Back to Nature" discoveries with a real outdoor experience, no matter how short or otherwise limited it must be. After this some of the other experiences given in "Procedure" may be planned. Some of your students may be experienced in these activities and can organize or help run field trips, expeditions or "clinics" designed to inform other interested class members. There is no need to feel that all must be serious! The idea is to develop an appreciation and enjoyment of the outdoor world.

MATERIALS REQUIRED:

The eight exercises which follow are very varied, and the class needs will vary. For a start, you will need access to the outdoors! This may be only a city park, or an arboretum, or someone's garden in the beginning. Number III suggests the use of blindfolds. Some maps and films and reference materials will be needed.

PROCEDURE:

I. 1. If there is grass on the campus, and the weather is fair, the class may go out and lie face down in the grass, propping the head in the hand. Ask them to try to see as much as they can in the grass within a few feet of their head in the next ten minutes. Discourage moving about and conversation. At first they may see "nothing," but after a minute or so they will begin to notice differences in the grass or weeds, insects, small stones, twigs, bare earth, perhaps a worm.

2. At the end of ten minutes, ask if anyone has seen anything the others might enjoy, or any insects they did not recognize. If subgrouping does not occur spontaneously, encourage it, asking some to investigate what others have found. If very little has been seen, team them in two's or three's to intensively investigate a different area. Since there is a real difference in what you observe at eye level from what you see walking or even sitting, encourage them again to get down into the grass.

3. After another 10—15 minutes, convene the group for a plenary to discuss first, very simply, what they saw. Some may introduce other sensory impressions, saying they "felt" the grass, or let an ant crawl over their hand, or "tasted" a blade of grass, or "heard" an insect. If they do not, ask for such input. Probably they will be surprised at how many things there were to experience in the small, relatively familiar area. Let them talk a bit about how they felt, lying silent in the grass.

II. 1. Take advantage of rain or snow, when possible. The temperature and clothing of the students will have to dictate when this is possible, but a short walk in rain or snow with the explicit purpose of really looking at it and hearing it and feeling it will provide sensory data often ignored, and will give pleasure.

2. Spend about twenty minutes on the walk, and then discuss the experience upon your return. Ask them to describe their experiences, what they liked and didn't like, which way the wind blew, puddles, how people they passed were reacting to the rain (snow). Did anyone open his mouth and tip his head back and drink in some of the rain? Do any members of the class enjoy rain (snow), or is it merely a nuisance? Did anyone take off his shoes and walk barefoot?

III. 1. Blind walk. The "led blind walk" described in "Freedom: Trust" may be used here for a different purpose. The technique is slightly different as the "guides" are asked to try to provide as many sensory experiences of the out-of-doors as possible for their charges. Ask them to try to find interesting things to feel, smell, taste, and hear. Ask them to be sure to make the experience a happy and pleasant one for the "blind" partner, being careful not to endanger or frighten them. Ask them to "try it themselves first" when it comes to tasting leaves, etc!

2. After about fifteen minutes, reverse roles, and repeat the experience.

3. Ask the students to discuss the experience with their partner. Did things seem different when they couldn't see? What did they notice? How did they feel? What did they enjoy most? . . . dislike most?

IV. 1. After the class has enjoyed one or more of the preceding experiences, have a planning session. This may be done in a number of ways. You may divide the class into subgroups of five or six, asking each group to plan one outdoor activity for the class, but giving each group a general category, so not all are simultaneously planning picnics! Have resource materials available for them, and indicate that you are available for help or suggestions, if they wish. Explain that all plans will be presented to the class, and the class may decide on one or more to carry out. Some possible categories might be: walks; camping trips; seashore walks; boating; skiing; swimming; trip to a cave. Their initial plans need not be all-inclusive, since after the class makes its decision there will be need for further planning involving others, as a rule. Give groups 20—25 minutes for initial planning, and then bring them together to decide which proposals are most appealing.

2. Each group explains its proposal. Important facts are listed on the chalkboard or newsprint. It may be that some plans sound attractive, but impractical. If the class really wants to carry them out, see if they are feasible with acceptable modifications. If they are going to require the assistance of others, be sure the group realizes that it must plan to obtain such assistance. They may require parental consent for some things, and anticipated objections should be examined and reasonable means of overcoming them designed. Possible expenses involved must be considered, and suitable dates which do not conflict with other student commitments.

3. An elaborate proposal may call for several further sessions. Committees may be developed to work on specific needs and discover suitable materials to be used in preparation for the event.

It is not necessary for the entire class to be involved in any one project, and several may be planned at once. It is important to help the class identify those in the class as well as outside who may be helpful resource people. A group which has never done any canoeing may plan an overnight canoe trip, while another member of the class with suitable experience may be more interested in a trip to a cave. The experienced canoe-resource-person should be temporarily available to the canoeing group.

4. Following any of these experiences, the entire class should have an opportunity to discuss them, sharing the experience and their feelings about it as well as any knowledge gained for future use. The practice in evaluation as well as in planning and decision making is helpful, students may prefer more spontaneity for one-day trips. Some students may not wish to participate, or may be prevented by other activities. The class should try to give them consideration and make them feel a part of one of the groups in some way, but should not expect them to do the "dumb work" in preparation if they are not going to be with the trip.

V. Several class members may be involved in outdoor sports or activities which might be of interest to the class. They may have collections of shells, slides, rock samples, be involved in bird tracking, know how to sail or have experience in wilderness camping. These resident experts should be encouraged to share their knowledge with interested class members and may win some new enthusiasts. A one-day show might be arranged in which a succession of showings of films and slides, plus table displays enable students to spend time with a new interest which appeals to them.

VI. Some members of the class, or perhaps the entire class, might be interested in taking a small group of young children on a "nature trip." This will possibly require adult supervision, and will certainly need advance planning and the cooperation of another teacher and/or institution. It may be possible to gather a group of younger brothers and sisters, trading siblings for the occasion. The class should have some grasp of the probable interests and abilities of the age group they plan to take. Some students may be interested in working with a group of handicapped children. If so, the students themselves should visit and talk with the appropriate personnel at the institution from which the children will come.

VII. A ferry-ride, if available, can be used as a trip if planned with specific goals in mind, such as observation of birds, water or shore life. Some students may have "ridden the ferry" often enough, but paid little attention to such things. Also, you may find that many students in riverside communities have never been "on" the river. It may be possible to charter a craft and crew for a day, or someone may know a boat owner who will entertain a small group if accompanied by a responsible adult.

VIII. Students may keep a one or two week record of all their physical activities, including sports, walking to and from school, cutting grass, etc. At the end of this time, small groups may discuss these activities with the purpose of trying to provide well-rounded programs for themselves. A few students may engage in a great deal of physical activity, and others in a bare minimum, or some may be involved in a good deal of activity, but of a limited range of types. Students may see possibilities for diversification.

Students may want to consider the body mechanics and muscular development and control involved in their activities. The result may be an awakened interest in the options provided by the community. A bulletin board or a dittoed "directory" may be prepared by some of the class members for distribution to all members, listing the various places in the community where facilities and/or instruction are available, a realistic explanation of costs involved, and names and addresses of class members interested and active in the sport or hobby. Experienced hikers and campers might add a list of "things you will need," or "foods which pack and carry well," or "places within 100 miles where you may build a fire, where camping is allowed, and where the water is safe."

SUGGESTED RESOURCES:

FILMS:

Moods of Surfing, 15 minutes, color, Pyramid Films. (It is not necessary to plan a surfing trip to enjoy this beautiful film.)

Green Years, 28 minutes, color, Center of Urban Education, available from Association Films. Educational and recreational uses of city parks, including cycling, running, kite-flying and boating.

Sky, 10 minutes, color, Contemporary Films/McGraw-Hill. (One of the best of the nature films.)

Quetico, 22 minutes, color. Contemporary Films. A canoe trip through Thunder Bay in Ontario and Minnesota.

Runner, 10 minutes, black and white. Long distance runner Bruce Kidd in action, with background reading of W.H. Auden's poetry.

Fishing in the Everglades, 30 minutes, color. Includes a commercial on Du Pont fishing line, but shows fishing trip through Everglades in a houseboat. E. I. Du Pont De Nemours & Co., Inc., Advertising Dept., Audio Visual Section, Wilmington, Del. 19898. No charge.

Thousand Mile Miracle, 22 minutes, color. Free loan from Public Affairs Office, Mississippi River Commission, U.S. Army Corps of Engineers, P.O. Box 80, Vicksburg, Miss. 39180. The Gulf Intracoastal Waterway from Apalachee Bay, Florida to Brownsville, Texas.

Big River, 15 minutes, color. Available as above from Mississippi River Commission.

Take Safety with You, 14 minutes, color. Recreation available on waterways and reservoirs, encouraging both use and safety. Available as above from Mississippi River Commission.

Carefree Boating, 14½ minutes, color. Free loan from Motion Picture Section, Aluminum Company of America, 1246 Alcoa Building, Pittsburgh, Pa. 15219. Send request 3—4 weeks in advance.

The Conservation Committee of the Garden Club of America has lists of films as well as booklets and leaflets. They have a listing of National Parks and some of our National Monuments such as Death Valley, Katmai Alaska and White Sands, New Mexico.

The U.S. Department of Agriculture has a complete catalog of films, some of which will be of

interest, and will also send the "Forest Service Films" catalogue, most of which are concerned with Forest Rangers and fire-fighting, but some of which will be of interest. They will also provide information on the 154 national forests administered by the U.S. Forest Service and the National Seashore Areas such as Cape Cod and Assateague Island.

Write to the American National Red Cross for a list of their publications, including *FIRST AID TEXTBOOK, CANOEING TEXTBOOK, BASIC SAILING, SWIMMING AND WATER SAFETY TEXTBOOK.* You may obtain materials from your local chapter, or write General Supply Office, American National Red Cross, Washington, D.C. 20006.

Write to the following organizations for literature:

American Youth Hostels, Inc., 20 W. 17th St., New York, N.Y. 10011.

National Campers and Hikers Association, Inc., 7172 Transit Rd., Buffalo, N.Y. 14221.

The Wilderness Society, 729 15th St., N.W., Washington, D.C. 20005.

BOOKS, PAMPHLETS AND ARTICLES:

Angier, Bradford, *HOW TO STAY ALIVE IN THE WOODS*, New York: Collier, 1956. (This $.95 paperback was originally published as *LIVING OFF THE COUNTRY*. It lacks an index and some information is buried where you might not look for it. Read it through quickly in advance, and then take it along.)

MISSISSIPPI RIVER NAVIGATION, Write Public Affairs Office, Mississippi River Commission, U.S. Army Corps of Engineers, P.O. Box 80, Vicksburg, Miss. 39180. (Although designed primarily for commercial users of the river and its tributaries, contains much information of value for small craft, including chart of small boat facilities and "picnic areas.")

"Rural Recreation Opportunities on Private Land," U.S. Dept. of Agriculture, Miscellaneous Publ. #930. Superintendent of Documents, U.S. Government Printing Office, Washington, D.C. 20¢.

Brainerd, John W., *NATURE STUDY FOR CONSERVATION (A HANDBOOK FOR ENVIRONMENTAL EDUCATION)*, New York: Macmillan, 1971.

Milliken, Hamer, and McDonald, *FIELD STUDY MANUAL FOR OUTDOOR LEARNING*, Minneapolis, Minn.: Burgess, 1968.

Wood, Beverly, J., "Backpacking to Paradise", *WOMAN'S DAY*, July 1971, pp. 56ff. (How-to-do-it by the mother of a backpacking family.)

Yankelovich, Daniel, "The New Naturalism," *SATURDAY REVIEW*, April 1, 1972, pp. 35, 37.

PURPOSE:

To experience a meal as a celebration, and to investigate the reasons why we serve food at parties, why celebrations often include a meal, why eating together is both a cause and a sign of happiness.

GROUP SIZE:

12—15

TIME SUGGESTED:

Some preparations should be made in advance, but the actual "meal time" can be 30—60 minutes. Some time should be set aside at a later session for a discussion of the event.

GENERAL DIRECTIONS:

This meal may be very simple or quite elaborate, depending on the group and the situation. The meal may be a "surprise," planned by a few members of the group, or the entire group may participate in its planning and preparation. The group should have met together for a number of sessions so they are fairly comfortable together, and so that they have something to celebrate. The "cause for celebration" may be something good which has recently happened to a class member, to the community or the school, "the end of our first 6 weeks," or an idea such as "our desire for peace," or even, "food is good!" You may, of course, plan special meals around a holiday, but they may be more greatly appreciated at a time when few such treats occur.

MATERIALS REQUIRED:

This will vary considerably depending on the group and its plans, but some physical arrangements should be made to enable the group to sit in a circle or oval around a large table, or around several tables grouped to form one, or on the floor around or on the edge of a mat, rug, etc. In some cases it may be possible to use a kitchen or at least a hot plate, which will increase the possibilities for variety in the foods served.

PROCEDURE:

1. A committee may be selected secretly, or the class may constitute itself a committee of the whole to plan for a meal for the entire group. Depending on the group and the situation, the meal may be as simple or elaborate as seems desirable. If a subgroup is preparing the meal for the entire group, it should be kept simple, in the interests of not putting too much burden on the subgroup. If the entire class is involved, each member should have a part in planning and executing the meal. There should be no planned entertainment, and any "decorations" should be kept to an absolute minimum, although attractive paper plates, cups and napkins would be helpful. Try to encourage the group to actually prepare the food themselves, rather than settling for "pretzels and potato chips and sodas." Tell them that food preparation is an art, and one deserving of loving care. Various members of the class may have "specialties"—many girls and some boys these days bake bread or have particular "main dishes" or "salads" which they will be happy to prepare. As part of the pleasure is sampling the foods prepared by others, it is better to have individuals prepare reasonably small amounts—for four to six people—rather than having one person make enough salad for the entire group, for instance. Planning should be done a week before the meal to allow plenty of time for purchasing and preparation.

2. On the day of the meal, help the group arrange the food attractively on the table, or floor mat, and have everyone sit down quietly. Start the meal with an informal grace, perhaps starting it yourself, and inviting others to add what they wish. You will want to strike the note of happy anticipation, as well as pleasure in the company of friends. Allow everyone to talk informally during the meal, but ask that all remain seated until the meal ends. Do not try to have a formal discussion of any kind during the meal, but encourage leisurely enjoyment of the appearance as well as the taste and texture, of the various foods. The meal may end with a song, if this seems appropriate.

3. At the following session of the group, take about twenty-five minutes to discuss the meal, how they felt about its preparation and the act of eating together. It will be interesting to explore the question of why food is always such an important part of celebrations, festivals, holidays, parties, religious "feasts"—after all, people obviously *could* get together for games, dancing, entertainment, conversation without the need for any food, and there are

relatively few such occasions when it is really necessary to eat because of hunger. If you are at home for the evening, you probably wouldn't eat anything after dinner, except for a possible "bedtime snack," and yet it would be a very unusual party at which nothing at all was served. —Why is it that—when we have guests, we almost always offer them something, if it is only a cup of coffee?—so many religious celebrations involve some sort of food or drink?—at holiday dinners we make a special effort to have more, or fancier food? What kinds of food are served at various holidays? Why?

VARIATIONS:

1. Prior to the planning of the meal, the class might have a session of talking about "meals I remember." In small groups of 5—8 ask them to think about a meal they remember from childhood. Ask them to think back to the early years of elementary school, and see if they can remember any meal from that time they particularly enjoyed—a summer picnic, a Thanksgiving dinner with relatives, even a meal at a restaurant with their parents. Ask them to describe these occasions to one another, trying to remember as much about it as possible—what food they had, who was there, was it a happy occasion, and if they had any part in its preparation. Some may remember a series of meals, rather than a single one, such as "Sunday at my grandparents," or "afternoons in the summer when the Good Humor truck came around the neighborhood." Some may remember particular dishes, reserved for "party" occasions in their family, or how good a plain hot dog and roll tasted at a beach picnic. It is possible to do this in the large group, if desired, but not everyone will have an opportunity to participate. If you are working with the full class, it may be necessary for you to recount such a memory first, to set the pattern and help others feel comfortable about speaking up. This technique is discussed in Dubois and Li's book in "Suggested Resources."

2. If desired, each person may bring only enough to share with one other person of some food he likes very much. There is no need for the selections to be announced in advance, and planning is done on an individual basis, so it is not a "meal" in the sense that all share in a series of different kinds of food. All sit around the table together, partners seated next to each other. Partners will begin by talking with one another, and conversation will never become as general as in the basic meal pattern described above, but there will be a spreading of the conversation beyond the pairs.

3. The class may wish to have a meal made up of foods from other countries, and may wish to print the name of the dish and the country of origin on 3 x 5 file cards, placing these on the table in front of the serving dish. The meal, however, should not be developed into a travelog or geography session— its purpose of enjoying the food and companionship together should not be weakened.

4. The class may be interested in doing some research on the symbolism of the various foods and beverages associated with rites, rituals and holidays. Weiser's book in "Suggested Resources" is a good source, and there are numerous "holiday cookbooks" which give such information. See also the exercise, "Life: Bread Day."

5. You may wish to follow this experience with other meals at intervals, exploring foods of other cultures, with the emphasis less on symbolism and more on simply the pleasure and interest of enjoying different food experiences together. Some students may be able to prepare a family recipe from another country, some may have an international student as a house guest or family friend who might help with this.

SUGGESTED RESOURCES:

Dubois, Rachel Davis, and Mew-Soong Li, *REDUCING SOCIAL TENSION AND CONFLICT,* New York: Association Press, 1970.

Weiser, Francis X., *HANDBOOK OF CHRISTIAN FEASTS AND CUSTOMS,* New York: Harcourt, Brace, 1958.

Helpful booklets are available without charge to teachers from Educational Service, Standard Brands Incorporated, P.O. Box 2695, Grand Central Station, New York, N.Y. 10017. Ask for "Mr. Peanut's Guide to Entertaining," "Five Great Cuisines" (recipes and menus for foods from other cultures), "The Blue Bonnet Margarine Book of Creative Cookery," "Appliance Cooking for All Seasons."

You may also write to Consumer Service Dept., Best Foods, International Plaza, Englewood Cliffs, N.J. 07632, for "Cook with Love." They will also send you on request an excellent little series of recipe folders including "America's Favorite Pies," "Creative Cooking with Corn Syrup," "Sandwiches Plain and Fancy" and folders on chicken, fish, salads, candy, and cooking with corn starch.

FUTURING

PURPOSE:

To begin to plan the future, rather than "letting it happen," examining the meaning of some of the probable or possible changes in the human body now in the foreseeable future.

COMMENT:

"Man is now in the position of actually creating the total world in which he lives, what the ethnologists refer to as his biotope. In creating this world he is actually determining *what kind of organism* he will be. This is a frightening thought in view of how very little is known about man" (Hall, *HIDDEN DIMENSION*).

". . . (W)hat kind of future world would we be structuring if we stopped technical progress and diverted all our efforts to the feeding of hungry people! As we peer into the midst of such a future, we see only more and more people living in more and more squalor. Our technical progress has stopped, and along with it future growth in knowledge, in education and productivity. The choice of options leading to such a future would create disaster beyond all comprehension!" H. W. Ritchey, president of Thiokol Chemical Corporation, address delivered at the Center of American Living, Inc. seminar on "The Victory in Space—the New Option, 2-18-70," reprinted in *AEROSPACE FACTS*, Thiokol Chemical Corp., April-June, 1970.

GENERAL DIRECTIONS:

There are two basic ways in which you may prepare this exercise: (1) you may make a selection of "possible futures" yourself, and prepare a set of cards to be distributed at random, one to each student; (2) you may provide either a reading list or the literature itself, and allow each student to make his own selection of items. In either event, you will wish to develop a situation in which each student has a paragraph which briefly describes some possible or probable innovation which will change our lives radically within the next twenty years. Two general classes are recognizable, those which will probably come about, and those which are felt to be "unforeseeable within the next 20 years." Of the latter it

may be said that since they are considered theoretically possible, their actual development will depend upon the interest and needs of some sufficiently powerful segment of the world's population. Nuclear energy, lasers, DNA, transistors, television and many other things came about without previous anticipation, and it is very risky to say "it won't happen" about anything which science can state, "Probably some day . . ." Furthermore, "science" is not the only field in which new thinking is going on, and from which very real results are occurring. The items to be selected may be from either class, or the "probables" might be used at one session, and the "unforeseeables" at a later session. The object is to have the students try to think through the probable results of such innovations and decide whether they want them. For the purpose of this exercise, items should be selected which are directly related to the human body, such as some of those suggested in "Suggested Resources."

MATERIALS REQUIRED:

Either (1) a set of previously prepared cards, each of which bears a descriptive paragraph concerning an innovation, or

(2) student prepared paragraphs, resulting from the investigation of literature provided or recommended in advance.

See "Suggested Resources" for these materials.

PROCEDURES:

1. Each student with the exception of the student-leaders and the Moderator has a card bearing a paragraph which describes one innovation, or possible new invention, process, technology, etc. He is given a few minutes to read and study this item, after which he will be asked to offer a defense of its promotion or use. Whether he really likes the idea or not, he will be asked to try to make a good case for its use by man, with the understanding that he will be "a person of importance whose voice will definitely be listened to."

2. Groups of five or six will now form for the purpose of selecting one from among all the items held by their group. They are to choose the one that they think would be best, most helpful, most productive of the general good of mankind. It will be best if each group has a leader to see that everyone gets a chance to make his case, and that the other members of the group really listen to the items pre-

sented. He will not have an item of his own to present, so he will be able to take a neutral position more easily. He will encourage the exploration of any possible "side-effects" of the items discussed, in an effort to help the group choose the best possible innovation to offer the class as "their choice." They will require 15—25 minutes for this discussion, depending on the degree of preparation—students who are well prepared for the discussion will require more time to make the decision.

3. The leader of each group will now form part of a panel which will present their item, first reading the paragraph which describes it, and then briefly telling the class why his group felt it was good or important. Following this, the panel members will discuss among themselves the possible implications of the development of all of the "first choice" items they have presented. The Moderator will help the group by seeing to it that everyone has a chance to speak, that no one dominates the discussion, and that the group discuss the possible interaction of the various innovations proposed. If it is believed that no student is adequate to the task of Moderator, the teacher may play this role.

SUGGESTED RESOURCES:

Boguslaw, Robert, *THE NEW UTOPIANS: A STUDY OF SYSTEM DESIGN AND SOCIAL CHANGE*, Englewood Cliffs, N.J.: Prentice-Hall, Inc., 1965, espec. pp. 1-28, and 112-126.

Bronwell, Arthur N., *SCIENCE AND TECHNOLOGY IN THE WORLD OF THE FUTURE*, New York: Wiley-Interscience, 1970. (See particularly chapter 9 on biomedical engineering. Both student and instructor will find this book sound, useful and fact-filled.)

Bugge, William A., "Highway Transportation after 1975," *CIVIL ENGINEERING*, Jan., 1962.

Calder, Nigel, *THE MIND OF MAN: AN INVESTIGATION INTO CURRENT RESEARCH ON THE BRAIN AND HUMAN NATURE*, New York: Viking, 1970.

Calder, Nigel, (ed.), *THE WORLD IN 1984: THE COMPLETE NEW SCIENTIST SERIES*, Vol. 1 and 2, Baltimore, Md.: Penguin, 1964. Almost 100 international authorities make predictions within their own fields. The articles are brief and the table of contents indicative of range, rather than of a specific "item," for instance, "Manufacture by Tissue Culture," "Changing Cell Heredity," "Bioengineering: Opportunity without Limit."

Fabun, Don, *DYNAMICS OF CHANGE*, Englewood Cliffs, N.J.: Prentice-Hall, Inc. This is available in a college paperback edition, and may be obtained by writing Mr. Paul Buralli, Trade Sales,

Prentice-Hall, Englewood Cliffs, N.J. 07632. The price is $4.95. A hardcover edition is also available at $8.95. This material was originally published in 1966 as six issues of the Kaiser News, and provides a wealth of material on probable and "unforeseeable" changes, as well as an excellent bibliography. Some free single copies of individual issues may still be obtained on request by writing Kaiser News, 866B Kaiser Center, 300 Lakeside Drive, Oakland, Calif. 94604.

Frank, Pat, *ALAS, BABYLON*, Philadelphia, Pa.: Lippincott, 1959.

Gordon, Theodore J., *IDEAS IN CONFLICT*, New York: St. Martin's Press, 1966. "Commercial Resurrection: Frozen Death and You," pp. 192-205.

Hall, Edward T., *HIDDEN DIMENSION*, p. 4.

Handler, Philip, (ed.), *BIOLOGY AND THE FUTURE OF MAN*, New York: Oxford Univ. Press, 1965. (See especially ch. 20. This encyclopaedic product of the National Academy of Sciences will provide the teacher with a summary of the knowledge of major experts in the field. Although addressed to the layman and well written, will overwhelm all but the seriously interested high school student.)

Hilton, James, *LOST HORIZON*, New York: Morrow, 1933.

Keyes, Daniel, *FLOWERS FOR ALGERNON*, New York: Harcourt, Brace & World, Inc., 1966.

Negley, Glenn, and J. Max Patrick, *THE QUEST FOR UTOPIA: AN ANTHOLOGY OF IMAGINARY SOCIETIES*, New York: Henry Schuman, 1952.

Platt, John Rader, *THE STEP TO MAN*, New York: John Wiley & Sons, 1966, particularly pp. 37-86. (Gives an overall view of the processes of change.)

Taylor, Gordon Rattray, *THE BIOLOGICAL TIME BOMB*, New York: World Pub. Co., 1968. "Is Death Necessary?" pp. 91-124. All chapters in this book are relevant, and a glance through the table of contents will provide more than one item per chapter.

Smith, Harmon L., *ETHICS AND THE NEW MEDICINE*, New York: Abingdon, 1970.

Vogt, William, "Conservation and the Guaranteed Income," *THE GUARANTEED INCOME*, Garden City, N.Y.: Doubleday Anchor, 1966, pp. 147-168, and see also Taylor's *THE BIOLOGICAL TIME BOMB*, pp. 22-55.

Walsh, Chad, *FROM UTOPIA TO NIGHTMARE*, New York: Harper & Row, 1962.

Asimov, Isaac, (ed.), *WHERE DO WE GO FROM HERE?*, Garden City, New York: Double-

162   day & Co., 1971.

Drucker, Peter F., "The Surprising Seventies," *HARPER'S MAGAZINE,* July, 1971 (Vol. 243. No. 1454), pp. 35ff.

FILM:

T.H.X. 1138 4EB, 15 min., 16 mm color. Prod. by Univ. of S. Calif. 1967. (This allegory of the impersonalism of modern technology stands as a warning to what could possibly happen in a future world where all is sterile, computerized, and artificial.)

BIOLOGICAL RHYTHMS

PURPOSE:

To explore our feelings and understandings about some of the rhythms of life.

COMMENT:

Where is time? What is rhythm? Why are we so sure about the difference between *now* and *then*? Many living organisms, including man, seem to have an "inner clock" which regulates body functions. These inner clocks apparently have a relationship to the world around us. For some people, the relationship to the rhythm of day and night works out very well—they awake early, refreshed and ready to work. Others seem to struggle against the day in the morning hours, but are full of energy in the evening when the "day people" are ready for sleep. Apparently everyone, however, suffers some disorientation when forced to reverse the day/night pattern. Workers going on the night-shift take six to eight weeks to adjust, but a very short time to make the opposite adjustment when they "go back on days." Jet passengers who can sleep "on demand" fare better than others, but the peculiar feelings suffered by most of these passengers are not imaginary, and physicians who care for crews of long-distance jet flights find serious disturbances of function in the men and women who must move too fast too often.

Physiological processes and environmental conditions interact to determine behavior. The discipline of behavioral biology seeks to understand the ways in which such internal processes as those of the nervous and endocrine systems affect human behavior and the reactions of the body to environmental conditions. Biological rhythms have been studied in the past by specialists in various fields, for instance, rhythms of the heart by cardiologists, of the brain by neurophysiologists, ovarian cycles by endocrinologists. During recent years more attention has been paid by biologists and physiologists to basic similarities and interactions of internal rhythms and their relation to environmental rhythms, such as the pattern of days and nights, of the tides, the moon and the year. Only the rhythm of the days as reflected in man's "circadian" rhythms have been sufficiently studied for scientific evidence to be available in mathematical form. This evidence shows these circadian rhythms are of internal origin in the human body, although affected by environment, by the pattern of day and night. Recently evidence has begun to accumulate showing relationships between tidal, lunar and annual rhythms and internal "circa-periods."

These rhythms are of practical importance, since recent findings show a relationship between circadian rhythms and sensitivity to drugs, X-ray treatments and other harmful stimuli. These are of importance to the practice of medicine, and also to industry and government in planning and management of space flights and even ordinary jet flights or work shifts on the land. For a good many years there has been an interest in trying to apply some of the apparent findings of researchers in biological rhythms, though much more investigation must be done before a sound scientific base is developed. European studies by physicians and psychologists have seemed to indicate patterns in three biological rhythms which they have called the physical, the sensitivity, and the intellectual, and their findings have been applied to such things as the scheduling of operations in hospitals and work assignments for employees of the transportation system of Zurich. More recently some American firms have begun to use these theories in similar ways.

GROUP SIZE:

Up to 20

TIME SUGGESTED:

45—60 minutes

MATERIALS REQUIRED:

None (Optional: a supply of graph paper and calendars for past, present and future years, or calendar "patterns," such as those on the inside covers of the *NEW YORK TIMES ENCYCLOPEDIC ALMANAC,* 1972.)

PROCEDURE:

1. You may wish to give your students more background than the following before the students calculate and discuss their "physical rhythms," but it is often better to defer additional input until the completion of the exercise, including at least a short discussion.

In your own words, explain to the students:

When you were born your physical cycle of twenty-three days started its upward swing. During the sixth day (actually 5.75 days later) it hit a peak and started down again, reaching the base line, or birth-start point 11.50 days later. Dropping below this point, it fell to a low on the 17th day (17.25 days from birth-start point), and then rose again, reaching the birth-start point on the 23rd day, and began all over again. This 23-day cycle has repeated itself ever since, slowly rising and falling in a wave-like pattern. It is believed that this pattern creates "highs" and "lows" in your physical condition. On "high" days you feel very well, full of energy, and can take minor stresses in your stride. On "low" days you are apt to feel more lethargic, are more susceptible to infections and less able to handle stress situations. Some researchers believe that the days on which the wave crosses the birth-start point line are times of vulnerability to accidents and stress.

2. You can plot your own pattern by counting the total number of days you have lived and dividing by 23 to find your cycle-start point. For instance, let us suppose that you were born September 20, 1956. By September 20, 1972 you will have lived 5844 days (365 x 16 + 4 leap year days = 5844). Dividing the number of days by the length of the cycle (23 days) tells you that you have lived through 254 cycles and 2 days (the remainder) into another cycle. You'll then start your next cycle in 9 days (23 - 2 = 21), or on October 11th.

If you wish you may chart your cycle on graph paper, making your wave peaks about 3—5 blocks above and below a base line across the middle.

3. You can calculate backwards to see what important events in your life happened at various high and low periods, and you can calculate forward to see when you should be at a high point or a low point. (If calendars are available, these may be distributed for use.)

4. When students have had the time to complete their calculations for Step No. 2 and an opportunity to experiment a bit with Step No. 3, divide the class into dyads or other small groups and let them compare findings for 10—15 minutes.

5. In a plenary session discuss the experience and how they feel about experimenting with "unproven" theories such as this.

—How much importance would you attach to a system like this?

—How much weight do you think should be given to the idea that such systems promote self-fulfilling prophecies?

—What did you notice about your own cycle patterns?

—What other biological rhythms do you think you are often aware of? . . . Do you "pay attention" to any of these? . . . why?

If desired, other data may be brought into the discussion. Students may suggest a relationship between astrology and biological rhythms (there is no apparent foundation for such a connection), or may be aware of the other two rhythms, the sensitivity and the intellectual. If they are interested in also plotting these, the same method of calculation is used, for a 28 day cycle for the sensitivity (or emotional) cycle and 33 days for the intellectual cycle. Students may be interested in doing some reading about these presumed cycles and other findings in biological rhythms, in keeping various charts for a time and in discussing some of their findings with the class at a later date.

SUGGESTED RESOURCES:

Handler, Philip, (ed.), *BIOLOGY AND THE FUTURE OF MAN*, New York: Oxford University Press, 1970, pp. 397-399.

Lewis, Maxine, "Biorhythm: How to Cope with Your Ups and Downs", *FAMILY CIRCLE*, June, 1971, pp. 36f. (*FAMILY CIRCLE* magazine offers a "do-it-yourself" *CYCLGRAF KIT* with an explanatory booklet containing key figures for finding your three biorhythm patterns through 1981, a supply of charts, and a ruler guide for drawing the "waves." (This may be obtained by sending $3.50 to *FAMILY CIRCLE KITS*, Dept. 525, P.O. Box 450, Teaneck, N.J. 07666.)

Luce, Gay Gaer, *BODY TIME: PHYSIOLOGICAL RHYTHMS AND SOCIAL STRESS*, New York: Pantheon, 1971.

Marteka, Vincent, *BIONICS*, Philadelphia, Pa.: Lippincott, 1965.

Ward, Ritchie R., *THE LIVING CLOCKS*, New York: Alfred A. Knopf, 1971.

Some students might be interested in material offered by the Bulova Watch Company on "Timekeeping in the Space Age" and "The Pursuit of Accuracy: A Brief History of Fifty Centuries of Timekeeping," available to schools by writing Director of Public Relations, Bulova Watch Co. Inc., 630 Fifth Ave., New York, N.Y. 10020.

"NEW TWISTS FOR OLD TOOLS"

PURPOSE:

To encourage an understanding of tools as extensions of man; to help students learn to select well designed tools and implements; to encourage creativity.

COMMENT:

Dr. Erwin Tichauer, Professor of biomechanics at New York University has designed a number of new hand tools to replace old-fashioned implements whose shape was ill fitted to the way man's muscles actually work. Such simple things as a paint scraper, a shovel, a child's spoon have benefited from his attention, and those who work with these new tools will find they become less sore and tired because the tool works with them, not against them.

GROUP SIZE:

Up to 20

TIME SUGGESTED:

60 minutes

GENERAL DIRECTIONS:

Students bring in tools which are "handy" and those which are not, and analyze the good and bad features, seeking to remedy the latter.

MATERIALS REQUIRED:

(Students bring in samples of tools from home.)

PROCEDURE:

1. A few days before the session, ask the class members to look around their homes and garages and make inquiries of the family regarding the comfort and efficiency of various hand tools and utensils. Ask them to select *one* which the class member or his family uses and rate as "comfortable to use and efficient," and *one* rated, "uncomfortable and inefficient." These may be kitchen utensils, e.g., mixing spoon, hand eggbeater; cleaning equipment, e.g., dustpan, broom; outdoor or indoor carpenters' and mechanics' tools, e.g., shovel, wrench. They are to bring these to the assigned session.

Tell them to be sure to find out how the tool is used and for what purpose if they are not the primary user, particularly if it is *not* used for the purpose for which it was designed, (for instance, a family may have found a small scalpel an excellent tool for sectioning oranges or grapefruit).

2. On the day of the session, each student brings his tools and is assigned to a subgroup in which he is to demonstrate the "good" tool and explain why it is superior to others for the same purpose. He should allow other members of the group to handle it, showing them its correct position for use. Students consider how tools cooperate with normal muscle position and action. Each subgroup selects one tool they consider "best of class" or "best of show," either because of frequent need for use, or generally superior design.

3. Each member then shows his subgroup his "poor" tool, and students investigate same factors as in Step No. 2. Remind them to think in terms of actually holding and using the tool over a long period of time, to help them gauge its faults.

4. Each subgroup selects one of the poor tools and attempts to re-design it for comfort and efficiency. The group product may be a sketch, a written list of suggestions, or the tool itself, bent in a different shape, if this is permissible.

5. A member of each group then presents to the entire class the tool they selected as "best" in Step No. 2, and another member presents the re-designed tool, explaining faults and features in each case.

6. In a plenary discussion, and in keeping with the general knowledge of the class, some consideration of specific anatomical and physiological factors should be given. Size, shape, surface texture, weight and balance may all affect comfort and efficiency. Some students may have brought in tools which are aesthetically pleasing, and this may also be discussed as contributing to the user's pleasure and therefore possibly to his judgment of it as "comfortable and efficient."

VARIATION:

1. If any class members have "shop," or belong to a craft club which owns suitable tools, some students may be interested in making new tools to the designers' specifications. It is not impossible that these could become saleable objects! A great many things we use everyday are poorly designed—felt-tip markers, toothbrushes, spoons, hammers, brooms, etc. In some cases it is a matter of being selective in our purchases, but in others it is because there is no better available. It is possible to save time, temper and energy by finding and using the "best" design.

2. Another session might be based on the "aesthetically pleasing" tool or utensil. Many objects we use daily and which cost from 25¢ to $5.00 are ugly and unpleasant to see and touch, and yet others in the same price range are equally or even more efficient and are also beautiful.

PURPOSE:

To exercise our memory; to loosen up the tension in the group with a humorous exercise.

COMMENT:

There is evidence for three different kinds of memory mechanisms: a short-term memory, a medium- and long-term memory, or at least some additional attention-focusing process necessary to establish long-term memory. Our senses, particularly vision, are continually offering "snapshots" to the control centers of the brain. Some of these the attention-focusing process selects as important, and these linger for varying lengths of time. There has been some evidence to suggest that all these "snapshots" are collected—are in the files somewhere, but it is also that some stored memories fade, disappear, and free the storage elements for new information. There is still much that is unknown about the process by which memories are created and stored, but there seems general agreement that physical changes in neuronal material occur when a memory trace is established, but it is not certain that the neuron itself is the basic storage element, or the only storage element. Each neuron supports up to 1000 synaptic connections, and memory probably is stored in these in some way.

The available memory storage mechanisms in the brain are probably startlingly large. Probably the most extreme projection is that of von Neumann (*THE COMPUTER AND THE BRAIN*), whose figures included the estimate of 30 billion on/off switches of memory capacity, each switch able to store a single bit. More modest estimates have ranged from 6 million on/off switches per neuron down to a total of 50 billion bits for all neurons combined. Our own experience tells us that we can only "take in" about 5 or 10 items in a list or similar stimuli. Psychological tests indicate that under the best conditions, 25 "bits" per second is the amount of information that we can take in and pass on immediately to another person. These "5 or 10 items" might total 75 to 150 bits. Much more than this is presented to our sensory organs, or even comes in through them to us, at any one time, but is not attended to.

The work of W. Ritchie Russell, a neurologist of Oxford University, suggests that memories moved into the long-term type of storage are actually strengthened by the passage of time, since there occur randomly generated discharges of current which are more apt to travel along established conduits, automatically increasing their strength. This would indicate that the folk-wisdom of the student who crams for exams, but stops in time to allow for a several hours or even days respite before the test itself, is based in fact. Continued studying might even be harmful, in that fatigue might cause inaccuracies in intake if the student continued, and the sound information laid down in the memory when the student is fresh may well dig deeper roots if given time to do so.

GROUP SIZE:

Up to 20

TIME SUGGESTED:

20—60 minutes

GENERAL DIRECTIONS:

A number of brief and simple exercises are suggested which may be tried at various times, together or separately. If a serious discussion of "memory" is desired, this may follow, or the exercises may be done without discussion, "just for fun," or to allow individual thinking about them without further comment.

MATERIALS REQUIRED:

1. None
2. A nearby room, previously unseen by students
3. A tray of ten different items, selected at random, or chosen for variety.

PROCEDURE:

1. Auditory. Group sits in circle.
2. In order, the first person repeats the first word given, the second person the first word plus the second, the third person repeats the two preceding words plus the third word, etc. The instructor speaks first, using a pattern to memorize words: e.g., the alphabet—a sentence using the first letter of each word, etc. Sometimes the more intent person will be able to pick up the pattern and anticipate the next word. (Examples: (1) apples, beets, carrots, dill pickle, etc.)

3. Visual. The prepared tray of objects is presented to students either in a group or one student at a time. The tray is exposed for 10—15 seconds, then covered or removed. Students either write down or report verbally on the contents of the tray, giving as many details as they can remember in addition to naming all items on the tray.

4. Students enter an unfamiliar room, one at a time or in small groups. After studying the room intently for a few minutes, they close their eyes and try to describe the room as fully as possible. The same exercise may be carried out with a film by running a segment which shows a room interior.

SUGGESTED RESOURCES:

Halacy, D.S., Jr., *MAN AND MEMORY,* New York: Harper & Row, 1970.

Wooldridge, Dean E., *THE MACHINERY OF THE BRAIN,* New York: McGraw-Hill, 1963, ch. 9.

DREAMING

PURPOSE:

To discover something about ourselves through our dreams.

COMMENT:

"Dreams portray the unconscious condition of the dreamer and contain a compensatory or complementary picture of the psychic situation." It is necessary to be aware of ourselves in order to be fully aware, fully conscious, and capable of seeing the "brother's situation as clearly as" one's own (Harding, THE 'I' AND THE 'NOT-I'). In the introduction to Jung's MAN AND HIS SYMBOLS, John Freeman points out that Jung believed that the communications of dreams "are of the highest importance to the dreamer—naturally so, since the unconscious is at least half of his total being—and frequently offers him advice or guidance that could be obtained from no other source." Jung said "Two fundamental points in dealing with dreams are these: First, the dream should be treated as a fact, about which one must make no previous assumptions except that it somehow makes sense; and second, the dream is a specific expression of the unconscious" (MAN AND HIS SYMBOLS). He stressed the fact that no dream could be understood apart from the dreamer, and that he himself could "never understand somebody else's dream well enough to interpret it correctly" (MAN AND HIS SYMBOLS). He also warned that there are some people whose mental condition is so unbalanced that to try to help them understand their dreams could be very dangerous without specific professional help.

Scientists have found that every night we dream about once every ninety minutes, and these dreams become progressively longer, the last one of the night enduring for about forty-five minutes. We remember our dreams best immediately upon rising, although the beginning of a dream may be lost beyond recall, and unless we tell someone our dream, or write it down, we usually forget it before the day is over. However, we can learn to remember our dreams, and to recall them upon awakening. In some cultures where dreams are given more importance, dreams are remembered quite well. Dr. Frederick Snyder, Chief of the Section on Psychophy-siology of Sleep, National Institute of Health, speaks of dreaming as "a third basic biological mode of existence, of the same order yet different from sleep or waking." In the Hindu and Buddhist worlds, this third is considered as important as the waking-mind. Writing in *LIFE*, Will Bradbury says, "Some theorists even suggest that sleep is the basic state of the brain, and to them consciousness is a mere servant of the unconscious mind, the time the brain takes out for food, sex, physical security and the other essentials for survival." ("The Brain: Part III," *LIFE*, Vol. 71, No. 20, Nov. 12, 1971, p. 61)

Renee Nell writes, "The dream is a part of our nature, working towards health and the kind of balance that we refer to as normality . . . We are now rediscovering the use of symbols and dream imagery as a guide to fruitful inner conversation with our Self, and as a means of growth." Her suggestions form the basis for the following exercise ("Guidance through Dreams," *WAYS OF GROWTH*).

GROUP SIZE:

Up to 20

TIME SUGGESTED:

Two sessions, several weeks apart, of 45—60 minutes each.

GENERAL DIRECTIONS:

The first session consists of a lecture or readings by the teacher, giving information on current ideas on dreams. Students are then asked to keep a dream diary for several weeks, and to share some of their findings with a friend at the last session. There is a brief discussion in a plenary on the subject of dreams.

MATERIALS REQUIRED:

You may prefer to read some of the materials in "Suggested Resources" as part of your initial lecture.

PROCEDURE:

1. We suggest you invite a few comments on "dreams," indicating that you are going to talk on the subject at this session. In "Suggested Resources" you will find the first section devoted to materials

for this purpose. After your lecture, ask students to keep a "dream diary" for 2—3 weeks, trying to write down each morning upon awakening all the dreams they can remember of that night. They may find in the beginning that they can remember no dreams at all, but by the third week all should be able to recall one occasionally. Ask them to include the date, and to jot down anything of importance that occurred the previous day, or any problem they had been trying to solve during that day.

2. A few days prior to the second session, assign the students to the task of going back over their dream diary and making a few notes as follows:

—Re-read all your dreams, and see if you can find a common theme or themes. Give each dream a title, like a short story.

—Examine the feelings expressed in the dream, by yourself or any other persons or animals in each dream. Try to relate these feelings to your notes about the experiences of the preceding day.

—Think about the other characters in your dreams as parts of your own psyche or personality, and see if this helps you understand the meaning of the dream.

—Remember that Jung said, "it is plain foolishness to believe in ready-made systematic guides to dream interpretation, as if one could simply buy a reference book and look up a particular symbol" *(MAN AND HIS SYMBOLS)*.

—Examine your dream to see if other people or characters are trying to give you advice or opposing you. If this was another "side" of your personality, what might it mean?

3. Ask the students to bring their dream diaries with them to the second session, but assure them they will not have to show them to anyone else. At this session ask each student to sit with a friend with whom he would like to share some of his dreams or some of the ideas he has gained from his dreams. Depending on the productivity of this session of sharing, decide how much time to allow, reserving some portion for a final plenary.

4. In the plenary avoid probing for personal revelations, but encourage any general observations, and discuss the validity of the experiment, its usefulness to the students, and any recommendations they would want to make to others. You may wish to conclude with a few minutes' reading from other source material.

SUGGESTED READINGS:

MATERIALS FOR THE FIRST SESSION:
Harding, M. Esther, *THE 'I' AND THE 'NOT-I'*, Princeton, N.J.: Princeton University, 1965. (Dr. Harding is a Jungian psychoanalyst and interpreter of Carl Jung. You may wish to read selections from pages 22-23, 35.)

Jung, Carl G., (ed.), *MAN AND HIS SYMBOLS*, New York: Dell, 1964. (Portions of the introduction by Freeman, and selections from Jung's article on pp. 5, 9, 12, 18, 28, and 42.)

Calder, Nigel, *THE MIND OF MAN*, New York: Viking, 1970, pp. 38-40.

de Ropp, Robert S., *THE MASTER GAME*, New York: Delta, 1968, pp. 55-56.

Stewart, Kilton, "Dream Exploration among the Senoi," *CREATIVE PSYCHOLOGY AND DREAM EDUCATION*, reprinted in *SOURCES*, Theodore Roszak (ed.), New York: Harper & Row, 1972, pp. 20ff.

Nell, Renee, "Guidance through Dreams," *WAYS OF GROWTH*, Herbert Otto and John Mann (eds.), New York: Viking, 1968, p. 188.

ADDITIONAL MATERIALS:
Luce, Gay Gaer, *CURRENT RESEARCH ON SLEEP AND DREAMS*, Washington, D.C.: U.S. Public Health Service Pub. #1389, 1966. Available for 65¢ from Superintendent of Documents, U.S. Government Printing Office, Washington, D.C. 20402.

Luce, Gay Gaer, and Julius Segal, *SLEEP*, New York: Coward-MacCann, 1966.

Handler, Philip, (ed.), *BIOLOGY AND THE FUTURE OF MAN*, New York: Oxford University, 1970, pp. 370-373; 408-411.

Eckstein, Gustav, *THE BODY HAS A HEAD*, New York: Harper & Row, 1969, 1970, see index, "Dreams."

FALL-OUT SHELTER

PURPOSE:

To introduce the problem of death in the course of exploring some values.

COMMENT:

Because the "Death Inquiry" exercise which follows may tend to induce resistance to discussion of the subject, a preliminary exercise such as this will open some doors for continuing discussion and provide more input both for the Death Inquiry discussion and any subsequent discussions on the subject of death.

GROUP SIZE:

Subgroups of 5—10

TIME SUGGESTED:

1 hour

GENERAL DIRECTIONS:

The "Directions" given below should be reproduced and distributed. If desired you may give a time limit for the individual decision, and also reserve some time at the end of the session for a plenary, if the class is large enough to have been subgrouped. By selecting the seven who are to stay in the shelter they are condemning three to death. As the exercise is written this will have little place in their consciousness—stress will be on valuing, on deciding who should stay because of their value to this particular community, or to the future of mankind, or even to their original "society."

If desired, this could be followed by one of the "urban design" exercises. Students may wish to go on to "build the new city," and can discuss how to go about it.

MATERIALS REQUIRED:

Copies of the following for each student.

PROCEDURE:

DIRECTIONS:

There is to be an atomic blast in three days. There are ten people who want to get into this particular fall-out shelter. Only seven can fit into this shelter. There is only enough food, water and oxygen for seven people. After discussing the choice for several days, the ten cannot come to any conclusion. They ask an impartial board (you) to make their decision for them. They will abide by whatever decision you make.

They are to stay in this shelter for three months, at the end of which time, there is a possibility that they will be the only people left alive on this planet or that they will be rescued and be able to move back into safety or society. They do not know which will be the case.

You are to select the seven people whom you think should be in this shelter. You are to do it INDIVIDUALLY at first and then COLLECTIVELY to agree on it. You are to come to a group CONSENSUS.

1. a woman, six months pregnant
2. her husband, an accountant
3. a 70 year old priest
4. a two-year pre-med student, a negro
5. a Hollywood movie starlet, singer & dancer
6. a famous writer
7. a biochemist
8. a nun, teacher
9. an armed policeman
10. an All-American athlete (all sports)

(NOTE: Each woman is in her twenties)

VARIATIONS:

1. The sex is not given in the above directions for 4, 6, 7 or 10, although the description seems to indicate a male. If you prefer, you can assign a sex to each of these people. If you do not do so, part of the discussion will focus on deciding whether to consider one or more of these people as women. At first the group may assume these individuals are men, but soon the more sophisticated will begin to question this assumption.

2. If the group has not had any previous experience in consensus seeking it will be necessary to explain the difference between consensus and majority rule prior to starting the exercise. On the other hand, you may wish to allow the groups to function as they choose, assuming that there will be some discussion of the meaning of consensus or that possibly students may not know the difference.

3. You may redesign this exercise as you wish, of course, substituting other roles for those

given here, or changing the circumstances of the disaster, e.g., a plane crash on a mountain peak, only one rescue helicopter makes it to the peak, can take only seven, the current blizzard will surely kill the remaining three before another copter can make it in.

4. This is very effective when carried out as a "role play." Students become the characters in question and try to decide the answer from "inside" the group, rather than a panel of "judges."

SUGGESTED RESOURCES:

MOVIES
1. *RED TENT* (feature film)
2. *PHOENIX 2* (feature film)
3. *RUN* (short subject)
4. *OCCURRENCE AT OWL CREEK BRIDGE*

BOOKS
Frank, Pat, *ALAS, BABYLON*, Philadelphia, Pa.: J.B. Lippincott and Co., n.d.

Mitford, Jessica, *THE AMERICAN WAY OF DEATH*, New York: Simon and Schuster, 1963.

Shute, Nevil, *ON THE BEACH*, New York: Apollo Edition, 1964.

Waugh, Evelyn, *THE LOVED ONE*, Boston, Mass.: Little, Brown and Co., 1948.

McLuhan, T.C., (compiler), *TOUCH THE EARTH: A SELF-PORTRAIT OF INDIAN EXISTENCE*, New York: Outerbridge & Dienstfrey/E.P. Dutton & Co., 1971, p. 30.

DEATH INQUIRY

PURPOSE:

To examine our values and moral imperatives in regard to "death" *versus* "life."

COMMENT:

Jean Amery points out that there is "a great deal of killing in American movies, but death is for the most part absent." He says, "All metaphysics is banished from Hollywood, as it is from American philosophy, which either dulls it with the support of neopositivists or relegates it to the theologians and 'experts' in transcendental matters" (*PREFACE TO THE FUTURE: CULTURE IN A CONSUMER SOCIETY*). Our funerals are designed to avoid death, rather than dignify it. It is the "unacceptable act" which is hushed up, not discussed, concealed. Our newspapers and news magazines seem eager to publish photographs of the victims of accidents, death on the battlefield, or even the bloodstains on the floor or the street left after a victim is removed, and yet studies have shown that even those who deal with death daily, doctors and nurses in hospitals, have great difficulty in talking about death with patients or their families.

In *CHILDHOOD AND SOCIETY*, Erik H. Erikson quotes Webster's definition of trust, "the assured reliance on another's integrity," and adds, ". . . it seems possible to further paraphrase the relation of adult integrity and infantile trust by saying that healthy children will not fear life if their elders have integrity enough not to fear death."

In June, 1971 *PSYCHOLOGY TODAY* reported on its survey on "death," their findings on "who feels how about living, dying, funerals, autopsies, euthanasia, suicide and after life; who welcomes death, who postpones it, who fears it, who hastens it; and what society, culture, literature, drugs and religion have to do with it." It is suggested that the entire report be read. The following are some aspects worth discussing together with the conclusions of your own survey. To the readers of *PSYCHOLOGY TODAY*, death was a topic more important than sex. More than 30,000 readers replied, and more than 2,000 sent letters.

1. Two reasons suggested for the interest in

the topic: (a) the occasion to unburden oneself about death and feel somehow cleansed; (b) the urgency to talk about death.

2. Man today makes himself the center of his own world, looking upon dying as an aspect of living.

3. The threat of nuclear war influences attitudes toward death.

4. Attitudes toward death seem to change as one matures. The older person is more likely to be convinced that there is no life after death.

5. Secularization of death has taken place. For the most part, people die in hospitals rather than in their homes.

6. Most respondents prefer sudden, quiet and dignified deaths, not violent death. They would not want to know the day on which they are going to die. However, if they had a terminal disease, they would prefer to be told.

7. Funerals are overpriced. More than 50 percent believe that funerals should cost less than $300.

8. Rituals (funerals and wakes) are important for the survivors.

9. Fear of death puts excitement into living.

GROUP SIZE:

Up to 20

TIME SUGGESTED:

45—60 minutes

GENERAL DIRECTIONS:

Timing is extremely important. Do not use this exercise, for instance, on a good Spring day. If possible, use it following the death of a national figure. It is recommended that this exercise be used after "Life: Fall-Out Shelter." You may find that students are willing to complete the questionnaire, but not to discuss it in small groups (Step No. 2) but may accept a less emotional discussion in a plenary (Step No. 3).

MATERIALS REQUIRED:

Copies of the questionnaire, "You and Death." You may also wish to reproduce for distribution the statements on death quoted in Step No. 3, below.

PROCEDURE:

1. Distribute questionnaires. Ask the students to fill in independently.

2. In groups of 8—10, ask the class to discuss the differences and similarities in their answers. Ask them to share with each other their reasons for choosing the answer marked. Encourage them to ask others to clarify differences.

3. In a plenary session ask each group to report the major issues discussed and some conclusions arrived at. If the class has been resistant to Step No. 2, you may wish to provide some input from "Comment," and encourage general discussion of the points raised. You may wish to reproduce and distribute some statements and definitions of death, such as the following:

Rahner, Karl, and Herbert Vorgrimler, *THEOLOGICAL DICTIONARY*, New York: Herder & Herder, 1964, pp. 115ff. (Select excerpts you believe suitable for your class.)

"Death. A state of complete and irreversible cessation or absence of bodily processes, such as respiration and circulation, leading ultimately to dissolution of the organism." Dorland's *POCKET MEDICAL DICTIONARY*, 20th ed., Philadelphia, Pa.: W.B. Saunders, 1959.

"Death. 1. The act of dying; termination of life." *AMERICAN HERITAGE DICTIONARY OF THE ENGLISH LANGUAGE*, Boston: Houghton Mifflin.

"Death: As regards mundane affairs most Zenists share in the usual Buddhist beliefs. In this case the belief is that though the body dies, the skandhas live on, and are reborn, subject to constant modification. Zenists rarely write or think about this . . . Still, without this belief they may not see how all persons will some time realize Nirvana, even though they may not proceed to do so until after many lifetimes" (Ernest Wood, *ZEN DICTIONARY*, New York: Citadel Press, 1962, p. 34).

"Real death would be destruction, not of the body, but of the soul; for in the body work of destruction is ever going on" (*PHAEDO*, 91). "When a man thinks himself to be near death he has fears and cares which never entered into his mind before; the tales of a life below and the punishment which is exacted there of deeds done here were a laughing matter to him once, but now he is haunted with the thought that they may be true: either because of the feebleness of age, or from the nearness of the prospect, he seems to have a clearer view of the other world" (*REPUBLIC*, I, 330). "Death is good, for one of two things: either death is a state of nothingness and utter unconsciousness, or, as men say, there is a migration of the soul from this world to another. Now if you suppose that there is no consciousness, but an undisturbed sleep, death will be an unspeakable gain. But if death is the journey to another place, what good can be greater than this?" (*APOL-*

OGY, 40). "Being dead is the attainment of the separation of soul and body when the soul exists in herself, and is parted from the body and the body is parted from the soul" (*PHAEDO*, 64) . . . Plato.

"What do you think of death?"

"Well, I must say I have no fear of death. I faced it once about two years ago on an internal level. This is hard to explain. I've actually faced the risk of death a number of times but this one time I actually became paranoid. I was overcome by anxiety. It was unclear what was going on. I overcame that state purely on a mind level and realized that I had the power in me not to become paranoid. It's the paranoia, the living in constant fear of death, that is the real bad trip, not the death itself. I will be surprised if I get a chance to live out my life. Gleefully surprised, but surprised none the less."

"Isn't that sort of gloomy?"

"No! Not really. You can't deny there is a tremendous amount of violence in this country. People who are engaged daily in radical social change are always exposed to that violence. I would rather die fighting for change than surrender. Death in a physical sense is just not seen as the worst of all possible things" (Abbie Hoffman, "Talking in My Sleep", *REBEL CULTURE*, Robert S. Gold (ed.), New York: Dell, 1970, p. 215).

YOU AND DEATH

QUESTIONNAIRE:

1. Who died in your first personal involvement with death?
   —A. Grandparent or great-grandparent
   —B. Parent
   —C. Brother or Sister
   —D. Other Family member
   —E. Friend or acquaintance
   —F. Stranger
   —G. Public figure
   —H. Animal

2. To the best of your memory, at what age were you first aware of death?
   —A. under three
   —B. Three to five
   —C. Five to ten
   —D. Ten or older.

3. When you were a child, how was death talked about in your family?
   —A. Openly
   —B. With some sense of discomfort
   —C. Only when necessary and then with an attempt to exclude the children
   —D. As though it were a taboo subject
   —E. Never recall any discussion.

4. Which of the following best describes your childhood conception of death?
   —A. Heaven-and-hell concept
   —B. After-life
   —C. Death as sleep
   —D. Cessation of all physical and mental activity
   —E. Mysterious and unknowable
   —F. Something other than the above
   —G. No concept
   —H. Can't remember

5. Which of the following most influence your present attitudes toward death?
   —A. Death of someone close
   —B. Specific reading
   —C. Religious upbringing
   —D. Introspection and meditation
   —E. Ritual (e.g., funeral)
   —F. TV, radio or motion pictures
   —G. Longevity of my family
   —H. My health or physical condition
   —I. Other (specify)

6. How much of a role has religion played in the development of your attitude toward death?
   —A. A very significant role
   —B. A rather significant role
   —C. Somewhat influential, but not a major role
   —D. A relatively minor role
   —E. No role at all

7. To what extent do you believe in a life after death?
   —A. Strongly believe in it
   —B. Tend to believe in it
   —C. Uncertain
   —D. Tend to doubt it
   —E. Convinced it does not exist

8. How often do you think about your own death?
   —A. Very frequently (at least once a day)
   —B. Frequently
   —C. Occasionally
   —D. Rarely (no more than once a year)
   —E. Very rarely or never

9. If you could choose, when would you die?
   —A. In youth
   —B. In the middle prime of life
   —C. Just after the prime of life
   —D. In old age

10. What does death mean to you?
   —A. The end; the final process of life
   —B. The beginning of a life after death; a transition; a new beginning
   —C. A joining of the spirit with a universal cos-

mic consciousness
—D. A kind of endless sleep; rest and peace
—E. Termination of this life but with survival of the spirit
—F. Don't know
—G. Other (specify)

11. What aspect of your own death is the most distasteful to you?
—A. I could no longer have any experience
—B. I am afraid of what might happen to my body after death
—C. I am uncertain as to what might happen to me if there is a life after death
—D. I could no longer provide for my dependents
—E. It would cause grief to my relatives and friends
—F. All my plans and projects would come to an end
—G. The process to dying might be painful

—H. Other (specify)

12. How do you rate your present physical health?
—A. Excellent
—B. Very good
—C. Moderately good
—D. Moderately poor
—E. Extremely bad

13. In your opinion, at what age are people most afraid of death?
—A. Up to 12 years
—B. Thirteen to 19 years
—C. 20 to 29 years
—D. 30 to 39 years
—E. 40 to 49 years
—F. 50 to 59 years
—G. 60 to 69 years
—H. 70 years and over

14. When you think of your own death (or when circumstances make you realize your own mortality), how do you feel?
—A. Fearful
—B. Discouraged
—C. Depressed
—D. Purposeless
—E. Resolved, in relation to life
—F. Pleasure, in being alive
—G. Other (specify)

15. How often have you been in a situation in which you seriously thought you might die?
—A. Many times
—B. Several times

—C. Once or twice
—D. Never

16. To what extent are you interested in having your image survive after your own death through your children, books, good works, etc?
—A. Very interested
—B. Moderately interested
—C. Somewhat interested
—D. Not very interested
—E. Totally uninterested

17. For whom or what might you be willing to sacrifice your life?
—A. For a loved one
—B. For an idea or moral principle
—C. In combat or a grave emergency where a life would be saved
—D. Not for any reason

18. If you had a choice, what kind of death would you prefer?
—A. Tragic, violent death
—B. Sudden but not violent death
—C. Quiet, dignified death
—D. Death in line of duty
—E. Death after a great achievement
—F. Suicide
—G. Homicidal victim
—H. There is no "appropriate" kind of death
—I. Other (specify)

19. If it were possible would you want to know the exact date on which you are going to die?
—A. Yes
—B. No

20. If your physician knew that you had a terminal disease and a limited time to live, would you want
—A. Yes
—B. No
—C. It would depend on the circumstances

21. If you were told that you had a terminal disease and a limited time to live, how would you want to spend your time until you died?
—A. I would make a marked change in my life style; satisfy hedonistic needs (travel, sex, drugs, other experiences)
—B. I would become more withdrawn; reading contemplating or praying
—C. I would shift from my own needs to a concern for others (family, friends)
—D. I would attempt to complete projects; tie up loose ends
—E. I would make little or no change in my life style

—F. I would try to do one very important thing
—G. I might consider committing suicide
—H. I would do none of these

SUGGESTED RESOURCES:

SCRIPTURE REFERENCES:
 Luke 12:35
 John 8:51
 John 20:31f
 Romans 6:6f, 7:10, 5:12
 2 Corinthians 4:11
 Philippians 1:20
 Job 3, 7, 10, 14
 Psalms 89:46, 146:4, 38:12
 Wisdom 4:7

Kubler-Ross, Elisabeth, *ON DEATH AND DYING,* New York: Macmillan, 1969. ("It might be helpful if more people would talk about death and dying as an intrinsic part of life just as they do not hesitate to mention when someone is expecting a new baby . . . If this book serves no other purpose but to sensitize family members of terminally ill patients and hospital personnel to the implicit communications of dying patients, then it has fulfilled its task." pp. 141-142. An excellent book which deserves wide readership.)

Amery, Jean, *PREFACE TO THE FUTURE: CULTURE IN A CONSUMER SOCIETY,* trans. by Paul Hilty, New York: Frederick Unger Publ., 1964, p. 110.

Erikson, Erik H., *CHILDHOOD AND SOCIETY,* 2nd ed., New York: W.W. Norton, 1963, p. 169.

WHO SHALL LIVE?
WHO SHALL DIE?

PURPOSE:

To explore the criteria by which the citizen must decide who shall live, who shall die. To recognize that this is going to be increasingly a duty of the citizen, though indirectly exercised.

COMMENT:

Law, medicine and religion all have difficulty in defining "death." *When is a person dead?* This has become far more than an academic question—with increasing numbers of transplant operations, the doctor is faced with this question in a sometimes terrifying way.

Another very real question is *Who shall live?* When two candidates are waiting for a kidney transplant and one kidney is available, who should decide and how?

There is the further question of *When should the patient die?* In the case of infants, for instance, the parents and the doctor are sometimes faced with the question of whether to keep an infant alive by continuing life support processes such as respirators, feeding and drainage through tubes inserted in the body, etc. The same problems arise in the case of many adult patients.

Looking toward the future many complex questions arise: in the case of a person who has received numerous transplants, *When is "he" dead and a "new person" alive* instead? In the case of a person who has undergone brain surgery which changes the character, will he be the "same person"? Will he, for instance, be responsible for crimes committed prior to this surgery?

When life can be greatly prolonged by replacement of organs, *Should a limit be set on the length of life?* for whom? by whom? how should such decisions be made? what should be the criteria?

GROUP SIZE:

Subgroups of 3—7

TIME SUGGESTED:

1—4 sessions

GENERAL DIRECTIONS:

This exercise may follow the Fall-Out Shelter and Death Inquiry exercises. The exercise consists of the examination of a number of case histories, individual and group decisions as to the disposition of the case, and subsequent general discussion of principles involved. Each member receives a copy of the case history for his group.

MATERIALS REQUIRED:

Sets of case histories.

PROCEDURE:

1. Talk briefly to the class about some of the kinds of problems suggested in "Comment" above. Subgroup the class and distribute copies of Case Histories. Each group may work on a different case history, or all may work on the same one.

2. Tell the class that each member is to read his case history, and make a tentative decision before discussing it with other members of his group. The group should then have 15—30 minutes to arrive at a decision. In this situation it might be well to propose that in cases of disagreement, the group may also prepare a "minority opinion."

3. Each group reads its case history to the rest of the class, together with their decision, including the minority opinion, if any.

If desired, the actual decisions reached in a particular case history may be fed in during the discussion in instances where the case history is a fairly accurate statement of real-life cases.

4. General discussion follows, focusing on such questions as:

—What is *human* life?

—Under what conditions should a person be considered incompetent to make a decision involving his own life? (age, mental condition, intelligence, "unconsciousness", etc.)

—When a person is not considered competent to make such a decision, whose responsibility should it be? relatives, friends, physicians, the state?

—How should decisions be made as to who should receive available organs for transplants?

—How should decisions be made as to how long a patient should be kept alive by "artificial means"?

—How should decisions be made as to who should be allowed to be a donor in the case of transplants from healthy living persons of a paired organ (e.g., kidney)?

VARIATIONS:

1. If the exercise is carried on over several sessions, some independent research in regard to the complexity of some of these problems should be encouraged. Some suggestions are included in "Suggested Resources." Brief reports on some of this material may then constitute part of one or more sessions, or the material may simply be used as input for the decision making and discussions.

2. Other case histories may be more suitable for your group, or more pertinent or timely. A certain amount of oversimplification is necessary in almost all cases to make the case history manageable for a class.

SUGGESTED RESOURCES:

ON DEATH:

"At Massachusetts General Hospital . . . it is a rule of thumb that if the brain trace [on an EEG] has been flat for 24 hours and does not respond to stimuli, such as loud noises, and if the patient has no heartbeat and respiration of his own, he can be pronounced dead and the equipment disconnected" (Gordon Rattray Taylor, *THE BIOLOGICAL TIME BOMB,* New York: World Publishing, 1968, pp. 116-117).

"Many doctors think that brain function is a better criterion of death than heart function, and that death should be diagnosed on the basis of EEG (electroencephalograph) tracings of the brain's electrical activity. As the Boston neurosurgeon Dr. Hannibal Hamlin, puts it: 'Although the heart has been enthroned through the ages as the sacred chalice of life's blood, the human spirit is the product of man's brain, not his heart.' But in legal practice generally, as also by custom, the stopping of the heart is taken to be the sign of death.

". . . In May 1966, by a unanimous decision, the French National Academy of Medicine decided that a man whose heart is still beating may be ruled dead. The Academy's decision, which was based on the report of a special commission set up four months previously, has the effect of permitting doctors to remove living organs for transplantation purposes from people who have no hope of survival. And it recommended that the demise should be confirmed by the electroencephalograph: if the brain shows no activity for 48 hours, the brain, and the patient, are to be assumed to be dead" (. . . Taylor, *BIOLOGICAL TIME BOMB,* pp. 114-115).

"Dr. G. P. J. Alexandre, Head of the Department of Renal Transplantation at the University of Louvain, has used nine patients as kidney donors who were victims of severe craniocerebral injury but whose hearts had not stopped. (Five conditions were always met in these nine cases: (1) complete bilateral mydriasis (dilation of both pupils); (2) complete absence of reflexes, both natural and in response to profound pain; (3) complete absence of spontaneous respiration, five minutes after mechanical respiration has been stopped; (4) falling blood pressure, necessitating increasing amounts of vasopressive drugs . . . ; (5) a flat EEG." . . . Alexandre accepted Dr. J. Hamburger's point that a flat EEG can be caused by barbiturate poisoning and added that a gas embolism occurring in heart surgery can also produce a flat EEG. More important, he insisted that patients registering a flat EEG as the result of barbiturate poisoning or gas embolism would not fulfill the other four conditions, nor would they, in all likelihood, have severe head injuries.

"Dr. J. P. Revillard of Lyon has suggested that, in addition to Alexandre's five signs, two other criteria afford even more precise determination of death: (1) interruption of blood flow in the brain as judged by angiography, which we assume is a better sign of death than a flat EEG, and (2)—of less value —the absence of reaction to a tropine" (Harmon L. Smith, *ETHICS AND THE NEW MEDICINE*, New York: Abingdon, 1970, pp. 138-139).

CASE HISTORIES:

The following Case Histories are suggested:

I. "One doctor to another: About the terminating of a pregnancy, (performing an abortion) I want your opinion. The father was syphilitic. The mother tuberculous. Of the four children born, the first was blind, the second died, the third was deaf and dumb, the fourth also tuberculous. What would you have done?"

II. Thousands of babies were born without arms or legs or with very serious deformities of the limbs and with other defects as the result of their mothers having taken a tranquilizer, thalidomide, on the advise of their physicians. In some cases, after the dangerous character of the drug was discovered, therapeutic abortion was performed to prevent the birth of such infants. In one case, however, such an infant was killed after birth by her mother. The baby had no arms, her face was deformed, and her anal canal was diverted so that the contents emptied through the vagina. The mother was tried for murder. Was she guilty?

III. Under common law the decision of a minor is not considered "valid consent," and therefore their parents or guardians have had to make the decision when they are to serve as transplant donors. In the case of kidney transplants, statistics show that the one-year survival rate for recipients of renal homografts (kidney transplants) is about 80 percent with close relative donors, 60 percent with cadaveric donors, and less than 30 percent with living unrelated donors. Also, the increased mortality risk of the donor, who now has one kidney, viewed over a five year period, is 99.1 percent, as compared with a normal expectation of 99.3 percent (this is the same risk as that encountered by anyone who traveled eight miles to work and back each day during that time). A hospital received a request from the parents of 14 year-old twins to transplant one kidney from the healthy twin to his very sick brother who, due to irreparable damage to both kidneys, could not long survive without a transplant. Should the hospital and staff accept this request and perform the operation? Should the healthy twin be consulted? Should the hospital consider his views?

IV. (Some of the data from Case III will be needed by students working on this Case History.) Persons judged by the courts to be mentally incompetent are unable to give valid consent and, like minors, have decisions made for them by parents and guardians. A seriously ill man is in need of a kidney transplant. He has a healthy brother who is considered by medical authorities to be the most suitable donor. However, his brother is mentally incompetent, being institutionalized in a state hospital. The mother of the two men asked the hospital to use the institutionalized brother as a donor. However, the state appointed a guardian of the institutionalized brother. The case was taken to court. How would you decide?

V. The head of the psychology department of a large university and his wife, also a psychologist, are going to have a baby next month. They have announced their intention to raise the child for the first year of its life in total isolation in a sterile environment. They have arranged that the child will be observed almost constantly through a one-way mirror window and fed and kept clean by means of a number of arm-sleeve entry holes around the room such as are used in some infant incubators or industrial situations. Other members of the faculty have violently objected to this plan, including other members of the psychology department, stating that studies have shown that children deprived of affection, handling and contact with people are seriously deprived, may be permanently retarded mentally or emotionally, and sometimes die. The prospective parents state that these objections are irrelevant because no experiment quite like theirs has been tried, they intend to provide the child with sensory input by means of tapes, films and slides, and the child is theirs and therefore the decision is their's alone. The faculty is meeting to decide whether to take the case to court to have the parents declared incompetent or abusive, to take the case to the administration petitioning for the removal from the faculty of the prospective father, or whether to allow the parents to raise the child as they wish. What should they decide?

VI. A 32-year old man fell on his head when butted during a fight, and was admitted to the hospital with severe brain injuries. On June 16, fourteen hours after admission to the hospital, he stopped breathing. He was connected to an artificial respirator to allow time for preparation for an operation to remove one of his kidneys for a transplant to another patient. His wife's permission was obtained for the removal of the kidney for this purpose. After twenty-four hours the kidney was removed, the respirator disconnected, and there was no breathing or blood circulation. The attending physician obtained the coroner's permission for the kidney removal. When did the patient die? Was anyone guilty of his death?

VII. The attending physician of an elderly lady must decide whether or not to perform an operation to save her life. He knows that if the operation is "successful" she may live another ten years. However, he also knows that she will be hopelessly paralyzed and comatose, requiring the full time attention of two or three nurses (throughout the rest of her life until her death). Is it the doctor's duty to preserve "life" in this situation?

DECISIONS:

I. The other doctor replied, "I would have ended the pregnancy." The question-poser then said, "Then you would have murdered Beethoven" (Norman St. John-Stevas, *THE RIGHT TO LIFE,* New York: Holt, Rinehart and Winston, 1963, p. 16).

II. Mrs. Suzanne Van de Put was acquitted by a jury in Liege, Belgium, November, 1962. The jury stated that the baby, Corinne, was killed, but not murdered (Harmon L. Smith, *ETHICS AND THE NEW MEDICINE,* New York: Abingdon Press, 1970, p. 21).

III. Peter Bent Brigham Hospital in Massachusetts performed three such operations in 1956, two on 14-year-old twins and the other on 19-year-old twins. The staff and trustees requested judgments from the Supreme Judicial Court of Massachusetts. In 1957 the three cases were heard before three different justices, each justice wrote an individual opinion, and all three opinions were affirmative. Their statements included four factors: (1) consent of the parents; (2) necessity of the operation to save the sick twin; (3) understanding of the operation and voluntary consent by the healthy twin; (4) psychiatric testimony that the operation was necessary for the continued good health and future well-being of the *donor.*

IV. The Kentucky Court of Appeals upheld the decision of the lower court to approve the transplant on the ground that the well-being of the institutionalized brother "would be jeopardized more severely by the loss of his brother than the removal of a kidney" (Harmon L. Smith, *ETHICS AND THE NEW MEDICINE,* New York: Abingdon Press, 1970, p. 106).

V. (This is a hypothetical case, although the ingredients are not unknown or unthinkable.)

VI. In the case of David Potter, admitted to Newcastle General Hospital, England, in 1963, the following decisions were reported in medical and legal journals and at the inquest and the Magistrates Court. (1) Attending physician: the patient was medically dead June 16, legally dead June 17; (2) A neurologist: brain damage was so extensive and irreparable that the patient was dead before the operation (before June 17); (3) The coroner: the patient was alive at the time the kidney was removed (June 17) but hopelessly injured, and the operation did not contribute to his death; (4) The jury at the inquest: the removal of the kidney did not contribute to the patient's death; the assailant was guilty of manslaughter; (5) Magistrates Court: the assailant was convicted on a reduced charge of common assault. (Harmon L. Smith, *ETHICS AND THE NEW MEDICINE*)

VII. The English physician did perform the operation, but the patient did not survive it. He wrote to a medical journal asking his fellow doctors the question posed above. (Gordon Rattray Taylor, *THE BIOLOGICAL TIME BOMB,* New York: World Publishing Co., 1968, p. 114.)

Drake, Donald C., "Unwilling 'Gods': Doctors Must Decide if Babies Live," *THE PHILADELPHIA INQUIRER,* Vol. 285, No. 95, Oct. 3, 1971, Sect. A., p. 1f.

Fox, Renee C., "A Sociological Perspective on Organ Transplantation and Hemodialysis," *HARVARD UNIVERSITY PROGRAM ON TECHNOLOGY AND SOCIETY,* Reprint No. 7, Cambridge, Mass.: Harvard Univ. Press, 1970.

Fox, Renee C., "Yes, Yes, Doctor," *THE PENNSYLVANIA GAZETTE,* Vol. 69, No. 6, April, 1971, p. 28ff.

Spivak, Jonathan, "Probing the Cell: Some Scientists Seek to Alter Human Genes to Cure Many Diseases, but Critics Claim Research Could Lead to the Breeding of Physical, Mental Giants," *THE WALL STREET JOURNAL,* Vol. CLXXVIII, No. 108, Dec. 2, 1971, p. 1f.

Thompson, Thomas, "The Year They

Changed Hearts: A new and disquieting look at transplants," *LIFE,* Vol. 72, No. 12, Sept. 17, 1971, pp. 56ff. (An excerpt from Thompson's book, *HEARTS,* McCall Books.)

VATICAN II, "Pastoral Constitution on the Church in the Modern World," section 34 and 56, Walter M. Abbott (ed.), *THE DOCUMENTS OF VATICAN II,* New York: Guild, America and Association Press, 1966, pp. 232-233, 261-262.

EMERGENCIES AND CAREERS IN HEALTH

PURPOSE:

To provide needed information on "what to do in an emergency"; to stimulate interest in careers in various fields in "health."

COMMENT:

Many students still graduate from high school with no training in first aid, and a very sketchy knowledge of various medical emergencies. Students are often active in dangerous sports outside of school, and have been given little or no training in the necessary safety rules and precautions, or the handling of common emergencies in skiing, boating, etc. If your students are well trained in these areas, Part I may be gone through quickly, serving merely as a refresher for those students with little actual experience.

Some interest in possible careers in the field of health should be developed in Part I. Students should be aware of the wide range of possibilities of careers in health, and know that there are openings for people with many different levels of academic preparation. It is a field in which there are more apt to be job openings than candidates for them, and students often have a very limited view of the varied vocational opportunities.

GROUP SIZE:

Up to 20

TIME SUGGESTED:

One or more sessions of 45—60 minutes; possibly additional sessions of 25—60 minutes.

GENERAL DIRECTIONS:

Discussion, role plays, talks, panel presentations, films, literature and individual research offer a variety of approaches to increased knowledge. Following the "Life: Who Shall Live? Who Shall Die?" exercise, students may be particularly interested in this exercise.

MATERIALS:

You may wish to make available some literature, such as is suggested below, or films, speakers, etc., but the first session may be conducted without any materials.

PROCEDURE:

PART I

1. In a plenary session ask the students what kinds of "medical emergencies" they have had to deal with, and how they handled them. If suitable, ask students to role play some of these situations. Encourage class discussion of student experiences and role plays, seeking "further suggestions."

2. When actual, first-hand experiences run dry, ask the students how they would handle others, such as some of the following:

You are away from home, and one of the following situations arises:

a. Someone is drowning

b. There is a skiing accident; you think the unconscious victim may have some broken bones

c. Hiking through the woods, someone steps on glass and cuts his foot badly

d. You find someone lying unconscious on the pavement

e. You are home alone with someone who faints

f. It is night. You are alone with someone coming down from a bad trip (drugs)

g. You are the baby-sitter, and a small child is badly burned . . . or cuts her face falling on broken glass

h. You are the only one at home with a very sick parent. You call the doctor. He wants to know the patient's temperature and pulse rate. Can you cope?

i. You discover your next door neighbor is irrational ("crazy"), and may hurt herself or others. She has called you into the house to ask you to "turn off the electricity because it is attacking me."

Again, some of these may be role played. When controversy arises, or information provided by the class is inadequate or incorrect, suggest further

class investigation. The class may elect (a) to do individual research and make a report to the class on a specific problem; (b) to do small-group research on available literature, films, etc., and provide these for the class, together with a recommendation from the research group as to suitable class procedure to provide the greatest benefit to the class from their materials; (c) to invite a physician, public health nurse, school nurse, first aid instructor, etc., to speak on specific, pre-selected emergencies, chosen by the class.

PART II

Some interest may have developed in Part I, or this section of the exercise may be used independently, following another situation which has generated interest, such as an exercise on ecology, or an exercise dealing with various careers. One or more of the following possibilities may be used:

1. Some students may have decided on careers in health, and be willing to talk to the class about their personal interest and plans.

2. The students may be interested in a panel presentation using guest speakers. Allow the students to select first and second choices for a panel of four members, as there may be some scheduling difficulties. Some of the following suggestions may be introduced: a physician, a registered nurse, a practical nurse, a nurse's aide, a registered medical technologist, a medical technician, someone working in public health, a safety engineer from an industrial plant, a Ph.D. candidate from a local university doing research in some area of medicine, physiology, etc., a psychiatric social worker, a pharmacist, a dentist, a dental hygienist, a physical education teacher, a dietician, someone working with a suicide prevention organization.

3. Recent graduates from your local high school(s) who are studying in a field of health, or have just completed their training, are often enthusiastic spokesmen for their field and appealing to young people. If desired, a number of such people could be invited to give brief talks and answer questions during a portion of a series of class sessions.

4. Someone in guidance counseling could speak to the class, bringing films, literature, etc., and covering a wide range of vocational opportunities in health.

5. Students themselves may do individual research and give a panel presentation to the class, each speaker representing a different field or specialty. Encourage panel speakers to interview experts in the field in preparation for their presentation, as well as reading suitable material on their subject.

6. There may be sufficient interest, or need, in the class for a separate session on "Safety."

Various panelists could present "Safety in Sports," "Safety on the Highway," "Safety in the Woods," "Safety on the Job," etc. A good many films are available from industry and government which could be used with, or instead of, these speakers. Highway safety would be of particular benefit for students not taking Driver Education in school. Perhaps a truck driver would be a particularly good resource person, and possibly more acceptable than a speaker from the State Police or the local police force, although some forces have speakers specially trained for this work.

SUGGESTED RESOURCES:

On emergencies, safety and first aid, see "Suggested Resources" in exercise, "Happiness: Back to Nature"—American Red Cross first aid and safety materials, etc. Some additional materials are:

Three useful booklets and a film are available without charge from the Metropolitan Life Insurance Co., Health and Welfare Division, One Madison Ave., New York, N.Y. 10010. They are "Panic/or Plan: A Picture Primer on Emergencies, Their Prevention and Care," "On Your Own: with Safety," and a wallet size folder on mouth-to-mouth rescue breathing, "How to Restore the Breath of Life." The film is "Emergency 77," 16 mm., 14 minutes, black and white sound film. Also ask for their catalogue, "Aids for Health Teaching: A Catalog for Schools."

For students in rural areas, many films on safety produced and distributed by the U.S. Department of Agriculture will be useful. Ask for "Films of the U.S. Department of Agriculture," Agricultural Handbook No. 14, 1968. This catalogue is available without charge to teachers, as are also lists of Co-operating Film Libraries in all States, so that many films may be obtained from nearby locations.

A colorful booklet, "Cold Facts and Fiction about Safe Winter Driving" is available without charge from the National Safety Council, 425 N. Michigan Avenue, Chicago, Ill. 60611. Ask them about other literature for teenagers.

Safety films are available without charge from the Film Librarian, Public Relations and Advertising Department, Aetna Life and Casualty, Hartford, Conn. 06115. There are six films on recreation safety, three on safety on the job, and four on highway safety, including *Driving—or Driven,"* 16 mm., 14:40 minutes, color, sound, specifically addressed to the teenager.

On careers in health, see "Suggested Resources" in exercises: "Freedom: and Work," and "Happiness: and Work." Some additional materials are:

The Metropolitan Life Insurance Co., at the address listed above, can supply a number of booklets dealing with careers in health, including "The Challenge of Health Research."

Pfizer Laboratories has booklets and films available without charge. Write to Pfizer Laboratories Division, 235 East 42 St., New York, N.Y. 10017. Three helpful and attractive booklets offer a wide range of career possibilities, and include sources of further information: "Your Career Opportunities in Pharmacy," "Your Career Opportunities in Hospitals," and "Your Career Opportunities in Medicine." They also offer a number of films dealing with various aspects of careers in Agriculture. These are available on a free loan basis from Farm Film Foundation, 1425 H. St. N.W., Washington, D.C. 20005: *"Agriculture, Research and You,"* 16 mm., 28 minutes, color and sound; *"Dynamic Careers Through Agriculture,"* 16 mm., 28 min., color and sound; *"The Dynamics of Animal Agriculture,"* 16 mm., 26 min., color and sound.

Your local branch of the Mental Health Association, or the National Association for Mental Health, 10 Columbus Circle, New York, N.Y. 10019, will send you one copy of "Because You Like People . . . Choose a Career in Mental Health," and a "Catalog of Selected Mental Health Films," which lists six films suitable for career guidance in this field, available for a small rental fee from various listed sources, or possibly from your local film library.

The following films are prepared by various companies, associations and government agencies and made available on a free loan basis from Modern Talking Picture Service, Inc., 1234 Spruce St., Philadelphia, Pa. 19107. *"The Career Game"* (dietetics), 14 minutes; *"The Surgeon"* (surgeon's day at the hospital, 13 minutes; *"What about Tomorrow"* (careers in dentistry) 26 minutes; *"Horizons Unlimited"* (medicine and allied fields), 28 minutes.

ECOLOGY, CONSERVATION AND POLLUTION

PURPOSE:

To explore some of the problems of ecology and our values as they relate to conservation and pollution, and to take specific remedial steps.

COMMENT:

When Moses was about to die he called his sons about him and said to them, "See, today I set before you life and prosperity, death and disaster. If you obey the commandments of Yahweh your God that I enjoin on you today, if you love Yahweh your God and follow his ways . . . God will bless you in the land which you are entering to make your own. But if your heart strays, if you refuse to listen, if you let yourself be drawn into worshipping other gods and serving them, I tell you today, you will most certainly perish; you will not live long in the land you are crossing the Jordan to enter and possess . . . Choose life, then, so that you and your descendants may live, in the love of Yahweh your God, obeying his voice, clinging to him; for in this your life consists, and on this depends your long stay in the land which Yahweh swore to your fathers Abraham, Isaac and Jacob he would give them." (DEUT. 30:15-20)

Zen Buddhism teaches, "To squander is to destroy. To treat things with reverence and gratitude, according to their nature and purpose, is to affirm their value and life, a life in which we are all equally rooted. Wastefulness is a measure of our egocentricity and hence of our alienation . . ." (Philip Kapleau (ed.), THE THREE PILLARS OF ZEN, Boston: Beacon Press, 1965, p. 199)

This country has begun to awaken to the need to "choose life," "to treat things with reverence and gratitude," but we have had a long sleep and the wakening is slow and painful. We begin to see the need to reduce pollution and are concerned about the contamination and unbalancing of air and water by thermal pollution, detergents, sewage, pesticides, run-offs from fertilized fields, solid waste and radioactive wastes. We are worrying a bit about noise, the problem of population growth, the control, care, preservation and renewal of our wildlife, timber, soil, minerals and ocean resources. We recognize the need to preserve some open spaces and natural beauty for the sanity as well as the safety of men.

Since the passage of the Refuse Act of 1899, many laws have gone on the books to arrest the growth of these problems, and many conservationists have long pleaded the cause of our vanishing resources, but until lately the public has not worried. America was big, richly blessed with seemingly endless natural resources, and we wanted more, more, and more "good things." In a letter to James Madison, Thomas Jefferson wrote, "The earth belongs always to the living generation. They may manage it then, and what proceeds from it, as they please during their usufruct. They are masters too of their own persons, and consequently may govern them as they please." William D. Ruckelshaus, Administrator of the Environmental Protection Agency, points out that American "masters" have been strong on the "what they please" part of this statement, but weak on an understanding of "usufruct," a term referring to farm rental which implies the right to harvest, but the duty to leave resources intact and pass them on without damage. ("The Structure and Program of the Environmental Protection Agency," a talk given in Brussels, April 19, 1970.)

But University of Minnesota Social Anthropologist Luther Gerlach, who has made a study of mass movements, believes he sees a change of sufficient dynamism to be called "revolutionary." He says, "Soon—it is beginning on a small scale now—people will begin making personal sacrifices for the movement, like not driving their cars. When this takes hold I think you'll see a much more militant phase of the movement." He goes on to point out that the person who is consciously depriving himself of some comforts and conveniences will be much quicker to launch citizen complaints against industrial and governmental polluters, to vote for candidates who demonstrate their ability to make the needed changes, to boycott and to picket. He says, however, "The real revolution will be a revolution of attitudes. How we see things, how we value things. It must ultimately concern itself with the meaning of 'progress,' and, if it is successful, cause man to see himself as interdependent with, and not plundering master of, his environment" (reported by John Pekkanen, LIFE, Vol. 68, No. 3, January 30, 1970, pp. 29-30).

GROUP SIZE:

Up to 20

184

TIME SUGGESTED:

Time required depends on project selected.

GENERAL DIRECTIONS:

It is recommended that each activity be preceded by a 15—30 minute discussion, investigating the students' knowledge of the problem involved, and followed by one or more discussions to share information and to assist the students in individual value clarification and decision-making.

MATERIALS REQUIRED:

Varies with project. Some background materials should be made available, possibly films shown and bibliographies distributed. Student interest should determine particular areas of concentration.

PROCEDURES:

PART I.

Alerting Your Community

1. Develop "Fact Sheets" to be reproduced and distributed on street corners about pollution problems in your own community.

2. Have a "Dirty Pictures" contest, with prizes for the photographs showing the worst pollution problems in your community. Try to persuade your local newspaper to sponsor the contest, publish the winner and perhaps donate the prizes. It is possible that publication in the newspaper will be reward enough. Ask local TV and radio stations to publicize the event.

3. Investigate what business and industry are doing in your community to correct problems of pollution. Some companies may publicly advertise their plans and projects—encourage others to follow suit. By means of interviews and/or field trips, document actual projects in preparation or operation. Information should be disseminated through school or local newspapers.

4. Prepare posters of "The World 100 Years from Now." These may illustrate either positive or negative scenarios of the future of the community. Perhaps some local stores will display prize-winning posters, or they may be hung in school corridors or the cafeteria. Again, use the mass media to publicize the project.

5. Prepare a taped collection of songs dealing with problems of ecology and pollution and arrange to have them played over the P.A. system for the cafeteria or student lounges. If music is publicly

broadcast in your community during the Christmas holidays, see if the equipment is operable during the rest of the year, and ask if the tapes could be played. Local radio stations may be willing to broadcast some of the tapes on their "public service" time.

6. Hold a "gas mask" parade, with posters or signs, in the main shopping area at a popular shopping time. Prepare mimeographed statements asking for specific actions to distribute at this time.

7. Prior to local election campaigns, find out where potential candidates stand on conservation and anti-pollution measures, and publicize this information in one of the ways suggested above. Work during actual campaigns for candidates who have taken a public stand on bills and measures seeking to solve problems.

8. At peak shopping seasons, before Christmas and Easter, alert your community to avoid purchasing articles made from skins, furs or feathers of *endangered* species.

9. Talk to top people in city government responsible for solid waste management, and see what the community's needs are for improvement in processes and installations. Learn their plans and find out why needed changes have not been made. Help publicize their needs, or check with others in city government to see whether conflicting views exist. Promote a public forum to discuss this problem. If part of the difficulty is mishandling by specific local industry, publicize this, also.

PART II.

Direct Action by Individuals and Groups

Before undertaking direct action either individually or as a group or in concert with other groups, try to inform yourself as well as possible on the problems and possible solutions involved. Much misinformation has been circularized and popularized, diluting helpful action and distracting attention from serious problems needing immediate attention. Even small steps are helpful, but be sure they are in the right direction and do not create another, even more serious problem.

1. Find out if a local group is operating a glass-recycling project. If so, check with them to be sure they are meeting success in having their collected glass accepted by a glass factory. If so, get exact directions on how glass is to be handled, when and where it can be delivered to them, and any limitations on the weight of individual containers, sorting by color, whether bottles must be washed, whether metal caps, bands, etc., must be removed, and whether labels too must be removed. Establish collection centers in your school, providing suitable containers, such as cardboard drums. Be sure the student body is aware of their existence and purpose and of necessary regulations. Establish regular

means of collecting containers and delivering them to the local glass recycling collection agency. Tell the students responsible for pick-up and delivery to wear heavy work gloves. Be sure containers are small enough so that lifting them when filled is not too difficult. You might want to expand this project beyond the school to include a local shopping center. If so, check with the local collection agency first and work cooperatively with them.

If there is no such project in your community, see if there is a glass factory in your area which would accept glass for recycling and, if so, what the necessary conditions would be. It is best to start on a weekly or monthly basis, asking people to bring the glass at stated hours to the places which you have obtained permission to use for collection centers. Arrange with local businessmen for a supply of containers and see if a local trucking agency will donate the use of a truck and driver one hour once a week or once a month for pickup and delivery.

Publicize your project as widely as possible through the media, direct contact with people, flyers at shopping centers, churches and synagogues, posters in stores and libraries.

Arrange for temporary storage if you are unsure whether the trucking time available to you will be sufficient to collect and deliver all material collected on any given day. Avoid using elementary school children for jobs involving handling glass or lifting containers.

A number of the larger glass companies have been accepting glass for recycling. If there is a local branch of one of the following, contact them for advice in starting your project:

Anchor Hocking Corporation
Brockway Glass Co.
Glass Containers Corporation
Kerr Glass Mfg. Corporation
Owens-Illinois, Inc.
Tatcher Glass Mfg. Co.

2. Contact your local branch of the Bar Association and see if they have an Environmental Control or Air Pollution or Water Pollution sub-committee. Contact local law schools to see if they have a group interested in environmental law. Find out from them what laws to control pollution affect your local community. See if there are ways in which you can work to further their efforts at implementing these laws. Many people do not realize that without citizen cooperation, these laws do not do their intended job. Work first on problems where your advisors believe there is some possibility of success. Some cities have an air pollution center which responds to all citizen complaints of specific polluters, and can advise you as to the proper approach. Ask them if they want readings with a Ringelmann chart, or what specific information must be given to

them.

At the University of Pennsylvania, 60 law students make up the Environmental Law Group. These young men bring suit against local firms and individuals alleged to be in violation of the Commonwealth's Clean Streams Law. They work cooperatively with the State Department of Environmental Resources and the State District Attorney's Office. If your local law school does not have such a group, they might be interested in getting one started. Ask what you can do to help. (Patricia McLaughlin, " 'So sue me,' said the Polluter," *THE PENNSYLVANIA GAZETTE,* Vol. 69, No. 8, June, 1971, pp. 17ff.)

William D. Ruckelshaus, E. P. A. Administrator, speaking to the Indiana State Bar Association in Indianapolis on April 15, 1971, said, "Contrary to the view taken by some other persons in the private and governmental sectors, I am convinced that suits by public interest law firms to private lawyers often provide the only citizen recourse to adverse governmental or private action." The 1970 Clean Air Act gives concerned citizens standing to sue individual polluters, governmental units that pollute, and even the Administrator of the EPA in the event he does not carry out his duties under the Statute.

3. Start a tree planting campaign. Trees planted near homes, schools and other public buildings serve as a sound baffle and help purify the air by manufacturing oxygen from carbon dioxide. Your school may be opposed to planting trees on school property because of possible dangers to students tempted to climb them, and also because of maintenance costs. If this is the case, see if you can prepare a report to be submitted for consideration to your local school board. Check with your own school authorities and those of other schools in the same kind of areas to obtain actual statistics on such matters, and include this data in your report. Propose ways in which problems can be handled.

4. Encourage conservation planting in your community to specifically attract birds. Some suitable plants are Amur honeysuckle; crabapple; firethorn; autumn olive; holly; silky gray-stemmed, rodosier, and flowering dogwood; highbush blueberry; sumac; cherry; mountain-ash; hawthorn; redcedar; American cranberry bush; bittersweet; tatarian honeysuckle; Virginia creeper. For further information, send for the United States Department of Agriculture booklet, "Conservation Plantings . . . Invite Birds to Your Home," 1968. USDA PA-840, 20¢.

5. If you live in a rural area, start a campaign and assist in carrying it out, to increase the wildlife in your area. For detailed plans send for "Making Land Produce Useful Wildlife," Farmers' Bulletin

186 No. 2035, USDA, rev. 1969. For sale by the Superintendent of Documents, U.S. Government Printing Office, Washington, D.C. 20402, 20¢.

6. Do something to beautify your community while improving the ecology. Rene Dubos, writing in the *SMITHSONIAN* magazine, said, "The greatest crime committed in American cities may not be murder, rape or robbery, but rather the wholesale and constant exposure of children to noise, ugliness, and garbage in the street, thereby conditioning them to accept public squalor as the normal state of affairs." Investigate community ordinances regulating over-the-street signs and billboards and see if infractions are corrected. Work to see that suitable trash containers are available on the streets and are used. Report infractions of regulations regarding trash and garbage collection. Run a "work-day" to completely clean a small area, such as a block near the school, a small park, or other public area. Encourage plantings for concealing unsightly spots. Send for a copy of "Plants for Screening, Junkyards, Gravel Pits and Dumps," by the horticulturist Donald Wyman, available for 20¢ from the Arnold Arboretum, Harvard University, Jamaica Plain, Mass. 02130.

7. Sponsor a campaign to lessen the use of private automobiles in your community. Start with plenty of advance publicity for a one-week "car holiday," in which everyone will be urged to use public transportation as much as possible, to car-pool, to use bicycles, or to walk. In some communities it may even be possible to encourage "universal hitch-hiking," so that pedestrians of any age may feel free, when tired, to "thumb" their way around town. Since the U.S. Public Health Service says automobiles account for 60 percent or more of pollutants in the atmosphere, some such plan is going to have to be worked out until the internal combustion engine and its fuels can be drastically changed or a substitute created. After the first week, continue to encourage the use of public transportation and car-pooling, and try to get your local newspapers and radio and TV stations to make regular spot announcements, publish and broadcast human interest stories, and create and distribute handbills at regular intervals. The Environmental Protection Agency has published regulations for lead-control, requiring that lead-free or low-lead gasoline be available for 1975 cars, that there be a 90 percent reduction in the level of hydrocarbons and carbon monoxide emitted by automobiles by that date, and a 90 percent reduction in the level of nitrogen oxides by the following year. However, industry has already begun protesting that it cannot achieve this by the deadline given. Furthermore, some environmentalists say all this is "too little and too late," and, as with many of the other steps suggested in this exercise, active involvement by a sizable percentage of the population

in such measures will keep the ecological problems we face in the public mind.

8. Run a "less trash" week, using the same tactics as in No. 7 above. Starting with students, experiment with the many ways in which you can cut down on the amount of excess paper, glass and plastic which each person must put into the communities solid waste disposal systems. When shopping, carry shopping bags or string bags, and avoid taking home extra paper bags and plastic wrappers by asking for purchases unwrapped. Remembering that labor costs and losses from shoplifting are primary causes of much prepackaging, approach local merchants about the possibility of selling an increasing number of articles without packaging, or with minimal bagging. Publicize your findings, your efforts, and any successes. Refuse to purchase soft drinks in nonreturnable containers. Re-use your paper lunch bags, avoid using paper plates, cups and napkins, and be extremely thrifty in your use of paper towels. Enlist the cooperation of your families and of school personnel. Try to make some initial investigations of the quantities of these materials used before and during the experiment, and publicize these.

Ask a local store, bank or library to allow you space to display a fabric shopping bag, and its contents. Prepare the bag by purchasing as they are normally sold a variety of non-perishable items from local food, variety, and book stores, cramming items in as tightly as possible. Then remove the contents, unwrap and un-bag all the contents, leaving packaged only items which absolutely must be enclosed in some way, such as dry cereal, sold in a plastic bag, rather than a carton with a bag inside. Pile all packaging and paper bags on one side of your display area, place the empty shopping bag on the other side, and pile the articles on the shopping bag. Put a catchy slogan on a poster in front of your display. You may want to make a number of such large, sturdy, attractive shopping bags and offer them for sale near the display area, if you can obtain permission for this and can man the sale table with enough volunteers. Your bag may carry a stenciled slogan or reminder to further your publicity. Be sure your bags are large enough and the handles strong and well attached so they will be a desirable substitute for the usual shopping bag.

When the week is over, select those particular practices that you believe have been most helpful and urge their continuance. Repeat "less trash" week once a year, or even once a month, varying the approach to keep up public interest.

9. Start a "clean air" campaign in your community. Gain the cooperation of a number of suitable local organizations, perhaps the YMCA, YMHA, Boy's Club, Boy Scouts, Kiwanis, or a number of local churches and synagogues. Form subcommittees and attack a number of sources of pollution simultaneously. In addition to the use of private automobiles and motorcycles, remember that other equipment such as gasoline power mowers, boats and snow throwers also cause pollution. If motors are in top-notch condition, less pollution occurs. If you live near wooded areas, stress the importance of avoiding forest fires and campaign for safety measures. If your community allows domestic burning of leaves or trash, encourage passage of ordinances forbidding these actions and seeking municipal collection and proper disposal. Encourage homeowners to keep furnaces clean and working efficiently. Watch stacks of incinerators and report dark smoke, indicating inefficient firing. Write to the U.S. Public Health Service, Washington, D.C. 20201 for free literature and recommendtions for your campaign.

10. Work for better laws for your community, state and country by examining pending bills and talking with organizations and individuals who are actively promoting specific legislation for ecological improvement. Check proposals against known facts and back proposals you believe sound. Assist by signing and circulating petitions, attending public meetings and hearings, writing to elected officials. If you are eighteen or older, your vote counts! If you are younger, you can still influence many voters— too few people even try. Letters to Washington go to:

(your U.S. Senator)—Senate Office Building, Washington, D.C. 20510

(your U.S. Representative)—House Office Building, Washington, D.C. 20515

(your President)—The White House, Washington, D.C. 20006.

For more information on effective political action, write for information to the League of Women Voters, 1730 M Street, N.W., Washington, D.C. 20036; The National Association of Counties, 1001 Connecticut Ave., N.W., Washington, D.C. 20036 (ask particularly for their pamphlets on community action on air and water pollution); read Saul Alinsky's book, *RULES FOR RADICALS,* New York: Random House, 1971.

11. If your community borders a lake or river or seashore, you can campaign to protect or improve these waters. Check and publicize the sources of pollution. Have a "work day" to clean a portion of the area, being sure to get as much publicity as possible, and to select a small enough area so that your group can really make a very noticeable difference in its appearance. If trash is being dumped into the water at any point, alert the community and try to have the area posted. An excellent booklet "Clean Water: It's Up to You" is available from the Izaak Walton League of America, 1326 Waukegan Rd., Glenview, Ill. 60025. Send for copies which give a great deal of

sound information, specific actions and procedures, and further sources of assistance to your campaign. If you live near a swamp or other "wetlands," encourage their protection and campaign against draining or filling. Preserving wetlands helps maintain the local water table, aids flood control and provides a place for wildlife and rare plants. Write for "Swamp, Marsh or Bog, Nature's Rain Barrels," the Garden Club of America (see "Suggested Resources: Organizations").

Encourage thrifty use of water, perhaps using the slogan, "the well is running dry." Each of us uses about 100 gallons of water every day. Much of this is beyond our control, being used by industry to provide us with things we wish to purchase, but an enormous amount of water is wasted in domestic use, with half-filled dishwasher and clothes-washer loads, faucets left running unnecessarily, and twenty minute showers when four minute ones would do the job. Ask students who have lived on farms or vacation homes with wells to give suggestions for domestic water conservation. Again, such practices have the added benefit of making the public ecology-minded.

12. Noise abatement campaign. Many communities have laws on the books which would greatly reduce unwanted and sometimes dangerous noise, but these laws are often ignored or need updating. With increasing population and use of machinery, environmental noise at work, at home, and abroad in the community is a growing menace, causing tension, stress and, in some cases, actual hearing loss. Encourage your school or public health services to offer free audiograms to a sizable cross-section of a particular population (a class, school, industry, company, community). If significant hearing losses are found, ask for an investigation to determine whether there is a likelihood that this is due to environmental noise. Check local sources of noise and applicable legislation in the community to see if compliance with the law is being obtained. New laws direct industry to curtail excessive exposure to noise by employees, but these laws will not apply in all circumstances.

Outside of industry, in the community and private homes, noise levels are seldom such as to induce hearing loss, but can cause considerable irritation and frustration and sometimes cause accidents, particularly when sudden or intermittent. Unnecessary use of sirens and car horns should be curtailed. There is reason to believe that the ordinary noise present in the community does increase the rapidity of hearing loss due to aging.

Repeated exposure for six or more hours a day to a continuous sound exceeding 80—85 decibels can develop significant permanent loss of hearing for speech after a period of years. Individuals vary in their capacity to sustain such assaults on their hearing without damage, and some frequencies are more damaging than others.

Develop a "Sound-level Chart" for your community, including various common sources of noise, pinpointing their location, and ask your local newspaper to publish it, or prepare handbills and distribute them, asking for suggestions on abatement. Base your chart on those published in one or more of the following books: *HANDBOOK OF NOISE MEASUREMENT*, 5th ed., West Concord, Mass., General Radio Company, 1963; Philip Handler, *BIOLOGY AND THE FUTURE OF MAN*, New York: Oxford University Press, 1970, p. 877; Amos Turk, Jonathan Turk, and Janet T. Wittes, *ECOLOGY, POLLUTION, ENVIRONMENT*, Philadelphia, Pa.: W. B. Saunders, 1972, ch. 10.

13. Plan a teach-in for your school on world population control, food production, and famine. Try to get knowledgeable speakers to present a number of different points of view. For a brief overview of the problem send for a free booklet by David E. Bell, "Can World Famine Be Prevented?", available from the Ford Foundation, Office of Reports, 320 East 43rd St., New York, N.Y. 10017.

SUGGESTED RESOURCES:

This is a very big subject indeed, and we find it hard to select from among the many sources available. However, since there is much on the market which is poor, misleading, faddish and simply sensationalistic, we have prepared the following list of various kinds of materials which we believe to be sound and helpful. Many of the publications and organizations listed can provide extensive specialized bibliographies of films, books and pamphlets.

ORGANIZATIONS:

The following publish literature and provide assistance to groups and individuals seeking to learn more about the problems and implement solutions. Some also supply films and speakers. If you are interested in forming local support groups or doing something about a specific local problem, write to them. Some have local offices—check your telephone directory. Many colleges and communities have "ecology centers," and you may have such a helpful resource near you.

Air Pollution Control Association, 4400 Fifth Ave., Pittsburgh, Pa. 15213.

American Conservation Association, 30 Rockefeller Plaza, New York 10020.

American Shore and Beach Preservation Association, Box 1246, Rockville, Md. 20850.

The Conservation Foundation, Audio-Visual Center, 30 E. 40th St., New York 10016. Main Office: 1250 Connecticut Ave., Washington, D.C. 20036.

Environmental Protection Agency, Waterside Mall, 4th and M Sts., Washington, D.C. 20460. There are also Regional Offices—check your telephone directory.

The Garden Club of America, Conservation Committee, 598 Madison Ave., New York, N.Y. 10022. (Ask for "Our Natural Resources Educational Packet")

Izaak Walton League of America, 1326 Waukegan Rd., Glenview, Ill. 60025.

The Natural Area Council, 145 E. 52nd St., New York, N.Y. 10022.

Natural Science for Youth Foundation, 763 Silvermine Rd., New Canaan, Conn. 06840.

The Nature Conservancy, 1522 K. St., N.W., Washington, D.C. 20005.

The National Audubon Society, 1130 Fifth Ave., New York, N.Y. 10028.

National Parks Assoc., 1701 18th St. N.W., Washington, D.C. 20009.

National Wildlife Federation, 1412 Sixteenth St. N.W., Washington, D.C. 20036. A limited amount of material is available without charge to teachers, including helpful literature on "endangered species."

Sierra Club, 1050 Mills Tower, San Francisco, Calif. 94104.

U.S. Department of Agriculture: Soil Conservation Service, Washington, D.C. 20250; Motion Picture Service, Office of Information, Washington, D.C. 20250. Ask for a catalog, "Forest Service Films," and for a complete catalog of all films. Many films dealing with ecology, conservation, pollution, use of natural resources, careers in conservation.

Wildlife Preserves, Inc., P.O. Box 55, 24 County Rd., Tenafly, N.J. 07670.

Wilderness Society, 729 Fifteenth St. N.W., Washington, D.C. 20005.

BOOKS:

Carroll, James, *ELEMENTS OF HOPE*, New York: Paulist Press, 1971. Not a book of "information," but a beautiful collection of large colored illustrations and prayerful poetic writing on man's relation to his environment. Individual sections may be used with many topics.

Carson, Rachel, *SILENT SPRING*, Boston, Mass.: Houghton Mifflin, 1952. (Carson writes well, and her book is a classic in the field. Focus is on pesticides.) See also Whitten's book listed below.

Davies, J. Clarence, III, *THE POLITICS OF POLLUTION*, New York: Pegasus, 1970. (Background on attempts at pollution control; information on political forces at work; what pollution control involves in setting standards, enacting legislation and enforcing laws; allocating funds; from viewpoint of a political scientist.)

Hamilton, Michael P., (ed.), *THIS LITTLE PLANET,* New York: Scribner's, 1970. (Three theologians and three scientists on ecology, conservation and a constructive approach to man's rule over the earth.)

Handler, Philip, (ed.), *BIOLOGY AND THE FUTURE OF MAN,* New York: Oxford University, 1965, ecology—431ff, 731ff; 819-830—pesticides; environmental health—831ff; noise—876ff; food—585-626; population—897-909. (See note on this book in Happiness: Futuring.)

NATURALIST ENGAGEMENT CALENDAR, Massachusetts Audubon Society, Lincoln, Mass., 01773. (An "ecology workbook" for students working with younger children in northern half of country. Two versions: (1) undated—start year when you wish; (2) dated for current year. $2.50 plus 25¢ postage.)

NEW YORK TIMES ENCYCLOPEDIC ALMANAC (or *FAMILY ALMANAC* '72), Morris Harth (ed.), New York: New York Times, 1971, population—482; interest in conservation—436; air pollution in U.S. cities—310.

Smith, Guy-Harold *CONSERVATION OF NATURAL RESOURCES,* 4th ed., New York: Wiley, 1971. (For the serious conservationist, this latest edition of well-known resource offers the work of 21 specialists.)

Turk, Amos, Jonathan Turk, Janet T. Wittes, *ECOLOGY, POLLUTION, ENVIRONMENT,* Philadelphia, Pa.: W.B. Saunders, 1972. (Compact and helpful new ancillary text designed for early college years, but high school students have sufficient background to understand clear, well presented material.)

Whitten, Jamie L., *THAT WE MAY LIVE,* New York: Van Nostrand, 1966. (Those who read Carson's *SILENT SPRING* should read this "other side of the story"—proper use of pesticides to increase agriculture yield; soil and water included in survey of agriculture and food for the world.)

(See also: Brainerd's book suggested in "Happiness: Back to Nature".)

PAMPHLETS:

American Education Publications. Two booklets, sound, current and useful, although not very attractive in their newsprint format. 48 pages each, designed for grades 7—12, "Our Polluted World, The Conservation Story" 40¢/copy. American Education Publications, Education Center, Columbus, Ohio 43216.

Associated Petroleum Industries of Pennsyl-vania, "Conserving Our Waters and Clearing the Air," a 16 p. student booklet is accompanied by 28 p. "Teacher's Guide" and 28 p. "Research Materials" and a poster. Free. Also, ask for catalog of free materials, "Teacher's Resource Reference." Associated Petroleum Industries of Pennsylvania, P.O. Box 925, Harrisburg, Pa. 17108.

Conservation Foundation, "Citizen Action for Clean Water," Free. Conservation Foundation, 1250 Connecticut Ave., Washington, D.C. 20036.

League of Women Voters, "Getting Something Done. Political Effectiveness and Conference Techniques," 15¢, League of Women Voters of New York State, 131 E. 23rd St., New York, N.Y. 10010.

Lever Brothers. "Detergents and the Environment," although naturally presented from biased viewpoint, is factually correct and useful. Free. Lever Brothers Co., 390 Park Ave., New York, N.Y. 10022.

National Wildlife Federation. "National EQ Index: America Is In Trouble." Reprint from Oct.-Nov. 1970 *NATIONAL WILDLIFE MAGAZINE.* Data on "Environmental Quality" diagrammed with colored illustrations in series of 2-page spreads on: air, water, wildlife, timber, soil, minerals, living space and population, with final page, "What you can do about it." As is often the case, some suggestions are based on misunderstandings of findings, but most are sound. Students copies available at 15¢/copy for 10—29. One copy available free to teachers. National Wildlife Federation, Educational Servicing, 1412 Sixteenth St. N.W., Washington D.C. 20036.

The following pamphlets are available from Public Affairs Pamphlets, 381 Park Ave. South, New York, N.Y. 10016, for 25¢ each, or 21¢ each in quantities from 10 to 99 copies. They are brief and well written, and good for discussion.

Gladwin Hill, "Our Troubled Waters: The Fight Against Water Pollution," 1971, #462.

Edward Edelson, "The Battle for Clean Air," 1970, #403A.

Theodore Berland, "Noise—The Third Pollution," 1970, #449.

Raymond F. Dasmann, "An Environment Fit for People," 1968, #421.

AUDIOVISUALS:

Many of the organizations, books and pamphlets listed above give lists of films and sources. Following are a few good films which might be missed and a record and commentary.)

Alcoa. *"Land of the Sea,"* 16 mm., 55 minutes, color and sound. Made with assistance of U.S. Navy. Documentary on resources of sea will interest students in problems of protecting this new and vast natural resource before it, too, is plundered and destroyed. Free loan. Motion Picture Section, Alumi-

190 num Company of America, 1246 Alcoa Bldg., Pittsburgh, Pa. 15219.

Mass Media Ministries, *"The Hellstrom Chronicle,"* produced and directed by W. Green for David Wolper Productions. Distributed by Cinema V. 98 minutes, color. Insects are potential threat to man in case of upset to nature's balance. Beautiful, fascinating, somewhat frightening. For further information, Mass Media Ministries, 2116 N. Charles St., Baltimore, Md. 21218 or 1714 Stockton St., San Francisco, Calif. 94133.

Modern Talking Picture Service, 2323 New Hyde Park Rd., New Hyde Park, L.I., N.Y. 11040 has about 2000 titles of loan free films. Among their better films dealing with these topics are:

"The American Trail." Natchez Trace, seen through the eyes of a little boy. Voted world's most outstanding travel film at 1970 Lisbon Film Festival. Sponsored by Humble Oil and Refining Company.

"The Gifts," unusually fine film on sewage disposal. Sponsored by Federal Water Quality Office.

"To Walk the Divide." Four youths backpacking across topmost Colorado. Conveys notion that there was little ecological awareness a hundred years ago, but maybe things will be better now. Sponsored by Humble Oil and Refining Company.

"Wild Rivers." Cooperative undertaking of Humble Oil and U.S. Department of the Interior. Conservation film which has won four major awards.

A song by Malvina Reynolds has been popularized by Joan Baez—"What Have They Done to the Rain?" Shroder Music Company. See also Robert Heyer *et al.*, *DISCOVERY IN SONG*, rev. ed., New York: Paulist Press, 1969, p. 115.

ECOLOGY AND YOUR FUTURE HOME

PURPOSE:

To think about our own attitudes toward everyday problems of ecology, about our future plans, and to experience our own creativity.

COMMENT:

Is it possible in the U.S. to build and live in a home which assists, rather than harms, the ecology? Can it be done in the city? . . . in the country? What factors should be considered? Is it more possible in other countries? Bronson P. Clark, executive secretary of the American Friends Service Committee, writing about his recent trip to the People's Republic of China, says their agriculture shows "an almost inherent knowledge of the proper ecological balance between man and nature," and their landscape "is pleasing to the eye (and) would warm the heart of any ecologist."

What factors make possible this situation? Clark suggests one factor is the frugality of the Chinese. In addition, the idea of service to the people is taught at all educational levels, and their orientation is away from economic and personal incentive. He says, "The puritanical and collectivist society of China has produced a high degree of public morality, along with public cleanliness and order.

There are other contributing elements. Clark points out that their technology is far behind that of the United States and that 80 percent of China's largely rural population are involved in agriculture. ("If Ever the Twain Shall Meet," *SATURDAY REVIEW*, Dec. 18, 1971, pp. 14ff). Per capita income in the United States is $3,910 a year. It is easier to be frugal in a country where the annual per capita income is $125, as in China. China is still largely an agricultural economy, whereas only 6 percent of the U.S. GNP derives from agriculture, forestry and fisheries, combined. More than 95 percent of our labor force is engaged in nonagricultural industries and yet, with the exception of slight downward shifts in oats, beans, peaches and hogs, production of all leading United States farm food crops and livestock has increased since the early 1960's, and the federal government still pays large amounts of money to farmers for not raising certain crops. (*NEW YORK TIMES ENCYCLOPEDIC ALMANAC,* 1972, Morris Harth (ed.), New York: New York Times, 1971, pp. 573, 677, 807.) Are ecological practices tied to economics? . . . to industrialization? . . . to ideology?

GROUP SIZE:

6—20

TIME SUGGESTED:

One 20-minute session, followed by one 60-minute session; two or more 60-minute sessions.

GENERAL DIRECTIONS:

This exercise may be carried on entirely during class sessions, or some parts of it may be done outside of class. Following a brief discussion, students select a home site and design a home they would like to build for themselves which takes ecology into account. This is followed by more extensive discussion. Student designs may be simple or complex, very brief or more complete, but an elaborate architectural exercise is not intended here, but more a sort of "day-dreaming with a pencil." The exercise may be used before or after other exercises on ecology, conservation and pollution.

MATERIALS REQUIRED:

None

PROCEDURE:

1. A short discussion is held concerning the role of domestic dwellings in relation to pollution problems and ecology. Some tentative data are elicited on such matters as waste disposal, noise levels, temperature control, avoidance of pollution by heating systems, consideration of natural resources, and site comparisons among city, suburbs, small town and rural areas. Step No. 2 may follow immediately, or students told to think about the next phase, which will be done in class at the next session.

2. Each student is asked to decide on the kind of area in which he would like to live, and then to design a house he would like to live in. The design may include rough sketches of all or part of the house and surroundings. There should be brief descriptions or suggestions of features included to lessen pollution, conserve resources, and promote sound ecology. Any materials and methods of construction *now available* may be used.

3. In subgroups, or a plenary in a small class, each student explains his plan. Discussion of each plan follows immediately, with a general discussion at the end. If desired, additional input may be provided by previous student research, or by written materials or a talk by the instructor including such data and questions as in "Comment" above.

SUGGESTED RESOURCES:

See materials listed in "Life: Ecology, Conservation and Pollution," and "Urban Design."

URBAN DESIGN: WALK-AROUND

PURPOSE:

To discover what we like and don't like about physical conditions in our community, and how some improvements might be made.

COMMENT:

This exercise, with the three following, form a series, but each could be used by itself. Together with the "Variations" there is enough material for a considerable number of sessions.

The focus is on urban and suburban, rather than rural areas. In our first census in 1790, 95 percent of the population of the United States lived in rural areas. By 1920 we had crossed the line, and 49 percent lived in rural areas. If the current trend continues, by the 1980's only 25 percent will live in the country, while 25 percent will live in the cities and 50 percent in the suburbs. Students in small towns in rural sections can profit from these exercises, but the problems will have less immediacy for them.

The first exercise, "Walk-around," gives a rough, rather simple overview of spot-problems and their possible solutions. Little background is required. The "Variation" offers an experience in registering sensory input both for enjoyment and to further students' development of values as a possible preliminary to the investigation of physical conditions in the community.

"Village Plan" offers students an opportunity to think in terms of their "ideal." It is more intensive, involves recognition of communication problems and the need for overall *vs.* spot planning.

"Study Your Community" comes back to the real-life situation, and proposes an in-depth study of the students' actual community, its needs, and the possibilities and forces for change.

"Get the Facts" attempts to combine "ideal" and "real." If this exercise is done in isolation from the above, a preliminary step would be necessary. Using a modification of their plan from the second exercise, students investigate some of the economics of operating a community built according to their

desires. Kevin Lynch says, "For perhaps the first time in history we have the means of producing an enjoyable environment for everyone. It need not be saved for vacations but can be achieved in the world into which we wake every day." ("The City as Environment," *CITIES*, New York: Alfred A. Knopf, 1965, p. 200. This book contains articles published in the September, 1965 issue of *SCIENTIFIC AMERICAN*.)

GROUP SIZE:

10—20

TIME SUGGESTED:

An initial 20—40 minute session, two 60-minute sessions, one or two field trips.

GENERAL DIRECTIONS:

After the preliminary discussion, students take a field trip, a "walk-around," in their own town or city. Students look for "good" and "bad" physical environments. This is followed by team planning of improvements, and by another field trip and/or literature search. A final discussion explores plans developed by teams.

MATERIALS REQUIRED:

Each team will need—
2—3 large sheets of paper or poster board
1 black and 1 red felt-tip marker
1 or more large maps of the community to be investigated

PROCEDURE:

1. In a 20-40 minute session class is subgrouped in small groups of 3—5. These teams will work together for all sessions and field trips. Field trips are planned. These may be scheduled for the entire class at the same time, or teams may work independently. Exercise is explained and deadlines set. At least two quite different sections of the city should be included. Possibility of taking photographs is discussed.

2. Teams are instructed to investigate or make a survey of selected area, perhaps 1-4 blocks or squares. They are to look for and list "good" and "bad" physical conditions, looking for such things as

beauty/ugliness, noise/quiet, convenience/inconvenience, safety/danger, cleanliness/dirt. If possible, they should take photographs, and finished photos would be brought to next class session.

3. In class session, teams draw rough sketch-map on their large sheet or poster of the area as it is now, using black felt-tip marker. Photos should be mounted on another poster board, number-keyed to sketch-map, with descriptive captions. Teams plan how area could be physically improved, if possible including the same facilities or kinds of land-use, e.g., dwellings, stores, factories, gas stations, bars, etc. They may make any other changes they wish, including transportation changes, e.g., close streets or change their location within area, reroute public transportation. They need not consider cost, but should try to remember all needs of area, such as delivery of heavy goods to stores or plants, access for fire-fighting equipment, safety of pedestrians, gradients required for ramps or stairways, show-windows for merchants. Changes are sketched in on original sketch-map using red felt-tip. Tell students they will have an opportunity at a later class session to show their plans to other teams.

4. Students may do some research to get other ideas on possible improvements. If possible, students should be given opportunity to decide on area for second field trip, chosen on grounds of good use of land area, relationships to transportation facilities. Interviews or discussions with community people may be included in research.

5. On second field trip students look for better ways of handling some problems discovered on their original walk-around. If possible, another set of photographs should be taken demonstrating management of specific problems, sites, operations, etc. Students develop ideas they may wish to incorporate in their improvements of original sketch-map.

6. Second full class session: first 10 minutes allowed for teams to make last minute changes on their "maps". Rest of session is devoted to plenary for sharing of plans and general discussion. Teams should explain how their new plan improves the physical environment for those who use the area. Students should look for imaginative and creative solutions to problems.

NOTE: If the other exercises in this series are not used, some of the "Suggested Resources" should be made available in connection with this exercise.

VARIATIONS:

This walk-around is designed for sensory input. Students may be given the following list of suggestions in advance, and should make a written and photographic record, if possible. The written record may be made on a ruled sheet with headings such as the following: "Keep. . . . Get Rid of . . . Change"; "This I like . . . This I don't like"; or a more discursive record may be made by completing sentences such as: "I would like to spend more time here because. . . . I never want to come here again until this place is changed because . . . ; or "What surprised me the most was . . .". If photos are taken a brief record of WHY each snapshot was made is important . . . it is easy to forget some important details.

WHAT DO YOUR SENSES TELL YOU?

What do you see?
    what lines—shapes—vistas—textures—surfaces—planes—size contrasts and relationships—colors—materials—what moves and what is still—what flashes, flickers, shines, gleams, glows, glares—what waves, floats, drifts, soars—can you see beyond, over, through, behind, around, up, down . . .

What do you hear?
    what soft and loud sounds—what sharp and sudden sounds—what mumbles, murmurs, drones, hums—what bangs, clatters, rattles, creaks—what rhythms do you hear—what harmonies and discords —do you hear birds, animals, people, machines, rustling paper, banging cans, slamming doors, squeaking brakes, shrieking sirens—things far away, or only close by . . .

What do you smell?
    good things or bad things—interesting things or dull things—things to eat, drink—oil, gasoline, burning waste, hot machinery—sunshine, grass, flowers, salt water, seaweed, dampness—people . . .

What do you taste?
    dust, salt air, smoke, chemicals, food . . .

What do you feel?
    wind, rain, warm sun, cold snow—reflected heat from old bricks—cold drafts from fresh concrete —smooth pavement under your feet, rough cobblestones, uneven dirt, soft grass, dry slipping sand—pushing or jostling crowds—smooth wood railings, rough wood fences, cold metal railings, turnstiles, glass doors, metal door handles—a sense of wide space, close space, high space—can you run freely, quickly, must you step carefully, slowly—can you walk up and down, or only on a level—can you sit on a bench, lie on the ground, ride on an escalator, climb a tree, walk on a wall, lean on a fence—can

you pat a dog, smooth a cat, feed a duck or squirrel by hand. . . .

SUGGESTED RESOURCES:

(See also following exercises)

Bernard Rudofsky, *STREETS FOR PEOPLE: A PRIMER FOR AMERICANS,* N.Y.: Doubleday, 1969. (Students will enjoy just looking at the pictures in this delightful book, even if they do not read its enjoyable text.)

URBAN DESIGN: VILLAGE PLAN

PURPOSE:

To discover what we value and disvalue in town and city life; to plan cooperatively a town to meet our needs.

COMMENT:

What makes a town or community a good place in which to live, work, play? If you could build a real town, what would you have in it? Where would you put the houses, schools, factories, offices, jails, hospitals, libraries, police stations, the post office, telephone company, sewage plant, trash incinerator, city government offices, bakers, milk processing plants, etc.? Would you have a hill for skiing, a bridle path, a pond for ice skating, playgrounds, a football stadium?

"Roads, together with the main transit lines, power lines and drains, form the essential infrastructure of the community . . . Roads . . . are physically big, and have the same power as any big topographical feature, such as a hill or a river, to create geographical, and, in consequence social, divisions" (Chermayeff and Tzonis, *ORDINARINESS AND LIGHT*). Telecommunications increase in importance, but people and their products still must move along roads, and what McLuhan calls the "paper routes" of communication still transport information along these public ways. McLuhan says, "The alteration of social groupings, and the formation of new communities, occur with the increased speed of information movement by means of paper messages and road transport" (*UNDERSTANDING MEDIA: THE EXTENSIONS OF MAN*).

In your new town, how would you get to the movies, the park, the drug store? How would children get to school and men and women to work, to the doctor's office, the restaurants? How would the firemen get to your house, and the food delivery trucks to the supermarkets or grocery stores, and the raw materials to your factories, and the fuel to your power plants? What kind of public transportation would you have, where would the roads be, would you want a river, how would you use it, will you want an airport?

Can you make "your town" more attractive, more human, more comfortable, safer and cleaner than the one you live in now? Professor Jacqueline Tyrwhitt, speaking at the Yale Seminars in 1966, said, "The first new towns in Britain were planned according to what people thought everybody wanted. Two great things remained quite naturally out of their consideration: one was the enormous influence of television, the other was the very rapid advent of the second car in almost every middle class family" (Chermayeff and Tzonis, *SHAPE OF COMMUNITY: REALIZATION OF HUMAN POTENTIAL*). What are you forgetting?

GROUP SIZE:

20—24

TIME SUGGESTED:

60 minutes, or a series of 30—45 minute sessions.

GENERAL DIRECTIONS:

Each team of four works with a large sheet of paper, divided into four equal quadrants, negotiating with one another to plan a town—the location of its buildings and services and its transportation. The "rules" or "limitations" may be provided in light of the group's previous history, membership, etc. You might wish to suggest that there are to be approximately 5000 families in each of the four squares which together are to form an isolated community; that they are to share services wherever possible; that when their plan is completed, they must have all needed services; that each person is free to plan his quadrant as he pleases, provided his teammates agree. No costs need be stated when reporting, but students should be told to "keep costs and taxation in mind." In part, this is an exercise in negotiation and consensus, as disagreements will arise over location of services, and at quadrant borders over location of roads, etc. For this reason, observers may be desirable for feedback to the class following the exercise.

MATERIALS REQUIRED:

One large sheet of paper divided equally into four quadrants, for each team; additional sheets of paper should be available for "corrections."

If desired, scratch paper may be used in the initial planning, but it is better not to delay too long before getting information on the big sheet.

PROCEDURE:

1. The class is subgrouped in quartets, the materials distributed and the exercise explained. Some materials may be distributed or read to the students, such as excerpts from "Comment" above. Students are told that each foursome is to design a "new town," sketching the map and plan and writing on their large sheet of paper. The finished product is to be a cooperative venture, though each individual is responsible for, and "owns," the planning of his quadrant. The same number of people are to live in each quadrant, e.g., 5000 families. Try not to duplicate services unnecessarily. Try to remember the possible costs to citizens through taxation for public services. You will need to cooperate on your roads, to avoid "dead-ends," and be sure necessary access is provided to needed services. You may talk together at any time within your foursome, but you may not visit other teams of town-planners. Later in the session, or at another session, all plans will be exhibited and explained to the rest of the class.

2. It will probably take the entire session for this stage of the exercise. The instructor should be available to answer questions, but should decide in advance what kinds of questions he wishes to answer, and which he will ask each foursome to decide among themselves. At the next session all plans will be posted, and each group can explain its plan. If observers have been used, allow 10—15 minutes at the end of the session, prior to the plenary session for discussion of plans, for observers to report to groups and some discussion within each foursome of the way their group operated.

3. In a plenary session plans are explained and discussed, and the advantages and disadvantages and feasibility of each plan investigated. There may be considerable variety, some communities may have been planned as far more "independent" than others, and some may be basically "suburbs," depending for many services on some other community. Part of the discussion should focus on values. You may introduce this by asking, "Where would you rather live? . . . in a city? . . . a suburb? . . . a small town? . . . the country? Why?" Develop discussion on what the students value in environmental conditions, the advantages and disadvantages of the life styles possible in these places. What do some students emphasize or give more weight to? Why? Have they ever made any attempt or initiated any steps to help them realize these things? . . . why or why not? What are the

essential ingredients for the desired way of life? Do their plans reflect these desires?

An investigation of the possibilities for employment in the towns planned may also involve a discussion of values. Some of the following questions may start such a discussion:

—Do they want a "single-industry town? . . . What would this mean for the people in the town? . . . Do they want a number of small factories, plants, etc.? . . . How many people will be employed by government—town, county, state, federal?

—How do their plans for employment possibilities in their "new town" compare with employment in the community in which they now live? . . . If a segment of similar population size were considered, would their "new town" offer a larger or smaller number of different occupations? . . . How would percentages compare in some of the following?

—What percentage do they think are employed in industry? . . . retail trade? . . . construction? . . . transportation? . . finance? . . . restaurants? . . . food manufacture, such as bakeries, canneries? . . . entertainment? . . . education? . . . professions such as social workers, lawyers, medicine?

—What percentage work in city services? (street repairmen, tax officials, water treatment, inspectors, police, etc.) . . . What percentage work for the state or federal government?

VARIATIONS:

1. The rules and limitations of the above exercise may be varied considerably. As described above, the exercise is made fairly simple. It is obviously left vague, e.g., no acreage is given, no income level, no clue as to the resources of this "town," what part of the country is being considered. Some of these elements may be added, but many students will be overwhelmed by too many specifics.

2. Some fact sheets may be given the students, such as lists of factors or elements they might want to consider including. Using statistics from your own community, a set of cards may be prepared, shuffled and dealt at random within each group. Cards may assign responsibilities for specific services, for instance, such as a hospital to serve the entire town, the sewage plant, etc.

3. You may wish to arrange for "negotiations" with the instructor on certain details, e.g., a group might ask if they could move all 5000 people from one quadrant into another, freeing that quadrant for some specific purpose, such as a large recreation and/or industrial area. Or a team might ask if

they could reduce their total population, believing that a "good community" is not this large, or they might ask if they are to plan for an increasing population. If this is to be done, the instructor should advise the planners of this general possibility, and decide what kinds of requests he will grant, and why.

4. Teams may be made competitive within themselves, or cooperative within themselves and competitive with other teams. Internal competition is increased by giving each team member a role, e.g., 1. builder, or head of building trades; 2. mayor, or head of civic-minded group (representative homeowners, women, schools, recreation, shopping as major interests); 3. head of a powerful labor union, interested in industry, jobs, etc.; banker, wants to attract business into town; or industrialist. If desired, further details of the roles may be given, such as some specific goals. Competition among teams may be introduced by giving "prizes" for the "best product," using a panel of judges.

5. If stress on city services is desired as the main thrust of exercise, a preliminary discussion may center on the student's use of services during the previous 6—12 hours. Student's may be asked to jot down which of these services they have used today, and then center discussion on the good and bad features of the service—water, sewage, trash, streets (including street cleaning and maintenance, and traffic police, if used), school, possibly publicly owned transit system or school bus, library or museum, air (if "clean air commission"), licensing of food-handlers (if restaurant or school cafeteria was used or food brought to school), possibly park maintenance, possibly passed sculpture erected by the city, or walked along the street where over-the-street advertising signs are controlled by the city, etc.

SUGGESTED RESOURCES:

(See also next exercise)

Fairbrother, Nan, NEW LIVES, NEW LANDSCAPES: PLANNING FOR THE 21ST CENTURY, New York: Alfred A. Knopf, 1970.

Institute for Social Research, PLANNED RESIDENTIAL ENVIRONMENTS, Ann Arbor, Mich.: University of Michigan. (Report on the planned communities including Columbia, Md. and Reston, Va. Write Publications Division, Inst. for Social Research, University of Michigan, 426 Thompson St., Ann Arbor, Mich. 48106. Hardbound, $7.00, paperback, $5.00, 264 pages.)

Smithson, Alison and Peter, ORDINARINESS AND LIGHT: URBAN THEORIES 1952-1960, AND THEIR APPLICATION IN A BUILDING PROJECT 1963-1970, Cambridge,

Mass.: M.I.T. Press, 1970, p. 145.

McLuhan, Marshall, *UNDERSTANDING MEDIA: THE EXTENSIONS OF MAN*, New York: McGraw Hill, 1964, p. 90.

Chermayeff, Serge, and Alexander Tzonis, *SHAPE OF COMMUNITY: REALIZATION OF HUMAN POTENTIAL*, Baltimore, Md.: Penguin, 1971, p. 85-86.

Town Council of the Burgh of East Kilbride, 22 Markethill Rd., East Kilbride, Scotland. Write for booklets and information on this, the first "new town," built near Glasgow after the Second World War.

FILM:

"Rise of New Towns: Is Planning the Answer?", 16 mm., 60 minutes, black and white, produced by NET, 1966. Available from Mass Media Ministries.

"Automania 2000", 16 mm., 10 minutes, color. Halas and Batchelor Cartoon Films, Ltd., London, 1961. Mass Media Ministries. Uses proliferation of the automobile as an example of life in our "consumer society," giving a satirical view of planning for the product, rather than the person.

URBAN DESIGN: STUDY YOUR COMMUNITY

PURPOSE:

To discover the physical needs of your community, the forces available to meet them, and identify crucial improvements needed.

COMMENT:

No community is perfect. Some communities, however, meet the needs of the people more satisfactorily than others. How does your community measure up in such areas as pollution control, public health or health services delivery, safety control, or health education? What agencies and individuals are responsible for meeting physical needs? Are there any gaps? Are services conveniently located? . . . adequately staffed? . . . which services are provided by the public sector? . . . the private sector? . . . what part is played by volunteers? . . . are there neighborhood associations or civic associations addressing themselves to these problems? . . . how do local political leaders stand on these questions? . . . where should pressure be brought to bear to solve some of these problems? . . . are religious bodies in the community seeking to improve such services?

GROUP SIZE:

10—20

TIME SUGGESTED:

This activity could be extended over a full semester, or could be completed superficially in 4—6 weeks of sessions once or twice a week. Even superficial study will have benefit. Much of the work is done through independent research or study and field trips, although class discussions following data-gathering are important, and a final discussion must precede making recommendations or instigating or initiating programs.

GENERAL DIRECTIONS:

The basic plan: (1) study the physical needs of the members of your community; (2) count the forces within the city that are available, and evaluate the quality of services; (3) try to initiate changes where needed. Students will need assistance in discovering the sources of data, in compiling data in usable form for class discussion, and in planning for change. Suggestions are given below and also in "Suggested Resources." The focus of this study is "physical needs," but the project may be expanded to include all needs if desired. The skeleton plan of necessity includes some data relevant to all needs, e.g., the kind of government, the important people. If a limited amount of time is available, or you believe the topic of limited interest, a few segments of the total problem may be investigated, e.g., recreation and sports facilities, sewage and solid waste disposal, health education, transportation.

MATERIALS REQUIRED:

If possible, a film or collection of slides of your own community, showing some of the good as well as some of the bad things related to serving the people's physical needs. If you live in a large city you may wish to select your "neighborhood" as this is understood by your students.

Consult your school or local librarian and ask to have some materials put on reserve for your class during the time your students will be doing their initial data-gathering. Wherever possible obtain for class use whatever give-away materials are available from local government and other agencies.

A good detailed street map (base map) of your community.

PROCEDURES:

1. Show the film or slide collection at the first session.

2. Discuss briefly with the class what they have just seen. Outline the projected plan of investigation, including its purposes and the possible improvements or kinds of improvements which might result. If you plan a limited survey, offer the students a list of choices and let them decide on the issues in which they are most interested.

3. Subgroup the class to divide the work on specific issues, problems, or elements of the survey.

4. Search out information: Explain to students the possibilities:

A. The newspaper

(1) For two weeks read the city paper from cover to cover. This study of the local newspaper will give you the general "feel" of the city.

(2) If there is a neighborhood paper, this also will be helpful.

(3) In general, look for such things as the following:

    (a) What kind of government exists?
    (b) Who are the important people?
    (c) What specific ideas and developments are going on?
    (d) What organizations, civic and religious, exist?

(4) Watch the editorials and letters to the editors. Look for patterns and relationships. The needs of the city are often expressed openly in these columns.

NOTE: Subgroups will soon learn to find their area of interest in the paper. The same category of material is usually found in the same place day after day, e.g., crime, religion news, meetings of civic organizations, etc.

(5) What to do when you spot an important article

    (a) Clip the article, date it, mark the page reference.
    (b) File it under your topic, and subtopics as these develop.
    (c) For every key name, use a file card (this could be an individual or an organization, e.g., NAACP. As information is gathered, add short notes to this card.
    (d) As information is recorded in some way, discard articles unless deemed important. As you work with the material, relationships will start coming into focus. If you are alert and if you are beginning to remember key names and facts, apparently unrelated bits of news will now start to provide further insights into the city.

B. The city or county yearbook. Almost every city has one. It is an annual publication. Check your Chamber of Commerce, the local newspaper. Such a publication includes every important name and organization within the city, as well as invaluable statistics for your greater comprehension.

C. The telephone book may also be helpful.

D. Local agencies. Whether governmental or privately supported these agencies have received funds to make the very inquiries that we are interested in. They are generally willing to share this information with educators interested in forming students to social responsibility. Some agencies may be: City Planning Commission; Urban Renewal Programs; Census Bureau; Community Chest Agencies; School District; League of Women Voters.

E. Films, slides, photos. In addition to original visual presentation, further such materials will aid understanding.

5. Pinpoint information on your detailed map. Mark up information as it is obtained. Such data as the following may be included:

A. Local public health centers, hospitals, nursing homes
B. Community organizations such as the YMCA, YMHA, Boy's Club
C. Location of high-crime areas
D. Location of high traffic accident areas
E. Population distribution
F. Schools and other educational institutions
G. Locations where improvements are taking place: street repairs, new sewers, new or renovated housing, new recreation center.

6. Determine centers of influence and power.

A. Who are the key people?
(1) Check the Board of Directors of Community Chest and Community Welfare Councils. These are usually volunteers who form a prestige group.
(2) Know the men who head up the organizations that are having an impact on the community.
(3) Watch the financial section. Who influences the economic life of the city?
B. What are the key groups?
(1) Determine the "centers of influence." Does industry hold control or is the control determined by "neighborhood associations"?
(2) Do not be fooled by many groups working toward one end, e.g., drug abuse or control. The same people may be in many organizations. This often gives the impression of a vast multitude when there are only the same few, or the number served may be very low.
(3) Don't be taken in by noisy groups, either. For the same reasons as above. We must go beyond the surface. Who is the controlling influence? What changes have been accomplished? Who was responsible?
(4) Study the make-up of the Chamber of Commerce and, if there is one, the Junior Chamber of Commerce. If industry predominates then probably there is a power-structure organization within the city. If business predominates (and industry does not get involved in the Chamber of Commerce) then probably there exist small "centers of influence." For this latter type of structure, a grassroots approach is essential for solving the problems of the city. For the former (the power-structure type) it is important to know the key men.

7. Decide on a few issues which you believe are important and possible to improve, and prepare recommendations to present to individuals and organizations with influence.

A. Describe the problem as you see it and possible corrections briefly and simply but as factually as possible. You may find, for example, that there are two recreation centers in one area of your community and none in another where there is need for one. If there is a vacant lot in the latter area, recommend that it be made a recreation center, giving statistics as to the approximate number of people it will serve. If a recreation center is not possible at this time, can it be made a play-lot? Can one or two "play-streets" be created? Is there an empty store or building that could be used?
B. Write a covering letter describing your group, its plan of study, and your willingness to present more data on request.
C. Mail copies of the letter and the proposed improvement to identified sources of power, including such people as heads of local industry or business, city government, civic organizations, neighborhood associations, planning groups, religious organizations, churches and synagogues, etc. On the basis of your study of the centers of influence, make the best possible use of your material and postage!
D. You may also wish to enlist the assistance of local merchants in publicizing the need, preparing posters or displays for use in their windows.

SUGGESTED RESOURCES:

FILMS, SLIDES, PHOTOS:
    Try the public library, the school district center, the Chamber of Commerce or local industry. Local churches and synagogues may have prepared such material and be glad to share it, or students themselves may have very useful material.

MAPS:
    Chamber of Commerce, City Clerk's office, some stationery stores. Local politicians may be able to give you a Ward Map. This is very detailed, even listing all the homes, businesses, etc., within a given

area.

If more current information is not available locally, information may be obtained from the 1960 U.S. Census of Population and Housing. The OEO Community Action Program Guide, Vol. 1, pp. 43-45 indicates possible additional sources of information.

The following outline for a "Statistical Profile" is adapted from that used by HUD in describing neighborhood conditions for the Model Cities Program, and can be adapted for your use.

STATISTICAL PROFILE

ITEM	TOTAL	ITEM	TOTAL
POPULATION		**HOUSING**	
Total White Negro Other (specify) Percent nonwhite Born in Puerto Rico Born in Mexico Born outside U.S.		Total housing units Number of substandard units Percent of substandard units Number of dilapidated units Percent of dilapidated units	
POPULATION DENSITY		**WELFARE**	
Total housing units Housing units per acre Number overcrowded Percent overcrowded		Persons under 21 Percent under 21 receiving AFDC payments Persons 65 or over Percent over 65 receiving old-age assistance	
FAMILY INCOME		**CRIME AND JUVENILE DELINQUENCY**	
Total number of families Number of families with incomes less than $3,000 Percent of total with incomes less than $3,000		Total number of persons under 18 Under 18, arrests per 1,000 Total number of persons 18 and over Over 18, arrests per 1,000	
UNEMPLOYMENT		**HEALTH**	
Males 14 and over in civilian labor force Number unemployed Percent unemployed Females 14 and over in civilian labor force Number unemployed Percent unemployed		Infant deaths per 1,000 live births Incidence of tuberculosis per 1,000 population	
EDUCATION			
Total number of persons enrolled in elementary and secondary schools Total number of persons 16 and 17 Percent of 16 and 17 year olds enrolled in school Total number of persons 25 and over Percent over 25 with less than 8 years education			

URBAN DESIGN: "GET THE FACTS"

PURPOSE:

To discover what it costs to run a town, how money is raised for this purpose, and to investigate our own values about these matters.

COMMENT:

The previous exercises in urban design obviously will be less than realistic without some consideration of approximate costs. This can be an extremely complicated subject, and one with which students can be expected to deal in only a limited fashion. However, facts can be obtained on the annual budget of their own town or city, and calculations made to give a rough estimate of how much it would cost to run their proposed "New Town" designed in "Village Plan." Some of these figures will relate also to proposed local improvements.

The question of where the money is to come from introduces the subject of taxation. The town in "Village Plan" was probably described as "isolated," which presumes that it is designed to be self-supporting in many respects, although it does not mean that no trade or traffic takes place between "New Town" and other towns and cities. Students probably have a limited amount of information on such things as average income, local welfare costs, expenditures of city government, or how much land is required for any given purpose such as dwellings, industrial plants of various kinds, schools, churches and synagogues, city services, or food warehousing. Land use percentage figures can probably be obtained for your community from the local government or the chamber of commerce. If students consider real estate taxes as one way of raising money for their New Town, they will need such figures as percentages of taxable *vs.* nontaxable land use in their community, for purposes of comparison.

GROUP SIZE:

Up to 24

TIME SUGGESTED:

Two or more 60 minute sessions; some time for possible field trips, interviews and/or individual research.

GENERAL DIRECTIONS:

Students are given suggestions as to the sources of information and asked to develop some figures estimating the cost of operating their "New Town." Comparisons will usually be made with costs in their own actual community. The final discussion is concerned with the sharing of information and consideration of values and priorities.

MATERIALS REQUIRED:

Input from previous exercises, particularly "Village Plan," bibliographies, general guidelines, pamphlets or "fact sheets" if available from the local community (see "Suggested Resources").

PROCEDURE:

1. Students are asked to work in their teams of four as grouped for the "Village Plan," and to arrive at a rough estimate of what it would cost to "operate" (not build) the "New Town" they designed. They are directed to sources of information. They may also be asked to find out how their own community raises the money to pay for its operation, and how their "budget pie" is sliced. Simple bar graphs comparing their own community and their New Town on some points will be useful. To help them get started, some specific questions may be suggested:

—What percentage of their own community's income comes from home-owners, business and industry, state and federal government?

—What is done in their own community to attract business and industry to the town to broaden the tax base? . . . What do they plan in their New Town?

—How are certain city services paid for, e.g., water, sewage disposal? Do these departments bill their customers, or is a fixed amount included in real estate taxes? Is the amount metered and the charge made according to the amount used? How is the industrial use of water paid for?

2. One or two sessions are held in which each team once more displays its New Town and gives the total cost of its operation. If taxation has been included in their study, they will be able to give an estimate of the average cost per person or per household of the operation of their own community, and their New Town, and any ideas they have on how this money should be raised. Discussion may then center on the basic needs of a citizen, how these are best met, and what additional services they would want in a community in which they lived. What are the most important services a community government should render its citizens? What are top priorities? How are these best achieved?

VARIATIONS:

1. Instead of tackling the total problem of costs, teams may focus on a particular aspect such as transportation—including roads, public transportation, consideration of delivery needs of such things as water, trash collection, etc. Or the focus might be on building codes and licensing and inspection, on health care, or schools.

2. A comparison could be made of similar statistics on a town of comparable size in another industrialized country, such as West Germany, Sweden or Japan. Be sure consideration is given to the role of the federal government in budgetary considerations in these countries.

SUGGESTED RESOURCES:

Students may be interested in a fact sheet giving figures such as the following:

THE COST OF RUNNING CITIES OF VARIOUS SIZES IN DIFFERENT SECTIONS OF THE U.S.

CITY	POPULATION	TOTAL EXPENDITURES	PUBLIC SCHOOL EXPENDITURES PER PUPIL	CITY TAX BURDEN PER CAPITA
Charleston, S.C.	66,945	$ 5,696,000	$ 458.31	$150.00
Albuquerque, N.M.	243,751	40,382,677	780.00	417.00
Portland, Oregon	382,619	73,762,390	724.00	161.00
Atlanta, Ga.	496,973	70,773,218	485.66	39.95
Baltimore, Md.	905,759	570,795,000	750.69	158.00
Detroit, Mich.	1,511,482	583,161,163	620.00	180.00
Los Angeles, Calif.	2,816,061	1,113,153,215	1,025.00	98.00
Chicago. Ill.	3,366,957	842,947,960	856.92	249.00

(Figures derived from *NEW YORK TIMES EN-CYCLOPEDIC ALMANAC,* 1972, New York: New York Times, Morris Harth (ed.), 1971, pp. 209-229. This volume will be found to have numerous helpful statistics. In order to have some idea of the size of their "New Town" students might be interested in comparing it with the size of a nearby town with which they are familiar. A table of populations of U.S. towns and cities is given on pp. 141ff.

GOVERNMENT PUBLICATIONS that your library may have:
 THE STATISTICAL ABSTRACT OF THE U.S.
 THE COUNTY AND CITY DATA BOOK
 FEDERAL ROLE IN URBAN AFFAIRS (you may be able to obtain a free copy of this for class use from your Congressional representative).

PERIODICALS:
 ARCHIVES OF ENVIRONMENTAL HEALTH; METROPOLITAN MANAGEMENT TRANSPORTATION AND PLANNING; METROPOLITAN AREA PROBLEMS; ARCHITECTURAL RECORD; (local publications dealing with city government).

RESOURCE PEOPLE:
 Members of city government; chamber of commerce; teachers of city government in local schools and colleges; your school librarian or the librarian at your public library.

BOOKS:
 Students will enjoy at least browsing through the following:
 Gottmann, Jean, *MEGALOPOLIS: THE URBANIZED NORTHEASTERN SEABOARD OF THE U.S.,* Cambridge, Mass.: M.I.T. Press, 1961 (a condensed version is available: *THE CHALLENGE OF MEGALOPOLIS: A GRAPHIC PRESENTATION OF THE URBANIZED NORTHEASTERN SEABOARD OF THE U.S.* by Wolf von Eckardt, 1964).
 Jacobs, Jane, *THE ECONOMY OF CITIES,* New York: Random House, 1969.
 Starr, Roger, *URBAN CHOICES: THE CITY AND ITS CRITICS,* Baltimore, Md.: Penguin, 1966 (hardcover edition titled "The Living End").

PAMPHLETS:
 U.S. Department of Housing and Urban Development, Washington, D.C. 20410 offers the following:
 HUD, IMPROVING THE QUALITY OF URBAN LIFE: A PROGRAM GUIDE TO MODEL NEIGHBORHOODS IN DEMONSTRATION CITIES, HUD PG-47, Dec., 1967.
 PROGRAMS OF HUD, Aug., 1967.

FILMS:
 "Big City," 54 minutes. Originally a CBS-TV presentation as part of its *"Tomorrow"* Series, this features a group of architects talking with city planner Edmund Bacon and announcer Gary Moore, using as models Brasilia and Philadelphia.
 "The Changing City," 16 minutes, color. Produced by Churchill Films, 1962. Views of problems produced by growth.
 "Megalopolis—Cradle of the Future," 20 minutes, color. Based on Dr. Gottmann's *MEGALOPOLIS.*
 "Suburban Living: Six Solutions," 60 minutes. City planner Blanche van Ginkel and architect James Murray discuss the solutions to some of the problems of suburban living in other countries.

BLIND NATURE WALK

PURPOSE:

To discover how much our senses will tell us when we focus on those other than vision.

COMMENT:

In our highly visual society, our eyes reign supreme, the other senses suffer neglect. The blind teach us that much can be learned about our environment from the other senses. The gourmet, tea and wine tasters tell us we are missing a lot by neglecting our sense of taste, the musician, the birdwatcher and the skilled woodsman hear far more than others, the sculptor, weaver and craftsman show us a more highly developed sense of touch, the chemist and perfumer have trained themselves to detect fine distinctions lost to the average person, the dancer, acrobat and mime are aware of messages from their muscles which we never seem to receive. Those who have been working and studying "sensory awareness" tell us that we short change ourselves by forgetting to train all our senses.

This is the first of a series of exercises specifically directed toward discovering some of the more subtle wonders all of our senses can bring us.

GROUP SIZE:

Up to 20

TIME SUGGESTED:

45—60 minutes

GENERAL DIRECTIONS:

Using the basic pattern of "Freedom: and Trust (Blind Walk), partners take turns being led blindfolded on a "Sensing Exploration." This may be done indoors or out, and it is more interesting if no preplanning or arranging is done, and guides use only the material at hand. It is called a "Nature" walk because it usually is carried on outdoors, and offers special interest when a suitable "natural" area is available.

MATERIAL REQUIRED:

Enough blindfolds for half the class.

PROCEDURE:

1. Tell the class that the sighted partner will lead the blindfolded partner about for 15—20 minutes, finding as many interesting things for him to explore with his remaining senses as possible. Depending on the environment, he can find things for him to hear, touch, smell, and taste. This is done in silence, and the purpose is not to try to identify the things experienced, but simply to concentrate on the actual sensing experience. It is important that the guide partner move slowly, carefully and gently so that no fears or apprehensions interfere with the pleasure of the sensing experience. Each guide will seek to find as many pleasant experiences for his partner as possible, but without rushing. It is better to have a few unhurried concentrated experiences than many too quickly hurried through.

2. After about twenty minutes, the partners reverse roles.

3. When both partners have completed their Blind Walk, they sit down together and discuss their sensing experiences.

4. If desired, and if time allows, a plenary may be held for a brief general discussion of the experience.

AWARENESS OF BODY: "INWARD JOURNEY"

PURPOSE:

To develop increased awareness of our physical sensations, and to become more aware of others.

COMMENT:

When we pay attention to a stimulus we perceive something. *What* we perceive depends a good deal upon our mental set—our organization of past experiences, our beliefs and our theories about the world. When we pay attention we do so in terms for which our mental set is prepared. Our mental set acts as a screen or filter, letting through some data and screening out others in ways which often differ considerably from one culture to another. The anthropologist Edward T. Hall says, "Americans and Arabs live in different sensory worlds much of the time" *(THE HIDDEN DIMENSION)*.

The small child welcomes all stimuli in egalitarian fashion. He is neither prejudiced nor discriminating. Though his ability to appreciate many things is very limited, his short attention span and his underdeveloped mental set allow many stimuli to register with him, at least in some fashion and unless the experience is painful he usually enjoys it. Part of our learning is developing a sense of discrimination which shuns those stimuli not considered relevant or suitable by our culture. The average adult in our Western industrialized society has little respect for much of the data presented to his senses, particularly that which concerns his own body. We are willing to grant that our knowledge of the world comes to us through our senses, and we all believe that knowledge is "good" and to learn is "virtuous." However, in our visually oriented, nontouching society, to take pleasure in the senses, except for circumspect seeing and hearing, is considered rather indelicate, if not dangerous. We even have a special word, "sensual," which we use in regard to food and drink and sexual pleasure, and which has acquired pejorative connotations. Introspection is considered proper only when it deals with our "ideas," and to dwell on one's own physical sensations is regarded as less civilized, less good, less virtuous than to dwell on those secondary products of the senses, abstract ideas. Seeing and hearing seem to have escaped with least censure on the dubious grounds that they are "closer" to being "spiritual," "mental," or "intellectual," and yet it is the same brain that grasps the perception and judges the qualities of the products of the other senses. There is irony in the fact that it is considered "anti-intellectual" to pay attention to some of the goings-on in our brain. The results of this attitude have been a certain impoverishment and stagnation, an underdevelopment of our abilities, a curtailment of our joy in living, and unreasonable distress caused by ill-founded fear and guilt.

GROUP SIZE:

Up to 20

TIME SUGGESTED:

45—60 minutes

GENERAL DIRECTIONS:

Students are helped, slowly and purposefully, to pay attention to their own sensations, first individually and then with others. The experience is then briefly explored in discussion. This may be used with a new group. It serves as a general introduction to exercises dealing with the senses. A dimly lighted room is preferable, but not essential.

MATERIALS REQUIRED:

Floor mats, towels or carpeting (optional)

PROCEDURE:

PART I

1. Ask the group to either lie down comfortably on the floor, or, if this is impractical, to sit comfortably and easily in chairs. Slowly direct them through the following steps. Speak quietly and easily to the group as a whole; avoid direct comments to any particular individual.

How do your feet feel, as they rest on the floor? Are you pushing down? Is the floor holding them up? Try to relax your feet—let the floor push against them. Now, how do they feel? Wiggle your toes, then let them relax. Extend your heel, but concentrate on how the bottom of your heel feels, rather than your ankle. Relax—how does it feel? Can you visualize your foot without looking at it? Both feet? Does your foot feel warmer now than when you started this exercise?

2. Now think of your ankles, as distinct from your feet—how do your ankles feel? Try to see your ankle in your mind's eye, without looking at it. Close your eyes, now, and keep them closed for a while.

3. Now move slowly and thoughtfully up your body, one section at a time, trying to be very aware of each part of your body. Tense and then relax one muscle or group of muscles at a time, really feeling the sensations involved. (Allow the group time to do this. If further cues are necessary, you may mention the other parts of the body, allowing about five seconds between each word or term—lower leg, knee, thigh, sexual organs, hips or pelvis, waist, mid-section or stomach, chest, shoulders, upper arms, elbows, lower arms, wrists, hands, neck, chin, ears, face, head, scalp.)

4. Now pay attention to your senses and what they are receiving: Open your eyes: What do you see directly in front of you? What is coming to you through your sight? Without turning your head, move your eyes—what else can you see? Now pay attention to your hearing. Try to identify all the sounds you are hearing. Now, your sense of smell—what can you smell?—Taste? what can you taste? Now pay attention to your skin. Does your face feel —warm? Do you feel any air moving across your face?—across any other area of skin? Is your skin relaxed? Now, your hands—are they warmer or cooler than your face? Close your eyes again, and rub the fingers of one hand first against the palm of the other hand, then against the back of the other hand, then against the inside of the wrist.

5. Close your eyes again and think of the inside of your body. You also have senses inside you which give you signals about your internal states, and about the relationships in space of one part of your body to the other parts. How do your muscles feel? Are any of them still tense? Can you relax them a bit? How do your bones feel? Are you conscious of any of them? Can you feel how far apart your right arm is from your left? How are things in your stomach? Do you feel any digestion going on there—or in your intestines? Now, think of your breathing—the air coming in and going out of your nose, your throat, your lungs—how does it feel? Take a few deep, slow breaths. Try to listen to your heart beating—concentrate on the sensation in your chest of your heart beating. Can you feel the pulse beating in your neck?

6. Keeping your eyes closed, think of the AIR immediately surrounding your body—think of it as a private layer of air about two inches thick, completely surrounding each part of you—your *own* air or space.—Now, think of the air *beyond* your own air-space. How is your own air-space different from that public air beyond? Does it feel warmer? More active? quieter?

—Move your hand gently about six inches to the right or left, and then back to rest. Did you feel your own air-space staying right with your hand and arm? Did it lag behind? Did your hand move out of your own air-space?—What happens to your air-space where your arms touch your body?

PART II
1. Now, it is time to pay attention to someone else. Open your eyes, get up and rearrange your chairs to face each other a few feet apart, two by two. Or, if you have been lying on the floor, sit up and face a partner. Without talking for the moment, quietly observe him, as he observes you. How do you think the floor feels to his feet? how does the air feel against his cheek? What is he listening to?—*Imagine* yourself reaching out and touching the palm of his hand—stroking the back of his hand—how does it feel?

2. Reach out and lightly touch the back of his hand—the palm of his hand. Now let him touch your hand with his fingertips—is it as you imagined? (Repeat with hair on top of head, at side of head.)

3. *Imagine* yourself standing beside your partner. Think about his height—is he taller or shorter than you? If you stood back to back, where would his head and shoulders be? Would his shoulders touch yours? Would your heads meet back-to-back?

4. Stand up and stand back to back with your partner—lean gently together until your shoulders push against him—now your head—continue standing back-to-back and remember what your partner looks like. Imagine him speaking to you —how does his voice sound? If he spoke, would you *feel* anything in your shoulders, your head?

5. Now speak quietly to each other. In turn, ask your partner if he had guessed correctly about your comparative heights, or tell your partner what sounds or sensations impressed you most during the previous part of this exercise. How does his voice sound? Can you feel it, as well as hear it? Is his voice higher or lower than you thought? Ask him to hum a few bars of a song—how does it *feel*?—Share with your partner some of your successes and failures in trying to identify your sensations—in feeling your bones inside you—were you better able to feel some bones than others? some muscles better than others? how did the air in your air-space feel?

6. Can you lean against each other comfortably? Arrange your chairs side by side and sit with your backs together (or, sitting on the floor, move around in place a bit until you are comfortably leaning against each other—relax, but don't push. Probably you can now see at least one other couple that your partner can't see—describe them to your partner, taking turns.

7. Now, talk to each other about what kinds of terms you used in describing the other couple. Did one of you describe clothing, the other not?—did one of you mention positions? gestures? skin, hair or eye color? body build? shoes? did one of you mention what seemed to you to be apparent feelings or attitudes, such as "cheerful," or "stern" or "happy" or "timid" or "tense" or describe facial expressions? Did one of you talk about how you imagined their skin or hair might feel to your hand?—or their voice sound,—or feel? . . . did one of you describe how it might feel to lean against one of the people you described?

A general discussion, or small group discussions, may now follow. Why do we focus attention on certain aspects of ourselves and of others? Are we normally aware of certain bodily sensations, but not others? Why?

If this is a new group, it might be well to follow Step No. 7 with another step: turn around now so you are both facing the same direction, and focus your attention on the couple nearest to you—decide which two couples are now a foursome. Do you all know each other's first name? If not, introduce yourselves. Talk among the four of you about your experience during the last half hour. Were you comfortable? Uncomfortable? Did you laugh? What do you remember most clearly about the experience? Were you afraid of "what might come next"? Why?

If you wish you may continue group building in this way by asking each foursome to combine with another and share some of the things they have talked about. Continue combining until you have a single large group.

SUGGESTED RESOURCES:

Hall, Edward T., *THE HIDDEN DIMENSION,* Garden City, N.Y.: Doubleday—Anchor, 1966, p. 3.

Spolin, Viola, *IMPROVISATION FOR THE THEATER,* Evanston, Ill.: Northwestern University Press, 1963. For a number of excellent variations or follow-up exercises, see "Feeling Self with Self," p. 56; "Space Substance," p. 81f.

FILMS:

"Gateways to the Mind," 60 minutes, color. This is one of the Science series made by A.T.&T. and deals with the human senses and how they function. Call the Public Relations Department of your local Bell Telephone Company to arrange for a free loan. Not all local offices will have the film, but they may be able to arrange to get it for you.

"The Smile," 18 minutes, color. Produced by Serge Bourquignon, 1963. Available from Contemporary Films. Beautiful film of a young Buddhist monk, showing his state of open awareness of the world and the people around him as he walks along behind his master.

"Run," 16 minutes, black and white. Produced by Jack Kuper, 1965. Available from Mass Media Ministries. Although seemingly unrelated, this metaphor of modern man's harried life provides a stunning emphasis of contrast if used following this exercise.

TUNE
IN
ON
YOUR
SENSES

PURPOSE:

To discover how much we recall of recent sensory impressions; to consciously receive as many sensory impressions as possible in a short period of time.

GROUP SIZE:

Up to 20

TIME SUGGESTED:

45—60 minutes

GENERAL DIRECTIONS:

Working individually, the students try to recall and list sensory impressions received during the last few hours. They then try to "tune in" to sensory impressions being received then and there, and list these. Dyads compare lists; class totals are prepared, and a general discussion is held. In your own words, give the students the instructions in "Procedure."

MATERIALS REQUIRED:

None

PROCEDURE:

1. "What did your senses tell you today?" Close your eyes, and in your mind replay your memory-tape from the time you got up this morning (or "since lunch," or "since you left home," etc.). Try to recall all the sensations you can actually remember. Take a sheet of paper and make five columns, headed: "Smell," "Taste," "Touch," "Hearing," and "Sight." In each column jot down a word or two identifying any sensory input you recall. For instance, you may have been awakened by an alarm clock, but do you actually remember the sound of the bell ringing? If you do, put down "alarm," but if you "know it happened," but do not recall being conscious of the sound, do not put it down. Perhaps when you woke you smelled coffee, but do not write down "coffee" under "Smell" unless you really remember smelling it. Do you remember the taste of your toothpaste? . . . What your toast felt like in your hand? . . . How your orange juice tasted? . . . Do you remember your coffee feeling hot or cold in your mouth? . . . What pictures come to mind when you think of what you saw? Take about five minutes to make your list. Stop if and when your list totals twenty or thirty items.

2. Total the number of entries in each list. Put an "L" over the longest column and an "S" over the shortest. Draw a line under your totals, or take another sheet of paper and fill in in the appropriate column all the items which you are receiving RIGHT NOW. Tune in on each of your senses, one at a time. Take about three minutes for this.

3. Total your new lists, note the shortest and longest as before, and compare with your original columns.

4. Sit down with a partner and compare your totals.

—Are your largest totals in the same columns as your partner's? How do the shortest compare? Are your largest totals in the same columns for both your first and second list?

—Do you think you recall some sensory inputs more easily than others? . . . Which? . . . Does your partner agree?

—Which sensory impressions did you enjoy most? . . . least? . . . Do you remember more pleasant ones or more unpleasant ones?

—What does this tell you about your recall of sensory input?

—What does it tell you about your ability to tune in on your senses now? . . . Do you think you will remember these recent sensory impressions six hours from now? . . . Which? . . . Why?

—Do you think you actually "received" as much data through your senses in all the other 3-minute periods today, but forgot it? . . . Why or why not? . . . Do you think you actually did *not* "receive" as much data? . . . why? . . . In which portions of the day did you find the most recollections of sensations? . . . the least? . . . why? What was happening to your senses during those times when you have little or no recall?

—Why is it hard to sort out the sensory impressions you "really remember"?

—Did you put down any sensations of temperature? . . . weight? . . . balance? . . . Where did you put them?

5. Rule off sections of the chalkboard as follows:

	SENSORY RECALL				IMMEDIATE SENSORY RECOGNITION			
	LONGEST LIST CLASS TOTAL		SHORTEST LIST CLASS TOTAL		LONGEST LIST CLASS TOTAL		SHORTEST LIST CLASS TOTAL	
SMELL								
TASTE								
TOUCH								
AUDITION								
VISION								

Ask each class member to name his longest and shortest column in both lists. Put a check in each of the four applicable spaces. Add checks in each space for class totals.

6. In a plenary session discuss the experience and findings. You may also wish to discuss such questions as:

—What are the advantages of tuning in on your senses? . . . the disadvantages?

—Are our senses safety back-up systems? early warning systems?

—What needs do they serve other than self-preservation?

SENSES: EXPLORING THE FAMILIAR OBJECT

PURPOSE:

To develop deeper sensory awareness of the everyday objects around us.

COMMENT:

A small child spends much time exploring objects with all his senses, but as we mature we "use," "consume" or ignore most of the things with which we come in daily contact. We identify and classify, using primarily our vision. Even our vision has been trained along the straight and narrow path so that it is extremely selective, "seeing" only that which is "necessary." Some things we carry about with us we learn to identify by touch, for "practical" reasons—so that it is not necessary for us to get everything out of our pocket or handbag and look at it in order to find what we want. But, here again, our touch is selective; we learn only what is necessary for purposes of identification. To some extent we are "immunized" against the beauty or the ugliness of simple everyday objects, so that we choose without concern for good design, and fail to enjoy much that we have that is good.

GROUP SIZE:

Up to 20

TIME SUGGESTED:

30—60 minutes

GENERAL DIRECTIONS:

In both parts A and B the instructor "talks" the class through first a recollection and then an examination followed by recall, of a simple familiar object. Class members may work individually or in dyads. Discussion may follow, but is not essential.

MATERIALS REQUIRED:

A—none
B—one piece of fruit for each member of the class

PROCEDURE:

A. Pocket Object
1. In your own words, guide the students through the exercise, using the following pattern. Think of some object which you have in your pocket or handbag—something you usually use every day, such as a pen, glasses' case, comb, wallet, or a coin such as a penny or a dime. Do not get it out and look at it, but close your eyes and image what it is like. For the moment, forget what it looks like now, and concentrate on how it smells or tastes . . . Now imagine it in your hand—what does it feel like? In your imagination, strike it against another object at hand—what does it sound like? . . . Drop it on the floor—what is the sound? . . . Again, let your memory show you its appearance.
2. Get the object out and hold it in your hand. Really look at it, as though you had never seen it before. Hold it in different positions, look at it from different angles. Examine it very carefully and see if you can find things about it you did not recall. Smell it or taste it, tap it against something. Imagine it as an empty, colorless shape . . . as a series of planes or lines.
3. Close your eyes and slowly fill in all the features—its color, texture, shininess or dullness. Is it really all the same color? How many different colors do you now remember? Does its texture or finish vary at all in different parts? Are there any words on it? How does its weight compare with that of a piece of paper? Can you remember its taste or smell? . . . how it sounded? . . . Is it an object that is pleasing to your senses?

B. A Piece of Fruit
1. Distribute an apple or orange to each member of the class.
2. Close your eyes and experience your piece of fruit by touch—with the fingertips, clasp your hands around it, hold it against your cheek, in the crook of your arm, hold it under your chin by bending your head down to hold it in place. Hold it in your hands; feel its texture, the blossom end . . . the stem end. Are there any irregularities in its surface? Lift it for weight.

3. Open your eyes and look at it very carefully . . . Imagine yourself eating it—how will it taste? . . . smell? . . . sound? . . . as you bite into it? Very slowly and carefully, begin to peel it with your fingers (if an orange) or bite into it (if an apple). Eat your fruit slowly, continuing to look at how it changes as you eat it—how does it taste, smell, sound, feel, look?

4. If desired, have someone read a suitable poem, such as Aiken's suggested below.

SUGGESTED RESOURCES:

see also: "Freedom from Prejudice: First Hand Impressions"

Aiken, Conrad, "The Crystal," *COLLECTED POEMS 1916—1970,* 2nd ed., New York: Oxford University Press, 1970 (particularly the 22 lines beginning, "Easy enough, it would be, to find in the darkness . . .").

SENSES: DEPRIVATION

PURPOSE:

To become more aware of our senses, develop a deeper appreciation of them, and to become more compassionate of those lacking one or more of the senses.

COMMENT:

Experimentally induced sensory deprivation sometimes has severe, although temporary, effects on the subjects. Even a decrease in the amount of sensory stimulation can be a surprisingly disturbing experience. In one experiment conducted by W. H. Bexton and his associates, college students were paid to live for a time in a lighted room with a comfortable bed. However, they had to wear goggles which allowed the passage of diffuse light, but prevented them from seeing the outlines of objects, patterns, etc. Except when eating or in the bathroom, they wore cardboard cuffs or shields which extended downward from the wrist to the fingertips, preventing them from being able to touch anything with their hands. The room was partially soundproofed, and what few sounds penetrated the room were masked by the hum of equipment. Even at good pay, students usually would not remain more than 2—3 days. They became uncomfortably restless, their ability to think was reduced, and some suffered hallucinations. Immediately upon leaving the experimental room they had temporary visual difficulties and did less well on cognitive tests than before entering.

To think seriously about the loss of one of our senses can help us to be more aware, and to imagine ourselves with the loss of all of our senses is an affecting experience. This exercise allows the student to imagine in a meditation or fantasy what this might be like.

GROUP SIZE:

Up to 20

TIME SUGGESTED:

For larger groups it is best to assign this as

homework. In a small group of students whom you know very well, you may "talk" them through this experience in about twenty minutes. Writing about and/or discussing the experience may take from 10—30 minutes.

GENERAL DIRECTIONS:

This exercise is best offered to students who have had some of the preceding exercises on the senses, and who have had some of the relaxation or daydreaming exercises. If assigning the exercise for homework, describe the process, but do not suggest any possible effects or results, except as given below in Step No. 1. Explain that there will be an opportunity to talk about it at the following session. Following the exercise itself, the students write about their experiences and/or discuss them.

MATERIALS REQUIRED:

None

PROCEDURE:

1. Working with a very small group of students whom you know well, tell them that they are to fantasize what it would be like to lose the use of their senses. In a quiet perhaps darkened room ask the students to sit far apart from one another. Talk to them as follows: "Sit quietly and comfortably. Now your sense of sight has left you—you can close your eyes—things you have been able to see, you will never see again . . . (allow about two minutes) . . . Now your sense of touch has slipped— things you used to be able to feel, you no longer can. You can't tell where your feet are . . . you can't feel the floor . . . you can't feel things with your hands . . . (etc). . . ."

Last to go is hearing. During this, tell them to sit and think about how they felt . . . their reactions . . . because now you will stop talking, as they can no longer hear anything.

2. In small groups, ask the students to describe and discuss their reactions. It may be a good idea to have the students write their reactions before discussing them, in which case their written material would be for their own use. You may wish to suggest some questions for consideration in their written materials and for discussion.

—Which sense were you most aware of losing? . . . least aware of?

—If you were to be deprived of one sense, which would be hardest to do without?

—If no one had any sense of taste or smell, what would meals be like?

—What would the world be like if no one at all could see? . . . How would we arrange our lives? . . . What would happen to the race problem?

SUGGESTED RESOURCES:

Bexton, W. H., W. Heron, and T. H. Scott, "Effects of Decreased Sensory Variation," *BASIC CONTRIBUTIONS TO PSYCHOLOGY: READINGS*, Robert L. Wrenn (ed.), Belmont, Calif.: Wadsworth Publishing Company, 1966, pp. 168ff.

Foss, Brian M., (ed.), *NEW HORIZONS IN PSYCHOLOGY*, Baltimore, Md.: Penguin, 1966, pp. 46-47, 66, 190.

Keller, Helen, *THE STORY OF MY LIFE,* New York: Doubleday, 1954.

SENSES:
A
SENSE
OF
WONDER

ercise; discussion is deferred until the second part is completed. NOTE: The somewhat unusual arrangement of chairs in regular rows is important in this experience, as it encourages participants to concentrate on themselves and on the particular object they are immediately experiencing, rather than on others or on objects they have not yet received.

PURPOSE:

To heighten our awareness of the importance of things, objects, in our life.

COMMENT:

A sense of wonder is an experience to awaken the appreciation of nature and of life, to deepen an awareness of being, of existence. Many things that go into our daily living exist without our full appreciation. This experience is an attempt to heighten our awareness of the importance of things, objects in our life. We stop, look and listen to the sounds of being.

Each sense is brought into play—hearing, seeing, feeling, smelling, tasting. Many objects are used—the greater variety, the better. Association of both common and personal experiences are received and associations are made. Discussion of this experience can center on the experience, and its meaning for us.

GROUP SIZE:

Minimum of twelve participants. May be used with larger group, or subgroups of twelve may be used.

TIME SUGGESTED:

60 minutes

GENERAL DIRECTIONS:

This exercise may be used with a beginning group. Participants are seated in rows, facing front. Participants are asked not to talk to one another. Soft music is playing. There are two parts to the ex-

MATERIALS REQUIRED:

1. Record player or tape player.
2. Records or tapes of music selected. Suggested: "The Comedians" by Kabalevsky; "Le Carnaval des animaux," by Saint-Saens.
3. Objects. (See items listed under Discovery I. Items," "Discovery II. 1.")
4. One copy of the reading selection from Carson. (See "Discovery I. 2.")
5. One copy for each participant of the Psalm. (See "Discovery II. 2."), or an overhead projector and single prepared copy may be used. It is important that all be able to see this easily and clearly.

PROCEDURE:

DISCOVERY I

1. Soft music is playing. After a few moments, when the music creates an atmosphere of quiet, a number of items will be passed through the group. The items will be passed from back to front.

ITEMS: any object that is small enough to pass around: natural objects such as sticks or twigs, leaves, stones, flowers, etc.; man-made objects such as an umbrella, hair spray, lighter, articles of clothing, etc. Suggested number of items: twenty.

2. Allow a few moments after all items are passed forward from one to another. Begin the reading aloud of the selection from Rachel Carson, *THE SENSE OF WONDER*. Rachel Carson explains the thrill of enjoying nature that she found when rediscovering nature through the eyes of her nephew, Roger (see "Suggested Resources").

DISCOVERY II

1. Envelopes containing the following items are arranged ahead of time:
   a. cracker
   b. slice of lemon
   c. napkin
   d. egg shell
   e. a piece of paper, which states: ". . . eat the cracker . . . suck on the lemon . . . crunch the egg shell in your hand . . . wipe your face and hands

with the napkin. . . . Finally, tear this paper into small pieces and return all remaining items to the envelope."

These envelopes are passed out to all participants, and they are told to open their envelopes. Music continues to play in the background and, if necessary, participants are reminded not to talk.

2. When all are finished, copies of Psalm 104 are distributed, or the Psalm is projected on a screen, and all are invited to recite the Psalm together.

3. Discussion. Discussion can be held in several fashions: one-to-one, then groups of four, and finally the entire group sharing; groups of four to six discussing.

VARIATIONS:

1. The selection from Rachel Carson is very appropriate. However, a substitute reading could be made, e.g., from THE PROPHET by Kahlil Gibran, from PRAYERS, by M. Quoist. The reading should take about ten minutes.

2. The Discovery I and II experiences could be modified.

3. A different Psalm, or other prayer or reading may be substituted for "II.2."

4. Several people can be observers and record the reactions of people. This could be meaningful feedback.

5. No discussion may follow. Allow the people to simply enjoy the experience.

(Adapted from Monsignor Knox's translation of "Psalm 103," THE HOLY BIBLE, Sheed & Ward, Inc., New York, 1956, verses 1-15, 24.)

Bless the Lord, my soul
  O Lord, my God, what magnificence is yours!
Glory and beauty are your clothing.
  Light is a garment you wrap around yourself,
  the heavens are a curtain that your hands unfurl.
The waters of heaven are your ante-chamber,
  the clouds your chariot.
On the wings of the wind you come and go.
  You have planted the earth on its own firm base
  undisturbed for all time.
The deeps once covered it like a cloak
  the waters stood high above the mountains.
They cowered before your rebuking word
  and fled at your voice of thunder.
Leaving the mountain heights to rise,
  and the valleys to sink into their appointed
    places!
Yet there shall be torrents flooding the glens,
  water among the hills, to give drink to every

wild beast.
Grass must grow for the cattle,
  for man, she must also put forth her shoots,
  if he is to bring corn out from her bosom.
If there is to be wine, to rejoice man's heart,
  oil to make his face shine, and bread to keep
    man's strength from failing.
What diversity, Lord, in your creatures!
What wisdom has designed them all!
There is nothing on earth,
  That does not give proof of your creative power!
Glory be. . . . . Amen.

NOTE: This translation seems somewhat preferable for this exercise to that of the JERUSALEM BIBLE where the Psalm is numbered "104," but the JERUSALEM BIBLE could be used as a second choice.

SUGGESTED RESOURCES:

DISCOVERY IN PRAYER: "The World Is Womb," pp. 28-30; "Saying Yes", p. 50.
DISCOVERY IN WORD: "It's a Beautiful World," pp. 107-8.
DISCOVERY IN FILM: "Adventures of an *", p. 26.
(Discovery Series; Paramus, N.J.: Paulist Press.)

Carson, Rachel, THE SENSE OF WONDER, New York: Harper and Row, 1956.

SEEING AND PERCEIVING

PURPOSE:

To discover some of the relationships between what we see and what we perceive.

COMMENT:

Evolving man, fascinated with his multi-purpose eyes connected to his superior brain, has increasingly depended on sight for information and for pleasure. With the advent of printing, these eyes became even more important and, at the same time, more restricted by what McLuhan calls the "linear" mental set. In our society, "left to right," "from the top to the bottom," is the "proper" way to scan a visual field. We tend to "read" a view, a situation, a picture in terms of successive rather regular bits. Our eyes serve us very well and we use them all day long to help us decide what to wear, what to eat, where to go, to help us identify what or who is around us. Very often we use our eyes to decide not to pay any attention to something—that is, to identify or categorize it for our needs, but to ignore its appearance. We go down to breakfast in the morning, find a "plate," put food on it, eat the food, take the plate back to the kitchen, perhaps wash it, and that's that. We haven't *seen* the plate at all.

Our education has taught us that there is a special category of things called "art." When we are presented with something which we are told is "art," we look at it quite differently. If it is representational art, we look at it first, perhaps, to see "what it's a picture of." We then begin to look at line, shape, color and, perhaps, texture. Also, if a certain spot is described to us as "scenery," we pay some attention to the contours of the land, the colors visible, the sparkle of water or the sense of great distance.

What happens if, for a little while, we treat our everyday life as if it were "art" or "scenery"? What happens when we temporarily turn off our "identifying" and "categorizing" and simply describe something? What happens to us? What happens to those who hear our descriptions?

GROUP SIZE:

Up to 20

TIME SUGGESTED:

45—60 minutes

GENERAL DIRECTIONS:

For the first four steps, all students should sit facing the front of the room. These steps allow the student to use language to describe what he sees, but *not* to identify objects, and allows his listeners to try to identify what he is describing. The second portion of the exercise uses reproductions of paintings or other art forms as the basis for small group discussions working with the same vocabulary. If desired, the first four steps may comprise the exercise, ending with a discussion.

MATERIALS REQUIRED:

A brown paper bag with 1—3 objects in it.

A group of reproductions of paintings, etc., offering comparisons of similar and different lines, color, shapes, etc., (see "Suggested Resources").

PROCEDURE:

1. Ask a volunteer to look at a front corner of the room (define the limits of the "corner") and describe everything he sees there, *without* naming any of the objects or the materials of their composition or describing their use. He will have to do this in terms of line, shape, color, texture, size, apparent weight, translucence. The class tries to identify the objects he describes. They may do this by calling out what he is describing, if the group is very small, but it will usually be better if they write down the objects on a piece of paper as they believe they recognize them.

2. Ask for another volunteer to repeat the experiment, but this time ask him to describe one of the *back* corners of the room. The rest of the class remains facing front, again trying to identify the objects described.

3. Take the previously prepared paper bag containing 1—3 objects to the back of the room and ask for another volunteer "describer." Ask for 1—3 other volunteers to go to the chalkboard and draw what they hear described. The describer stands facing toward the back wall and takes the objects, one

at a time, from the bag and describes them as in Step No. 1, while those at the chalkboard attempt to draw the object from his description. NOTE: Discourage the "describer" from giving "drawing instructions," e.g., "Draw a line about a foot long . . . Now erect a perpendicular in the middle, making the perpendicular line about two feet high. . . ."

4. Ask for another volunteer and give him a slip of paper containing the following directions: "You are to describe a spiral staircase. You may not name the object or its parts, and you may not use your hands." Ask for 1—3 other volunteers to go to the chalkboard and draw the object as this person describes it.

5. Arrange the class in subgroups of 5—7 and distribute a pair of reproductions of paintings to each subgroup. Ask them to describe and discuss the pictures *in the same way* the room and the objects were described in Steps Nos. 1 and 4. Ask them to look for similarities and differences. Tell them they may point to and touch the pictures.

If there is sufficient time, additional pictures or pairs of pictures may be circulated for similar discussions.

SUGGESTED RESOURCES:

Kriesberg, Irving, *ART: THE VISUAL EXPERIENCE,* New York: Pitman, 1964, pp. 4-5. (Kriesberg suggests comparing the lines in Matisse's "Interior in Yellow and Blue" with Picasso's "Study for Bull's Head" (Museum of Modern Art, New York —a 1937 sketch for the "Guernica" mural), and comparing the lines, shapes and spaces in De Chirico's "The Anxious Journey" (Museum of Modern Art, New York) with Fra Angelico's "Road to Calvary" (San Marco Museo, Florence, Italy).

Lavin, Edward, and Terrence Manning, *DISCOVERY IN ART,* Paramus, N.J.: Paulist Press, 1969. (Students may compare the shape or form in Picasso's "Guernica" on pp. 22-23 and in the photograph by Sergio Larrain-magnum on p. 25; the line and color in Larry Zox' "Keobuk," p. 163 with that in Anuskiewicz's "Corona" on p. 185.)

Taylor, Joshua C., *LEARNING TO LOOK,* Chicago, Ill.: University of Chicago, 1957. (Taylor suggests a comparison of the colors and lines or forms in Perugino's "The Crucifixion with Saints" (Central Panel) and in Crivelli's "The Crucifixion," pp. 5 and 7, and see also pp. 50-54.)

SENSES: VISUAL ILLUSIONS

PURPOSE:

To explore some problems of perception through investigating some aspects of vision and illusion.

COMMENT:

"The world casts its reflection upon the mind, and this reflection serves as raw material, to be scrutinized, sifted, reorganized, and stored . . . (The) given world is only the scene on which the most characteristic aspect of perception takes place. Through that world roams the glance, directed by attention, focusing the narrow range of sharpest vision now on this, now on that spot, following the flight of a distant sea gull, scanning a tree to explore its shape. This eminently active performance is what is truly meant by visual perception . . ." (Arnheim, *VISUAL THINKING,* p. 14).

We have all had the experience of walking past some person, object or occurrence in apparent oblivion, and then doing a double-take. We stop, seem to undergo a moment of belief mixed with unbelief, turn and focus our attention on the thing of interest. Apparently, when the object first passed across our retinal screen our attention was focused elsewhere and we failed to "see" it, but there was something about this "picture" sufficiently unexpected or bizarre to trigger a delayed response in us. There are, of course, many other occasions on which we simply pass by, without the double-take, and "miss seeing" the surprising feature altogether.

Another time a friend hands us a picture or a printed page and says, "For heaven's sake—look at this!" We look, and look again very carefully, and see—nothing of interest, until our friend stabs the page with his finger and says, "That's Joe!" or "They've misspelled our names!"—and then we "see."

In these cases the object on our retina does not change, but there is considerable difference in what we "see."

Most people are intrigued by visual illusions which, by a kind of magic, fool us about what we see. Even when the illusion is "explained" or pointed out to us, we still are baffled by what seems a distortion of reality, and the question "why" nags us. Visual illusions are more than amusing tricks and have fascinated philosophers, psychologists and physiologists since the Greek empiricists tried to explain why a straight stick looks bent when plunged part way into the pool. Oddly enough, there is still such uncertainty about the answers to these problems that psychologist Josef Cohen flatly states "Most visual illusions are unexplained" *(SENSATION AND PERCEPTION: 1. VISION)*.

Rather than being able to say, "Seeing is believing," psychologists concerned with visual perception such as R. L. Gregory say, ". . . perceptual interpretation involves betting on the odds." *(EYE AND BRAIN*, p. 180), and Wilentz says ". . . the brain never adds up all the visual content available to it at any moment, but seizes bits and rejects others. It's as though the eye constantly samples the scene, compiling data that has been checked against some mentally stored image" *(SENSES OF MAN*, p. 275). Franklin Kilpatrick says, "the assessment of 'what is out there' depends in large degree on where the person is, what he is attending to, and his experience in decoding patterns of vervous impulses of that kind" *(EXPLORATIONS IN TRANSACTIONAL PSYCHOLOGY*, p. 317). Kilpatrick defines perception as ". . . that part of the transactional process which is an implicit awareness of the probable significance for action of present impingements from the environment, based on assumptions related to the same or similar impingements from the environment" (p. 4). Similarly, the authors of *PSYCHOLOGY TODAY: AN INTRODUCTION* point to the Necker cube as an example or demonstration of the fact that perception apparently involves a selection of data from among the possibilities proposed by any visual field. They ask why, among all the possible rectilinear figures in various poses, the figure is invariably identified as a "cube." After all, it could be "the flat projection, the retinal image, of an infinity of different objects—truncated pyramids and so on—and yet only two possibilities (both based on the cube assumption) are entertained" (p. 330).

The star of the Gestalt psychologists had alternately risen and fallen in the firmament of studies of perception. Reacting against nineteenth century "mechanistic" theories, such as those of Helmholtz, they posed a set of principles based on a belief which approximated Plato's "innate ideas," and stated that the human mind preferred, by nature, certain patterns to others and "wholes" or "Gestalts" to parts. Although they had little or no empirical evidence to support their views, they accused those they termed "Introspectionists" of an equal lack of evidence.

Their opponents, often reacting more strongly to Gestalt psychology's premises than to its findings, held that there was a one-to-one correspondence between what was presented to the retina and what was "seen," and that all else was the result of learning. Part of the source of the controversy is contained in Kohler's statement in *GESTALT PSYCHOLOGY*, "The Introspectionist's thesis that changes of attitude do not influence true sensory experience is also incompatible with actual facts. The thesis almost amounts to an arbitrary definition of true sensory experience" (p. 69). Helmholtz and his followers were closer to defining "seeing" in terms of stimulus-response, and, at least to some degree, accepting "retinal image" as the "response." Koffka, Kohler and such contemporary Gestalt psychologists as Arnheim define "seeing" in a way which comes closer to "perceiving." This is not, however, simply a question of semantics.

Both sides have modified their positions today, and additional physiological, primarily neurological, evidence has become available in the last ten years which gives some support to Gestalt views. Gregory in *THE INTELLIGENT EYE* says, ". . . there remains the possibility that some perceptual organizing processes are 'wired in' at birth . . . It is now clear from neurological studies that some visual feature-detectors are built in to retina and brain structure" (p. 22). Also, Dean E. Wooldridge, remarking on the problem of why we recognize the plate tipped on an angle as a disk, or select the cube as the rectilinear object when we see it presented with the Necker cube, says, ". . . some of the data processing involved may be carried out in the peripheral nervous system before the visual information is passed on to the brain . . . some processing of the primary visual data may be carried out by means of the detailed pattern of interconnection between the fibers of the optic nerve and the neurons of the visual cortex . . . If, as seems likely, man's visual system is organized much like the cat's, we would now appear to have a solid physiological explanation for this fact of perception; we are unusually sensitive to straight lines because each neuron in our visual cortex receives inputs from linear arrays of retinal receptors . . . (N)euronal elements, that do not much care where in the field of view a straight line of illumination is located but are very much concerned with its angular orientation, may well underlie the neural mechanisms that permit man . . . to identify triangles, squares, and other straight-edged geometrical figures, regardless of their distance or position in the field of view . . . (N)ot all the 'intelligence' of the nervous system resides in the brain" *(THE MACHINERY OF THE BRAIN)*.

GROUP SIZE:

Up to 20

TIME SUGGESTED:

There is sufficient material here for up to six sessions of 60 minutes each, but sections may be selected for any lesser number, or a number of 30 minute sessions could be derived.

GENERAL DIRECTIONS:

As an opener, students make certain judgments about an "ambiguous figure" and compare the results. In small groups the students first go through a series of exercises demonstrating some factors involved in vision and then examine and discuss briefly various types of visual illusions. Discussions on "perception" follow, dealing with some aspects of decision making, evidence, and distortion. If desired, independent research and reports on the eye, vision, perception, etc., may be presented at alternate or subsequent sessions.

MATERIALS REQUIRED:

If you are going to use the film, a film projector will be necessary. For showing copies of the various illusions an overhead projector may be used if you have prepared transparencies, or an opaque overhead projector will do a good job of showing many of them, but some will be difficult to see. Many books contain pictures of the illusions, and it may be possible to obtain a reasonable number and pass them around in small groups. Some of the books listed in "Suggested Resources" also suggest additional experiments, and illustrated directions for making other simple illusions. Page references throughout this exercise are to books listed in "Suggested Resources." You may wish to prepare some of the following simple illusions for your class:

1. Gray on black and white—contrast. Using one piece of black and one piece of white construction paper, mount them side by side, matching long edges closely, on a sheet of bristol board or fairly stiff stock. Cut a "doughnut" or hollow ring from a sheet of light gray construction paper, making the diameter of the ring about 8—9 inches overall, and the width of the ring about two inches. Mount the ring across the two sheets of black and white paper, centering it exactly on the line where the two sheets meet. Also provide a piece of black thread about 11—12 inches long.

2. Dot figure. Prepare a figure consisting of 36 identical dots spaced equidistantly in the shape of a square, six dots on each side. Use contact or pressure adhesive dots in black on a white sheet, or other strong contrast colors.

3. Perceptual set—letter diagram. On a sheet of white paper draw a large square crossed by a horizontal line at midpoint and by two diagonals forming a cross from the corners (an "X" across the square).

4. Draw and cut out the two "doughnut segments" of Jastrow's illusion of figures of geographically equal size which appear unequal when arranged above one another (see McKeller, p. 54).

I. Starter

Show the students the "young-old lady" (see "Suggested Resources"—Gregory, *INTELLIGENT EYE*, p. 39; McKeller, *EXPERIENCE AND BEHAVIOUR*, p. 44; Attneave, *SCIENTIFIC AMERICAN*, p. 66; (see also many psychology texts). Working individually, students are to jot down answers to such questions as the following:

—How old do you think this woman is?

—What kind of job do you think she has, if any?

—Do you think you would like to know her? Why or why not?

Allow only a few minutes for this.

Then ask the students to share some of their answers. As differences arise the ambiguity of the figure will be disclosed.

II. Exercises illustrating some elements or factors involved in vision and perception.

1. Using the gray circle mounted on black and white paper, as prepared in "Materials Required. 1.," show the class the exhibit. The evenly colored gray ring looks lighter against the black background. Hold the piece of black thread taut against the figure across the gray circle and over the line formed by the meeting of the black and white sheets. The contrast is enhanced.

Part of our ability to "see" things depends on contrast, on borders, and on our tendency to see patterns or figures, rather than disorganized parts or pieces. The thread enhances the contrast because of the "new border" and "new figures"—there is a greater tendency to see two figures, rather than one, when this new line is added. Apparently part of this recognition takes place in the retina and part in the brain.

2. Recognition of motion. Although more complex and "sophisticated," our visual apparatus shares many features with the eyes of lower animals. The edge of man's retina is more primitive, serving the more primitive needs of all animals to be alert to danger and to be aware of possible food. Therefore it responds to movement, even when no object can actually be recognized. The following experiments show this.

a. Ask two students to volunteer for this demonstration. "A" stands facing the class, both eyes open and looking toward the back wall. He is to continue to gaze straight ahead until this experiment is completed. "B" stands a few feet behind him, and very slowly moves forward and sideways, waving his hand up and down. Explain to "A" that he is to say "stop" the instant he is first aware of this movement, and announce on which side he sees it. Then give "B" a slip of paper, secretly instructing him to wave his "fist," rather than his open hand, and to hold perfectly still, fist in position, when "A" says "stop."

When "A" is conscious of "B" 's hand and says "stop," ask "A" to demonstrate with his own hand how "B" 's hand looked. He will probably say that he doesn't know, that he just was aware of "movement," which is the case. Ask him how "B" 's hand looks right now. If he has kept his eyes focused straight ahead, and "B" stopped promptly, "A" will no longer be able to see "B" 's hand. Now that it is stationary, it will have disappeared.

This is the kind of elementary vision of vital importance to most animals who must be ready to jump, swoop or spring when they become aware of motion—to escape from danger or to secure food. Our normal tendency is to swivel our head around or at least turn our eyes toward the perceived motion in order to get the moving object onto the portion of the retina capable of taking in details more complicated than simple motion. If desired, this last point may be demonstrated by having two students do a variation of "A" above. In this case explain to "A" that he is free to shift his gaze, but not his head, from side to side whenever he wishes, but not to "hunt" for "B" or anticipate "B" 's moves. "B" may move into "A" 's line of vision on either side, waving his hand in any way that he wishes, and must freeze when "A" says "stop," indicating that he has seen motion. In this case "A" will be able to identify the appearance of the signaling hand, if he reacts naturally, and will usually be unaware that he did not "see" an actual hand at first.

b. A variation of "A" may be performed involving the entire class. Send a boy and a girl to the back of the room. Ask the rest of the class to sit facing front and keep their eyes on the front of the room throughout the experiment. Ask the boy and girl to decide secretly which one is to walk to the front along the right side, and which one along the left. Ask the class to notice individually (a) when they are first aware of movement, and (b) when they are able to identify which of the two is on their right or left, as the two move very slowly and quietly to the front.

c. Recognition of motion and velocity without background. If it is possible to use a room that can be totally darkened, this experiment may be done. With the room illuminated, ask a student to walk slowly across the front of the room. Ask the rest of the class to watch him. They will obviously have no difficulty seeing that he moves. Why? The eyes follow the moving object, keeping the focus upon it in such a way that the image on the retina remains in the same spot—the figure is *not* moving across the retina. The students will respond that it is the changing background that they see which identifies the motion and speed of the moving figure.

However, something more is involved, somewhat mysteriously. Darken the room completely, and wave a lighted cigarette about in front of the students. They will be perfectly able to see that this light is moving, not fixed, and aware of its speed, despite the fact that their eyes will again follow the motion, and this time there is no visible background to provide the kind of knowledge available in the first instance. Apparently this awareness of speed motion is due to our sense of our eyes moving within their sockets.

d. Perceptual set. Using the "dot figure" as prepared in "Materials Required. 2.," show the students the figure and induce various "sets" by suggesting, "Look for fours," "Look for columns," "Can you see sixes?" In fact, if you simply gaze at the figures you will begin to organize them in similar ways without outside suggestion.

Another perceptual set exercise can be done with the letter diagram described in "Materials Required. 3." Show the diagram and suggest that they look for an "X", and "H", "L", "N", "Z", "E", "F". McKeller describes this exercise, indicating that our tendency to organize figures makes it easy to find these letters.

e. Stereoscopic vision. Some people are right-eyed, some are left-eyed, just as some people are right-handed, some left-handed, but apparently there is no connection—a right-handed person may be either right- or left-eyed. Students may easily discover which eye dominates their vision. Ask them to look at a fairly distant object, with both eyes open. Now, "close your right eye. Open it and close your left. Do it again, if necessary. If the distant object 'jumps' when you close your right eye, but remains stationary when you close the left, you are right-eyed."

Since our eyes are about two and one-half inches apart they receive slightly different images on the retina. This difference causes stereoscopic vision, which allows us to see depth. The difference between the two images is called "disparity." The old stereopticon worked on this principle. Two photographs were taken with two cameras separated by the distance between the eyes, and then looked at through a viewer shielded down the center so each eye saw separately its appropriate photograph, resulting in the "illusion" of depth. If the pictures were reversed, a strange reversal of depth appears, with distortion due to shadowing, perspective, etc. If the two cameras have been placed too far apart, a strange distortion occurs due to *retinal rivalry*—first one eye "wins," then the other, as parts of one picture are combined with parts of the other, or as one picture is totally rejected temporarily. The principle of stereoscopic photography is used today in a number of ways.

If possible, show the students some stereoscopic pictures. If an old stereopticon and its prepared photographs are available, these may be used. A few pictures which may be viewed with a small mirror are shown in the Time-Life book on *THE MIND*, and there are also some fascinating 3-D pictures in Gregory's *INTELLIGENT EYE* which may be viewed with the red and green spectacles included in the book.

f. Depth perception. In addition to our stereoscopic vision which, incidently is of little use beyond twenty feet, we have a number of other "monocular" cues which tell us about depth or distance. Leonardo da Vinci wrote a treatise for painters in which he said:

"The first thing in painting is that the object it represents should appear in relief, and that the grounds surrounding them at different distances should appear to extend (three dimensionally) right into the wall on which they are painted, with the help of the three branches of perspective, which are: the diminution of the forms of the objects; the diminution in their magnitude; and the diminution in their color.

"Shadows appear to me to be of supreme importance in perspective, because without them opaque and solid bodies will be ill defined."

He went on to talk about how color also aids in the perception of depth, saying, "There is another kind of perspective which I call Aerial Perspective, because by the atmosphere we are able to distinguish the variations in distance of different building, which appear placed on a single line . . . In an atmosphere of equal density the remotest objects seen through it, as mountains, in consequence of the great quantity of atmosphere between your eye and them—appear blue and almost of the same hue as the atmosphere itself when the sun is in the East. Hence you must make the nearest building above

the wall of its real color, but make the more distant ones less defined and bluer . . . If one is to be five times as distant, make it five times bluer" (*A DOCUMENTARY HISTORY OF ART*, Vol. I, Elizabeth G. Holt (ed.) .

A more recent student of depth perception, J. J. Gibson has made a study of textural or density changes, particularly in two-dimensional representations of scenes in which there are more or less regular rows of objects "receding" into the horizon—the horizontal lines of ploughed fields, stretches of stoney beach, brick streets or plazas, wheat fields, etc. These have come to be called "Gibson's gradients."

John Wilentz says, "It is dangerous to assume when you see a painting or examine the art of some past culture that this corresponds to the way people actually saw the world. Nor should the frontality of archaic art, the flatness of Egyptian paintings, the varied-sized persons of medieval art, the strange inversions of perspective in Chinese art, suggest that these were in any way lesser works of genius. The artist picks and chooses and his work is a manifestation of metaphysics rather than physics. So the medieval painter may seem to be preoccupied with verticals, with Gothic heights and proportions, but this may be his way of mirroring the hierarchical structure of life, the order imposed by church and feudalism" (p. 297).

Students may investigate depth perception as follows:

(1) Art students and photographers in your class may be interested in taking over the job of finding suitable pictures. An assortment of photographs, drawings, and reproductions of paintings might include some work of 5—6 year old children, art from various cultures and periods, shadowed drawings or photographs of landscapes, including mountains, craters, valleys or lakes are useful, as are street scenes and interiors. See "Suggested Resources" for suggested pictures illustrating "Depth perception."

(2) Prior to investigating the pictures, ask the subgroups to spend 5—10 minutes listing cues to depth, distance, solidity, and dimension—that is, when you look around this room, or out the window, how do you know something is flat, round, square, solid, near, far, small, large? Suggest that the students focus first on something nearby, and progressively shift their focus farther away, noting the clues that help them make the above judgments.

(3) Distribute the selected pictures. It is not necessary that each subgroup have the same pictures, but only that each has a suitable variety to demonstrate cues of size, contrast, parallax, interposition, texture, shadowing and light. If you wish, you may include color in this part of the exercise, demonstrating Leonardo da Vinci's rules. Ask the

students to examine the pictures and see how they demonstrate the factors they listed in "2" above, and if they can add to their list. Ask them to compare the children's drawings and primitive art with post-Renaissance art, and then with some contemporary works.

(4) Bring the groups together to share their findings and discuss the implications. Encourage members to demonstrate their statements with particular pictures. Some questions which may be discussed are:

—How does size help us to judge distance?

—How do shadows help us to judge shapes?

—If you turn a shadowed landscape upside down, what does it look like? Does it affect your judgment about shape?

—What colors are distant hills or mountains in the pictures?

—If they have pictures of a crowd scene, a parade of soldiers, the audience in a movie or a TV studio audience, a military cemetery, a housing development, or fields of grain or an orchard—How are the "back rows" different from the front?

—When you use the terms "look at" or "see" something, do you mean different things? . . . What do you mean by "seeing"?

—Do you feel you can "trust your eyes"? When, if ever, have they fooled you? . . . Or did you fool them?

g. What are known as *Shape* and *Size Constancy* are probably also involved in visual illusions. Students may see these in the following simple ways:

(1) *Shape Constancy:* Show the students a square box or cube and a plate or record, slowly turning these in your hands to present different views. Ask the students to observe closely what they actually see—what is the image presented to the retina? Some of the distinctions between "seeing" and "perceiving" become manifest as these assorted rectilinear and eliptical figures are accepted as cubes and disks.

(2) *Size Constancy:* (a) Ask the students to hold their hands in front of them, one stretched out away from them, and the other fairly close to the face, held so both are visible. They will look about the same, although the far hand is making a smaller image on the retina. Ask them now to overlap the near hand over the far one, and the size difference will become more apparent. (b) Ask two students of the same height to stand in front of the class, one against the wall and the other in the middle of the room, arranged so both are visible to the rest of the class which should stand across the back of the room. It will be quite obvious to the class that they have no difficulty recognizing these two figures as

approximately the same size, although in fact the image on the retina of the observer in this case is only half as large for the distant figure as for the closer one. There is apparently a good deal more involved here than "memory," and various theories have been advanced to explain how *Size* and *Shape Constancy* work for us.

(3) A more dramatic demonstration of *Size Constancy* employs a source of light strong enough to produce a good after-image, such as a photographic flash. Explain the steps prior to exposing students to the light source.

—Students gaze at a strong light source.

—Students shift their gaze to the palm of their hand or a book held in hand.

—Students shift their gaze to blank wall.

What will happen is that the after-image obtained from "a" will appear small on the hand and somewhat amazingly larger in "b", following an inversion of the same law as (2) above, doubling the size as the distance is doubled. *Size Constancy* helps us "see" things in reasonable size, despite varying distances.

h. Motion and time lag. To demonstrate the time lag in our vision, which allows us to see movies as a continuous, unbroken picture, students may be shown some footage from old films made at a speed less than the present 24-frames per second rate, and will be able to see the flicker effect. Another approach is the use of one of those books made to be flipped rapidly to produce the illusion of motion. One excellent example is *FLIX* by Robert Breer, published by La Cinematheque canadienne, film museum and archive, on the occasion of World Retrospective of Animation Cinema, 1967. A simple illustrated explanation is given in *THE WAY THINGS WORK: AN ILLUSTRATED ENCYCLOPEDIA OF TECHNOLOGY* (Vol. I), New York: Simon and Schuster, 1967, pp. 132-133.

III. Using the film in "Suggested Resources" and/or various books, articles or reproductions, show to students assorted visual illusions.

If desired, these may be given to the students in random lots, for suggested classification or categorization. In subgroups, students may decide which illusions seem to "go together" or be based on similar principles. One possible classification follows:

1. Those based on extreme redundancy, which is disturbing to our vision in some way not clearly understood, such as the "McKay rays" or the similar figure of closely spaced narrow parallel bands of black on white, such as are shown in Gregory, *EYE AND BRAIN*, pp. 134, 135. Some of the effect of movement in op art is apparently due also to redundancy. See also the figure on p. 336 of *PSY-*

2. Illusions where the confusion is apparently due to misapplied rules for perceiving three-dimensional objects seen on the flat page or sheet of paper. (1) Those which offer a distorted appearance in themselves, such as the Muller-Lyer arrow illusion. (2) Those which are so designed that the underlying features distort other elements placed upon them, such as the Ponzo railway lines illusion or the Hering fan illusions. (See Foss, pp. 73, 74, 78; McKeller, pp. 51, 52, 53; Wilentz, p. 301, 302, 303; the books by Gregory and the Attneave article in *SCIENTIFIC AMERICAN.*)

3. Ambiguous or "impossible" figures, in which depth clues are distorted, boundaries or borders ambiguous, and more than one object is hypothesized, such as Jastrow's duck-rabbit, the young-old lady, the two faces and the vase; and depth reversing objects such as the Necker cube. (See Foss, p. 72-73, 79, 81, 89; Gregory's books, Attneave's *SCIENTIFIC AMERICAN* article, and Wilentz pp. 276, 277, 278.)

4. Figural after-effects. An example of this is given in Foss, p. 75.

Ambiguous figures. Gregory says that possibly the illusion involved in depth-reversing figures is due to a kind of constancy scaling "set by perspective features which are inappropriate, because the figure in fact lies on a flat plain." (*NEW HORIZONS,* Brian M. Foss, (ed.), p. 88.) The Necker cube is one of the best known depth-reversing ambiguous figures. It is purposely drawn without the normal features of perspective, both the "back" and the "front" being the same size, so there is no clue as to which is which.

In viewing most ambiguous figures it is noticeable that only one of the possible versions or "object hypotheses" is apparent at any moment, the other(s) vanishing. Also, once alternative perceptions become visible, there is a tendency for the versions to alternate spontaneously as we continue to gaze at the figure. Furthermore, this alternation seems to continue in a regular "on/off" time sequence, and the rate of alternation tends to increase with time. One plausible explanation offered for the alternation and acceleration of rate is that each version follows different neural pathways, and as the structures of one path become fatigued they "turn off," allowing the other to "turn on." Fatiguing of these paths becomes more rapid with continued use, as is common in other sensory activities. This explanation is helpful in understanding the mutual exclusivity of the various possible versions or object hypotheses.

Perspective, coloring, shadowing and the total setting may all be used to contribute to ambiguity, and are demonstrated both in optical illusions, per

se, and in illusionism in art, including the exaggerations of trompe l'oiel paintings and decorations, which are perhaps more science than art. Students may be shown a collection of reproductions of paintings which demonstrate illusionism, a style recurrently popular since the early art of Pompeii. Examples may be found in Italian Baroque, nineteenth century art and even contemporary art, and some examples are given under "Suggested Resources." Students may discuss in small groups the effects of these paintings, why they like or do not like them, their differences and similarities, and how they compare with the "impossible figures," depth-reversing figures, and other typical optical illusions.

IV. Setting.

After the students have completed some of the above exercises they may wish to arrange for the viewing of objects in a variety of situations, to investigate differences in appearance. For instance, a vase, a small object such as a key, or a small piece of sculpture may be mounted for viewing in settings or environments which provide various effects. The following elements may be considered:
—lighting
—colored backgrounds
—differences in scale of setting
—high, low, of eye-level placement
—placement among or next to a variety of things which imitate or conflict in line, shape, bulk, etc.

These experiments may be done on table tops, or, if desired, a series of cardboard cartons or open cigar boxes may be used, or both types of general setting may be used. Objects so displayed may obviously be made to stand out, fade away, lose or gain in clarity of line, form and meaning. This may become an exercise in montage or "found art," a psychological experiment, a lesson in interior decorating, or an experiment in the physiology of vision.

V. Perceptual Set.

Students may observe what others see to discover kinds of perceptual set.

1. What does a dog or a cat "see"? Ask the students to observe and report.

2. What does a small child see? Suggest that students take a pre-schooler for a walk, encouraging him to tell "what he sees" along the way. If possible, walk with the child to a street where some of his friends or relatives live. Ask the child to show you which house he lives in, and then ask him how he knows that's the right house.

3. Invite an international student to talk to the class about what he remembers seeing when he first arrived. What caught his eye? What looked

"wrong" or "different"? If any of the students in your class have international students staying with them, particularly if they have recently arrived in the country, ask them to go with them on a shopping trip, and ask the student what he sees.

4. Interest and pupil dilation. What we are interested in or like is part of our perceptual set. One interesting aspect of this may be shown in a simple experiment which demonstrates a physiological reaction to an affective change. If someone is shown a series of pictures, his pupils will dilate at the sight of something he likes very much or is very interested in, and contract when presented with something he actively dislikes. This experiment may be done by mounting a series of suitable pictures on construction paper or other fairly heavy stock, and giving these to the student experimenter, who sits facing the student subject. The experimenter holds up one picture at a time for the subject to look at, meanwhile carefully observing the pupil size of the subject. The pictures should be held in such a way that the subject does not look down, as this would make the experimenter's observations difficult. The series may be numbered on the back of the set, starting with "neutral" pictures. As the experimenter slips the pictures, one at a time, to the front, he sees the number, but not the picture itself, so that he can more objectively determine which pictures change the pupil size. Problem solving will also cause pupil dilation, and if desired, one of the "pictures" shown could be a problem in math or logic, or a "find the hidden face in this picture."

The experiment may be explained in advance to the class or to a subgroup, which may then prepare suitable pictures, or the instructor may prepare the pictures, have the experiment performed by dyads, and the results discussed. It is better to go through the experiment prior to describing the expected effects. You and your students might be interested in reading a paper by the discoverer of this phenomenon, Dr. Hess—see "Pupil Size as Related to Interest Value of Visual Stimuli" by Eckhard H. Hess and James Polk, in SCIENCE, 132, 1960, pp. 349-50.

Students might be interested in trying this experiment at home, selecting suitable pictures to invoke various responses in family members. They may be surprised by some of the "liking" and "disliking" responses.

VI. Deja vu.

Many people have experienced the apparently visual phenomenon upon seeing something for the first time, of feeling that they have seen it before—that it is all familiar from a previous experience. McKellar, checking with 182 university students, found that 69 percent had experienced this, and also found that, despite its common occurrence, some people were rather frightened by it and were unaware that others have had the same experience. It is true that a somewhat exaggerated form of deja vu accompanies the onset of some epileptic attacks, but obviously many people with no organic or functional problems have this experience.

It is also interesting because opinion is still divided as to its cause, some psychologists believing it is related to memory and some confusion of memory traces. Freud thought it was due to unconscious fantasies and Jung thought it was another manifestation of the collective unconscious of mankind. On the other hand, in 1968 Eugene Guccione, associate editor of CHEMICAL ENGINEERING, said that it was neurophysiological in nature, and due to a kind of "neural misfiring." As we come around that bend in the road, sometimes the impulse wave from the left eye, for instance, reaches the brain first and produces a memory trace. When the lagging impulses from the other eye reach the brain, it finds a stored image already there. "The process occurs too quickly for the brain to 'frame' the image in a temporal context; and so you cannot remember whether you saw a particular image 5 minutes, or five years . . . earlier" (CHEMICAL ENGINEERING, January 15, 1968, p. 218).

Students may be interested in (a) comparing experiences of deja vu; (b) polling the class or some other group to see how their frequency of occurrence figure compares with McKellar's; (c) doing individual research to determine the latest findings and opinions on its cause.

VII. Discussion will follow many sections of this exercise, and can deal with problems in philosophy, physiology, psychology and art.

A few suggested questions are:

—What is the difference, if any, between the classical illusions and the illusion that the household light is steady, not flickering? . . . that although we sometimes see the flicker in home movies, we usually do not see it in commercial film except under conditions of very bright lighting?

—How do we decide the relationship between what we "see" and what is "out there"?

—When do we feel least secure about the reality of what we are seeing? why? . . . When do we feel most secure? . . . why?

—Why are most people somewhat fascinated by optical illusions?

—What do you think is the difference between such pictures as "impossible figures" and "figure-ground reversal"? What is the differences in its effect on you? . . . Which interests you most? . . . Why do you think this is so?

—Why do you think people are often fascinat-

224 ed by trompe l'oeil paintings and decorations? . . . Why do you think many contemporary artists are doing paintings with the "frontality" of old Egyptian wall paintings?

SUGGESTED RESOURCES:

THINGS TO MAKE.

In addition to the suggestions given in "Materials Required," the following may be used:

1. Attneave in his *SCIENTIFIC AMERICAN* article suggests you draw your own reversing figure by "scribbling a meaningless line down the middle of a circle. The line will be seen as a contour or a boundary, and its appearance is quite different depending on which side of the contour is seen as the inside and which as the outside." He points out that it is "impossible to see both sides of the contour as figures at the same time" and that a "third possibility is being able to see the line as a thing in itself, as a twisted wire rather than the boundary of a figure" (p. 63).

2. A fascinating version of the "impossible figure" is an actual photograph of the Penrose "impossible triangle" reproduced on pp. 55-57 on Gregory's *THE INTELLIGENT EYE.* Can one of your students make one of these, or can you?

FILM:

Visual Perception, 18 minutes, color, 1960. Made with the cooperation of Princeton University this shows the Ames "distorted room" etc. Available on free loan basis from Thiokol Chemical Corporation, Film Library, P.O. Box 27, Bristol, Pa. 19007. Book well in advance.

Two excellent sources of free literature on the anatomy and physiology of the eye for distribution to students are: Bausch and Lomb Inc., Dept. 6606, 635 St. Paul St., Rochester, N.Y. 14602; and National Society for the Prevention of Blindness, Inc., 79 Madison Ave., New York, N.Y. 10016. The latter also has free literature and free loan films on eye hygiene and safety; ask for their Catalogue of Publications and Films.

BOOKS AND ARTICLES ON VISUAL PERCEPTION AND ILLUSIONS:

Arnheim, Rudolf, *ART AND VISUAL PERCEPTION: A PSYCHOLOGY OF THE CREATIVE EYE,* Berkeley, Calif.: University of California, 1954. This and the following work by Arnheim, Professor of the Psychology of Art at Harvard, were reprinted in 1971 by the University of California, and deal with the application of principles of Gestalt psychology to perception, vision and the study of art.

Arnheim, Rudolf, *VISUAL THINKING,* Berkeley, Calif.: University of California, 1969.

Attneave, Fred, "Multistability in Perception," *SCIENTIFIC AMERICAN,* Vol. 224, No. 6, Dec., 1971, pp. 62ff.

Beeler, Nelson F., and Franklyn M. Branley, *EXPERIMENTS IN OPTICAL ILLUSION,* New York: Thomas Y. Crowell, 1951.

Carraher, R. G., and J. B. Thurston, *OPTICAL ILLUSIONS AND THE VISUAL ARTS,* New York: Reinhold, 1966.

Cohen, Josef, *SENSATION AND PERCEPTION: 1. VISION,* Chicago, Ill.: Rand McNally & Co., 1969, p. 67.

Culkin, John, "Telemobility: The World of Marshall McLuhan," *DISCOVERY PATTERNS: BOOK 1. PATTERNS OF SITUATIONS,* Robert J. Heyer and Richard J. Payne, (eds.), New York: Paulist, 1969, pp. 30-35.

Foss, Brian M., (ed.), *NEW HORIZONS IN PSYCHOLOGY,* Baltimore, Md.: Penguin, 1966, Section I. "Perception, Thinking and Communication."

Gregory, R. L., *EYE AND BRAIN: THE PSYCHOLOGY OF SEEING,* New York: McGraw-Hill, 1966.

Gregory, R. L., *THE INTELLIGENT EYE,* New York: McGraw-Hill, 1970. Available in paperback, complete with the fascinating 3-D stereo illustrations, and the necessary red-green spectacles for viewing. The illustrations are carefully designed to illustrate a number of principles about vision and perception, and other experiments are suggested in this and Gregory's previous entertaining and informative book. This volume also contains copies of the "Plateau spiral" and a modified "Benham's Disk" which may be removed for experimental use.

Holt, Elizabeth G., (ed.), *A DOCUMENTARY HISTORY OF ART, VOL. I,* Garden City, N.Y.: Doubleday Anchor, 1957, pp. 259-282.

Kilpatrick, Franklin P., *EXPLORATIONS IN TRANSACTIONAL PSYCHOLOGY,* New York: New York University, 1961. This book was reprinted in 1970. It contains illustrated papers on the Ames demonstrations in perception, including the distorted rooms and the rotating trapezoid by Ames, Cantril, Ittelson and others (see also the film listed above).

McKellar, Peter, *EXPERIENCE AND BEHAVIOUR,* Baltimore, Md.: Penguin, 1968, ch. 2, "Perception of the Outside World."

Tibbetts, Paul (ed.), *PERCEPTION: SELECTED READINGS IN SCIENCE AND PHENOMENOLOGY,* Chicago, Ill.: Quadrangle, 1969. Contains a number of useful papers including James J. Gibson's "The Stimulus Variables for Visual Depth Perception" from *THE PERCEPTION OF*

THE VISUAL WORLD, 1950.

Tolansky, S., *OPTICAL ILLUSIONS,* New York: Pergamon Press, 1964.

Wilentz, John Steen, *THE SENSES OF MAN,* New York: Thomas Y. Crowell, 1968. Excellent general book on senses. (Note: The "young-old lady" illustration in this book is a poor copy to use.)

Wilson, John Rowan, and the Editors of Time-Life Books, *THE MIND,* New York: Time-Life Books, 1969, pp. 48-54. Numerous illusions and ambiguities attractively presented in color. Page 49 contains a series of right- and left-hand scenes which may be viewed stereoscopically with the aid of a small mirror.

Wooldridge, Dean E., *THE MACHINERY OF THE BRAIN,* New York: McGraw-Hill, 1963, pp. 49-53.

Editors of Communications/Research/Machines, Inc., *PSYCHOLOGY TODAY: AN INTRODUCTION,* Del Mar, Calif.: CRM Books, 1970, chs. 16, 17.

Depth perception: (In addition to the suggestions given below for "illusionism in art," the following pictures from the *DISCOVERY* series will be helpful:

Heyer, Robert, and Anthony Meyer, *DISCOVERY IN FILM,* New York, N.Y.: Paulist Press, 1969, pp. 32, 35, 39, 42, 53, 73, 141, 145, 169 and 173. See also drawing on p. 115 and reproduction of "cave painting" on p. 187.

Heyer, Robert J., and Richard J. Payne, *DISCOVERY IN PRAYER,* New York, N.Y.: Paulist Press, 1969, pp. 10, 25, 37, 75, 85, 97, 98, and 109.

Heyer, Robert J., *et al., DISCOVERY IN SONG,* New York, N.Y.: Paulist Press, 1970, pp. 26, 95.

Baecher, Charlotte M., and Elizabeth M. Pierotti, *DISCOVERY IN SERVICE,* New York, N.Y.: Paulist Press, 1970, pp. 16-17, 25, 26, 27, 150, 155.

Frazier, Cliff, and Anthony Meyer, *DISCOVERY IN DRAMA,* New York, N.Y.: Paulist Press, 1969. Line drawings will be useful.

EXAMPLES OF ILLUSIONISM IN ART:

(Students may compare perspective, and its absence, in primitive drawings and paintings, early Egyptian art, pre-Renaissance European painting, Chinese paintings (which use a quite different set of perspective conventions), fourteenth century European paintings in which there were often converging lines, but neither light nor shadowing was used to indicate depth; early examples—as Crivelli's "The Annunciation" and the full blown and emphasized perspective of Canaletto. The following specific examples of various types of illusionism could be re-placed by many others. The classic illusionism of the Renaissance is often dependent upon being viewed in the buildings for which it was designed, and loses a great deal in reproduction.

Examples of depth:

Pieter de Hooch (1629—after 84); "The Mother" (Berlin Museum); use of light as well as perspective

Vincent van Gogh (1853—90); "The Railway Bridge of Arles" (1888—Porto Ronco, E. M. Remarque Collection)

Classic illusionism—combines strong use of perspective with depth enhancement through lighting, shadows, color, etc.

Giovanni Battista Gaulli, called Baciccia (1639—1709); ceiling of the Gesu church in Rome (1668—83) (combines painted figures and stucco figures)

Antonio Correggio, (1494, or 1489—1534); cupolas of S. Giovanni Evangelista (1420—23) and Cathedral (probably 1526—30) (illusionistic when seen from below)

Andrea Mantegna (c. 1431—1506); frescoes—Camera degli Sposi at Mantua (1474) (walls and ceilings—first completely illusionistic "Sotto in Su"); see also some paintings

Pietro (Berrettini) da Cortona (1596—1669); fresco—"Allegory of Divine Providence and Barberini Power" (1633—1639—ceiling Galleria Nazionale, Rome)

Andrea Pozzo (1642—1709); ceiling of Jesuit church of S. Ignazio (1691—94) (illusion "works" from only one point in the nave, photograph made from this position gives some of the Sotto in Su effect).

Trompe l'oeil:

Salvador Dali (contemporary); "Illuminated Pleasures" (Sidney and Harriet Janis Collection, Museum of Modern Art, New York) (*DISCOVERY IN ART,* p. 187)

William M. Harnett; —"Old Cremona" (1885) (Metropolitan Museum of Art, New York)

Charles Bird King; "Vanity of an artist's Dream (1830) (Foss Art Museum, Harvard University, Cambridge, Mass.)

Distorted perspective:

Roy Lichtenstein (contemporary); "Holly Solomon" (1966) (frontality (Collection of Mr. and Mrs. Horace Solomon, New York, 1970) (*DISCOVERY IN ART,* p. 62); "Blond 1," (1965) (ceramic—use of 3-dimensional conventions painted on a 3-dimensional object—shadows, etc.) (Collection of Mr. and Mrs. Roger Davidson, Toronto; *POP ART,* p. 96)

Richard Hamilton (contemporary); "Transition IIII" (1955) (multiple perspectives) (Collection of the artist) (Michael Compton, *POP ART,* New

York: Hamlyn, 1970, p. 44)

Giorgio de Chirico (contemporary); "The Lassitude of the Infinite" (deviates from normal perspective through isometric base of central statue, distortion of horizon, etc.); "Melancholy and Mystery of a Street" (Arnheim, *ART AND VISUAL PERCEPTION*, p. 290)

Jasper Johns (contemporary); "Three Flags" (1958) (ambiguity through use of two-dimensional objects as subject matter) (Collection of Mr. and Mrs. Burton Tremaine, New York) (Michael Compton, *POP ART*, New York: Hamlyn, 1970, p. 10)

Peter Phillips (contemporary); "Tiger-Tiger" (1968) (two-dimensional subject matter (Galerie Bischofberger, Zurich) (Michael Compton, *POP ART*, p. 75)

Allan D'Arcangelo (contemporary); "Highway Series," five pictures (1963) (Museum of Modern Art, New York, and private collections) (Michael Compton, *POP ART*, pp. 128-129)

Distorted Size Constancy:

Rene Magritte (contemporary); "Personal Values" (1952), (collection Harry Torczyner, New York)

Ambiguous depth clues:

Maurits C. Escher (contemporary Dutch); "Belvedere" (collection of C. V. S. Roosevelt, Washington, D.C.); (see others in which waterfalls run uphill and buildings form "impossible figures," M. C. Escher, *THE GRAPHIC WORK OF M. C. ESCHER*, New York: Duell, Sloan and Pearce, 1960)

Josef Albers (contemporary); "Structural Constellation: N-34" (1964); (*SAT. REV.* Jan. 29, 1972, p. 53)

Depth reversal:

Frank Stella, "Wolfboro II" (contemporary); (Leo Castelli Gallery, New York) (*DISCOVERY IN ART*, p. 87)

Figure-ground reversal:

Pablo Picasso (1881-1973); "Girl Before a Mirror" (ambiguity or visual contradiction combined with figure-ground reversal in face of girl) (Museum of Modern Art, New York)

Salvador Dali (contemporary); "Slave Market with Apparition of the Invisible Bust of Voltaire" (Dali Museum, Cleveland, Ohio) (Attneave, *SCIENTIFIC AMERICAN*, p. 62)

Maurits C. Escher (Dutch contemporary); "Circle Limit IV" (woodcut of angels and devils) (*THE GRAPHIC WORK OF M. C. ESCHER*)

Ambiguity or visual contradiction of shared borders:

Pablo Picasso (1881-1973); "Guernica" (Museum of Modern Art, New York) (*DISCOVERY IN ART*, pp. 22-23)

Op Art:

Anuskiewicz (contemporary), "Corona" (Sidney Janis Gallery, New York) (*DISCOVERY IN ART*, p. 185)

Bridget Riley (contemporary), "Fall" (Gregory, *INTELLIGENT EYE*, p. 89)

ADDITIONAL RESOURCES:

Robert Froman, *SCIENCE, ART AND VISUAL ILLUSIONS*, New York: Simon and Schuster, 1970. Reproductions of works of art used to demonstrate visual illusions in this study of scientific observations about perception.

Louis G. Brandes, *AN INTRODUCTION TO OPTICAL ILLUSIONS*, Portland, Maine: J. Weston Walch, Publisher. A collection of 24 common optical illusions which people normally experience: such as height-width, contour, perspective and contrast. Printed in a handy 8 1/2 x 11 booklet, these drawings may be mounted or passed among the students. A brief explanation of each illustration is printed on the back for the convenience of the teacher.

DISTORTED ROOM; ROTATING ILLUSION, (model PT-12); *HIDDEN CHAIR ILLUSION* (model PT-13); *SEEING IS DECEIVING*, a series of overhead transparencies on visual perception. Contact Research Media, Inc., 4 Midland Avenue, Hicksville, N.Y. 11801.

Wolfgang Köhler, *GESTALT PSYCHOLOGY*, New York: Mentor, 1947.

SENSES: VISION: SERIAL REPRODUCTION

PURPOSE:

To explore perceptual set and memory through "serial reproduction" of simple line drawings.

COMMENT:

A visual form of "Whisper Down the Lane" will exhibit some of our tendencies toward interpretation and/or distortion of a visual message. A simple drawing of an ambiguous nature will be reproduced in such a way that the original receiver organizes the material in a comprehensible pattern, in some cases retaining data, in others eliminating it, and in others changing it to correspond with some view of reality. F. C. Bartlett, a British psychologist, carried on a number of experiments demonstrating many aspects of this experience, including the differences induced by giving the subjects a name for the drawing at the time the drawing was shown the subjects. This is again an illustration of the way in which perceptual set influences the message our senses send to our brain, or perhaps the way our brain affects the message our senses receive and transmit.

GROUP SIZE:

Up to 20

TIME SUGGESTED:

45—60 minutes

GENERAL DIRECTIONS:

If desired, this exercise may be used in connection with one of the exercises on "Freedom: from Prejudice," or it may be used with some of the other exercises on "Vision" or on "Memory." Students are allowed a minute or so to study a simple drawing, and then are to reproduce it. Their reproduction, in turn, is shown to another student, and the process is repeated through a series. Students examine the completed series, looking for simplification, elaboration and organization toward the familiar. More than one series may be in progress simultaneously.

MATERIALS REQUIRED:

Several simple and somewhat ambiguous line-drawings, such as those reproduced here. Several copies of each may be needed.

A table and chair for the student examining the picture and doing the sketching should be placed at a distance from the class. Additional similar set-ups will be required if more than one series is carried on simultaneously.

PROCEDURE:

1. A student is shown one of the line draw-

PORTRAIT OF A MAN

EGYPTIAN MULAH

228

ings and allowed a few minutes to study it, being told he will be asked to draw it afterward. Other students are not allowed to see the picture. NOTE: It may be better to allow the student to actually copy, although not trace, the picture, rather than removing it. Other students are not allowed to see the picture at this point.

2. The picture is removed, concealed from all, and the student given a few minutes to complete his sketch, which he numbers "1". He returns to his group, leaving his sketch on the table.

3. A second student is taken to the table and shown the first student's drawing, and the procedures of Steps Nos. 1 and 2 are repeated, this student labeling his drawing "2". The process is continued until 12—15 students have made a drawing, numbering them in order.

4. The original drawing is produced, the entire series posted, in order, and examined by the class.

5. Discussion of the "gallery" will include an examination of the possible factors causing changes in the drawings. Stress is on "perception" rather than on quality of the "art" or "good or bad memory." Results demonstrate perceptual set, a tendency to organize toward the familiar, and the contrasting tendencies toward simplification and elaboration. Those sketches which carry a name will be seen to quickly take on "suitable attributes" in accordance with the set introduced by the name—a form of self-fulfilling prophecy. Ambiguous and unnamed sketches such as the Egyptian "mulak" may become birds, cats or other figures. Simple but straightforward drawings may lose or acquire characteristics.

VARIATION:

One or more series may be used which include a "name" for the original sketch, as suggested above ("Portrait of a Man," "Egyptian Man," etc.) Also, halfway through the series a student may be asked to omit the name in copying the drawing, and the instructor may substitute another name, for instance, "Portrait of a Man" may be changed to "Egyptian Man." If the same students work on more than one drawing, the results may be distorted to some extent by their memory of the other drawings on which they have been working. This consideration may be discussed when the "gallery" is exhibited.

SUGGESTED RESOURCES:

The original source of this exercise is work done by F. C. Bartlett, and published in *REMEMBERING,* (rev. ed.), New York: Cambridge University, 1950, pp. 177-185. Portions of this work are reprinted in *BASIC CONTRIBUTIONS TO PSYCHOLOGY: READINGS,* Robert L. Wrenn (ed.), Belmont, Calif.: Wadsworth Publishing, 1966, pp. 172ff.

Fred Attneave, "Multistability in Perception," *SCIENTIFIC AMERICAN,* Vol. 225, No. 6, Dec., 1971, p. 62. The "man-girl" figures of Gerald Fisher are here reproduced. If used for this exercise, the last figure in the top row should be reproduced.

SENSES: VISION: COLOR AND FEELING

PURPOSE:

To discover some of our emotional responses to color.

COMMENT:

Most people demonstrate some degree of color preference, of an emotional response to color. However, there is a wide range of opinion as to why this is so. Although many studies have been carried out, it still cannot be stated positively that color, *per se*, evokes genuine affective responses.

A study of 500 Chinese high school students showed that the color they most liked was white, and the one they most disliked was violet; Japanese children in the upper grades liked blue best, and green least, and 1300 American university students also liked blue best, but liked yellow least, and so did 200 German children, 1000 American Negroes, and a group of European adults. Another collection of groups agreed with yellow as least liked, but liked red best, rather than blue: 15 American graduates, 200 German schoolgirls, 1000 Filipino children, 550 full-blooded Indians, a group of mixed-blood Indians, and 1032 "young children." A group of Bengali students liked green best, and one group of European adults preferred violet. "Nobody didn't like" blue or red, but lots of people didn't like yellow, a good number didn't like orange, a small number didn't like green, and a very few listed purple or violet as least liked. However, these figures are drawn from a very small amount of evidence derived from 31 studies. (Robert W. Burnham *et al.*, *COLOR: A GUIDE TO BASIC FACTS AND CONCEPTS,* p. 210.)

N. F. Dixon, a psychologist whose field is perception, believes there is sufficient experimental evidence to indicate that red, at least, "tends to evoke an emotional reaction." However, whether this is innate or acquired is still an open question, he believes. (N.F. Dixon, "The Beginnings of Perception," *NEW HORIZONS IN PSYCHOLOGY,* Brian M. Foss (ed.), Baltimore, Md.: Penguin, 1966, p. 60.

There are some psychologists working in the field of color who believe not only that color very definitely does affect emotion, but even that one's personality can be accurately determined by investigating the colors one prefers and dislikes. Dr. Max Lüscher, formerly a professor of psychology at the University of Basel in Europe, and now a color consultant in many fields, has devised an easily administered color preference test for the use of psychologists and psychiatrists. B. J. Kouwer, a Dutch psychologist, has said, "The fact that a certain relationship exists between character and color preferences has become evident from so many experiments that further proof is hardly required" (quoted by F. Birren in *COLOR IN YOUR WORLD*). Faber Birren, who has been a color consultant to industry and to the U.S. Government, says, ". . . color preferences are innate in most individuals . . . and will probably last throughout your life." (*COLOR IN YOUR WORLD,* p. 17-18). On the other hand, Burnham *et al.* state that "children's color preferences develop and shift with age, showing a tendency to move from warm to cool colors with increasing years" (p. 212).

How much of our color preference is due to education? It does seem to be a fact that certain hues seem to advance and make objects appear nearer or larger, and that others seem to recede and make objects look further away. It is also a fact that white reflects light, and black absorbs it, so that white clothing is "cooler" in the summer. How much do these facts affect our feelings about colors? How much does color symbolism—ecclesiastical, academic, national flag, sports uniforms, and colors associated with marriage and mourning—affect our feelings? In our culture, for instance, black is often associated with death and mourning. Does this affect our feelings about the color black? What if, as in some other cultures, white mourning were worn? Dark blue, grey, and yellow are all colors selected by particular cultures for mourning. If we used one of these colors for mourning, would we feel differently about black?

GROUP SIZE:

Up to 20

TIME SUGGESTED:

60 minutes

GENERAL DIRECTIONS:

Using questionnaires and color samples, students make various determinations of their own color preferences and associations. Discussion focuses on possible reasons for particular affective responses, and heightened awareness of color in our lives.

MATERIALS REQUIRED:

One copy for each student of each of the two questionnaires.

One set of color samples. These may be prepared in a number of ways. Samples may be cut from various kinds of construction, craft or art papers and identical numbered sets made up for each student. Color effects differ with the light reflecting qualities of the surface of the paper, and you may want to prepare two sets—one of a flat, nonreflecting finish and the other of a glossy, highly reflecting finish. It is better to number the colors, rather than give them names. "Color Association Questionnaire, II" indicates a set of 8 colors, but any number may be chosen and the questionnaire adjusted accordingly.

PROCEDURE:

1. Distribute copies of the "Color Association Questionnaire, I", and ask the students to fill them in individually.

2. Distribute sets of numbered color samples prepared as suggested in "Materials Required." Distribute copies of "Color Association Questionnaire, II", and ask the students to fill in individually, using the *numbers* given on the color samples, *not names* of the colors.

3. In dyads or other small groups, ask the students to share the results of their questionnaires. Encourage them to explore the possible reasons for their associations.

4. In a plenary session the class may discuss their opinions and beliefs about color and emotion. Some of the following questions may be explored:

—Were there similarities in your subgroup as to colors "most liked" and "least liked"? . . . Do you have any ideas on why this is so?

—Were there similarities in the "word and color association" lists? . . . Why do you think this was so?

—Were there similarities in the list of products and package colors? . . . If you were responsible for choosing the package color for a new product, what color would you choose? . . . Why? . . . How much relation does color attractiveness have to the product? . . . Would it matter whether the product were a food, say "butter," or a perfume?

—If you were choosing a color scheme for the room for someone who was very depressed, what color would you choose? . . . why?

—How much effect do you think society has on your liking or not liking certain colors?

—Scientists in West Berlin have found you are safer driving a bright red, orange or yellow car, because other drivers see and react more quickly to these colors. Do you think this would be true everywhere? Why or why not?

VARIATIONS:

1. If desired, students may be encouraged to experiment with the books by Lüscher and Birren, and report to the class. People are often fascinated by the Lüscher "personality analysis," but if this is carried out in the classroom some students will be made very uncomfortable. Instead, talk briefly and informally with students about the controversial nature of the "scientific findings" in regard to color preference, color and personality, and color therapy. Ask the students to investigate the Lüscher and Birren books given in "Suggested Resources," and report to the class. Ask other students to see what they can find on the subject. After reports have been given, general discussion by the class will be worthwhile.

2. Film. Run a short black and white film. Subgroup the students and help them discuss the use of color in film. Would they have liked the film they just saw more if it had been in color? . . . Why? . . . Why do you think it was done in black and white? . . . Do you usually like color films better than black and white films? . . . Do you think most people do? . . . Why? . . . Do you think all films would be better in color? . . . Why do you think some film makers choose black and white? . . . If you were to do the film you just saw in color, what colors would you use? . . . Would it matter what color clothing was worn? . . . (etc., depending on the specific film used).

3. Color in prints and paintings. Various methods may be used for examining our own reactions to the artists' use of color: (a) A series of slides may be shown, reproducing paintings, lithographs and other graphics in color, with concentration on the use of color. Students may be asked to react in written form and then in discussion, or direct verbal response may be used. If desired, slides may be numbered, rather than named, or even shown upside down, asking students to react only to the colors they see. (b) Students may be subgrouped and small collections of reproductions given each subgroup for similar reactions. (c) Students may work individually with small collections of reproductions, or books containing reproductions—DISCOVERY IN ART is particularly well suited to this. Ask the students to

go through their pictures rather rapidly, jotting down a page or number to identify the pictures that particularly struck them because of color. Ask them to note their immediate, off-the-top-of-the-head reaction to the color or colors—like, dislike, makes me feel happy, sad, rather frightened, confused, etc. In subgroups, members share their reactions and discuss them, concentrating on color.

4. Students may be given sets of color samples, such as paint chips, and asked to select colors they would want to use in decorating their own room—wall, ceiling, other furnishings. Discussion in subgroups on why they believe they have selected these colors and how a room in these colors might make them feel.

5. A wide selection of oil pastels may be made available, and students asked to select one or two colors to work with. On large sheets of paper encourage free use of the color selected by individuals working alone. Ask them to concentrate on the color, their reactions to it, and any forms that seem to flow spontaneously from the color itself. This is an experience in awareness, spontaneity and possibly day dreaming, and need not be followed by sharing or discussion. It is important to stress the need for care in the selection of the desired color at the beginning of this experience—sampling paper may be provided, and indicate that there will be plenty of time to select the color "you really want to work with." The following is a suggested questionnaire for use with this exercise. You may prefer to prepare your own with your particular group in mind.

COLOR ASSOCIATION QUESTIONNAIRE, I
Try to put down the color which first comes to your mind as you read each question.

1. What color do you associate with the following words?

WORD	COLOR
mystery	
importance	
school	
Fall	
joy	
dignity	
Summer	
freedom	
breeziness	
fear	
hope	
Winter	
love	
home	
Spring	
power	

2. Suppose you were going into a store to buy the following things. Each item is packaged in a container on which one color dominates. None of the brand-names are known to you in this store and, except for color, all packages look identical and contain equal amounts. As you go down this shopping list, try to picture these boxes in your mind's eye and decide which you would buy. Check your choices.

PRODUCT	COLOR OF PACKAGE
sugar	brown___; blue___; green___
flour	purple___; white___; orange___
detergent	red___; blue___; black___
hand soap	yellow___; purple___; red___

COLOR ASSOCIATION QUESTIONNAIRE, II
Some people associate vowel sounds with particular colors. Do the following vowel sounds bring any color to your mind? Say the sound silently in your head, and if a color comes spontaneously to mind, put it down. Do not put down anything if you have to "hunt" for an association:

SOUND	COLOR
ah	
a as in "way"	
ee	
I	
o as in "row"	
oo	
u as in "unicorn"	

Spread out the numbered color samples you have received, select the one you like best, and put the number down in the list below. Put that color sample aside, and select the one you like next best, and put that number down. Continue until all your color samples have been ranked.

1. (like best)
2. (like next best)
3.
4.
5.
6.
7.
8.

Choose the color that makes you think of death, and put its number here ___
Choose the color you associate with jealousy, and put its number here ___
Put here the color you associate with purity ___
Which color do you think is most calming? ___
Which color do you think is most exciting? ___

SUGGESTED RESOURCES:

The art department of your school or local library may be able to offer helpful material for use with this exercise.

Birren, Faber, *COLOR IN YOUR WORLD,* New York: Collier-Macmillan, 1962.

Burnham, Robert W., Randall M. Hanes and C. James Bartleson, *COLOR: A GUIDE TO BASIC FACTS AND CONCEPTS,* New York: John Wiley & Sons, 1963.

Evans, Ralph M., *AN INTRODUCTION TO COLOR,* New York: John Wiley, 1948 (physics, psychology, physiology, colorimetry, color systems, color aesthetics).

Lavin, Edward, and Terrence Manning, *DISCOVERY IN ART,* New York, N.Y.: Paulist Press, 1969.

Scott, Ian A., translator and editor, based on text by Max Lüscher, *THE LÜSCHER COLOR TEST,* New York: Random House, 1969.

SENSES: TOUCH: 2-POINT THRESHOLD AND LOCALIZATION ERROR

PURPOSE:

To examine our variations in touch perception in different areas of the skin.

COMMENT:

All of our senses have a "threshold" point, "a point or a region on an intensity scale below which we do not detect the stimulus and above which we do" (Conrad G. Mueller, *SENSORY PSYCHOLOGY*). Common sense tells us that an odor has to be strong enough before we smell it, a star bright enough before we see it, a sound loud enough before we hear it. There are also "discrimination thresholds"—points below which we can see "something," but not be able to describe or identify it, for instance. This is also true of our sense of touch, and since the quality of our sense of touch varies in different areas of the body, and can be demonstrated with fairly simple equipment, this exercise can introduce a number of concepts about our senses.

GROUP SIZE:

Subgroups of 2—4, or larger groups with a small demonstration team may be used.

TIME SUGGESTED:

45 minutes

GENERAL DIRECTIONS:

The subject being tested is blindfolded, and the investigator, working with simple equipment, checks his "Two-Point Threshold" (or "tactile acuity") and "Localization Error" on various parts of the skin. If there is sufficient equipment, each person may have a turn being "subject" and "investigator"; otherwise, demonstration teams may show the process to small or large groups. General discussion follows. If desired, the equipment may be kept out of sight until the first set of subjects is blindfolded, so that the subjects may try to identify the object, or type of object touching them by feel alone.

MATERIALS REQUIRED:

For each subject, a blindfold.

For each investigator, a pair of calipers, a ruler (a six-inch plastic ruler is best), pencil and paper, and a bottle of liquid cosmetic (eye-liner), lash-liner or similar harmless liquid with a fine brush.

A clean-up method should be available, such as a liquid or cream cosmetic remover.

Papers are prepared as follows:

Object	Two-Point Threshold	Localization Error
Leg	_____	_____
Forearm	_____	_____
Forehead	_____	_____
Lips	_____	_____

PROCEDURES:

1. The subject to be tested is blindfolded. He is instructed that he will be lightly touched with various harmless objects on the bare skin of his leg, forearm, forehead and lips.

2. The investigator is provided with the above listed equipment. He announces to his subject that he is about to touch him on one of the announced areas. Taking the lash-liner bottle, he carefully withdraws the brush, wiping excess fluid on the rim of the bottle, and puts a tiny dab on one of the areas listed in Step No. 1. He asks the subject: "Will you please put your finger on the spot where I touched you?" The subject is to keep his finger on that spot while the investigator measures the distance, if any, from the spot of dye-stuff to the subject's finger-tip. He writes down the resulting figure in the "localization error" column. He may then ask the subject: "Can you identify the object with which I touched you?" He may write down the answer, if one is forthcoming. The procedure is repeated for the other 3 areas named in Step No. 1. If the subject

does not feel the touch at all, as may be possible on some parts of the leg or even the forearm, another spot is touched.

3. Without removing the blindfold, or commenting in any way on the procedure, the investigator puts aside the lash-liner, and takes up the calipers, adjusting them so the tips are touching. He touches the tips very gently to a different portion of one of the same four areas of skin. He asks the subject: "Did I touch you at one spot then, or at two spots at the same time?" Presumably the subject will answer "One." If he answers "Two," the subject is asked to point to the "two" spots, and the procedure is repeated until the subject answers "One." These initial "errors" need not be recorded.

4. The calipers are then adjusted so that the tips are separated by 1/16 of an inch—if the calipers are not calibrated in this way, the ruler may be used each time in adjusting them. The subject is touched and the question repeated. If the subject continues to answer "One," the calipers are re-adjusted, moving the points apart in 1/16 of an inch increments until the answer "two" is elicited. The distance between the tips of the calipers is recorded in the correct place on the "Two-Point Threshold" column. Another one of the areas listed in Step No. 1 is chosen, and the process repeated from the beginning of this step. If desired, the subject may at some point be asked if he can identify the object with which he is being touched.

5. If desired, subject and investigator may trade roles. The knowledge of the procedures may slightly distort the perceptions of the subject, but it is still worth the experience.

6. The entire class may compare their findings and discuss its meaning in terms of the sense of touch, in terms of the concept of sensory threshold, and in terms of the relation between "sensation" and "perception." This discussion may take a physiological, a psychological, or even a philosophical direction. It will be found that there is a correlation between the two columns, as might be expected. The lips are the most sensitive, the leg the least sensitive, and the forehead considerably more sensitive than the forearm.

VARIATION:

As an opener, or follow-up, an old "parlor trick" will mildly entertain students, and provide additional input. Tell students, working with a partner, to lay palm surface of their index finger against the palm surface of their partner's index finger, and then, with the thumb and two fingers of the other hand stroke up and down both surfaces of this "combined finger." The resulting sensation is

234 somewhat strange and unexpected. Why is this so, when we know and can see what is happening?

SUGGESTED RESOURCES:

Mueller, Conrad G., *SENSORY PSYCHOL-OGY*, Englewood Cliffs, N.J.: Prentice-Hall, 1965, pp. 5, 92-93.

Wilentz, Joan Steen, *THE SENSES OF MAN*, New York: Thomas Y. Crowell, 1968, pp. 66-68.

SENSES: TOUCH: SKIN SLAP/TAP

PURPOSE:

To tune in to our skin as a means of seeing tension and developing a sense of well being.

COMMENT:

During the time of Queen Victoria, women's magazines such as *GODEY'S LADIES' BOOK,* recommended a certain amount of cheek slapping and even "pinching" to stimulate the skin of the face and bring a "healthy glow" to the cheeks. Since then, women's magazines have often suggested gentle slapping, along with various kinds of massage, for the skin of the face, neck and scalp. Exercises such as those below help us in more than cosmetic ways. They help us tune in to our sensations and make us feel more awake, more alive. They can wake us up when we feel sleepy at the wrong time, and while energizing us can also reduce tension. Once learned, they may be done individually as desired, much as one might do any other sort of exercise.

GROUP SIZE:

Up to 20

TIME SUGGESTED:

10—15 minutes

GENERAL DIRECTIONS:

It is best for the instructor to demonstrate the exercise briefly to the group, allow the group to try each exercise following its demonstration, and avoid talking during the students' performance of the exercise. There is no need for discussion, and the exercises are best performed in peaceful silence, but the instructor may talk as he demonstrates.

MATERIALS REQUIRED:

None

PROCEDURE:

1. Face. Sit quietly. Concentrate on how your face feels. After about 30 seconds, flex the fingers of both hands slightly. Raise both hands to the face and gently and rapidly tap the face, with the cushions of the fingers. Start with the cheeks, one hand on each cheek. After about 15—20 seconds, move to the jaw line, then the chin and lips, then the forehead. Spend about the same amount of time on each area. (Do not tap eyelids.) Use only one finger of each hand against each side of the nose. Rhythm should be steady and fairly rapid (for most people a comfortable pace is about four taps per second). Exert enough pressure for the taps to be audible, but never uncomfortable. Now rest quietly for about one minute, experiencing how your face feels.

2. Head and neck. Tapping as in "1", cover various areas of the head, starting with the back of the head, moving to the sides, top, then front. Spend about 20 seconds on each. Tilt the head gently forward and tap the neck, starting with the middle at the hairline and moving out until the fingers begin to touch the ears, then down the neck to the shoulder, then back to the middle. Rest for a minute. Concentrate on how the head and neck feel.

3. Slap. Although known as "slapping," this might better be called "vigorous patting." There should be no discomfort at any time. Curve the hand slightly, keeping fingers together. Rapidly pat the forehead with both hands for about 15 seconds. Move down to the cheeks, where the palms of the hands will also make contact with the cheeks. Move a bit more vigorously along the jaw, then more gently over the chin and lips. Keep the eyes closed, take your time, spend about 15 seconds on each area. (Again, do not slap eyelids.) Keep the eyes closed for minute or two while you rest and experience sensations of the face.

SUGGESTED RESOURCES:

Gunther, Bernard, *SENSE RELAXATION BELOW YOUR MIND*, New York: Collier, 1968.

Keen, Sam, "Sing the Body Electric," and "My New Carnality," *PSYCHOLOGY TODAY*, Oct., 1970, Vol. 4, No. 5, pp. 56ff, 59ff.

SENSES: TOUCH: WATER

PURPOSE:

To experience the "feel" of water, and to discover some of our "feelings" about water.

COMMENT:

Loren Eiseley begins one of the chapters of his book, *THE IMMENSE JOURNEY*, with the words, "If there is magic on this planet, it is contained in water." He goes on to describe his experience when, one day on a solitary walk along a shallow stretch of the Platte River, he slipped in and floated downstream. He says that as he pulled himself out of the river, he "knew once more the body's revolt against emergence into the harsh and unsupporting air, its reluctance to break contact with that mother element which still, at this late point in time, shelters and brings into being nine tenths of everything alive" (pp. 19-20). He speaks, as many poets have spoken, of man's affinity with water.

From the embryo cozily rocking in amniotic fluid, through the infant, splashing happily in the tub and the children playing in the backyard wading pool to the swimmer, the surfer, and the sailor, we all show an enthusiasm for water derived from something more than its ability to cleanse or sustain exercise. People will pay more for housing which offers a view of river or sea, will seek out a restaurant beside the water, want fountains in their parks and decorative pools in their gardens. Man's earliest experiences with agriculture taught him the necessity of rain and he therefore invested water with magic properties, sometimes worshiped it as a god, and often devised elaborate water rites to ensure its needed presence. Water quenches thirst, makes crops grow, puts out fires, and washes people and things, but it has pleasure giving qualities accessible to hearing, sight, and touch and even to our kinesthetic sense which is not directly related to these practical aspects.

236 **GROUP SIZE:**

Up to 20

TIME SUGGESTED:

45—60 minutes

GENERAL DIRECTIONS:

The object of the exercise is to consciously experience the feel of water on the hands and to follow this up by either meditation, discussion or creative writing. If desired, students may be told a few days before the exercise to look for a favorite poem or bit of writing that deals with "water" as a mysterious and fascinating element. These would then be brought to class for use during this session.

MATERIALS REQUIRED:

Containers for water
Water
Towels
(Optional: soap; marbles)
(If possible, both hot and cold water should be available)

PROCEDURE:

1. Running water. When a sink is available, partners can work together, with the first person turning on the spigot and adjusting the water to a comfortable temperature, and his partner then holding his hands under the spigot, simply letting the water flow over the back, side and palm of the hand, cupping his hands, and then letting the water escape. The entire exercise should be done in silence, to allow for concentration on the experience. Partners then switch roles and repeat. The experience may be initiated with the eyes closed, and then with the eyes opened when the hands are cupped.

Variation: Soap may be provided and a careful washing of the hands may end the experience. Each person may wash his own hands, or those of his partner—the experience is different. This should be done slowly, feeling the water, the soap, the lather, the towel. Also, the temperature of the water may be varied.

2. Still water. If running water is not available, or to provide an additional experience, pails of water of different temperatures are provided. Sug-

gest the following procedure: Dip your hand straight down into the cold water and move it about gently, feeling the water swirl around your hand. Let your hand go limp and move your arm slowly back and forth. Lift your hand out of the water and let the water run off your hand for a few seconds. Dry your hand and plunge it into the hot water, repeating the above actions. This experience should be completed in silence. Sit and think a minute about how your hand felt and experience how it now feels. Contrast this with the way your other hand feels, which did not participate in the experience. Do you want to repeat the experience with your other hand?

Variation: If the pails are shallow a few marbles may be placed in the bottom of the pails.

3. Meditation. This may be carried on in several ways, depending on the group and its experience. (1) Students may precede meditation with 5—10 minutes for individual meditation, with no further input. (2) Students may precede meditation with 5—10 minutes of readings, using some of the poems and other writings they have brought in, or some of the material in "Suggested Resources." (3) Music or "the environment record" may be used as a background for individual meditation. (4) You may use group meditation, in which individuals may speak if they wish, contributing some of their thoughts, or may remain silent.

4. Discussion (optional). If individual meditation has been used, individuals may contribute some of their thoughts as input for group discussion. Questions may center on the symbolism of water, if desired.

VARIATIONS:

1. In warm weather students may be encouraged to go individually or as a group to listen to a fountain, a waterfall, a lapping lake, a rushing river or stream, a gently moving bay, an ocean. Students may wish to tape some of these sounds for later playback to the class.

2. Students may be encouraged to do individual research on the symbolism of water in the East as well as in the West. They may also investigate the decorative use of water in their own community in fountains, pools, etc.

SUGGESTED RESOURCES:

Dickey, James, "Inside the River," *POEMS*, 1957-1967, New York: Collier, 1968, pp. 105-106.

Eiseley, Loren, *THE IMMENSE JOURNEY*, New York: Vintage, 1957, ch. 2.

Frost, Robert, "Spring Pools"; "Once by the Pacific"; "West-Running Brook" (particularly lines 38-44); "Neither Out Far Nor in Deep"; "The Wind and the Rain" (particularly part II); THE POETRY OF ROBERT FROST, Edward C. Lathem (ed.), New York: Holt, Rinehart and Winston, 1967, pp. 245, 250, 259, 301, 337.

McNaughton, William, THE TAOIST VISION, Ann Arbor, Mich.: University of Michigan Press, 1971, p. 3.

Record

Environment and Environment II, Syntonic Research Inc., 663 Fifth Avenue, New York 10022.

SENSES: KINESTHESIS: SOCIAL SPACE

PURPOSE:

To discover some of our feelings about private space and social distance.

COMMENT:

Our "distance receptors"—eyes, ears, nose—are augmented by touch and the two principle proprioceptor systems when we move closer to objects. One set of proprioceptors are those which tell us what our muscles are doing and where our arms and legs are in space, and the organs of the inner ear tell us whether we are going fast or slow and how gravity is acting upon us. Touch is not a simple sense, but includes receptors for heat, cold, pain, pressure and somehow enables us to make the fine distinctions involved in knowing whether it is velvet or satin that is brushing against us. Our reaction to other people in our environment involves all these. Our sense of our own private space is probably closely related to our sensing of body heat. When other bodies are close enough to our own for us to be aware of the infrared heat generated, we feel crowded, and when our hands move far enough from our bodies to lose immersion in our generalized body heat, we tend to feel we are moving them out of our own private space. However, heat alone is not the whole story.

Edward T. Hall, an anthropologist who has done considerable work on man's reaction to the spaces about him, has carefully classified the senses involved in our perception of four general categories of "proxemic perception" of spaces or distances: intimate, personal, social-consultive and public. Ours is not a very "touching" society—we like a rather large balloon of private space around us, we are uncomfortable when people stand close to us in conversation, if men walk about with their arms around one another's shoulders they are looked at with suspicion, and in buses we tend to pull away from contact with others when possible. We are even rather disturbed by sitting down on a chair still warm with residual heat from someone who has just vacated the

238 spot. Aggressive responses are generated by too much touching—"invasion of personal space" and "overcrowding" are two of the causes of violence suggested by some of the people studying the problem of violence in our society today (R. C. Boelkins and Jon F. Heiser, *VIOLENCE AND THE STRUGGLE FOR EXISTENCE*, Daniels, Gilula and Ochberg [eds.]). At the same time, we share mankind's common need for the physical touch of others—babies can die without it, the lonely adult suffers from its absence, and we are all aware of the importance of physical contact with those we care about.

GROUP SIZE:

Up to 20

TIME SUGGESTED:

45—60 minutes

GENERAL DIRECTIONS:

Select several of the following exercises or experiments. Follow this with discussion of the experience. The "Variations" offer a considerably expanded investigation, including some individual research, if students are interested in further sessions.

MATERIALS REQUIRED:

None

PROCEDURE:

I. Feeling space.

In groups of about 12 members, students follow these steps:

1. Stand or sit on the floor in a circle, close together.

2. Close your eyes.

3. Stretch out your arm and, with your hands, "feel your space"—in front of you; over your head; behind your back; below you; beside you.

4. After about 5 minutes, discuss the experience. What sort of things happened? . . . What did you notice? . . . How did you feel? . . . Some of the following findings may develop: (1) Some will stay in their own space and resent any contact with others; (2) Some will be cautious about intruding into another's space for fear of being rejected; (3)

Some will touch and run; some will be inviting, others forbidding; (4) Some will mention feelings of loneliness; some will talk about physical contact.

II. Crowding.

1. Divide the class in half and ask both groups to "sit in a group on the floor."

2. After they are seated, ask them to make a mental note of how far apart they are from one another—how many are actually touching one another.

3. Now ask them to "crowd in close together," and again notice any remaining space between themselves and others. Give them a minute or so to experience the mild crowding.

4. Ask one group to remain on the floor while the other helps to crowd or herd them together by slowly moving chairs up against them. Ask the chair-movers to move slowly and carefully, but firmly, gradually reducing the space available for those seated on the floor. Allow them to experience this situation for a minute or so.

5. Now have the chairs removed, and allow the group to "move back to a position in which you feel comfortable." Ask them to again note how much space they have around them and how it compares with the previous experiences, including their first seating arrangement.

6. Discuss the experience. Among other things, ask, "Why do we feel pretty comfortable crowding with someone we know well, but rather uncomfortable crowding with strangers or casual acquaintances? . . . What do you think would happen if you were crowded like that for an hour? . . . How would the experience differ if you were outdoors? . . . If it were hotter? . . . colder? . . . pitch dark?

III. In the following brief role plays, ask those observing to note the following: voice loudness; direction of the gaze of role players—do speakers look at the other's eyes, mouth, hands, where?—actual distance apart—could speakers actually touch one another's hands? . . . are they close enough to put their arms around one another? . . . are they close enough to feel the heat from one another's body? . . . to smell one another?

1. Ask a student to volunteer to "get up and address the class" for one minute on _____ (suggest a topic of known interest, such as a hobby, a political conviction, a topical controversial matter, etc.). Do not give any specific directions as to where the student is to stand, but suggest that he stand "so that all can see and hear him."

2. Ask one student to explain something to a second student; directions to a specific building or town; how to make something simple, such as

scrambled eggs; a description of a movie he saw recently. Start the two conversationalists about 12 feet apart, at the front of the class, and ask them to move in as they talk until they feel comfortable.

3. Ask two students to argue opposite sides of a question on which they know they actually differ. As in Step No. 2, ask them to start 12 feet apart and move in as they wish.

4. Student "A" has fallen down several steps, and is hurt. Student "B" is to comfort her.

5. Class discusses the experience, including the feelings of the role players and the observations of the rest of the class.

VARIATIONS:

1. If the environment permits, the class may play "Sardines." This is a game of Hide and Seek in which the person who is "It" is given time to hide, and then all the rest try to find him. As each person finds "It," he quietly, and without disclosing his position to the rest of the seekers, crowds in with "It." This continues until all are squeezed into It's hiding place as best they can. Discuss.

2. *Crowding.* Ask 6—8 students to "form a line in front of the room, facing the door." Ask them and the rest of the class to note how much space there is between them. Now help them squeeze tightly together—ask two students to gently push the two end people by the shoulders, and to finish by acting as "bookends." Discuss.

3. *Myths and legends.* As individuals, or in subgroups, ask the students to compose a myth or legend to explain: "Why ours is not a 'touching' society"; or "Why physical contact with others is important to our well being."

4. *Public spaces.* Arrange the chairs to form spaces which may be designated "elevator," "bus" (bus should have both seating and standing room); and "church or synagogue seats." Ask for volunteers to people these spaces, one at a time. Try with both uncrowded and crowded situations. Ask for perceptions of both role players and observers.

5. As a follow-up to *I. Feeling space,* above. Milling about. You may wish to play music as a background for this. Ask the students to do the following: (1) Stand in a circle, eyes closed, no talking. (2) Stretch out your hands. (3) Begin to move about slowly. (4) Explore. (5) Discuss: What added ideas and feelings do you have? . . . What differences do you perceive between "talking about" a feeling and acting it out?

6. Ask a subgroup of students to devise some exercises for the class using material in Hall's *THE HIDDEN DIMENSION.*

7. Ask a subgroup of students to prepare a small collection of short films, or of footage, to demonstrate various situations and behaviors of people and their use of space. It would be interesting to show several "conversations" of people from various cultures—United States, United Arab Republic, South America, Italy, England. If several projectors are available, short sections of a number of different films could be shown.

SUGGESTED RESOURCES:

Daniels, David N., Marshall F. Gilula, and Frank M. Ochberg (eds.), *VIOLENCE AND THE STRUGGLE FOR EXISTENCE,* Boston, Mass.: Little, Brown & Co., 1970.

Hall, Edward T., *THE HIDDEN DIMENSION,* Garden City, New York: Doubleday Anchor, 1966.

Montagu, Ashley, *TOUCHING: THE HUMAN SIGNIFICANCE OF THE SKIN,* New York: Columbia University Press, 1971.

Morris, Desmond, *THE HUMAN ZOO,* New York: Dell, 1969. (Some rather free-wheeling deductions regarding human beings, made from a zoologist's observations of animals.)

SENSES: KINESTHESIS AND BALANCE

chological benefits of increased privacy, choice of companions, choice of route, radio programs on the car radio, etc., help to compensate the driver for the aggravations of bumper-to-bumper driving ("Sick Transit", an interview with Dr. Richard Evans, *THE HUMBLE WAY,* First Quarter, 1970, Vol. IX, No. 1, pp. 20-23).

PURPOSES:

To explore our kinesthetic senses in muscular activity.

COMMENT:

"A centipede was happy quite
Until a toad in fun
Asked it which leg came after which?
This wrought it up to such a pitch
It fell exhausted in a ditch
Not knowing how to run . . . (Taoist verse)"

(quoted by Serge Chermayeff and Alexander Tzonis, *SHAPE OF COMMUNITY,* Baltimore, Md.: Penguin, 1971, p. 135).

There is probably a relationship between our kinesthetic senses and our apparent need for freedom of locomotion. Although there are cultural and psychological factors at work here, a certain amount of the discomfort felt by those confined to their beds in the hospital for long periods of time, or forced to take long subway rides daily, is apparently due to a real need for greater muscular freedom. Dr. Richard I. Evans, professor of psychology at the University of Houston, has said that city planners must be aware of the dangers of enforced mass transportation, sometimes recommended as an answer to some of the problems of our large cities. He states that "when people lose control over their locomotion, they may develop various psychosomatic reactions." He cites studies made by the Cornell University Medical School, showing that "citizens of New York are under tremendous pressures, and the levels of tension, anxiety, unhappiness, and distress are very high. If enforced use of mass transit should come, it would be undesirable from this standpoint." When asked if there was anything that could be done about people's need to control their own locomotion, he said, "Not really . . . It is innate. The need can be modified or sublimated, but not eliminated." He says that in riding a horse or driving a car the individual retains essential control, and the added psy-

GROUP SIZE:

Up to 20

TIME SUGGESTED:

30—45 minutes

GENERAL DIRECTIONS:

The exercise does not attempt to reproduce situations in which locomotion is limited, but rather promotes conscious awareness of kinesthesis. A balance exercise and an exercise in "conscious walking" may be followed by a period of attempted concentration on the sensing of internal operations.

MATERIALS REQUIRED:

None

PROCEDURE:

1. *Balance exercise:* This exercise requires close cooperation to avoid tipping the partner or being tipped over. Instruct the students as follows:

a. Select a partner of about the same height and weight.

b. Stand facing one another, toes touching. Grasp your partner's hands. Now, working together, gently lean back, striving for balance or equilibrium.

c. Once in a position of balance, try shifting your weight slightly, explaining to your partner each time just what you are going to try to do. Feel the changes in your muscles.

d. Change partners, deliberately seeking a partner with whom it will be more difficult to balance. Repeat "b" and "c".

e. Think: Is your mind telling your muscles what to do? Are your muscles telling your mind what is happening?

2. *Conscious walking.* Ask for a volunteer, or if the group is fairly large, subgroup the class and

ask for a volunteer for each subgroup.

The volunteer is asked to walk about, but told that before each step he must stop and think and explain exactly what he is going to do. For instance: "lift leg"—How far? . . . "Extend foot"—How far? . . . "Put foot down"—Where? . . . Heel or toe first? . . . or whole foot?, etc.

3. *Internal sensations.* Tell the students they are to "shut down" on vision and hearing by closing their eyes and cupping their hands over their ears, so that they can sit quietly for a few minutes, paying attention to internal reports from their bodies. Can they feel their heart beating? . . . The muscles of the chest moving, the ribs moving in and out as they breathe? . . . Can they feel any sensations below the surface of the skin of their arms or legs? . . . Ask them to note that they are quite aware of the location of their arms and legs without having to see them or touch them.

Allow about three minutes of silence for this experience, then signal that time is up.

4. Discuss with the entire group or in subgroups of 2—5 the foregoing experiences. Start with some questions about No. 3, and then move on to others.

—How did you feel?

—What did you notice?

—Did you like it or not?

—Did you find it frightening in any way?

—Did your mind wander away from your body to something else? . . . why?

—Did you feel your body was a friend or a foe? . . . why?

—Have you ever had the experience of entering a room and then saying, "I know I came in here for *something,* but I can't remember what," and then retracing your steps in order to remember it? . . . Why do you think this recalls it to your mind?

—Why did you have trouble explaining how you walked?

SENSES: OLFACTION: "SMELLS OF CHILDHOOD"

PURPOSE:

To discover and explore the relationship between aromas and memory.

COMMENT:

Fish can smell their dinner, and go looking for it. They can also smell an enemy or a potential mate. As life inched up out of the water, smell became even more important, particularly to those animals whose heads are fairly close to the ground. As man's ancestors took to the trees, however, the usefulness of the sense of smell was largely replaced by that of vision, and man himself is a relatively poor "smeller."

However, for some reason, odors have a powerful effect on our emotions, and are closely related to memory. Investigators have recently become more interested in this relatively neglected sense because of their desire to better understand memory. Some of the processing of olfactory input in the brain involves structures known to be related to long-term memory. John Wilentz says, "Were you to smell an odor tomorrow that you hadn't smelled for twenty years, the chances are that it would not only be instantly recognized, but that it would trigger a whole flood of memories and emotional associations" (*THE SENSES OF MAN,* p. 110).

GROUP SIZE:

Up to 20

TIME SUGGESTED:

This may be part of another exercise, combined with one of the other exercises on olfaction, or completed alone in 30—45 minutes. Time is somewhat dependent on which of the "Options" is used.

GENERAL DIRECTIONS:

This may be conducted as a discussion or "group conversation," or it may be a combination of sharing materials brought in by students, followed by discussion. The atmosphere is deliberately relaxed and informal, stress is not on identification, classification or valuing, but on "reminiscing."

MATERIALS REQUIRED:

Option I: none

Options II and III: materials brought in by students. If this option is chosen, the students are told of the exercise in advance and asked to bring to class something which conveys an aroma they remember with pleasure from their childhood. This may result in such things as: a can of cinnamon, a ginger-cookie, a piece of sandalwood, a tobacco humidor, chocolate icing, a piece of cedar wood, freshly sharpened pencils, a new notebook, a jar of paste, or a sprig of "Christmas tree." Ask the students to try to find some way to re-create the smell itself, as the casing object may not be available to them. This can present an opportunity for imaginative creativity. Tell them they will share their objects with the class.

Option III: materials brought in by students. If this option is chosen, tell the students in advance that they will participate in an exercise of smelling various interesting things, just for fun. Ask each student to bring in three objects, separately packaged in small white paper bags or other odorless opaque containers. Tell them to put their initials on each of their three packages, and not disclose their contents to others. Suggest that both natural and artificial aromas will be welcome, and, if necessary, suggest things such as herbs and spices, drugs, cleaning fluid, perfume, candles, incense. Liquids should be bottled, of course, before being placed in their bags.

PROCEDURES:

OPTION I

1. Ask the students to take a few silent moments to think back to their early childhood. "What particular odor, aroma, or smell comes to mind connected with a happy event?" . . . You may wish to start the ball rolling yourself by recalling and briefly describing such a situation.

2. After everyone has had an opportunity to speak, ask the group to think back to the *recent* past and recall a smell connected with a happy event.

3. There is no effort in this exercise to intellectualize the experience or to develop "findings,"

although students will discover it is difficult to actually recall a specific smell. They will remember that it existed and may be able to name it and its associations but they will find it very hard to re-create the experience of smelling.

OPTION II

1. The students are asked to share the samples they have brought with them of aromas they remember from childhood. These may be passed around in subgroups, or in the entire class if it is small enough, and anyone who wishes may comment. You will find that some objects brought in by one student will spark reminiscences in other students, and they will want to talk about them briefly. The tone of the experience should be one of enlarging our awareness and exploring the relationship of memory and smell, and judgmental remarks should be discouraged.

2. Following the rather easy-going experience of Step No. 1, students may be interested in hearing something about the physiology of olfaction, and be interested in discussing the relation of smell and memory from the scientific standpoint.

OPTION III

1. The concealed odor-producing substances are passed around with the tops of the bags rolled down and held squeezed together, leaving an opening just large enough for the nose. For bottled liquids, tape the bag around the bottle neck. The object is not to identify the odor, but simply to enjoy the experience, although the temptation to identify it will persist. Tell the students to keep their guesses to themselves in order to avoid prejudicing anyone for or against a particular smell, and to think of the smells as "interesting" rather than "good" or "bad."

SUGGESTED RESOURCES:

Handler, Philip, (ed.), *BIOLOGY AND THE FUTURE OF MAN,* New York: Oxford University Press, 1970, p. 417.

Otto, Herbert A., "An Adventure with Your Sense of Smell," *WAYS OF GROWTH,* Herbert A. Otto and John Mann, (eds.), New York: Viking, 1968, pp. 68ff.

Wilentz, John Steen, *THE SENSES OF MAN,* New York: Thomas Y. Crowell, 1968, ch. VI.

SENSES: OLFACTION: CLASSIFYING

PURPOSE:

To discover some of the intricacies of odor classification and identification.

COMMENT:

The classification and description of odors are a difficult matter. The old rule about defining words, "Do not use the word itself in the definition," should apply in describing odors, but this is a problem. What does chocolate smell like? What does coffee smell like? What does leather smell like? roses? roast beef? There is a difference between *identifying* odors and *describing* them. It is even a bit difficult to decide which are "pleasant" and which "unpleasant" odors—even a panel of expert "smellers" will differ. One authority said that the use of such terms as leathery, woody or grassy, although common in the perfumer's vocabulary, are a poor substitute for their practice "of communicating with one another by means of absorbent strips saturated with the perfume concerned." This activity, of course, does not constitute a classification. It has been claimed that "the skilled perfume chemist can recognize . . . something of the order of 8,000 to 10,000 different substances by their smell alone."

GROUP SIZE:

Subgroups of 5—7. Total number depends on equipment and space available.

TIME SUGGESTED:

One or more sessions of 60 minutes each.

GENERAL DIRECTIONS:

Three or more separate kinds of experiments may be done: sniffing odors to attempt to describe them; classifying odors; identifying odors by smell alone.

MATERIALS REQUIRED:

Samples are prepared in advance, in suitable amounts and strengths, and placed in opaque containers with easily removed lids. Your school's chemistry department, your druggist, and your grocery store are good sources. If desired, student subcommittees may be assigned the job of selecting and preparing samples. If committees work separately, one committee may participate in the sniffing of the samples of other committees. Or a single small committee may prepare all the samples and participate in administering the "tests," rather than in the "sniffing." They may learn as much or more from their work as the rest of the class.

Lists are prepared and reproduced, containing "suggested descriptive phrases" and "suggested classifications." Other lists should be prepared identifying the substances, and, if desired, duplicate but scrambled lists may be prepared for use in Step No. 5.

LIST OF SUGGESTED DESCRIPTIVE TERMS OR PHRASES

Moods[1]	*Moods*[2]
agreeable	anti-erogenic
stimulating	stimulating
brisk, alerting	exalting
full harmonious	erogenic
restrained	sultry
strong	narcotic
fruity	soothing
fresh	
unpleasant	
depressing	
spicy	
inharmonious	
primitive	
artificial	
bitter	
resinous	
course	

A Step toward Classification[3]

sulfurous	pungent
goaty	warm
oily	musty
smoky	sweet
spicy	sour
cool	etherish
fishy	putrid
medicinal	heavy
dry	tarry
burnt	metallic
flowery	rancid

A Comparison of Four Major Systems of Classification, 1752-1964 [5]

Linnaeus (1752—Botany materia medica)	Zwaardemaker (1895—Physiology & Perfumery)	Amoore (1952/62—Physical Chemistry)	Schutz (1964—Psychology & Food Science)
Aromatic	Aromatic	* * *	* * *
* * *	Ethereal	Ethereal	Etherish
Fragrant	Fragrant (floral as subgroup)	* * *	* * *
		Floral	* * *
* * *	* * *	Pepperminty	* * *
* * *	* * *	Camphoraceous	* * *
* * *	* * *	* * *	Spicy
* * *	* * *	* * *	Oily
Ambrosial	Ambrosial	Musky	* * *
* * *	Empyreumatic (or burnt)	* * *	Burnt
Alliaceous	Alliaceous	* * *	* * *
Hircine (goaty)	Hircine	* * *	* * *
* * *	* * *	* * *	Sulphurous
* * *	* * *	* * *	Rancid
* * *	* * *	Pungent	* * *
Foul	Repulsive	Putrid	* * *
Nauseating	Foetid or Nauseous	* * *	* * *
* * *	* * *	* * *	Metallic

garlicky   woody
fragrant   acid
fruity

SUGGESTED CLASSIFICATIONS

A Perfumer's Classification[4]

Floral—rose, jasmin, hyacinth, lilac, orange flower, tuberose, violet

Woody—spicy (pepper), sandal, clove (carnation)

Rural (Pastoral)—menthol (peppermint), camphor (rosemary), herbaceous (lavender), green (violet leaves), vegetable (methyl heptenone)

Balsamic—vanilla, galbanum, olibanum (incense), resinous

Fruity—hesperidean (bergamot), aldehydic (fatty aldehydes), almond (bitter almond), anisic (aniseed), fruit (raspberry)

Animal—musky, castoreum, skatolic (civet), fresh fish and sea fish (sea weed), ambered note (ambergris)

Empyreumatic—smoky (birch tar), tobacco

Fatty—butyrates

A Perfumer's Classification, defined in terms of particular substances[2]

Sour (oil of lemon)
Resinous (pine needle oil)
Camphor-like (borneol)
Minty (oil of peppermint)
Aromatic/spicy (safrole)
Woody (oil of vetiver)
Mossy (oakmoss extract)
Of burning/empyreumatic (phenolic)
  (birch tar oil)
Dusty (choking, powdery)
Rancid (sweaty) (octaldehyde)
Greasy, fatty (waxy) (nonylalcohol)
Cheesy (rotten, decayed) (ginger grass oil)
Herb-like (oil of sage)
Bitter (isobutylquinoline)
Like urine (paracresyl derivatives)
Faecal (indole)
Honey-like (phenylacetic acid and its esters)
Alkaline (ammoniacal) (tonquin moss)
Balsamic (balsam of Peru)
Sweet (rose oil)
Flowery (hydroxycitronellal)
Fruity (geranyl formate)
Watery (dimethylbenzyl-carbinol)
Green (phenylacetaldehydedimethylacetal)

Suggested List of odors to be judged "pleasant" or "unpleasant"[6]

1. anethole
2. safrole
3. jasmin
4. amyl acetate
5. amber
6. rose
7. benzaldehyde
8. camphor
9. chocolate
10. ethyl acetate
11. cardamom
12. guaiacol
13. caprylic acid
14. butyric acid
15. pyridine

Another list to be judged "pleasant" or "unpleasant"[7]

1. methyl salicylate
2. menthol
3. camphor
4. o-bromotoluene
5. heptyl aldehyde
6. vanillin
7. distilled water
8. phenol
9. ethyl cinnamate
10. n-capric acid
11. geraniol
12. p-dichlorobenzene
13. acetophenone
14. quinoline

Groups of odorous substances may include perfumes, spices, and general substances. It is important to prepare the samples so that the odors are sufficiently strong and distinct, but not overpowering. They must be in a form that can be conveniently sniffed, i.e., liquid or gaseous. They may be placed in numbered 30 ml. wide-mouth reagent bottles, with ground glass stoppers, and students may sniff the stoppers, or the students may sniff numbered slips of blotting paper, dipped in the substance. Some dry spices release their aromas readily, and these may be placed in reagent bottles without treatment. However, the contents of the bottle must be sniffed, not merely the stopper.

PROCEDURES:

1. The easiest and simplest determination is "liking" and "not liking." Students may be presented with 6—12 substances to sniff, and either asked to arrange them in order of preference, or to rate each one on a scale such as the following:[8]

+3 *Very pleasant*
+2 *Moderately pleasant*
+1 *Weakly pleasant*
 0 *Indifferent*
−1 *Weakly unpleasant*
−2 *Moderately unpleasant*
−3 *Very unpleasant*

Two or more rounds or "tries" may be used, if desired, and the students may average their own scoring before comparing them with those of other members of their subgroup.

2. The same or a different group of substances may then be presented, and the student asked to spontaneously write a descriptive word or two, trying to avoid describing it as "like" something else, for instance: "like onions," or "onion-y," or "like fruit," or "fruity." Again, one or more rounds may be tried before subgroup members compare their findings.

3. This time, students may be provided with a set of descriptive words or phrases, and asked to select from these in describing the odors sniffed. Compare findings within the subgroups.

4. Using the same substances presented before, or a different group, students are given one or more systems of classification and asked to place each odor sniffed in one of these classifications. Compare findings within the subgroups.

5. Now the students may try to identify odors. For this exercise it is best if no more than ten odors are used. Each student is presented with the sample and may write down what he thinks it is. He is allowed 30 seconds for one to three sniffs, and 45 seconds between each sample. If he is unable to identify the substance, ask him instead to write down what he associates with that smell or, if all else fails, at least whether it is "familiar," and whether it is "pleasant," "unpleasant" or "neutral." This last step may be repeated at later sessions, as in itself it constitutes a "training" experience— usually the student's ability will improve. At the end of each session he is given a copy of the correct list of odors, numbered in the order in which he sniffed them. In comparing them immediately with his list, it will help him form a memory of the odor. They may be interested to know that it is usually believed to take between 2—6 years to become reasonably proficient as a perfumer or flavor chemist.

6. *Adaptation* or *fatigue* will occur, raising the sensory threshold, so that the first sniff is often the "clearest" with any given substance. There is also the possibility that a "central" fatigue occurs. If students will hold one nostril closed, sniff the same odor a number of times with one nostril, then switch nostrils, they may notice that the odor is no more sharp and distinct on the first sniff with the "new" nostril than it was on the last sniff with the "old" nostril. Did recovery from fatigue occur, or not? Students may experiment with this problem with a few fairly "strong" odors, and tabulate their results.

There are certain substances which quickly dull our sense of smell, making us less able to detect other odors. Experiments may be tried with some of these, sniffing them first in a series. Some of the "smell-dullers" are ether, camphor, gasoline and oil of cloves.

7. Perhaps partly because our sense of smell is nonintellectual, as evidenced by our difficulty in finding ways to talk about odors, it is strongly tied to our emotions. Students may be allowed to make a single "round" of the odors available, stopping whenever any feelings or images come to mind to write them down. They may then share any of these experiences they wish with a partner or in a subgroup. Smell is the most "nostalgic" of our senses.

8. Paper finishes and printers' inks have distinctive odors. With practice, it is possible to recognize particular books or magazines when they are new and fresh by smell alone. In order to experiment with this, it would be necessary to collect six to eight newspapers and magazines with which students may be fairly familiar. The students should be blindfolded, the magazine opened quickly to a fresh page, and the page held close to the student's nose. Students who may not have been aware of these odors may learn fairly quickly to distinguish at least a few. They may also become more aware of the smell of new books, and begin to associate certain smells with certain books.

SUGGESTED RESOURCES:

Harper, R., E. C. Bate Smith and D. G. Land, *ODOUR DESCRIPTION AND ODOUR CLASSIFICATION*, New York: American Elsevier Publishing Co., 1968. References above are from this volume:

1. Adaptation from Paukner, p. 79.
2. Adaptation from Jellinek, p. 75.
3. Adaptation from Pilgrim and Schutz, p. 128.
4. Adaptation from Billot, p. 81-2.
5. From Linnaeus Onwards, p. 21.
6. From Engen and McBurney, p. 150.
7. From Young, p. 146.
8. From Young, p. 143.

Moncrieff, R. W., *ODOUR PREFERENCES*, New York: John Wiley, 1966.

You and your students may be interested in some on the materials available from the American Spice Trade Association, Information Bureau, 350 Fifth Ave., New York, N.Y. 10001, such as "Standard Guide to Spice Terminology," "A History of Spices," and "A Glossary of Spices."

SENSES: OLFACTION: "WHAT SMELLS SELL?"

PURPOSE:

To explore our reactions to our "re-odorized society," and our feelings about "natural odors."

COMMENT:

Western Society has cut itself off from "natural" smells to a great degree. American tourists frequently report becoming extremely conscious of odors when they travel in other parts of the world, and people from southern Europe, Asia, Africa and the Middle East are sometimes amused and sometimes annoyed when they encounter America's bland aroma and note our fearfulness about contact with odors they consider proper, normal and often enjoyable.

If man's sense of smell were as keen as that of a dog, for instance, he would probably suffer greatly from our crowded living conditions, and perhaps our increasing banishment of all smells connected with the human body is influenced by increased population and urbanization, but aside from a greater use of incense such crowded countries as India seem not to spend so much time, money and energy banishing the smell of their fellow man as we do.

What we do in most cases is re-odorize, rather than de-odorize—we mask many smells with other smells which please us better. We have even decided, or been taught, that the smell of a good meal cooking is something to which we should not subject our guests, and so we use room deodorizers or scented sprays or candles. Dozens of compounds are sold to insure an "odor free" bathroom, some of which have very strong odors themselves. The list of preparations for use on and in the person to remove all trace of natural odors is long indeed. What is the cause of all this? To what do advertisers appeal in their campaigns to sell these products? What is the effect on us?

GROUP SIZE:

Up to 20

TIME SUGGESTED:

45—60 minutes

GENERAL DIRECTIONS:

Students prepare by monitoring radio and TV, collecting advertisements from magazines and newspapers, advertising flyers, etc. Some resources may be provided in the classroom. Students prepare lists of their own reactions to odors and discuss collected materials.

MATERIALS REQUIRED:

Students provide materials as in "General Directions," and other resources should be available in the classroom, such as magazines, etc. If possible, old TV commercial videotapes may be used, and perhaps some materials may be viewed with an opaque projector. See also "Suggested Resources" for suggestions.

PROCEDURES:

1. At a previous session assign the collection of suitable materials. Ask the students to seek samples of advertising which stress both good and bad odors, products sold, at least in part, by advertising their ability to cover, conceal or "remove" personal and environmental odors. Students with tape recorders may make a record from TV or radio, but these should be edited before use to limit playing time to relevant material.

2. Ask the students to make individual lists of two columns: (1) "good smells I remember"; (2) "bad smells I remember."

3. In subgroups of 5—7, students may share some of the information from their lists in Step No. 2. If desired they may make a common record of their findings. Ask the groups to spend a few minutes looking for reasons or explanations of why these smells were appealing or unappealing. They may talk about such questions as:

—What did you associate with that smell?

—Do you think that smell was naturally displeasing, or were you taught that it was "bad"? . . . If so, by whom? . . . Why?

4. Ask the students to share their collected materials, either with the entire group or in their subgroups, depending on the size of the class and the amount of collected material. If input is slight, provide old magazines, etc., for inspection, show material on an opaque projector, or screen videotapes, if available.

5. In subgroups students now discuss the material inspected, looking for answers to:

—What sells smells?

—What smells sell?

—What appeals are used? . . . Why do they work? . . . What associations are made or implied by advertisers?

Students may be asked to introduce material from their lists in Step No. 2 for comparison.

6. In a plenary session the entire class shares its findings and investigates the questions posed at the end of "Comment," above.

VARIATIONS:

1. Subgroups may prepare copy for an advertisement for a new product which makes a "bad" smell, or introduces a "good" smell into the environment. You may remind them that it is possible to purchase a spray can of a substance with the "new car" smell, with a "leather" smell, etc. What would they like to introduce? . . . a "new book" smell? . . . a "seashore" smell? . . . How would they sell it? . . . To whom would it appeal? . . . What would they say? . . . What kind of pictures would sell it? . . . Would it be possible to change the image of a "bad" smell? . . . What smell? . . . How could they sell it?

2. Students may bring in spray cans of various room deodorizers, or slips of blotting paper sprayed at home with such preparations and brought to school in sealed jars or plastic sandwich bags. Students try to identify and characterize the odors and explore possible associations with these odors.

3. Students may compile a record of the various kinds of deodorizers, maskers and scented additives used in their own homes, in the school, and in various local businesses, churches or synagogues and institutions to which they have easy access.

—How many different kinds of products are used?

—What explanations do they receive in answer to, "Why do you use a product like this?"

—Suppose all such products were abolished . . . what would be the result?

SUGGESTED RESOURCES:

Hall, Edward T., *THE HIDDEN DIMEN-*

SION, Garden City, New York: Doubleday Anchor, 1966 (see index, "olfaction").

Payne, Richard J., and Robert Heyer, *DISCOVERY IN ADVERTISING*, New York, N.Y.: Paulist Press, 1969.

Rasschaert, William M., "Appeals to Selected Emotions: A Semantic Study of Advertising Techniques," *MONOGRAPHS FOR ENGLISH TEACHERS*, New York: Harper & Row, n.d., reprinted in *CRITICAL READING*, Martha L. King, Bernice D. Ellinger, Willavene Wolf, (eds.), Philadelphia, Pa.: J.B. Lippincott, 1967, pp. 321ff.

SENSES: OLFACTION: JAPANESE INCENSE-SMELLING

PURPOSE:

To enjoy the pleasure of smelling various kinds of incense, and thus increase sensory awareness.

COMMENT:

Incense has a long and interesting history. It was burned or added to oil for lamps in ancient Egypt in religious ceremonies and for the pleasure of its aroma in the homes of the wealthy, and also used, usually for religious purposes, in Persia, Assyria and Babylonia. It has been used from early times in India, China and Japan and the smaller countries of the East. It is frequently mentioned in the Old Testament because of its use in religious ceremonies of the neighboring tribes and its eventual use in the rituals of Judaism. Its importance and relative scarcity made it a product of considerable economic importance.

It was not part of the regular services of the synagogue at the time of Christ and therefore was not used by the primitive Christian church. In fact, its use was frowned upon as a pagan practice, particularly during the Roman persecutions when one way in which a Christian could disavow Christianity and escape punishment was to offer a few grains of incense in front of the Emperor's altar. However, by the fifth century it was becoming common to use it in eucharistic services.

In early times it was believed that the gods would be pleased with the sweet smell wafted up to them, as with the odor of other "burnt offerings," but later its use was symbolic, standing for sacrifice, for prayer, the virtues of the saints, and the goodness and purity for which men strive. Contemporary Zen masters recommend the use of incense to convey a sense of the holy and to help develop the concentration necessary for meditation.

Its early use in many countries in connection with ceremonies for the dead was doubtless encouraged by the fact that the odor of the corpse rapidly became extremely unpleasant. Also, it is only in very recent times that man has been able to keep himself and his clothing really clean, particularly in cold climates. The wealthiest kings of Tudor England could not have as many baths or clean clothes as someone just above the poverty level in the United States today. Cold winters, few garments and those not always washable, lack of sufficient hot water and soap or dry cleaning materials resulted in a distinctly unpleasant aroma when groups of people gathered together, and burning incense certainly helped. It was a pleasure to go into a building which smelled "good."

In England after the Reformation the use of incense in church services was frequently prohibited, but it was still sometimes used as a "health" measure to "fumigate" the churches, as though it were believed that what you can't smell won't hurt you. Incense has enjoyed a rising popularity in this country, partly as a means to mask the odor of burning marijuana and partly because of increasing interest in Eastern religions and a growing appreciation of the pleasures of the senses. At the same time that the younger members of the family are burning incense, their parents are finding scented candles a pleasant adjunct to social gatherings and a perhaps more esthetic approach to drowning "household odors" than the omnipresent spray can of "air-freshener."

The Japanese have cultivated sensory awareness for centuries—the eye, through flower arrangement—the taste, through the tea ceremony—the nose through incense-smelling. The last is less well-known, and is primarily a form of entertainment for the upper classes in Japan at the present time.

GROUP SIZE:

10—12

TIME SUGGESTED:

45 minutes

GENERAL DIRECTIONS:

Various incense products are burned, students try to identify the fragrances and discuss the experience.

MATERIALS REQUIRED:

Sticks or blocks of incense and/or scented candles.

Metal containers such as incense burners, small aluminum foil tart pans or ash trays or candle holders.

"Prizes"—perhaps some of the unburned incense left after the exercise.

(optional: Japanese fans, or a portable electric fan)

PROCEDURE:

1. The classic Japanese procedure involves the "host" who lights and passes the incense to his "guests" who sit in a semicircle around him. The atmosphere is rather formal, and suitable decorations enhance the experience. The principal object is the pleasure of the experience itself, plus training of the olfactory sense. Prizes are awarded to the person who correctly identifies the largest number of fragrances.

2. As the incense is passed around, each student-guest writes down his guess as to its identity. The one with the highest score may be awarded the remaining incense or candles. Since the fragrance will linger in the air, this exercise is best done outdoors or in a large, well-ventilated room. If this is not possible, fans may be used to create a small breeze to disperse each fragrance before the next stick or block of incense is lighted.

3. General discussion follows. Students talk about the experience, express preferences, and may also talk about the general use and symbolism of incense and their own associations with it.

4. If you wish you may distribute some information on incense, provide books or articles on the subject, or ask the students to read aloud previously researched material.

VARIATIONS:

1. Air fragrances are available in a number of forms. In addition to incense to be burned and candles, there is also potpourri—mixtures of specially dried flower petals and herbs and spices, and there are "burning perfumes" which may be burned in special little "lamps" or containers. Other fluid fragrances may be heated in metal rings which rest around the top of ordinary light bulbs or in lamps with special tops which serve as fragrance containers. Most of these fragrances tend to be rather expensive and more difficult to find than the incense or candles, but some students or their friends may have some at home they would be able to share with class members. Some herbs and other plant leaves have a pleasant fragrance when dried, crumpled and

burned in small amounts, and students might enjoy experimenting with some of these.

2. A similar exercise, though perhaps lacking some of the glamour of the incense smelling party, may be carried out with a collection of spices and herbs. These may be prepared in opaque sniffing bottles or similar containers and numbered. Even some of the common household spices are hard to identify sight unseen. See "Suggested Resources" for "Life: Senses: Olfaction: Classifying."

SENSES: TASTE AND SIGHT

PURPOSE:

To discover how what we see affects what we taste.

COMMENT:

The psychologist H.H. Ferguson conducted an experiment in which he colored "jellies" (could substitute gelatin) and found people identified the product according to the color, thus raspberry jelly, colored yellow, tasted like lemon, and lemon jelly, colored red, tasted like raspberry to the subjects.

GROUP SIZE:

Up to 20

TIME SUGGESTED:

45—60 minutes

GENERAL DIRECTIONS:

Students taste foods while blindfolded, first without the food being identified, then with prior identification. Students without blindfolds are then offered a choice of unusually colored foods.

MATERIALS REQUIRED:

Enough blindfolds for half the class.

An assortment of food: milk, bread, butter, cream cheese, hard-boiled egg, salt, sugar, water, dry cereals, plain cooked noodles, gelatin desserts, etc.

An assortment of some of the same foods as above, but prepared with the addition of inappropriate food coloring (small bottles of food coloring

252

are available at most supermarkets).

You may also wish to use some food flavorings.

Paper plates, napkins, plastic spoons.

NOTE: Foods should be prepared prior to the session. A committee may be asked to do this, keeping their activity secret, and bring the foods in closed containers. You might want to ask the Home Economics Department of your school to cooperate in preparing these materials.

PROCEDURE:

1. Before any of the foods are brought into the room, the students are told that they are going to have a "food-tasting" experience. Select half the class, including those who were on the "food preparation committee" if used, which colored the foods. Blindfold these students.

2. Bring in the uncolored (normally colored) foods on small paper plates. The plates should be numbered, the food served first from plates numbered "1". The blindfolded students are fed small portions of the food by the "sighted" students, who do not tell them what the foods are. After each spoonful, the taster is asked to identify the food and a record made of his answers.

3. The procedure in Step No. 2 is repeated, but this time the student being fed is told what the food is each time before he tastes it. His reactions, if any, are recorded.

4. Blindfolds are removed, and the class told that the rest of the students will have an opportunity to taste some foods. The artificially colored foods are brought in on similar paper plates, without comment, and placed on the table. The formerly blindfolded students watch while the rest of the class make a free selection from the available foods, *not including* the normally colored foods, which are set aside.

5. Students discuss the experience.

VARIATION:

It is well-known that much of our sense of taste is actually very dependent on our sense of smell. Students may be asked to "hold your nose" while being fed some of the sample foods, if desired. This is more noticeable, of course, if some hot foods can be included, as more of the "flavor molecules" escape into the air from hot coffee, for instance, than from cold coffee.

SENSES: TASTE: JAPANESE TEA CEREMONY

PURPOSE:

To experience the pleasure of the tea ceremony, with its appeal to the various senses.

COMMENT:

The tea ceremony, "Cha No Yu," is considered a cultural activity by the Japanese, and is much more than the mere drinking of tea. By the fifteenth century it was an aesthetic practice, involving some of the aspects of religion and philosophy. It is sometimes called "the religion of the art of life." To be correctly carried out there should be a tea house, complete with small garden and stone path, the proper equipment and utensils, and a hanging scroll or "kakemono" to be enjoyed by the guests as they enter. However, some aspects of the ceremony may be reproduced. There is more than one school of thought on the exact procedures, and rivalry exists between the proponents. All aim, however, at a "rite in which a beautiful but simple setting; a few fine pieces of old pottery; a slow, formalized, extremely graceful ritual for preparing and serving the tea; and a spirit of complete tranquility all combine to express the love of beauty, the devotion to simplicity, and the search for spiritual calm which characterized the best of Zen" (Reischauer, *JAPAN: THE STORY OF A NATION*).

GROUP SIZE:

The "proper" number of guests is about five. Depending on the availability of skilled "hosts," one group may participate while the rest of the class watches, or all may participate in fairly small groups.

TIME SUGGESTED:

45—60 minutes

GENERAL DIRECTIONS:

If possible, ask someone who knows how to perform the tea ceremony to do this for the class—perhaps one or more Japanese students from a local university, or visiting students passing through the community on a travel program such as the Experiment in International Living. Not all Japanese have learned the procedure. You may wish to make inquiries about the availability of such people and schedule your class at a time when you may take advantage of their services. If your city has a Japanese consul he may be able to suggest someone. When making arrangements, ask what equipment you should provide.

If no trained people are available, your local museum may have a volunteer guide who is familiar with the materials used in the ceremony and would be willing to serve as "host." He may be able to bring some things with him, or can guide you as to what you should provide.

If all else fails, perhaps someone in the community has at least participated in the tea ceremony in Japan, or even here in the States, and will help plan the event.

Properly done, the tea ceremony is rather long and tedious for students, particularly without the proper setting, but it is likely that, however it is managed, they will actually get a speeded-up version.

MATERIALS REQUIRED:

If you cannot obtain expert assistance in the selection of materials, the following list provides a rough guide:

powdered tea, preferably green
a ceramic bowl
a whisk to stir or beat the tea in the bowl
a tea kettle of boiling water
Japanese tea cups or mugs—these come in various shapes and sizes, but characteristically have no handles
a hanging scroll—if nothing suitable is available, an attractive Japanese poster or a reproduction of a Japanese print may be hung on a piece of neatly trimmed burlap
(optional: an incense-burner and a vase with a single flower; also, small, simple cookies; straw mats for the floor area to be used)

NOTE: Since the appearance of the utensils used is so important in this experience, it is essential that some effort be made to have attractive cups, bowl, and kettle, and to arrange a portion of the room to be used in a simple but attractive fashion.

PROCEDURES:

NOTE: If someone familiar with the ceremony has agreed to assist your class, they will guide you in planning the procedures. In case this is not possible, students may be asked to do some research, or a committee appointed. The following brief guide outlines the usual steps.

1. Guests enter the low-doored tea house through the garden, passing the hanging scroll by the entrance. They pause to admire and comment on the scroll. They take their places in a semicircle, kneeling on the floor (mats), and resting on their heels.

2. When the guests are in place, the host enters, bowing to his guests. He prepares the tea in silence, placing the powdered tea in a bowl, adding the boiling water, and beating the mixture with the whisk. He pours the tea and serves his guests, as they enjoy the appearance of the bowl and cups.

3. If an "expert" has joined the class as "host," he may talk to the students about the tea ceremony. Otherwise, the students may discuss the experience together. Other aspects of Japanese art and culture may be shown and discussed, if desired.

VARIATIONS:

1. If no outside expert is available, the students might prefer a "tea-tasting" session. Students may research some of the possibilities and bring in recipes and ingredients. A variety of teas may be prepared, if boiling water is available. Paper cups may be used, although they tend to add their own flavor. Some of the possibilities are:

Lemon-rind Tea. Wash and dry one lemon. Cut off the yellow part of the peel, avoiding the white rind, and put it in a teapot. Add boiling water and steep five minutes. Sweeten with honey or brown sugar.

Melissa Tea. Add boiling water to melissa in the pot and steep five minutes. Sweeten with honey.

Melissa Blend. Use equal parts of melissa, hawthorn and sweet marjoram, for a total of one teaspoonful of the mixture per cup. Add boiling water and steep three to five minutes. Sweeten with honey or sugar.

Orange-flower Tea. Put a small handful (about 9—12 blossoms) of orange flowers in the pot, add boiling water and steep three minutes. Strain. Sweeten with honey or brown sugar.

Many other teas are available commercially, and health food stores have a considerable variety.

SUGGESTED RESOURCES:

Dilts, Marion M., *THE PAGEANT OF JAP-*

254   *ANESE HISTORY*, 3rd ed., New York: Longmans Green, 1961, pp. 143-145; 314.

Reischauer, Edwin O., *JAPAN: THE STORY OF A NATION*, New York: Alfred A. Knopf, 1970, p. 72.

Suzuki, D.T., *ZEN BUDDHISM*, ed. by William Barrett, Garden City, N.Y.: Doubleday Anchor, 1956, pp. 293-294. NOTE: This final rather brief section might be read to students while they sip their tea. It is a delightful description of the ceremony.

Waldo, Myra, *TRAVEL GUIDE TO THE ORIENT AND THE PACIFIC*, New York: Macmillan, 1965, pp. 234-236.

SENSES: TASTE: BREAD DAY

PURPOSE:

To explore the taste of a variety of breads, and to consider the symbolism of bread and of special kinds of breadstuffs.

COMMENT:

Bread is made of many different kinds of materials, with a wide variety of flavorings, and in a great many shapes. Every country has its typical breadstuffs, and many special breads have symbolic significance, particularly those for holidays. Sometimes the symbolism is associated with the basic ingredients, sometimes with the special flavorings added, sometimes with the shape, and sometimes with the way in which it is presented for eating.

People are usually more willing to sample the bread of another country than almost any other of its foods, and therefore it is a good place to start sampling foreign cuisine. Even within the United States there are breads which are common in one region and little known in others, and within any area many families use only a few of the numerous breads commercially available.

Both men and women often enjoy bread baking, and it has become a popular kind of "fun" cooking for many people. Some cool Fall or Winter day, students may enjoy baking bread at home to bring to class for sampling.

GROUP SIZE:

Up to 20

TIME SUGGESTED:

45—60 minutes

GENERAL DIRECTIONS:

Talk over the possibilities of this session with

the class in advance. Suggest that they might enjoy baking a special kind of bread, keeping half at home for the family and bringing half to school to share. Some may prefer to purchase ready-made products more difficult to make at home, such as pretzels, matzos, etc. Suggest that they look at home or in the library for interesting recipes for breads from other countries, and find out something about the history of the bread or its special uses or significance. Remind them that if they have a freezer at home, the bread may be baked at any time, wrapped and frozen until the day of the session. To help them get started you may wish to provide some of the materials listed in "Suggested Resources."

MATERIALS REQUIRED:

Breads brought in by students
Bread knives to cut the loaves, and one or more bread boards.
Paper plates and napkins.
(Optional: butter and/or cheeses, small knives or spreaders.)

PROCEDURE:

1. There is hardly a need for a "procedure" in this. The breads are cut or torn and served. Each person who has brought a bread should be asked to tell the group something about it. Grace may be said.

2. A general discussion of the experience may follow, either in subgroups or with the entire class. The discussion may focus on symbolism, on the foods of other cultures, or on any of the things that have interested the students in the material they used in looking for their recipes.

VARIATIONS:

1. Students may wish to repeat the experience at a later date, specifically focusing on breads with symbolic significance. At this time it would be best if the students brought suggestions to class before making their final decisions, in order to avoid duplication and provide a wide variety.

2. Students may wish to follow this experience with participation in a symbolic meal. Local churches and synagogues may have special meals in connection with holidays or holy days, and arrangements may be made for students to attend. Sometimes the YMCA, YWCA or YMHA and YWHA also have special meals which are open to the public. It might be possible to arrange for your students to prepare a special meal in your school's Home Economics Department. Religious bookstores carry pamphlets describing the food and procedures and giving recipes for such meals as a Christian Passover dinner, a Jewish Seder for Pesach, or simple meals for Ash Wednesday or Good Friday. A number of cookbooks contain menus and recipes for special holidays, and books on cooking in other countries may be used.

3. Students may wish to explore the cuisine of a number of other countries or cultures. Sometimes meals of cold foods may be prepared at home and brought to school, or sometimes arrangements may be made as in Variation 2 above.

SUGGESTED RESOURCES:

Weiser, Francis X., *HANDBOOK OF CHRISTIAN FEASTS AND CUSTOMS*, New York: Harcourt Brace, 1958. (This contains considerable information on the symbolic use of various breads and other foods, both within Christianity and also in pagan societies from which some of the uses of special foods were derived.)

Free recipes for your students may be obtained from the following sources:

American Spice Trade Association, Information Bureau, Empire State Building, New York, N.Y. 10001. (Their booklet "Spice Recipes from Many Lands" contains Australian Curry-Cheese Biscuits, Poppy Seed Rolls from the Netherlands.)

Educational Service, Standard Brands, Inc., P.O. Box 2695, Grand Central Station, New York, N.Y. 10017. ("Fleischmann's New Treasury of Yeast Baking" contains a section of recipes for holidays with brief descriptions of the symbolism and country of origin. They will also send a guide to the science and nutrition of bread, "Our Daily Bread," and "Yeast Dough Shaping Made Easy" which contains recipes for Hoska, Moravian Sugar Cake and Italian Easter Bread, among others. Ask also for their Planters Peanut recipes which include a Groundnut Bread from North Africa.)

FILMSTRIP:

This Sustaining Bread, 72 frames, color, record. Friendship Press, 1959. (Bread as the symbol of brotherhood and the Body of Christ. Suitable for meditation or liturgy. An unusually beautiful presentation.)

SENSES: TASTE NUTRITION

PURPOSE:

To explore some of the relationships between taste, belief, hunger, nutrition and health.

COMMENT:

The present concern about correct diet is justified. In a land of plenty we eat poorly—perhaps half the population below par because of too little food, too much food, or the wrong food. Many teenagers suffer from malnutrition, including some of those who eat too much. Our consumption of potato chips, soft drinks and alcohol has gone up in the last fifteen years, while our consumption of fruits, vegetables and milk has gone down. Among teenagers this is a result of following diets believed to have special virtues, but in all probability it is most often due to bad food habits, or a miseducated taste. We have learned to yearn for the wrong foods!

It is believed that most people in the United States get over 40 percent of their calories from fats, a percentage which is far too high. *LIFE* magazine recently published a picture of what looked at first glance to be a nutritious, balanced day's menu. Breakfast consisted of bacon, eggs, toast, orange juice and coffee with cream. Lunch was a cheeseburger with sliced tomatoes and lettuce, french fries and a coke, and dinner was steak, a baked potato, peas, green salad, apple pie, coffee with cream, wine and pretzels. However, without any additional snacks, the calorie total was 3,256—over 400 more than a man with a sedentary job should have, and 49 percent of this was fat.

Teenagers are usually better off than the middle-aged, simply because they are more active and burn up more excess calories, and also because their activity helps their appetite controls to function normally. However, they may be setting poor eating habits which will be harmful later, with diets including excess sugar and fat. The soft drink habit, for instance, adds carbohydrates without providing the minerals and vitamins of milk and fruit or vegetable juices.

Food fads which recommend *adding* certain items to the diet, such as yogurt, or "tiger's milk," or wheat germ are seldom harmful, and often of value, though they may result in too much of the food budget being used for unnecessary items, but those which *subtract* whole classes of foods can be hazardous. The dangers of the microbiotic diet, consisting primarily of brown rice, seaweed and very small amounts of meat and fish, have been well publicized since the death of one convert from undernourishment. Part of the problem is that although research has shown that a normal "well-balanced" diet of a certain number of servings of the basic four food groups will nourish us properly, there are an insufficient number of studies to allow equal certitude when substitutions from other groups replace the meat and milk groups. Food prejudices and the habit of eating only a limited number of kinds of food compound the teenager's problem at a time when his nutritional needs are high.

Some food fads depend on views so extreme that improvement within the fad guidelines is impossible, but these are the exception. Most teenagers have been raised in a society which stressed high protein intake, fresh fruits and vegetables, and it is usually possible to persuade them to approximate these standards. Those who do not eat meat, for instance, are frequently aware of the need for more protein, and interested in how to get enough of the right amino acids in pleasant form. The extreme vegetarian who avoids all meat products, including milk, eggs, gelatin and food additives believed to be possibly derived from meat sources has a very difficult problem, particularly since his own guidelines prohibit supplementary dietary products such as vitamin pills. It is still not impossible to be adequately nourished on such a diet, but it takes considerable knowledge and persistent effort, and requires a large volume of food in most cases. Most physicians in the United States are not knowledgeable in the field of nutrition, and even many professionally trained nutritionists lack knowledge in some areas. Although much is being learned about the relation between food and health, much is still unknown.

GROUP SIZE:

Up to 20

TIME SUGGESTED:

This will vary according to the projects selected. An introductory session based on one or two may be completed in 45—60 minutes. Further sessions may be planned depending on group needs and interests, and other projects expanded or combined.

GENERAL DIRECTIONS:

Interviews outside of class, a quiz and discussion form the basis of the following projects. Informational input may be provided in several ways.

MATERIALS REQUIRED:

You may wish to reproduce some "Fact Sheets" and have available for distribution some of the literature in "Suggested Resources."

POSSIBLE PROJECTS:

1. Special diets. Ask the students to interview friends on special diets, trying to collect as many diets as possible. Suggest that they ask, "Are you on any kind of special diet? . . . Would you tell me about it? . . . What do you eat, and what don't you, and why? . . . How much of any special foods do you eat?" Ask them to make their notes as accurate as possible and bring the information to class to share with others. Ask them to approach this as an anthropological study, and to avoid critical remarks to those they interview. Ask them to include themselves in their sample, if they are on a special diet.

Data is brought to class to be shared in subgroups or with the entire class. Ask the students to avoid identifying those they interviewed, but to give such information as their age, occupation, general body build, and general appearance of health. Remind them it is possible that, despite their efforts to achieve an adequate interview, those with whom they talked accidentally omitted important information.

Distribute literature or Fact Sheets as needed, or spread them on a table and indicate what is available for class use. Tell the students that you realize they may have reason to disbelieve the usefulness of the material you have provided—"science" itself is being called into question these days as a way to either "truth" or "the good life."

Discussion should focus first on trying to understand the diets and their purposes. Students should then try to evaluate their quality in terms of meeting known nutritional needs, cost, availability, and ease of preparation. In open discussion a good deal of disagreement will arise as to what is and what is not "good for you." It might be well to discourage discussion of food additives, saving this for another session concentrating on this problem. If students find some diets inadequate in some respects, ask them to see if they can find ways to make them nutritionally sound *without* including foods banned by the guidelines of the particular diet. Ask them to respect the beliefs underlying the diets, but also to respect the beliefs of the medical profession and of nutritionists. Can they figure out ways to satisfy both?

2. Folk-sayings about foods. A list of folk-sayings, such as those listed below, is given to the class, and they are encouraged to add to this before continuing with a discussion of their validity. If the class has not had previous information on nutrition they may have difficulty sifting the wheat from the chaff. This could serve as a starter or introductory exercise at a session preceding the one during which information could be provided through assigned student reports on research or by materials provided by the teacher. The folk-sayings may be discussed in small groups, and ideas so developed shared in a plenary.

a. *Fish is brain food.*

b. *An apple a day keeps the doctor away.*

c. *Bread is the staff of life.*

d. *Only eat oysters in months with an 'r' in them.*

e. *Don't eat fish and ice cream in the same meal.*

f. *Natural foods are better for you. (this currently popular saying could lead to a later session on food additives, "organic foods," etc.)*

g. *Jack Sprat could eat no fat, his wife could eat no lean,*
And so, between the two of them, they licked the platter clean.

h. *"Those were our macaroni years."*

3. Calorie quiz. Students fill in a simple quiz, the correct answers are given and students check their own papers. The quiz can be in two parts: (1) a list of foods to be ranked in order of the caloric content of an average serving. Such a list can be composed of 10—15 items of foods currently popular in your own area. Students would not be asked to give the number of calories per serving, but simply rank them from "highest caloric content" to "lowest"; (2) a list of activities to be ranked according to caloric expenditure, such as "sleeping," "playing tennis," "eating," etc.

The quiz can serve as the starting point for a discussion on weight control, as some students will be interested in gaining or losing weight, or for a discussion on world poverty and malnutrition, or for a discussion on the diet of welfare recipients.

4. Weight control. The session can begin with a general discussion on problems of weight control, eliciting suggestions from class members as to the best ways to achieve an ideal weight. If the class has done project No. 1, input from this will be useful, as will information from No. 3. This initial discussion should be followed by an examination of some typical popular weight loss diets, perhaps some which have been tried by the students, and an effort to determine whether they are nutritionally sound. Data

may be provided by student research or by the distribution of some of the available literature. An initial 30 minute session might be followed by a 45—60 minute session wherein subgroups could compare and evaluate diets using this data. Student groups might also take one or more popular diets and make necessary changes to bring them up to nutritional standards.

Diets for weight loss often fail because of lack of appeal. Can the students suggest ways in which the taste of such diets might be improved? "Diet farms" and "health spas" help patrons by providing low-calorie foods with high taste and eye appeal—what suggestions do the students have?

Why is breakfast important? Why do people often skip breakfast, particularly when trying to lose weight? Would the class like to experiment with using two sample breakfast menus, one the "ideal breakfast," the other a light breakfast without sufficient nourishment and low on protein? Will groups volunteer to try one diet for one week and then switch to the other for one week, and report to the class on how they felt, and also how these diets affected their food intake the rest of the day?

5. Welfare recipients and food. Ask the students to make up a week's menus for a welfare recipient, trying to provide correct nutrition. Specify family size (or they may use their own family as a base). Price lists may be derived from ads in local papers, or students may make "dry-run" food shopping trips to local stores. If there are food cooperatives in your area, students may investigate these, finding out how many hours work, if any, are required of members, or whether initial or monthly "membership charges" are made. Remind them to include in their calculations all snacks and food eaten away from home.

Ask the members of the class to live for three days on the food allowance of a welfare mother for a child their age. Ask if any family would volunteer to live for a week on the welfare food allowance, and then come in a group, or with as many family members as possible, and report their experiences to the class.

SUGGESTED RESOURCES:

You may wish to reproduce some of the following information on "Fact Sheets" for your students.

VEGETARIAN DIETS:

The vegetarian needs additional sources of iron, niacin and protein. A particular problem for the teenager is his high need for protein during these years, combined with the tendency toward acne which is exacerbated by excess fat intake such as occurs when a good many nuts or peanut butter are used to try to increase the protein in the diet.

The vegetarian who eats meat products, such as milk and eggs, will have an easier time replacing his "2 servings a day of meat" advocated in the Basic Four Food Guides. The 4—6 ounces of lean meat, poultry or fish may be replaced by one cup of cooked dried beans, four tablespoons of peanut butter or two eggs or increased amounts of milk and cheese. The four cups of milk or the equivalent, satisfying his intake from the "milk group," should still be included. A 1-inch cube of cheddar cheese equals 2/3 cup of milk in calcium, and 1/2 cup of ice cream provides the same calcium as 1/4 cup of milk. He may substitute 1/2 cup of cottage cheese for 1/3 cup of milk.

Without adding vitamins and minerals in the form of pills or food additives, an adequate diet may be designed for these vegetarians by including sufficient quantities of the following each day:

Protein: A teenager needs approximately 1/2 gram of protein per pound of body weight per day, or approximately 85 grams from age 13—15 and approximately 100 grams from age 16—19. However, if a 15—19 year old is pregnant, she probably needs about 40 additional grams, according to recent studies by Dr. Janet C. King of the University of California at Berkeley.

1 cup milk = 8 grams of protein (1 quart = 32 grams)

3 oz. (generous 1/2 cup) cooked soy beans = 20 grams (NOTE: More iron is absorbed when beans are cooked than when eaten raw, and the protein may be better utilized by the body.)

2 tablespoons peanut butter = 7 grams

1 egg = 7 grams

1 oz. cheese (cheddar, swiss, particularly good) = 7 grams

1 slice bread = 2 grams

3/4 cup dry cereal = 2 grams (NOTE: *Total, Special K* have more, and also have minimum daily requirements of most vitamins and minerals. Despite their claims, most dry cereals are often of less value than a slice of enriched bread.)

1/2 cup cooked cereal such as oatmeal = 2 grams

Iron: Teenagers need 15—18 milligrams of iron.

3 oz. (generous 1/2 cup) *cooked* soy beans = 8 milligrams

3 oz. peanuts = 2 mg.

2 eggs (3 oz.) = 2 mg.

(Other good sources are leafy green vegetables, dark molasses, whole grain and enriched bread.)

NOTE: For those who may be concerned for fear the iron in vitamin products is prepared from animal sources, they can be reassured that such is not the case. Iron for food products and vitamin and mineral capsules is prepared from mineral salts.

Calcium: The teenager needs 1.3 to 1.4 grams.
1 cup of milk = 288 mg.
1-inch cube of cheddar cheese = 192 mg.
1/2 cup ice cream = 72 mg.

Riboflavin: (Vitamin B-2)

The primary sources are liver, mushrooms, milk, cheddar cheese, milk, meat, eggs, deep-green leafy vegetables, fortified cereals and enriched bread and almonds. If the vegetarian avoids fortified cereals and enriched bread, he will need considerable quantities of green leafy vegetables, mushrooms and almonds to obtain sufficient riboflavin.

Niacin and Niacinamide: (nicotinic acid and niacinamide)

Generous portions of whole grain cereals, peanuts, corn and yeast will compensate for the lack of meat, tuna fish, milk, chicken and enriched flour and bread, even for complete vegetarians.

Cyanocobalamin: (B-12) Normal sources are liver, milk, meat, fish and eggs, but yeast is also a good source, and sufficient quantities will meet the needs of the vegetarian.

Vitamin D: Most young people are exposed to sufficient sunshine to manufacture their own vitamin D. Young people are usually protected by drinking milk fortified with D (or irradiated to produce it), but even without this, the average young person spends enough time outdoors to take care of his vitamin D needs.

Vitamin A: The increased amounts of fruits and vegetables usually eaten by the vegetarian will supply adequate vitamin A.

Iodine: Iodine is found in fish and seafood, and in the water in many parts of the country. However, in the Great Lakes area those who do not eat fish or seafood from other parts of the country or the ocean need iodized salt. Again, those who follow a strict vegetarian diet are also apt to be those who feel that adding iodine to salt is adding something "unnatural" to it, and will select noniodized salt. A severe lack of iodine may result in enlargement of the thyroid, a goiter.

Thiamine: (Vitamin B-1) This will usually be ingested in sufficient quantities even on a vegetarian diet, as it is found in whole grains, potatoes, dry peas and beans, enriched bread and products made with enriched flour. (NOTE: In the case of severely restricted diets, the coating consumed with "brown rice" is an additional source.)

Diets which also eliminate meat products—milk, cheese, eggs, butter, etc., will contain insuf-

ficient riboflavin, and possibly vitamin A, vitamin D, calcium and phosphorus, and will obviously need even more bolstering with protein and iron. It is not impossible to provide these missing factors on such a diet, but it is difficult. Vitamin and mineral supplements in the form of pills and capsules would be helpful, although probably not as nutritionally sound as a balanced diet, but those who eat a strict vegetarian diet are usually opposed to taking "artificial products." No commercial vitamins are prepared from animal products, but it is perfectly true that they come out of a laboratory or factory, rather than the ground.

A high-protein food supplement such as Multi Purpose Food (MPF) which contains a soy base with added minerals and vitamins would be a very helpful adjunct to a vegetarian diet, and possibly be acceptable to at least some teenagers. It was developed years ago for an organization called Meals for Millions which ships food to starving people overseas under the sponsorship of a number of religious organizations and individual donors. It can be ordered either from Modern Protein Foods, 1820 Olympic Boulevard, Santa Monica, Calif. 90404, or General Mills, Box 300, Minneapolis, Minn. 55460.

In addition to the above, you may wish to consult some of the following, or make available to students some of the free literature available from the following sources:

Burns, Marjorie, "Nutrition Books: A Guide to Their Reliability," rev. 1967, New York State College of Human Ecology, Cornell University, Ithaca, New York. Single copies free to New York State residents; additional copies 15¢ each. Excellent annotated bibliography.

(For booklets similar to above, contact your local State Agricultural Extension Service or State College.)

"The Big Stretch: A Guide for Teachers on Teen-age Nutrition Education," 1970. Available without charge to teachers from Metropolitan Life Insurance Co., Health and Welfare Division, One Madison Ave., New York, N.Y. 10010.

"A Complete Summary of the Iowa Breakfast Studies," available to teachers without charge from the Cereal Institute, Inc., 135 S. LaSalle St., Chicago, Ill. This study of several years ago overemphasizes the use of cereals, but the basic data presented is interesting and important.

"What is a balanced diet?", Sealtest Consumer Service, 605 Third Ave., New York, N.Y. Useful single sheet, 3-hole punched, available in quantity for class distribution. Ask for other literature of use to your class.

"The wonder of you," and "Food and you," 1961, available from the American Institute of Baking, 400 E. Ontario St., Chicago, Ill. 60611, in classroom quantities. However, we suggest you send for single copies and see if they would be suitable for your class. They are useful and contain a good deal of information, but would probably be more acceptable to 9th and 10th graders than to upper classmen in high school.

"Choose Your Calories Wisely," 1971, available in classroom quantities from Department of Home Economics Services, Kellogg Co., Battle Creek, Mich. 49016. Useful and attractive folder with chart of calorie values of average servings of many common foods, plus estimates of calorie needs, etc.

Other sources include:

United States Department of Agriculture, Washington, D.C. 20250.

WHITE HOUSE CONFERENCE ON FOOD, NUTRITION AND HEALTH, 1969, available for $3.00 from the U.S. Government Printing Office, Washington, D.C. 20402. This 341 page report contains considerable information.

Council on Foods and Nutrition, American Medical Association, 535 N. Dearborn St., Chicago, Ill. 60610.

National Dairy Council, 111 N. Canal St., Chicago, Ill. 60606.

Deutsch, Ronald M., *THE NUTS AMONG THE BERRIES: AN EXPOSE OF AMERICA'S FOOD FADS,* rev. ed., New York: Ballantine Press.

Katz, Marcella, *VITAMINS, FOOD AND YOUR HEALTH,* Public Affairs Pamphlet #465, 1971. This pamphlet contains a number of helpful charts and considerable information in its 28 pages. It is available for 25¢ a copy (21¢ in quantities from 10—99), from Public Affairs Pamphlets, 381 Park Ave. South, New York, N.Y. 10016.

SENSES: TASTE: FOOD ADDITIVES

PURPOSE:

To discover something about food additives, their sources, the purposes for which they are used, and their effect on the flavor and texture of foods.

COMMENT:

Writing in *FAMILY CIRCLE,* Ronald M. Deutsch suggests we examine a nonexistent label which reads: "acetone, methyl acetate, furan, diacetyl, butanol, methyl-furan, isoprene, methylbutanol, caffeine, essential oils, methanol, acetaldehyde, methyl formate, ethanol, dimethyl sulfide and propionaldehyde." Does it sound tasty? . . . safe? . . . natural? What is it? It is pure coffee, with no additives. Here's another: "actomyosin, myogen, nucleo-proteins, peptides, amino acids, myoglobin, lipids, linoleic acid, oleic acid, lecithin, cholesterol, sucrose, adenosine, triphosphate (ATP), glucose, collagen, elastin, creatine, pyroligineous acid, sodium chloride, sodium nitrate, sodium nitrite, and sodium phosphates." This one is sugar-cured ham, the old fashioned kind, with no "man-made" chemicals added. Deutsch goes on to point out that preservatives added to foods are among the substances often feared by the label-readers, and that these are usually substances naturally found in "natural" foods, and are harmless.

For instance, sodium and calcium propionate are salts of propionic acid, produced naturally in Swiss cheese, and these salts are completely metabolized by natural digestive processes. Vitamin E and citric acid are also used to prevent spoilage, and occur naturally in many foods. Other substances frequently added to foods do not occur naturally, but are close chemical relatives of others which do, and are apparently handled by the body in the same way as their naturally occurring cousins. Without the use of additives such as these, long-distance shipping, warehousing, and even relatively short-term storage on your kitchen shelf would be attended with many dangers as foods changed in composition, frequently developing toxic substances. (Ronald M. Deutsch, "Are Chemicals Poisoning Our Food?," *FAMILY CIRCLE*, Vol. 80, No. 1, Jan. 1972.)

But those strange polysyllabic words appearing with increasing frequency on our food packages may cause us more than literary distress. We sometimes read them because we are disturbed by the possibility of long-range damage from some additives which the government and many individuals believe may not have been adequately tested. The FDA deputy commissioner James D. Grant instituted an extensive literature search to be completed in 1972 on no less than 700 food additives. This will result in new guidelines for the food industry which may be more strict than those in force since 1958. Some people feel that one cause of our poor food habits is a dulling of our sense of taste by the increasing use of artificial flavorings and the changing of the natural taste and texture of some foods due to the use of preservatives and various kinds of softeners or texturizers. After having welcomed the increased variety of foods available in our markets, and foods which seemed to look, taste, and keep better, many people now feel they have been sold a bill of goods by the food industry. Some even feel the government has aided the industry in fooling the public. The result is that many young people are easily influenced by any self-appointed expert who starts his appeal for changed food habits by downgrading the regular food producers and distributers and government controls and recommendations.

GROUP SIZE:

Up to 20

TIME SUGGESTED:

45—60 minutes

GENERAL DIRECTIONS:

Using food package labels, students attempt preliminary judgments of additives, and then receive some additional information. An attempt is made to decide on the relative merits of specific additives, their purposes, sources and possible health hazards.

MATERIALS REQUIRED:

Food packages (or labels from food packages or cans) brought in by students.

Leaflets, books, charts, Fact Sheets, etc., to provide additional information (see "Suggested Resources").

PROCEDURE:

1. Prior to the session ask the students to plan to bring in sample food packages or labels from home which show a number of additives. If possible, demonstrate by reading from some packages you have brought for the purpose.

2. In subgroups ask the students to compile a list of additives from their labels, indicating next to each the particular foods in which they were to be found. Ask them to leave enough space after each additive to add information later, or use a separate sheet or card for each additive.

3. Give each subgroup a copy of the following, asking them to fill in as much information as they think they feel pretty sure of in their group. Ask them to add appropriate information to their list from No. 2.

—After the name of each additive on your list, write its purpose, or the reason you think it was added to the food.

—If you know the source of any of the additives, fill that in.

—If you know of any possible health hazards connected with the use of an additive, fill that in.

—Is this product normally found in any foods? . . . if so, what? . . . add this information.

—Are there any additives on your list that you would call "natural"? If so, mark them "N".

4. You may wish to distribute some "Fact Sheets" at this point, or have students check some of the literature available in class. Ask the subgroups to add to or change their information if necessary, in order to share their answers with other class members.

5. In a plenary session compare and collate findings. Tell students the information they have gathered may be reproduced for them and, if desirable, make arrangements with class members for this.

The following questions may also be explored at this time:

—Do you read labels as a rule? . . . why?

—What additives, if any, do you usually avoid? . . . why?

—At present the government controls the use of additives . . . do you think this should be? . . . If so, do you think they are doing a good job? . . . If not, what do you think they should do?

—Do you think you could purchase food for a week which would provide adequate nourishment but would not contain any addi-

Additive	Foods to which this is often added	Purpose for which this is usually added
agar	chocolate products, ice cream	thickener and stabilizer
amyl acetate	candy, dessert mixes	banana flavor
ascorbic acid	canned peaches, other fruit products	antioxidant (prevent browning)
benzaldehyde	sweets	cherry, almond flavor
butylated hydroxyanisole (BHA)	fats	antioxidant, to inhibit development of rancidity
butylated hydroxytoluene (BHT)	fats	antioxidant, to inhibit development of rancidity
calcium propionate	sweets	inhibitor, to prevent growth of molds and bacteria
carboxymethylcellulose	ice cream	thickener, stabilizer
carotene	margarine	yellow coloring
cinnamic aldehyde	soft drinks, candy	cinnamon, cola, flavor
citral	dessert mixes, candy	lemon flavor
citric acid	fruit products	antioxidant, prevent browning, etc.
diglycerides	salad dressing, cake mix	emulsifiers, to prevent separation
gelatin	ice cream	thickener and stabilizer
glycerine	candy, coconut	humectant (moisturing agent, to prevent drying out)
gum arabic	ice cream	thickener and stabilizer
gum tragacanth	ice cream	thickener and stabilizer

hydrolyzed plant protein (an early step in production of MSG)	soup, sauces	flavor enhancer
lecithin	cake mix, salad dressing	emulsifier, to prevent separation
methyl cellulose	chocolate products	thickener and stabilizer
mineral oil (white)	dehydrated fruits and vegetables, raw fruits and vegetables	as a "release agent," protective coating
monoglycerides	cake mixes, shortening	emulsifier, to prevent separation
monosodium glutamate (MSG)	meat products, soups	flavor enhancer
pectin	ice cream, jellies	thickener and stabilizer
petrolatum	candy; raw fruits and vegetables	release agent, sealing and polishing agent; protective coating
propyl gallate	fats	antioxidant, to inhibit development of rancidity
propylene glycol	candy	humectant (moisturizing agent, to prevent drying out)
sodium benzoate	sweets	inhibitor, to prevent growth of molds and bacteria
sodium propionate	sweets	inhibitor, to prevent growth of molds and bacteria
sodium sulfite	dehydrated poatoes	to prevent browning
sorbic acid	sweets	inhibitor, prevent growth of molds and bacteria
sulfur dioxide	dried apricots	to prevent browning
Vitamin E	fats, fruit products	antioxidant, inhibit development of rancidity, browning

tives? . . . What sorts of things would you buy? . . . Are there any foods with additives which you would want to include? . . . why?

—Are you more concerned about food additives, or about possible residual amounts of fertilizers and pesticides? . . . why? . . . What should be done about these problems? . . . Who should do it? . . . What would be the possible results? . . . Who would be affected? . . . How?

—How would you distinguish between a "natural" and an "unnatural" food? . . . What oils, for instance, would you consider "natural"? . . . why? . . . What oils are "unnatural"? . . . why? . . . Are there any soft drinks which you would consider "natural"? . . .

VARIATIONS:

Students may be interested in pursuing this subject further, and individual research papers may be assigned for reporting to the class at a later date.

Students may also wish to make a field trip to a local market and report on their success in "filling an order" without buying any foods with additives. They may wish to do this on the basis of "food for a week," or "food for a dinner they like."

SUGGESTED RESOURCES:

Burns, Marjorie M., and Ruth N. Klippstein, "Food Additives: Their Role Today," Cornell Extension Bulletin 1106, New York State College of Home Economics, single copies free to New York State residents; additional copies 10¢ each.

Trager, James, "What Adelle Davis and Others Say About Eating Right," *FAMILY CIRCLE,* Vol. 80, No. 2, Feb., 1972, pp. 50ff.

LIFE magazine, "The Move to Eat Natural," *LIFE,* Vol. 69, No. 24, Dec. 11, 1970.

American Institute of Baking, "Enriched Bread," rev., 1970, available without charge from American Institute of Baking, 400 E. Ontario St., Chicago, Ill. 60611.

"Sonneborn Products for Food Processing and Handling," available without charge from Witco Chemical, Sonneborn Division, 277 Park Ave., New York, N.Y. 10017.

Deutsch, Ronald M., "Are Chemicals Poisoning Our Food?", *FAMILY CIRCLE,* Vol. 80, No. 1, January, 1972.

The following information might be used in preparing a "Fact Sheet" for students:

FOOD AND FAMINE

PURPOSE:

To examine the problem of hunger on the national and international level.

COMMENT:

ACCORDING TO EXPERTS . . .

There are from 10—20 million people in the United States who are malnourished.

Only about a third of the low-income families in the United States have an adequate diet.

An estimated 10,000 people somewhere in the world, mostly children, die *each day* from undernutrition and malnutrition.

Since 1961 food per capita has been decreasing.

The *majority* of people in underdeveloped countries must be assumed to suffer from some degree of undernutrition and/or malnutrition.

In many countries poverty, the population explosion, low yields per acre of food crops and low productivity of labor produce an increasingly tragic picture.

Simply producing more of the same foods and using them in the same ways will not solve the problem within the period of time in which we can realistically envision sufficient decreases in population.

BUT IT IS ALSO SAID . . .

There is enough food in the United States for everyone in this country to eat well.

Since 1961 there has been a yearly increase in food production on a world-wide basis.

If we actually ate all the food we raised in the world today there would be enough nourishment for more than ten times the number of people now living.

Plant breeders have developed new seeds and new ways of growing them which have resulted in enormously increased yields of cereals—wheat, corn and rice. India's wheat crop increased 50 percent between 1965 and 1969, and Ceylon's rice crop increased 34 percent between 1967 and 1968.

Technological discoveries now available could wipe out the protein, vitamin and mineral deficiencies all over the world right now if put into practice.

WHICH GROUP OF STATEMENTS IS CORRECT?

Apparently all these things are true—it is the "yes, but . . ." statements which should follow each of the above that make the tragic difference.

Although poverty, both here and abroad, is the most important cause of malnourishment and the only really important cause of hunger and famine, lack of education, miseducation, misleading advertising and labeling practices have led to malnutrition in the higher income brackets as well as contributing to malnourishment among the poor. The 1969 White House Conference on Food, Nutrition, and Health declared malnutrition and undernourishment a national emergency, and recommended such measures as a guaranteed income, increased Social Security benefits for the elderly, a better food stamp program and school breakfast and lunch programs, compulsory enrichment and fortification of many common foods, better education in nutrition for the medical profession and general public, and more helpful labeling and advertising by the food industry. The United States has the money, the food, the technology and the personnel to carry out such programs.

The picture is much less bright in the underdeveloped nations. Increased yields of better quality cereals or grains in these countries have required large-scale mechanized farming, sophisticated methods of fertilization, irrigation, pest control and harvesting requiring high initial capital investment, large tracts of land, heavy equipment and new, suitable roads. This has had little effect on the "small" farmer, and some of that effect has been harmful.

Technology can make certain "inedible" foods appealing and digestible. Sources of animal and fish protein could be improved through development of new species and proper management of existent supplies. Synthetically produced amino acids and vitamins could be added to many foods and the quality of protein in plants can be improved. For instance, 5—10 percent of Fish Protein Concentrate added to any cereal raises the protein quality to that of milk, meat or eggs, and sunflower seed meal can be made into food products containing more and better quality protein than that in commonly used cereals supplying most of the protein in many countries.

The increase in population rate in underdeveloped countries does not indicate an improved standard of living but a decline of the mortality rate brought about by advances in medicine which cure and prevent fatal diseases that previously curbed population growth. The impact of these factors will increase. Children who suffer protein deficiencies are usually short on vitamins and minerals as well. The combination results in apathetic, low-energy adults, incapable of sustained productive work and sometimes suffering damaged metabolic processes which prevent proper utilization of food ingested. Long-term, world-wide programs are needed to insure adequate nourishment of all children, including pre-natal nourishment through proper maternal diet.

Gunnar Myrdal, after years of study of these problems, says that "huge reforms in the interest of greater equality and a more rapid rise of production must be carried out by the underdeveloped countries themselves." He says the major roles of developed countries should be: (1) "not to strengthen the powerful vested interests that have been delaying . . . those reforms"; (2) "to focus their efforts on research"; and (3) to make themselves responsible for "emergency aid to prevent hunger" (THE CHALLENGE OF WORLD POVERTY). Myrdal states that on both a national and international level drastic changes must be made on a moral basis with acceptance of the fact that this will mean a sacrifice on the part of the more developed nations.

In all probability, in addition to a decrease in the rate of population growth, it will be necessary to change people's food habits and farming practices, increase international government control of the food industries and possibly of migration, and redistribution of land and other resources. If sweeping changes are not made, the present trends will eventually bring us all to "general retrogression." Development must be "a movement upward of a whole system of interdependent conditions" (pp. 407-408).

GROUP SIZE:

Up to 20

TIME SUGGESTED:

One or more sessions of 45—60 minutes.

GENERAL DIRECTIONS:

It is not possible to give students the experience of starvation or even of acute prolonged hunger. For one thing, the ill effects might be irreversible. If students wish, they may experiment with such things as fasting for a few days, or eating a very limited diet for a week, but they should realize that these experiences are extremely weak imitations of starvation. Their memories of times in their lives when they were quite ill are a better basis for consid-

eration of the problem. If they will think of how they felt then, and at the same time think of all their family and most of their friends being simultaneously in the same condition, and also realize that, for the starving, these feelings usually are accompanied by the realization that there will be very little food, if any, available to them in the future, and that they will probably never feel any better—then they may have some idea of what "starving" feels like.

Films and reading materials will be helpful. Whatever materials are used for the Step No. 1 suggestions, Step No. 2 should be concerned with the investigation of possible solutions to the problem and possible action which they may take.

MATERIALS REQUIRED:

Selections from "Suggested Resources" should be available to students.

PROCEDURE:

Select one of the following for Step No. 1.

a. Ask the students to read in advance, or read to them in class, a report of experimentally induced hunger, such as the report by Guetzkow and Bowman (see "Suggested Resources"). Follow with discussion, considering such questions as:

—How do the men in this experiment differ from starving people in conditions of poverty here and in other countries?

—How do you think the "semi-starvation" described here differs from "starvation"?

—Would any of you be willing to undergo such a six-month experiment? . . . Why or why not? . . . What is the use of experiments like this?

—Would you be willing to live on their diet for a while if you could replace just one item with another food? What food would you eliminate? . . . What would you substitute for it? . . . Why?

b. Show one of the films exposing the problem ("Suggested Resources"). After the film ends, ask the students to think about it quietly for a few minutes, and then to write a short letter. Ask them to imagine that they are starving. They know they have not long to live . . . To whom would they want to write this letter? . . . What would they want to say? . . . Since they are very weak, they can only write a short letter . . . what are the most important things they would want to say? . . . Or would they only be able to write about how they felt, in such a situation?

Letters can be shared and discussed in small

groups, or saved for a future discussion.

c. Read students the short narrative of the wreck of the *Essex*, from *CALL ME ISHMAEL* by Charles Olson. This deals in a very matter of fact way with cannibalism among the survivors of an early nineteenth century shipwreck. Discussion should focus on what it must be like to eat human flesh, the reasons for man's aversion to it, and why starving people do not use this means of survival. What are the differences between the starvation of these men or the snow-bound immigrants in the Donner Pass, and the starvation of people in poverty or caught in a famine?

Select one of the following for Step No. 2.

a. Distribute copies of the question form below, or put questions on the board. Ask the students to fill in their answers.

1. Is the problem of increasing hunger in the world insoluble?

   Yes _____

   No _____

2. If it were possible to solve this problem, I don't think the people of the world would get together and solve it.

   True _____

   False _____

3. Do you think there is anything *you* can do about the problem?

   Yes _____

   No _____

4. If there is anything you might be able to do, what would you need in order to do this? _____

   _____

   _____

5. What hinders you from doing anything about it now? _____

   _____

6. How could these hindrances or interferences be removed? _____

   _____

7. As a voter, or potential voter, is there anything you could do through your vote? What? _____

   _____

   _____

After the students have completed questionnaires, ask them to share their answers and discuss them in subgroups. A plenary session can pool results.

b. Show one of the films dealing with possible solutions to the problem ("Suggested Resources"). Discuss, trying to develop the pros and cons of the suggested solutions.

c. Provide students with input from some of the written materials in "Suggested Resources," either by individual research and reporting by student panels using panelists who have studied some of the materials, or by assigning readings to the entire class. Discuss findings as in "b".

d. Provide input on possible careers in research which would seek solutions. Speakers may be invited, or films or written materials used as above. In a plenary discuss the advantages and disadvantages of such careers.

e. If there is a drive for money in your area to be given to starving people somewhere in the world, discuss the pros and cons of this effort.
Such questions as the following may be raised:

—How much of this money will benefit the hungry? . . . How can someone find out about this? . . . If only a small percentage will reach those for whom it is intended, what can or should be done about this?

—If these people live in a part of the world where malnutrition is very common, is it only prolonging their agony to send them food? . . . Would it be better to let some of the weaker ones die during this emergency in order that those with a better chance of "making it" have less competition?

—If you have been trying to help raise money for this drive, what have been the reactions of people you approached? . . . What do you think is behind any negative reactions you got? . . . Why did you decide to help in this drive? . . . If you were asked to help and didn't, why?

—What do you think will happen to the recipients of this fund next year?

—What do you know about the causes of their problem?

—What do you think is the responsibility of the United States to these people? . . . If you think our government should give more help, how should this be done?

—Suppose there were drives every month for people starving in different parts of the world, what would be the result? . . . Why?

—Do you think if our conflicts in Southeast Asia ended this year our government would do more to help these people than it did *before* we got involved? . . . Why or why not?

f. Show a film dealing with hunger in the United States ("Suggested Resources"). Ask the students to fill in their answers to the following questions: (Distribute forms or put on board, as in "a" above).

1. Do you think there are any families in your community without sufficient food? Yes _____ No _____

2. If you answered "yes," how many families are there, would you guess? _____

3. How should their needs be met?_____

_____

4. What would be the effect on your family of the steps you suggested in "3"?_____

_____

5. If you answered "no" to question No. 2, can you name the nearest community where there are hungry families?_____

_____

6. How should their needs be met?_____

7. What would be the effect on your family of the steps you suggested in "6"? (fill this in ONLY if it differs from your answer to question "4")_____

_____

Students may share and discuss their answers in subgroups, pooling findings in a plenary afterward.

g. Place signs across the front of the room to form a continuum as follows:

1.	2.	3.	4.
Not my problem.	I am interested, but can do nothing.	I might be interested in doing something.	I am personally very concerned about this problem, and plan to do something about trying to solve it.

Ask the students to "take a stand" under the statement which reflects their feelings at the present time about the problem of world hunger. Ask the students in groups Nos. 1 and 2 to sit down and explain their positions to each other, and ask the students in groups Nos. 3 and 4 to do the same. After a few minutes, ask the students to again "take a stand," in case some wish to change their positions. Ask all but group No. 4 to be seated, and then ask those in group No. 4 to hold a brief panel discussion in front of the rest of the class. Ask members of groups Nos. 1, 2 and 3 to question the panel on such things as feasibility of their plans, possible negative results of projected actions, etc. NOTE: It is possible that you will have no students in group No. 4. If so, ask students in group No. 3 to form the panel, and proceed. If all students are in groups Nos. 1 and 2, discuss with the class why Nos. 3 and 4 are "empty sets."

SUGGESTED RESOURCES:

WRITTEN MATERIALS:

Don Fabun (ed.), *FOOD: AN ENERGY EXCHANGE SYSTEM:* Number Four of "The Markets of Change Series," Kaiser News, 1970. Kaiser Center 866: Dept. 470, 300 Lakeside Drive, Oakland, Calif. 94604.

Don Fabun (ed.), *ECOLOGY: THE MAN-MADE PLANET,* Number One of "The Markets of Change Series," 1970. Kaiser News (see above).

Guetzkow, H., and P. H. Bowman, *MEN AND HUNGER: A PSYCHOLOGICAL MANUAL FOR RELIEF WORKERS,* Elgin, Ill.: The Brethren Press, 1946, pp. 23-43. An abridged version is available in *BASIC CONTRIBUTIONS TO PSYCHOLOGY: READINGS,* Robert L. Wrenn (ed.), Belmont, Calif.: Wadsworth Publishing Co., 1966, pp. 96ff.

Handler, Philip, (ed.), *BIOLOGY AND THE FUTURE OF MAN,* ch. 15, "On Feeding Mankind," New York: Oxford Univ. Press, 1970.

Leinwand, Gerald, (General Editor of Problems of American Society series), *HUNGER,* New York: Washington Square (Simon and Schuster), 1971. Text on starvation and the United States, aimed at high school students and adults.

Myrdal, Gunnar, *THE CHALLENGE OF WORLD POVERTY: A WORLD ANTI-POVERTY PROGRAM IN OUTLINE,* New York: Pantheon/Random House, 1970.

Olson, Charles, *CALL ME ISHMAEL,* N.Y. City Lights, 1947. (The story of the wreck of the *Essex* was reprinted in *THE 1970 FIRESIDE CALENDAR AND ENGAGEMENT BOOK,* Robert Gottlieb (ed.), New York: Simon and Schuster, 1969).

Horwitz, Julius, *THE DIARY OF A.N.: THE STORY OF THE HOUSE ON WEST 104th STREET,* New York: G. P. Putnam's Sons, 1970. An excellent novel for young people, written as the diary of a young black girl in Harlem caught in the dehumanizing situations of life "on the welfare."

Public Affairs Pamphlets. A number of these well-done pamphlets deal with related problems and are a good basis for discussion. See particularly

"Hunger in America" and "A New Look at Our Crowded World" (#393), both by Maxwell S. Stewart, 381 Park Ave. South, New York, N.Y. 10016.

Hopcraft, Arthur, *BORN TO HUNGER*, Boston, Mass.: Houghton Mifflin, 1968. Hunger in Africa, Asia, Central and South America.

FILMS:

HUNGER IN THE U.S.:

Hunger in America, black and white, 50 min., 1968. Produced by CBS-TV. Available for low rental fee from AFL-CIO.* Despite length, excellent presentation of the problem, including investigation of food stamp program, welfare. Interviews some of the people of the Citizens' Board of Inquiry into Hunger and Malnutrition found living in 265 counties in 20 states.

Poverty in Rural America, #4910, black and white, 28½ minutes. 1965. Free loan from U.S.D.A. The people tell their own story. Excellent portrayal of poverty among White, Black, Indian and Mexican people. Stresses need for education among poor.

Christmas in Appalachia, black and white, 29 min., CBS Reports. Available at low rental fee from AFL-CIO.* This is *not* a "Merry Christmas" film— use it any time. A documentary. No solutions suggested, but direct, simple moving statements by residents. People subsist on surplus foods.

The Captive, black and white, 28 min., 1965. Produced by National Council of Churches. Available at low rental from AFL-CIO.* Case study of young unemployed coal miner in West Virginia. Emphasis is on loss of dignity, lack of opportunity and lack of training. Family finally accepts surplus foods and welfare. (Film was made before OEO programs.)

Depressed Area, black and white, 14 min., 1962. Produced by NBC-TV. Available for low service charge from AFL-CIO.* Brinkley narrates story of West Virginia mining town. One of men interviewed has five children suffering from malnutrition. Presents no answers but raises many basic problems. (Film is even older than preceding one. Although these films are out of date in some respects, problems remain.)

The Harvester, 19 min., 1961. Produced by Franciscan Films. Available for low service charge from AFL-CIO.* Migratory workers in California. Competition between Mexican and United States workers (see also next listing).

Harvest of Shame, black and white, 54 min., 1960. CBS-TV. Available at low rental from AFL-CIO.* Edward R. Murrow's TV report on migratory workers, produced by David Lowe. Although long, a fine film which includes discussion of pros and cons of use of migratory workers and possible solutions.

Misery, despair, child neglect. Contains some of first pictures of fruit pickers in California at organizing meeting, conducted by AFL-CIO. Conditions have changed somewhat since 1960.

The Last Menominee, black and white, 30 minutes. Mass Media Ministries. Menominee Indians are interviewed about their plight as they face coming termination of reservation status by Bureau of Indian Affairs. Lack of food is part of their problem.

The Poor Pay More, Part I., black and white, 27 min., 1967. Produced by National Educational Television, Indiana University. Available for low service charge from AFL-CIO.* Consumer education as part of recognition and solution of one reason why poor families eat poorly.

The Battle of Newburgh, black and white, 55 min., 1962. Produced by NBC White Paper. Available at low rental fee from AFL-CIO.* Documentary on controversial welfare program in Newburgh, N.Y., allegedly instituted to eliminate "chiselers" from welfare rolls. All the old cliches about the welfare recipients are contrasted with the tragic situations of cases explored in this film.

HUNGER IN THE WORLD:

The Population Explosion, black and white, 43 minutes. Mass Media Ministries. Although filmed in India when Nehru was Prime Minister, is unfortunately up-to-date in presentation of problem. Some of the conversation is difficult to understand, but mature students will find coverage of actual conditions interesting.

Forgotten Indians, 28 min., 1958. Produced by British Broadcasting Corp. Available at low service charge from AFL-CIO.* South American Indians, problems of land distribution, overcrowded and over-worked land, poor seed and low yields. Classic problems still internationally abundant. Features work of UNESCO, FAO, WHO and other UN agencies.

The Food Crisis, black and white, 60 min. Mass Media Ministries. Contrasts seen of abundance and starvation. History, causes and possible solutions. Sequences made in India, Libya, the Philippines, South America, Canada, Europe and the United States.

FILMS WHICH CONCENTRATE ON POSSIBLE SOLUTIONS:

Who Shall Reap?, color, 28 minutes, 1969. Free loan from U.S.D.A. Focus on recent research efforts with awareness of world problems, but some of the ecology minded will object to use of word "safe" in connection with pesticides as "government propaganda."

The Riddle of Photosynthesis, color, 14½ minutes, 1965. Produced by Handel Film Corp. Free loan from U.S. Atomic Energy Commission. For

270 your nearest outlet write: Technical Information, U.S.A.E.C., Oak Ridge, Tenn. 37830. Shows how research with radioactive carbon-14 has begun to solve this "riddle," and ends with discussion of future plans for artificial food production to feed the world's hungry.

The Only War We Seek, 28 min., 1963. Produced by Agency for International Development. Available for low service charge from AFL-CIO.* Some students will be turned off by the title and by government sponsorship, but for others film is good presentation of the needs. Does good selling job on helping underdeveloped nations for our own long-range self-interest. Where the money comes from, where it is spent, why money for foreign aid is needed.

Harvest, color, 28 min., produced by Willard Van Dyke. Staff members of Rockefeller Foundation in Mexico and Columbia discuss hybrid corn, rust-resistant wheat and blight-resistant potatoes in a beautiful film showing technical research in relation to progress in agriculture.

Agriculture, Research and You, available in both black and white and color, 28 minutes. Free loan from Farm Film Foundation, 1425 H St. N.W., Washington, D.C. 20005. Won number of awards in 1965. Deals with such areas as animal disease prevention and control of crop diseases and pests, emphasizing need for research.

Food or Famine, color, 28 minutes, appeals for greater international cooperation in expanding food production world wide. It factually presents the impending threat of mass starvation; then covers the globe to report what is being done to prevent it—through land reclamation, improvement of seed crops, soil enrichment through fertilization, improved range management, better fishing methods, and insect and weed control. Free loan from Shell Oil Company, Houston, Texas.

The Rival World, color, 27 minutes, is an on-the-spot account of the endless, costly war between man and insects. An unusual blend of scientific objectivity and great visual impact has won acclaim for this film. Free loan from the Shell Oil Company.

Unseen Enemies, color, 32 minutes, shows the threats to health in frank and sometimes shocking views of the causes and effects of infectious disease that maim and destroy the people of the earth. Produced with the support of the World Health Organization. Free loan from the Shell Oil Company.

The Living Soil, color, 20 minutes, explores the life that abounds in the earth's thin layer of top soil. Most of this life is beneficial to mankind, but intensive farming provides a rich environment for the pests that can destroy the crops upon which man so heavily depends. Free loan from the Shell Oil Company.

*For AFL-CIO film outlet nearest you, write AFL-CIO, 816 16th St., Washington, D.C. 20006.

FILMSTRIPS:

Tomorrow the Moon, but When Do We Get to Earth?, 73 frames (15 min.), color, guide, record with automatic inaudible and nonautomatic audible signals. Produced by Thomas S. Klise Co., 1967. Suggests some solutions, controversial. Interesting art work compensates for preachy ending unsuitable for some groups.

Let's Get Together, 72 frames (or individual slides), color, guide, record with non-automatic audible signal. Produced by OEO, 1967. Free loan from Dept. of Public Affairs, Office of Economic Opportunity, 1200 19th St. N.W., Washington, D.C. 20036.

PROJECT:

Students might like to make a contribution to the Meals for Millions project. Meals for Millions, 1800 Olympic Boulevard, P.O. Box 1666, Santa Monica, Calif. 90406. This organization was started quite a few years ago and is sponsored by a number of religious organizations as well as individual donors. It ships high-protein food supplement (MPF, Multi Purpose Food), to starving people overseas. Write them for information.

SENSES:
AUDITION
(HEARING):
TAPES AND VOICES

MATERIALS REQUIRED:

Tape recorder, tapes and take-up reel. If possible, one set-up per group.

PROCEDURE:

1. In subgroups of 5—6, tape a 10 minute discussion.

2. Each subgroup replays once or twice the tape it has just made to enable everyone to hear his own voice on tape. Subgroups may discuss how their own voices sounded to them, compare this with other members' perceptions, talk about why they often react, "That doesn't sound like me!"

3. Each group may select a member, listen to a segment of tape carrying his voice, and then ask him to say something "live" about the same subject, and compare the sound differences. What is it that is "missing" in the taped sound—not facial expressions, or gestures, but in the sound itself? What differences does he himself feel are there? This may be repeated for all members of the group.

4. Each subgroup makes another short tape, using one or more of the following suggestions:

a. Each member repeats a single word three or four times.

b. A simple short sentence is decided upon, and each member separately repeats this sentence on the tape. The entire subgroup then repeats the sentence simultaneously, in choral style, several times on the tape. As a last step, a particular pitch and stress pattern is decided upon for the sentence, and the sentence is taped again.

c. Each member whispers the chosen word separately, then in chorus. Each member speaks the word quietly, then loudly, first individually, then in chorus.

d. Each member individually, decides on a particular note or tone, silently. All members, at a signal, hum that note for a few seconds. All members then try to come together in a "common note" or "tone"—no direction is given as to how this note is to be chosen. The final tone is held for a few seconds.

e. Each member, individually, recites a series of nonsense syllables. Students should decide in advance what these are to be, and write them down, so that they can be repeated later. The subgroup then chooses one set, and recites them in chorus. The subgroup members all recite their own nonsense statement simultaneously.

5. These tapes are played back and examined as in "3". It will be more possible to concentrate on the sound, rather than the sense, in the tapes made in Step No. 4.

PURPOSE:

To investigate and identify differences in pitch and tone of the voice, "live" and on tape; to better understand and enjoy sounds.

COMMENT:

The human ear is remarkable in its ability to pick up fine shades of difference. We all know that we can "recognize a familiar voice," but seldom stop to think "how?" We know we can recognize a familiar voice on a tape, and yet "somehow" it doesn't sound just exactly the same as it does when talking person-to-person. Students are interested in listening to their own voices and those of friends on tape, and can begin to consider some of the fine discriminations made by the ear. Even those students who have heard themselves on tape before usually are interested in the experience.

GROUP SIZE:

Up to 20

TIME SUGGESTED:

60 minutes

GENERAL DIRECTIONS:

Students tape their own voices, play them back, make comparisons of various kinds between voices on tape and between taped and "live" voice sounds. If desired, additional discussion on communication problems may be a part of this exercise as speech patterns are examined.

6. Each subgroup may now make a five minute stretch of "blank" tape, in which no one is to speak. When this is played back, the groups should listen carefully to pick up any sounds which appear. Ask each member to listen silently, and jot down on a piece of paper each sound he hears and, where possible, what he believes is its source. All may now discuss their findings. They will probably find that they are not aware, as a rule, of these sounds which are all around them, even in a quiet room.

7. In a plenary the class discuss their findings. This may include some investigation of the fine distinctions which make recognition of voice sounds possible.

VARIATIONS:

1. A group of tongue-twisters may be selected for taping, and each subgroup member may have an opportunity of reading one or more of these. In playback, individual members should first listen to their own voices, paying particular attention to clarity, and then to others. The subgroups may discuss what sounds were most difficult to hear, which words were most commonly twisted and in what ways. If desired, this may be followed by the reading of "sensible" statements, for concentration on clarity of sound. In this case, each group member should be given a separate slip of paper containing a statement, unknown to other members. Statements should be sufficiently simple so that "stumbling" in reading will not be an important factor. Group members may be able to help one another pick up communication problems due to speech habits or patterns. It should be discovered that sound problems in communication are not due to the *sense* of what is being said, but to the sound.

2. Subgroups may choose a short choral reading, perhaps from a play or a poem, and rehearse it briefly. They may wish to try more than one taping to get the sound quality they want. These tapes may then be played back to the entire group. The listeners may be asked to pay particular attention to the sound, rather than the selection read. It might be interesting if this is done in various foreign languages, the selections having been reproduced with an interlinear of phonetic pronunciation. This will help the listeners concentrate on sound.

3. Subgroups may wish to examine some "pictures" of voice sounds, such as those made by the Bell Telephone Company. They may also be interested in studying something about the anatomy and physiology of the ear, or the physics of audition (see references below).

4. Students may wish to tape a variety of voice sounds and patterns outside the classroom situation. Some students will have tape recorders, and may be able to bring in tapes with voices of individuals of various ages, or of dinner table conversations. They may also wish to tape a few snippets of radio or TV broadcasts of well-known people. These tapes may be played in class, both for identification and for discrimination of voice sounds and patterns.

5. This exercise may be combined with the "Life: Audition: Spaces" taping voices in spaces with different accoustical properties and comparing the differences.

6. Using a metronome, students read a sentence, one word per beat. This eliminates one variable, rate of speed, enabling listeners to concentrate on other factors. It also allows an individual the opportunity to hear his voice sounds at different rates, and often to pick up specific "flaws," or sounds which cause communication difficulties.

SUGGESTED RESOURCES:

"Mechanical Principles of the Human Ear," a brief pamphlet, and two charts, "Sectional Diagram of the Human Ear," and "How We Hear," both of which are available in wall chart and notebook size, may be obtained without charge for your students from the Sonotone Corporation, Saw Mill River Road, Elmsford, N.Y. 10523.

Van Bergeijk, William A., John R. Pierce, and Edward E. Davis, Jr., *WAVES AND THE EAR,* New York: Doubleday, 1960. Students interested in pursuing this subject can understand this presentation of the physiology of hearing, problems of communication and speech, etc., given in this paperback.

Stevens, S. S., and F. Warshofsky, *SOUND AND HEARING, LIFE SCIENCE LIBRARY,* New York: Life-Time, 1965.

SENSES:
AUDITION: SOUNDS
AND SPACES

PURPOSE:

To listen to the accoustical properties of various spaces, and become aware of the effect on the sound of known voices, to increase our understanding of the sounds of voices in our lives.

COMMENT:

This exercise involves some of the properties of touch, as well as sound, since spatial data is registered by our bodies in more ways than by sound alone. We also react cognitively and affectively to different kinds of spaces, and to conversations carried on in these spaces. The exercise may combine investigation of this combined data, and then seek to break it down into its components.

GROUP SIZE:

6—20

TIME SUGGESTED:

This exercise may be carried out in segments as part of a field trip, or may be completed in about an hour.

GENERAL DIRECTIONS:

A variety of kinds of spaces is necessary. Students will move about, holding brief discussions in various places. The route may be planned in advance, or if the exercise is part of a field trip, you may take advantage of various situations as they present themselves.

MATERIALS REQUIRED:

Suggested "spaces": elevator, closet, shower stall, gym, auditorium, stairwell, boiler room, rooftop, street, classroom, etc.

PROCEDURE:

1. Before starting the experiment, explain to the students that they are to notice how they feel, how they move, how others with them seem to be feeling, and how their voices sound, in the various places in which they will be working. Tell them that they will hold a brief discussion under various circumstances, and will try to identify and explain the differences in the way their voices sound. Ask them to enter each new "space" silently—to stop and "listen to the space itself" each time, before continuing their discussion. Select a simple, interesting topic on which all can speak easily, as their starting point. As the exercise continues, the conversation will primarily concern itself with the exploration of the data of the experience, rather than the original "topic." Work in subgroups of 5—6.

2. Start wherever you are, right now. Listen to the space. Now, carry on your discussion for 5—10 minutes. While in the same space, ask the students to turn their backs on other members of their subgroup, while continuing their discussion for a few minutes.

3. Move the groups from one location to another, following essentially the same pattern throughout. As they move about, ask the groups to allow each member to speak while the other members listen, trying to pinpoint differences in the sound of that single voice in the various locations. After their initial period of silence in each new location, ask them to try to describe the "sound of the space" before they take up their voice sound exploration.

4. At the end of the exercise, reconvene the class for a general discussion, pooling their findings. Where was communication best? How much of the effect was due to the sound itself? Were they more aware of their own voices in some places than others? why?

VARIATIONS:

See exercise in "Life: Senses: Kinesthesis: Social Space."

SUGGESTED RESOURCES:

Students who have worked with rock or folk

groups, who have recorded their own music or have worked with other kinds of recordings will be able to contribute considerable information to such a session. You may wish to enlist their assistance in planning the experience.

Hall, Edward T., *THE HIDDEN DIMENSION*, Garden City, N.Y.: Anchor-Doubleday, 1966.

SENSES: AUDITION: BACKGROUND MUSIC

PURPOSE:

To consider and enjoy our affective response to music and other sounds, to express our reactions, and to consider "background music" in our lives.

COMMENT:

You have probably used music as a background to other activities in your class. "Background music" is very much part of our lives these days, for good and for ill, and should be given some examination. Piped-in music is used in stores to encourage buying, in factories and offices to encourage work, and in waiting rooms, restaurants and other public places to develop a mood, provide company for the lonely, avoid awkward silences for the non-talkative, or mask less pleasant sounds. It is also supposed to provide pleasure, and is frequently used by students as a background to study. Dr. Thomas J. Scott studied hyper-active 7-11 year-old boys in the House of the Good Shepherd, Utica, N.Y., and found their ability to concentrate and study improved when background music was added to normal class conditions (*AMERICAN JOURNAL OF ORTHOPSYCHIATRY:* Vol. 40, p. 667). It is not often that an individual who objects to this "instrusion of privacy" or "manipulation" is able to silence these sounds, and perhaps for most of us they are helpful.

We normally distinguish between "listening to music," as at a concert, and "background music." What are the differences? What are the effects? When we listen to the "background music," what happens? How do we feel about these things?

GROUP SIZE:

Up to 20

TIME SUGGESTED:

One or more sessions of 45—60 minutes.

GENERAL DIRECTIONS:

Students experiment with such activities as "painting to music," and discuss the effect of background music on our lives.

MATERIALS REQUIRED:

Tapes, records, tape and record players.

Art materials, such as drawing paper; long scrolls of paper such as shelf paper; paints, crayons, felt-tip markers; clay; materials for collages.

PROCEDURE:

1. Distribute art materials; explain procedures. One approach is to have rolls of paper and wide felt-tip markers, suggesting that students use color, line and shape to respond to music to be played. Music is started after suggesting that, in order to compare responses, a signal will be given at the end of each minute of playing-time, at which point students will draw a straight line from top to bottom of their paper before continuing. Students will work individually.

2. In subgroups of 5—6, students spread painted rolls on the floor, one above another, matching segments of time by the "minute marks." Subgroups discuss experience, including:

—What is your reaction to "seeing the music" as expressed by your group?

—What similarities and differences do you notice in color, line and shape?

3. If desired, each subgroup may select one roll to compare with the selected rolls of other groups. These may be posted in front of the room for all to see. The music may be played through once more, while students examine their own and the posted rolls.

4. In a plenary, discuss the rolls, data from their subgroup discussion, and feelings from this last experience of re-hearing the music while looking at the rolls. Such questions as the following may be discussed:

—What kinds of feelings do we get from music? . . . why?

—How much of this do you think is from association with certain kinds of sounds?

—Why do some sections (minute-segments) seem similar, while others vary a good deal?

—On the rolls, is a mood expressed? . . . Is it consistent?

—Do some colors seem consistently related to some sounds? . . . lines? . . . forms? . . . Are some segments blank?

—How do you think you have reacted in the past when music was played as a background to class activities?

—How do you feel about "background" music in general?

—Do you think we are always "aware" of it?

—How do you think music in stores affects you? . . . others?

—What is the effect of background music in other public places? . . . in your home?

—Do you think background music in public places is a good idea?

—Do you consider it an invasion of privacy?

—Do you feel you are manipulated by background music?

—Do you think background music in the school cafeteria is a good idea?

—If you had control of a store, would you play background music? What kind? . . . why?

—Do you like background music in the dentist's office?

—If you worked in an office, would you want background music?

VARIATIONS:

1. Tapes may be prepared in which individual notes, and then individual chords, are played. Each note or chord is repeated steadily for 15—30 seconds, and followed by thirty seconds of silence. This is more interesting to listen to if a variety of instruments is used. Response here is to pitch and tone without rhythm or melody, or with minimal rhythmic effect. This may be used as part of Step No. 1, or at another session. Discussion should follow as in Step No. 4 above.

2. Following the general outline given in "Procedure," eliminate the "time-lines." Students. may draw, paint, color or sculpt during and immediately following playing the music.

3. Play record of background music; follow the outline in "Procedure," eliminating time lines if desired.

4. Other art media may be used, such as individual or group collages, and combined with any of the suggestions given here.

5. A field trip involving visits to places where there is moving water, such as the edge of a lake or river, a fast-rushing stream, a waterfall, a fountain may be used instead of music, and students provided with sketch pads and a few crayons for on-site sketching. Explain that they are to react to the sound, rather than the sight, of the moving water. Suggest they listen with eyes closed for a few min-

utes before starting their artistic expression of the experience.

6. Repeat the following word slowly, three times, and ask the students to respond with appropriate lines or shapes: "maluma."

Now repeat "takete" slowly, three times, and ask the students to respond.

Students will be interested to know that these two words were used by the Soviet psychologist Uznadze in combination with a series of "hard" and "soft" lines, and found a common response among people of various cultures—all felt "maluma" was "soft" and "takete" "hard" in terms of lines associated with the sound. If you prefer, you may use the two sketches prepared by the Gestalt psychologist, Wolfgang Kohler, and ask the students, "Which is 'Maluma'?", and "Which is 'Takete'?" (McKellar, *EXPERIENCE AND BEHAVIOUR*). This may be combined with some of the above experiences.

7. Play a record with suitable background music and encourage students to meditate during this time. Some relaxation exercises, such as those given in "Freedom: Stretch Exercises" may be used before starting the record, if desired. This may be used independently with students who have previously done some meditating, "day-dreaming," etc., or may be used as a last step in an exercise in which they seem ready to give some time to individual consideration of a point, a problem, an issue, or a theme.

SUGGESTED RESOURCES:

McKellar, Peter, *EXPERIENCE AND BEHAVIOUR*, Baltimore, Md.: Penguin, 1968, pp. 70-71.

SENSES: AUDITION: IDENTIFYING SOUNDS

PURPOSE:

To increase our ability to be purposively selective in listening; to heighten awareness of differences in sound in order to improve our ability to identify specific sounds.

COMMENT:

Most sighted people rely very little on their sense of hearing in identification, but the heightened sensitivity of the blind to small differences in sounds shows the reservoir of ability we seldom tap. We can "tune in" a lot more sounds if we try, and train ourselves to distinguish and identify their sources.

Gertrude Jekyll writes that she can tell what trees she is near by the sound of the wind in the leaves. She says, "The birches have a small, quick, high-pitched sound; so like that of falling rain that I am often deceived into thinking it really is rain, when it is only their own leaves hitting each other with a small rainlike patter. The voice of oak leaves is also rather high-pitched, though lower than that of birch. Chestnut leaves in a mild breeze sound much more deliberate; a sort of slow slither. Nearly all trees in gentle wind have a pleasant sound, but I confess to a distinct dislike of the noise of all the poplars; feeling it to be painfully fussy, unrestful, and disturbing. On the other hand, how soothing and delightful is the murmur of Scotch firs both near and far." *(THE 1970 FIRESIDE CALENDAR AND ENGAGEMENT BOOK).*

GROUP SIZE:

Up to 20

TIME SUGGESTED:

45—60 minutes

GENERAL DIRECTIONS:

A series of brief experiments in identifying sounds is followed by the playing of some tapes prepared by students in advance of the session. The session can be ended by reading a selection from literature dealing with the awareness of sounds.

MATERIALS REQUIRED:

Tapes prepared by students as in Step No. 1.
One copy of material to be read to students—see "Suggested Resources."

PROCEDURE:

1. Arrange to have several students tape a few local "environments" prior to the session. Students may be interested in knowing that the Leisure Data company in New York sells an "Alibi Series" of four tapes or cassettes which offer background sounds of an office, airport, busy highway, subway station, hospital, train station, a wild party and the sounds of long distance phone operators from eight major cities. The purpose is to play these tapes as a background to phone calls according to your special needs! They also have a twenty minute cassette of a barking and snarling German shepherd, for "protection." Ask the students to tape "environments" with which they believe most students in the class are familiar, explaining that they will be played in class. Ask the students to edit the tapes to allow 60—90 seconds of each environment.

2. Start the actual session by spending a few minutes with simple sounds you can produce by handling materials in the classroom. Ask the students to close their eyes and see if they can tell what you are doing. Your actions may include such things as closing a door, opening a window, opening a drawer, moving a chair, tearing a piece of paper, cutting a piece of paper with scissors, eating an apple, etc. If desired, you could simply start the experiment, and then let volunteers take over the "sound production."

3. Explain the "environment tapes," without identifying any of the places included, and let students try to identify the locations. This may be handled in a plenary, with students either calling out their guesses or writing them down, or in subgroups, with group members talking *quietly* as they try to identify the various environments.

4. After all tapes have been played, ask their makers to re-play them, identifying each segment this time.

5. Ask the students to sit quietly with their eyes closed and notice what seems to be the *loudest* sound around them—in the room or nearby. Each should do this individually, not speaking but making a mental note. Each should now try to notice the *quietest* sound around them. Again, this is to be done silently. After a few minutes of this, start the reading.

6. Read a short passage dealing with sound from one of the sources in "Suggested Resources," or from something you yourself have discovered.

SUGGESTED RESOURCES:

Merton, Thomas, "Rain and the Rhinoceros," *RAIDS ON THE UNSPEAKABLE,* New York: New Directions, 1966. (Use pp. 9-14, ending with "There is no clock that can measure the speech of this rain that falls all night on the drowned and lonely forest." If you feel your class would enjoy more, select additional passages and close with the last section on p. 23.)

Clare, John, (Written in Northampton Asylum), "Pleasant Sounds," *A BOOK OF PEACE,* Elizabeth Goudge (ed.), New York: Coward-McCann, 1967, p. 110.

Joyce, James, "All day I hear the noise of waters," *A TUNE BEYOND US: A COLLECTION OF POEMS,* Myra Cohn Livingston, (ed.), New York: Harcourt, Brace and World, 1968, p. 206.

Jekyll, Gertrude, *THE 1970 FIRESIDE CALENDAR AND ENGAGEMENT BOOK,* (Robert Gottlieb, compiler, New York: Simon and Schuster, 1969, December 14).

SENSES: AUDITION: A MUSICAL HAPPENING

PURPOSE:

To take advantage of a moment when some sort of musical expression is appropriate, and involve everyone in the class in actual participation.

COMMENT:

In *THE FEAST OF FOOLS* Harvey Cox presents a strong argument for the revival of fantasy and festivity in our lives, saying that to celebrate events of the past and hopes for the future is a vitally important step in humanizing our lives. He says, "Man is by his very nature a creature who not only works and thinks but who sings, dances, prays, tells stories, and celebrates." He points out that our young people seem to have grasped this more clearly than their elders and have reinstated "expressive play and artistic creation . . . in the center of life" rather than pushing them out to the edge, or ignoring them completely. He points out that true celebrations "celebrate *something* . . . our joy *about* something . . . that has a place in human history, past or future . . . As both an affirmation of history-making and a temporary respite from it, festivity reminds us of the link between two levels of our being—the instrumental, calculating side, and the expressive, playful side" (New York: Harper and Row, 1969, pp. 10, 16, 46). There are times in the life of a community, a school and a class when some sort of celebration or ritual is a felt need, but this need is seldom expressed, let alone met.

Most celebrations of the past included music as a vital part of their expression, and song and dance are a natural means of expressing the "other side" of our feelings—that side which can come through strongly in artistic expression, but may crumble to dust and ashes when analyzed and "logically" pronounced. Most of us are used to having "professionals" do whatever celebrating is allowed, and feel hesitant and mistrustful of our own ability, and self-conscious about doing anything much more

expressive than clapping our hands to applaud the work of others. It will take some courage to plunge into spontaneous creative celebration, but once the first step is taken the others are fairly easy.

GROUP SIZE:

Up to 20

TIME SUGGESTED:

15—60 minutes

GENERAL DIRECTIONS:

It is important that everyone be involved in some way, and that the moment chosen be appropriate. Groups which have had previous experience together in daydreaming or fantasy, meditation or prayer may be able to go into such a musical happening or celebration in a time of stress or sorrow, but other groups will find a first experience of this sort more acceptable in a time of joy or good fortune. If there would be too great a time lapse between the moment of the event—the high pitch—and the time when a celebration could take place, it would be better to work with what is available, rather than trying to prolong a feeling. If the event to be celebrated is of sufficient importance and involves the group members deeply, a day or so could elapse, allowing time for gathering musical instruments.

MATERIALS REQUIRED:

If the event is such as to lend itself to some previous planning, students may bring their own musical instruments, or objects with which they can create fairly musical sounds, such as jugs, pans, bells, sticks or glassware.

If the event is to be completely spontaneous, gather together anything suitable which the environment provides.

PROCEDURE:

1. Talk very briefly about the theme of the celebration. Distribute any instruments available to those who can play them, and give out any other suitable "noisemakers." Seat everyone in a circle, explaining that they may move about later if it seems appropriate.

2. Try to develop a phrase from group comments which can be the first line of a song or chant, or select a few suitable words yourself, e.g., "We're glad we won," or "Spring is here," or "Glory, what a snow," or "John is back." Repeat the line softly a few times, perhaps clapping your hands or tapping gently on a flat surface.

3. Encourage the group to find a melody for the line, and repeat it as others join in.

4. Try for a second line, encouraging group members to suggest words.

5. Using your first line as a chorus or refrain, develop a free-flowing song or chant. An occasional interlude of wordless music will be helpful. You may find you will want to repeat the first two or three lines as a chorus after a few minutes.

6. Depending on how things are going, the group may end on its feet, dancing or stamping, or may rise briefly and then sit down and slowly, quietly end the celebration. It is usually best when you do this for the first time to keep it short and work for a definite closure or ending.

VARIATION:

After a group has had a few successful experiences of this kind they may wish to plan a multimedia celebration which could be of the nature of a liturgy or religiously oriented festival. This could include some planned experiences, such as readings, slides, group singing with a guitar, or meditation, but try to include some period of time for spontaneous group music of some kind.

SENSES: AUDITION: SILENCE

PURPOSE:

To investigate silence—its various meanings and effects upon us.

COMMENT:

"The first American mingled with his pride a singular humility. Spiritual arrogance was foreign to his nature and teaching. He never claimed that the power of articulate speech was proof of superiority over the dumb creation; on the other hand, it is to him a perilous gift. He believes profoundly in silence—the sign of a perfect equilibrium. Silence is the absolute poise or balance of body, mind and spirit. The man who preserves his selfhood is ever calm and unshaken by the storms of existence—not a leaf, as it were, astir on the tree; not a ripple upon the surface of the shining pool—his, in the mind of the unlettered sage, is the ideal attitude and conduct of life.

"If you ask him: 'What is silence?' he will answer: 'It is the Great Mystery!' 'The holy silence is His voice!' If you ask: 'What are the fruits of silence?' he will say: 'They are self-control, true courage or endurance, patience, dignity, and reverence. Silence is the cornerstone of character' " (Ohiyesa, in *TOUCH THE EARTH: A SELF-PORTRAIT OF INDIAN EXISTENCE*).

"We love quiet; we suffer the mouse to play; when the woods are rustled by the wind, we fear not" (Indian Chief to the governor of Pennsylvania, 1796, in *TOUCH THE EARTH: A SELF-PORTRAIT OF INDIAN EXISTENCE*, p. 5).

The contemporary musician of "chances," John Cage, has long been interested in silences in music. When he was a young man the interest in percussion music stirred up in the 1920s led him to consider that of the four characteristics of sound—pitch, timbre, loudness and duration—the only one that relates to both sound and silence is duration. He thought of silence as the other side of the mold, the enclosing form, the "negative volume" of the sculptor. He said, "any structure for percussion music—for a situation in which harmony does not exist

—must be based on duration, or *time*."

Later he was surprised to find that in a soundproof room in the physics laboratory at Harvard he actually was conscious of two sounds, one high and one low, and that in this room what he had imagined as "silence" did not really exist. He was told that the "high sound was his nervous system in operation and the low one was his blood circulating. If true silence did not exist in nature, then the silences in a piece of music . . . could be defined simply as 'sounds not intended,' and Cage made up his mind to write a piece composed entirely of just such sounds." He called it *4'33"*—the number of minutes and seconds the piece takes to perform. David Tudor played the composition by closing the keyboard cover at the beginning of each of the three movements and opening it at the end, sitting quite still during the "duration" of each movement. The first performance was at the Maverick Concert Hall in Woodstock, N.Y. in 1952, and Cage found that in the open-backed hall the audience could hear rain on the wind in the trees during the first movement, rain on the roof during the second, and during the third the audience themselves provided the 'sounds not intended' by their puzzled murmurs of conversation." (From *THE BRIDE AND THE BACHELORS* by Calvin Tomkins. Copyright © 1962, 1964, 1968 by Calvin Tomkins. Reprinted by permission of The Viking Press, Inc.)

John Hotchkin points out the "pregnant pause" as "a simple but intriguing example of man's power to extend his life energy into a void and in so doing to transform the void into a medium." ("Metabolic Man Radiant," *THE CRITIC*, Sept.-Oct., 1970, Vol. XXIX, No. 1, pp. 29). Christina Rossetti had called silence "more musical than any song" ("Rest"). Shakespeare speaks of "silence sad" in *MIDSUMMER NIGHT'S DREAM*, but the Rev. Sydney Smith said of Macaulay that, "He has occasional flashes of silence, that make his conversation perfectly delightful" *(MEMOIR)*. Robert Louis Stevenson said, "The cruelest lies are often told in silence" *(VIRGINIBUS PUERISQUE)* but Swinburne said, "For words divide and rend; But silence is most noble 'til the end" *(ATALANTA IN CALYDON)*. Silences around us, in nature and among people can "mean" many things. Francis Bacon said "Silence is the virtue of fools," but Thomas Carlyle said "Speech is human, silence is divine, yet also brutish and dead: therefore we must learn both arts."

Serge Poliakoff, the Russian-born abstract painter, said, "When a painting is silent, it means it is successful."(*N.Y. TIMES*, 11/16/70). We use the term "silence" in reference to things other than the absence of sound, equating it to a mood, a feeling, sometimes to a certain kind of stillness or peace.

What is the connection? How will our lives and feelings change in this world in which any degree of silence is a rarity?

GROUP SIZE:

Up to 20

TIME SUGGESTED:

45—60 minutes

GENERAL DIRECTIONS:

The group attempts to experience silence in various ways—by being "silent" themselves, by listening to tapes or records which include silence, by reacting to the idea of "silence" in forms other than auditory. They explore their own meanings of silence and discuss its various aspects and relationships.

MATERIALS REQUIRED:

Records or tapes of music in which there are periods of silence.

Reproductions of paintings; magazine pictures of interiors, landscapes, etc.

Color samples (large enough to be seen easily—sheets of construction paper, for instance).

Fabric swatches of various textures.

Some materials on noise as a pollutant may be used, if desired.

PROCEDURE:

1. Subgroups of 6—10 sit silently in a circle for five minutes, making no effort to communicate.

2. The subgroups discuss this experience briefly. At this point there will be little attention paid to the "sound of the silence," as most discussion will concern their emotional response to the unusual and often discomfiting experience. The problems of "where to look," "what to do," self-conscious smiling and even giggling will be brought out. The idea of the quality of the silence experienced may be introduced, if you wish, by asking, "What kind of silence was it? What did it sound like? Was it the lack of conversation, or the silence that affected you? If you had been alone in the room, how would the silence have been different?"

3. Play a few short musical selections in which there are moments of silence of various dura-

tions. Ask the students to listen for the silences.

4. Discuss the quality of the silences in the music and compare the experience with that of the experience of silence in Step No. 1.

5. A short plenary session may be held to bring together the findings of the subgroups up to this time, and to begin to explore the students' own views of silence—what it is, how they would define it, how it affects them in various circumstances. They may discuss the silence in the situation of non-verbal communication which they have experienced in other exercises, and the silences of this session. They begin to try to differentiate between "silence" as a sensory experience, and "silence" as part of communication.

6. Subgroups now examine reproductions of paintings and sculpture, selecting several which to the individuals, represent "silence." Still in subgroups, they should explore their choices, trying to explain to themselves and others why these paintings seem to say "silence" to them. You might introduce the quotation from Poliakoff at this point, and ask them to look at the paintings again and see how they interpret his statement.

7. The subgroups now examine a variety of pictures torn more or less at random from old magazines, all of which show "places"—either landscapes, building exteriors, or interiors. Ask them to again consider the question of which ones seem "silent," and why, and compare their criteria with those they used in Step No. 6.

8. Swatches of fabric of a variety of textures are distributed to the subgroups. They are asked to select those they react to as "silent," once more comparing their judgments with those made in Steps Nos. 6 and 7.

9. In a plenary session hold a general discussion of "silence." They may discuss its various meanings, their reactions to it in various situations, and how they translate the idea of "silence" from one sensory mode to another, as in comparing paintings (visual), fabrics (tactile), music (auditory), as well as their own "silence" (emotional?) in Step No. 1.

—What is "silence"?
—What is the value of silence?
—When is it helpful? . . . why? When is it harmful?
—Is it possible to create a sort of personal silence in the midst of noise? . . . why or why not? . . . how?
—Are there some kinds of sounds in which it is more difficult to find silence than others? if so, which? . . . why?
—Is this just a matter of semantics—are we playing with words, or is something more involved?

—When we say, "Listen to how *quiet* it is!" what do we mean?
—How can we "listen" to "silence"?
—Can you recall times in which you were very aware of silence? What kinds of experiences were these? . . . What did these experiences mean to you?
—Is there any place within walking distance where you can experience true "soundlessness"?
—Is there a difference between "soundlessness" and "silence"? If so, what is it?
—How much sound can be present and still allow for a feeling of silence? Do some sounds destroy silence more for you than other kinds of sounds?
—What is "noise"? . . . Does noise always destroy silence?
—Do you think the increasing noise level in our world makes us more or less *aware of* silence? . . . more or less *in need of* silence?

SUGGESTED RESOURCES:

Environmental Protection Agency, *ENVIRONMENTAL NEWS: THE NOISE PROBLEM*, FS-A-1, 5/1/71, Environmental Protection Agency, Washington, D.C. 20460. Copies of this pamphlet may be requested for your class members.

Handler, Philip, (ed.), *BIOLOGY AND THE FUTURE OF MAN*, New York: Oxford, 1965, pp. 876-881, on environmental noise. Includes table of "Typical Over-all Sound Levels" also available in *HANDBOOK OF NOISE MEASUREMENT*, 5th ed., 1963 by General Radio Co., West Concord, Mass.

Lavin, Edward, and Terrence Manning, *DISCOVERY IN ART*, New York, N.Y.: Paulist Press, 1969, for reproductions of paintings and sculpture.

Ohiyesa, *TOUCH THE EARTH: A SELF-PORTRAIT OF INDIAN EXISTENCE*, compiled by T.C. McLuhan, New York: Outerbridge and Dienstfrey/E.P. Dutton and Co., 1971, p. 110.

PEACE

AMERICAN HISTORY

PURPOSE:

To examine the association in our minds between American history and violence, aggression, and war.

COMMENT:

It has become a cliche to say with Rap Brown, "Violence is as American as cherry pie" or "The history of the U.S. is the history of violence." However, when most of us think back to our courses in school on American history, the large events or important occurrences which come to mind are, indeed, usually linked with some act of violence or aggression, if not war itself. Seldom do we think of those people or actions which led to a greater degree of peace in our country or in the world. Perhaps we need to re-think our history and search for such steps, placing the wreath of laurel on the head of the peacemaker. Perhaps we should celebrate holidays of peace, not merely in the sense of the old "Armistice Day," which celebrated the cessation of war, but with the intention of honoring those small steps by which man may eventually reach true peace in society.

GROUP SIZE:

Up to 20

TIME SUGGESTED:

45—60 minutes

GENERAL DIRECTIONS:

Students jot down lists in answer to two successive questions, examine these lists individually and then in subgroups, and discuss their findings. Following this the students attempt to make other lists, and discuss them. A plenary pulls together findings and suggestions.

MATERIALS REQUIRED:

None

PROCEDURE:

1. Ask the students to jot down quickly any ten events from American history which they remember having learned in school. They are to retain these lists, so their notes may be quite brief.

2. Ask the students to make another list of 3—5 items they remember from news reports during the last few days—TV, radio or newspaper items.

3. Ask the students to examine their lists and put a check beside those items on their lists which relate to war, violence or aggression.

4. In subgroups of 5—7, ask the students to share lists, and prepare a single list for the group, eliminating duplicates. As a group, ask them to check this list for violence, as in Step No. 3. Ask the groups to discuss some of the following questions among themselves:

—Is history necessarily the consideration of war and violence?

—What kinds of violence are reflected in your lists?

—What were the causes of these acts of violence?

—Was this violence a good thing?

—Was the result good? . . . What was accomplished by it?

—Could the result have been achieved in some other way?

—Is "news" usually the reporting of violence? . . . why?

—What is violence?

5. Ask the students to prepare another list of ten things they remember from American history which did *not* include violence. This may be done individually, or by the groups as seems best at the time, but if done individually, should be discussed by the subgroups. Some of the following questions may be considered:

—Were these events of equal importance to those in your first list?

—How many items from your first list can be included in this one?

—Do you think American history should stress non-violence? . . . If so, wouldn't this distort the truth of our history? . . . What is the purpose of studying history? . . . Should the violence in our history be taught, but in a different way? . . . If so, how?

6. In a plenary, gather findings and suggestions from the groups for brief discussion.

SUGGESTED RESOURCES:

Bernstein, Barton J., (ed.), *TOWARDS A NEW PAST: DISSENTING ESSAYS IN AMERICAN HISTORY*, New York: Pantheon/Random House, 1968. A collection of essays by a group of young American scholars who seek a more objective history of our country. It would be interesting for students to examine this volume to determine whether violence plays the same role in their thinking as in the more traditional views.

Finn, James, *PROTEST: PACIFISM & POLITICS: SOME PASSIONATE VIEWS ON WAR AND NONVIOLENCE*, New York: Random House, 1967.

Lewin, Leonard C., *REPORT FROM IRON MOUNTAIN ON THE POSSIBILITY AND DESIRABILITY OF PEACE*, New York: Delta, 1967. Students who have not been exposed to this book will find it a fascinating experience. Do not tell them in advance that it is a put-on.

Sibley, Mulford Q., (ed.), *THE QUIET BATTLE: WRITINGS ON THE THEORY AND PRACTICE OF NON-VIOLENT RESISTANCE*, Garden City, N.Y.: Anchor, 1963. An excellent collection of classics.

Reed, Edward, (ed.), *PEACE ON EARTH: PACEM IN TERRIS: THE PROCEEDINGS OF AN INTERNATIONAL CONVOCATION ON THE REQUIREMENTS OF PEACE.* Sponsored by the Center for the Study of Democratic Institutions, New York: Pocket Books, 1965.

Hofstadter, Richard, and Michael Wallace (ed.), *AMERICAN VIOLENCE, A DOCUMENTARY HISTORY*, New York: Knopf, 1970. Four centuries of violence in the United States.

DEFINING PEACE

PURPOSE:

To explore the meaning of peace and man's tendency toward both war and peace.

COMMENT:

"John XXIII says, as Thomas Aquinas did before him, that peace is the work of charity and justice. Peace is not merely the absence of war; it is the nurture of human life everywhere" (Robert M. Hutchins, "Preface," *PACEM IN TERRIS: PEACE ON EARTH*, Edward Reed, (ed.), New York: Pocket Books, 1965).

"War is not, as is widely assumed, primarily an instrument of policy utilized by nations to extend or defend their expressed political values or their economic interests. On the contrary, it is itself the principal basis of organization on which all modern societies are constructed." (Leonard C. Lewin, *REPORT FROM IRON MOUNTAIN ON THE POSSIBILITY AND DESIRABILITY OF PEACE*, New York: Delta, 1967, p. 79.)

"So long as war does not become psychologically impossible, it will remain, or, if banished for a while, return . . . Only when man has developed not merely a fellow-feeling with all men, but a dominant sense of unity and commonality, only when he is aware of them not merely as brothers—that is a fragile bond—but in a large universal consciousness, can the phenomenon of war, with whatever weapons, pass out of his life without the possibility of return" (Aurobindo Ghose, Indian philosopher, in *WAR AND SELF-DETERMINATION*, Calcutta; S. Ghose, 1922; quoted in *THE QUIET BATTLE*, Mulford Q. Sibley (ed.), Garden City, N.Y.: Doubleday-Anchor, 1963, p. 70 n.5).

The following statements by Gandhi, Schweitzer and Martin Luther King are to be found in *A BOOK OF PEACE*, Elizabeth Goudge (ed.), New York: Coward-McCann, 1967.

"A non-violent man can do nothing save by the power and grace of God. Without it he won't have the courage to die without anger, without fear and without retaliation. Such courage comes from the belief that God sits in the heart of all, and that there should be no fear in the presence of God . . .

"I am a man of peace. I believe in peace. But I do not want peace at any price. I do not want the peace that you find in stone; I do not want the peace that you find in the grave; but I do want the peace which you find embedded in the human breast, which is exposed to the arrows of the whole world, but which is protected from all harm by the power of Almighty God" (Mahatma Gandhi, p. 199).

"We have tolerated the mass killings of men in time of war . . . the annihilation by atomic bombing of whole cities and their populations . . . We have learned of these things by radio or from the newspapers, and we have judged them according to whether they signify achievements accomplished by the society we belong to, or whether they were done by our enemies. When we admit that all these things are direct results of acts of inhumanity, we qualify the admission that 'war is war', and there is nothing we can do about it. So, by offering no resistance and by resigning ourselves, we become guilty of a crime against humanity.

"The important thing is that all of us should acknowledge that we are guilty of inhumanity. The horror of the avowal must arouse us from our torpor, and compel us to hope and work for an age when there will be no war. These hopes, these determinations, can have only one object: the attainment, through the growth of the spirit, of a state of superior reason in which we shall no longer put to deathly uses the vast powers which now lie at our disposal" (Albert Schweitzer, from the Nobel Prize Speech, p. 201).

"I am no doctrinaire pacifist. I have tried to embrace a realistic pacifism. Moreover, I see the pacifist position not as sinless but as the lesser evil in the circumstances. Therefore I do not claim to be free from the moral dilemmas that the Christian nonpacifist confronts. But I am convinced that the church cannot remain silent while mankind faces the threat of being plunged into the abyss of nuclear annihilation. If the church is true to its mission it must call for an end to the arms race" (Martin Luther King, p. 201).

GROUP SIZE:

Up to 20

TIME SUGGESTED:

45—60 minutes

GENERAL DIRECTIONS:

Students define "peace" through various approaches, discussing the meaning of their definitions.

MATERIALS REQUIRED:

None

PROCEDURE:

1. Working individually, each student writes a definition of "peace." Their statements will be read by other class members. Allow 6—10 minutes. Definitions may be a few words or a paragraph.

2. In subgroups of 5—7 statements are piled together, shuffled and re-distributed. Working with the copies of definitions they have received, subgroup members try to reach a consensus on a single definition. Groups which have difficulty reaching agreement may include a "minority report" in their statement. Ask the groups to print their statements on newsprint and post them on the wall. Assign a number to each statement.

3. Ask class members to circulate, reading the posted definitions and noting the ones they prefer.

4. Class votes on preferred definition.

5. In a plenary, class discussion focuses on such questions as the following:

—Why is this the preferred definition?

—Does being able to define peace have anything to do with being able to achieve it?

—Can an individual be "at peace" if his country is at war? . . . if there is internal violence in the country? . . . why?

—If a nation were attacked and did not resist, would it be "at peace" or "at war"?

—Is peace negative or positive?

—The Preamble of the Constitution of the United States says that one of the reasons for its establishment is to "insure domestic tranquility". . . does this mean "peace"? . . . If so, how would this peace be described? . . . If not, what does it mean? . . . How does this meaning relate to peace?

—Is peace an absolute good, so that anything should be sacrificed to achieve it? . . . If one country, such as the U.S.A., U.S.S.R., or the Republic of China became strong enough to rule the world, would this be peace? Would it be worth the necessary sacrifices to achieve this peace?

—Do you think most people want peace? . . . Why does it not exist, if the majority want it? . . . Do they mean different things by peace?

—Is there a relationship between "peace of

mind" and "peace"? . . . If you were engaged in combat, do you think you could have peace of mind? Is this a different use of the same word? . . . Is physical peace necessary for mental peace? . . . Is mental peace necessary for physical peace?

—Do you think there is a relationship between physical violence at home and abroad? . . . Do you think that a nation at war is more, or less, likely to have peace within its borders? . . . Do you think that if all wars between nations stopped, there would be more, or fewer, instances of violence among the citizens? . . . Do you think carrying on a war uses up some of a people's aggression?

—Do you think substitute activities should be encouraged by a country to use up aggressive tendencies? . . . If so, what are some possibilities?

—Is war inevitable?

—Is man naturally aggressive? . . . Does this mean he is violent? . . . Is this a cause of war?

—There are drugs available which inhibit aggressiveness—do you think everyone should take them? . . . Why or why not?

—What purposes are served by aggressiveness? . . . Is it good, bad, neutral?

—What is the opposite of "aggression" or "aggressiveness"?

—What is the opposite of "violence"?

—What is the opposite of war?

SUGGESTED RESOURCES:

Bronwell, Arthur N., *SCIENCE AND TECHNOLOGY IN THE WORLD OF THE FUTURE*, New York: Wiley Interscience, 1970. See particularly ch. 17 on war, peace, and technology.

Daniels, David N., *et al.* (eds.), *VIOLENCE AND THE STRUGGLE FOR EXISTENCE*, Boston, Mass.: Little Brown & Co., especially ch. 1, "The Biological Bases of Aggression," and ch. 3, "Environmental Theories of Violence."

Handler, Philip, *BIOLOGY AND THE FUTURE OF MAN*, New York: Oxford University Press, 1970. See pp. 402, 889 on fighting and antagonistic behavior.

Huberman, Edward and Elizabeth, (eds.), *WAR: AN ANTHOLOGY*, New York: Washington Square. A fine anthology of short stories, poetry, essays on brutality.

Lorenz, Konrad, *ON AGGRESSION*, New York: Bantam, 1963, 1966.

FILMS:

The War Game, black and white, 47 min., produced by Peter Watkins for BBC-TV, 1966. This is a powerful and horrifying film based on facts of nuclear warfare. It may in some cases result in a feeling of despair, but it can lead to a fruitful discussion of the necessity of working for peace.

Language of Faces, black and white, 17 min., produced by the American Friend's Service Comm., 1961. Some of the scenes of this film are out of date —children singing during H-bomb drills, businessmen inspecting bomb shelters—but the underlying idea of the peace and war which exist within each individual are very pertinent. Tries to set a hopeful and positive tone useful for developing a discussion on the possibilities of furthering peace.

Happy Birthday, Felisa, color, 13 min., produced by J. Dell. Available from Mass Media Ministries. Shots of a five-year old's interracial birthday party are contrasted with the children's future— peace and happiness with war and hatred. Does it have to be this way?

CONFLICT

PURPOSE:

To examine the useful side of conflict, and distinguish between useful conflict and destructive violence at the verbal level.

COMMENT:

"There is a general superstition that conflicts are harmful, and that hence they should be avoided. The opposite is true. Conflicts are the source of wondering, of the development of strength, of what one used to call 'character'." (Erich Fromm, *THE CREATIVE ATTITUDE*, quoted in "Walking through your community with your senses turned on" by Inez Seagle, LCA YOUTH MINISTRY, 2900 Queen Lane, Philadelphia, Pa. 19129.

GROUP SIZE:

Up to 20

TIME SUGGESTED:

45—60 minutes

GENERAL DIRECTIONS:

Students experiment with several kinds of discussion in situations of conflict, and discuss the implications; "real" arguments are used and also role playing.

MATERIALS REQUIRED:

None

PROCEDURE:

1. Select a topic on which there is current disagreement among class members. It should be a subject on which strong feelings are held. Ask two members holding opposite opinions to volunteer to discuss the problem together in front of the class. Allow enough time for the main points to be made, and then stop the discussion temporarily.

2. Ask another member of the class who is undecided on the issue to join the two at the front. Ask the two members to try to persuade this third party to their own point of view.

3. After a few minutes ask the class to discuss what they saw and heard. Some of the following questions may be considered:

—Did anyone change his mind? . . . Why or why not?

—Did anyone get angry or annoyed, or were the discussants not very serious about their argument?

—What other ingredients would have been necessary in order for violence to have occurred? . . . What inhibited the violence?

—Why do some arguments end in blows while others do not?

—Why do people sometimes change their mind as the result of an argument? . . .

4. Tell class that they are going to try a listening exercise in which small groups of 3—7 will be used. When groups are seated, ask for a volunteer in each group to act as "Moderator." The Moderator's role is simply to see that the one "rule" is kept: each time a person speaks he must first sum up in his own words the views of the previous speaker, before he adds his own opinion. His "summing up" must be to the satisfaction of the previous speaker.

5. Assign a non-controversial topic, and allow 4—5 minutes of discussion.

6. Keeping the same Moderators in each group, assign a current controversial topic for discussion, arbitrarily assigning "sides" in each group —e.g., ask groups to "count off," and odd numbers take one side, even numbers the opposite. Discussion is to follow the rule as explained in Step No. 4.

7. After about 6—8 minutes, stop the discussion and explain that it will continue on the same topic but that this time everyone is to "change sides" except the Moderator who continues in the same role.

8. After another six minutes or so, stop the discussions and ask the moderators to report to their groups on what they noticed.

9. Ask the groups to discuss the experience. Some of the following questions may be considered:

—Did people listen to each other?

—Was it hard to argue for a side with which you disagreed?

—Did the moderators notice differences in what was said or done in the three different discussions? . . . What differences did the participants notice?

10. In a plenary session ask the groups to

share their findings and explore the relationships between the resolution of conflict and listening. If there is time, ask the students to role play a recent "unsuccessful" argument they have experienced. The one describing the argument may assign the roles and explain them. The class may then examine what happened.

VARIATION:

The role play may be deferred until a later session, and several different situations of conflict may be role played and discussed. After the students have examined the various factors involved in producing these conflicts, they may wish to re-play the argument or situation of conflict, trying to resolve it by means of listening and other suggestions which have been developed in their discussions. Some attention should be paid to nonverbal communication, openness, and possible "underlying problems" or hidden agenda.

CONFLICT AND PUNISHMENT

PURPOSE:

To examine our ideas of the use of punishment in our society as an attempt to resolve conflict.

COMMENT:

"Habits of violence are acquired largely through imitation, . . . or through the direct rewarding of destructive aggressive behavior. Preceding frustration is not necessarily required. In sum, physical punishment by parents does not inhibit violence and most likely encourages it. . . . This is not to say that punishment does not have its place in child-rearing, only that it should take a secondary role in socialization and be used selectively. Punitive parental behavior might be reduced through public opinion against violence and through more effective parental education about child-rearing practices" (pp. 80, 81, 84).

"Man's inherent potential for aggressive behavior suggests that effective controls upon the expression of destructive forms of aggression are necessary and that reduction of violence depends upon teaching constructive means of expressing aggression" (p. 413).

"Unfortunately, opportunities for destructive, manipulative behavior; relationships based upon power and exploitation; and gratification of dependency by a controlling, unloving, authoritarian parent-surrogate often occur in prisons. In these ways such institutions actually play into and reinforce rather than overcome antisocial defenses. Unwholesome old patterns must be blocked, and the individual helped with the conflicts that then emerge. The traditional mental hospital is not well equipped to cope with violent and antisocial behavior, and the prison traditionally has been concerned with retribution rather than with treatment and rehabilitation. New treatment methods and settings must be evolved" (pp. 386-87).

"Although preservation of the self and reproduction of the species have been the organizing principles of organic evolution, there is no reason to assume that our collective consciousness must now serve only these same ends. For man adaptation no longer involves merely reacting to environmental changes. *Adaptation today requires producing changes through envisioning ultimate consequences.* One of these changes may be the necessity to counter excessive competitiveness resulting from biological evolution by replacing it with moral concern for the welfare of our fellows" (p. 115) (David N. Daniels, *et al.*, *VIOLENCE AND THE STRUGGLE FOR EXISTENCE,* Boston, Mass.: Little, Brown & Co., 1970).

GROUP SIZE:

Up to 20

TIME SUGGESTED:

One or more sessions of 45—60 minutes.

GENERAL DIRECTIONS:

Using the Case Study method, students examine instances in the press of conflict and punishment and attempt to devise alternatives to violence. The exercise may include the writing of "Letters to the Editor," if desired.

MATERIALS REQUIRED:

Copies of the day's newspaper.

PROCEDURE:

1. Ask the students to bring newspapers to class. Distribute sections of the papers if there is a shortage, and ask the subgroups to select a single item which reflects conflict in their community. Allow a few minutes for subgroups to familiarize themselves with the content.

2. Ask the subgroups to discuss possible ways in which the conflict could be resolved. They are to consider themselves a "Citizens' Special Board," charged with the duty of settling the problem, but *avoiding punishment* of the parties concerned. What steps should be taken, by whom, and whose cooperation would be needed to achieve a resolution of the conflict? Ask the students to try to be realistic, dealing with this particular problem rather than totally restructuring society!

3. After about 20 minutes, ask each group to explain its problem and solution to the rest of the

class. If desired, students may vote for the "best solution" or "best analysis of the problem," or a "panel of judges" may be appointed prior to Step No. 2.

4. In a plenary discuss the use of "punishment" in our society in dealing with conflicts. Such questions as the following may be raised:

—Why do we tend to want to "punish" people whose acts displease us?

—Who is punished in our society? . . . For what? . . . With what results?

—Why do we call our jails and prisons "correctional institutions"?

—What is the relationship between "punishment" and "correction"?

—What other kinds of punishment does our society use? . . . What is the result?

—Do you think it would be possible to have a society without any means of punishment? . . . Would such a society have laws? . . . How would they be enforced?

—What kinds of punishment do parents use with their children? . . . Why? . . . What are the effects? . . . Are there alternate means of teaching children? . . . What are they? . . . Do you think they are effective? . . . If you have children, how will you teach them such things as: not to run out in the street; not to play with matches; not to chew on electric wires? . . . If you have done any baby-sitting or helped care for younger brothers and sisters, what controls, restraints or punishments have you used? . . . Why?

—What are the differences between a parent punishing his child and society punishing a citizen?

—When nations go to war, is there an element of punishment involved? . . . If so, what are the common strains or elements? . . . If not, how would you characterize the aggression present in punishment? . . . How does it differ from that present in war?

—What distinctions would you want to make between "violence" and "aggression"? . . . If violence is not punished, how should society deal with it? . . . With other forms of aggression?

—If those who commit criminal acts are mentally ill, how should they be dealt with? . . . Who should decide if they are mentally ill? . . . If they do not "recognize their illness," should they be forced into treatment? . . . Should drugs be used to reduce their aggressiveness? . . . Behavior therapy?

VARIATIONS:

1. The above questions obviously provide

enough material for a number of discussions. Those factors of interest to the students may be pursued in various ways. For instance, ask an ex-convict to speak to the class on his experiences in a "correctional institution"; ask a social worker to speak on his experiences with people who have been imprisoned; ask a psychiatric social worker, a clinical psychologist or a psychiatrist to speak on their views on "punishment," or "imprisonment," or "patients who are legally committed"; ask students to read and report on some of the materials in "Suggested Resources," or have subgroups read excerpts from a single work and discuss them.

2. As a follow-up to their attempt to resolve the conflict situations in the newspaper, ask students to write letters to the "Editor," recommending specific steps to be taken. If desired, these letters could be reproduced and serve as the basis for a class discussion. See to it that the letters, or those the class chooses, are actually sent to the newspaper.

SUGGESTED RESOURCES:

Gordon, Thomas, *PARENT EFFECTIVENESS TRAINING,* New York: Peter H. Wyden, 1970, especially ch. 11 "The No-lose Method for Resolving Conflicts."

Ilfeld, Frederic W., Jr., and Richard J. Metzner, "Alternatives to Violence: Strategies for Coping with Social Conflict," in *VIOLENCE AND THE STRUGGLE FOR EXISTENCE,* David N. Daniels *et al.* (eds.), Boston, Mass.: Little Brown & Co. 1970. (Note: A number of the other articles in this volume will interest the serious student of these problems.)

Schrank, Jeffrey, *TEACHING HUMAN BEINGS: 101 SUBVERSIVE ACTIVITIES FOR THE CLASSROOM,* Boston, Mass.: Beacon, 1972, especially ch. 3 "Violence and the Violated."

Silberman, Charles E., *CRISIS IN THE CLASSROOM: THE REMAKING OF AMERICAN EDUCATION,* New York: Random House, 1970, especially ch. 4 "Education for Docility."

Henry, Jules, *ON EDUCATION,* New York: Vintage/Random House, 1966, 1971, ch. 1 "Vulnerability in Education."

Szasz, Thomas S., *PSYCHIATRIC JUSTICE,* New York: Macmillan, 1965. This book by a controversial psychiatrist gives his reasons why he believes no one should be committed for psychiatric treatment against his will, and why those who commit criminal acts should be imprisoned rather than given psychiatric care.

The following booklets are available from Public Affairs Pamphlets, 381 Park Ave. South, New York 10016, at 25¢ each or 21¢ for 10 to 99 copies.

Dorothy Baruch, *HOW TO DISCIPLINE YOUR CHILDREN,* #154, 1949.

Irvin Block, *VIOLENCE IN AMERICA,* #450, 1970.

Joseph L. Sax, *LAW AND JUSTICE,* #433, 1969.

Monrad G. Paulsen, *EQUAL JUSTICE FOR THE POOR MAN,* #367, 1964.

Robert Rice, *THE CHALLENGE OF CRIME,* #425, 1968.

Ruth and Edward Brecher, *THE DELINQUENT AND THE LAW,* #337, 1962.

Junius L. Allison, *THE JUVENILE COURT COMES OF AGE,* #419, 1968.

WAR AND PEACE: PERCEPTION CHECK

MATERIALS REQUIRED:

Nine signs, each representing a point on a 25-point interval scale ranging from —100 (representing highly negative feelings) to 0 (neutral feelings) to +100 (highly positive feelings).

Perception Check Sheets for each class member.

PURPOSE:

To check the accuracy of our perceptions of others' feelings about issues of war and peace, and discuss the reasons for differences.

COMMENT:

War and peace are probably issues of some concern to all members of the group, and yet how much understanding do we have of others' feelings on these issues? The use of a valuing continuum and "stimulus words" can help both to clarify our own values and to check our perceptions of others. The following exercise is based on one prepared by Anthony T. Palisi.

GROUP SIZE:

10—20

TIME SUGGESTED:

45—60 minutes

GENERAL DIRECTIONS:

A list of stimulus words of phrases is prepared by the class, e.g., "The Resistance," "American Revolution," "Conscientious Objector," "The War in Vietnam," "Nuclear Warfare," etc. Class members predict others' positive and negative reactions to terms, and enter these and their own reactions on a chart. Predictions are checked against some actual responses by using a valuing continuum along which volunteers take a position. Findings are discussed. For a group which has been talking about these issues through some of the other exercises on "Peace" this exercise will need no other preparation.

PERCEPTION CHECK SHEET

INDIVIDUAL NAMES

Stimulus
Words

Pred.											
Act.											
Pred.											
Act.											
Pred.											
Act.											
Pred.											
Act.											
Pred.											
Act.											
Pre.											
Act.											
Pred.											
Act.											
Pred.											
Act.											

PROCEDURE:

1. Before starting the exercise, post the nine signs across a wall of the room as follows:
—100—75—50—25   0   +25+50+75+100

As a warm-up, suggest to the class another issue or area of interest, such as "poverty" or "women's rights" or "racism," and explain that there are certain "stimulus words" which evoke feelings in connection with this topic. Either ask the class to suggest a few such words, or suggest one or two yourself. Ask for three volunteers to stand at the "0" sign. Then ask the rest of the class to call out one of these words, and ask each of the volunteers to move from "0" to the point on the scale which expresses his feelings. Of course, if he feels he should remain at "0", he may do so.

2. Help the class develop a list of stimulus words connected with "peace" and/or "war." Write this list of 6—12 words on the board.

3. Give each student a copy of the Perception Check Sheet, and ask them to fill in the names of the class members across the top on the slanting lines. Ask them to write the stimulus words down the left hand column in the same order in which they appear on the board. Now ask them to make a judgment about each member of the class in relation to each term—at which point on the continuum do they think each student would stand? Ask them to fill in these numerical values opposite "Pred." (Predicted Response). Show them an example on the blackboard or newsprint.

4. Ask for 3—5 volunteers to position themselves at "0" as before. Erase the list of words on the chalkboard. The rest of the class now calls out one word at a time, in random order, allowing plenty of time after each word for the volunteers to re-position themselves in accordance with their feelings about the word or term, and for the rest of the class to enter the actual responses across the "Act." line under the names of the volunteers. NOTE: Volunteers will not be able to fill in the "Act." line for those class members volunteering in the same round.

5. After all the stimulus terms have been used, another round of volunteers takes its position under the "0", and the process is repeated.

6. Completed Perception Sheets are retained by owners and used in the course of a discussion. If the class is larger than ten, subgroups may compare findings and discuss misperceptions and differences in responses. In a class of ten or less, the entire class may discuss together.

VARIATIONS:

1. If this is used as a first discussion on "peace," a short film may be used first, but the "stimulus words" will tend to be primarily those used in or aroused by the particular film. See "Suggested Resources."

2. A composite chart may be made of the entire class. If the class is interested, Perception Check Sheets may be brought to the next session. The chart outline may be prepared in advance and posted. Fill in by asking, for instance, "On the first word, how many filled in John's "Predicted Response" as +100 . . . as +75 . . ." etc. This is time consuming, and in working with a large class is better done in subgroups. This procedure requires a somewhat higher trust level than the original exercise, as the feelings of all are necessarily "exposed."

3. Subgrouping for discussion may be made on the basis of either divergence of views, or misperceptions, grouping together those who most misperceived one anothers' responses, or who may have perceived and predicted correctly, but who strongly disagree.

4. Another session may be scheduled for discussion of particular issues of disagreement. If desired the Perception Check might be repeated following this, using terms which developed as "stimulus words" during this particular discussion.

SUGGESTED RESOURCES:

FILMS:

(See also films listed in exercise, "Peace: Defining Peace")

The Hat, black and white, 18 minutes, John Hubley, 1964. Animated story of two soldiers guarding a line. One drops his hat over the line, but cannot retrieve it. A conversation starts in which questions of war and peace are raised without drawing conclusions.

Which Way the Wind, black and white, 29 minutes, Produced by American Friends Service Committee, 1962. Pacifist film which raises many issues connected with "making peace."

CONFLICT: SCAVENGER HUNT

PURPOSE:

To examine our feelings about competition as "conflict," and possible relationships to war and peace.

COMMENT:

Both "conflict" and "competition" usually imply that someone is expected to "win" and someone else to "lose." This is not the necessary resolution of conflict, but our "American way" of thinking about it usually places it in this competitive framework. This is also the "way" of many other, but not all, cultures. Once the American child passes the age of "ring-around-a-rosy" where *all* fall down, he enters a world of competition—in games, in school, in business. The natural competition existant within a family situation is amplified in our society, either consciously or unconsciously, so that the child is usually fairly well prepared for this competitive atmosphere by the time he starts school.

We are apt to say, "It is good for a child to face competition—it will teach him what the real world is like," or "Children can be motivated in the classroom by pitting one team, for instance, against another." This exercise starts with an activity which in itself can be interesting, fun and thought-provoking without any element of competition or conflict. However, competition is deliberately introduced via the pitting of team against team. Conflict is intensified by the need for classmates to make necessarily subjective judgments in deciding "who wins."

GROUP SIZE:

10—20

TIME SUGGESTED:

1—2 hours.

GENERAL DIRECTIONS:

Students are told how the Scavenger Hunt is to be organized and judged, are given lists of things to find and sent out of class for thirty minutes or longer to find their objects. Upon returning, each group judges another group, which in turn judges them. Items are rated to determine the winner. Discussion of items follows. Discussion is presumably on how choices demonstrate our feelings about our bodies, but will be affected by the judging procedure or the atmosphere of "combat," "conflict," or "competition," and these elements will then be discussed, relating them to war and peace.

MATERIALS REQUIRED:

Lists of items, one copy for each member. Items should pertain to the body and our feelings about it. Following is a suggested list:

1. something good to eat
2. something that smells good
3. something intimate and feminine
4. something intimate and masculine
5. something with a texture interesting to touch
6. something that makes a funny noise
7. something that makes a sound you enjoy
8. something you would, or do, hate to wear
9. something threatening to your physical well-being
10. something that would improve your physical well-being

PROCEDURE:

1. Subgroup class, give each member a copy of the list. Subgroups may decide how they will "hunt"—whether dividing the list, or hunting as a "pack." Class is told that their items will be judged by class members to determine the winning team. Time limit; 20—30 minutes.

2. As each group starts to return, a spot in the room is designated for their collection. A "lateness penalty" may be invoked, if desired.

3. A point scale is announced. For instance, "Each item is to be rated on a scale of 1—3 for suitability, originality, or inventiveness, with '3' as the highest score (best)." Group One now sits in judgment on Group Two's items, taking one item at a time. Group Two is to sit silently and watch this procedure. One member of Group Two silently presents each item in turn for judgment.

4. The process is now reversed, and Group Two judges Group One's items. Other groups should

be similarly paired.

5. Each member of the class is now given 4—5 minutes to write down their feelings about the way in which the judging was done.

—How did you feel when the other group was judging your team?

—What influence, if any, did this judging have on you when you, in turn, judged this group?

6. The original subgroups now discuss among themselves how they feel about their bodies as demonstrated by the items selected.

7. After a few minutes, combine Groups One and Two (Three and Four, etc.), so that the groups which judged each other are now a single group. Ask them to continue their discussion together. There will soon be comments about the "judging." When this happens, change the discussion to one about the "judging"—about the "competition."

Ask them to get out the papers they wrote in Step No. 5 and share with the group whatever they wish. As the discussion progresses, feed in additional questions such as the following:

—What effect did the knowledge of the competition have on your own "hunt"? . . . selection of items?

—How did you feel when items you were pleased with were downgraded by the other group? . . . or:

—Did collaboration occur, so that all items on all lists were rated "3"? . . . If so, why?

—Was the game more "fun" because you were competing? why?

—Would a prize have made it still more fun? . . . why?

—Do activities like this have to be competitive to be fun?

—Is competition in other areas of our society "fun"? why?

—Is competition necessary in our society?

—Do you think competition is more natural to man than cooperation?

—How would you describe the differences, if any, between "competition" and "conflict"? . . . Does one always imply the other?

—What are the causes of international competition? . . . Are these useful or harmful?

—What is the relationship between international competition and war?

—Is a competitive society necessarily more apt to go to war?

VARIATIONS:

1. If the class is large enough for four, five or six groups, various situations of conflict/no-conflict, competition/no-competition may be set up.

—Two groups may operate in a no-competition, no-conflict situation, simply explaining and discussing their items, without any scoring or judging procedures.

—Two groups may be paired in a competition and conflict situation, in which Group One judges Group Two, and Group Two judges Group One, as in the original exercise.

—An alternate arrangement is for three groups to handle their judging as follows: Group One judges Group Two; Group Two judges Group Three; Group Three judges Group One. There is less conflict among these three, although there is still an element of competition. This arrangement may be used in combination with one or more of the above.

A discussion of the differences in feelings in the various situations is very important.

MEDIA MONITORING

PURPOSE:

To investigate how the media helps or hinders the promotion of a peaceful society.

COMMENT:

Jerome Ellison, writing in *THE NATION*, December 21, 1963, characterized the United States as "the most murderous industrial nation in the world." He wasn't talking about our involvement in Southeast Asia, but our activities at home. He went on to point out that our homicide rate was three and a half times that of Canada, twice that of England, France and Japan, four times that of West Germany, six times that of Spain, seven times that of Sweden and Belgium, nine times that of Denmark, sixteen times that of the Netherlands.

However, we are more dangerous to ourselves than to others—our suicide rate is about twice our homicide rate.

For a while, things in this country seemed to be improving. Murder decreased for twenty years between 1937 and 1957, but in 1959 it started up again. Has there been any improvement in recent years? No, on the contrary. The National Center for Health Statistics issued a report at the end of 1971 which showed that murder has increased sharply as a cause of death among the young since 1963, suicide is increasing in all races and all age groups, and motor vehicle accidents are the leading cause of death among young white men, having increased 20.8 percent during these years. Black men are ten times more likely to be homicide victims than white men, and for some of the younger age groups it has become a leading cause of death. Despite advances in medicine, there has been an actual decrease in life expectancy for males in the United States. It is important to note that these statistics do not include war deaths, which would have made the picture even worse among young males. The death rate for women has dropped, particularly for black women. Many blame the media for encouraging violence. Others exonerate the media, seeing its products as the proper and accurate reflection of our society. America has a violent history. America has a violent society. What is the proper role of the media under these circumstances? What is the responsibility of the press, of film makers, or TV producers?

Television is educating our children, probably at least as much, if not more, than their formal schooling. Child psychologist Alberta E. Siegel says "The evidence that we do have indicates that film and TV are profoundly educative for their viewers, teaching them that the world is a violent and untrustworthy place and demonstrating for them a variety of violent techniques for coping with this putatively hostile environment" (*VIOLENCE AND THE STRUGGLE FOR EXISTENCE*, David N. Daniels *et al.* [eds.], p. 227).

The television industry has consistently demanded the right to self-regulation and, following the deep national concern awakened by the assassination of three national leaders and the wave of "civil disorders," instituted through the various networks a series of internally directed studies. The National Broadcasting Company set up a Division of Environmental Study of Television and Violence. In April of 1971 the first Progress Report was released, but there has been much criticism of the validity and usefulness of the research, and even more of the lack of improvement of the medium's content.

The universality of TV viewing, particularly among the young, the strength of its impact and the desperate need of the world for ways to peace and lessened violence would seem to require a reorientation of TV programming, designed to teach alternatives to violence as a means of problem solving. How much of this is being done? By whom? How can such efforts be increased?

GROUP SIZE:

Up to 20

TIME SUGGESTED:

One session of 15—30 minutes; one or more sessions of 45—60 minutes; students are expected to spend some out-of-class time monitoring TV.

GENERAL DIRECTIONS:

In an initial brief discussion students talk about "peace" as they think it is reflected in the media. Monitoring assignments are made, and a week later findings are reported and discussed.

MATERIALS REQUIRED:

None

PROCEDURE:

1. An initial discussion explores students' views on "peace" as expressed in the media, particularly TV. The terms "violence," "non-violence," "conflict," "conflict resolution," and "peace" are introduced through such questions as the following:

—Do you think the media in general give more information about "peace" or "non-peace"?

—What kinds of "peace" are described and shown? . . . What kinds of violence? . . . What kinds of war?

—How are problems of conflict resolved, according to the media?

—Is TV more or less violent than other mass media?

—What kinds of violence are shown on TV?

—What kinds of conflicts are shown on TV? . . . How are they resolved, as a rule? . . . Is "peace-making" stressed? . . . If so, how?

2. Students may help prepare two kinds of forms or charts for use in TV monitoring, one showing instances of various types of violence and the other showing instances of various types of peace-making. The examples on p. 298 should be modified to suit the class.

PEACE-MAKING ON TV

The article by Dr. Siegel, referred to in "Comment," including the following questions that could make a good basis for a chart.

"—How many instances were there of constructive intervention to end disagreement?

—What other methods of resolving conflict were exampled?

—How many instances of tact and decency could an avid televiewer chronicle during the same hours?

—How often was reconciliation dramatized?

—How many adult acts of generosity were provided to children for modeling?

—What strategies for ameliorating hate were displayed?

—How many times did the child viewer see adults behaving in loving and helpful ways?

—What examples of mutual respect did he view?

—What did he learn about law and order?

—How many episodes of police kindness and considerateness did he see?

—How frequently did the glow of compassion illuminate the TV screen?" (p. 228).

3. Students are asked to keep their charts handy and whenever they watch TV during the next week, check both charts in the appropriate boxes. If preferable, specific time slots may be assigned. Students should also make a few notes, which they can use to refresh their memory during discussion at the next session. Monitoring should cover a variety of programs, e.g., news broadcasts, serials, talk shows, drama, "games," sports broadcasts, films.

4. In a plenary session students report results of monitoring, and discuss how they think televiewing affects our society's handling of its problems of conflict.

VARIATIONS:

1. Students may wish to concentrate on the use of the human body to symbolize force or violence. For instance, why is a knight in armor used to sell a household cleanser?

Some students may wish to concentrate on the violence in our language, the words commonly used which have been adopted from the vocabulary of war or aggression, such as the language of the sportscaster. What "violent" words are used to describe products, and why? (Examples: "this really packs a punch"; "send for your free 'Getaway Kit' "; "don't knock it till you've tried it"; "fight cavities two ways"; "saddle up and hit the trail.") Why are car names so often symbols of force and/or violence? (names of models?) This could be explored without TV monitoring, but the question is not, "Do these terms exist in our language?" but "Does TV encourage a way of thinking and living by using and illustrating these terms?"

2. If the students are interested in knowing about some of the studies which have been done on the effects of TV violence on viewers, you may suggest that they read and report on some of the available material. The class might be interested in hearing a panel of students discuss some of the pros and cons as the basis for a discussion at another session.

VIOLENCE ON TV

TYPES OF VIOLENCE	TIME SLOTS AND NUMBER OF INSTANCES				
	WEEKDAY 3-5	WEEKDAY 5-8	WEEKDAY 9-midnight	WEEKEND before 8 p.m.	WEEKEND after 8 p.m.
Physical violence					
men to men					
women to women					
men to women					
women to men					
children to adults					
women to children					
children to children					
men to children					
Emotional violence					
to sense of self					
by authorities					
by the frustrated					
about sex					
in sex					
Institutional violence					
by remote control					
for conflict resolution					
for vengeance					
in war					

SUGGESTED RESOURCES:

Cook, Fred J., *THE WARFARE STATE,* New York: Macmillan, 1962.

Daniels, David N., Marshall F. Gilula, and Frank M. Ochberg, (eds.), *VIOLENCE AND THE STRUGGLE FOR EXISTENCE,* Boston, Mass.: Little, Brown & Co., 1970. An excellent collection of articles dealing with many aspects of violence from the psychiatric point of view.

Endleman, Shalom, (ed.), *VIOLENCE IN THE STREETS,* Chicago, Ill.: Quadrangle, 1968. Section II deals with the role of the media, and includes a report on some of the research studies by Albert Bandura and associates on the effects on aggressive behavior in children of TV violence.

Goldsen, Rose K., "NBC's Make-Believe Research on TV Violence," transACTION, Vol. 8, No. 12, Oct. 1971, pp. 28ff.

Thayer, George, *THE WAR BUSINESS: THE INTERNATIONAL TRADE IN ARMAMENTS,* New York: Simon and Schuster, 1969.

LIFE magazine, "Tracks That Violence Leaves," Jan. 30, 1970, pp. 57-58. Brief report on studies by Dr. Victor Bailey Kline, University of Utah.

LIFE magazine, "TV: A Special Section," Vol. 71, No. 11, Sept. 10, 1971, pp. 35ff. Articles by Daniel J. Boorstin, a report on a poll by Louis Harris, a report by Thomas Thompson on how the CBS programming director puts a season together, an article by Joan Barthel on popular shows of the past twenty years.

REPORT OF THE NATIONAL ADVISORY COMMISSION ON CIVIL DISORDERS, New York: Bantam, 1968. See index for sections dealing with TV, also "Media."

FILM:

M*A*S*H. This full-length commercial film deals with life in an Army Field Hospital (Mobile Army Surgical Hospital) during the Korean war, and surfaces many topics for discussion on war, aggression, the human body, and our feelings and beliefs and values connected with these.

Johnson, Nicholas, *HOW TO TALK BACK TO YOUR TELEVISION SET,* Boston, Mass.: Little, Brown, 1970. A member of the F.C.C. looks at the influence of T.V. policies and programs and suggests citizen action.

"TV Ratings; What They Are, How They Work," *CHANGING TIMES: THE KIPLINGER MAGAZINE,* Vol. 26, No. 3, March 1972, pp. 39-40. In addition to this article, "Changing Times" has a teaching unit pamphlet reprinted from *CHANGING TIMES TEACHER'S JOURNAL,* which includes a form for students to fill in and other suggestions. Write to *CHANGING TIMES* Education Service, 1729 H Street, N.W., Washington, D.C. 20006.

MIME AND GESTURES OF PEACE

PURPOSE:

To examine the meaning of some of the nonverbal communication we use to express "peace" and "non-peace."

COMMENT:

In one of the exercises on "Communication" we investigated some of the meaning of the handshake as a nonverbal communication. We have a few other gestures of peace in our society, but we seem to have many more ways of nonverbally communicating aggression and violence. It is interesting to look at Lionel Tiger's definitions of "aggression" and "violence," and the behaviors and gestures he associates with these terms.

He says, "I define 'aggression' as a process of more or less conscious coercion against the will of any individual or group of animals or men by any individual or group of people. At its broadest, the process is similar to chopping a tree, damming a river, or uprooting a yam—it involves the intervention by a human agency in a situation or pattern. In its more complex meaning, the definition implies the imposition of martial law, religious orthodoxy, the establishment of consumer needs through advertising campaigns, the killing of enemy troops, winning a game of football, promoting a pop song to the hit parade, or fighting an election. There is no necessary element of ferocity, viciousness, or destructiveness; the only necessary condition is that there be 'willed agency'. . .

" 'Aggression' is a social-organizational term referring to a process, while 'violence' describes an event which is only one possible outcome of the aggressive process. Aggression occurs when an individual or group see their interest, their honour, or their job bound up with coercing the animal, human, or physical environment to achieve their own ends rather than (or in spite of) the goals of the object of their action. Violence may occur in the process of the interaction. Violence is most obvious when it is physical . . . Obviously it is difficult to create a

hard and all-embracing distinction between violence and aggression. Is the group of hunters aggressive or violent who bring down an ungulate with poison arrows? Is the manager of an electric console aiming missiles aggressive or violent? What is the driver in a hurry who passes another driver in a hurry on a crowded highway? . . . What is significant is the statement of difference between effective action which is part of a process of mastery which involves the violation of an organism's personal space and the infliction of physical pain . . . I want to regard aggression as a 'normal' feature of the human biologically based repertoire, a type of behaviour intrinsic to man's being and to his effective interaction with his social environment. Violence is not necessarily part of all or any of these" (*MEN IN GROUPS*, New York: Random House, 1969, pp. 158-159).

GROUP SIZE:

Up to 20

TIME SUGGESTED:

45—60 minutes

GENERAL DIRECTIONS:

This exercise is best used after a class has had some experience with pantomime, or at least with role playing, and has also been through some of the other exercises on "peace." A brief mime or two is presented and used as the basis of a discussion of gestures and physical attitudes relating to peace and non-peace, and the discussion continues with a further exploration of the relationships of aggression, violence, and peace.

MATERIALS REQUIRED:

If "hand" or "foot" mimes are used, an adjustable half screen of some sort is desirable.

PROCEDURE:

1. Prior to the session ask a few volunteers interested in theater and/or acting to prepare a brief mime or two to be performed before the class. These should last only a few minutes and there will be no dialogue. The following are only suggestions:

—a group tableau or "stabile" illustrating first "violence or war," and second "peace"

—hand mime (only hands and forearms are exposed above the screen)—two people may act out violence or war

—feet mime—as above, with bare feet, or leg from the calf down, exposed below the screen (this is apt to cause laughter unless the group is fairly serious about mime and has had some experience).

2. When the class meets, explain that a pantomime is to be performed. Ask the class to watch closely and try to decide what is going on. If you think it better with your particular class, give the mimes titles, or ask mimers to prepare and announce titles. These may give strong hints, but need not necessarily use the words "peace" or "war."

3. After the performance ask the class what they understood the mimes to mean, if they have not already spontaneously called out explanations. Ask the class to try to think of the specific gestures which told them what was going on, and then move discussion into some of the following question areas:

—Why do we associate these attitudes, gestures, etc., with "peace" or "non-peace"?

—What were the most violent moments of the mimes? . . . why?

—Did anyone laugh? . . . why? . . . Why do we sometimes laugh at a fight scene, even when it is a "serious" fight? . . . Why are Punch-and-Judy type shows "funny"? . . . Why do we laugh at clowns hitting each other?

—What gestures or physical attitudes often lead to violence? . . . why? . . . What do they represent? . . .Why do they make people angry? . . . or do they make people afraid? . . . What is the difference?

—Could you re-play the hand mime of "violence" or "war," and intervene physically to "make peace"? (Have students do this and ask the class to examine carefully what actually happens, why, and what it means.)

—Is peace "passive"? . . . Is "non-peace" active?

—Martin Luther King once said that if a man has nothing he would die for he has nothing to live for . . . Could you agree? . . . Does this involve "violence"? . . . Is "dying for a cause" a violent act?

—What does religion teach about peace and war? . . . why? . . . Which of these positions do you agree with? . . . why?

—Are there "gestures" which nations make which tend to bring on war? . . . peace? . . . What is the relation between the meaning of "gesture" used about a nation, and used about our own actions?

SUGGESTED RESOURCES:

Students may be interested in reading about the "gestures" of animals which invite attack or placate a potential enemy as described by Konrad Lorenz in *ON AGGRESSION,* trans. by Marjorie Kerr Wilson, New York: Bantam, 1963.

LOVE

LOVE IN THE COMIC STRIP

PURPOSE:

To explore society's views on love and marriage as reflected in the comic strip.

COMMENT:

"America is the land of friendship, not of love. America is a paradise of pretenders; love cannot exist on pretense. America is a land of equalities; equals are friends and unequals are lovers. America worships machines, the machines of steel or the machines of the mind; love is of humans and machines are eunuchs . . ." (one of the students quoted by Kenneth Keniston, *THE UNCOMMITTED: ALIENATED YOUTH IN AMERICAN SOCIETY,* New York: Dell, 1967, p. 51.)

GROUP SIZE:

Up to 20

TIME SUGGESTED:

Two 45—60 minute sessions, plus work outside of class.

GENERAL DIRECTIONS:

Students collect examples of comic strip or cartoon portrayals of love and marriage and combine these to form a film strip. These are shown at a later session. Discussion follows.

MATERIALS REQUIRED:

An assortment of individual cartoons and/or frames from comic strips, collected and brought to class by students.

Movie camera, projector and screen (Note: See "Variation No. 3" for carrying out this exercise with an opaque overhead projector instead of film).

Roll of shelf paper, 1 bottle of casein glue, or rubber cement, or paste for each subgroup.

PROCEDURE:

1. In advance of the first session, ask students to select 6—8 individual frames from comic strips or newspaper cartoons during the next week which illustrate society's views of (1) love before marriage; (2) love in marriage; (3) marriage. Each student is to bring his selection to class on the day appointed.

2. In subgroups of 6—8, students select from their entire subgroup's collection arranging them in what they believe is a meaningful sequence. When they have decided on their sequence, they receive a strip of shelf paper of sufficient length to mount their cartoons or frames, leaving sufficient space in between to enable each frame to be photographed separately. They may wish to separate some frames by a frame of their own captions or statements, printed in ink or with a narrow felt-tip marker.

3. Each subgroup's "strip" is filmed, allowing adequate time for viewing each frame. Students with previous film experience can handle this part of the project. Have the film processed.

4. At the second session each subgroup's film is shown to the entire class, and is discussed. Each subgroup may wish to explain why it selected particular frames and their particular sequence.

VARIATIONS:

1. If desired, photographic slides could be used instead of movie film.

2. Students may wish to prepare a running commentary to accompany their film strip. This may be written out and read by a member of the group. It is possible to tape this instead of having it read "live," but would require a "rehearsal" with the finished film to get timing correct. It is also possible to provide a "sound track" for the cartoons by taping student actors reading the lines provided by the cartoons, or by using a specially prepared tape made by re-recording portions of appropriate songs, etc. Since the speed of the film, once it is processed, cannot be controlled, slides would be preferable if students desire an extensive sound track.

3. If photographic equipment is not available, but an opaque overhead projector is, the latter may be used to show the original pasted-up strip.

LEARNING TO LOVE

may be posted around the room to serve as thought-starters.)

PURPOSE:

To explore some of the ways in which we learn how to love others.

COMMENT:

"Learning to love another human being is the greatest challenge in human experience because it makes the most fundamental moral and psychological demands. Loving another person challenges our most deeply-rooted tendencies toward spiritual and psychological narcissism. Love raises concern for others onto an equal plane with concern for ourselves. And as a man's relations with others deepen, he comes to see that all phases of his loving constitute a single experience, whether the loved one be friend, spouse, child, or God" (E. Mark Stern and Bert G. Marino, *PSYCHOTHEOLOGY*, New York: Newman Press, 1970, p. 55).

GROUP SIZE:

Up to 20

TIME SUGGESTED:

45—60 minutes

GENERAL DIRECTIONS:

Students diagram on a time-line their collective experiences which they believe have helped or hindered their growth in the ability to love. Discussion follows.

MATERIALS REQUIRED:

Roll of shelf paper.
Felt-tip markers.
(Optional: posters and collections of pictures

PROCEDURE:

1. Post a long strip of shelf paper across one wall of the room. Draw a continuous line through the center from one end to the other. Bisect the line with a vertical line, and mark this vertical with the present date or year.

2. Ask students to jot down on a piece of paper those events in their lives which they think have influenced their ability to love, putting those which "helped" in one column, and those which "hindered" in another. Allow about ten minutes for students to work individually on these.

3. Ask the students to consider which *kinds* of experiences they believe would be common to most members of the class, e.g., "parents," "school," "particular teachers," "grandparents," "brothers and sisters," "prayer or meditation," "the war in Vietnam," "a friend of the opposite sex," "women's liberation." They may wish to include some historical events which happened before their own birth, but which they believe have had an influence on their ability to love.

4. Students now fill in along the horizontal time-line the kinds of experiences that have affected most, though not necessarily all, of the class, putting those which "helped" above the line and those which "hindered" below the line. Several students may print in the items as class members call them out, or students may go up and print them along the line, or subgroups may decide on which items should be included. A rough chronology should be followed.

5. The class may now discuss for 15—20 minutes. Without trying to arrive at a definition of "love," students can explore such questions as:
   —Do you have to learn how to love, or do you think it is natural and inevitable?
   —Can everybody love?
   —Are some people just naturally more loving than others? . . . why?
   —Can our capacity for love diminish? . . . can it increase?

6. Students should now fill in the right side of the line with those imagined future events which they think may help them be more loving people.

7. Rather than a final discussion, a period of silent meditation would provide a suitable closure for this exercise, or the class might listen to music or a reading for a few minutes.

PUBLIC INTERVIEW

PURPOSE:

To explore some of our own meanings of "love."

COMMENT:

"I exist only to the extent that I exist for others. At the ultimate limits of the possible, to be means to exist in love" (Emmanuel Mounier, quoted by Jean Amery, *PREFACE TO THE FUTURE*, New York: Frederick Ungar, 1964, p. 43).

"Love I said dies in contact with the impersonal and anonymous" (Teilhard de Chardin, *THE PHENOMENON OF MAN*).

GROUP SIZE:

10—15

TIME SUGGESTED:

45—60 minutes

GENERAL DIRECTIONS:

The teacher asks for a volunteer for a public interview, to be conducted by the teacher, on "love," following certain rules. General discussion follows.

MATERIALS REQUIRED:

None

PROCEDURE:

1. The teacher announces that it will be helpful to the group if they start their discussion of love by holding a "public interview". The rules are as follows:

a. Any question may be passed, that is, need not be answered.

b. Interview may be terminated whenever the person being interviewed wishes.

c. Any question the teacher asks the person interviewed, that person may in turn ask the teacher.

2. The teacher asks for a volunteer for the interview.

3. The person to be interviewed is seated comfortably in front of the teacher. If physical arrangements permit, it may be preferable if the teacher changes his seat to accomplish this, rather than having the student move. While the class listens, the teacher asks questions until either the interviewee terminates the process, or the teacher feels a change of activity is preferable. The following questions are only suggestions. You will develop your own for your own group.

—What is your meaning of "love"?

—Have you ever loved anybody?

—Has this person really loved you?

—Is it possible to love more than one person?

—Have you ever fallen out of love? . . . Can you tell us how it felt?

—What do you look for in a person that you would like to love?

—What is it that attracts you most toward that person?

—Are you in love now?

—What have you done for that person?

—If someone you loved moved far away, would you continue to love them?

4. General discussion follows. Others will usually have something they wish to contribute in response to the questions and ideas developed in the interview, or other questions may be introduced concerning various kinds of love.

VARIATION:

A general discussion may precede the public interview and the interview take place when a natural need for it seems to exist. In this case, two sessions might be used, as further discussion would probably be indicated.

SUGGESTED RESOURCES:

Raths, Louis E., Merrill Harmin, Sidney B. Simon, *VALUES AND TEACHING,* Columbus, Ohio: Charles E. Merrill, 1966.

Lewis, Clive S., *FOUR LOVES,* New York: Harcourt Brace Jovanovich, 1960.

May, Rollo, "When Love Becomes THE Problem", *SEXUALITY ON THE ISLAND*

EARTH, David Darst and Joseph Forgue (eds.), New York, N.Y.: Paulist Press, 1970, abridged from LOVE AND WILL by Rollo May, New York: W.W. Norton & Co., 1969.

Fromm, Erich, THE ART OF LOVING, New York: Bantam, 1970.

FILM:
The Tender Game, 7 minutes Contemporary Films, Inc.

"I LOVE YOU!"

PURPOSE:

To explore technological advancements and interpersonal relationships.

COMMENT:

"To be cut off from other human beings and
     their love,
to be cut off from all sense of God and of his
     love,
to be cut off from what one believes to be
     one's real self
and to be lodged in the body of a ghost who
     has lost the power to love:
this is loneliness."
(Hubert Van Zeller, LISTEN TO LOVE, Louis M. Savary (ed.), New York: Regina Press, 1971, p. 28.)

GROUP SIZE:

Up to 20

TIME SUGGESTED:

60—120 minutes

GENERAL DIRECTIONS:

Students read the short article included in this exercise and react to it individually and then in small groups. Each subgroup develops a presentation of the content of the article and shares it with the class. General discussion follows.

MATERIALS REQUIRED:

Each student receives a copy of the article, "I love you . . . this is a recording" (The title, "Ma Bell Saves the Day" may be used, if desired).

PROCEDURE:

1. Students read the article individually, making notes of their reactions, feelings, etc.

2. In subgroups of 6—8, students share their notes.

3. Each subgroup plans a presentation of the contents of the article. This presentation may take any form the group wishes. It is usually more effective, however, if dramatized or a role play is developed. Allow no more than twenty minutes to prepare the presentation.

4. Each subgroup makes their presentation to the entire class.

5. General discussion follows, exploring reactions, different approaches. It is not necessary that the group or groups come to any final conclusion.

I LOVE YOU—
THIS IS A RECORDING
by Arthur Hoppe

Herewith is another unwritten chapter from that unpublished text, "A History of the World, 1950 to 1999." Its title: "Ma Bell Saves the Day."

By the early 1970s, the old morality had crumbled. The old certitudes had vanished. Wars, riots and revolutions flourished. Neighbor mistrusted neighbor. People no longer touched each other. Conversations were icily polite.

And from the look in the eyes of mankind, it was clear that the human race was on the brink.

It was the telephone company that preserved civilization.

With people retreating inward on themselves, the number of telephone calls placed daily had dropped alarmingly. To stimulate business, it was suggested that the company provide another recorded message as a public service.

"We already give our subscribers the time and the weather," said the Board Chairman irritably, "What else do people need these days?"

"Sympathy?" suggested a vice president, half jokingly.

The new service was an instant success. At first people were hesitant to dial "S-Y-M-P-A-T-H-Y." "That's silly," they'd say, shaking their heads. Then, when they were sure no one was listening, they'd pick up the phone in embarrassed secretiveness.

"Poor dear," the recording began in a gentle voice of sweet consolation. "I'm so terribly sorry for you. Oh, the pain you must be suffering! But how brave you are not to show it. How very proud of you I am. Poor dear."

After one month, studies showed each subscriber was making an average of 3—4 calls to the number daily. The company immediately announced plans for new recorder services. Next came, "I- L-O-V-E- Y-O-U":

"Oh, dearest, how deeply I love you—with my whole soul, my whole being. You are everything on earth to me—my sun, my moon, my stars . . ."

This was quickly followed by "F-R-I-E-N-D-S-H-I-P" ("Hi, there, old buddy . . ."), "C-O-N-F-I-D-E-N-C-E" ("Gosh, you're just about the greatest . . ."), and "S-E-C-U-R-I-T-Y" ("There, now, there's absolutely nothing to worry about as long as we have each other").

Special messages were added for those with special needs, such as "M-O-T-H-E-R" ("Oh, it's so good to hear your voice, son. Are you getting enough to eat? Are you wearing your galoshes? Are you . . .").

Surprisingly, one of the most popular was "A-U-T-H-O-R-I-T-Y." ("When you hear the signal, you will have 60 seconds to state your dilemma." After 60 seconds, a stern voice came on to thunder: "You know what's right. Now, by God, do it!"

Thus humanity came to have everything that man had always wanted from his fellow man—sympathy, love, friendship, confidence, security and authority. And yet, oddly enough, deep down people were still uneasy.

Further studies were made. And at last the telephone company came up with the solution: "U-L-T-I-M-A-T-E- N-E-E-D."

"You are a singular human being, unique among all living creatures, different from all other men. You are that God-created miracle: you are, above all else, an individual."

"This is a recording."

WALL HANGING

PURPOSE:

To explore nonverbal expressions of love in an art medium.

GROUP SIZE:

Up to 20

TIME SUGGESTED:

One session, 30 minutes; later session of 45—60 min.

GENERAL DIRECTIONS:

Students have a brief preliminary discussion of "kinds" of love, and subgroups are assigned to work on each category. Using various techniques and "found art," subgroups prepare wall hangings illustrating kinds of love.

MATERIALS REQUIRED:

Squares and strips of felt, burlap, etc.

Balls of macrame yarn or string, heavy sewing thread or crewel yarn.

Dowels or lath or other straight strip of rigid, lightweight composition objects brought in by students.

Box of straight pins.

Glue, heavy yarn needles, scissors; you may also wish to use a stapler.

PROCEDURE:

1. A short general class discussion on the kinds, types or categories of "love" develops a list including perhaps such headings as: "Membership: friends, parents and child, engaged couple, etc."; "Characteristics: selfish, smothering, creative, sharing, etc." Taking into account class interest, help the students refine list to select 3—4 categories.

2. Each category is put on a slip of paper. Subgroups are formed, and one member of each subgroup comes forward to draw a slip giving the category on which his group will work. Explain to the class that each subgroup will create a wall hanging illustrating or demonstrating that "kind" of love. Wall hangings may be suspended from a dowel or bar if knotted hangings of the macrame type are desired. Each student is to bring in some small object which he believes helps him understand the particular kind of love on which his subgroup is focusing, and these objects will be included as part of the wall hanging.

3. Give subgroups about fifteen minutes for a planning session to decide on the materials or make some very general plans for the hanging they will create at the next session. Encourage the groups to be flexible enough to allow for any good ideas individuals may bring to the next session.

4. At the second session materials are made available, and groups are given 20—25 minutes to prepare their hangings. Small objects may be pinned, sewed, tacked, tied or pasted into or on the background material.

5. The last part of the session is devoted to viewing the other subgroups' work. There is no formal discussion, but there will be informal conversations about the hangings.

THE FAMILY CAVE

PURPOSE:

To examine some of the values on which or around which families focus or which they find very important.

COMMENT:

"Sometimes you have to go a long way out of your way in order to go a short way correctly. I mean, most of what we're doing here should be magnificently obvious. Like the trip with things. Now there's a constant master-slave relationship: Do I own my things or do they own me? What kind of nonsense do I have to go through in order to have my fifty-thousand-dollar house, my Stingray with dual carbs, and my eighty-watt fifteen-channel stereo set? It's pretty obvious that it's hard to have all those things and not get attached to them. So what we're doing here is to get back to something really simple: The fewer things you have, the easier it's going to be to figure out what's important" (quoted by Keith Melville, *COMMUNES IN THE COUNTER CULTURE,* New York: William Morrow & Co., 1972, p. 166).

GROUP SIZE:

Up to 20

TIME SUGGESTED:

45—60 minutes

GENERAL DIRECTIONS:

After a brief introductory talk, students work individually to express family values as demonstrated in "possessions," using a simple art medium. Results are shared and discussed.

MATERIALS REQUIRED:

Large sheets of drawing paper, or construction paper or, instead of drawings, students may use cardboard boxes and 3 x 5 file cards and/or magazine pictures. This approach will require paste and scissors, or pictures may be roughly torn and contact tape used.

PROCEDURE:

1. Talk briefly to the students about primitive man's "home," mentioning that caves were sought out and lived in for both comfort and safety, and eventually were "furnished" and "decorated" to some extent. Ask the students to think of their own families furnishing a "cave" for a more or less permanent home. What things would they consider essential? Recognizing that some students may not live with their own families, tell them they may either do this exercise on the basis of their own family, or of a family with whom they now live.

2. This project may now be carried on in a number of ways.

—Students may sketch their "family cave" on a large sheet of paper and draw in the items, or they may write the names of the articles on slips of paper, at least temporarily, and lay them on their drawing. The latter method permits students to change their minds more easily.

—Students may use cardboard boxes, "furnishing" them with items printed on tent-folded 3 x 5 cards, or make a collage on the inner walls of their box using pictures cut from old magazines, or a combination of the two.

3. In a large group form subgroups to share their completed work with one another. Each student may explain his own family cave.

4. A general discussion focuses on such questions as the following:

—Why are these "essential" for your family?

—What do these things mean to your family? . . . to you?

—What kinds of things you actually have at home did you eliminate?

—Which members of your family did you think of in making your selection?

—Do you think other family members would have chosen different items?

—Do you value these items as much as your family does?

—What values do you see in common with other family members?

—What values are different? . . . why?

—What do you see as the relationship between these values and "love" in your family?

—Did any students furnish their family cave with non-material things? If so, what and why?

—Are the non-material or the material things more valued in your family? . . . What is the relationship between these values and "love" in your family?

—Do you think your family's life together is based on the material or non-material things? . . . Without the material things, would the non-material things exist in your family?

VARIATIONS:

1. Students may be interested in making a new "cave" on the basis of "If you were going to live alone in the cave, what would you add? . . . what would you take out? . . . Would you want any of the things you actually have in your home now? . . . If you wanted to start a new family, what would you add?"

2. Tell students about the "bower bird." The Australian bower-bird not only builds a rather elaborate "cave," hut or "bower," but furnishes it as a "playground" for himself and his mate, bringing to it and carefully arranging various bright and colorful objects. Depending on the species, he may have a playground without a bower, or a variety of kinds of bowers, but in any case this area never serves as the nest, but is part of his sexual display. Fruits and flowers which are sometimes included are not to be eaten, but along with shells, stones and other objects are selected for bright color or on some other aesthetic basis, known to the bower bird alone.

Ask students to walk around their own homes and mentally select those few objects they would really want for their "bower"—things of no "practical" use, but cherished because of beauty, sentimental appeal, etc. Ask them to bring their lists and put them at the entrance to their "cave." Ask students to share their lists with a friend, thus dividing class on the basis of self-selecting dyads.

In a general discussion ask students to talk about the general kinds of things they and their partner chose, avoiding revealing anything which might be considered confidential information. Discussion might include exploration of some of the following questions:

—Why do we want to share things we are fond of with people we are fond of?

—What do other people's "cherished objects" tell us about them as people?

—Do we want to share everything we like with someone we love? . . . why? . . . Is this a good thing?

—What happens when someone we love dislikes something we are very fond of?

—Is it a good idea to try to "sell" someone we love on our favorite things?

—Do you cherish some things simply because someone you love admires them? . . . Is this good or bad?

FAMILY COMMUNICATION

PURPOSE:

To examine aspects of loving and unloving conversation within the average family.

COMMENT:

"From the moment of birth, when the Stone Age baby confronts the twentieth-century mother, the baby is subjected to these forces of violence, called love, as its mother and father, and their parents before them, have been . . . love and violence, properly speaking, are polar opposites. Love lets the other be, but with affection and concern. Violence attempts to constrain the other's freedom, to force him to act in the way we desire, but with ultimate lack of concern, with indifference to the other's own existence or destiny" (R. D. Laing, *POLITICS OF EXPERIENCE*, New York: Ballantine Books, 1967, p. 58).

GROUP SIZE:

Up to 20

TIME SUGGESTED:

Preliminary session of 30—60 minutes; second session of 45—60 minutes.

GENERAL DIRECTIONS:

After a brief preliminary discussion of family communication and its relationship to love, students are asked to tape a family dinner conversation and report on their findings. Some students may volunteer to bring in tapes for class listening, with or without discussion.

MATERIALS REQUIRED:

Students will need to use tape recorders at home, and a player may be needed in class for the second session.

PROCEDURE:

1. In a brief general discussion explore student views of characteristics of "loving" and "unloving" conversation, and of the kinds of conversation they believe typical of the average family's dinner table. Ask students to tape three dinner-time conversations at home, reminding them to ask permission first of all members present at the time. Ask them to play back these conversations for their families and to notice the kinds of comments the family members make about the playback. If you wish you may give them a list of questions such as the following to help them listen to the tape and the family comments:

—Did you feel you learned anything about your family? . . . about how love is expressed by family members? . . . about your own role in the family?

—Did you find you play a different role with friends or at school than the one you play at home?

—What did you learn about your family's communication patterns? . . . Who speaks? . . . Who doesn't? . . . Who interrupts whom? . . . Who is listened to? . . . Who is ignored? . . . Who introduces new topics for discussion? . . . Who makes decisions? . . . How? . . . Who encourages the expression of opinions? . . . of feelings? . . . Who discourages these?

2. At the following session ask the students to compare their original ideas expressed in the discussion at the last session with the reality of their own family conversation on these tapes. Ask them to share some of their findings with a subgroup or the class.

With family permission, some students may wish to play tapes for the class. Such tapes are often a confusion of noise and sometimes are incomprehensible to listeners outside the family. Ask the students who volunteer to be sure to play understandable segments for the class. It may be best to play some of these segments toward the end of the session, and avoid discussing them.

If tapes are not played, a general discussion on how love is expressed in families can be built on some of the findings students express.

VARIATION:

Students who are interested in the problems of communication in the family and among people who love one another may be interested in reading and reporting on all or part of one of the books in "Suggested Resources." Discussion in subgroups or a general class discussion following such a report will be helpful.

SUGGESTED RESOURCES:

Lederer, William J., and Don D. Jackson, *THE MIRAGES OF MARRIAGE,* New York: W. W. Norton & Co., 1968.

Gordon, Thomas, *PARENT EFFECTIVE-NESS TRAINING,* New York: Peter H. Wyden, Inc., 1970.

FILM:

Adventures of an *, 10 minutes, color, animated, Storyboard, Inc., 1957. See also Robert Heyer and Anthony Meyer, *DISCOVERY IN FILM,* New York, N.Y.: Paulist Press, 1969, pp. 26-28, which discusses this film and suggests a discussion related to the Generation Gap; *DISCOVERY PATTERNS, BOOK 2: DYNAMICS AND STRATEGIES* Robert J. Heyer and Richard J. Payne (eds.), New York, N.Y.: Paulist Press, 1969, suggests additional questions on p. 166, dealing with "creative love."

SEXUAL CODES

PURPOSE:

To explore some of the codes of ethics concerned with sexual behavior and consider our own code.

COMMENT:

In our society there is not one, but several sexual codes or sets of rules concerning sexual behavior. Many of our rules, both spoken and unspoken, are directed toward the control of behavior considered "sexual," although we are often unaware that this is the concern.

"The weakening of conviction and belief in the established value systems also contributes to the inconsistency between proclaimed attitudes and observable behavior. For better or worse the 'official' standards always change more slowly than actual behavior. Whereas attitudes favoring greater sexual freedom can be discerned among some of the clergy as well as others who seriously appraise the morality of our culture, the long-established, prohibitive standards continue to be vigorously defended. The virtue of virginity, the ideal of sexual abstinence and 'purity' until marriage, the concepts of carnal sin and 'dirty' sex still are a part of the proclaimed ethic in a large proportion of our society. The same is true of the strong taboo against the direct expression of aggression, although aggression does not carry the same degree of reproach as does sexuality.

"Middle-class culture, of course, is not monolithic in sexual attitudes. There are sizable segments of the population, particularly the more sophisticated adults in the larger urban areas, that openly disagree with the prohibitive morality of their parents and grandparents and try to rear children accordingly. But most observers would regard these elements as exponents of change rather than as arbiters of current majority attitudes. Middle-class culture, for the most part, does not provide for a guilt-free orgastic sexual outlet between puberty and marriage.

"One result of this kind of morality is that the adolescent has both the tremendous task of controlling his sexual feelings and urges, and the heavy burden of guilt arising from the almost inevitable failure to do so. Referring again to the emphasis middle-class culture places on the nuclear family, it seems likely that this plays an important role in intensifying the adolescent sexual conflict by focusing virtually all of the developing child's sexual feelings on his biological parents.

"Adolescents find it very difficult to live by the culturally prescribed sexual morality, and they often pay a high price emotionally in attempting to do so. Many have just about given up making the effort, for no one whose childhood was lived on the context of a prohibitive morality can be really free of its legacy of sexual guilt. The nature of the dilemma determines the standard variations of adolescent efforts at solution of the problem: rebellion against sexual ethics and denial of conscience; early dependent marriage; early marriage with withdrawal from the socio-economic struggle; repudiation of sexual prohibitions in good faith and sincerity but with unavoidable unconscious guilt; subordination of sex to, and contamination of sex with, competitive goals; or strong repression of sexuality, with the likelihood of subsequent mental or emotional disorder. The attitudes of middle-class culture make it very nearly impossible for adolescents to employ in a healthy way, the alternatives to such modes of behavior, namely, masturbation or sexual intimacies with the opposite sex, appropriate to the individual's age and degree of emotional maturity.

"This generalized view of middle-class morality as being prohibitive and inhibitive may seem to be contradicted by the obvious current emphasis upon sex in our culture. Note the content of much of what is expressed through the media of mass communication and the child-rearing practices of many parents who condone and sometimes foster such things as dating and the wearing of make-up and sexually provocative clothing at a very early age. These attitudes usually are more sexually stimulating than truly permissive, however, and they tend only to add to the sexual conflict. In most families, particularly in some subcultural groups, the line is firmly drawn at sexual intercourse, or even at masturbation. The degree of sexual behavior which is permitted also differs for boys as against girls. For the girl it is competitive 'sexiness,' not functional sexuality, that is fostered. The attitude of many adults is paraphrased in the expression, 'Hang your clothes on a hickory limb but don't go near the water.'" (Committee on Adolescence, Group for the Advancement of Psychiatry, "Discontinuity of the Adolescent Experience," *DISCOVERY PATTERNS, BOOK 1: PATTERNS OF SITUATIONS*, Robert J. Heyer and Richard J. Payne (eds.), New York, N.Y.: Paulist Press, p. 132. (We suggest you read this entire article, and also "Changing Morality: A TIME-Louis Harris Poll," p. 65ff.)

GROUP SIZE:

Up to 20

TIME SUGGESTED:

A preliminary session of about 30 minutes, and a 45—60 minute session. Work is also done outside of class time.

GENERAL DIRECTIONS:

Several students form a panel to present previously researched material on codes of sexual behavior, and the class discusses and evaluates the material presented.

MATERIALS REQUIRED:

None, unless students wish to play portions of tape, in which case a player will be needed at the second session.

PROCEDURE:

1. Ask a group of students to volunteer to research codes or rules and regulations concerned with the control of sexual behavior. Indicate that because there are a number operating in our contemporary society, each student should research a different group and be prepared to discuss his findings as a panel member in front of the class at a subsequent session. Ask students for suggestions as to specific groups, such as "our parents", "upper middle class", "the counter-culture", "the poor", "recent Spanish-American immigrants"; "students' code", "women's liberation code", "codes of various religious denominations". Point out that a "parents' code", for instance, might fit only *some* parents, as might a "students' code".

2. Assign subgroups to work with each panel member, helping in doing the research, which may be reading and/or interviews. Students should be encouraged to examine both the "stated rules" and what they can discover about "actual behavior". Remind researchers to approach their particular group's code sympathetically, and to try to develop as good a case as possible for that code. Ask subgroups to apportion task so as many different resources are tapped as possible. Interviews may be taped, with the interviewee's permission, or the student can take notes which should then be reviewed and approved by the person interviewed.

3. Panelists hold a 20 minute discussion in front of the class. This should not be conducted as a debate, but as an information sharing session under the guidance of a moderator whose task is primarily to see that all views get a hearing, that interrupting is avoided and that vague or ambiguous statements are clarified.

4. A few minutes may be allowed for students to question panel members for further information on a particular code, and then a general discussion is held. Some of the following questions might be explored:

—Which code appeals to you? . . . why?

—What effects do some of these codes have on the ability of a couple to achieve a loving relationship? . . . or of an individual?

—Why are there so many different codes within our single society?

—What happens when a person brought up in one code falls in love with someone brought up in another code?

—Which codes demonstrate a "double standard"? Is this good or bad? . . . Why do you think it exists?

—What factors influence your own selection of a code? . . . What makes a code "good" or "bad"?

—If "love" is an important factor in a code, toward whom is this love directed? . . . How does this affect others with whom one has a close relationship?

SUGGESTED RESOURCES:

For interviews: local ministers, priests, rabbis as well as laymen; teachers in fields of social studies, home economics, religion; parents; friends with a particular point of view; students and teachers in nearby colleges or universities, particularly in fields of psychology and sociology.

Darst, David, and Joseph Forgue, *SEXUALITY ON THE ISLAND EARTH*, New York, N.Y.: Paulist Press, 1970. (A small paperback which includes articles by Gregory Baum, Sydney Callahan, Rollo May and James M. Gustafson.

Kirkendall, Lester A., and Elizabeth Ogg, "Sex and Our Society", Public Affairs Pamphlet No. 366, 1964, 381 Park Ave. S., New York, N.Y. 10016.

FILM:

Help! My Snowman's Burning Down, 10 minutes, Contemporary Films, Inc.

MARRIAGE

PURPOSE:

To discover some of the reasons for success and failure in marriage.

COMMENT:

It is certainly no secret from young people that marriage as an institution is in a bad way. Perhaps there actually are no fewer unhappy or broken marriages today than in the past and perhaps people are simply more outspoken about it, or quicker to take steps to change the situation, but the picture is gloomy. In addition to the over 400,000 divorces per year in the United States, the rate per thousand married women rose steadily during the sixties, and this trend apparently continues. This figure does not include, of course, annulments, separations, desertions or the many marriages which remain so in name only.

Lederer and Jackson say, "We . . . are *for* marriage—workable, harmonious marriage. If this end is to be achieved, current mirages about marriage must be eliminated . . . The most easily apparent causes (of failure) are the failure to pick a suitable mate, and the failure—once a mate has been chosen—to work out relationship rules that will be durable and equitable." The authors go on to list seven of the "mirages" or "false assumptions," including, "That people marry because they love each other," "That most married people love each other," "That love is necessary for a satisfactory marriage." They believe that societal conditions have changed and that although the family unit is still appropriate, the forms and processes of marriage need revision. They also hope that the day will come when elementary school children will take "Human Relationships" along with "Arithmetic" and "English". In the meantime they offer an analysis of the "mirages" and concrete methods for dealing with marital conflict as well as questionnaires to help couples decide if they are good prospects as partners and to help married couples diagnose their difficulties. (William J. Lederer and Don D. Jackson, *THE MIRAGES OF MARRIAGE*, pp. 7, 14, 15).

GROUP SIZE:

Up to 20

TIME SUGGESTED:

Two or more 45—60 minute sessions.

GENERAL DIRECTIONS:

The first session starts with either viewing a film, reading a "Fact Sheet" or a pamphlet, and a brief discussion at the end of which subgroups accept an assignment in data gathering. The second session shares the data and discusses the problems. Subsequent sessions may explore in greater depth one or more problems according to class need.

MATERIALS REQUIRED:

A film, pamphlet or "Fact Sheet" for first session (see "Suggested Resources").

A tape player may be needed for the second session, if student-made tapes are available (see "Possibilities: b and c").

PROCEDURE:

1. Show a film such as one of those suggested below; or hand out a "Fact Sheet" on marriage and divorce giving some statistics from your own community, county or state or excerpts from published materials; or distribute copies of pamphlets such as suggested below and have the students read selected portions.

2. Engage the students in a brief discussion, 10—15 minutes, on the material in Step No. 1, raising the questions, "What is marriage?", "Why do some marriages succeed?", "Why do some marriages fail?"

3. To gather data for the next session, ask students to pursue one of the following "possibilities." You may wish to subgroup the class and have each subgroup work on a different possibility.

Possibilities:
a. WATCH FIVE TV shows. Using just what you can learn from these five shows, describe marriage in a few paragraphs.
b. INTERVIEW one member of at least three different married couples, asking, "What is marriage?" Tape these or make notes.
c. INTERVIEW four people (married or single) and ask them to think of one or two successful marriages of people they know fairly well. Ask them what are the most important reasons for the success of these marriages. Tape or make a few notes.

d. SEE a movie or READ a novel about a marriage that failed. Make a list of the principal reasons for the failure. (NOTE: "Failure" may be judged by your own standards, or by those of the people in the film or novel.)

4. At the second session, in subgroups, have students share their feelings, notes, tapes and lists. Those who used "Possibility d" may be asked to illustrate with examples from the film or novel.

5. In a plenary session share findings and ideas. You may want to list on the chalkboard some themes or ideas that recur frequently. If interest is high, help students plan at least one more session in which data already gathered may be further pursued, some research done and reports given, additional films shown and discussed, or speakers invited to address the class. Further suggestions are given in "Suggested Resources."

SUGGESTED RESOURCES:

FILMS:
(For the first session)
David and Hazel, 28 minutes, Contemporary Films. (Communication problems in a marriage.)
Engagement—Romance and Reality, 15 min., color. McGraw-Hill, 1964. (Can two young people who differ greatly love one another?)
The Tender Game, 7 min., color, John Hubley, 1962, Contemporary Films. (Beautiful film about "falling in love.")
(For subsequent sessions)
Below the Fruited Plain, 9 min., black and white, Leonard Lipton, Creative Film Society. (Sound track of unseen quarreling American couple on a trip to Mexico accompanies picturing of sandal-making in a village.)
The Couple, 16 min., black and white, Michael Wadley.
For Better, for Worse, 25 min., black and white, FRAFCO, 1966. (Explores some of the problems of a teenage marriage.)
Handling Marital Conflicts, 14 min., color, McGraw-Hill, 1964.
Point of View, 4½ min., Family Theater. (Straightforward presentation of some of the causes of divorce and its effects.)
Prometheus Bound, 27½ min., Paulist Productions. (Childless couple with marital problems work through their difficulties when they have a mentally retarded child.)

BOOKS, PAMPHLETS AND ARTICLES:
(For the first session)
David R. Mace, "What Makes a Marriage

Happy?" Public Affairs Pamphlet 290, 1959. (Since this is twenty pages in length, you may wish to ask students to read only a few sections for this initial discussion, finishing it at another time.)
(For subsequent sessions)

Elizabeth and William Genne, "Building a Marriage on Two Altars," Public Affairs Pamphlet #466.

Richard H. Klemer and Margaret G. Klemer, "The Early Years of Marriage," Public Affairs Pamphlet #424.

Evelyn Millis Duvall, "Building Your Marriage," Public Affairs Pamphlet #113.

William J. Lederer and Don D. Jackson, *THE MIRAGES OF MARRIAGE*, New York: W. W. Norton & Co., 1968. Suggest that students considering marriage take the tests in chapter 52, together with their prospective partner.

Thomas A. Harris, *I'M OK—YOU'RE OK: A PRACTICAL GUIDE TO TRANSACTIONAL ANALYSIS*, New York: Harper & Row, 1969. (Not specifically about marriage or the family, but attempts a "how-to-do-it" manual for human relationships which seek to prevent and cure the kinds of problems on which marriage often founders.)

NEW FAMILY PATTERNS

PURPOSE:

To investigate contemporary variations on the nuclear family pattern and to explore our own reactions to them.

COMMENT:

"Well, the Beatles are a new family group. They are organized around the way they create. They are communal art. They are brothers and, along with their wives and girl friends, form a family unit that is horizontal rather than vertical, in that it extends across a peer group rather than descending vertically like grandparents-parents children . . . The Beatles are a small circle of friends, a tribe." (Abbie Hoffman, "Talking in My Sleep," *THE REBEL CULTURE*, Robert S. Gold (ed.), New York: Dell, 1970, p. 212.) Perhaps the fact that the Beatles are no longer a "family group" makes them a good model of the current unstable, ephemeral "tribe."

On December 28, 1970, *TIME* magazine hit the newsstands in this season of holiday jollification with a cover showing a father, mother and two children, the girl holding a doll with prominent breasts. These well-groomed, well-dressed characters were portrayed in wood with a few plastic decorations, but rather than evidencing the dignity, stability, and naturalness which this medium usually carries, these wooden figures managed to look cheap, unstable and artificial. The caption read, "The U.S. Family: 'Help!' " The feature article had many unhappy things to say about the state of marriage and family life today.

" 'America's families are in trouble—trouble so deep and pervasive as to threaten the future of our nation,' declared a major report to last week's White House Conference on Children . . . The family, says California psychologist Richard Farson, 'is now often without function. It is no longer necessarily the basic unit in our society.' " The article goes on to explore some alternatives—communes, "trio marriages," various man-woman "arrangements," "single-parent families," and also a few proposals for strengthening the nuclear family

318   (*TIME,* Vol. 96, No. 26, December 28, 1970, pp. 34ff).

In *FUTURE SHOCK,* Alvin Toffler quotes Ferdinand Lundberg: "The family is 'near the point of complete extinction,'," and psychoanalyst William Wolf, who says, "The family is dead except for the first year or two of child raising." He goes on to report some of the alternatives to the nuclear family such as attempts to put into practice the proposals of Robert Rimmer in *THE HARRAD EXPERIMENT* and in *PROPOSITION 31,* underground polygamous families, and "aggregate families" "based on relationships between divorced and remarried couples, in which all the children become part of 'one big family'." He also describes temporary and trial marriages, including the proposals of German theologian Siegfried Keil of Marburg University and Father Jacques Lazure of Canada. (Alvin Toffler, *FUTURE SHOCK,* New York: Bantam, 1970, pp. 238, 248, 253-254.)

Margaret Mead, addressing Barnard students and their parents in 1970, told them that the family is not going to disappear, that children will continue to be raised in families, but that in twenty years we will have fewer families. However, she also jolted a good many by saying that although the family as an institution will endure, "everybody won't have to live in it all the time." By this she obviously meant "families" quite different in theory, if not in fact, from those we now have. Our "theory" presents the monogomous, "closed," life-enduring husband and wife. Our "fact," of course, is that about fifty percent of our marriages end in divorce, extra-marital "affairs" are common, and even serial monogamy seems less common than in the past. You might want to read your students Margaret Mead's speech which was reproduced in transACTION, Vol. 8, No. 11, September, 1971, pp. 50ff.

Both Toffler and Keith Melville point out the tendency of today's communards to look toward the past rather than the future—sometimes to a past that never was. Melville, drawing on many historians and sociologists, surveys the changes in family life in the past four centuries, pointing out that life used to be more "communal" for all families, and that the present family life-style began in the eighteenth century when the nuclear family began to seek greater privacy, gave greater importance to the individual, and began to live a less public life. The enormous number and variety of "organizations" in the life of the average American often seek to fulfill some of the needs of the old "communal" family, but fail to satisfy emotional needs, leaving an enormous burden for the nuclear family at a time when it is particularly unfitted to carry it, especially in the arid wasteland of suburbia.

Off-beat marital arrangements have charac-terized many of our most famous intentional communities of the past. Along with several other nineteenth-century "communes," the Oneida Community was middle-class, somewhat middle-aged, economically successful, lasted more than a quarter of a century, and practiced group marriage for several decades. Melville spells out some of the major differences between the nineteenth century communes and those of today as follows:

"Where those communes were large groups cemented by strong leadership, today's communes are small and anarchistic. Where many of them were highly structured communities in which individual behavior was strictly regimented, the communities of today are consciously unstructured, the lives of their members purposefully unregulated. Where those groups consisted of men, women, and children of all ages, the communes of today consist mainly of young people in their late teens and early twenties. Yet, in a curiously unutopian sense, the communes of the counter culture are a revival of the nineteenth-century theme, attempts to effect radical change through small communitarian experiments" (Keith Melville, *COMMUNES IN THE COUNTER CULTURE,* New York: William Morrow & Co., 1972, p. 51).

GROUP SIZE:

Up to 20

TIME SUGGESTED:

One or more sessions of 45—60 minutes.

GENERAL DIRECTIONS:

We believe this subject is of sufficient interest and importance to most students to warrant some serious reading and, if possible, talks by speakers who have experienced some of the alternatives: life in a commune, the extended family, single-parent households, couples living together without the formality of marriage. Students should be given reading lists judged suitable for their needs, and reports and discussions comprise the exercise.

MATERIALS REQUIRED:

Reading lists (see "Suggested Resources").
Services of guest speakers, if available. (Sources: nearby colleges and universities; religious movements and innovative churches and syna-

gogues; also, ask the students themselves if they can recommend local people who can speak from personal knowledge.)

PROCEDURE:

1. In a brief preliminary session, discuss with students their knowledge of existing alternatives to the nuclear family and its typical life-style. Ask them if they can recommend local speakers—they may know students and young adults living in communes in your area, or have older brothers and sisters who can suggest speakers. Distribute suitable reading lists. You may wish to assign specific books and articles to be reported on, arrange for a student panel, or offer to lecture yourself on one or two topics or areas. Arrange for the date or dates on which the subject will be discussed and encourage students to prepare lists of questions in which they are interested to be addressed to guest speakers or student reporters. You may wish to give them a few of the questions suggested in Step No. 2.

2. Following the reporting or talks or lectures, some of these questions may be investigated:

—What are the advantages and disadvantages of intentional communities, the extended family, communes, group marriage, couples living together without marriage, single parenthood? (These should, of course, be pursued individually.)

—In what ways can some of the above arrangements or life-styles eliminate or help to solve some of the problems of the nuclear family?

—How does the tribal life of some other culture avoid or solve some of the problems of the nuclear family? (See "Suggested Resources".)

—Is it possible to transfer these aspects of tribal life to an industrialized society?

—Is life on a commune a way of coping, or of copping out? If the latter, is it useful? . . . to whom?

—Since most communes are parasitical, depending on "money from home," food stamps, etc., does this help or hinder the society at large?

—If we consider the poorer nations, as well as the United States, does life in a commune here help or hinder these nations?

—Are Toffler's suggestions of a "computer software company whose program writers live and work communally," or an "education technology company whose members pool their money and merge their families" in line with your understanding of communes? (See Toffler, *FUTURE SHOCK*, p. 468.)

—What do you see as the differences between the intentional communities of the nineteenth century and the communes of today?

—How does Erich Fromm's "watch case factory" group fit into the nineteenth-century mold, or today's patterns?

—Which alternative family life-style has most appeal for you? . . . Which has least? . . . Why? . . . Do you prefer the nuclear family? . . . Why? . . . What do you think can be done to make the nuclear family a more livable situation today?

3. At a subsequent session, subgroups may be asked to arrive at a design for a family pattern and life-style which they think would be ideal. Allow for a "minority opinion." Ask subgroups to describe their pattern to the rest of the class and handle questions from class members.

4. At the end of the time devoted to this subject, students may be asked to write a brief paper, summing up their own views, expressing their hopes and fears about their own future family life and stating what steps they plan to take now to help them develop a satisfactory family life of their own.

SUGGESTED RESOURCES:

(Comparative studies of family and tribal life in various cultures.)

Blitsten, Dorothy R., *THE WORLD OF THE FAMILY: A COMPARATIVE STUDY OF FAMILY ORGANIZATIONS IN THEIR SOCIAL AND CULTURAL SETTINGS*, New York: Random House, 1963.

Brown, Ina Corinne, *UNDERSTANDING OTHER CULTURES*, Englewood Cliffs, N.J.: Prentice-Hall, 1963, especially chapter 3.

Lewis, Oscar, *LA VIDA: A PUERTO RICAN FAMILY IN THE CULTURE OF POVERTY—SAN JUAN AND NEW YORK*, New York: Random House, 1966.

Elwin, Verrier, *THE TRIBAL WORLD OF VERRIER ELWIN*, New York: Oxford University, 1964. (An Englishman's life with the Christa Seva Sangha in India, a Christian missionary group that allied itself with Mahatma Gandhi.)

Embree, John F., *SUYE MURA: A JAPANESE VILLAGE*, Chicago, Ill.: Univ. of Chicago, 1939.

Myrdal, Jan, *REPORT FROM A CHINESE VILLAGE*, New York: Signet, 1965.

Warner, W. Lloyd, *A BLACK CIVILIZATION: A STUDY OF AN AUSTRALIAN TRIBE*, New York: Harper & Row, 1958.

Turnbull, Colin M., *THE LONELY AFRICAN*, New York: Simon and Schuster, 1962.

Gatheru, R. Mugo, *CHILD OF TWO WORLDS*, Garden City, N.Y.: Doubleday Anchor, 1965. (Tribal upbringing in Africa.)

320

Duvignaud, Jean, *CHANGE AT SHEBIKA: REPORT FROM A NORTH AFRICAN VILLAGE*, trans. by Frances Frenaye, New York: Random House, 1970. (Life in a primitive village of Islam in Tunisia, especially pp. 69-158; 184-200.)

Leftwich, Joseph, (ed.), *YISROEL: THE FIRST JEWISH OMNIBUS*, rev. ed., New York: Thomas Yoseloff, 1963. (Life in the extended family of villages and cities in Europe.)

(Studies of family life in various sectors of society in the U.S.)

Warner, W. Lloyd, *AMERICAN LIFE: DREAM AND REALITY*, rev. ed., Chicago, Ill.: University of Chicago, 1962, ch. 4, "The Family in a Class System."

David, Jay, (ed.), *GROWING UP BLACK*, New York: Pocket Book, 1968.

Perrucci, Robert and Marc Pilisuk, (eds.), *THE TRIPLE REVOLUTION: SOCIAL PROBLEMS IN DEPTH*, Boston, Mass.: Little, Brown and Co., 1968, pp. 431-468 (two articles on the black family), and 407-430 (article on migrant workers).

Seeley, J.R., R.A. Sim, and E.W. Loosley, *CRESTWOOD HEIGHTS*, New York: John Wiley & Sons, 1963. (Although not new, and about a Canadian suburb, this classic description of life in suburbia is one of the best.)

Binzen, Peter, *WHITE TOWN USA*, New York: Vintage, 1970. (White working-class family and neighborhood life.)

Salisbury, Harrison E., *THE MANY AMERICAS SHALL BE ONE*, New York: W. W. Norton, 1971, chs. 8, 13, 14. (Communes, intentional communities, and the future.)

Hedgepeth, William, and Dennis Stock, *THE ALTERNATIVE: COMMUNAL LIFE IN NEW AMERICA*, New York: Macmillan, 1970. (About the "old" communes or intentional communities.)

Boguslaw, Robert, *THE NEW UTOPIANS: A STUDY OF SYSTEM DESIGN AND SOCIAL CHANGE*, Englewood Cliffs, N.J.: Prentice-Hall, 1965, pp. 112-126.

Fitzgerald, George R., *COMMUNES: THEIR GOALS, HOPES, PROBLEMS*, New York. N.Y.: Paulist Press, 1970.

Fromm, Erich, *THE SANE SOCIETY*, New York: Fawcett Premier, 1955, pp. 139-147; 267-278. (Descriptions of a U.S. suburb and of "communities of work" in Europe.)

Greeley, Andrew M., "The Risks of Community," *THE CRITIC*, Vol. XXVIII, No. 6, July-Aug., 1970, pp. 18ff. (An interesting, though quite unsympathetic article which deals in part with "encounter groups" as well as communes and "tribalism".)

LeShan, Eda J., "Mates and Roommates: New Styles in Young Marriages," Public Affairs Pamphlet, No. 468, 1971. (381 Park Ave. S., New York, N.Y. 10016.)

LIFE Magazine, "The Youth Communes", Vol. 67, No. 3, July 18, 1969, pp. 16B-23. Also, "The Marriage Experiments," Vol. 72, No. 16, April 28, 1972, pp. 42-76.

Melville, Keith, *COMMUNES IN THE COUNTER CULTURE: ORIGINS, THEORIES, STYLES OF LIFE*, New York: William Morrow & Co., 1972.

Toffler, Alvin, *FUTURE SHOCK*, New York: Bantam, 1970, pp. 245-259.

SEX EDUCATION

PURPOSE:

To discover what kind of "sex education" students feel younger children should have.

COMMENT:

"Today's preoccupation with sexuality, while a sign of immaturity, is at least a step forward from the world where it could not be mentioned even though it had a vigorous subterranean life. Howsoever ill-framed and confused are today's questions and answers, they at least show man shedding his hypocrisy, and attempting to understand his sexuality as a rich and rightful part of himself. He has, in other words, dropped the awful defensive system that allowed him to lead a divided life, permitted him to reassure himself of his propriety on the one hand while he guiltily enjoyed an isolated sexuality on the other. He is still having enormous difficulty in integrating his sexuality, but man is more open and less ready to be deceitful about it." (Eugene Kennedy, "It Shows Up in Sex," *THE CRITIC*, Vol. XXVIII, No. 6, July-August 1970, p. 34). "(T)he thing that bothers Americans most about obscenity is that they don't know about sex. The American people have a tremendous hangup on the subject. The problem is a lack of information. Obscene materials satisfy a basic craving for information. We recommend programs in the schools—with the consent of the local community—and community regulated. Professionals, like doctors and priests, whom people turn to for information, need to be educated themselves. Parents should talk about sex with their children" (Paul Bender, in an interview by Lillian R. Kohn, "Counsel to the Commission on Pornography," the *PENNSYLVANIA GAZETTE*, Vol. 69, No. 3, December 1970, p. 24).

GROUP SIZE:

Up to 20

TIME SUGGESTED:

Two or more sessions of 45—60 minutes.

GENERAL DIRECTIONS:

Students are asked to develop a plan of sex education for children from birth through 12th grade. The exercise may be started with a brief discussion or the examination of some materials. In subgroups they put together an outline which is later shared with the class. Interest may indicate further sessions developing some portions of the outline in depth. Proposals for sharing their data with others are suggested.

MATERIALS REQUIRED:

Some literature should be made available to the class (see "Suggested Resources").

PROCEDURE:

1. Explain the exercise, telling the students that when it is finished each student will receive a copy of the product—an overall plan for sex education of the child up to and including 12th grade. To get things started, students may wish to examine in subgroups some materials such as those in "Suggested Resources," or examine some of the questions given in Step No. 4, or may wish to start from "scratch."

2. Allow students about twenty minutes in subgroups of 5—7 to prepare an overall outline of what they see as the essential ingredients of sex education. They may wish to block out their outline in time-spans such as "Pre-school," "Elementary School," "High School," or in shorter time periods. Their outline should consider such things as: kinds of information to be conveyed, by whom, how; attitudes to be instilled; "do's and don'ts"; relationship to other kinds of education or educational experiences. Tell them they will have another opportunity later to refine their outline. Ask each subgroup to put their outline in written form.

3. Ask each subgroup to explain their outline briefly to the rest of the class.

4. In a plenary session help students discuss some questions such as the following in the light of their prepared outlines.

—What do you see as the relationship between love and "sex"? (or "sexual relationships")

—What kinds of sexual behavior do you think are instinctive? . . . learned?

—Do you think the relationship between love and sex is learned or instinctive? . . . How could this opinion affect the kind of sex education you would advocate?

—Do you think most young people you

know have learned the same things about sex that you have?

—Do you think it would be a good thing if all the young people you know shared the same sexual standards? . . . why?

—Where do conflicts in standards occur? . . . why? . . . Is this good or bad?

—How do "dirty jokes" differ from other jokes? . . . why?

—What is the relationship, if any, between sex education and dirty jokes? . . . and dirty graffiti? . . . and pornography?

—What do you think are the most influential sources of learning about sex for children and young people?

—What kind of sex education do you think children and young people should have? . . . If you have children some day, what kind of sex education will you give them? . . . why? . . . what kind will you want their schools to give them? . . . other agencies or institutions, such as churches and synagogues?

—How would the sex education you advocate differ from that which you received? . . . why?

5. Collect the outlines of the subgroups to hold for students until the next session, and ask students to write a paragraph to be shared with their own subgroup and then handed in to you on "Changes I would want to make in our outline on sex education." If desired, some outside reading or interviewing may be assigned for the next session.

SESSION II

1. Distribute ditto masters on which students may write or print their final version of their subgroup's outline. More than one sheet per subgroup may be needed, of course. Explain that their product will be reproduced for the entire class.

2. Ask each student to read to his subgroup his paragraph of suggestions, and also to provide any additional input he can from outside reading or interviews with parents, friends, etc. (NOTE: This may result in some joking and silliness, but since the "paragraphs" are to be handed in, they themselves should provide a stabilizing influence.)

3. The subgroups spend the rest of the session refining and perhaps enlarging their outlines.

4. If possible, arrange to have products of each subgroup made available to an audience wider than the class—copies might be sent to parents, given to the Home and School Association, posted on faculty bulletin boards, sent to an educational journal or society. If students know that their work will receive a more public hearing they may find it more worthwhile to put serious effort into their plan.

VARIATION:

1. If students are interested, more literature and films could be explored at subsequent sessions. Students might wish to prepare individual or group reports on the good and bad points of various plans and materials designed for various age levels.

2. If a student-parent meeting can be arranged, ask a representative from each subgroup to present his group's outline and then invite parent questions and comments.

3. A speaker from your school's Home Economics, Physical Education, or Health department or from your city or district school system, may be asked to give a talk to the class on sex education as it is and as they would want it to be. The class may wish to give this speaker copies of their outlines in advance of the talk and invite comments by the speaker. There should be time for questions and/or discussion following the talk.

4. Following the first session students may feel they need to know a bit more about child development and particularly about child psychology. In this case they may wish to defer their second session until after one or more sessions dealing with children. If they have done the exercise, "Communication: Learning As," they may wish to refer to some of their findings from that session. They may wish to have one or more lectures on child development and child psychology or do some reading on the subject such as that suggested in "Love: and Children."

SUGGESTED RESOURCES:

Contact your State Agricultural Extension Service, explaining your needs and ask them to send you literature suitable for your students in their project.

Write the American Social Health Association, 1740 Broadway, New York 10019. Briefly explain your project and ask for copies of "About Family Life Education," the reprint, "Family Life and Sex Education in the Turbulent Sixties" by Rose M. Somerville, from the *JOURNAL OF MARRIAGE AND THE FAMILY*, Feb., 1971, and a catalogue of their publications. The first pamphlet named gives an excellent list of names and addresses of other sources, and their publications are inexpensive.

Kirkendall, Lester A., "Sex Education, *SIECUS* Study Guide No. 1," New York: SIECUS, 1965. Write to *SIECUS* Publications Office, 1855 Broadway, New York 10023 for this pamphlet (single copy, 50 cents, ask for prices on quantity shipments) and a catalogue of their materials.

Hymes, James L., Jr., "How to Tell Your Child about Sex," Public Affairs Pamphlet, No. 149, 1949. (Despite the age of this pamphlet, it is still a very popular one, being in its thirtieth printing in 1971.)

The following two booklets are presented from within the Christian perspective, and present a number of viewpoints. They are addressed to the young adult.

Darst, David, and Joseph Forgue (eds.), *SEXUALITY ON THE ISLAND EARTH*, New York, N.Y.: Paulist Press, 1970.

Frisbie, Richard, *THE SIX PARADOXES OF SEX*, Chicago, Ill.: Claretian Publications, 1969, 221 W. Madison St., Chicago, Ill. 60606.

Mandel, William K., "The Birds, the Bees, and Medical Expertise: What your doctor doesn't know about sex may surprise you," *PENNSYLVANIA GAZETTE*, Vol. 69, No. 8, June, 1971, pp. 20ff.

JUDEO-CHRISTIAN RELIGIONS

PURPOSE:

To explore the idea of love in Judaism and Christianity, and see how it relates to our ideas of "religion."

COMMENT:

"Brothers, have no fear of men's sin. Love a man even in his sin, for that is the semblance of Divine Love and is the highest love on earth. Love all God's creation, the whole and every grain of sand in it. Love every leaf, every ray of God's light. Love the animals, love the plants, love everything. If you love everything, you will perceive the divine mystery in things. Once you perceive it, you will begin to comprehend it better every day. And you will come at last to love the whole world with an all-embracing love." (p. 382, *THE BROTHERS KARAMAZOV*, by Fyodor Dostoyevsky, translated by Constance Garnett. The Modern Library, New York: 1950. Random House, Inc., copyright.

GROUP SIZE:

Up to 20

TIME SUGGESTED:

45—60 minutes

GENERAL DIRECTIONS:

The teacher reads some or all of the quotations from the Bible given in Step No. 1, and then distributes a questionnaire. When the students have completed the questionnaire, they share portions with their subgroup.

MATERIALS REQUIRED:

Copies of the Questionnaire.

1. Most of your students will be familiar with the following quotations from the Bible, but ask them to listen to them with the idea of trying to see what is meant by the word "love" in these passages.

"But now, thus says Yahweh, who created
  you, Jacob, who formed you, Israel
Do not be afraid, for I have redeemed you;
I have called you by your name, you are mine.
. . . Because you are precious in my eyes,
because you are honoured and I love you . . .
Do not be afraid, for I am with you."
(*ISAIAH* 43:1-4)

"Hatred provokes disputes,
  love covers over all offenses." (*PROVERBS*
10: 12)

"Better a dish of herbs when love is there
  than a fattened ox and hatred to go with
it." (*PROVERBS* 15: 17)

"Yahweh, your love fills the earth . . ."
(*PSALMS* 119: 65)

"What does Yahweh your God ask of you? Only this: to follow all his ways, to love him, with all your heart and all your soul,"

". . . Yahweh your God is God of gods and Lord of lords, the great God, triumphant and terrible, never partial, never to be bribed. It is he who sees justice done for the orphan and the widow, who loves the stranger and gives him food and clothing. Love the stranger then, for you were strangers in the land of Egypt." (*DEUTERONOMY* 10: 17-19)

In the SONG OF SONGS, the bridegroom says, "Set me like a seal on your heart, like a seal on your arm. For love is strong as death, jealousy relentless as Sheol." (*SONG OF SONGS,* 8: 6)

"Yahweh says this:
They have found pardon in the wilderness,
those who have survived the sword.
Israel is marching to his rest.
Yahweh has appeared to him from afar;
I have loved you with an everlasting love
so I am constant in my affection for you."
  (*JEREMIAH* 31: 2-3)

"Yahweh spoke to Moses; he said: 'Speak to the whole community of the sons of Israel and say to them: Be holy, for I, Yahweh your God, am holy . . . You must not bear hatred for your brother in your heart. You must openly tell him, your neighbor, of his offense; this way you will not take a sin upon yourself. You must not exact vengeance, nor must you bear a grudge against the children of your people. You must love your neighbor as yourself. I

am Yahweh.' " (*LEVITICUS* 19: 1, 17-18)

"I may speak in tongues of men or of angels, but if I am without love, I am a sounding gong or a clanging cymbal. I may have the gift of prophecy, and know every hidden truth; I may have faith strong enough to move mountains, but if I have not love, I am nothing. I may dole out all I possess, or even give my body to be burnt, but if I have not love, I am none the better.

"Love is patient; love is kind and envies no one. Love is never boastful, nor conceited, nor rude; never selfish, not quick to take offense. Love keeps no score of wrongs; does not gloat over other men's sins, but delights in the truth. There is nothing love cannot face; there is no limit to its faith, its hope, and its endurance." (*1 CORINTHIANS*, ch. 13, 1-7).

"Dear friends, let us love one another, because love is from God. Everyone who loves is a child of God and knows God, but the unloving know nothing of God. For God is love; and his love was disclosed to us in this, that he sent his only Son into the world to bring us life. The love I speak of is not our love for God, but the love he showed to us in sending his Son as the remedy for the defilement of our sins. If God thus love us, dear friends, we in turn are bound to love one another. Though God has never been seen by any man, God himself dwells in us if we love one another; his love is brought to perfection within us . . . God is love; he who dwells in love is dwelling in God, and God in him . . . There is no room for fear in love; perfect love banishes fear . . . We love because he loved us first. But if a man says, 'I love God,' while hating his brother, he is a liar. If he does not love the brother whom he has seen, it cannot be that he loves God whom he has not seen." (*JOHN* 4, 7-20)

"Then what can separate us from the love of Christ? Can affliction or hardship? Can persecution, hunger, nakedness, peril, or the sword? 'We are being done to death for thy sake all day long,' " as Scripture says; "we have been treated like sheep for slaughter"—and yet, in spite of all, overwhelming victory is ours through him who loved us. For I am convinced that there is nothing in death or life, in the realm of spiritist or superhuman powers, in the world as it is or the world as it shall be, in the forces of the universe, in heights or depths—nothing in all creation that can separate us from the love of God in Christ Jesus our Lord." (*ROMANS* 8, 35-39)

Ask the students to jot down on a piece of paper the words that they think would be the best synonyms for "love" in these various passages, as you read them. The selections from *ISAIAH, PROVERBS, PSALMS, DEUTERONOMY, JEREMIAH* and *LEVITICUS* are from the *JERUSALEM BIBLE*, those from *CORINTHIANS, JOHN*, and *ROMANS* are from the *NEW ENGLISH BIBLE*.

2. Give students a few minutes to complete their jottings, and then distribute a Questionnaire. *Select* those questions from the following which you think would be best suited to your class. Include question No. 1.

3. When students have completed the questionnaire, divide the class in subgroups of 5—7. Ask each subgroup to start by discussing their answer to the first question, and then go on to talk about the relation between "love" and "religion" as they see it, using whatever data they wish from their questionnaires.

4. Students would probably be interested in reading the replies of their fellow class members, but may wish to preserve anonymity. If so, you may offer to compile the data and duplicate it for distribution.

QUESTIONNAIRE

Please answer the following questions to the best of your ability. You will retain possession of your paper, but will be asked to share some of your ideas later. There are no right or wrong answers to these questions which are asking for your own ideas and opinions.

1. What do you think is the meaning of "love" expressed in the passages read to you?

2. What do you think is the place of religion in the world? . . . in your life?

3. What is the most important job of religion in the world today?

4. Why is this the job of "religion," rather than of some other part of life (or society)?

5. How could the job be done? . . . Who should do it?

6. What do you think is the function or purpose of religion for the individual? . . . How do the religions you know try to fulfill this purpose? . . . What helps them succeed? . . . What sometimes causes them to fail?

7. Since all religions try to help the individual reach a higher plane of existence and a happier life, why do so few people achieve these?

8. Have you known anyone who was "religious" in what you would consider the "right" way? . . . What was this person like? . . . Did he or she appeal to you, personally? . . . why? . . . Would you want to be like him to some extent?

9. Do you ever believe you see some evidence of God in the world? . . . in your own life?

10. What do you think are your parents' religious values or beliefs?—could you list 5—10 words or phrases that would characterize them? . . . Do you agree with these beliefs or values? . . . If not,

do you have different ones?

11. Which of the following elements of religion do you think most important? . . . least important?
public worship
prayer or meditation
scriptures or other sacred writings or stories
mystical or spiritual experiences
ethical or moral teachings and acts
beliefs about God and his relationship to man
fellowship of a community of believers
sacraments

12. What is the difference between a religious belief and some other kind of belief?

13. Why do you think all religions apparently have stories about some of their first members? . . . Do you think there are common elements in the lives of these people? . . . Do you think this tells us anything about God? . . . about man?

14. How would you describe the difference between ideas and actions which are "religious" and those which are not?

15. Do you consider yourself a member of a religious faith? . . . If so, do you feel yourself a member of a church or synagogue?

16. Are there any ways in which you would like to see your religious group improve? . . . If so, can your ideas get a hearing? . . . To whom would these ideas apply? . . . Have you tried to put them into practice yourself in any way?

17. Do you approve of religion for others, but not for yourself? . . . for whom?

VARIATION:

Students may be interested in comparing the quotations from the Bible with statements on love from other sacred writings. The following might be read to them at a later occasion, and further discussion might include compiled data from Step No. 4 above.

The Bhagavad-Gita, sometimes called the Song of God, is regarded by Ananda K. Coomaraswamy as a compendium of Vedic doctrine, including the most basic and important ideas from the Hindu Vedas, Brahmanas and Upanishads. Krishna is an incarnation of the Divine Ground, or God in somewhat the same way that Jesus is considered by Christians to be the Incarnation of divinity, or Gautama the Buddha an Incarnation by Buddhists. The Gita contains the teachings of Krishna, and is usually dated about the third or fourth century, B.C. In this work, Krishna sometimes speaks of himself as Brahman, or God Himself, and says to his disciples:

326

"Whatever man gives me
In true devotion:
Fruit or water,
A leaf, a flower:
I will accept it.
That gift is love,
His heart's dedication."

"Those whose minds are fixed on me in steadfast love, worshipping me with absolute faith, I consider them to have the greater understanding of yoga."

"He who is free from delusion, and knows me as the supreme Reality, knows all that can be known. Therefore he adores me with his whole heart."

"And he who dwells
United with Brahman,
Calm in mind,
Not grieving, not craving,
Regarding all men
With equal acceptance:
He loves me most dearly."

"Give me your whole heart,
Love and adore me,
Worship me always,
Bow to me only,
And you shall find me:
This is my promise
Who love you dearly."

"A man should not hate any living creature. Let him be friendly and compassionate to all." (BHAGAVAD-GITA, trans. by Swami Prabhavananda and Christopher Isherwood, New York: Mentor, 1951, pp. 83-84; 97; 128; 129; 99.)

The Upanishads are those portions of the writings of the ancient Hindu seers and saints which are concerned with the knowledge of God. They also include some teachings on "right conduct," such as the following:

"Whatever you give to others, give with love and respect. Gifts must be given in abundance, with joy, humility, and compassion." (THE UPANI-SHADS, trans. by Swami Prabhavananda and Frederick Manchester, New York: Mentor, 1957, p. 54.)

The Gautama Buddha, born into the world of the Vedas and belief in Brahman, accepted some of these teachings and rejected or transformed others. He thought of the goal of man's religious quest as Nirvana instead of union with Brahman. The following is from early Buddhist writings and is part of a selection sometimes called the Buddhist "Thirteenth Chapter of First Corinthians."

"Just as with her own life
a mother shields from hurt
her own, her only, child,—
let all-embracing thoughts
for all that lives be thine,
—an all-embracing love
for all the universe
in all its heights and depths
and breadth, unstinted love,
unmarred by hate within,
not rousing enmity."
(E. A. Burtt, [ed.], THE TEACHINGS OF THE COMPASSIONATE BUDDHA, New York: Mentor, 1955, p. 47.)

THE NEW RELIGIONS

PURPOSE:

To explore the contemporary spiritual quest, particularly among the "new religions" from the East.

COMMENT:

Young people turning to new religions, spiritual quests and even drugs, experience the world around them as "bad" in some way. Our traditional major religions have usually taught that this sense of dissatisfaction with the world and our place in it is our own fault, either directly, through personal failure to live and worship correctly, or indirectly through the heritage of original sin. These religions tried to make sense of our world and guide our choices in such a way that we could find peace and acceptance of the world and of ourselves. However, many young people feel these religions have failed, either by inadequately explaining the world they see around them, or by offering moral precepts which run counter to their desires, or to what seems good and right to them.

The physical sciences, which seemed to offer so much, had within them the seeds of their own downfall as a cure for man's unhappiness. As man's scientific knowledge grew and was turned to practical use in technology, his dissatisfactions and uncertainties seemed to increase. The threat of pollution and ecological destruction, an unpopular war, and the pressures under which their parents live and work have given young people a distrust of and even a fear of science.

Philosophy offered mental constructs, often of great beauty and appeal, and many ethical systems designed to help man believe that the following of certain principles would yield the satisfaction of being "right." The discipline of philosophy as a way of life had a very limited appeal, however, and although its overflow affected the lives of most people, its teachings were unsatisfying without the substance acquired only through discipline. Existentialism denied the existence of "sense" in the universe, positing a senseless or absurd world, and offered instead the urging of choice upon man as a free decision which he must make without help from supernatural resources and without hope of finding any meaning other than that which he created for himself. As an explanation and a guide it was a cold, unfriendly path. To accept the feeling of "fallenness" without explanation or cure appealed to only a limited number.

Both science and philosophy have increasingly stressed the "rational," ignoring or discounting feeling and emotion and thus displacing happiness, peace or "feeling good" as legitimate goals for man. If these elements of man were considered at all they were posed as distant goals to be achieved when "all" was "known."

Psychology and psychiatry were both more than willing to deal with these "irrational" facets of man, and offered various explanations for man's unhappiness based on the individual's inability to accept his own needs and desires and offered help in retraining toward such acceptance. However, many found the cure as painful as the disease and the end-product was not a guaranteed peace or happiness. Some of the best known followers of this path were forced to the conclusion that something "more" was needed: Jung felt no one was really "cured" unless he found some sort of religious faith or beliefs; Freud and later R. D. Laing believed that essentially all of society was so "sick" that only analysis or a complete and painful journey to the central core of one's being, on the part of everyone, would produce a society in which a well man could find some measure of happiness.

In despair of finding adequate answers among these choices, and with an increasing realization that there are more people outside of mainstream Western society than within it, young people have turned toward some of the solutions offered by other cultures. Since many of these religions and philosophies have persevered in societies which have never experienced the problems found in the United States, or deny the values of our swiftly changing, materialistically successful culture, they seem to address the frustrations of youth. In place of a freedom which insists on constant individual decision making they offer the hard discipline of *zazen* in Zen Buddhism or the unquestioning obedience to Meher Baba. In place of technological overkill of nature, they offer the acceptance and tutelage of nature in Tao or the religions of the American Indians. In place of intellectualism they offer the emotions of Hasidism and Hare Krishna. In place of a distrust of the senses or demands for self-denial, they offer the transcendental meditation of the Maharishi or the drug experience. For the confusion and diffusion of thought and energy required to follow a normal day on an urban campus, they substitute the separation from the world, the quiet and the monotonous concentration on a few acts and thoughts as in Hinayana Buddhism or the Bhum-nda of Tibetan Buddhism. In place of the uncertainty of both precepts and predictions, they offer the assurance and certainty of the Tarot cards or astrology. Instead of the sense of guilt and personal responsibility, they recommend the freedom and release of a belief in *karma*. In exchange for the boring routine of the largely non-participative services of the church or synagogue, they hold out the totally involving, ever changing activities of a *latihan* of Subud or an encounter group. Instead of a striving to change and improve oneself, they offer the calm acceptance taught by Krishnamurti, or the energetic proselatizing of the "Jesus freaks." In place of a distant, unknown religious leader of the past, they offer a visible, touchable guru or a shaman.

In every case, of course, there is a tendency to skim the surface, to distort the basic teachings of these faiths by an oversimplification, to create, in effect, a "heresy," or a brand new religion formed by combining certain features of various older faiths. However, even in this, there are models for the young, both because many of the religions of the East tend to be inclusionist, rather than exclusionist, and do not think in terms of heresy, and because young people find among their elders many who are involved in offbeat religious activities such as Pentecostalism without feeling in any sense that they are heretical or are leaving their religious denomination. In such a time of rapid change, cross cultural impact, and loss of a sense of certainty it is not surprising that young people should question and even leave the faith of their parents. It is rather impressive, however, to find so many searching so actively for something to take its place. Some will find their way back on other paths to the faith they once left, some will not, but all who are willing to search will profit from their journey.

GROUP SIZE:

Up to 20

TIME SUGGESTED:

One or more sessions of 45—60 minutes, depending on class interest.

GENERAL DIRECTIONS:

It will be best if convinced members of various religious or spiritual-thought groups can speak with your class about their beliefs and activities. In some cases there will be near-by centers of worship or study available which students may visit. Some members of your class may be members of such groups. If such human resources are not available, ask interested students to research the subject and present brief papers or talks to the class. Some recorded materials are available.

MATERIALS REQUIRED:

This will depend on the particular religion being investigated. You might want some reproductions of Zen art, a few hand bells, incense, copies of some of the periodicals of some of the groups, a mandala, some selections of Tao poetry, tapes or records.

PROCEDURES:

1. Explain to your students that you would like to investigate, with them, some of the Eastern religions and other strains of religious or spiritual thought that have recently become more popular in the United States. Ask if they know of such groups in their own community, if they themselves have attended any meetings, or if they know young people or adults who are members. Plan with them how your class may best learn about some of these ideas.

2. If a talk has been arranged by a member of a particular faith or "way," help your students prepare to make their visitor welcome, and encourage them, if necessary, to approach the experience in a spirit of sincere learning, not of argument and certainly not of disdain. If possible, arrange to have your speaker bring with him some of the materials used by his group and to demonstrate their use to your students. Also, ask him if he will allow time for questions at the end of his talk. If a discussion is planned, it may be best to hold it at the following session. If appropriate, your speaker may teach the group a prayer or chant or song.

3. If possible arrange a few trips to nearby places of worship or study centers of some of these groups.

4. Some students may be interested in further guided study. Some of the materials in "Suggested Resources" may be made available or recommended.

SUGGESTED RESOURCES:

The following books offer a broad basis for exploration. Many of them have extensive bibliographies for those who wish to explore further.

THE CLASSIC ROOTS:

Radhakrishnan, *THE HINDU VIEW OF LIFE*, New York: Macmillan, 1927.

BHAGAVAD-GITA: THE SONG OF GOD, trans. by Swami Prabhavananda and Christopher Isherwood, New York: Mentor, 1944, 1951.

THE UPANISHADS, trans. by Swami Prabhavananda and Frederick Manchester, New York: Mentor, 1948, 1957.

THE TEACHINGS OF THE COMPASSIONATE BUDDHA, E. A. Burtt (ed.), New York: Mentor, 1955.

Creel, H. G., *CHINESE THOUGHT FROM CONFUCIUS TO MAO TSE-TUNG*, New York: Mentor, 1953.

Lao Tzu, *THE WAY OF LIFE*, trans. by R. B. Blakney, New York: Mentor, 1955.

Parrinder, Geoffrey, *RELIGION IN AFRICA*, Baltimore, Md.: Penguin, 1969, Part One: Traditional Religions.

Black Elk, *THE SACRED PIPE*, Joseph Epes Brown (ed.), Baltimore, Md.: Penguin, 1971.

BLACK ELK SPEAKS, as told through John G. Neihardt, Lincoln, Nebr.: University of Nebraska, 1961.

McLuhan, T. C., (compiler), *TOUCH THE EARTH: A SELF-PORTRAIT OF INDIAN EXISTENCE*, New York: Outerbridge & Dienstfrey, 1971.

CONTEMPORARY CLASSICS:

Kapleau, Philip, (ed.), *THE THREE PILLARS OF ZEN*, Boston, Mass.: Beacon, 1965.

Suzuki, D. T., *ZEN BUDDHISM*, William Barrett (ed.), Garden City, N.Y.: Doubleday Anchor, 1956.

McNaughton, William, *THE TAOIST VISION*, Ann Arbor, Mich.: University of Michigan Press, 1971.

REPORTS ON CONTEMPORARY RELIGIOUS GROUPS AND APPROACHES:

Maslow, Abraham H., *RELIGIONS, VALUES, AND PEAK-EXPERIENCES*, New York: Viking, 1964, 1970.

Lanternari, Vittorio, *THE RELIGIONS OF THE OPPRESSED: A STUDY OF MODERN MESSIANIC CULTS*, trans. by Lisa Sergio, New York: Alfred A. Knopf, 1963.

Melville, Keith, *COMMUNES IN THE COUNTER CULTURE*, New York: William Morrow & Co., 1972, ch. 9, "The Search for Alternative Realities."

Needleman, Jacob, *THE NEW RELIGIONS*, rev. ed., New York: Pocket Books, 1970.

Maupin, Edward W., "Meditation," *WAYS OF GROWTH*, Herbert A. Otto and John Mann (eds.), New York: Viking, 1968, pp. 189ff.

Peterson, Severin, *A CATALOG OF THE WAYS PEOPLE GROW*, New York: Ballantine, 1971.

de Ropp, Robert S., *THE MASTER GAME: BEYOND THE DRUG EXPERIENCE*, New York: Delta, 1968, Sections III and IX.

Roszak, Theodore, *THE MAKING OF A COUNTER CULTURE*, Garden City, N.Y.: Doubleday Anchor, 1969, chapters IV, V and VIII.

Roszak, Theodore, (ed.), *SOURCES: AN ANTHOLOGY*, New York: Harper & Row, 1972, Section V., and also pp. 341-353 and 373-387.

Watts, Alan W., *PSYCHOTHERAPY EAST AND WEST*, New York: Ballantine, 1961.

Clark, Walter Houston, *CHEMICAL ECSTASY: PSYCHEDELIC DRUGS AND RELIGION*, New York: Sheed & Ward, 1969.

INNOVATIONS AMONG THE MAJOR U.S. TRADITIONS:

Cox, Harvey, *THE FEAST OF FOOLS*, New York: Harper & Row, 1969.

Keen, Sam, *TO A DANCING GOD*, New York: Harper & Row, 1970.

Merton, Thomas, *MYSTICS & ZEN MASTERS*, New York: Delta, 1967.

O'Connor, Edward D., *THE PENTECOSTAL MOVEMENT: IN THE CATHOLIC CHURCH*, Notre Dame, Indiana: Ave Maria Press, 1971.

Sleeper, James A., and Alan L. Mintz, (eds.), *THE NEW JEWS*, New York: Vintage, 1971, especially "Along the Path to Religious Community" by Alan Mintz, "Psychedelics and Kabbalah" by Itzik Lodzer, and "New Metaphors: Jewish Prayer and Our Situation" by Alan L. Mintz.

Stern, E. Mark, and Bert G. Marino, *PSYCHOTHEOLOGY*, New York: Newman Press, 1970.

MEDITATION

PURPOSE:

To discover ways of meditation.

COMMENT:

"Words and sentences are composed of silences more meaningful than the sounds. The pregnant pauses between sounds and utterances become luminous points in an incredible void: as electrons in the atom, as planets in the solar system. Language is as a cord of silence with sounds the knots—as nodes in a Peruvian *quipu,* in which the empty spaces speak. With Confucius we can see language as a wheel. The spokes centralize, but the empty spaces make the wheel.

"It is thus not so much the other man's words as his silences which we have to learn in order to understand him . . . Just as with our words, there is an analogy between our silence with men and with God. To learn the full meaning of one, we must practice and deepen the other.

"First among the classification of silences is the silence of the pure listener, of womanly passivity; the silence through which the message of the other becomes 'he in us,' the silence of deep interest.

"The next great class . . . we will call the silence beyond words. The farther we go, the farther apart does good and bad silence grow in each classification. We now have reached the silence which does not prepare any further talk. It is the silence which has said everything because there is nothing more to say. This is the silence beyond a final *yes* or a final *no,* This is the silence of love beyond words, as well as the silence of *no,* forever; the silence of heaven or of hell . . . At the pole opposed to despair there is the silence of love, the holding of hands of the lovers. The prayer in which the vagueness before words has given place to the pure emptiness after them. The form of communication which opens the simple depth of the soul. It comes in flashes and it can become a lifetime—in prayer just as much as with people. Perhaps it is the only truly universal aspect of language, the only means of communication which was not touched by the curse of Babel . . ." (Ivan Illich, *CELEBRATION OF AWARENESS, A CALL FOR INSTITUTIONAL REVOLUTION,* Garden City, N.Y.: Anchor, 1970, pp. 31-37.)

GROUP SIZE:

Up to 20

TIME SUGGESTED:

45—60 minutes

GENERAL DIRECTIONS:

Students are asked to bring in something which they believe helps them meditate. Depending on the class and its needs, the session is simply a silent period of meditation, or a combination of this plus some shared meditation.

MATERIALS REQUIRED:

Materials brought in by students.

PROCEDURE:

1. Explain to students the purpose of the exercise, and ask them to bring to the designated session something they believe will be helpful to them, or possibly to others in the class, in meditation. This may be a piece of writing, a picture, even a tape or record. Explain that any sounds used in the class will occupy only a brief portion of the time.

2. Open the session with some brief relaxation or stretch exercises, such as those given in "Freedom: Breathing", "Freedom: Stretch", "Happiness: Dreaming". Some students may have forgotten to bring anything with them, and for their sakes it may be best to ask one or two students to read their selection or to play a tape or record they have brought—the "Birds in the Forest" side of the "Environment" record is an example, as are short selections from "Jesus Christ—Superstar" or "Godspell" or some of the materials in "Suggested Resources". Some students may have brought a picture or a small art object which may be displayed in front of a small group.

3. Depending on your group, you may wish the entire session to be one of silent meditation after Step No. 2, or you may wish to introduce new elements part way through the time. There should be no discussion.

SUGGESTED RESOURCES:

Avant Garde Records, 250 W. 57th St., New

York, N.Y. 10019 has an excellent selection of contemporary religious music of a wide variety of types. Write for their catalogue.

In addition to the sacred writings mentioned in the accompanying exercises in this section, here are a few more suggestions:

Goudge, Elizabeth, (ed.), *A BOOK OF PEACE,* New York: Coward-McCann, 1967.

Hammarskjold, Dag, *MARKINGS,* trans. by Leif Sjoberg and W. H. Auden, New York: Alfred A. Knopf, 1964.

Herberg, Will, *JUDAISM AND MODERN MAN: AN INTERPRETATION OF JEWISH RELIGION,* New York: Meridian, 1951.

Kresh, Paul, (ed.), *THE AMERICAN JUDAISM READER,* New York: Abelard-Schuman, 1967. (Selections from within Reform Judaism. See particularly, pp. 35-37; 44-46; 70-75; 345-366.)

Livingston, Myra Cohn, *A TUNE BEYOND US: A COLLECTION OF POEMS,* New York: Harcourt, Brace & World, 1968. (A wide-ranging selection from many cultures, some of which are given in the original language as well as in English, and all of which have a quality of "otherness", although some are simply nonsense or "fun" rhymes.)

Wolf, Arnold Jacob, (ed.), *REDISCOVERING JUDAISM: REFLECTIONS ON A NEW THEOLOGY,* Chicago, Quadrangle, 1965.

Bush, Roger, *PRAYERS FOR PAGANS,* Dayton, Ohio: Pflaum, 1968. (Illustrated prayer-poems dealing with problems of today.)

Carroll, James, *ELEMENTS OF HOPE,* New York, N.Y.: Paulist, 1971. (Photographs and writings suitable for Christian meditation.)

Chagneau, Francois, *STAY WITH US: PRAYERS FOR WORSHIP AND CONTEMPLATION,* New York, N.Y.: Paulist Press, 1970.

Heyer, Robert J., and Richard J. Payne, (eds.), *DISCOVERY IN PRAYER,* New York, N.Y.: Paulist Press, 1969. (A collection of writings and pictures from many sources.)

Padovano, Anthony T.. *DAWN WITHOUT DARKNESS,* New York, N.Y.: Paulist, 1971. (Photographs and writings suitable for Christian meditation.)

Savary, Louis M., (ed.), *LISTEN TO LOVE: REFLECTIONS ON THE SEASONS OF THE YEAR,* New York: Regina Press, 1971. (Another collection of photographs, poems and readings.)

APPENDIX

APPENDIX

The following outline shows how the exercises may be incorporated into a typical high school course or subject offerings.

COMMUNICATIONS

ADVERTISING:
Freedom: Mass Media and "Good" and "Bad" Bodies
Life: Senses: Olfaction: "What Smells Sell?"
Peace: Media Monitoring

ART:
(See exercises listed under "Art" in the "Humanities" section of this appendix.)

AUDITION:
(See exercises listed in "Psychology" section of this appendix.)

COLOR:
(See exercises listed in "Psychology" section of this appendix.)

COMMUNICATIONS:
NOTE: In addition to the exercises in the section of the book titled "Communications," the following will be useful:
Life: Senses: Audition: Tapes and Voices
Life: Senses: Sounds and Spaces
Love: and Family Communication
Peace: Conflict, see Step No. 4

FAMILY:
Love: and Family Communication

FEELINGS AND EMOTIONS:
(See exercises listed in "Psychology" section of this appendix.)

LANGUAGE:
Peace: Media Monitoring, see Variation No. 1
(See also "Speech" below.)

MASS MEDIA:
Freedom: Mass Media and "Good" and "Bad" Bodies
Happiness: Photographs
Life: Senses: Olfaction: "What Smells Sell?"
Love: in the Comic Strip
Love: and Marriage, see Step No. 3
Peace: Conflict and Punishment, see Step No. 1
Peace: Media Monitoring

MOVIES:
(See "Mass Media" above.)

MUSIC:
(See exercises listed in "Humanities" section of this appendix.)

NOISE:
(See exercises listed in "Psychology" section of this appendix.)

NONVERBAL COMMUNICATION:
Freedom: Eyeball to Eyeball, see Step No. 2
Love: Wall Hanging

SENSORY AWARENESS:
(See exercises listed in "Psychology" and "Life: Senses" sections of this appendix.)

SPEECH:
Life: Senses: Audition: Tapes and Voices

SYMBOLISM:
(See exercises listed in "Humanities" section of this appendix.)

TV:
(See "Mass Media" above.)

THEATER:
(See exercises listed in "Humanities" section of this appendix.)

VIOLENCE AND:
Peace: Media Monitoring

FAMILY LIFE, HEALTH EDUCATION

ABORTION:
(See exercise listed in "Social Studies" section of this appendix.)

ADVERTISING:
(See exercises listed in 'Communications" section of appendix.)

AGGRESSION:
(See exercises listed in "Psychology" section of this appendix.)

ALCOHOLISM:
(See exercise in "Social Studies" section of this appendix.)

BABY-SITTING:
(See exercise listed in "Guidance" section of this appendix.)

BODY RHYTHMS:
Life: Biological Rhythms

BREAD:
(See exercise listed in "Religion" section of this
appendix.)

BREATHING:
Freedom: Breathing

CALISTHENICS:
Communication: Paraverbal and Silent Communi-
cation
Freedom: Stretch
(See also "Breathing," above.)

CHILDREN:
Communication: as Learning
Happiness: Back to Nature, see Section VI
Love: and "Sex Education"
Peace: Conflict and Punishment
Peace: Conflict: Scavenger Hunt
Peace: Media Monitoring
Life: Emergencies and Careers in Health

CLOTHING:
(See exercises listed in "Guidance" section of this
appendix.)

COMMUNAL LIVING, COMMUNES:
(See exercises listed in "Social Studies" section of this
appendix.)

COMMUNICATION:
Communication: Our Multiple Selves
Love: Family Communication

COMMUNITY:
(See exercises listed in "Social Studies: City
Planning" section, and "Social Studies:
Community" section of this appendix.)

COOKING:
(See "Food," below.)

DEATH:
(See exercises listed in "Religion" section of this
appendix.)

DIETS:
Life: Senses: Taste: Nutrition

DREAMS:
(See exercise listed in "Psychology" section of this
appendix.)

DRIVER EDUCATION:
Life: Emergencies and Careers in Health
Communication: Giving Directions and "Successful"
Communication

Life: Ecology: Conservation and Pollution, see Part II,
Step No. 7

DRUG ABUSE:
(See exercise listed in "Psychology" section of this
appendix.)

ECOLOGY:
(See exercises listed in "Social Studies" section of this
appendix.)

EMPATHY:
(See exercise listed in "Psychology" section of this
appendix, and also exercises on "Nonverbal
Communication" in section of book, "Communication.")

FEELINGS AND EMOTIONS:
(See exercises listed in "Psychology" section of this
appendix.)

FIRST AID:
Life: Emergencies and Careers in Health

FOOD:
Happiness: Meal
Life: Senses: Olfaction: Classifying
Life: Senses: Olfaction: Japanese Incense-Smelling,
Variation No. 2
Life: Senses: Taste . . . and Sight
Life: Senses: Japanese Tea Ceremony, and see also
Variation
Life: Food and Famine
Life: Senses: Taste: Food Additives
Life: Senses: Taste: Nutrition

GENERATION GAP:
Happiness: Body as "Good" or "Bad"

GROUPS:
(See exercises listed in "Social Studies" section of
this appendix.)

HEALTH:
Life: Senses: Taste: Nutrition
Life: Senses: Taste: Food Additives
(NOTE: Most exercises in this "Family Life"
section concern health.)

JOBS:
(See "Vocational Guidance" below.)

LOVE:
(See exercises in section of book titled "Love.")

MARRIAGE:
Freedom: from Prejudice: Male/Female Roles

Love: in the Comic Strip
Love: and Marriage
Love: New Family Patterns

MEDICINE:
(See exercises listed in "Social Studies" section of
  this appendix.)

MEMBERSHIP, FAMILY:
Communication: Effect on Our Bodies of Group
  Membership
Happiness: What is Community?, Section IV

MENTAL ILLNESS:
(See exercises listed in "Psychology" section of this
  appendix.)

MONEY MANAGEMENT:
Freedom: from Prejudice: Male/Female Roles
Happiness: Money and Work

NUDITY:
Freedom: and Nudity

NUTRITION:
Happiness: Poise: Trying On
Life: Senses: Taste: Nutrition
Life: Senses: Taste: Food and Famine

PHYSICAL DEPENDENCIES:
(See exercises listed in "Psychology" section of this
  appendix.)

PHYSICAL HANDICAPS:
(See exercises listed in "Psychology" section of this
  appendix.)

PHYSIOLOGY:
Freedom: Breathing
Life: Biological Rhythms
Life: Death: Who Shall Live: Who Shall Die:
Life: Senses: Visual Illusions
Life: Senses: Touch: 2-Point Threshold and Local-
  ization Error

PSYCHOLOGY:
(The following are selected as particularly applicable
  to this subject section—for further exploration, see
  all listings in "Psychology" section of this
  appendix.)
Communication: Physiognomy
Communication: Graphology
Freedom: and Trust
Happiness: Self-Image: Art Media
Happiness: Acceptance/Rejection
Happiness: Belonging
Happiness: Group Excursions

Life: Biological Rhythms
Life: Memory
Life: Dreaming
Life: Death Inquiry

PUNISHMENT:
(See exercise listed in "Psychology" section of this
  appendix.)

RECREATION:
(See exercise listed in "Guidance" section of this
  appendix.)
(See also exercises listed under "Religion": Celebrations" in this appendix.)

RELAXATION:
(See exercises listed in "Psychology" section of
  this appendix.)

REPONSIBILITY:
Freedom: and Responsibility
Happiness: the Handicapped and
Happiness: Group Excursions
Happiness: What is Community?
Life: Food and Famine, see Step No. 2, e

SAFETY:
(See exercise listed in "Guidance" section of this
  appendix.)

SELF:
(See exercises listed in "Psychology" section of this
  appendix.)

SEX:
(See exercises listed in "Psychology' section of this
  appendix.)

SLEEP:
(See exercise listed in "Psychology" section of this
  appendix.)

SMOKING:
(See exercise listed in "Psychology" section of this
  appendix.)

TEACHING:
Communication: as Learning

TV:
(See exercises listed in "Humanities: Mass Media"
  section of this appendix.)

TRUST:
(See exercises listed in "Psychology" section of this
  appendix.)

VALUES:
(See exercises listed in "Humanities" section of this appendix.)

VEGETARIANS:
Life: Senses: Taste: Nutrition

VOCATIONAL GUIDANCE:
(See exercises listed in "Guidance" section of this appendix.)

WEIGHT CONTROL
Life: Senses: Taste: Nutrition, see "Possible Options," No. 4
Happiness: Poise: Trying On

WELFARE RECIPIENTS:
(See exercise listed in "Social Studies" section of this appendix.)

WOMEN'S LIBERATION:
Freedom: from Prejudice: Male/Female Roles
Life: Death: Fall-Out Shelter, see Variation No. 1

WORK:
(See exercises listed in "Guidance: Vocational Guidance" section of this appendix.)

GUIDANCE, ORIENTATION, "UPWARD BOUND"

ABORTION:
(See exercise listed in "Social Studies" section of this appendix.)

ADVERTISING:
(See exercises listed in "Communications" section of this appendix.)

AGGRESSION:
(See exercises listed in "Psychology" section of this appendix.)

ALCOHOLISM:
(See exercise listed in "Social Studies" section of this appendix.)

ASTROLOGY:
Life: Biological Rhythms, see Step No. 5

BABY-SITTING:
(See exercise listed in "Family Life" section of this appendix.)

BALANCE:
Life: Senses: Kinesthesis and Balance

BODY RHYTHMS:
(See exercise listed in "Family Life" section of this appendix.)

CHILDREN:
(See exercises listed in "Family Life" section of this appendix.)

CLOTHING:
Communication: Apparel as Symbolic Speech
Happiness: Clothing: The Insurance Company

COMMUNAL LIVING, COMMUNES:
(See exercises listed in "Social Studies" section of this appendix.)

COMMUNICATION:
Communication: Paraverbal: "Harry"
Communication: Voice and Intelligibility
Life: Senses: Audition: Tapes and Voices
(For further exploration, see section of book titled, "Communications.")

COMMUNITY:
(See exercises listed in "Social Studies" and "Psychology" sections of this appendix.)

CONFLICT:
(See exercises listed in "Social Studies" section of this appendix.)

CONFORMITY:
Freedom: from Prejudice—Identity and Difference
Freedom: from Prejudice: Male/Female Roles
Communication: Apparel as Symbolic Speech
Happiness: Photographs
Happiness: Values and Life Styles
Happiness: Acceptance/Rejection

CONSENSUS:
(See exercises listed in "Psychology" section of this appendix.)

COOPERATION:
(See exercises listed in "Psychology" section of this appendix.)
(NOTE: Almost all exercises in this book can be used as examples of "cooperation.")

COUNTER CULTURE:
(See exercises listed in "Social Studies" section of this appendix.)

DRUG ABUSE:
(See exercise listed in "Psychology" section of this appendix.)

ENERGIZING:
Life: Senses: Touch: Skin Slap/Tap

FAMILY LIFE:
(See exercises listed in "Family Life" section of this appendix.)

FEELINGS AND EMOTIONS:
(See exercises listed in "Psychology" section of this appendix.)

FREEDOM:
Communication: Apparel as Symbolic Speech
Communication: Pantomime
(See also exercises in section of book titled "Freedom.")

FUTURING:
(See exercise listed in "Humanities" section of this appendix.)

GROUPS:
(See exercises listed in "Social Studies" section of this appendix.)

JOBS:
(See "Vocational Guidance" below.)

LEARNING:
(See exercises listed in "Psychology" section of this appendix.)

MARRIAGE:
(See exercises listed in "Family Life" section of this appendix.)

MASS MEDIA:
(See exercises listed in "Communications" section of this appendix.)

MEDITATION:
(See exercises listed in "Religion" section of this appendix.)

MENTAL ILLNESS:
(See exercises listed in "Psychology" section of this appendix.)

MONEY MANAGEMENTS:
(See exercises listed in "Family Life" section of this appendix.)

NONVERBAL COMMUNICATION:
(See exercises listed in "Psychology" section of this appendix.)

NUDITY:
(See exercise listed in "Family Life" section of this appendix.)

NUTRITION:
(See exercises listed in "Family Life" section of this appendix.)

PHYSICAL DEPENDENCIES:
(See exercises listed in "Psychology" section of this appendix.)

PHYSICAL HANDICAPS:
(See exercises listed in "Psychology" section of this appendix.)

POISE:
(See exercises listed in "Psychology" section of this appendix.)

PREJUDICE:
(See exercises listed in "Social Studies" section of this appendix.)

PUNISHMENT:
(See exercise listed in "Psychology" section of this appendix.)

RACISM:
(See exercises listed in "Social Studies: Prejudice" section of this appendix.)

RECREATION:
Happiness: Back to Nature
(See also listings under "Religion: Celebrations" in this appendix.)

RELAXATION:
(See exercises listed in "Psychology" section of this appendix.)

RESPONSIBILITY:
(See exercises listed in "Family Life" section of this appendix.)

SAFETY:
Happiness: Back to Nature
Life: Emergencies and Careers in Health

SELF:
(See exercises listed in "Psychology" section of this appendix.)

SENSORY AWARENESS:
(See exercises listed in "Psychology" section of this appendix.)

SEX:
(See exercises listed in "Psychology" section of this appendix.)

SLEEP:
(See exercise listed in "Psychology" section of this appendix.)

SMOKING:
(See exercise listed in "Psychology" section of this appendix.)

SPEECH:
(See exercises listed in "Communications" section of this appendix.)

SPORTS:
Happiness: Back to Nature

TRUST:
(See exercises listed in "Psychology" section of this appendix.)

VALUES:
(See exercises listed in "Humanities" section of this appendix.)

VOCATIONAL GUIDANCE:
Freedom: and Work
Freedom: from Prejudice: Male/Female Roles
Happiness: The Handicapped and
Happiness: Money and Work
Life: Emergencies and Careers in Health
Life: Food and Famine, see Step No. 1, d

WEIGHT CONTROL:
(See exercises listed in "Family Life" section of this appendix.)

WOMEN'S LIBERATION:
(See exercises listed in "Social Studies" section of this appendix.)

WORK:
Life: New Twists for Old Tools
(See also "Vocational Guidance" above.)

YOGA:
(See exercises listed in "Religion" section of this appendix.)

HUMANITIES

ANTHROPOLOGY:
Life: Senses: Taste: Nutrition, see "Possible Projects", No. 1

Cultures, Foreign:
Freedom: Nudity
Communication: Hand Clapping, Dance
Happiness: Meal, see Variation Nos. 3 and 5
Life: Ecology and Your Future Home, see "Comment"
Life: Senses: Visual Illusions, see "Perceptual Set", 3
Life: Senses: Vision: Color and Feeling, see "Comment"
Happiness: Back to Nature
Life: Senses: Kinesthesis: Social Space, see Variation No. 7
Life: Senses: Olfaction: Japanese Incense-Smelling
Life: Senses: Taste: Japanese Tea Ceremony
Life: Senses: Taste: Bread Day, see Variation No. 3
Love: the New Religions
Communication: Nonverbal: Handshake, Fist

Cultures, Counterculture:
(See exercises listed in "Social Studies" section of this appendix.)

ART:
(NOTE: This listing does not include exercises involving "art work" or "art projects" by students, of which there are many.)
Communication: Hand Clapping, Dance
Freedom: and Nudity
Life: New Twists for Old Tools, Variation No. 2
Life: Senses: Seeing and Perceiving
Life: Senses: Visual Illusions
Life: Senses: Vision: Color and Feeling, Variation No. 3
Life: Senses: Japanese Tea Ceremony
Life: Senses: Audition: Silence, see Step No. 6
(See also "Music", "Theater", below)

CELEBRATIONS:
(See exercises listed in "Religion" section of this appendix.)

COLOR:
(See exercises listed in "Communications" section of this appendix.)

DANCE:
Communication: Hand Clapping, Dance

FREEDOM:
Communication: Apparel as Symbolic Speech
Communication: Pantomime
(See also all exercises in section of book titled, "Freedom.")

FUTURING:
Happiness: Futuring

GOVERNMENT:
(See "Politics" below)

HISTORY, AMERICAN:
(See exercise listed in "Social Studies" section of this appendix.)

INDIANS, AMERICAN
Communication: Hand Clapping, Dance
Life: Senses: Audition: Silence, see "Comment"

LANGUAGE:
(See exercise listed in "Communication" section of this appendix.)

LAW:
Life: Ecology, Conservation and Pollution, see Part II Steps Nos. 2 and 10

MASS MEDIA:
(See exercises listed in "Communication" section of this appendix.)

MUSIC:
Communication: Hand Clapping, Dance
Happiness: Sound
Life: Senses: Audition: Background Music
Life: Senses: Audition: A Musical Happening
Life: Senses: Audition: Silence

PHILOSOPHY:
(See most of the exercises in book sections titled, "Freedom", "Love", "Peace", "Happiness" and "Life" for concept development.)

POLITICS:
Freedom: Break Through
Life: Ecology, Conservation and Pollution, see Part I, Step No. 7; Part II, Step No. 10
Life: Urban Design: Study Your Community
Life: Urban Design: Get the Facts

RELIGION:
(See exercises listed in "Religion" section of this appendix.)

SCIENCE:
(NOTE: Following exercises deal with concepts of science, "What is science?", "What is the 'scientific method'?", etc.)
Communication: Physiognomy
Communication: Graphology
Happiness: Futuring
Life: Biological Rhythms
Life: Senses: Vision: Color and Feelings, see especially Variation No. 1

SOUND:
Happiness: Sound
Life: Senses: Touch: Water, see Variation No. 1
Life: Senses: Audition: Tapes and Voices
Life: Senses: Audition: Sounds and Spaces
Life: Senses: Audition: Background Music
Life: Senses: Audition: Identifying Sounds

SYMBOLISM:
Communication: Apparel as Symbolic Speech
Communication: Nonverbal: Handshake, Fist
Happiness: Meal, particularly Variation No. 4
Life: Senses: Touch: Water, see Variation No. 2
Life: Senses: Taste: Bread Day, particularly Variations Nos. 1 and 2
Peace: Media Monitoring, Variation No. 1

THEATER:
(Note: This listing does not include exercises which involve dramatizations or role plays used for other purposes.)
Communication: Paraverbal—"Harry"
Communication: Paraverbal, and Silent Communication
Communication: Nonverbal: Handshake, Fist, see especially Step No. 6
Communication: Mirror, mirror on the wall . . .
Communication: Pantomime
Freedom: Breathing, see Step No. 2
Peace: Mime and Gestures of,
  (See also other listings under "Communication" section of this appendix such as "Speech", "Nonverbal Communication.")

TV:
(See exercises listed in "Communication: Mass Media" section of this appendix.)

TIME:
Life: Biological Rhythms

VALUES:
Freedom: and Valuing
Freedom: and Responsibility
Freedom: Mass Media and "Good" and "Bad Bodies"
Happiness: Photographs
Happiness: Faces
Happiness: Values and Life Styles
Happiness: Clothing: the Insurance Company
Happiness: Body as "Good" or "Bad"
Life: Death: Fall-Out Shelter
Life: Death Inquiry
Life: Death: Who Shall Live? Who Shall Die?
Life: Urban Design: Village Plan
Life: Food and Famine, see Step No. 2
Love: The Family Cave
Love: Sexual Codes

ZEN
(See exercises listed in "Religion" section of this
   appendix.)

PSYCHOLOGY

ADVERTISING:
(See exercises listed in "Communications" section
   of this appendix.)
Freedom: Mass Media and "Good" and "Bad"
   Bodies
Life: Senses: Olfaction: "What Smells Sell?"

AGGRESSION:
Peace: American History
Peace: Mime and Gestures of,

ALCOHOLISM:
(See exercise listed in "Social Studies" section of this
   appendix.)

ANTHROPOLOGY AND PSYCHOLOGY:
Life: Senses: Taste: Nutrition, see "Possible Projects"
   No. 1
Communication: Nonverbal: Handshake, Fist
Communication: Apparel as Symbolic Speech

ART AND PSYCHOLOGY
Communication: Hand Clapping, Dance
Freedom: and Nudity
Life: New Twists for Old Tools, Variation No. 2
Life: Senses: Seeing and Perceiving
Life: Senses: Visual Illusions
Life: Senses: Vision, Color and Feeling
Life: Senses: Audition: Silence

ASTROLOGY:
Life: Biological Rhythms, see Step No. 5

AUDITION:
Life: Senses: Audition: Tapes and Voices
Life: Senses: Audition: Sounds and Spaces
Life: Senses: Audition: Background Music
Life: Senses: Audition: Identifying Sounds
Life: Senses: Audition: Silence

BALANCE:
Life: Senses: Kinesthesis and Balance

BODY RHYTHMS:
(See exercise listed in "Family Life" section of this
   appendix.)

BREAD:

(See exercise listed in "Religion" section of this
   appendix.)

CHILDREN:
(See exercises listed in "Family Life" section of this
   appendix.)

CLOTHING:
(See exercises listed in "Guidance" section of this
   appendix.)

COLOR:
Happiness: Self-Image: Art Media, Variations Nos.
   1 and 2
Life: Senses: Visual Illusions, See II.f
Life: Senses: Color and Feeling

COMMUNAL LIVING, COMMUNES:
(See exercises listed in "Social Studies" section of this
   appendix.)

COMPETITION:
Peace: Conflict: Scavenger Hunt

CONFLICT:
(See exercises listed in "Social Studies" section of this
   appendix.)

CONFORMITY:
(See exercises listed in "Guidance" section of this
   appendix.)

CONSENSUS:
Happiness: What is Community?
Life: Death: Fall-Out Shelter, see also Variation
   No. 2
Peace: Defining Peace, see Step No. 2 (includes
   possibility of a "minority report")

COOPERATION:
Peace: Conflict: Scavenger Hunt
(NOTE: Most exercises may be used as examples of
   "cooperation.")

CRIME:
(See "Punishment," below.)

DEATH:
(See exercises listed in "Religion" section of this
   appendix.)

DREAMS:
Life: Dreaming

DRUG ABUSE:
Freedom: from Physical Dependencies

EMPATHY:
Freedom: from Prejudice: First Hand Impressions
Peace: War and Peace: Perception Check
(See also listings in section of book, "Communication," on "Nonverbal communication.")

FEELINGS AND EMOTIONS:
Communication: Examining Nonverbal Behavior
"Mirror, mirror on the wall . . ."
Freedom: Breathing, see Step No. 2
Communication: Alter Ego
Happiness: Giving
Life: Senses: Vision: Color and Feeling
Life: Senses: Touch: Water
Life: Senses: Audition: Background Music
Peace: War and Peace: Perception Check
Peace: Conflict: Scavenger Hunt

FOOD AND FEELINGS:
Happiness: Meal
Life: Senses: Olfaction: Japanese Incense-Smelling,
    see Variation No. 2
Life: Senses: Taste . . . and Sight
Life: Senses: Taste: Japanese Tea Ceremony and
    see "Variations"
Life: Senses: Taste: Nutrition (see "fads")

FREEDOM:
Communication: Apparel as Symbolic Speech
Communication: Pantomime
(See also section of book titled "Freedom.")

FUTURING:
(See exercise listed in "Humanities" section of this
    appendix.)

GRAPHOLOGY:
Communication: Graphology

GROUPS:
(See exercises listed in "Social Studies" section of this
    appendix.)

GUIDANCE:
(See exercises listed in "Guidance" section of this
    appendix.)

HEARING:
(See "Audition", above.)

ILLUSIONS:
Life: Senses: Visual Illusions

KINESTHETIC SENSE:
Life: Senses: Touch: Water
LIfe: Senses: Kinesthesis: Social Space
Life: Senses: Kinesthesis: and Balance

LANGUAGE:
(See exercise listed in "Communication" section of
    this appendix.)

LEARNING:
Communication: as Learning
Love: Learning to Love

MARRIAGE:
(See exercises listed in "Family Life" section of this
    appendix.)

MASS MEDIA:
(See exercises listed in "Communications" section of
    this appendix.)

MEMORY:
Life: Memory
Life: Senses: Olfaction: "Smells of Childhood"
Life: Senses: Olfaction: Classifying, See Step No. 7

MENTAL ILLNESS:
Happiness: the Handicapped and
Peace: Conflict and Punishment, see Step No. 4 and
    Variation No. 1

NOISE:
Life: Ecology, Conservation and Pollution, Part II,
    Step No. 12

NONVERBAL COMMUNICATION:
(See exercises in section of book titled, "Communication.")

NUDITY:
(See exercise listed in "Family Life" section of this
    appendix.)

OLFACTION:
Life: Senses: Olfaction: "Smells of Childhood"
Life: Senses: Olfaction: Classifying
Life: Senses: Olfaction: "What Smells Sell?"
Life: Senses: Olfaction: "What Smells Sell?"
Life: Senses: Olfaction: Japanese Incense-Smelling

OPTICAL ILLUSIONS:
(See "Illusion" above)

PERCEPTION:
Happiness: Montage of Physical Self, Variation No. 4
Happiness: Sound
Life: Senses: Seeing and Perceiving
Life: Senses: Vision: Serial Reproduction
Life: Senses: Audition: Identifying Sounds
(NOTE: All in the "Life: Senses" section of the book
    apply, but above are particularly good for dealing

with certain concepts and principles about perception.)

PHYSICAL DEPENDENCIES:
Freedom: from Physical Dependencies
Happiness: Dreaming—"Tripping without Drugs"

*PHYSICAL HANDICAPS AND
SENSORY DEPRIVATION:*
(See exercises listed in "Social Studies" section of this appendix.)

POISE:
Happiness: Belonging
Communication: Pantomime
Freedom: Eyeball to Eyeball
Happiness: Self-Confidence, Poise and Self-Image
Happiness: Poise: Trying On
Happiness: Poise: Contrary Directions
(See also "Relaxation" below.)

PREJUDICE:
(See exercises listed in "Social Studies" section of this appendix.)

PHYSIOGNOMY:
Communication: Physiognomy

PUNISHMENT:
Peace: Conflict and Punishment

QUESTIONNAIRE DESIGN:
Freedom: and Work

RACISM:
(See exercises listed in "Social Studies: Prejudice" section of this appendix.)

RELAXATION:
Freedom: Breathing, see Step No. 3
Freedom: Stretch
Life: Senses: Touch: Skin Slap/Tap

SELF:
Communication: and Our Multiple Selves
Communication: Apparel as Symbolic Speech
Freedom: from Prejudice—Identity and Difference
Happiness: Belonging
Life: Dreaming
Life: Senses: Audition: Tapes and Voices

SENSORY AWARENESS:
Freedom: and Trust
Freedom: from Prejudice: First Hand Impressions, see Variation
Happiness: Sound
Happiness: Back to Nature

Life: Urban Design: Walkaround, see Variation
Life: Awareness of Body: "Inward Journey"
Life: Blind Nature Walk
(In addition, see section of book titled "Life" for exercises on "Senses.")

SENSES
(See separate listings in this section: Audition, Kinesthetic sense, Perception, Sensory Awareness, Touch, Vision.)

SEX:
Freedom: from Prejudice: Male/Female Roles
Freedom: Nudity
Freedom: Mass Media and "Good" and "Bad" Bodies
Love: Sexual Codes
Love: and "Sex Education"

SIGHT:
(See "Perception", "Vision.")

SLEEP:
Life: Dreaming

SMELL, SENSE OF
(See "Olfaction.")

SMOKING:
Freedom: from Physical Dependencies

SOCIAL SPACE:
(See exercises listed in "Social Studies" section of this appendix.)

SYMBOLISM:
(See exercises listed in "Humanities" section of this appendix.)

TASTE:
Life: Senses: Taste . . . and Sight
Life: Senses: Taste: Japanese Tea Ceremony
Life: Senses: Taste: Bread Day
Life: Senses: Taste: Nutrition

TEACHING:
(See exercise listed in "Family Life" section of this appendix.)

TOUCH:
Life: Senses: Touch: 2-point Threshold and Localization Error
Life: Senses: Touch: Skin Slap/Tap
Life: Senses: Touch: Water
Life: Senses: Touch: Sound and Space, see "Comment"
(See also "Kinesthetic Sense.")

TRUST:
Freedom: and Trust
Happiness: Self-Image: Art Media
Happiness: Meal, see Variation No. 2

VALUES:
(See exercises listed in "Humanities" section of this
   appendix.)

VIOLENCE:
(See exercises listed in "Social Studies" section of this
   appendix.)

VISION:
(See "Perception.")

WAR:
(See exercises listed in "Social Studies" section of this
   appendix.)

WEIGHT CONTROL:
(See exercises listed in "Family Life" section of this
   appendix.)

WOMEN'S LIBERATION:
(See exercises listed in "Social Studies" section of this
   appendix.)

YOGA:
(See exercises listed in "Religion" section of this
   appendix.)

RELIGION

ABORTION:
(See exercise listed in "Social Studies" section of this
   appendix.)

ASTROLOGY:
Life: Biological Rhythms, see Step No. 5

BELIEF:
Communication: Physiognomy, Variation No. 4
(See also "Faith" below.)

BREAD:
Life: Senses: Taste: Bread Day

CELEBRATIONS:
Life: Senses: A Sense of Wonder
Happiness: Sound
Happiness: Group Excursions
Happiness: Meal
Life: Senses: Olfaction: "Smells of Childhood,"
   see Options Nos. 2 and 3
Life: Senses: Olfaction: Japanese Incense-Smelling

Life: Senses: Taste: Japanese Tea Ceremony
Life: Senses: Taste: Bread Day
Life: Senses: Audition: A Musical Happening

COMMUNAL LIVING:
(See exercises listed in "Social Studies" section of this
   appendix.)

COMMUNITY:
(See exercises listed in "Social Studies" section of this
   appendix.)

DEATH:
Life: Death: Fall-Out Shelter
Life: Death: Inquiry
Life: Death: Who Shall Live? Who Shall Die?

EUTHANASIA:
Life: Death: Who Shall Live? Who Shall Die?

FAITH:
Freedom: Trust
(See also "Belief" above.)

FUTURING:
Happiness: Futuring

HUNGER:
Life: Food and Famine

LOVE:
Love: the New Religions
Love: in Judeo-Christian Religions
(See also section of book titled "Love.")

MEDITATION:
Life: Senses: Touch: Water
Life: Senses: Auditon: Background Music, see
   Variation No. 7
Life: Senses: Audition: Identifying Sounds
Love: Learning to Love, see Step No. 7
Love: Meditation

POVERTY:
(See exercises listed in "Social Studies" section of this
   appendix.)

PREJUDICE:
(See exercises listed in "Social Studies" section of this
   appendix.)

RACISM:
(See exercises listed in "Social Studies: Prejudice"
   section of this appendix.)

RITUAL:
Communication: Hand Clapping, Dance

Life: Senses: Olfaction: Japanese Incense-Smelling
Life: Senses: Taste: Bread Day, see Variation No. 2

RESPONSIBILITY:
(See exercises listed in "Family Life" section of this appendix.)

SELF:
(See exercises listed in "Psychology" section of this appendix.)

SYMBOLISM:
(See exercises listed in "Humanities" section of this appendix.)

TAOISM:
Life: Senses: Kinesthesis and Balance
Love: the New Religions

TRUST:
(See exercises listed in "Psychology" section of this appendix.)

VALUES:
(See exercises listed in "Humanities" section of this appendix.)

WAR:
(See exercises listed in "Social Studies" section of this appendix.)

YOGA:
Freedom: Breathing
Happiness: "Dreaming"
Love: the New Religions

ZEN:
Freedom: Breathing, see Step No. 6
Life: Death Inquiry, see Step No. 3
Life: Ecology, Conservation and Pollution
Life: Senses: Olfaction: Japanese Incense-Smelling
Life: Senses: Taste: Japanese Tea Ceremony
Love: the New Religions

SOCIAL STUDIES, SOCIOLOGY, URBAN STUDIES

ABORTION:
Life: Death: Who Shall Live? Who Shall Die?

AGGRESSION:
(See exercises listed in "Psychology" section of this appendix.)

ALCOHOLISM:
Freedom: from Physical Dependencies

BODY RHYTHMS:
(See exercise listed in "Family Life" section of this appendix.)

CANNIBALISM:
Life: Food and Famine, Step No. 1, c

CITIZEN ACTION:
Peace: Conflict and Punishment, Variation No. 2
(See also listings under "City Planning", "Ecology", "Politics" below.)

CITY PLANNING:
Life: Urban Design: Walkaround
Life: Urban Design: Village Plan
Life: Urban Design: Study Your Community
Life: Urban Design: Get the Facts

COMMUNAL LIVING, COMMUNES:
Happiness: What Is Community?
Love: New Family Patterns

COMMUNITY:
Communication: Effect on Our Bodies of Group Membership
Communication: and Community
Communication: Apparel as Symbolic Speech
Happiness: the Handicapped and,
Happiness: What Is Community?
Life: Ecology, Conservation and Pollution
Peace: Conflict and Punishment
(See also "City Planning" above.)

COMPETITION:
(See exercise listed in "Psychology" section of this appendix.)

CONFLICT:
Peace: and Conflict
Peace: Conflict and Punishment
Peace: Conflict: Scavenger Hunt

CONFORMITY:
(See exercises listed in "Guidance" section of this appendix.)

CONSENSUS:
(See exercises listed in "Psychology" section of this appendix.)

CONSERVATION:
(See exercises listed in "Ecology" below.)

COOPERATION:
(See exercises listed in "Psychology" section of this appendix.)
(NOTE: The majority of the exercises in this book

may be used as examples of "cooperation.")

COUNTER CULTURE:
Communication: Apparel as Symbolic Speech
Freedom: from Physical Dependencies
Happiness: Values and Life Styles
Life: Senses: Taste: Nutrition, see data on Vegetarian Diets
Life: Senses: Taste: Food Additives
Love: New Family Patterns
Love: the New Religions
Freedom: Breathing; see also Step No. 6 (Zen)
Happiness: Dreaming (Yoga)
Life: Death Inquiry, see Step No. 3 (Zen)
Life: Senses: Olfaction: Japanese Incense-Smelling
Life: Senses: Taste: Japanese Tea Ceremony (Zen)

CRIME:
Peace: Conflict and Punishment
(See also "Violence" below.)

"CROWDING":
Life: Senses: Kinesthesis: Social Space, Variation No. 2

CULTURES, FOREIGN:
(See exercises listed in "Humanities: Anthropology" section in this appendix.)

DRUG ABUSE:
(See exercise listed in "Psychology: Physical Dependencies" section of this appendix.)

ECOLOGY:
Life: Ecology, Conservation and Pollution
Happiness: Back to Nature
Life: Ecology and Your Future Home
Life: Senses: Food Additives

FAMILY LIFE:
(See exercises listed in "Family Life" section of this appendix.)

FOOD ADDITIVES:
Life: Senses: Taste: Food Additives

FREEDOM:
(See section of book titled "Freedom.")

FUTURING:
(See exercise listed in "Humanities" section of this appendix.)

GOVERNMENT:
(See "Politics" below.)

GROUPS:
Communication: Effect on Our Bodies of Group

Membership
Communication: and Position Change
Communication: Alter Ego
Freedom: from Prejudice: Group Rejection
Freedom: Eyeball to Eyeball, see steps Nos. 4-7
Happiness: Group Excursion
Happiness: What Is Community?
Happiness: Meal, see Variation No. 1
Peace: Conflict: Scavenger Hunt
(Since most of the exercises in this book involve working at least part of the time in small groups, many may be used as the basis for an examination of the behavior of groups.)

HISTORY:
Peace: American History

LAW:
(See exercise listed in "Humanities" section of this appendix.)

MARRIAGE:
(See exercises listed in "Family Life" section of this appendix.)

MASS MEDIA:
(See exercises listed in "Communications" section of this appendix.)

MEDICINE:
Life: Death: "Who Shall Live?" Who Shall Die?"
Life: Emergencies and Careers in Health

MENTAL ILLNESS:
(See exercises listed in "Psychology" section of this appendix.)

MONEY MANAGEMENT:
(See exercises listed in "Family Life" section of this appendix.)

NOISE:
(See exercises listed in "Psychology" section of this appendix.)

NUTRITION:
Life: Sense: Taste: Nutrition
Life: Senses: Taste: Food and Famine
(For further exploration, see exercises listed in "Family Life: Food" section of this appendix.)

PHYSICAL DEPENDENCIES:
(See exercises listed in "Psychology" section of this appendix.)

PHYSICAL HANDICAPS:
Freedom: and Trust

Freedom: and Physical Handicaps
Happiness: Faces, see Step No. 4
Happiness: the Handicapped and,
Life: Senses: Deprivation

POLITICS:
(See exercises listed in "Humanities" section of this appendix.)

POLLUTION:
(See "Ecology" above.)

POPULATION GROWTH:
Life: Food and Famine

POVERTY:
Life: Senses: Taste: Nutrition, see "Possible Options" No. 3
Life: Senses: Taste: Food and Famine

PREJUDICE:
Communication: Physiognomy, see Variation Nos. 1-3
Freedom: from Prejudice—Identity and Difference
Freedom: from Prejudice: First Hand Impressions
Freedom: from Prejudice: Male/Female Roles
Freedom: from Prejudice: Group Rejection
Happiness: Acceptance/Rejection
Life: Senses: Deprivation
Life: Senses: Vision: Serial Reproduction
(See also some of the exercises listed above under "Physical Handicaps.")

PRIVACY:
Life: Senses: Audition: Background Music
(See also "Crowding" above.)

PUNISHMENT:
(See exercise listed in "Psychology" section of this appendix.)

QUESTIONNAIRE DESIGN:
Freedom: and Work

RACISM:
(See "Prejudice" above.)

RECREATION:
(See exercise listed in "Guidance" section of this appendix.)

RESPONSIBILITY:
(See exercises listed in "Family Life" section of this appendix.)

SAFETY:
(See exercises listed in "Guidance" section of this appendix.)

SMOKING:
(See exercise listed in "Psychology" section of this appendix.)

SOCIAL PROBLEMS:
(See specific listings, such as "City Planning", "Ecology", "Marriage", "Physical Dependencies", "Poverty", "Population Growth.")

SOCIAL SPACE:
Communication: Walking
Life: Senses: Kinesthesis: Social Space
Life: Senses: Audition: Sounds and Spaces

URBAN DESIGN:
(See "City Planning" above.)

VIOLENCE:
Peace: American History
Peace: and Conflict
Peace: Conflict and Punishment
Peace: Media Monitoring
Peace: Mime, and Gestures of,

VOCATIONAL GUIDANCE:
(See exercises listed in "Guidance" section of this appendix.)

WAR:
Peace: American History
Peace: Defining Peace
Peace: War and Peace: Perception Check
Peace: Conflict: Scavenger Hunt

WELFARE RECIPIENTS:
Life: Senses: Taste: Nutrition, see "Possible Options" No. 5

WOMEN'S LIBERATION:
Freedom: from Prejudice: Male/Female Roles
Life: Death: Fall-Out Shelter, see Variation No. 1

WORK:
(See exercises listed in "Guidance" section of this appendix.)

358

U.S. Dept. Labor, Bureau of Labor Statistics, Washington, D.C. 20212, p. 94

U.S. Public Health Service, Washington, D.C. 20201, p. 187

Wilderness Society, 729 15th St. N.W., Washington, D.C. 20005, pp. 157, 188

Wildlife Preserves, Inc., P.O. Box 55, 24 County Rd., Tenafly, N.J.

07670, p. 188

WITCO Chemical, Sonneborn Div., 277 Park Ave., New York, N.Y. 10017, p. 264